U.S. Regulation of Hedge Funds

Second Edition

Shartsis Friese LLP

Douglas L. Hammer • Carolyn S. Reiser • Geoffrey W. Haynes

Neil J. Koren • James J. Frolik • Christina M. Hamilton

Ellyn T. Roberts • Joan L. Grant

AMERICAN BAR ASSOCIATION

Business Law Section

Cover design by Anthony Nuccio/ABA Publishing.

Page layout by Quadrum Solutions.

Printed in the United States of America.

17 16 15 14 13   5 4 3 2

Library of Congress Cataloging-in-Publication Data

U.S. regulation of hedge funds, second edition / Shartsis Friese LLP, Douglas Hammer … [et al.].

pages cm

Includes index.

ISBN 978-1-61632-811-5 (alk. paper)

1. Hedge funds—Law and legislation—United States. 2. Pension trusts—Law and legislation—United States. 3. Mutual funds—Law and legislation—United States. I. Hammer, Douglas L., and Carolyn S. Reiser, eds. II. Shartsis Friese LLP. III. Title: US regulation of hedge funds. IV. Title: United States regulation of hedge funds.

KF1078.U14 2013

346.73'0922—dc23

2013039154

Discounts are available for books ordered in bulk. Special consideration is given to state bars, CLE programs, and other bar related organizations. Inquire at Book Publishing, ABA Publishing, American Bar Association, 321 N. Clark Street, Chicago, Illinois 60654-7598.

www.ShopABA.org

Summary of Contents

Contents

CHAPTER **1**

Introduction

§ 1.1 The Nature of Hedge Funds

"Hedge fund" has no uniformly accepted meaning, but commonly refers to a professionally managed pool of assets used to invest and trade in equity securities, fixed-income securities, options, futures and other derivatives, and other financial instruments. Participation in a hedge fund typically is restricted to relatively wealthy individual and institutional investors that satisfy private offering standards.[1] The adjective "hedge" is useful for distinguishing hedge funds from other types of investment pools (such as mutual funds, venture capital funds, private equity funds, and commodity pools), but it has little descriptive value—hedge funds may or may not hedge against risks.

Indeed, some hedge funds invest only in securities and only for the long-term. Some hedge funds never invest at all, but only trade to profit from market or security depreciation (this subspecies of hedge funds is sometimes called "short funds"). Some long-short hedge funds sell securities short to guard against risks in their long investments; some sell securities short opportunistically to profit from expected declines in the prices of the securities; and some do both. Some hedge funds trade in put and call options or futures contracts to hedge; others do so hoping to profit from directional security or market bets. Some hedge funds are fundamental investors, while others rely on technical analysis. Some hedge funds invest and trade only distressed debt instruments. Some hedge funds attempt to take advantage of pricing discrepancies between different markets in the same instruments through any of an array of arbitrage strategies. Some hedge funds specialize in currency trading, while some refuse even to consider securities that are not denominated in U.S. dollars. Some hedge funds eschew any kind of borrowing, while others margin their portfolios to the maximum extent allowed by law.[2] At least one hedge fund based trading decisions on its interpretation of astrological charts.

Hedge funds thus do not represent an asset class or any particular style of portfolio management. The investment philosophies of hedge funds are as diverse as their portfolio managers. Hedge funds' investment techniques and

1. *See* Chapter 5, *infra*.

2. *See* Implications of the Growth of Hedge Funds, Staff Report to the U.S. Securities and Exchange Commission, § IV.A, at 33-43 (Sep. 2003), (hereinafter "Staff Report"), *available at* http://www.sec.gov/news/studies/hedgefunds0903.pdf (last visited May 2, 2013).

methods represent their managers' individual experiences, backgrounds and biases. If any common thread runs through the hedge fund community, it is that hedge fund managers retain flexibility to manage their portfolios in ways they consider most likely to achieve returns for their investors and concomitantly for themselves. They generally are subject only to their fiduciary obligations and such investment restrictions as they impose on themselves. Hedge funds are excepted from regulation as mutual funds under the Company Act[3] and as a result are not constrained by the Company Act's rigid rules about such matters as hedging, leverage and diversification, leading some unknowing pundits to suggest that hedge funds are unregulated or lightly regulated.[4] Hedge fund managers are, however, subject to requirements and constraints of a panoply of federal and state laws, including the Adviser's Act,[5] the Securities Act,[6] state securities laws,[7] the Exchange Act,[8] ERISA,[9] the Tax Code[10] and (depending on investment choices) the Commodity Exchange Act.[11]

§ 1.2 Some Regulatory History and Prospects

Alfred Winslow Jones organized the first hedge fund in 1949.[12] When we began our practice representing hedge fund managers in the early 1980s, U.S. hedge funds numbered fewer than 100 and managed only a few billion dollars of assets,[13] but the hedge fund business generally escaped (or avoided) public notice and its magnitude was largely unexamined.[14] After the stock market crash in October 1987, the government briefly shone a low-wattage light on hedge funds,[15] but did not implement major regulatory initiatives directed at them. U.S. hedge funds held assets valued at $39,000,000,000 in 1990, which grew to a peak of $1,870,000,000,000 in 2007 (when a recession began), and by April 2012 were around $2,130,000,000,000.[16]

---

3. *See* Chapter 3, *infra.* This book does not address hedge funds or funds of hedge funds that are offered to the public in offerings registered under the Securities Act; such offerings typically are promoted by large brokerage firms for small investors. This book also does not generally address funds of hedge funds, or the special considerations that may arise for them.
4. *See, e.g.*, William Safire, *Watch the Hedgehogs*, N.Y. Times, Apr. 12, 2004, at A19.
5. *See* Chapters 2, 6, 8, 9, 12, 14 and 15, *infra.*
6. *See* Chapters 5, 6, 8 and 9, *infra.*
7. *See* Chapters 2 and 7, *infra.*
8. *See* Chapters 10, 13 and 14, *infra.*
9. *See* Chapter 11, *infra.*
10. *See* Chapters 4, 11 and 16, *infra.*
11. *See* § 2.9 and Chapter 6, *infra.*
12. Staff Report § II.A, at 3.
13. Hennessee Group LLC, *10th Annual Manager Survey – 2004.*
14. *See* Ralph S. Janvey, *Hedge Funds*, Rev. of Sec. & Commodities Reg., Vol. 21, No. 11, at 91 (June 8, 1988), and authorities cited there.
15. *Id.*
16. Juliet Chung, *Hedge-Fund Assets Rise to Record Level*, The Wall Street Journal (Apr. 19, 2012).

The SEC's first substantial regulatory initiative aimed at hedge funds began in 2002. Inspired by the growth of hedge funds and notorious financial scandals since 2001, especially those involving managers of large mutual fund complexes, the SEC and other regulatory agencies became highly motivated (whether for political or other reasons) at least to appear to be pursuing remedies to perceived regulatory and institutional weaknesses. In an avowed effort to learn more about the theretofore veiled hedge fund business, the SEC in 2002 directed its staff to examine it and convened a "Roundtable" in May 2003 to provide a public forum for discussion and debate about the implications of hedge fund growth.[17] The resulting Staff Report recommended additional registration, disclosure, and compliance requirements for hedge funds and their managers.[18]

In 2004, the SEC proposed a new rule under the Advisers Act (the "2004 Rule"), which eliminated the so-called "private adviser exemption" from registration on which many hedge fund managers had relied, and required most of them to register by 2006.[19] This set off a flurry of activity in 2005 by unregistered investment advisers (and a spike in salaries of compliance professionals), as they scrambled to formalize compliance policies and procedures required of SEC-registered advisers.

From the time it was proposed, the 2004 Rule was met with vociferous opposition from within the SEC itself, other public officials, and hedge fund industry participants. The stated purposes of the 2004 Rule were, among other things, to collect data about hedge funds and their managers, prevent unfit persons from managing hedge funds, deter fraud, and protect investors by imposing additional compliance requirements on managers.[20] Critics claimed that the data the 2004 Rule collected would not have any useful purpose, registration would not determine whether an adviser was unfit or deter fraud, and the SEC did not have the resources to oversee more advisers.

The SEC adopted the 2004 Rule by a divided vote,[21] and promptly thereafter an investment advisory firm and a hedge fund it managed sued the SEC on grounds that it had exceeded its authority and acted arbitrarily and unreasonably in adopting the rule. The District Court agreed and a panel of the Court of Appeals unanimously affirmed, vacating the 2004 Rule in 2006.[22] The SEC did not seek *en banc* review of the Court's decision, stating that it would instead move "aggressively on an agenda of rulemaking and staff guidance," in furtherance of its "goal of advancing investor protection."[23]

---

17. Staff Report § I, at 2. *See generally*, Sec. Reg. & L. Rep. (BNA), Vol. 35, No. 20, at 851-856 (May 19, 2003).

18. Staff Report § VII, at 88-103.

19. Advisers Act Release No. 2266 (July 20, 2004, 69 F.R. 45, 172 (July 28, 2004).

20. *Id.*

21. Advisers Act Release No. 2333 (Dec. 2, 2004), 69 F.R.72,054 (Dec. 10, 2004), which includes the dissent of the 2 Commissioners who opposed the new rules.

22. Goldstein v. SEC, 451 F.3d 873 (D.C. Cir. 2006).

23. Statement of Chairman Cox Concerning the Decision of the U.S. Court of Appeals in Phillip Goldstein, et al. v. SEC (August 7, 2006), *available at* http:\\www.sec.gov/news/press/2006/2006-135.htm.

Between 2006 and 2010, the SEC, as promised, adopted several new rules under the Advisers Act, including new anti-fraud rules, another overhaul of the custody rules, and multiple rules regulating short sales.[24] Through early 2010, however, the registration requirements for investment advisers to hedge funds were essentially the same as they were before the 2004 Rules.

More fundamental changes to hedge fund regulation came only at Congress's direction, in the aftermath of the dramatic events that shook the U.S. financial sector starting in 2007. The fraud of Bernard Madoff, the Lehman Brothers insolvency, fire sales of other troubled brokerage firms, government bailouts of "too big to fail" banks and insurers, and severe contraction of the credit markets collectively disrupted both the U.S. economy and the psyches of the legislators and agency officials charged with regulating it. Most observers attributed the financial crises of that period to some combination of abusive practices by banks and other lenders, rating agencies, insurers and investment banks, the failure of the self-regulating market hypothesis, and the purposeful inattention of lawmakers and regulators. Few identified unregistered hedge fund managers as a principal source of such systemic dysfunction. Calls for comprehensive reform and greater oversight, however, extended to all market participants.

In July 2010, Congress passed the Dodd-Frank Act,[25] which outlined sweeping regulatory changes intended to bring greater transparency and oversight to the financial markets. It encompassed derivatives, credit rating agencies, securitized financial products, proprietary trading by banks and their affiliates, capital requirements of banks and brokerage firms, compensation of corporate executives, and much more. Drafted precipitately, due in part to legislators' need to appear to be acting quickly and decisively, it included some 90 provisions requiring the SEC and other agencies to craft rules within an unrealistically short time that would accomplish some of Congress's objectives, and dozens of other provisions authorizing them to tackle the rest.

Although Congress was responding most proximately to crises in which investment advisers and hedge funds were relatively minor players, it did not overlook them. Mandated by the Dodd-Frank Act, the SEC adopted new rules in 2011 that eliminated (again) the private adviser exemption, required more hedge fund managers to register with the SEC or a state authority, and required much more detailed and frequent reporting from most managers. SEC chairman Mary Schapiro stated that the new rules would "fill a gap in the regulatory landscape, [giving] the Commission and the public insight into the hedge fund and other private fund managers who previously conducted their work under the radar and outside the vision of regulators." In response to various Dodd-Frank directives, the SEC and the Commodity Futures Trading Commission (CFTC)

---

24. *See, e.g.*, Advisers Act Release No. 2628 (Aug. 3, 2007), 72 F.R. 44,756 (Aug. 9, 2007); Advisers Act Release No. 2968 (Dec. 30, 2009), 75 F.R.1,456 (Jan. 11, 2010); Exchange Act Release No. 56212 (Aug. 7, 2007), 72 F.R. 45,544 (Aug. 14, 2007); Exchange Act Release 58774 No. (Oct. 14, 2008), 7.3. F.R. 61,666 (Oct. 17, 2008); Exchange Act Release No. 58785 (Oct. 15, 2008), 73 F.R. 61,678 (Oct. 17, 2008); Exchange Act Release No. 61, 595 (Feb. 26, 2010), 75 F.R. 11,232 (Mar. 10, 2010).

25. Pub. L. 111-203 (July 21, 2010).

issued thousands of pages of proposals for new rules that directly or indirectly regulate investment advisers and hedge funds; many have been adopted.

The hedge fund industry's reactions to the proposed Dodd-Frank rulemaking were predictable: costs of complying with increased regulation would drive out existing players and deter new entrants; cumbersome compliance requirements would undermine the global competitiveness of U.S. managers; increased reporting would put highly confidential trading data at risk of being discovered by competitors; and regulatory agencies would not be able to process or make use of the vast new data reported to them. The continuing economic uncertainty, however, along with protestations that financial institutions had not borne nearly their fair share of the economic pain of the prior two years, deterred some objections to the new regulations. Although many proposed rules received numerous comments, overall most were greeted with some sense of inevitability.

In practice, so far, new registration, disclosure and reporting requirements have significantly increased hedge fund managers' compliance costs. The complexities of compiling and processing data into SEC- and CFTC-specific reporting formats have spawned a technology boomlet of consultants offering regulatory software solutions. Investment advisers without substantial assets under management may not be able to afford the compliance infrastructure needed to comply with increased regulation. Industry observers have noted the increasing consolidation of the hedge fund business: at the end of 2012, U.S. investment advisers with more than $1,000,000,000 under management managed more than 85 percent of the total hedge fund assets managed by all U.S. investment advisers.[26] Regulators are grappling with how to process and make timely use of the data now required to be reported to them.[27]

Across the table, investors—especially larger ones—are requesting more oversight and transparency from hedge fund managers. Institutional investors such as corporate and public pension plans, endowments and foundations are demanding more portfolio transparency, more liquidity, more detailed risk reporting, more independent fund governance, and more sophisticated compliance protocols within advisory firms. In the wake of 2007-2009, with lawsuits against Madoff's fund clients still pending and the global economy still in disarray, institutional investors are more aware than ever of their investment risks. Perhaps skeptical of the efficacy of regulation, they are making their own demands on hedge fund managers. In light of the regulatory and market forces

---

26. Global Assets: Hedge fund assets pick up again as momentum builds, HedgeFund Intelligence (April 12, 2013), *available at* http://www.hedgefundintelligence.com/IssueArticle/3189486/GLOBAL-ASSETS-Hedge-fund-assets-pick-up-again-as-momentum-builds.html?ls=GR_Top_site.

27. Discussing in March 2013 the CFTC's receipt of swaps data required to be reported beginning January 1, 2013, CFTC Commissioner Scott O'Malia noted that "the Commission's progress in understanding and utilizing the data in its current form and with its current technology is not going well. The Commission now receives data on thousands of swaps each day. So far, however, none of our computer programs loads this data without crashing." The Financial Times Limited (Mar. 19, 2013).

at work, Commissioner Schapiro's 2011 observation that hedge fund managers conduct their work "under the radar and outside the vision of regulators" seems to look back to a distant era.

§ 1.3 Glossary

Depending on the context, we use "limited partnership," "limited liability company" and "corporation" interchangeably in referring to hedge funds, and use "investment adviser," "manager", and "general partner" interchangeably in referring to the person or entity that manages a hedge fund. For convenience, we also use the following abbreviations:

Advisers Act	Investment Advisers Act of 1940[28]
CEA	Commodity Exchange Act[29]
CFTC	Commodity Futures Trading Commission
Company Act	Investment Company Act of 1940[30]
CPO	Commodity Pool Operator
CTA	Commodity Trading Adviser
Dodd-Frank Act	Dodd-Frank Wall Street Reform and Protection Act[31]
DOL	Department of Labor
ERISA	Employee Retirement Income Security Act of 1974[32]
Exchange Act	Securities Exchange Act of 1934[33]
FinCEN	Financial Crimes Enforcement Network of the U.S. Department of Treasury
FINRA	Financial Industry Regulatory Authority[34]
FTC	Federal Trade Commission
GAAP	U.S. generally accepted accounting principles

28. 15 U.S.C. §§ 80b-20 *et seq.*
29. 7 U.S.C. §§ 1 *et seq.*
30. 15 U.S.C. §§ 80a-51 *et seq.*
31. Pub. L. 111-203 (July 21, 2010).
32. 29 U.S.C. §§ 1001 *et seq.*
33. 15 U.S.C. §§ 78a *et seq.*
34. In 2007, FINRA was created by the consolidation of the NASD, NASDR and NYSE Member Regulation.

GLBA	Gramm-Leach-Bliley Act (Financial Services Modernization Act of 1999)[35]
IARD	Investment Adviser Registration Depository of FINRA
IRS	Internal Revenue Service
JOBS Act	Jumpstart Our Business Startups Act[36]
NASD	National Association of Securities Dealers, Inc.[37]
NASDR	National Association of Securities Dealers Regulation, Inc.[38]
NFA	National Futures Association
NYSE	New York Stock Exchange, Inc.
SEC	Securities and Exchange Commission
SEC-Exempt Adviser	An investment adviser exempt from registration with the SEC[39]
Securities Act	Securities Act of 1933[40]
Tax Code	Internal Revenue Code of 1986[41]

All footnote references in this book to "C.F.R." (the Code of Federal Regulations) or "U.S.C." (the United States Code), as well as footnote references to state statutes, regulations or rules, are to those most recently published before this edition was prepared in early 2013. The reader should consider any changes or amendments in later publications of those materials.

35. Pub. L. No. 106-102, 114 stat. 3928 (codified as amended in scattered sections of 12 U.S.C. and 15 U.S.C.).

36. Pub. L. 112-106 (Apr. 5, 2012).

37. *See* note 34, *supra*.

38. *Id.*

39. *See* § 2.1.2, *infra*.

40. 15 U.S.C. §§ 77a *et. seq.*

41. 26 U.S.C. § 1 *et. seq.*

CHAPTER **2**

Investment Adviser Registration and Regulation

§ 2.1 Federal Definition of "Investment Adviser"

The Advisers Act defines "investment adviser" as any person (whether a natural person or an entity) who for compensation is engaged in the business of advising others or issuing reports or analyses regarding securities.[1] Many financial planners, pension consultants and agents (for example, of athletes or entertainers) are investment advisers.[2]

Whether a person is "in the business" depends on the frequency and regularity with which that person gives advice about securities or engages in other advisory activities. A person giving advice about securities will be deemed to be in the business unless the advice is solely incidental to a nonadvisory business, the advice does not specify particular securities, and the person does not receive special compensation for the advice.[3] Investment advice need not be a person's primary or even a major activity for that person to be in the business of providing investment advice.[4]

"Compensation" includes any economic benefit a person receives, whether advisory fees, commissions on the sale of financial products, or indirect economic or other benefits, including fees or benefits received from sources other than the recipient of the advice. If an adviser receives compensation for providing several types of services to clients, it will be deemed to receive compensation for investment advisory services if the services it provides include investment advisory services.[5]

"Securities" include any note, stock, treasury stock, security future, bond, debenture, evidence of indebtedness, certificate of interest or participation in any profit-sharing agreement, collateral trust certificate, preorganization certificate or subscription, transferable share, investment contract, voting trust certificate, certificate of deposit for a security, fractional undivided interest in oil, gas or

---

1. Advisers Act § 202(a)(11), 15 U.S.C. § 80b-2(a)(11).
2. *Id.*
3. Advisers Act Release No. 1092 (Oct. 8, 1987), 52 F.R. 38,400 (Oct. 16, 1987).
4. *Id.*
5. *Id.*

other mineral rights, or put, call, straddle, option or privilege on any security or group or index of securities or entered into on a national securities exchange relating to foreign currency, or in general any interest or instrument commonly known as a "security," or any certificate of interest or participation in, temporary or interim certificate for, receipt for, guaranty of, or warrant or right to subscribe to or purchase any of the foregoing.[6] Advice about securities need not relate to specific securities. The advice can be as general as recommending investing in securities rather than other types of investments,[7] market timing,[8] or selecting or evaluating investment advisers.[9]

1. Exclusions from the Investment Adviser Definition

The following persons and entities are not defined as investment advisers under the Advisers Act:[10]

- banks and bank holding companies that are not investment companies, except for banks and bank holding companies, or separately identifiable departments or divisions of banks or bank holding companies, that act as investment advisers to registered investment companies;[11]
- lawyers, accountants, engineers and teachers who give investment advice that is solely incidental to the practice of their respective professions;
- brokers who give investment advice that is solely incidental to their brokerage business and who receive no special compensation for giving investment advice;

---

6. Advisers Act § 202(a)(18), 15 U.S.C. § 80b-2(a)(18).

7. New Directions Group, Inc., SEC No-Action Letter (Mar. 6, 1985, reconsidered and reaffirmed May 2, 1985).

8. Maratta Advisory, Inc., SEC No-Action Letter (July 16, 1981).

9. Greater Cleveland Hospital Ass'n, SEC No-Action Letter (May 11, 1995); Advisers Act Release No. 1092 (Oct. 8, 1987), 52 F.R. 38,400 (Oct. 16, 1987).

10. Advisers Act § 202(a)(11), 15 U.S.C. § 80b-2(a)(11).

11. Advisers Act § 202(a)(11)(A), 15 U.S.C. § 80b-2(a)(11)(A). A "separately identifiable department or division" of a bank is a unit (a) that is under the direct supervision of an officer designated by the bank's board of directors to be responsible for the day-to-day conduct of the bank's investment adviser activities for one or more investment companies, including the supervision of all bank employees performing such activities, and (b) for which all records relating to its investment adviser activities are separately maintained or extractable from the unit's own facilities or the facilities of the bank, and for which the records are so maintained or otherwise accessible to permit independent examination and enforcement by the SEC of the Advisers Act or the Company Act and the rules and regulations thereunder. Advisers Act § 202(a)(26), 15 U.S.C. § 80b-2(a)(26).

- publishers of bona fide newspapers, magazines, or business or financial publications of general and regular circulation that are not primarily vehicles for distributing investment advice;[12] and
- persons whose investment advice relates solely to U.S. government securities (including securities issued by government-sponsored enterprises or federal agencies).

The SEC has provided limited guidance on when investment advice is "solely incidental" to another business. The staff has noted that if a broker establishes a limited partnership and provides investment advice as its general partner, those activities may not be solely incidental to the broker's conduct of a brokerage business.[13] In addition, "special compensation" may include reimbursement for expenses incurred in offering the limited partnership's securities.

In 2005, the SEC adopted Rule 202(a)(11)-1, which excepted from the definition of "investment adviser" certain brokers that provide nondiscretionary advice solely incidental to their brokerage services, regardless of the form of compensation (for example, an asset-based fee versus a fixed fee).[14] Two years later, the D.C. Circuit Court vacated Rule 202(a)(11)-1, agreeing with the Financial Planning Association that the SEC did not have the authority to alter the protections established by Congress under the Advisers Act.[15] The Court ruled that anyone being paid a fee to provide financial advice must make certain disclosures, such as conflicts of interest and the cost structure of the investments or other financial products recommended to clients, and must register as an investment adviser under the Advisers Act.

2. Investment Advisers Exempt from Registration

Some persons that the Advisers Act defines as investment advisers are nevertheless exempt from registration as such under the Advisers Act by virtue of specific exemptions in the Advisers Act and the rules under it (each, an "SEC-Exempt Adviser"). An SEC-Exempt Adviser generally is not subject to the Advisers Act provisions relating to registration, record-keeping or performance

12. *See* Lowe v. SEC, 472 U.S. 181 (1985). The exemption for publishers also extends to the publisher of a website, if the website is bona fide and of general and regular circulation. A website is "bona fide" if it contains disinterested commentary and analysis (that is, the publisher is not encouraging readers to invest in securities in which the publisher has invested or intends to invest) and does not promote a security in which the publisher has an interest or for which the publisher is compensated. A website may not be considered bona fide when the publisher e-mails advice to its subscribers or answers questions in a chatroom. A website may not be of "general and regular" circulation if updates to it are triggered by specific market activity or events affecting or having the ability to affect the securities industry. *See* SEC v. Park (a/k/a "Tokyo Joe"), 99 F. Supp. 2d 889 (N.D. Ill. 2000).

13. John Terwilliger, SEC No-Action Letter (June 27, 1977).

14. Advisers Act Rule 202(a)(11)-1, 17 C.F.R. § 275.202(a)(11)-1.

15. Financial Planning Association v. Securities and Exchange Commission, 375 U.S. App. D.C. 389 (D.C. Cir. 2007).

fees, but is subject to the anti-fraud provisions of Advisers Act section 206.[16] Persons that are not defined as investment advisers are not, however, subject to Advisers Act section 206.[17] The activities of both SEC-Exempt Advisers and persons excluded from the definition of "investment adviser" are subject to other federal securities laws and regulations, such as Rule 10b-5[18] under the Exchange Act. The categories of SEC-Exempt Adviser are described below.

i. Intrastate Investment Advisers

An investment adviser is an SEC-Exempt Adviser if all of its clients are residents of the state in which it maintains its principal office and place of business and it does not advise about securities listed or admitted to unlisted trading privileges on any national securities exchange.[19]

ii. Investment Advisers with Only Insurance Company Clients

An investment adviser whose only clients are insurance companies is an SEC-Exempt Adviser.[20]

iii. Other Organizations

Charitable and religions organizations and some non-U.S. advisers that conduct no activities in the United States are SEC-Exempt Advisers.[21]

iv. Exempt Reporting Advisers

The Dodd-Frank Act[22] repealed section 203(b)(3) of the Advisers Act, which had exempted from registration certain private advisers, and replaced that exemption with new, more limited exemptions for investment advisers to venture capital funds, investment advisers that solely advise private funds and that manage less than $150,000,000 (the "Private Fund Adviser Exemption"), and certain foreign private investment advisers.

The Dodd-Frank Act defines "private fund"[23] as a fund that would be an investment company, as defined in Company Act section 3, but for Company Act section 3(c)(1) or 3(c)(7). Under this definition, most hedge funds, private equity funds and venture capital funds are private funds. Private fund advisers and venture capital fund advisers (as defined below and, together, "Exempt Reporting Advisers") are exempt from SEC registration. Exempt Reporting

16. *See* §§ 2.7.1, 8.4, 9.3.1 and 9.4, *infra*. Exempt reporting advisers are subject to certain reporting requirements; *see* § 2.1.2.iv, *infra*.

17. *See* § 2.1.1, *supra*.

18. 17 C.F.R. § 240.10b-5. *See* Chapter 6, *infra*.

19. Advisers Act § 203(b)(1), 15 U.S.C. § 80b-3(b)(1).

20. Advisers Act § 203(b)(2), 15 U.S.C. § 80b-3(b)(2).

21. Advisers Act § 203(b)(4), 203(b)(5), 203(a), 15 U.S.C. §§ 80b-3(b)(4), 80b-3(b)(5), § 80b-3(a); Advisers Act Release No. 1710 (Mar. 27, 1998), 63 F.R. 14,806 (Mar. 23, 1998); 1 E. Greene, et al., *U.S. Regulation of the International Securities and Derivatives Markets* (9th ed. 2009), at § 11.03[3][b].

22. The Dodd-Frank Wall Street Reform and Consumer Protection Act, Pub. L. 111-203, 124 Stat. 1376 (July 21, 2010) (codified in various sections of the U.S. Code).

23. Advisers Act § 202(a)(29), 15 U.S.C. 80b-2(a)(29).

Advisers are nevertheless required to file information reports with the SEC and remain subject to SEC examination, the anti-fraud provisions of Advisers Act section 206 and Advisers Act Rule 206(4)-5, which prohibits certain advisers from engaging in pay-to-play practices.[24]

a. Venture Capital Fund Advisers

The Dodd-Frank Act amended Advisers Act section 203,[25] by adding new subsection (l) exempting from SEC registration investment advisers that manage only venture capital funds. A "venture capital fund" is defined as a private fund that:

- invests no more than 20 percent of its total capital in assets other than qualifying investments[26] and short-term holdings,
- is not leveraged (other than short-term borrowing no greater than 15 percent of the fund's total capital and with a nonrenewable term of no longer than 120 days),
- does not offer its investors liquidity rights except in extraordinary circumstances,
- is not registered under the Company Act and has not elected to be treated as a business development company, and
- represents that it follows a venture capital strategy (as determined by all of the statements and omissions made by the fund).[27]

Under a grandfather provision, a preexisting private fund may be regarded as a venture capital fund if it (i) represented to initial investors that it was a venture capital fund, (ii) sold securities to at least 1 investor before December 31, 2010, and (iii) does not sell securities or accept capital commitments after July 21, 2011. A grandfathered fund would thus include any fund that has accepted all capital commitments by July 21, 2011, (including capital commitments from existing and new investors) even if none of the capital commitments has been called by then.

---

24. Advisers Act § 204(b), 15 U.S.C. 80b-4(b); Advisers Act Rules 204-1, 204-2, 204-3 and 206(4)-5, 17 C.F.R. §§ 275.204-1, 275.204-2, 275.204-3 and 275.206(4)-5. The North American Securities Administrators Association ("NASAA") has proposed a model rule similarly exempting such advisers at the state level. *See* § 2.3.2, *infra*.

25. 15 U.S.C. § 80b-3.

26. Advisers Act Rule 203(l)-1, 17 C.F.R. § 275.203(l)-1, defines "qualifying investment" as an equity security issued by (a) a qualifying portfolio company that has been directly acquired from the qualifying portfolio company, (b) a qualifying portfolio company in exchange for an equity security issued by the qualifying portfolio company described in the preceding clause (a), or (c) a company of which a qualifying portfolio company is a majority owned subsidiary or predecessor company, if acquired in exchange for an equity security described in the preceding clause (a), or (b). Rule 203(l)-1 also defines "qualifying portfolio company" as any company that (a) when the private fund invests, is not (and is not in a control relationship with) a reporting or foreign traded company, (b) does not borrow in connection with the private fund's investment, and (c) is not an investment company, private fund or commodity pool.

27. Advisers Act Rule 203(l)-1, 17 C.F.R. § 275.203(l)-1.

b. Private Fund Advisers

Advisers Act Rule 203(m)-1[28] exempts from registration an investment adviser solely to private funds, with its principal office in the United States and with aggregate assets under management of less than $150,000,000. An investment adviser that has 1 or more clients that are not private funds is not eligible for the exemption.[29] A non-U.S. investment adviser may rely on the exemption, if all of its clients that are U.S. persons[30] are qualifying private funds.

In calculating assets under management, an adviser must, among other things:

- include all proprietary assets, assets managed without receiving compensation and non-U.S. clients' assets,
- include the value of the assets (including nonsecurities) of any private fund to which the adviser provides continuous and regular supervisory or management services,
- include uncalled capital commitments of each such private fund,
- value private fund assets at fair value,
- value private fund assets on a gross basis (that is, without deducting any outstanding indebtedness (such as margin balances) and other accrued but unpaid liabilities), and
- if providing subadvisory services to a private fund, include only the portion of the private fund assets under management for which the adviser provides subadvisory services.

c. Reporting Requirements

Each Exempt Reporting Adviser is required to file with the SEC reports on Part 1A of Form ADV, disclosing organizational and operational information, including:

- Item 1 - basic identifying information about the Exempt Reporting Adviser and its owners or affiliates,
- Item 2B - basis for exemption from registration,

---

28. 17 C.F.R. § 275.203(m)-1.

29. The adopting release notes that, depending on facts and circumstances, the SEC may view 2 or more separately formed advisory entities that each has less than $150,000,000 in private fund assets under management as a single adviser for purposes of assessing the availability of the exemption. Likewise, whether a single-investor fund could be a private fund for purposes of the exemption depends on the facts and circumstances; an adviser could not convert client accounts to single-investor funds in order to avoid registration. On the other hand, a fund that seeks to raise capital from multiple investors but has only a single, initial investor for a period of time could be a private fund, as could a fund in which all but 1 of the investors have redeemed their assets. Advisers Act Release IA-3221, 76 F.R. 42950 (July 19, 2011), notes 314 and 506, and notes 323-325 and accompanying text.

30. Advisers Act Rule 203(m)-1, 17 C.F.R. § 275.203(m)-1, defines "United States person" by incorporating the definition of "U.S. person" in Regulation S under the Securities Act; *see* § 5.4.3.iii, *infra*.

- Item 3 - form of organization,
- Item 6 - details regarding the adviser's and its affiliates' other business activities,
- Item 7 - financial industry affiliations and private funds managed,
- Item 10 - the identities of the Exempt Reporting Adviser's direct and indirect owners and control persons,
- Item 11 - disciplinary actions against the Exempt Reporting Adviser and its employees, and
- Schedules A, B, C and D (which include ownership information).

A private fund adviser that has complied with all of its reporting obligations as an Exempt Reporting Adviser may continue to rely on the exemption for up to 90 days after filing its annual updating amendment indicating that it has $150,000,000 or more in assets under management. This 90-day transition period is not available, however, to an investment adviser that otherwise would not qualify for the Rule 203(m)-1 exemption, including an investment adviser relying on the venture capital adviser exemption. An investment adviser seeking to rely on the venture capital adviser exemption may not accept a client that is not a venture capital fund without first registering under the Advisers Act. Similarly, the transition period is not available to an investment adviser relying on the private fund adviser exemption that takes on a client that is not a private fund.

v. *Foreign Private Advisers*

A "foreign private adviser"[31] is any investment adviser that:

- has no place of business in the United States,
- has, in total, fewer than 15 clients in the United States and investors in the United States in private funds advised by the investment adviser,[32]
- has aggregate assets under management attributable to clients in the United States and investors in the United States in private funds advised by the investment adviser of less than $25,000,000, and
- neither holds itself out generally to the public in the United States as an investment adviser nor acts as an investment adviser to an investment company or a business development company.

"Investor" includes any person that would be included in determining the number of beneficial owners of the outstanding securities of a private fund under Company Act section 3(c)(1) or determining whether the outstanding

---

31. Advisers Act § 202(a)(30), 15 U.S.C. § 80b-2(a)(30).

32. An investment adviser need not count a private fund as a client if the investment adviser counted any investor in the private fund as an investor in the private fund for purposes of determining the availability of the exemption. Advisers Act Rules 202(a)(30)-1(b)(4) and 202(a)(30)-1(c)(2), 17 C.F.R. § 275.202(a)(30)-1(b)(4) and 275.202(a)(30)-1(c)(2). Likewise, an investment adviser is not required to count a person as an investor if the investment adviser counts such person as a client of the investment adviser. Advisers Act Rule 202(a)(30)-1(b)(5), 17 C.F.R. § 275.202(a)(30)-1(b)(5).

securities of a private fund are owned exclusively by qualified purchasers under Company Act section 3(c)(7).[33] A beneficial owner of short-term paper issued by the private fund also is an investor, however, notwithstanding that holders of short-term paper need not be counted for purposes of Company Act section 3(c)(1).[34] "Knowledgeable employees" are not treated as investors.[35]

To avoid double-counting, an investment adviser may treat as a single investor any investor in 2 or more private funds advised by the investment adviser. The investment adviser to a master fund in a master-feeder arrangement would treat as investors all of the investors in any feeder fund formed or operated for the purpose of investing in the master fund, instead of counting only the feeder funds, which act as conduits. In addition, an investment adviser must count as an investor an owner of a total return swap on a private fund, because that arrangement effectively provides the risks and rewards of investing in the private fund to the swap owner.[36] Assets under management are determined by reference to an investment adviser's regulatory assets under management, which are reported in Item 5 of Form ADV.[37]

vi. Family Offices

The Dodd-Frank Act and SEC rules adopted under it exclude family offices from the definition of "investment adviser" in the Advisers Act.[38] The exclusion contains 3 general conditions:

- it is limited to family offices that provide advice about securities only to family clients;
- it requires that family clients wholly own the family office and family members or family entities control the family office; and
- it precludes a family office from holding itself out to the public as an investment adviser.

"Family clients" include current and former family members, certain employees of the family office (and, under certain circumstances, former employees), charities funded exclusively by family clients, estates of current and former family members or key employees, trusts existing for the sole current benefit of family clients or, if both family clients and charitable and nonprofit organizations are the sole current beneficiaries, trusts funded solely by family clients, revocable trusts funded solely by family clients, certain key employee trusts, and companies wholly owned exclusively by, and operated for the sole benefit of, family clients (with limited exceptions).

---

33. Advisers Act Rule 202(a)(30)-1(c)(2), 17 C.F.R. § 275.202(a)(30)-1(c)(2); 15 U.S.C. §§ 80a-3(c)(1) and 80a-3(c)(7).

34. *Id.*

35. Advisers Act Release No. 1A-3222, F.R. 39646 (July 6, 2011).

36. *Id.*

37. *See*, § 2.2.3, *infra*.

38. Advisers Act § 202(a)(11), 15 U.S.C. § 80b-2(a)(11); Advisers Act Rule 202(a)(11)(G)-1, 17 C.F.R. § 275.202(a)(11)(G)-1.

"Family members" include all lineal descendants of a common ancestor (living or deceased), as well as current and former spouses or spousal equivalents of those decendents, if the common ancestor is no more than 10 generations removed from the youngest generation of family members. All children by adoption and current and former stepchildren also are considered family members. Involuntary transfers of assets to a person who is not a family client does not cause the family office to lose its exclusion; a family office may continue to provide advice with respect to such assets for a transition period of up to 1 year. The exclusion does not extend to family offices serving multiple families.[39]

§ 2.2 Federal and State Registration of Investment Advisers

1. Mandatory SEC Registration

The Investment Advisers Supervision Coordination Act, a part of the National Securities Markets Improvement Act of 1996 ("NSMIA"),[40] allocates regulatory responsibilities for investment advisers between the SEC and the states.[41] NSMIA generally prohibits an investment adviser regulated by the state in which it maintains its principal office and place of business from registering with the SEC unless it has at least $25,000,000 of assets under management. NSMIA preempts certain state laws regulating investment advisers registered with the SEC. Consequently, NSMIA makes the states the primary regulators of smaller investment advisers (that is, investment advisers with less than $25,000,000 in assets under management), and the SEC the primary regulator of larger investment advisers.

The Dodd-Frank Act delineated a new category of midsized investment advisers and shifted primary responsibility for their oversight to the states by prohibiting a midsized investment adviser from registering with the SEC if it has assets under management between $25,000,000 and $100,000,000 and is required to be registered as an investment adviser in the state in which it maintains its principal office and place of business and, if registered, is subject to examination as an investment adviser by state investment adviser regulatory authorities.[42] A midsized investment adviser must register with the SEC if (a) it is not required to register with the securities administrator (or any agency or office performing like functions) of the state in which it maintains its principal

39. *Id.*

40. Pub. L. No. 104-290, 110 Stat. 3416 (1996) (codified in various sections of the U.S. Code).

41. 15 U.S.C. § 80b-3a.

42. Advisers Act § 203A(a)(2)(B), 15 U.S. C. 80b-3a(a)(2)(B). The laws of the state where an investment adviser has its principal office and place of business may exempt the investment adviser from state registration, even if the investment adviser's assets under management are between $25,000,000 and $100,000,000. In that case, the investment adviser may be required to register with the SEC.

office and place of business; or (b) if registered with that state, the investment adviser would not be subject to examination as an investment adviser by such securities administrator.[43] In addition, an investment adviser must register with the SEC if it:

- has any client that is an investment company or a business development company;[44]
- maintains its principal place of business in a state that does not require registration of investment advisers (currently, only Wyoming);[45]
- maintains its principal place of business outside the United States, but has U.S. clients;[46]
- is a pension consultant with respect to assets of plans (employee benefit plans, governmental plans and church plans under certain sections of ERISA) with an aggregate value of at least $200,000,000 as of the end of the investment adviser's last fiscal year;[47] or
- is affiliated (in a control relationship) with an SEC-registered investment adviser, with which it shares a principal office and place of business.[48]

"Control" is the power to direct or cause the direction of the management or policies of the investment adviser, whether through ownership of securities, by contract or otherwise. A person or entity that directly or indirectly owns at least 25 percent of an investment adviser's voting securities or is entitled to at least 25 percent of its profits is presumed to control the investment adviser. An investment adviser's "principal office and place of business" is the executive office from which the officers, partners or managers of the investment adviser direct, control and coordinate its activities.[49]

An investment adviser with more than $100,000,000 in assets under management is required to register as such with the SEC, unless it is eligible for an exemption.[50]

---

43. In 2011, the SEC asked all states to inform it if they subject registered investment advisers to examination. By mid-2011, New York, Wyoming and Minnesota had not responded. See Advisers Act Release No. IA-3221, 76 F.R. 42950 (July 19, 2011). Consequently, an investment adviser with its principal place of business in New York, Wyoming or Minnesota and with assets under management between $25,000,000 and $100,000,000 must register with the SEC.

44. Advisers Act § 203A(a), 15 U.S.C. § 80b-3a(a). Advisers Act Rule 203A-1(a), 17 C.F.R. § 275.203A-1(a).

45. Advisers Act § 203A(a)(1), 15 U.S.C. § 80b-3(a)(1).

46. *See* Advisers Act Release IA-3222, F.R. 39646 (July 6, 2011).

47. Advisers Act Rule 203A-2(a), 17 C.F.R. § 275.203A-2(a). In determining the aggregate value of plan assets, the investment adviser may include only that portion of the plan's assets for which the investment adviser provides investment advice, including any advice with respect to the selection of an investment adviser to manage the assets. *Id.* As used in Rule 203A-2(b), "assets of plans" is not limited to securities portfolios.

48. Advisers Act Rule 203A-2(b), 17 C.F.R. § 275.203A-2(b).

49. *Id.*; Advisers Act Rule 203A-3(c), 17 C.F.R. § 275.203A-3(c).

50. *See* § 2.1.2, *supra*.

2. Optional SEC Registration

An investment adviser that is not otherwise required to register with the SEC and that has assets under management between $100,000,000 and $110,000,000 may, but is not required to, register with the SEC.[51] If an SEC-registered investment adviser's assets under management, as reported on its annual updating amendment to its Form ADV,[52] are less than $90,000,000, and it is not otherwise eligible to register with the SEC, it must withdraw from SEC registration within 180 days, unless its assets under management increase to at least $90,000,000 within the 180-day period.[53]

An investment adviser may elect to register with the SEC if it would otherwise be required to register as an investment adviser with at least 15 states.[54] Such an investment adviser must maintain a record of the states in which it would be required to register for at least 5 years from the date on which the application or amendment is filed.[55] An investment adviser relying on the rule must withdraw from SEC registration when it is no longer required to be registered with 15 states.[56]

A newly formed investment adviser that reasonably expects to be eligible for SEC registration within 120 days of the effective date of its registration may elect to register with the SEC.[57] If the investment adviser's assets under management are not at least $100,000,000 within 120 days after its SEC registration becomes effective, it must withdraw its SEC registration.[58]

Any investment adviser that does not register with the SEC may be required to register under applicable state law. An investment adviser that is eligible but not required to register with the SEC may desire to avoid SEC registration to reduce its exposure to the SEC's inspections and regulations. Alternatively, some investment advisers choose to register with the SEC to gain whatever marketing cachet SEC registration might afford or to avoid potentially more burdensome or less predictable state regulation. Under no circumstances, however, may an investment adviser ever claim that it has been sponsored, recommended or approved, or that the investment adviser's abilities or qualifications have in any

---

51. Advisers Act Rule 203A-1(a)(1), 17 C.F.R. § 275.203A-1(a)(1).
52. *See* §§ 2.4.1 and 2.5.1, *infra*.
53. Advisers Act Rule 203A-1(b)(2), 17 C.F.R. § 275.203A-1(b)(2).
54. Advisers Act Rule 203A-2(d), 17 C.F.R. § 275.203A-2(d).
55. *Id.* In its application or amendment, the investment adviser must undertake to withdraw from SEC registration if it is required to register in fewer than 15 states at the time of filing its next annual updating amendment.
56. Advisers Act Release No. IA-3221, 76 F.R. 42950 (July 19, 2011).
57. Advisers Act Rule 203A-2(c), 17 C.F.R. § 275.203A-2(c). In its initial application, the investment adviser must undertake to withdraw from SEC registration if it is not eligible for SEC registration on the 120th day after its SEC registration becomes effective. Such an investment adviser may choose to register under applicable state law during the 120-day period if it is not certain whether it will be eligible to be SEC-registered at the end of the 120-day period, because no grace period for state law registration is provided at the end of that period.
58. *Id.*

respect been passed on, by the United States, the SEC, any other federal agency or any of their officers.[59]

3. Assets Under Management

For the purpose of determining whether an investment adviser must register with the SEC or under state law, the investment adviser's assets under management include all securities portfolios with respect to which it provides "continuous and regular supervisory or management services."[60] A "securities portfolio" is an account or accounts of which securities represent at least 50 percent of the total value.[61] Cash and cash equivalents may be treated as securities for this purpose.[62] The entire value of the account or accounts, and not only the value of the securities portion, is included in determining the amount of the investment adviser's assets under management.[63]

Accounts over which an investment adviser has discretionary authority and for which it provides ongoing supervisory or management services, as reported on the investment adviser's Form ADV, must be included in its assets under management.[64] Nondiscretionary advisory arrangements may also be required to be included under specified circumstances.[65]

Assets under management include accounts of clients that do not pay fees to the investment adviser.[66] For example, a hedge fund must include capital provided by the investment adviser, its affiliates, family members and other investors for whom fees are waived. Assets under management also include assets of clients who are not U.S. persons.[67] An investment adviser must calculate its assets under management on a gross basis, without deducting any outstanding indebtedness or other accrued but unpaid liabilities.[68] Accordingly, an investment adviser may not deduct accrued fees, expenses or the amount of any borrowing.

An investment adviser must include the value of any private fund over which it exercises continuous and regular supervisory or management services, regardless of the nature of the assets held by the private fund. If an investment adviser provides continuous and regular supervisory or management services for only part of a securities portfolio (for example, as one of several subadvisers to a hedge fund), the investment adviser should include in its assets under management only the portion of the portfolio with respect to which it provides such services.[69] An investment adviser also must include the amount of any

59. Advisers Act § 208, 15 U.S.C. § 80b-8.
60. Advisers Act § 203A(a)(3), 15 U.S.C. § 80b-3A(a)(3).
61. Form ADV, Instructions for Part 1A, Item 5(b)(1).
62. *Id.*
63. *Id.*
64. *Id.*
65. *Id.*
66. Form ADV, Instructions for Part 1A, Item 5.b(1).
67. *Id.*; Form ADV, Appendix C, Item 43.
68. Form ADV, Instructions for Part 1A, Item 5.b(2).
69. *Id.*

uncalled capital commitments made to a private fund that it manages.[70] The SEC reasoned in the adopting release that investment advisers to such funds typically earn fees based on the total amount of capital commitments.[71] An investment adviser must use the market value of private fund assets, or the fair value of private fund assets where market value is unavailable.[72]

4. Transition between State and SEC Registration

Form ADV requires an investment adviser registering with the SEC to specify the amount of assets it manages.[73] As discussed below,[74] an SEC-registered investment adviser must amend and update its Form ADV within 90 days after the end of each fiscal year.[75] If an SEC-registered investment adviser files an annual updating amendment showing that its assets under management have fallen below $90,000,000, so that it is no longer eligible for SEC registration, it must file Form ADV-W[76] to withdraw from SEC registration within 180 days of the end of its preceding fiscal year, and it must register with the applicable state authority, if required by state law.[77] If the investment adviser's assets under management increase to more than $90,000,000 during this 180-day period, it may remain SEC-registered.[78]

An investment adviser that is not otherwise subject to mandatory SEC registration becomes eligible to register with the SEC if its assets under management increase to $100,000,000.[79] A state-registered investment adviser that reports year-end assets under management of $110,000,000 or more must register with the SEC within 90 days of such filing unless it is an SEC-Exempt Adviser.[80] If the investment adviser's assets under management decrease to less than $100,000,000 within that 90-day period, it is prohibited from registering with the SEC.

5. State Regulation of Investment Adviser Representatives

NSMIA established that state laws requiring the registration, licensing or qualification of an investment adviser or supervised person of an investment adviser may not be applied to an SEC-registered investment adviser or its supervised persons, except that a state may license, register or otherwise qualify any investment adviser representative who has a place of business in

---

70. Form ADV, Instructions for Part 1A, Item 5.b(1).
71. Advisers Act Release No. 1A-3221, 76 F.R. 42956 (July 19, 2011).
72. *Id.*
73. *See* §§ 2.4.1 and 2.5.1, *infra*.
74. *Id.*
75. Advisers Act Rule 204-1(a)(1), 17 C.F.R. § 275.204-1(a)(1).
76. 17 C.F.R. § 279.2; *but see* § 2.2.1, note 43, *supra*.
77. Advisers Act Rule 203A-1(a)(2), 17 C.F.R. § 275.203A-1(a)(2).
78. *Id.*
79. Advisers Act Rule 203A-1(a)(1), 17 C.F.R. § 275.203A-1(a)(1).
80. Advisers Act Rule 203A-1(b)(1), 17 C.F.R. § 275.203A-1(b)(1).

that state.[81] An "investment adviser representative" of an investment adviser is a supervised person of the investment adviser (a) who has more than 5 clients who are natural persons (other than "excepted persons") and (b) more than 10 percent of whose clients are natural persons (other than excepted persons).[82] An investment adviser that only manages 1 hedge fund would not have any investment adviser representatives, since the hedge fund counts as a single client and thus fewer than 10 percent of the investment adviser's clients are natural persons. An investment adviser that manages separate accounts may, however, have investment adviser representatives.

A "supervised person" is a partner, officer, director or employee of an investment adviser, or other person who provides investment advice on behalf of the investment adviser and is subject to the supervision and control of the investment adviser.[83] A supervised person is not an investment adviser representative of an investment adviser if the supervised person (a) does not on a regular basis solicit, meet with or communicate with clients of the investment adviser, or (b) provides only impersonal investment advice (advice that does not purport to meet the objectives or needs of specific individuals or accounts).[84] A "place of business" is an office at which the investment adviser representative regularly provides or is held out to the public as providing investment advisory services, or solicits, meets with or otherwise communicates with clients.[85]

An "excepted person" is a client who is a natural person and (a) has at least $1,000,000 under the investment adviser's management, (b) has a net worth (together with his or her spouse) of more than $2,000,000, (c) is an executive officer, director, trustee or general partner of the investment adviser, (d) is an employee of the investment adviser who participates in the investment activities of the investment adviser as part of his or her regular functions or duties and has been performing such duties or functions for the investment adviser or another investment adviser for at least 12 months, or (e) has (together with his or her spouse) at least $5,000,000 in investments.[86] Persons who solicit clients for investment advisers may be investment adviser representatives. Rules of various states define "investment adviser representative" differently, sometimes mirroring the Advisers Act definition, and sometimes not.

6. National *de Minimis* Exemption

Even if an investment adviser is exempt from SEC registration, a state may require the investment adviser to register only if it has a place of business (as defined above) in the state or has more than 5 clients that are residents of

81. Advisers Act § 203A(b)(1), 15 U.S.C. § 80b-3A(b)(1).
82. Advisers Act Rule 203A-3(a)(1), 17 C.F.R. § 275.203A-3(a)(1).
83. Advisers Act § 202(a)(25), 15 U.S.C. § 80b-2(a)(25).
84. Advisers Act Rule 203A-3(a)(2), 17 C.F.R. § 275.203A-3(a)(2).
85. Advisers Act Rule 203A-3(b), 17 C.F.R. § 275.203A-3(b).
86. Advisers Act Rules 203A-3(a)(3)(i) and 205-3(d)(1), 17 C.F.R. §§ 275.203A-3(a)(3)(i) and 275.205-3(d)(1). The definition of "investments" for this purpose is complex. *See* § 3.3.2, *infra*.

the state during any 12-month period.[87] This exemption is not relevant for SEC-registered investment advisers, because a state may not require registration of any investment adviser that is registered or required to be registered with the SEC.[88] It may be useful, however, to an investment adviser that has clients, either limited partnerships or separate accounts, in several states but is not SEC-registered in reliance on an exemption or because it has less than $100,000,000 in assets under management.

7. State Notice Filings

Even an investment adviser that is SEC-registered or exempt from both SEC and state registration may be required to make state notice filings and pay related state fees. State notice filing requirements vary from state to state. Generally, notice filings are made through the IARD system.

§ 2.3 State Requirements

1. Registration

i. Filings

All states (except Wyoming), the District of Columbia and Puerto Rico have registration or licensing requirements for investment advisers. These requirements may include:

- registration or licensing of the investment adviser (unless the investment adviser is SEC-registered);
- notice filings by SEC-registered investment advisers;[89]
- exam requirements for each individual acting as an investment adviser or investment adviser representative; many states require investment adviser representatives to pass either the FINRA Series 65 or Series 66 examination, although many states exempt individuals with certain industry certifications (such as certified financial planners, chartered financial analysts and chartered financial consultants);[90]
- payment of fees for processing the applications;
- certain disclosures to the securities agency or the public;
- registration of branch offices; and
- bonding or minimum net capital.

87. Advisers Act § 222(d), 15 U.S.C. § 80b-18a(d).
88. Advisers Act § 203A(b), 15 U.S.C. § 80b-3(b).
89. *See* § 2.2.7, *supra*.
90. *See, e.g.*, 10 Cal. Code of Reg. § 260.236; N.Y. Gen. Bus. Law § 359-e.

ii. Licensing Period

An investment adviser and its investment adviser representatives ordinarily must renew their registration and licenses annually. In many states, the term is from January 1 through December 31, although some states have different renewal periods.

2. NASAA Model Rule for Exempt Reporting Advisers

In response to the Dodd-Frank Act and the SEC's rules governing Exempt Reporting Advisers,[91] the North American Securities Administrators Association ("NASAA") published for comment a model rule that would exempt from state registration investment advisers to certain types of private funds.[92] As proposed, the model rule would exempt an investment adviser from state registration if (a) neither the investment adviser nor any of its advisory affiliates is subject to a disqualification described in Rule 262 of SEC Regulation A;[93] (2) the private fund adviser files with the state each report and amendment thereto that an Exempt Reporting Adviser is required to file with the SEC pursuant to SEC Rule 204-4;[94] and (3) the private fund adviser pays the specified fees. An investment adviser to a 3(c)(1) Fund[95] that is not a venture capital fund would also be subject to the following requirements:

- the investment adviser must advise only 3(c)(1) Funds (other than venture capital funds) whose outstanding securities (other than short-term paper) are beneficially owned entirely by persons who, after deducting the value of their primary residences from their net worth, would each meet the definition of "qualified client" in SEC Rule 205-3[96] when the interests in the hedge fund are purchased;
- at the time of purchase, the investment adviser must disclose the following in writing to each beneficial owner: (a) that the 3(c)(1) Fund, not the individual beneficial owners, is the investment adviser's client; (b) all services, if any, to be provided to individual beneficial owners; (c) all duties, if any, the investment adviser owes to the beneficial owners; and (d) any other material information affecting the rights or responsibilities of all beneficial owners;
- the investment adviser must obtain annual audited financial statements of the 3(c)(1) Fund and deliver copies of them to each beneficial owner of the 3(c)(1) Fund.

---

91. *See* § 2.1.2.iv, *supra*.

92. *See* www.nasaa.org/wp-content/uploads/2011/08/10-Private_Fund_Adviser_Model_Rule_061311.pdf (last visited May 2, 2013).

93. 17 C.F.R. § 230.262.

94. 17 C.F.R. § 275.204-4.

95. *See* Chapter 3, *infra*.

96. 17 C.F.R. § 275.205-3.

Like an Exempt Reporting Adviser, an investment adviser claiming this exemption would file the report described above through the IARD. An investment adviser to a 3(c)(1) Fund with nonqualified clients would be grandfathered if the 3(c)(1) Fund existed before the effective date of the regulation and, commencing with that date, the 3(c)(1) Fund ceases to accept beneficial owners that are not qualified clients.

Some states, such as California, have proposed rules that follow NASAA's model rule. As a result, in those states, an investment adviser with less than $150,000,000 in regulatory assets under management that only advises private funds (and otherwise meets the requirements of the SEC and state exemptions) could file as an Exempt Reporting Adviser with both its state regulatory authorities and the SEC. Alternatively, if such an investment adviser desires to register with the SEC, it could file as an Exempt Reporting Adviser with the state and register with the SEC.[97]

3. Record-Keeping

States may impose record-keeping requirements.[98] The Advisers Act, however, prohibits a state from imposing requirements related to books, records, net capital or bonding that are beyond the requirements imposed by the state in which an investment adviser is registered and has its principal place of business (as long as the investment adviser complies with its home state's requirements).[99] An investment adviser's principal place of business is the office at which it regularly provides investment advisory services and solicits, meets with, or otherwise communicates with clients.[100]

4. Custody

If an investment adviser has direct or indirect access to client funds or securities, it is considered to have custody[101] of client assets and may be subject to additional state regulatory requirements. For example, the state in which it is registered may require it to maintain specified net capital.[102]

5. Fiduciary Duty

The Advisers Act anti-fraud provisions[103] and most state laws[104] impose on state-registered investment advisers fiduciary duties to their clients.

---

97. *See* § 2.2.1, *supra*.

98. Advisers Act § 222(c) and (d), 15 U.S.C. §§ 80b-18a(c) and (d).

99. Advisers Act § 222(c), 15 U.S.C. § 80b-18a(c).

100. Advisers Act Release No. 1633 (May 15, 1997), 62 F.R. 28,112 (May 22, 1997); 17 C.F.R. § 275.222-1.

101. *See* Chapter 12, *infra*.

102. *See, e.g.*, 10 Cal. Code of Reg. § 260.237.2.

103. Advisers Act § 206, 15 U.S.C. § 80b-6; *see also* SEC v. Capital Gains Research Bureau, Inc., 375 U.S. 180 (1963).

104. *See, e.g.*, 10 Cal. Code of Reg. § 260.238.

6. Inspections

State-registered investment advisers are subject to periodic, sometimes unannounced, inspections by state regulatory authorities, to determine compliance with the applicable licensing, books and records, and anti-fraud requirements.

§ 2.4 SEC and State Registration Processes

1. Federal

An applicant registering as an investment adviser with the SEC (or an exempt reporting adviser) must file an application on Form ADV electronically through the IARD, operated by FINRA,[105] unless the applicant receives a temporary or continuing hardship exemption.[106] Part 1 was revised in 2011 to incorporate changes required by the Dodd-Frank Act.

Form ADV includes substantial disclosure, such as disciplinary information, background information about portfolio managers and controlling persons, fees charged, brokerage allocation practices and other aspects of an investment adviser's business. The Advisers Act does not require an investment adviser or its associated persons to pass any exam or otherwise demonstrate competence to become SEC-registered. It does, however, disqualify an individual from registering with the SEC as an investment adviser or serving as an associated person of an investment adviser if the individual has been convicted of any of several specified crimes, violated federal or state securities laws or filed false or misleading statements with the SEC.[107]

105. Advisers Act Rule 203-1, 17 C.F.R. § 275.203-1. Additional information about filing on the IARD can be obtained at the IARD website, www.iard.com, and at the SEC website, www.sec.gov/iard.

106. Advisers Act Rules 203-1(b) and 203-3, 17 C.F.R. §§ 275.203-1(b) and 275.203-3. An applicant may request a temporary hardship exemption when it experiences unanticipated technical difficulties that prevent it from filing on the IARD system, but the applicant nevertheless must file Form ADV electronically within 7 business days after the filing is due. Advisers Act Rule 203-3(a), 17 C.F.R. § 275.203-3(a). A continuing hardship exemption permits the applicant to submit its Form ADV to FINRA on paper. Advisers Act Rule 203-3(b), 17 C.F.R. § 275.203-3(b). The continuing hardship exemption is available only to small businesses that are able to demonstrate that the electronic filing requirements are prohibitively burdensome or expensive. *Id.* A "small business" for purposes of this exemption is a business that (a) had total assets of less than $5,000,000 on the last day of its most recent fiscal year, (b) is not in control of, controlled by or under common control with another person (other than a natural person) that had total assets of $5,000,000 or more on the last day of that person's most recent fiscal year and (c) is not in control of, controlled by or under common control with another investment adviser that had assets under management of $25,000,000 or more on the last day of that investment adviser's most recent fiscal year. Advisers Act Rule 203-3(b)(5), 17 C.F.R. § 275.203-3(b)(5); Form ADV, General Instructions 17 and 18, *available at* http://www.sec.gov/about/forms/formadv-instructions.pdf.

107. Advisers Act § 203(c)(1)(G), 15 U.S.C. § 80b-3(c)(1)(G). *See* Chapter 8, *infra*.

Part 2 of Form ADV consists of Part 2A and Part 2B. Part 2A is a narrative brochure written in "plain" English.[108] Part 2A is filed with the SEC electronically via the IARD. An investment adviser must deliver a copy of Part 2A to each client before entering into an advisory contract[109] and should also furnish a copy of Part 2A to each prospective investor in a hedge fund that the investment adviser manages.[110] An investment adviser whose Part 2A has materially changed since its last annual updating amendment must deliver to each client, within 120 days after its fiscal year-end, either a current amended Part 2 (which contains a "Material Changes Summary") or a separate document containing the Material Changes Summary and an offer to provide the relevant current Part 2A without charge.[111]

Part 2 of Form ADV also includes a Part 2B supplement for each supervised person that formulates investment advice for and has direct contact with any client of the investment adviser, or who makes discretionary investment decisions for any client (even with no direct contact).[112] New clients must receive the most current version of Part 2B. Existing clients must receive updates of Part 2B only if there are material changes to the disciplinary information. Unlike the Part 2A brochure, Part 2B is not filed through the IARD and thus is not publicly available.

An Exempt Reporting Adviser is not required to prepare and file Part 2.[113]

2. State Laws

Investment advisers registering with state authorities ordinarily complete Form ADV, like SEC-registered investment advisers. Application for state registration or licensing typically includes, in addition to filing Form ADV:

- providing required state-specific forms and evidence of compliance with any examination requirements for investment adviser representatives;
- filing a Form U-4 application for each investment adviser representative who will provide services on behalf of the investment adviser; and
- paying registration fees for the investment adviser and its investment adviser representatives.

---

108. Advisers Act Release No. 3060 (July 28, 2010), 75 F.R. 49,234 (Aug. 12, 2010).

109. Advisers Act Rule 204-3, 17 C.F.R. § 275.204-3. Before the 2010 amendment, an investment adviser was required to offer clients a 5-day termination right if the brochure was not delivered at least 48 hours before entering into the advisory contract.

110. Even though the Form ADV requires an investment adviser to deliver its brochure only to each "client," the instructions state that, as a fiduciary, an investment adviser may be required to deliver similar information to hedge fund investors, which disclosure could be made by delivering Part 2 of Form ADV. Form ADV, Instructions for Part 2A for Form ADV; *see also* Advisers Act Rule 204-3(f), 17 C.F.R § 275.204-3(f).

111. Advisers Act Rule 204-3, 17, C.F.R. § 275.204-3.

112. Form ADV, Part 2B; *see also* Advisers Act Release No. 3060 (July 28, 2010), 75 F.R. 49,234 (Aug. 12, 2010).

113. See § 2.1.2.iv, *supra*.

Some states allow or require an investment adviser registering with them to file Form ADV and Forms U-4 electronically via the IARD. An SEC-registered investment adviser that is required to make a notice filing in a state generally does so by:

- filing a complete copy of its Form ADV as filed with the SEC;
- filing a Form U-4 application for each investment adviser representative who will provide services on behalf of the investment adviser; and
- paying filing fees.

An SEC-registered investment adviser must make any required state notice filings electronically via the IARD, rather than on paper.

§ 2.5 Reporting Requirements and Annual Fees

An investment adviser must update its Form ADV when certain changes occur and at least annually.

1. Federal

An SEC-registered investment adviser must:

- Offer to provide Part 2 of its Form ADV or a brochure containing equivalent information at least annually to each advisory client.[114] The offer should also be made to each investor in a hedge fund that the investment adviser manages. The offer can conveniently be made by including a sentence to that effect in an individual account client's first quarter bill or in a letter to hedge fund investors reporting the preceding year's results.
- Promptly amend its Form ADV if any information provided in response to Item 1, 3, 9 or 11 of Part 1A or Item 1, 2.A through 2.F or 2.I of Part 1B becomes inaccurate in any way, or any information provided in response to Item 4, 8 or 10 of Part 1A or Item 2.G of Part 1B becomes materially inaccurate.[115]
- Amend its Form ADV within 90 days of the end of its fiscal year.[116]
- Promptly amend Part 2 of its Form ADV if any information in Part 2 becomes materially inaccurate.[117]

An Exempt Reporting Adviser must:

- Promptly amend its Form ADV if any information provided in response to Item 1, 3 or 11 of Part 1A becomes inaccurate in any way, or any

114. Advisers Act Rule 204-3(b)(2), 17 C.F.R. § 275.204-3(b)(2).
115. Advisers Act Rule 204-1(a), 17 C.F.R. § 275.204-1.
116. Advisers Act Rule 204-1(a), 17 C.F.R. § 275.204-1(a).
117. Form ADV General Instruction 4, *available at* http://www.sec.gov/about/forms/formadv-instructions.pdf.

information provided in response to Item 10 of Part 1A becomes materially inaccurate.[118]

- Amend its Form ADV within 90 days of the end of its fiscal year.[119]

Amendments to Form ADV are made electronically using the IARD system.

2. States

States may also require annual renewals, amendments and fee payments. For example, California and New York require an investment adviser to pay an annual fee and amend its Form ADV within 90 days of its fiscal year-end and within 30 days after a change occurs.[120]

3. Surprise Inspection by Accountant

If an investment adviser has custody of any of its clients' funds or securities,[121] federal and some states' rules may require the investment adviser's independent accountant to conduct annually a surprise inspection of the investment adviser to verify the funds and securities held by it in accounts within its custody. The accountant must file a report of such inspection on Form ADV-E[122] with the SEC or the appropriate state regulatory authority.[123]

4. Filings Required Under the Exchange Act

If an investment adviser, its control persons or its discretionary clients acquire security positions of a certain size, they may be required to report such positions to the SEC, and possibly also to the issuer and the exchange on which the securities are listed.[124]

§ 2.6 Disclosure of Financial and Disciplinary Information

Federal and state anti-fraud laws apply to hedge fund managers and other investment advisers whether or not registered with the SEC or in any state.[125] The Advisers Act and some state laws obligate an investment adviser to disclose facts relating to legal or disciplinary events that occurred in the last 10 years and that are material to an evaluation of the investment adviser's business or

118. *Id.* Advisers Act Rule 204-1, 17 C.F.R. § 275.204-1.

119. *Id.*

120. 10 Cal. Code of Reg. § 260.231(e); 13 N.Y. C.C.R. § 11.4(f).

121. *See* Chapter 12, *infra*.

122. Advisers Act Release No. 1181 (July 26, 1989), 54 F.R. 32,049 (Aug. 4, 1989).

123. Advisers Act Rule 206(4)-2(i), 17 C.F.R. § 275.206(4)-2(i); *see also* 10 Cal. Code of Reg. § 260.237(e).

124. *See* § 13.1, *infra*.

125. *See, e.g.*, Advisers Act § 206, 15 U.S.C. § 80b-6; Advisers Act Release No. 2203, 2003 SEC LEXIS 2958 (Dec. 15, 2003).

the integrity of its management.[126] If an investment adviser has discretionary authority over client accounts, has custody or control of clients' funds or securities, or requires payment of fees of more than $1,200 6 months or more in advance, it must also disclose to any client or prospective client all material facts about its financial condition that are likely to impair its ability to meet its contractual commitments to its clients.[127]

§ 2.7 Fiduciary Duties; Policies and Procedures

1. General Duty

The federal fiduciary duty requirements apply to all investment advisers, whether or not registered with the SEC or in any state. An investment adviser has a fiduciary duty to act in the best interests of its clients, to put its clients' interests before its own interests, and to deal fairly with its clients in all respects.[128] An investment adviser's fiduciary duties under federal law include, among other things:

- having a reasonable, independent basis for its investment advice;[129]
- obtaining best execution for client securities transactions if the investment adviser determines or recommends the broker used;[130] and
- being loyal to clients.[131]

An investment adviser has a duty to provide advice that is suitable for the client based on the investment adviser's knowledge of the client, and the investment adviser is obligated to inquire about the client's investment objectives, financial situation and needs.[132] An investment adviser may not exceed the authority the client grants it.[133] An investment adviser should not cause trading in a client's account that is excessive in magnitude and frequency in view of the financial resources, investment objectives and other characteristics of the client.[134]

---

126. Form ADV, Instructions for Part 1A, Item 11, Part 1B, Item 2, Part 2A, Item 9, Part 2b, Item 3.

127. Form ADV, Instructions for Part 2A, Item 18.

128. For example, an investment adviser may breach its fiduciary duty by granting special rights to some investors, without informing others. *See* § 6.6, *infra.*

129. Advisers Act Release No. 897, 1984 SEC LEXIS 2429 (Jan. 11, 1984); Advisers Act Release No. 1689, 1997 SEC LEXIS 2628 (Dec. 23, 1997).

130. *See* § 14.1, *infra.*

131. Advisers Act Release No. 40 (Feb. 4, 1945), 11 F.R. 10,997 (Feb. 5, 1945); Advisers Act Release No. 232, 1968 SEC LEXIS 251 (Oct. 16, 1968).

132. *In re* John G. Kinnard & Co., Inc., SEC No Action Letter (Oct. 30, 1973); *see, e.g.*, 10 Cal. Code of Reg. § 260.238(a).

133. *See, e.g.*, 10 Cal. Code of Reg. §§ 260.238(b), (c) and (d).

134. *See, e.g.*, 10 Cal. Code of Reg. § 260.238(e).

States may impose additional duties on investment advisers registered under state laws.[135] For example, a California-registered investment adviser may not (a) borrow money or securities from a client unless the client is a broker-dealer, an affiliate of the investment adviser or a financial institution engaged in the business of lending funds or securities,[136] (b) lend money to a client unless the investment adviser is a financial institution engaged in a lending business or the client is an affiliate of the investment adviser,[137] or (c) provide a report or recommendation to any client prepared by someone other than the investment adviser without disclosing this fact (although this prohibition does not apply if the investment adviser uses published research reports or statistical analyses to render advice or if the investment adviser orders such reports in the normal course of providing service).[138]

Advisers Act Rule 206(4)-8[139] makes it a fraudulent, deceptive or manipulative act, practice, or course of business for any investment adviser to a pooled investment vehicle to (a) make any untrue statement of material fact or omit to state a material fact necessary to make the statement made, in the light of the circumstances under which it was made, not misleading to any investor or prospective investor, or (b) otherwise engage in any act, practice or course of business that is fraudulent, deceptive or manipulative with respect to any investor or prospective investor in the pooled investment vehicle. The Rule is aimed at addressing the perceived regulatory gap left by a U.S. District Court's 2006 decision that vacated the SEC's broader registration rule.[140] Rule 206(4)-8 applies to any investment adviser to a pooled investment vehicle, whether or not registered or required to be registered under the Advisers Act or state law.

"Pooled investment vehicle" includes any investment company under Company Act section 3(a) or any company excluded by Company Act section 3(c)(1) or 3(c)(7).[141] Unlike other federal anti-fraud rules, such as Exchange Act Rule 10b-5,[142] Rule 206(4)-8 is not limited to fraud in connection with the purchase and sale of a security. In addition, the SEC does not need to demonstrate that an investment adviser acted with scienter, so an investment adviser could be liable for an inadvertent misstatement in a hedge fund offering circular provided to a prospective investor that never invested in the hedge fund. No private cause of action is available, however, for violation of Rule 206(4)-8.

---

135. *See, e.g.*, Cal. Corp. Code § 25235; N.Y. Gen. Bus. Law § 352-c.

136. *See, e.g.*, 10 Cal. Code of Reg. § 260.238(f).

137. *See, e.g.*, 10 Cal. Code of Reg. § 260.238(g).

138. *See, e.g.*, Title 10, Cal. Code of Reg., § 260.238(i).

139. 17 C.F.R. § 275.206(4)-8; Advisers Act Release No. 2628, 72 F.R. 44756 (Aug. 9, 2007). *See* § 6.5.1, *infra.*

140. Goldstein v. Securities and Exchange Commission, 451 F.3d 873 (D.C Cir. 2006); Advisers Act Release No. 2576 (Aug. 3, 2007), 72 F.R. 400 (Aug. 9, 2007).

141. *See* Chapter 3, *infra.*

142. 17 C.F.R. § 240.10b-5. In addition, the U.S. Supreme Court has held that a mutual fund investment adviser cannot be held liable in a private action under Rule 10b-5 for false statements included in its prospectuses because it did not actually make those statements. Janus Capital Group, Inc. v. First Derivative Traders, 566 F.3d 111 (June 13, 2011).

Investment advisers to investment companies are subject to additional fiduciary duties under the Company Act, but those duties are not addressed in this book.

2. ERISA

Investment advisers to ERISA Plans and to hedge funds whose assets constitute "plan assets" owe fiduciary duties under ERISA to such plans and hedge funds.[143]

3. Compliance Programs for SEC-Registered Investment Advisers

Advisers Act Rule 206(4)-7[144] requires every investment adviser that is registered or required to be registered with the SEC to (a) adopt and implement written policies and procedures reasonably designed to prevent violations of the federal securities laws, (b) review those policies and procedures annually, and (c) designate a chief compliance officer to administer the policies and procedures. Failure to adopt and implement adequate compliance policies and procedures is by itself unlawful, independent of any other securities law violation.

Under Rule 206(4)-7, such an investment adviser must adopt and implement written policies and procedures reasonably designed to prevent violation of the Advisers Act by the investment adviser or any of its supervised persons. In preparing these policies and procedures, an investment adviser should identify conflicts of interest and other compliance factors that create risk exposure for the investment adviser and its clients in light of its operations and design policies and procedures to address those risks. At a minimum, the policies and procedures should address the following issues, to the extent that they apply to the investment adviser:

- portfolio management processes, including allocation of investment opportunities among clients and consistency of portfolios with clients' investment objectives, disclosures by the investment adviser and applicable regulatory restrictions;
- trading practices, including procedures by which the investment adviser satisfies its best execution obligation, uses client brokerage to obtain research and other services ("soft dollar arrangements"), and allocates aggregated trades among clients;
- proprietary trading by the investment adviser and personal trading activities of its supervised persons;
- the accuracy of disclosures made to investors, clients and regulatory authorities, including account statements, advertisements and published prior performance;
- safeguards to protect client assets from conversion or inappropriate use by investment advisory personnel;

143. *See* Chapter 11, *infra*.

144. 17 C.F.R. § 275.206(4)-7.

- accurate creation of required records and their maintenance in a manner that secures them from unauthorized alteration or use and protects them from untimely destruction;
- marketing practices, including the use of solicitors;
- procedures to value client holdings and assess fees based on those valuations;
- safeguards to protect the privacy of client records and information; and
- business continuity plans to protect client interests if the investment adviser becomes unable to provide advisory services (for example, after a natural disaster).

This list is not exhaustive and does not include matters required by other laws and rules to be addressed in written policies and procedures, such as insider trading, privacy, anti-money laundering, and proxy voting.[145]

An investment adviser is required to review its policies and procedures annually to determine their adequacy and effectiveness. The review should consider any compliance matters that arose during the previous year, any changes in the business activities of the investment adviser or its affiliates and any changes in the Advisers Act or applicable regulations. Investment advisers also should consider interim reviews in response to significant compliance events, changes in business arrangements and regulatory developments.

An investment adviser is required to designate a chief compliance officer to administer its policies and procedures. The chief compliance officer should be competent and knowledgeable about the Advisers Act and should have full responsibility and authority to develop and enforce appropriate policies and procedures.

Investment advisers are required to maintain copies of all policies and procedures in effect during the preceding 5 years. Investment advisers also are required to keep records documenting the annual review. Investment advisers may maintain these records electronically.

On January 15, 2009, the Asset Managers' Committee to the President's Working Group on Financial Markets issued a report entitled "Best Practices for the Hedge Fund Industry,"[146] which provided additional guidance to investment advisers on compliance and other matters. According to the Committee, an investment adviser should establish a comprehensive and integrated compliance and business practices framework that is supported by adequate resources. This framework should include:

- a written code of ethics;
- a written compliance manual;

---

145. Advisers Act Release No. 2204 (Dec. 17, 2003), 68 F.R. 74714 (Dec. 24, 2003). *See* §§ 2.7.4-2.7.8, *infra*.

146. *Available at* www.amaicmte.org/Public/AMC%20Report%20-%20Final.pdf (last visited May 13, 2013).

- a conflicts committee;
- regular training of personnel with respect to compliance issues; and
- a compliance function that includes a chief compliance officer, appropriate discipline and sanctions to address departures from the compliance program, and an annual review of the compliance program.

The Committee emphasized that a culture of compliance is critical to the framework's success. Creating a culture of compliance requires, among other things, having senior management participate in compliance meetings and training sessions, giving employees the ability to communicate concerns to senior management, and making the role of chief compliance officer institutionally significant.

4. Code of Ethics

Advisers Act Rules 204A-1[147] and 204-2[148] require SEC-registered investment advisers to adopt and enforce codes of ethics applicable to their supervised persons.[149] These rules are intended to prevent fraud by reinforcing the fiduciary principles that govern the conduct of investment advisory firms and their personnel. An investment adviser's code of ethics must, at a minimum:

- establish standards of conduct that are expected of the investment adviser's supervised persons and that reflect the investment adviser's fiduciary duties;
- require each supervised person to acknowledge, in writing, receipt of a copy of the code of ethics and any amendments;
- require supervised persons to comply with applicable federal securities laws;
- require certain supervised persons, called "access persons," to report their personal securities holdings and transactions, including transactions in mutual funds advised by the investment adviser or an affiliate;
- require access persons to pre-clear any personal investments in initial public offerings and limited offerings; and
- require supervised persons to report, promptly, any violations of the investment adviser's code of ethics to the investment adviser's chief compliance officer or to other designated persons.

An investment adviser should require each of its employees to acknowledge receipt of its policies and procedures, including its code of ethics, when the employee becomes an access person. At that time, the investment adviser should require the access person to disclose any personal securities holdings. Thereafter, the investment adviser should require the access person to arrange for the chief compliance officer to receive duplicate confirmations or brokerage statements,

147. 17 C.F.R. § 275.204A-1.
148. 17 C.F.R. § 275.204-2.
149. Advisers Act Release No. 2256 (July 2, 2004), 69 F.R. 41,696 (July 9, 2004).

or at least to provide quarterly transaction reports. At least once a year, each employee should sign a certificate certifying his or her compliance with the investment adviser's policies and procedures and informing the investment adviser of any changes to the information previously provided.

5. Insider Trading

An investment adviser that is registered or required to be registered with the SEC must (and every investment adviser should) establish, maintain and enforce written policies and procedures that are reasonably designed, taking into consideration the nature of the investment adviser's business, to prevent insider trading and the misuse of material, nonpublic information by the investment adviser or any person associated with the investment adviser.[150]

The investment adviser should establish procedures for handling inside information, including the steps access persons should take if they come into contact with such information (such as, for example, placing the issuer on a restricted list). The investment adviser should restrict physical access to areas where material nonpublic information might be discussed and employ security measures to protect information on computers, such as passwords. The investment adviser also should consider the extent to which it should impose trading restrictions when certain employees are in possession of material nonpublic information. The investment adviser's policies and procedures should address situations when an access person or investor is an officer, director or consultant to a company and therefore could be exposed to material nonpublic information.

6. Privacy

i. In General

SEC and FTC rules under the Gramm-Leach-Bliley Act (the "GLBA")[151] establish standards for investment advisers and investment limited partnerships to (a) insure the security and confidentiality of their customer records and information, (b) protect against any anticipated threats or hazards to the security or integrity of such records, and (c) protect against unauthorized access to or use of such records or information that could result in substantial harm or inconvenience to any customer.[152] The SEC's rules apply only to SEC-registered investment advisers; the FTC's rules apply to state-registered and unregistered investment advisers.

Both sets of rules require investment advisers to adopt policies and procedures to protect the privacy of the personal information about their customers and to provide their customers with initial and annual privacy notices describing their policies and procedures for collecting and disclosing nonpublic

---

150. Advisers Act § 204A, 15 U.S.C. § 80b-4a; Advisers Act Rule 204A-1, 17 C.F.R. § 275.204A-1. *See* §§ 13.10 and 13.11, *infra*.

151. 15 U.S.C. §§ 6801-6827.

152. 15 U.S.C. § 6801(b).

personal information.[153] "Customer" generally includes any individual who obtains financial services for personal, family or household purposes.

Under SEC Regulation S-P, SEC-registered investment advisers must adopt policies and procedures that address administrative, technical, and physical safeguards for the protection of customer records and information. These policies and procedures must be reasonably designed to:

- ensure the security and confidentiality of customer records and information;
- protect against any anticipated threats or hazards to the security or integrity of customer records and information; and
- protect against unauthorized access to or use of customer records or information that could result in substantial harm or inconvenience to any customer.[154]

Under the FTC's rules, every state-registered or unregistered investment adviser must "develop, implement and maintain a comprehensive information security program that is written in one or more readily accessible parts." Such an investment adviser must:

- designate an employee or employees to coordinate the program;
- identify reasonably foreseeable internal and external risks to the security, confidentiality and integrity of customer information and assess the sufficiency of any safeguards in place to control these risks;
- design and implement information safeguards to control the risks and regularly test or otherwise monitor the effectiveness of the safeguards;
- oversee service providers; and
- evaluate and adjust its information security program in light of the results of testing and monitoring.

A CTA or CPO[155] that is registered with the SEC as an investment adviser or securities broker may comply with the privacy regulations by complying with the SEC's Regulation S-P.[156] Similarly, a CTA or CPO that is registered or required to be registered with the state in which it maintains its principal office and place of business may comply with the privacy regulations by complying with the FTC's regulations.[157] Otherwise, CTAs and CPOs must comply with the CFTC's privacy rules. The CFTC's privacy regulations require every CTA or CPO to:

- provide an initial notice to each of its customers disclosing the types of nonpublic personal information the CTA or CPO collects and the extent to which such information may be disclosed;[158]

---

153. 17 C.F.R. §§ 248.4, 248.5; 16 C.F.R. § 313.6(a)(8).
154. 17 C.F.R. § 248.30.
155. *See* § 2.9, *infra.*
156. SEC Privacy of Consumer Financial Information, 17 C.F.R. §§ 248, *et seq.*
157. FTC Privacy of Consumer Financial Information, 16 C.F.R. §§ 313, *et seq.*
158. 17 C.F.R. §§ 160.4 and 160.6.

- provide an annual notice to its existing customers;[159]
- amend (if necessary) existing agreements with nonaffiliated parties under which the CTA or CPO discloses nonpublic personal information about customers to require the nonaffiliated parties to protect the confidentiality of customers' nonpublic personal information, and include the same protections in new agreements;[160]
- establish policies and procedures to protect the confidentiality of customer records;[161] and
- on an ongoing basis, determine whether disclosure to nonaffiliated third parties of nonpublic personal information about customers or individuals who have applied to be customers triggers other requirements of the privacy regulations.

To comply with the privacy rules of the SEC, the FTC or the CFTC, an investment adviser should protect customer information by employing electronic safeguards (such as passwords) to limit access to confidential information stored on computers and limiting physical access to nonelectronic confidential information by locking or monitoring access to the offices and storage areas where this information is located. If the investment adviser shares office space, it may need to take additional precautions. If the investment adviser engages any third-party service providers, it should ensure that those service providers are obligated to protect the investment adviser's and its customers' confidential and proprietary information.

ii. Protection from Identity Theft

Effective May 20, 2013, with compliance required by November 20, 2013, the SEC and the CFTC jointly issued rules and guidelines to require certain registered entities to establish programs to address risks of identity theft, implementing provisions of the Dodd-Frank Act that amended the Fair Credit Reporting Act (the "FCRA").[162] Of relevance to managers of hedge funds, the rules require financial institutions and creditors that offer or maintain one or more covered accounts to develop and implement written identity theft programs designed to detect, prevent and mitigate identity theft in connection with certain existing accounts or the opening of new accounts.

The CFTC's rules apply to financial institutions, as defined in the FCRA, and explicitly include, among others, any CPO or CTA.[163] The SEC's rules include any financial institution, as defined in the FCRA, that is an investment adviser registered or required to be registered under the Advisers Act.[164] The FCRA defines "financial institution" to include certain banks and credit unions, and "any other person that, directly or indirectly, holds a transaction account . . .

159. 17 C.F.R. § 160.5.
160. 17 C.F.R. §§ 160.13(a)(ii), 160.18(c).
161. 17 C.F.R. § 160.30.
162. 78 F.R. 23,638 (Apr. 19, 2013).
163. CEA Rule § 162.3(b)(7), 17 C.F.R. § 162.3(b)(7).
164. Advisers Act Rule 201(a), 17 C.F.R. § 248.201(a).

belonging to a customer."[165] For example, a private fund adviser would hold a transaction account if it has the authority to direct an investor's redemption proceeds to other persons on instructions received from the investor.[166]

The CFTC's and the SEC's identity theft rules also apply to creditors, as defined in the FCRA, which are persons that regularly extend, renew or continue credit or make those arrangements.[167] The CFTC rules specifically state that any CTA or CPO that "regularly and in the course of business . . . advances funds to or on behalf of a person, based on an obligation of the person to repay the funds or repayable from specific property pledged by or on behalf of the person" is a creditor for purpose of the rules. Some investment advisers may be treated as creditors under the rules; for example, an investment adviser could qualify as a creditor if it regularly and in the ordinary course of business lends money, short-term or otherwise, to investors to allow them to invest in a fund, pending the receipt or clearance of their subscription funds.[168]

Under these rules, a financial institution or creditor must establish a red flags program if it offers or maintains covered accounts. A "covered account" is an account that (a) a financial institution or creditor offers or maintains, primarily for personal, family or household purposes, that involves or is designed to permit multiple payments or transactions, or (b) the financial institution or creditor offers or maintains for which there is a reasonably foreseeable risk to customers or to the safety and soundness of the financial institution or creditor from identity theft, including financial, operational, compliance, reputation or litigation risks (for example, a margin account or brokerage account).[169] The rules require a financial institution or creditor to:[170]

- Assess whether it offers or maintains covered accounts. As part of this periodic determination, an entity must conduct a risk assessment that takes into account (a) the methods it provides to open its accounts, (b) the methods it provides to access its accounts, and (c) its previous experiences with identity theft.[171]
- Develop and implement a written program designed to detect, prevent and mitigate identity theft in connection with opening a covered account or any existing covered account. Each program must be appropriate to the size and complexity of the organization and the nature and scope of its activities. The program must include reasonable polices and procedures to identify, detect and respond appropriately to red flags and must be periodically reviewed and updated as appropriate.[172] The final rules include guidelines and examples.

---

165. 15 U.S.C. 1681a(t).
166. 78 F.R. 23,638 at 23, 642 (Apr. 19, 2013).
167. 15 U.S.C. 1681m(e)(4)(A)(iii).
168. 78 F.R. 23,638 at 23, 644.
169. CEA Rule § 162.3(b)(3), 17 C.F.R. § 162.3(b)(3); Advisers Act Rule 201(b)(3), 17 C.F.R. § 248.201(b)(3).
170. 78 F.R. 23,638 at 23, 646 (Apr. 19, 2013).
171. *Id.* at 23, 645.
172. 78 F.R. 23,638 at 23, 645-46 (Apr. 19, 2013).

- Obtain approval of the initial written program from its board of directors or, if it does not have a board of directors, from a designated senior management employee (such as an investment adviser's chief compliance officer). In addition, the board of directors or senior management employee must be involved in the oversight, development and administration of the program. Financial institutions and creditors must also exercise appropriate and effective oversight of service provider arrangements.

The rules identify 5 categories of red flags that financial institutions and creditors must consider including in their programs:[173]

- alerts, notifications or other warnings received from consumer reporting agencies or service providers, such as fraud detection services;
- presentation of suspicious documents, such as documents that appear to have been altered or forged;
- presentation of suspicious personal identifying information, such as a suspicious address change;
- unusual use of, or other suspicious activity related to, a covered account; and
- notice from customers, victims of identity theft, law enforcement authorities or other persons regarding possible identity theft in connection with covered accounts held by the financial institution or creditor.

7. Anti-Money Laundering

The Financial Crimes Enforcement Network ("FinCEN") of the U.S. Treasury Department proposed rules on April 29, 2003, that would have required registered and certain unregistered investment advisers to establish anti-money laundering programs pursuant to section 352 of the ironically named Uniting and Strengthening America by Providing Appropriate Tools Required to Intercept and Obstruct Terrorism Act (the "USA PATRIOT Act"). The notice of proposed rulemaking was withdrawn, however, effective November 4, 2008.[174] Given the passage of time since the original rulemaking, FinCEN determined that it would not proceed with an anti-money laundering requirement for investment advisers without publishing a new proposal.

The proposed rules would have required every investment adviser to:

- establish and implement policies, procedures and internal controls reasonably designed to detect and prevent money laundering and terrorist financing;
- provide for independent testing for compliance;

173. *Id.* at 23647.
174. 73 F.R. 65,568 (Nov. 4, 2008).

- designate a person or persons responsible for implementing and monitoring the investment adviser's anti-money laundering program; and
- provide for ongoing employee training.[175]

Although these rules were not adopted, investment advisers should adopt policies that address money laundering risks. For example, the investment adviser could periodically compare its investor list to the government watch lists prepared by the Office of Foreign Assets Control (www.ustreas.gov/ofac) and by the SEC (www.sec.gov/news/headlines/recordsearch.htm). The investment adviser also should consider red flags, such as:

- wire transfers being sent from a country or territory that is neither a member of the Financial Action Task Force (the "FATF") nor a member of a regional organization that is a member of the FATF, or transactions occurring with a person located in such a country or territory (a list of FATF members can be obtained from the FATF web site, www.fatf-gafi.org);
- an investor bank or other institution acting as an agent for an undisclosed principal;
- an investor making frequent investments or withdrawals, or making investments followed by withdrawals within a short time;
- an investor that is a senior foreign political figure, immediate family member of a senior foreign political figure or close associate of a senior foreign political figure;
- an investor seeming unusually concerned about the investment adviser's compliance with its anti-money laundering policies or other governmental reporting obligations;
- an investor being reluctant to reveal identifying information about itself;
- an investor seeming unusually unconcerned about investment performance; or
- an investor asking the investment adviser to process its transactions in an unusual manner.

In addition, a hedge fund should obtain appropriate anti-money laundering documentation from prospective and existing investors. For example, if the investor is a natural person with whom the adviser has not previously established a substantive relationship, the investment adviser should consider requiring the investor to have his or her signature notarized on the subscription agreement or to provide a certified or notarized copy of his or her driver's license or passport. If the investor is an entity, the investment adviser should consider obtaining a certified copy of the entity's charter documents and certificates of good standing. If the investor is an investment fund, the investment adviser should consider

175. 68 F.R. 23646 at 23649-23651 (May 5, 2003); *see* § 2.10, *infra*.

requiring additional representations from the investor that it has and follows its own anti-money laundering policies and procedures. An investment adviser to an offshore hedge fund should require the fund's administrator to obtain similar representations and warranties from the fund's existing and prospective investors.

8. Proxy Voting

i. SEC-Registered Investment Advisers

An SEC-registered investment adviser with voting authority over its clients' securities must:

- Establish a written proxy voting policy reasonably designed to ensure that the investment adviser votes client securities in the best interests of clients. The policy should be tailored to the investment adviser's particular situation, but must, among other things, describe how the investment adviser addresses material conflicts that may arise between its interests and its clients' interests. An investment adviser may include its policy in Part 2A of its Form ADV, or maintain it in a separate document.[176]
- Disclose to clients (for example, in Part 2A of Form ADV) how they may obtain information about how the investment adviser voted proxies.
- Describe its proxy voting policy to clients (again, in Part 2A) and furnish the policy to any client on request.
- Keep records of proxy votes that the investment adviser casts on behalf of its clients and copies of (a) its policy, (b) each proxy statement it receives regarding its clients' securities, (c) any document that is material to a voting decision of the investment adviser or that describes the basis for that decision and (d) each written client request for information about how the investment adviser voted proxies and each written response by the investment adviser to such a client request (written or oral). An investment adviser may rely on a third-party (such as a broker) to keep voting records and copies of proxy statements, or may rely on obtaining those copies through the SEC's Electronic Data Gathering, Analysis, and Retrieval ("EDGAR") system.[177]

An investment adviser with no voting authority over any of its clients' securities is not required to comply with these rules. An investment adviser that desires not to have voting authority should expressly provide in its investment management agreements that the clients reserve all voting rights with respect to their securities, and should forward all proxy statements to the clients. An investment adviser that is the general partner of a hedge fund cannot avoid proxy voting authority, because the investment adviser, as general partner, controls the "client."

176. Advisers Act Rule 206(4)-6, 17 C.F.R. § 275.206(4)-6.
177. Advisers Act Rule 204-2(c)(2)(ii), 17 C.F.R. § 275.204-2(c)(2)(ii).

ii. State-Registered Investment Advisers

Although the foregoing proxy voting policy rules apply only to SEC-registered investment advisers, some states require investment advisers registered or doing business there to comply with record-keeping and other rules that are the same as or similar to those for SEC-registered investment advisers, including rules relating to proxy voting policies. An investment adviser in any such state must adopt such a policy and maintain the required records, even if the investment adviser is not registered with the SEC.

iii. FINRA Requirements

A broker that is a FINRA member is required to forward proxy solicitation and certain other materials to the beneficial owner of securities held in the broker's name, if that owner requests and gives the broker satisfactory assurance that it will reimburse the broker for the cost of forwarding.[178] The broker must include a letter with proxy solicitation materials noting the time limit for completing and returning the proxy. A FINRA member may vote proxies where it holds the stock as executor, administrator, guardian, trustee, or in a representative or fiduciary capacity with authority to vote. A FINRA member designated by a named ERISA plan fiduciary as the investment manager of stock held as assets of the ERISA plan may vote the proxies in accordance with the ERISA plan fiduciary responsibilities if the ERISA plan expressly grants discretion to the investment manager to manage, acquire or dispose of any plan asset, and has not expressly reserved the proxy voting right for the named ERISA plan fiduciary.[179] Any designated investment adviser may also vote such proxies.

§ 2.8 Books and Records Requirements Under the Advisers Act

1. General Rule

Under Advisers Act Rule 204-2,[180] an SEC-registered investment adviser is required to keep true, accurate and current the following books and records relating to its investment advisory business:

- a journal or journals, including cash receipts and disbursements records, and any other records of original entry forming the basis of entries in any ledger;
- general and auxiliary ledgers (or other comparable records) reflecting asset, liability, reserve, capital, income and expense accounts;
- a memorandum of each order given by the investment adviser to buy or sell any security, of any instruction received by the investment

178. FINRA Rule 2251, "Forwarding of Proxy and Other Issuer-Related Materials."
179. *See also* Chapter 11, *infra*.
180. 17 C.F.R. § 275.204-2.

adviser concerning the purchase, sale, receipt or delivery of a particular security, and of any modification or cancellation of any such order or instruction; each such memorandum must (a) show the terms and conditions of the order, instruction, modification or cancellation, (b) identify the person connected with the investment adviser who recommended the transaction to the client and the person who placed the order, and (c) show the account for which the order was entered, the date of entry, and the bank, broker or dealer by or through which the order was executed, where appropriate, and orders entered pursuant to the exercise of discretionary power must be so designated;

- all check books, bank statements, canceled checks and cash reconciliations of the investment adviser;
- all bills or statements (or copies thereof), paid or unpaid, relating to the business of the investment adviser as such;
- all trial balances, financial statements and internal audit working papers relating to the business of the investment adviser;
- originals of all written communications the investment adviser received and copies of all written communications the investment adviser sent that relate to any recommendation the investment adviser made or proposed to make and any advice it gave or proposed to give, any receipt, disbursement or delivery of funds or securities, or the placing or execution of any order to buy or sell any security, except that (a) the investment adviser need not keep any unsolicited market letters and other similar communications of general public distribution not prepared by or for the investment adviser, and (b) if the investment adviser sends any notice, circular or other advertisement offering any report, analysis, publication or other investment advisory service to more than 10 persons, the investment adviser need not keep a record of the names and addresses of the persons to whom sent (except that if the notice, circular or advertisement is distributed to a list of persons, the investment adviser must keep with the copy of the notice, circular or advertisement a memorandum describing the list and its source);
- a list or other record of all accounts over which the investment adviser has any discretionary power with respect to any client's funds, securities or transactions;
- all powers of attorney and other evidences of granting any discretionary authority to the investment adviser (or copies thereof);
- all written agreements (or copies thereof) between the investment adviser and any client or that otherwise relate to the investment adviser's business;

- a copy of each notice, circular, advertisement, newspaper article, investment letter, bulletin or other communication that the investment adviser circulates or distributes, directly or indirectly, to 10 or more persons not connected with such investment adviser, and if such communication recommends the purchase or sale of a specific security and does not state the reasons for such recommendation, a memorandum by the investment adviser indicating the reasons therefor;
- a copy of the investment adviser's code of ethics[181] that is in effect or that was in effect at any time within the past 5 years; a record of any violation of the code of ethics, and of any action taken as a result of the violation; and a record of all written acknowledgments as required by the code of ethics rule[182] for each person who is currently, or within the past 5 years was, a supervised person of the investment adviser;
- a record of each report made by an access person as required by the investment adviser's code of ethics, including any information provided in lieu of such reports; a record of the names of persons who are currently, or within the past 5 years were, access persons of the investment adviser; and a record of any decision, and the reasons supporting the decision, to approve any access person's acquisition of securities, for at least 5 years after the end of the fiscal year in which the approval is granted;[183]
- a copy of each written statement and each amendment or revision thereof, given or sent to any client or prospective client of the investment adviser in accordance with Advisers Act Rule 204-3,[184] and a record of the dates that each written statement, amendment and revision was given or offered, to any client or any prospective client who subsequently becomes a client;
- all written acknowledgments of receipt obtained from clients pursuant to the solicitors rule and copies of the disclosure documents delivered to clients by solicitors pursuant to that rule;[185]
- all accounts, books, internal working papers and other records or documents that are necessary to form the basis for or demonstrate the calculation of the performance or rate of return of any or all managed accounts or securities recommendations in any notice, circular, advertisement, newspaper article, investment letter, bulletin or other communication that the investment adviser circulates or distributes, directly or indirectly, to 10 or more persons not connected with such investment adviser, except that, with respect to the performance of a managed account, this requirement is deemed to be satisfied by the retention of all account statements, if they reflect all debits, credits and

---

181. *See* § 2.7.4, *supra*.
182. *Id.*
183. *See* §§ 2.7.3 and 2.7.4, *supra*.
184. 17 C.F.R. § 275.204-3.
185. *See* §§ 8.8 and 10.1.3, *infra*.

other transactions in the client's account for the period of the statement and all worksheets necessary to demonstrate the calculation of the performance or rate of return of the managed account; and

- a copy of the investment adviser's policies and procedures[186] that are in effect, or were in effect at any time within the past 5 years, and any records documenting the investment adviser's annual review of those policies and procedures.

If an investment adviser has custody or possession of securities or funds of any client account,[187] the investment adviser must also keep the following:

- a journal or other record showing all purchases, sales, receipts and deliveries of securities (including certificate numbers) for such account and all other debits and credits to such account;
- a separate ledger account for each such client showing all purchases, sales, receipts and deliveries of securities, the date and price of each purchase and sale, and all debits and credits;
- copies of confirmations of all transactions effected by or for the account of such client; and
- a record for each security in which such client has a position, showing the name of each client having any interest in the security, the amount or interest of each such client, and the location of the security.

An SEC-registered investment adviser who renders any investment supervisory or management service to any client must also keep the following records, with respect to the client's portfolio it supervises or manages, if the information is reasonably available to or obtainable by the investment adviser:

- records showing separately for each such client the securities purchased and sold, and the date, amount and price of each such purchase and sale; and
- for each security in which any such client has a current position, information from which the investment adviser can promptly furnish the name of each such client and the current amount or interest of such client.

An SEC-registered investment adviser that exercises voting authority with respect to client securities must, with respect to those clients, keep the following:

- copies of all policies and procedures required by Advisers Act Rule 206(4)-6;[188]
- a copy of each proxy statement that the investment adviser receives regarding client securities, either directly or by relying on a third-party to make and retain, on the investment adviser's behalf, a copy of a proxy

---

186. *See* § 2.7, *supra*.
187. *See* Chapter 12, *infra*.
188. 17 C.F.R. § 275.206(4)-6.

statement (if the third-party has undertaken to provide a copy of the proxy statement promptly on request) or relying on obtaining a copy of a proxy statement from the SEC's EDGAR system;

- a record of each vote cast by the investment adviser on behalf of a client, either directly or by relying on a third-party to make and retain, on the investment adviser's behalf, a record of the vote cast, if the third-party has undertaken to provide a copy of the record promptly on request;
- a copy of any document the investment adviser created that was material to a proxy voting decision it makes on behalf of a client or that memorializes the basis for such decision; and
- a copy of each written client request for information on how the investment adviser voted proxies on behalf of the client, and a copy of any written response by the investment adviser to any such written or oral client request.

An investment adviser may maintain any of the required books or records in a manner that indicates the identity of its client by numerical or alphabetical code or some similar designation.

Generally, an investment adviser must maintain and preserve the required books and records in an easily accessible place for at least 5 years from the end of the fiscal year during which the last entry was made, the first 2 years in an appropriate office of the investment adviser. An investment adviser must, however, maintain its and its predecessor's charter documents, minute books and stock certificate books in its principal office and preserve them until at least 3 years after termination of the business. Records relating to any notice, circular, advertisement, newspaper article, investment letter, bulletin or other communication must be maintained and preserved in an easily accessible place for 5 years (the first 2 years in an appropriate office of the investment adviser) from the end of the fiscal year during which the investment adviser last published or otherwise disseminated such communication.

An investment adviser that was exempt from registration under the "private adviser" exemption, but that was required to register after the exemption was eliminated on July 21, 2011, is not obligated to keep certain performance-related records for any period when it was not registered with the SEC, but if the investment adviser preserved such performance-related records even though not required to keep them, it must continue to preserve them.[189]

The documents used to organize a hedge fund and solicit investments in the hedge fund are within the scope of Advisers Act Rule 204-2.[190] The hedge fund's offering circular, agreement of limited partnership or other charter documents, subscription agreements, offering questionnaires and other documents (discussed in Chapters 4, 5 and 6) constitute records subject to the rule.[191]

---

189. Advisers Act Rule 204-2(e)(3)(ii), 17 C.F.R. § 204-2(e)(3)(ii).

190. 17 C.F.R. § 275.204-2.

191. *See* § 8.11, *infra*.

2. Storage Media; Electronic Records

All of the foregoing records may be maintained on paper, micrographic or electronic media. Advisors Act Rule 204-2(g)[192] governs electronic record-keeping. If the investment adviser keeps the required records in electronic format, it must:

- arrange and index the records in a way that permits easy location, access and retrieval of any particular record;
- provide promptly at the SEC's request (a) a copy of the records in the medium and format in which they are stored, (b) a printout of the records, and (c) means to access, view and print the records; and
- separately store a duplicate copy of the records in an electronic, micrographic or paper medium.

The investment adviser must also establish and maintain procedures to (a) maintain and preserve the electronic records reasonably to safeguard them from loss, alteration or destruction, (b) limit access to the records to properly authorized personnel and the SEC, and (c) reasonably ensure that any reproduction of a nonelectronic original record on an electronic storage medium is complete, true and legible when retrieved.

§ 2.9 Commodity Trading Activities

1. General

Securities markets and futures and commodity option markets are regulated under separate statutory schemes. The CEA[193] and the regulations promulgated thereunder ("CEA Regulations")[194] govern the trading of futures and commodity option contracts and most over-the-counter swaps (collectively, "commodity interests"), and are administered by the CFTC.[195] The CFTC has delegated significant authority and responsibilities to the NFA, the self-regulatory organization for the commodity futures trading business.[196]

An adviser that invests its clients' advisory accounts in commodity interests is generally required to register with the CFTC as a CTA. An operator of an investment fund that invests in commodity interests must generally register as a CPO. The CEA and CEA Regulations provide various exclusions and exemptions from CTA and CPO registration, however, and many investment advisers to separate accounts and investment funds rely on them to avoid such registration.

192. 17 C.F.R. § 275.204-2(g).
193. 7 U.S.C. §§ 1, *et seq.*
194. 17 C.F.R. Ch. 1.
195. CEA § 2, 7 U.S.C. § 2.
196. *See, e.g.*, 62 F.R. 36,050 (July 3, 1997).

Investment advisers and general partners of investment funds are generally subject to regulation under the CEA even if they trade only non-U.S. commodity interests, if they do so on behalf of clients in the United States or its territories and possessions.[197]

The discussion below is based in part on formal and informal interpretations of the CEA and CEA Regulations by the CFTC and the NFA. These interpretations are not necessarily binding and might be modified by the CFTC, the NFA or their respective staffs.

2. Jurisdiction of the CFTC

Under the CEA, the CFTC generally has jurisdiction over the trading of commodity futures, financial futures (such as interest rate futures and futures on broad-based securities indices) and options on futures. The Dodd-Frank Act expanded the CFTC's jurisdiction to include commodity options and most financial swaps.[198]

"Swap" is defined in both the CEA and the Exchange Act as, generally, an agreement, contract or transaction that (a) is an option of any kind (including puts, calls, caps, floors, collars and similar arrangements) for purchase or sale of, or based on the value of, one or more interest or other rates, currencies, commodities, debt instruments, indices, quantitative measures, or other financial or economic interest or property, (b) provides for any purchase, sale, payment or delivery (other than a dividend on an equity security) that depends on the occurrence, nonoccurrence or extent of occurrence or nonoccurrence, of an event or contingency associated with a potential financial, economic or commercial consequence, or (c) provides on an executory basis for an exchange of payments based on the value or level of any instrument or measure described in clause (a) above, and transfers some or all of the financial risk associated with a future change in any such value or level without changing ownership of the asset or liability that incorporates that risk.[199] Swaps include most over-the-counter derivatives, such as rate caps, floors and collars; commodity, basis, equity, debt, total return and credit default swaps; and foreign exchange swaps and forwards.

---

197. CEA Rule 30.4, 17 C.F.R. § 30.4.

198. Dodd-Frank Wall Street Reform and Consumer Protection Act, Public Law 111-203, 124 Stat. 1376 (2010). The Dodd-Frank Act also created registration requirements and compliance obligations for certain categories of participants in swap transactions, including "swap dealers," "security-based swap dealers," "major swap participants" and "major security-based swap participants." The CFTC and the SEC have, however, adopted rules that define those terms narrowly, to capture mainly only traditional dealers in over-the-counter swap markets and very large buy-side participants. Accordingly, investment advisers to hedge funds, and most hedge funds, are unlikely to be within any of those categories, and neither those categories nor their associated registration requirements are discussed in this book. CEA § 1a(49), 7 U.S.C. § 1a(49); CEA § 1a(43), 7 U.S.C. § 1a(43); CEA § 1a(33), 7 U.S.C. § 1a(33); CEA § 1a(32), 7 U.S.C. § 1a(32).

199. CEA § 1a(47), 7 U.S.C. § 1a(47); Exchange Act § 3(a)(69), 15 U.S.C. 78c(a)(69).

The CFTC has jurisdiction over swaps other than security-based swaps and the SEC has jurisdiction over security-based swaps.[200] "Security-based swap" is defined in both the CEA and the Exchange Act as a swap that is based on (a) a single security or loan (such as a single-name credit default swap), (b) a narrow-based security index (one with no more than 9 component securities, subject to certain weighting requirements), or (c) the occurrence, nonoccurrence or extent of occurrence or nonoccurrence of an event relating to a single issuer of a security or the issuers of securities in a narrow-based security index, if the event directly affects the issuer's financial statements, condition or obligations.[201] Security-based swaps are included in the definition of "security" under the Exchange Act.[202]

"Security-based swap agreements" are a subset of swaps over which the CFTC has regulatory and enforcement authority but shares anti-fraud and certain other authority with the SEC. A security-based swap agreement is generally a swap agreement with a material term that is based on the price, yield, value or volatility of a security or security index, and is not a security-based swap.[203] Although the CFTC and the SEC have indicated that it is not possible to provide a bright-line distinction between security-based swap agreements and other types of swaps, they have stated that security-based swap agreements include swaps based on securities indices other than narrow-based security indices, and index credit default swaps that are not based on narrow-based security indices or the issuers of securities in a narrow-based security index.[204]

The CFTC and the SEC also share jurisdiction over security futures and mixed swaps. "Security futures" are futures on single securities and narrow-based security indices, and options on such futures.[205] A "mixed swap" is a security-based swap that also has characteristics of a swap, in that it is also based on the value of one or more interest or other rates, currencies, commodities, debt instruments, indices, quantitative measures, or other financial or economic interest or property, or the occurrence or nonoccurrence of an event associated with a potential financial, economic or commercial consequence.[206]

Investments advisers that trade CFTC-regulated swaps are CPOs and CTAs even if they do not trade futures or commodity options. Although the particular characteristics of each instrument must be examined carefully to classify it reliably, the following generally are swaps regulated by the CFTC:

- swaps on broad-based security indices;

---

200. CEA § 2(a)(1)(A), 7 U.S.C. § 2(a)(1)(A); CEA § 2(a)(1)(G), 7 U.S.C. § 2(a)(1)(G).

201. CEA § 1a(42), 7 U.S.C. § 1a(42); Exchange Act § 3(a)(68), 15 U.S.C. 78c(a)(68).

202. Exchange Act § 3(a)(10), 7 U.S.C. 78c(a)(10).

203. CEA § 1a(47)(A)(v), 7 U.S.C. 1a(47); Exchange Act § 3(a)(78), 15 U.S.C. 78c(a)(78).

204. Further Definition of "Swap," "Security-Based Swap," and "Security-Based Swap Agreement;" "Mixed Swaps;" Security-Based Swap Agreement Recordkeeping: Proposed Rule, 76 F.R. 229818 (May 23, 2011).

205. CEA § 2(a)(1)(D)(i), 7 U.S.C. § 2(a)(1)(D)(i).

206. Exchange Act § 3(a)(68)(D), 15 U.S.C. 78c(a)(68)(D); CEA § 1a(47)(D), 7 U.S.C. § 1a(47)(G). Few instruments qualify as mixed swaps; an example would be a contract in which the underlying references are both the price of an oil company's stock and the price of oil.

- swaps on U.S. government securities, including swaps on rates or yields of U.S. Treasuries;
- swaps based solely on interest rates or other monetary rates that are not based on securities (such as LIBOR and other interbank rates, money market rates, the Federal Reserve discount rate, prime rates and the consumer price index);
- swaps on yields based on interest rates or monetary rates;
- credit default swaps, other than single-name credit default swaps;
- certain index credit default swaps on security indices that are not narrow-based;
- total return swaps based on two or more nonsecurity loans, or based on broad-based security indices;
- forward rate agreements;
- foreign currency options, foreign exchange options and foreign exchange rate options (other than foreign exchange or currency options traded on a national securities exchange);
- currency swaps and cross-currency swaps;
- swaps on futures other than futures on single securities or narrow-based security indices; and
- options on instruments that are swaps ("swaptions").

Transactions that are generally not subject to CFTC regulation include:

- swaps on single stocks or loans;
- swaps on narrow-based security indices;
- swaps on portfolios where the parties have discretion to change the composition or weighting of the securities in the portfolio;
- swaps on single foreign government securities or narrow-based indices composed of foreign government securities;
- swaps on yields based on a single debt security, single loan or narrow-based security index, where "yield" is a proxy for price or value (except for swaps on yields of U.S. Treasuries, which are subject to CFTC regulation);
- single-name credit default swaps (that is, those based on a single entity, security or loan);
- index credit default swaps on narrow-based security indices;
- total return swaps based on single securities, single loans or narrow-based security indices (although if the swap incorporates elements that create interest rate or currency exposures that are unrelated to the financing of the security-based swap, the swap may be a mixed swap subject to the jurisdiction of both the SEC and the CFTC);

- options on security-based swaps (which include the preceding 8 categories);
- swaps on futures on a single security or narrow-based security index;
- exchange traded foreign currency options; and
- bona fide foreign exchange spot transactions (that is, transactions that are settled within the customary timeline of the relevant spot market).

Whether a transaction is documented using an industry standard form agreement that is typically used for swaps may be a relevant factor, but is not dispositive, in determining whether the transaction is a swap subject to CFTC regulation. The specific terms of each transaction under an International Swaps and Derivatives Association ("ISDA") Master Agreement must be analyzed to determine whether it is a swap.

As evidenced by the above lists, the distinction between broad-based indices and narrow-based indices is important, because swaps on broad-based indices are typically subject to CFTC regulation, while those on narrow-based indices are not. The distinction is complex. In general, however, a security index is "narrow-based" if any of the following applies: (a) it has 9 or fewer component securities, (b) 1 of its component securities accounts for more than 30 percent of the index's weighting, (c) 5 of its component securities together comprise more than 60 percent of the index's weighting, or (d) the lowest weighted component securities that together comprise 25 percent of the index's weighting have an aggregate average daily trading volume of less than $50,000,000 (or $30,000,000 if the index has more than 15 components). Different criteria apply for classifying as narrow-based or broad-based debt security indices, volatility indices and credit default swap indices.

3. Commodity Pool Operators

i. Definition

Under the CEA, a CPO is:

> any person engaged in a business that is of the nature of a commodity pool, investment trust, syndicate, or similar form of enterprise, and who, in connection therewith, solicits, accepts, or receives from others, funds, securities, or property, either directly or through capital contributions, the sale of stock or other forms of securities, or otherwise, for the purpose of trading in commodity interests.[207]

The definition goes on to specify that commodity interests include commodity futures, commodity options, security futures products, swaps regulated by the CFTC, and other instruments under the CFTC's jurisdiction. The CFTC regards any pooled investment vehicle (whether organized as a trust, partnership, limited liability company, corporation or other entity) as a commodity pool if it invests

207. CEA § 1a(11), 7 U.S.C. § 1a(11).

to any extent in commodity interests.[208] Generally, CPOs include the trustees of a pool organized as a trust, the officers and directors of a pool organized as a corporation, the managers of a pool organized as a limited liability company, and the general partners of a pool organized as a partnership, if those persons solicit investors for the pool and accept capital contributions on behalf of the entity.

Therefore, an investment adviser that acts as the general partner of a hedge fund that invests in commodity interests is generally the hedge fund's CPO.[209] The investment adviser of an offshore hedge fund organized as a corporation, however, usually is not technically a CPO, because its relationship with the fund is, at least on paper, limited to providing investment management services pursuant to an investment management contract. An offshore hedge fund's directors and administrator are responsible for much of an offshore hedge fund's operations, including accepting and receiving contributions from investors. Those parties, however, are often neither willing nor licensed to serve as the offshore hedge fund's CPO.[210] The CFTC has indicated that the directors of the fund may delegate their rights and obligations as CPO to another person, such as the fund's investment adviser, if that person agrees to assume such rights and obligations and is registered as a CPO, but the directors must remain jointly and severally liable with respect to any violations of the CEA.[211]

ii. Exclusions from CPO Definition

CEA Rule 4.5 excludes the following entities and their principals and employees (collectively, "Rule 4.5 Accounts") from the definition of "CPO": investment companies registered under the Company Act that do not market themselves as commodity pools or vehicles for trading commodity interests, and whose trading in commodity interests other than for bona fide hedging purposes does not exceed specified *de minimis* thresholds; insurance companies, with respect to separate accounts they establish or maintain; banks, with respect to the assets of trusts,

208. CEA § 1a(10), 7 U.S.C. § 1a(10); CEA Rule § 4.10(d), 17 C.F.R. § 4.10(d).

209. The CFTC has on occasion issued special exemptive relief deeming a commodity pool's investment adviser, rather than its general partner, to be the pool's CPO, if the general partner received performance allocations from the pool but the investment adviser performed all management and solicitation activities. CFTC Letter No. 07-19, 2007 CFTC Ltr. LEXIS 19; Comm. Fut. L. Rep. (CCH) P30,697 (Sep. 13, 2007).

210. In the context of registered investment companies, the CFTC has expressly acknowledged the difficulty of identifying the CPO. The CFTC has advised that, although a registered fund's directors or trustees generally perform the functions described in the definition of a CPO, the investment adviser is the most appropriate party to serve as the CPO, because requiring a director or trustee to be the CPO would create operational concerns by effectively piercing the limits on liability that apply to those persons when they act in their capacities as directors and trustees. The same argument would presumably apply to directors and trustees of a private fund that is organized as a corporation or trust, although the CFTC's comments were made only with regard to registered funds. Commodity Pool Operators and Commodity Trading Advisors: Amendments to Compliance Obligations, 77 F.R. 11252 (Feb. 24, 2012).

211. Division of Swap Dealer and Intermediary Oversight Responds to Frequently Asked Questions—CPO/CTA: Amendments to Compliance Obligations, August 14, 2012, *available at* www.cftc.gov/LawRegulation/DoddFrankAct/GuidanceQandA.

custodial accounts and other separate units for which they act as fiduciaries and are vested with investment authority; and trustees or named fiduciaries of plans subject to Title I of ERISA, with respect to such plans. A person or entity claiming this exclusion must file a notice of eligibility electronically with the NFA before trading commodity interests for any Rule 4.5 Account, furnish prospective participants in such account with written disclosure about the exclusion from the CPO definition, submit to any special calls for information that the CFTC requires to determine compliance with Rule 4.5,[212] and make annual notice filings with the NFA reaffirming its reliance on the exclusion.

A CPO that relies on the CEA Rule 4.5 exclusion with respect to some of its accounts may also qualify for an exemption from CPO registration (for example, under CEA Rule 4.13, as discussed below) with respect to pools or accounts that are not covered by Rule 4.5.[213]

iii. Exemptions from CPO Registration[214]

a. Noncompensated and Small Pool Operators

A CPO is exempt from CFTC registration if (a) it receives no direct or indirect compensation for operating a pool (other than reimbursement of ordinary administrative operating expenses), (b) it operates only 1 commodity pool at a time, (c) it is not otherwise required to register with the CFTC and is not affiliated with any person or entity required to register with the CFTC, and (d) no advertising occurs in connection with the pool.[215] For this purpose, advertising includes the systematic solicitation of prospective participants by telephone or seminar presentation.[216]

A person or entity is also exempt from CPO registration if the aggregate capital contributions to all of its pools do not exceed $400,000, and none of its pools has more than 15 participants at any time (excluding each pool's CPO and CTA and their principals, those persons' children, siblings, parents and spouses, and those persons' spouses and relatives who live in the same residence).[217]

A CPO relying on either of the above exemptions must furnish participants in each pool with copies of the pool's monthly statements from the futures commission merchant that executes transactions in commodity interests for the pool, showing net profits and losses from transactions in commodity interests.[218] The CPO must affirm the exemption annually within 60 days after the end of each calendar year, through an electronic filing with the NFA.

---

212. CEA Rule § 4.5, 17 C.F.R. § 4.5.
213. CEA Rule § 4.5(g), 17 C.F.R. § 4.5(g).
214. An exemption from CPO registration formerly available to many investment advisers to hedge funds was revoked by the CFTC in 2012. That exemption, in CEA Rule 4.13(a)(4), was available to CPOs of hedge funds that were offered only to certain highly sophisticated investors. It is not discussed in this book.
215. CEA Rule § 4.13(a)(1), 17 C.F.R. § 4.13(a)(1).
216. CEA Rule § 4.13(a)(1)(iv), 17 C.F.R. § 4.13(a)(1)(iv).
217. CEA Rule § 4.13(a)(2)(i), 17 C.F.R. § 4.13(a)(2)(i).
218. CEA Rule § 4.13(c)(3), 17 C.F.R. § 4.13(c)(3).

b. Limited Trading Exemption

CEA Rule 4.13(a)(3) (the "Limited Trading Exemption") exempts a CPO from CFTC registration with respect to any pool:

- whose interests are exempt from registration under the Securities Act and are offered and sold without marketing to the public in the United States;
- that satisfies 1 of the following tests: either (a) the aggregate initial margin and premiums required to establish positions in commodity interests, measured when the most recent position was established, do not exceed 5 percent (excluding the in-the-money amounts of options that are in-the-money at the time of purchase) of the liquidation value of such pool (after taking into account unrealized profits and losses on such positions) or (b) the aggregate net notional value of the pool's commodity interest positions, measured when the most recent position was established, does not exceed the liquidation value of the pool's portfolio (after taking into account unrealized profits and losses on such positions);[219]
- that is not marketed to the public as a commodity pool or as a vehicle for trading in commodity futures or commodity options markets; and
- in which participation is limited to (a) accredited investors, as defined in Securities Act Rule 501,[220] (b) trusts formed by accredited investors for the benefit of family members, (c) knowledgeable employees as defined in Company Act Rule 3c-5,[221] and (d) certain qualified eligible persons ("QEPs"), as defined in CEA Rule 4.7(a)(2)(viii)(A)[222] (which includes only the pool's CPO, CTA, investment adviser, and certain of their employees, principals and family members).

In an interpretative letter, the CFTC stated that the investor sophistication standards in CEA Rule 4.13(a)(3)[223] apply only to U.S. investors, and thus a CPO claiming the Limited Trading Exemption with respect to a pool may admit non-U.S. persons who do not meet those standards.[224]

It is difficult to determine how to apply the trading limits of the Limited Trading Exemption to funds of funds. The CFTC previously promulgated special guidance that described alternative methods for imposing and calculating the

---

219. Rule 4.13(a)(3) specifies the method of calculating the "net notional value" of futures, options and cleared swaps. It provides for netting of futures contracts with the same underlying commodity across designated contract markets and foreign boards of trade, and netting of swaps that are cleared on the same designated clearing organization. Over-the-counter swaps may not be netted. CEA Rule § 4.13(a)(3)(ii)(B), 17 C.F.R. § 4.13(a)(3)(ii)(B).

220. *See* § 5.3.2.ii, *infra.*

221. *See* §§ 3.2.2.iv and 3.3.2.xiii, *infra.*

222. 17 C.F.R. § 4.7(a)(2)(viii)(A).

223. 17 C.F.R. § 4.13(a)(3).

224. CFTC Letter No. 04-13, 2004 CFTC Ltr. LEXIS 9; Comm. Fut. L. Rep. (CCH) P29,753. (Apr. 14, 2004).

trading limits at the investee fund level.[225] It revoked that guidance in 2012 but has stated that it expects to issue new guidance in the future.

c. Additional Conditions of Exemptions

A CPO that relies on any of the exemptions from CPO registration described above in sections 2.9.3.iii.a and b must file a notice of eligibility with the NFA before delivering a subscription document for the pool to any prospective investor. This notice must be filed electronically through NFA's electronic exemption filing system and must include, among other things, representations that each eligible pool will be operated in accordance with the requirements of the applicable exemption. Within 60 days after the end of each calendar year, the CPO must file, electronically, a notice with the NFA reaffirming its reliance on the exemption it has claimed.[226] The CPO must also provide specified disclosure to each prospective participant in a pool with respect to which the CPO is exempt from registration, describing the criteria of the exemption and noting that, unlike a registered CPO, it is not required by the CEA to deliver a disclosure document or certified annual report to pool participants.[227] The CPO must also retain specified records and submit to special calls by the CFTC.[228]

If a CPO operates pools that are eligible for the Limited Trading Exemption, and also operates pools with respect to which it must register as a CPO, it must register as a CPO, but is exempt from all other requirements imposed on a CPO under the CEA with respect to the eligible pools, except the anti-fraud and anti-manipulation provisions. Such a CPO must, however, furnish certain additional disclosures to participants in the exempt pools. If an existing pool operated by a CPO would qualify as an eligible pool but for the fact that the CPO has not filed the required notice, the CPO may convert the pool into an eligible pool by notifying all participants in the pool of the CPO's intention to convert the pool into an eligible pool and giving them the right to withdraw prior to such conversion. The CPO may then file a notice of eligibility with the CFTC.[229]

A CPO claiming an exemption from CPO registration under CEA Rule 4.13(a) with respect to some pools may rely concurrently on an exclusion from the CPO definition under CEA Rule 4.5 with respect to other accounts that are Rule 4.5 Accounts.[230]

4. Commodity Trading Advisers

i. Definition

In general, a CTA is any person or entity that engages for compensation in the business of giving advice about trading in commodity interests.[231] An investment

225. CEA Rule, Appendix A to Part 4 - Guidance on the Application of Rule 4.13(a)(3) in the Fund-of-Funds Context, 17 C.F.R. Part 4, Appendix.

226. CEA Rule § 4.13(b), 17 C.F.R. § 4.13(b).

227. CEA Rule § 4.13(a)(6), 17 C.FR. § 4.13(a)(6).

228. CEA Rule § 4.13(c), 17 C.F.R. § 4.13(c).

229. CEA Rule § 4.13(e), 17 C.F.R. § 4.13(e).

230. CEA Rule § 4.13(f), 17 C.F.R. § 4.13(f). *See* § 2.9.3.ii, *supra*.

231. CEA § 1a(12), 7 U.S.C. § 1a(12).

adviser that desires to cause any of its clients to invest in any commodity interests should comply with the regulations applicable to CTAs. CTAs must comply with CEA rules on registration, disclosure, reporting, record-keeping and fraudulent practices. A CTA generally must register with the CFTC, unless it qualifies for an exemption from registration.[232]

ii. Exclusions from CTA Definition

Any person or entity excluded from the definition of "CPO" by CEA Rule 4.5,[233] and any of its principals or employees, is also excluded from the definition of "CTA" if its advice about commodity interests is solely incidental to its management of CEA Rule 4.5 Accounts, it files a notice of eligibility with the NFA to claim relief under Rule 4.5 with respect to its Rule 4.5 Accounts before providing trading advice about commodity interests to those accounts, and it submits to the CFTC's special calls to demonstrate compliance with this exclusion.[234] A person or entity relying on the Rule 4.5 exclusion must also make annual notice filings with the NFA reaffirming its reliance on the exclusion.

iii. Exemptions from CTA Registration

a. Private CTA Exemption

A CTA is exempt from CTA registration if during the preceding 12 months it has not furnished commodity trading advice to more than 15 persons and it does not "hold [itself] out generally to the public" as a CTA.[235] For this purpose, a pool counts as a single person. In addition, a natural person, that person's minor children, spouse, relatives living in the same residence, and accounts and trusts of which such persons are the only primary beneficiaries, collectively count as a single person.[236]

b. Registered Investment Adviser Exemption

A CTA is exempt from registration if it is registered as an investment adviser under the Advisers Act, its business does not consist primarily of acting as a CTA, and it does not act as a CTA to any investment trust, syndicate or similar form of enterprise that is engaged primarily in trading commodity interests.[237] The CFTC has not offered guidance on how much a pool may invest in commodity interests before it is deemed to be engaged primarily in trading commodity interests.[238]

---

232. CEA § 6m(1), 7 U.S.C. § 6m(1).
233. 17 C.F.R. § 4.5; *see* § 2.9.3, *supra.*
234. CEA Rule § 4.6(a)(2), 17 C.F.R. § 4.6(a)(2).
235. CEA § 4m(1), 7 U.S.C. § 6m(1).
236. CEA Rule § 4.14(a)(10)(i), 17 C.F.R. § 4.14(a)(10)(i).
237. CEA § 4m(3), 17 U.S.C. § 6m(3).
238. Similarly, a CTA registered as such is exempt from registration as an investment adviser if its business does not consist primarily of acting as an investment adviser and it does not act as an investment adviser to an investment company registered under the Company Act or a business development company under the Company Act. Advisers Act § 203(b)(6), 15 U.S.C. § 80b-3(b)(6).

c. Registered/Exempt CPO Exemption

A person or entity that is registered as a CPO or exempt from CPO registration, and whose commodity trading advice is directed solely to the pools it operates, is exempt from registration as a CTA.[239] Thus, an investment adviser that registers as a CPO and confines its trading advice regarding commodity interests to U.S. and offshore hedge funds that it manages would not also be required to register as a CTA.

d. Section 4.14(a)(8) Exemption

A CTA that is registered as an investment adviser under the Advisers Act or state law, or that is exempt from registration as an investment adviser, or that is excluded from the definition of "investment adviser" under Advisers Act section 202(a)(11) (such as a securities broker or publisher), is exempt from registration as a CTA,[240] if:

- the investment adviser's trading advice regarding commodity interests is directed solely to: (1) Rule 4.5 Accounts with respect to which a notice of eligibility has been filed; (2) certain ERISA plans defined in CEA Rule 4.5(a)(4); (3) pools organized and operated offshore that were not so organized to enable their CPO to avoid registration, that are not marketed from within the United States or to U.S. persons, and that limit participation by U.S. persons to the pools' CPO, CTA and their principals, who may own in the aggregate no more than 10 percent of each such pool; and (4) pools whose CPO is relying on or is eligible to rely on the Limited Trading Exemption from CPO registration;
- the investment adviser's trading advice regarding commodity interests is solely incidental to its business of providing securities investment advice;
- the investment adviser does not otherwise hold itself out as a CTA; and
- the investment adviser files an initial notice of exemption with the NFA and annual notices reaffirming its reliance on the exemption.

The investment adviser must also retain certain records and submit to special calls by the CFTC.

A CTA may rely on the Private CTA Exemption with respect to one set of clients, and on the section 4.14(a)(8) Exemption with respect to other clients. Similarly, a CTA may rely on the Registered Investment Adviser exemption with respect to some clients, and on the exemption under CEA Rule 4.14(a)(8) with respect to other clients.[241]

e. Non-U.S. Accounts

In certain circumstances, a U.S. investment adviser that advises only non-U.S. clients (including offshore hedge funds) that are not directly or indirectly

239. CEA Rule §§ 4.14(a)(4) and 4.14(a)(5), 17 C.F.R. §§ 4.14(a)(4) and 4.14(a)(5).
240. CEA Rule § 4.14(a)(8), 17 C.F.R. § 4.14(a)(8).
241. 52 F.R. 41,975, 41,978 (Nov. 2, 1987).

owned by any U.S. citizens or residents may obtain from the CFTC a special exemption from CTA registration. The CFTC issues such relief on a case-by-case basis. Investment advisers that have received such exemptions have generally satisfied some or all of the following conditions: are registered with the SEC as investment advisers, provide commodity interest trading advice to non-U.S. clients in a manner solely incidental to their securities advice to those clients, invest in commodity interests solely for bona fide hedging purposes, and invest no more than 5 percent of each client's assets under their management in initial margin and option premiums on positions in commodity interests.

5. CTA and CPO Registration

i. Registration Requirements for CTAs and CPOs

The CFTC has delegated the review of CTA and CPO registration applications to the NFA.[242] An applicant for registration as a CTA or CPO or both must complete NFA Form 7-R and file it with the NFA,[243] with a Form 8-R and fingerprint card for each of its principals and associated persons. Registered CPOs and CTAs must also join the NFA. Form 7-R includes an application for NFA membership. The NFA assesses application fees and annual membership dues.

Registration forms must be filed electronically with the NFA using its Online Registration System ("ORS").[244] An applicant may not act as a CPO or CTA until the registration is granted.[245] The NFA may deny or revoke the registration of any CTA or CPO if it determines that the applicant or registrant is not fit to be a CTA or CPO or for good cause.[246]

ii. Registration Requirements for APs and Principals

An associated person (an "AP") of a CPO or CTA is any person who solicits investors or clients for the CPO or CTA or who directly or indirectly supervises those persons (such as the CPO's or CTA's president, chief executive officer, managing director or managing partner).[247] Thus, marketing personnel and persons who supervise them, up to the highest level executives of the firm, may be APs. An individual who does not solicit clients or supervise anyone else who solicits clients is not an AP, even if he or she makes investment decisions regarding commodity interests.

"Principal" is a broader category that includes any owner of at least 10 percent of the CPO or CTA, any contributor of at least 10 percent of the CPO's or CTA's capital (measured on an ongoing basis), any officer whose duties relate to commodity interest activities, any director or general partner of the CPO or CTA, or any person who has the ability, directly or indirectly, to exert

242. CEA Rule § 3.2, 17 C.F.R. § 3.2.
243. CEA Rule § 3.10(a)(1), 17 C.F.R. § 3.10(a)(1).
244. NFA Registration Rule 801(a)(5).
245. *Id.*
246. NFA Registration Rule 501.
247. CEA Rule § 1.3(aa), 17 C.F.R. § 1.3(aa).

a controlling influence over the activities of the CPO or CTA.[248] A person may be both an AP and a principal. The NFA may refuse to register or may register conditionally any person applying to register as an AP and may suspend or revoke the registration of such person based on standards of fitness under the CEA.[249]

Each principal or AP of a CPO or CTA must file a Form 8-R with the NFA using the ORS,[250] as well as a fingerprint card. Each AP must generally pass the Series 3 examination administered by FINRA or obtain an exemption from this requirement.[251]

iii. Exemptions from Registration as an AP

a. Certain Principals

CEA Rule 3.12(h)[252] exempts a person in the supervisory chain of command of a CPO or CTA (such as the general partner, manager or chief operating officer), who would otherwise be an AP, from registration as an AP and from the FINRA Series 3 examination requirement if:

- that person is registered as a principal of the CPO or CTA;
- the CPO or CTA has not been found to have committed fraud or failed to supervise an employee under the CEA or the CEA Regulations and is not subject to any pending proceeding alleging such fraud or failure;
- that person is not authorized to solicit or accept client funds, solicit funds for a pool, solicit clients or supervise persons engaged in such activities;
- that person has no authority with respect to hiring, firing or other personnel matters involving employees of the CPO or CTA who are engaged in activities related to commodity interests;
- at least 1 other person is registered as an AP of the CPO or CTA and exercises full and final supervisory authority over client activities of the CPO or CTA relating to commodity interests and over hiring and firing personnel of the CPO or CTA who engage in such activities (if such person ceases to have such authority, the CPO or CTA must notify the NFA within 20 days of such occurrence and the identity of such person's successor); and
- commodity interest activities account for no more than 10 percent of the CPO's or CTA's annual revenues.[253]

This exemption requires the CPO or CTA to file appropriate resolutions with the NFA indicating compliance with the foregoing requirements.[254]

---

248. CEA Rule § 3.1(a), 17 C.F.R. § 3.1(a); NFA Registration Rule 101(t).
249. NFA Registration Rule 501.
250. NFA Registration Rule 801.
251. NFA Registration Rule 401.
252. 17 C.F.R. § 3.12(h).
253. CEA Rule § 3.12(h)(1)(iii), 17 C.F.R. § 3.12(h)(1)(iii).
254. *Id.*

b. APs of Certain CTAs

A person who is exempt from registering as a CTA or is associated with a person who is exempt from registering as a CTA under the exemptions described above in section 2.9.4.iii is not required to register as an AP of that CTA.[255] This exemption is not available for any person who solicits or supervises persons who solicit discretionary client accounts for a CTA that does not qualify for the exemptions described above in section 2.9.4.iii or that does qualify for an exemption but is registered as a CTA.[256]

c. Registered Representatives and Principals of FINRA Members

A registered representative, registered principal, limited representative or limited principal of a member of FINRA is exempt from registration as an AP of a CPO if he or she only solicits pool participants or supervises any person who does so for that member and does not engage in any other activity regulated by the CFTC.[257]

d. Non-U.S. APs

A non-U.S. individual who solicits for a CTA or a CPO only potential clients or investors who are not U.S. persons and conducts such solicitations entirely outside the United States is exempt from registration as an AP of that CTA or CPO.[258] Such an individual cannot undertake any marketing activity that could reasonably be expected to have the effect of soliciting U.S. persons.[259]

---

255. CEA Rule § 3.12(h)(2)(ii), 17 C.F.R. § 3.12(h)(2)(ii).

256. *Id.*

257. CEA Rule § 3.12(h)(l)(ii), 17 C.F.R. § 3.12(h)(1)(ii).

258. CFTC Interpretive Letters No. 88-8, 1988 CFTC Ltr. LEXIS 25; Comm. Fut. L. Rep. (CCH)) P24,227 (Apr. 8, 1988) (concerning APs of CTAs) and Nos. 90-4, 1990 CFTC Ltr. LEXIS 25, Comm. Fut. L. Rep. (CCH) P24,588 (Jan. 31, 1990), and 93-106, 1993 CFTC Ltr. LEXIS 135 (Oct. 12, 1993) (concerning APs of CPOs).

259. CFTC Interpretive Letter No. 93-106, 1993 CFTC Ltr. LEXIS 135 (Oct. 12, 1993). The term "U.S. person" includes:

- a natural person who is a resident of the United States;
- a partnership, corporation or other entity that is organized under the laws of the United States or has its principal place of business in the United States;
- any estate or trust, the income of which is subject to U.S. income tax regardless of source; or
- any entity organized principally for passive investment such as a commodity pool, investment company or other similar entity (other than a pension plan for the employees, officers or principals of an entity organized and with its principal place of business outside the United States), in which U.S. persons hold units of participation representing in the aggregate 10 percent or more of the beneficial interest in the entity, or which has as a principal purpose the facilitating of investment by a U.S. person in a commodity pool with respect to which the operator is exempt from certain requirements of Part 4 of the CEA Regulations by virtue of its participants being non-U.S. persons. CFTC Interpretive Letter No. 92-3, 1992 CFTC Ltr. LEXIS 22, Comm. Fut. L. Rep. (CCH) P25,221 (Feb. 4, 1992).

iv. *Waivers and Exemption from Examination Requirement*

The NFA may waive the FINRA Series 3 examination requirement for APs of a CPO, if (a) the CPO or its pools are regulated by a federal or state regulatory authority or the pools are privately offered pursuant to an exemption from registration under the Securities Act and (b) the CPO limits its commodity interest activities to operating pools that (1) engage principally in securities transactions, (2) commit no more than 10 percent of their assets (measured on an ongoing basis) as initial margin and premiums for commodity interests, and (3) use commodity interests only for hedging or risk management purposes. A similar waiver is available to APs of a CTA if the CTA is regulated by a federal or state regulatory authority, and the CTA's advice to each client regarding commodity interests is incidental to the securities advice it provides and is for hedging or risk management purposes.[260]

An AP of a CPO or CTA that is required to register as such only because of activities involving swaps is automatically exempt from the examination requirement. In addition, an AP of a CPO that trades commodity interests but that would be excluded from the CPO definition under Rule 4.5(c)(2)(iii)(A) or (B) or exempt from CPO registration under Rule 4.13(a)(3) were it not for its swaps activities (that is, it would meet the *de minimis* standard except for its swaps activities) may apply for a waiver of the examination requirement.[261] This exemption and waiver are based on the fact that the FINRA Series 3 examination does not relate to swaps; they may be revoked in the future if FINRA or the NFA develops an examination more directly relevant to swap activities.

6. Amendments to Forms 7-R and 8-R

Registration as a CPO or CTA remains effective for 1 year.[262] Accordingly, each registered CPO or CTA must file a Form 7-R with the NFA annually on a date specified by the NFA. If the CPO or CTA does not make this filing on time, the NFA will regard the failure as a request to withdraw from registration.

CPOs, CTAs and APs of a CPO or CTA must report promptly, on Form 3-R, any changes in the information on their respective Forms 7-R or Forms 8-R.[263] If the change is the addition of a new principal who is a natural person, the CPO or CTA must file a Form 8-R and fingerprint card for the new principal.[264] The CPO or CTA must report an additional nonnatural person on Form 3-R.[265] If an AP or principal of a CPO or CTA terminates its relationship with the CPO or CTA, the CPO or CTA must file a notice of that termination on Form 8-T with

260. NFA Registration Rule 402.
261. NFA Registration Rule 401(e)(2)(ii).
262. CEA § 4f(a)(1), 7 U.S.C. § 6f(a)(1).
263. CEA Rule § 3.31, 17 C.F.R. § 3.31.
264. CEA Rule § 3.31(a)(3), 17 C.F.R. § 3.31(a)(3).
265. *Id.*

the NFA within 20 days of the termination.[266] Forms 3-R and 8-T must be filed electronically using the ORS.[267]

If a registered CPO or CTA changes its form of organization from one entity to another (such as from a partnership to a corporation), the CPO or CTA must report such change on a Form 3-R but generally is not required to file a new registration application for the reorganized entity. If a CPO or CTA changes from a sole proprietorship to a business entity, or from a business entity to a sole proprietorship, however, the CPO or CTA must file a Form 7-W electronically using the ORS to withdraw the registration of the original entity or sole proprietorship and file a Form 7-R to register the successor entity or sole proprietorship.[268] The reorganized entity will be liable for the obligations of the pre-existing entity under the CEA and CEA Regulations.[269]

7. Disclosure Requirements

Disclosure requirements for registered CPOs and CTAs are discussed in Chapter 6.

8. Required Reports to Clients and Pool Participants

A registered CTA is not required to send periodic reports to its clients. A futures commission merchant, which conducts business as a broker in commodity interests, is required to send confirmations and month-end account statements directly to the clients of a CTA and to the CTA that controls the accounts.[270]

In contrast, a futures commission merchant sends confirmations directly to CPOs, not to pool participants.[271] Accordingly, a registered CPO must send pool participants a monthly or quarterly (depending on the size of the pool) account statement within 30 days following the end of each reporting period, which includes financial statements prepared in accordance with GAAP and any previously undisclosed material business dealings between the pool and its CPO, CTA, futures commission merchant or any of their respective principals.[272] In addition, the CPO must send pool participants an annual report, within 90 days after the end of the pool's fiscal year, that includes performance data and financial statements prepared in accordance with GAAP and audited by an

266. CEA Rule § 3.31(c), 17 C.F.R. § 3.31(c).

267. *See* http://www.nfa.futures.org/nfa-registration/online-registration-system-overview.html (last visited May 5, 2013).

268. CEA Rule § 3.31(a)(1), 17 C.F.R. § 3.31(a)(1).

269. CEA Rule § 3.31(a)(2), 17 C.F.R. § 3.31(a)(2).

270. CEA Rule § 1.33, 17 C.F.R. § 1.33.

271. CEA Rule § 1.33(b)(4), 17 C.F.R. § 1.33(b)(4).

272. CEA Rule § 4.22, 17 C.F.R. § 4.22.

independent public accountant.[273] CEA Rule 4.22[274] identifies the information that must be disclosed in the account statement and annual report.

If the annual report is sent to pool participants within 45 days of the end of the pool's fiscal year, the CPO is not required to deliver an account statement for the final month of that fiscal year.[275] A copy of the annual report must be filed with the NFA.[276] If a CPO cannot distribute the report within 90 days from the end of the pool's fiscal year, the CPO may request an extension from the NFA.

9. Reports of Substantial Market Positions

Registered CTAs and CPOs are required to report to the CFTC their positions in commodity interests that exceed thresholds set forth in CEA Regulations and must maintain books and records detailing their positions and transactions in commodity interests.[277] CEA Regulations also limit a registered CTA's or CPO's speculative trading and the size of the positions it may hold.[278] Generally, all accounts controlled by a CTA or a CPO are aggregated for reporting and position-limit purposes.[279]

10. Systemic Risk Reports

Registered CPOs and CTAs are required to file reports with the CFTC that are intended to allow the CFTC to monitor systemic risk.[280] Form CPO-PQR reports various identifying and operating data of the CPO and is similar to SEC Form PF.[281] The amount of information that a CPO must report on Form CPO-PQR depends on the aggregate gross assets under management ("AUM") of the funds that the CPO operates and any separate accounts that it manages using substantially the same strategy as any of its funds.

Every CPO must complete Schedule A, which requires disclosure of the CPO's total AUM, its service providers, and information about each fund it operates, including monthly performance and redemption terms. A CPO with commodity pool AUM of $150,000,000 or more must furnish additional information on Schedule B of Form CPO-PQR, including information about its investment strategy, borrowings, types of creditors, counterparty credit and exposure, and investments. A CPO with commodity pool AUM of $1,500,000,000 or more must also complete Schedule C, which solicits

273. CEA Rule § 4.22(c), 17 C.F.R. § 4.22(c). The SEC has no similar audit requirement. Thus, investment advisers that do not trade commodity interests are not required to provide their hedge fund investors with audited financial statements, although they may do so to comply in part with the custody rules. *See* Chapter 12, *infra.*

274. 17 C.F.R. § 4.22.

275. CEA Rule § 4.22(b), 17 C.F.R. § 4.22(b).

276. CEA Rule § 4.22(c), 17 C.F.R. § 4.22(c); NFA Compliance Rule 2-13.

277. CEA Rule §§ 15 and 18, 17 C.F.R. Parts 15 and 18.

278. CEA Rule § 150, 17 C.F.R. Part 150.

279. CEA Rule §§ 18.01, 150.4 and 150.5(g), 17 C.F.R. §§ 18.01, 150.4 and 150.5(g).

280. CEA Rule § 4.27, 17 C.F.R. § 4.27.

281. *See* § 13.2.

information about the aggregate portfolios of the pools, including geographic breakdowns of investments, and certain risk metrics about each large pool.

In an effort to harmonize the CFTC and SEC reporting requirements, the CFTC provides that a CPO that is also registered with the SEC as an investment adviser and files SEC Form PF does not need to complete the items on Form CPO-PQR that request the same information that the CPO reports on its Form PF.

A registered CPO with AUM of $1,500,000,000 or more must file Form CPO-PQR within 60 days after the end of each calendar quarter. A registered CPO with AUM under $1,500,000,000 must file Form CPO-PQR within 90 days after the end of each calendar year. Form CPO-PQR is not subject to public disclosure, except for portions of Schedule A.

A registered CTA must file a report on Form CTA-PR within 45 days after the end of each calendar year. Form CTA-PR is similar to, but much less extensive than, the Form CPO-PQR, soliciting basic demographic information about the CTA and the names of any pools it advises. Form CTA-PR is subject to public disclosure, except for the names of pools the CTA advises.

Registered CPOs and CTAs are also required to make quarterly and annual filings with the NFA, which include part of the information on Forms CPO-PQR and CTA-PR, information about service providers and specified financial and performance data. The forms for the NFA filings are consolidated with Forms CPO-PQR and CTA-PR; a CPO or CTA files a single set of forms with the NFA, and the NFA forwards the relevant sections to the CFTC.

11. Record-Keeping Requirements

A registered CTA or CPO must maintain the following records:

- acknowledgments from clients that they received the CTA's or CPO's disclosure document;
- copies of each confirmation of a commodity interest transaction, each purchase and sale statement, and each monthly statement from a futures commission merchant concerning each client account, the CTA's or CPO's own account and the accounts of its principals;
- copies of all materials sent to clients and prospective clients, including the text of oral presentations, showing the date of first distribution;
- itemized daily records of all transactions in commodity interests by the CTA or CPO; and
- books and records of other transactions and business dealings by the CTA or CPO and its principals relating to trading commodity interests or engaging in cash market transactions.[282]

A CTA must also maintain all powers of attorney and other documents authorizing it to trade commodity interests on behalf of clients; copies of all written agreements between the CTA and its clients; and a list or other record of all commodity interest accounts directed by the CTA and of all transactions

282. CEA Rule §§ 4.23 and 4.33, 17 C.F.R. §§ 4.23 and 4.33.

effected for those accounts.[283] A CPO must maintain additional records, including journals, ledgers, periodic income statements and balance sheets of each pool operated by the CPO and all other records, data and memoranda prepared or received by the CPO in operating the pool.[284] CTAs and CPOs must maintain the required records for 5 years.[285]

12. Exemptions from Certain Disclosure, Record-Keeping and Reporting Requirements

CEA Regulations afford registered CPOs and CTAs relief from some of the CEA's disclosure, record-keeping and reporting requirements with respect to certain commodity pools and separate accounts that they manage.[286] Such relief applies only to qualifying pools and accounts, rather than to the CPO or CTA generally, and the CPO or CTA must file a notice with the NFA to claim such relief. Those pools and accounts, which include "4.12(b) Pools," certain offshore funds, "QEP Pools" and "QEP Accounts," are described in Chapter 6, along with certain CEA disclosure, record-keeping and reporting requirements that apply to them.

13. Anti-Fraud Provisions

CTAs and CPOs are subject to broad anti-fraud provisions under the CEA, similar to those under Exchange Act section 10(b) and Rule 10b-5 discussed in Chapter 6. CEA section 4b prohibits fraudulent activity and material misrepresentation in connection with commodity futures contracts and swaps.[287] CEA section 4o provides further that a CTA or CPO may not:

> employ any device, scheme, or artifice to defraud any client or participant or prospective client or participant or ... engage in any transaction, practice, or course of business which operates as a fraud or deceit upon any client or participant or prospective client or participant.[288]

Examples of fraudulent practices include false and deceptive advertising, unauthorized trading, churning, taking the other side of a client's order without prior consent, crossing orders between clients in lieu of competitive market execution, and misrepresentations and omissions in disclosure documents (such as, for example, concealing commission kickbacks and failing to disclose certain risks of trading in commodity interests).

CEA section 6c prohibits the use or attempted use of any manipulative or deceptive device in connection with any commodity interest in interstate commerce, including knowingly transmitting false, misleading or inaccurate

283. CEA Rule § 4.33, 17 C.F.R. § 4.33.
284. CEA Rule § 4.23, 17 C.F.R. § 4.23.
285. CEA Rule § 1.31(a), 17 C.F.R. § 1.31(a).
286. CEA Rule §§ 4.22, 4.33 and 4.34, 17 C.F.R. §§ 4.22, 4.33 and 4.34.
287. CEA § 4b, 7 U.S.C. § 6b.
288. CEA § 4o, 7 U.S.C. § 6o.

information concerning the price of any commodity interest or conditions affecting such price.[289] CEA Rule 180.1[290] makes it unlawful to: (a) employ any manipulative device, scheme or artifice to defraud; (b) make or attempt to make any untrue or misleading statement of a material fact or to omit to state a material fact; (c) engage in any act, practice, or course of business, which operates or would operate as a fraud or deceit on any person; or (d) deliver a false or misleading or inaccurate report concerning crop or market information.

In modeling Rule 180.1 on SEC Rule 10b-5, the CFTC stated that it "will be guided, but not controlled, by the judicial precedent applying comparable language in Rule 10b-5."[291] In doing so, the CFTC provided that it intends to interpret the rule "not technically and restrictively, but flexibly to effectuate its remedial purposes" and notes that proof of a market or price effect is not required. Rule 180.1 adopts a recklessness scienter standard consistent with precedent interpreting SEC Rule 10b-5. It thus creates a lower scienter threshold and prohibits fraud and fraud-based manipulative devices employed intentionally or recklessly, regardless of whether the suspect conduct was intended to create an artificial price.

The CFTC's enforcement authority includes nationwide subpoena powers and the ability to seek sanctions, including civil monetary penalties, restitution, and industry bars.[292]

14. Other Considerations

A pool must operate as a separate entity from its CPO. All funds received by the CPO for use in pool activities must be received in the pool's (not the CPO's) name. The CPO may not commingle funds of the pool with funds of another person.[293] CTAs and CPOs, as such, are not subject to net capital requirements. CTAs and CPOs are subject to restrictions on advertising and rules regarding supervisory procedures for preparing and reviewing promotional materials.[294] CTAs and CPOs may be subject to additional requirements under state law.[295]

The CFTC's Statement of Acceptable Practices for ethics training[296] is a safe harbor, outlining acceptable procedures for ethics training programs and topics that ethics training programs should address. Because the Statement is general, the NFA adopted Compliance Rule 2-9, "Ethics Training Requirements."[297] The NFA's rule requires firms to have written procedures that outline their ethics training programs. NFA members may obtain ethics training from third-party

---

289. CEA § 6c, 7 U.S.C. § 6c.
290. 17 C.F.R. § 180.1.
291. 76 F.R. 41398 (July 14, 2011).
292. CEA § 6c, 7 U.S.C. § 6c.
293. CEA Rule § 4.20, 17 C.F.R. § 4.20.
294. CEA Rule 4.41; NFA Compliance Rule 2-29.
295. *See, e.g.*, Cal. Corp. Code § 29500, *et seq*; NY Gen'l Bus. Law § 359-e.
296. 17 C.F.R. Ch. 1, Pt. 3, App. B.
297. NFA Interpretive Notice 9051, NFA Compliance Rule 2-9: Ethics Training Requirements (July 1, 2003), *available at* http://www.nfa.futures.org/nfamanual/NFAManual.aspx?RuleID=9051&Section=9 (last visited May 5, 2013).

providers, although members are still responsible for ensuring that the provider is qualified. Training format and frequency depends on the member's specific business operations and workforce. Members must document compliance with their procedures.

§ 2.10 Anti-Money Laundering

See section 2.7.7 above regarding proposed and withdrawn anti-money laundering rules. Legislation has been introduced in Congress that would require hedge funds to implement anti-money laundering programs. Whether or not legislation is enacted, the U.S. Department of the Treasury may propose new rules, and investment advisers should consider adopting anti-money laundering programs in the interim based on the withdrawn rule.

CHAPTER 3

Exclusions from "Investment Company" Definition

The Company Act defines an investment company as, among other things, an issuer that "is or holds itself out as being engaged primarily ... in the business of investing, reinvesting, or trading in securities."[1] Hedge funds engage in that business, but avoid most of the regulations applicable to investment companies under the Company Act by relying on the exclusions from the definition of "investment company" in Company Act sections 3(c)(1) and 3(c)(7).[2]

§ 3.1 Summary of Registration Requirements

1. Key Limitations on Registered Investment Companies

An investment fund that does not qualify for an exclusion from the definition of "investment company" may not offer or sell a security in the United States,[3] unless the company is registered under Company Act section 8.[4] A registered investment company is subject to technical, complex and extensive substantive regulation of its activities. For example, a registered investment company must have a board of directors or similar body, at least 75 percent of the members of which must be independent of the company.[5] A registered investment company must disclose to its investors those of its investment policies that it believes are fundamental,[6] and those policies can only be changed by a shareholder vote. The Company Act also limits a registered investment company's ability to employ leverage, sell securities short and engage in transactions with affiliates.[7]

---

1. Company Act § 3(a)(1), 15 U.S.C. § 80a-3(a)(1).
2. 15 U.S.C. §§ 80a-3(c)(1) and 80a-3(c)(7).
3. Company Act § 7(a), 15 U.S.C. § 80a-7(a).
4. 15 U.S.C. § 80a-8.
5. Company Act § 10(a), 15 U.S.C. § 80a-10(a); Company Act Rule 0-1(a), (7), 17 C.F.R. § 270.0-1(a)(7).
6. Company Act § 8(b), 15 U.S.C. § 80a-8(b).
7. Company Act § 18(f), 15 U.S.C. § 80a-18(f); Company Act Release No. 10666 (Apr. 18, 1979), 44 F.R. 25,128 (Apr. 27, 1979).

2. Consequences of Failure to Register and to Comply with Limitations

If a fund is required by the Company Act to register as an investment company and does not do so, the fund and the fund's general partner, manager or promoter would be subject to criminal or civil penalties, administrative actions, injunctive relief that would prohibit the fund from continuing to do business until it registers under the Company Act, or private actions to require refunds of market losses or advisory fees.[8]

§ 3.2 Section 3(c)(1) Exclusion

1. General Statement of Rule

Company Act section 3(c)(1)[9] excludes any pooled investment vehicle from the definition of "investment company" if it does not have more than 100 beneficial owners of its outstanding securities (the "100-Owner Limit") and does not make or propose to make a public offering of its securities. A hedge fund that relies on this exclusion is commonly called a "3(c)(1) Fund."

2. Determination of Beneficial Ownership

i. Partnerships, Corporations, Trusts and Other Entities

The Company Act and SEC rules promulgated under it prevent in certain circumstances the use of multitiered pooled investment vehicles to avoid the 100-Owner Limit, by looking through an entity (an "Investing Entity") that invests in a 3(c)(1) Fund and counting the beneficial owners of the Investing Entity's outstanding securities as if they were direct beneficial owners of outstanding securities of the 3(c)(1) Fund. The SEC and its staff have established standards for determining whether to look through an Investing Entity. Those statutory provisions, rules and other standards and their applications are described below.

---

8. Company Act § 42(d), 15 U.S.C. § 80a-42(d) ("... a court of equity may, to the extent it deems necessary or appropriate, take exclusive jurisdiction and possession of the investment company or companies involved and the books, records and assets thereof, wherever located; and the court shall have jurisdiction to appoint a trustee, who with the approval of the court shall have power to dispose of any or all such assets ..."). Company Act section 42(d), 15 U.S.C. § 80a-42(d), also authorizes the SEC to transmit evidence of any violation of the Company Act to the U.S. Attorney General for institution of criminal proceedings. Company Act § 42(e), 15 U.S.C. § 80a-42(e), authorizes the SEC to impose monetary penalties for violations of the Company Act.

9. 15 U.S.C. § 80a-3(c)(1).

a. The 10 Percent Look-Through Test

Under Company Act section 3(c)(1)(A),[10] each beneficial owner of outstanding securities of an Investing Entity is counted as a beneficial owner of outstanding securities of a 3(c)(1) Fund for the purpose of the 100-Owner Limit, if both of the following conditions (the "3(c)(1)(A) Tests") exist:

- The Investing Entity is an investment company, as defined in the Company Act (such as a mutual fund), or is a 3(c)(1) Fund or a hedge fund that relies on Company Act section 3(c)(7) (a "3(c)(7) Fund") (each, a "Covered Company"); and
- The Investing Entity owns 10 percent or more of the 3(c)(1) Fund's outstanding voting securities (the "10% Test").[11]

If only one of the 3(c)(1)(A) Tests is met, no look-through is required. In addition, the analysis described above is necessary only when an Investing Entity acquires a voting security of the 3(c)(1) Fund, and no look-through is necessary if the interest of an Investing Entity that is a Covered Company increases to 10 percent of a 3(c)(1) Fund's outstanding voting securities solely because of the redemption of other voting securities of the 3(c)(1) Fund.[12] If an Investing Entity is a fund of funds (that is, its business is to invest a pool of investor funds in 3(c)(1) Funds and other professionally managed accounts), the Investing Entity may be expected in most cases to meet the first 3(c)(1)(A) Test. In such case, a 3(c)(1) Fund in which it invests should either limit the Investing Entity's investment to less than 10 percent of the 3(c)(1) Fund's investor assets or assume that each of the Investing Entity's direct and indirect owners will be deemed to be a beneficial owner of the 3(c)(1) Fund.

Section 3(c)(1)(A) does not require a look-through unless the Investing Entity is an investment company, as defined in the Company Act, or a private investment company. Before accepting an investment from any Investing Entity that is not a natural person, a 3(c)(1) Fund should require that Investing Entity to disclose whether or not it is a Covered Company. If the Investing Entity is a Covered Company, the 3(c)(1) Fund should determine whether the Investing Entity exceeds the 10% Test.

The 10% Test refers to ownership of 10 percent or more of the 3(c)(1) Fund's voting securities. Most 3(c)(1) Funds are organized as limited partnerships. The SEC generally considers limited partner interests to be voting securities.[13] In

---

10. 15 U.S.C. § 80a-3(c)(1)(A).

11. Company Act Rule 3c-1, 17 C.F.R. § 270.3c-1, provides, however, that a Covered Company that owns 10 percent or more of a 3(c)(1) Fund's outstanding voting securities is considered to be only one beneficial owner of the 3(c)(1) Fund (that is, the Covered Company is not subject to a look-through), if (a) the Covered Company owned 10 percent or more of the 3(c)(1) Fund's outstanding voting securities on April 1, 1997, and (b) on each date that the Covered Company invests in the 3(c)(1) Fund, no more than 10 percent of the Covered Company's total assets are invested in the 3(c)(1) Fund and other Covered Companies.

12. Company Act Release No. 22597 (Apr. 3, 1997), 62 F.R. 17,512 (Apr. 9, 1997) (hereinafter, "1997 Release"), at § III.A.2.

13. Horsley Keogh Venture Fund, SEC No-Action Letter (Apr. 27, 1988).

certain instances, however, limited partner interests may not be voting securities, so that no investor owns outstanding voting securities of the 3(c)(1) Fund and the 10% Test is not met.

The SEC staff has stated that a limited partner interest generally is not considered to be a voting security if: (1) the Investing Entity is not formed for the purpose of investing in the (3)(c)(1) Fund and does not contribute the majority of the 3(c)(1) Fund's capital; (2) no limited partner takes part in the conduct or control of the business of the (3)(c)(1) Fund or has the right to vote on the election, replacement or removal of the general partner or investment manager (even if the general partner or investment manager withdraws from the 3(c)(1) Fund); and (3) no limited partner itself relies on section 3(c)(1) to avoid registration under the Company Act.[14]

Even if these conditions are met, the SEC may consider a limited partner interest to be a voting security if a limited partner can seek to amend or renew the partnership agreement at regular intervals or if a limited partner exercises sufficient control through economic power that the limited partner interests are the functional equivalent of voting securities.[15] A general partner's interest ordinarily is excluded in determining the total amount of voting securities of a 3(c)(1) Fund.[16]

If both 3(c)(1)(A) Tests are met, all of the beneficial owners of the Investing Entity are deemed to be beneficial owners of the 3(c)(1) Fund. If a beneficial owner of the Investing Entity is another entity, the SEC may determine whether that other entity by itself meets both 3(c)(1)(A) Tests, and, if it does, the SEC may look through to that entity's beneficial owners.[17] The SEC has not specified the manner in which such a second look-through might be calculated.

b. Investing Entity's Owners That Can Vary the Size of Their Indirect Investments in a 3(c)(1) Fund

If the investors in an Investing Entity have the right or authority to specify the amount of their participation in particular investments made by that Investing Entity, each participating owner of that Investing Entity is considered, for purposes of the 100-Owner Limit, a beneficial owner of a 3(c)(1) Fund in which the Investing Entity has an interest.[18]

---

14. Rogers, Casey & Associates, Inc., SEC No-Action Letter (June 16, 1989); Weiss, Peck & Greer Venture Associates II, L.P., SEC No-Action Letter (Apr. 10, 1990); Clemente Global Growth Fund, Inc. v. Pickens, 705 F. Supp. 958, 967 (S.D.N.Y. 1989); Kohlberg Kravis Roberts & Co., SEC No-Action Letter (Sep. 9, 1985); MMC Fund, L.P., SEC No-Action Letter (Mar. 31, 1989); Laifer Inc., SEC No-Action Letter (Jan. 5, 1993); Standish Equity Investments, Inc., SEC No-Action Letter (Dec. 15, 1993).

15. Rogers, Casey & Associates, Inc., SEC No-Action Letter (June 16, 1989). Devonshire Capital Corp., SEC No-Action Letter (Feb. 15, 1976); Pierce, Lewis & Dolan, SEC No-Action Letter (Apr. 21, 1972).

16. *See* § 3.2.2.vi, *infra*.

17. Clemente Global Growth Fund, Inc. v. Pickens, et al., 705 F. Supp. 958, 965 (S.D.N.Y. 1989).

18. Tyler Capital Fund, L.P./South Market Capital, SEC No-Action Letter (Sep. 28, 1987); Six Pack, SEC No-Action Letter (Nov. 13, 1989).

Some Investing Entities, such as funds of funds and family partnerships, treat their limited partners differently based on their different investment objectives. A limited partnership whose general partner consults with its limited partners to determine their investment objectives and apportions each limited partner's participation in the partnership's investments in accordance with those investment objectives will not be considered a single beneficial owner of a 3(c)(1) Fund, even if the general partner (and not the limited partners) makes the ultimate investment allocation decisions.[19] Such an Investing Entity probably would be ignored for purposes of section 3(c)(1) and each of its participating beneficial owners probably would be deemed a beneficial owner of a 3(c)(1) Fund in which the Investing Entity invests. It is unclear, however, whether a 3(c)(1) Fund should count a beneficial owner of such an Investing Entity that directs the Investing Entity not to invest any of the owner's capital in the 3(c)(1) Fund.

The SEC staff has indicated that an employee benefit plan that permits participants to direct their investments will be disregarded and all of its participants will be counted as beneficial owners of any 3(c)(1) Fund in which the plan invests.[20] On the other hand, the SEC staff has allowed a 3(c)(1) Fund to count as a single beneficial owner a participant-directed defined contribution plan whose participants could allocate their capital to generic investment options, but had no role in deciding whether assets allocated to a particular option would be invested in the 3(c)(1) Fund.[21] In the case of a participant-directed plan sponsored by the investment adviser and general partner of a 3(c)(1) Fund, the SEC staff allowed the 3(c)(1) Fund to count the employee benefit plan as a single beneficial owner of the 3(c)(1) Fund's securities.[22] The SEC staff's decision depended particularly on the employee plan's participants' high level of access to information about the 3(c)(1) Fund's operations and investments.

c. Entity Formed for the Purpose of Investing in a 3(c)(1) Fund—40-Percent Test

The SEC staff has indicated that for purposes of the 100-Owner Limit, a 3(c)(1) Fund's owners include each of the investors in any Investing Entity that was formed for the purpose of investing in the 3(c)(1) Fund. The SEC staff has also indicated that an Investing Entity usually will be deemed to have been formed for the purpose of investing in a 3(c)(1) Fund if 40 percent

---

19. WR Investment Partners Diversified Strategies Fund, L.P., SEC No-Action Letter (Apr. 15, 1992).

20. The PanAgora Group Trust, SEC No-Action Letter (Apr. 29, 1994).

21. The Standish, Ayer & Wood, Inc. Stable Value Group Trust, SEC No-Action Letter (Dec. 28, 1995).

22. Caxton Corp., SEC No-Action Letter (Dec. 28, 1994).

or more of its committed capital is invested in the 3(c)(1) Fund.[23] Except in unusual circumstances, an Investing Entity should not be regarded as having been formed for the purpose of investing in a 3(c)(1) Fund, and should not be looked through on that basis, if less than 40 percent of its committed capital is invested in the 3(c)(1) Fund, even if one of its express purposes is to invest in the 3(c)(1) Fund.[24] The SEC staff has not addressed whether the 40-percent test would be applied to an Investing Entity formed a significant time before making a 40-percent or greater investment in a 3(c)(1) Fund.

d. Trusts

In other contexts, the SEC has indicated that the main factor in determining whether a trust can be considered one investor is whether one or more of the beneficiaries or trustees can revoke the trust.[25] If the SEC applies a similar analysis in deciding how to count revocable trusts toward the 100-Owner Limit, the SEC would count only the persons possessing that power, and not all of the trust's beneficial owners, against the 100-Owner Limit. An irrevocable trust that is not a Covered Company and does not have more than 40 percent of its assets invested in a 3(c)(1) Fund is usually counted as one beneficial owner of the 3(c)(1) Fund for the purposes of section 3(c)(1).[26]

---

23. Merrill Lynch & Co., Inc., SEC No-Action Letter (Apr. 23, 1992); CMS Communications Fund, L.P., SEC No-Action Letter (Apr. 17, 1987). *But see* Cornish & Carey Commercial, Inc., SEC No-Action Letter (June 21, 1996) (allowing an Investing Entity that invests more than 40 percent of its capital in a 3(c)(1) Fund to be counted as one beneficial owner of the 3(c)(1) Fund, provided that, among other things, the Investing Entity is not structured or operated to circumvent § 3(c)(1)). *See also* American Bar Association Section of Business Law, SEC No-Action Letter (Apr. 22, 1999) (hereinafter "American Bar Association"), Answer D (noting that, in determining whether an Investing Entity is formed for the purpose of investing in a 3(c)(7) Fund, the percentage of the Investing Entity's assets invested in the 3(c)(7) Fund is relevant, but not determinative).

24. In Clayton and Dubilier Associates IV Limited Partnership, SEC No-Action Letter (Nov. 2, 1992), the SEC staff stated that it would consider a family partnership created to invest in a particular 3(c)(1) Fund, and other funds, for estate planning purposes, to be only one beneficial owner, when the family partnership's capital invested in the 3(c)(1) Fund represented less than 40 percent of the family partnership's assets and less than 10 percent of the 3(c)(1) Fund's capital. *See also* Cornish & Carey Commercial, Inc., SEC No-Action Letter (June 21, 1996).

25. The SEC has determined that certain revocable trusts, which (due to powers retained by the grantors) would be deemed not to exist as a legal entity, will be disregarded for purposes of Advisers Act Rule 205-3, 17 C.F.R. § 275.205-3 (the so-called "Performance Fee Rule"). *See* § 15.2.3.i, *infra*, and Securities Act Rule 501(a)(8), 17 C.F.R. § 230.501(a)(8) (an entity is an "accredited investor" if all of its equity owners are accredited investors). The SEC will look instead to the grantors of the trust to determine if they meet the net worth requirements of those sections. Securities Act Release No. 6455 (Mar. 3, 1983), 48 F.R. 10,045 (May 10, 1983); and Capital Technology Fund, SEC No-Action Letter (Mar. 10, 1989). The SEC might apply a similar analysis to the 100-Owner Limit under § 3(c)(1).

26. Nemo Capital Partners, L.P., SEC No-Action Letter (July 28, 1992); Handy Place Investment Partnership, SEC No-Action Letter (July 19, 1989); OSIRIS Mgmt., Inc., SEC No-Action Letter (Feb. 17, 1984).

If a trust invests more than 40 percent of its assets in a 3(c)(1) Fund, a beneficiary who does not contribute to the trust and does not elect to be a beneficiary of the trust probably would not be considered a beneficial owner of the trust.[27] Accordingly, even if such a trust were to be looked through, involuntary noncontributory beneficiaries probably would not be counted against the 100-Owner Limit.

Investing Entities that are trusts can create complicated issues. For example, because it is not always clear who, if anyone, is the beneficial owner of a trust, it may be impossible to look through a trust to its beneficial owners.

ii. Spouses and Other Family Members

The SEC considers securities of a 3(c)(1) Fund owned jointly by both spouses (directly or through an entity) to be owned by only one beneficial owner,[28] but spouses with separate interests count as two beneficial owners.[29] In addition, investors who are related other than by marriage, such as a parent and children, count as separate beneficial owners.[30] Therefore, to minimize the number of beneficial owners, investments by parents and minor children could be made through the parents or a single entity, such as an appropriate trust or partnership that qualifies as a single investor.[31]

iii. Multiple Ownership Interests of an Investor

If an investor has a direct interest in a 3(c)(1) Fund and also has an indirect interest in the same 3(c)(1) Fund through a wholly owned subsidiary or an affiliate or as the sole beneficiary of a trust or individual retirement account (an "IRA"), such multiple interests should be considered to be owned by only one investor. Similarly, if several Investing Entities all have the same beneficial owner, they should be counted as only one investor.

Generally, if the owners of a subsidiary or affiliate or the beneficiaries of a trust are not identical to the individual investors, then each record holder of an interest in a 3(c)(1) Fund is counted separately. This is the result even for trusts having the same trustee, if their beneficiaries differ in any respect.[32] If a group of investors owns interests in a 3(c)(1) Fund through various Investing Entities and no one else has an interest in those Investing Entities, the 3(c)(1) Fund may count only the individual investors, and not the separate Investing Entities, even if their ownership proportions in the Investing Entities are not identical.[33]

---

27. Long-Term Capital Mgmt., L.P., SEC No-Action Letter (Apr. 28, 1994).

28. 1997 Release (*see* n. 12, *supra*) at note 69; American Bar Association (*see* n. 23, *supra*) at Answer I.2.

29. American Bar Association (*see* n. 23, *supra*) at Answer I.1.

30. American Bar Association (*see* n. 23, *supra*) at Answer A.4(i).

31. *But see* § 3.2.2.i.c, *supra.*

32. OSIRIS Mgmt., Inc., SEC No-Action Letter (Feb. 17, 1984); Railbox Co., SEC No-Action Letter (Sep. 10, 1984); Nemo Capital Partners, L.P., SEC No-Action Letter (July 28, 1992).

33. Nemo Capital Partners, L.P., SEC No-Action Letter (July 28, 1992); Wm. S. Barnickle & Company, SEC No-Action Letter (Nov. 1, 1994).

iv. Knowledgeable Employees

For purposes of the 100-Owner Limit, the following owners of the 3(c)(1) Fund's securities are excluded:

- a person who at the time he or she acquired such securities was, or who subsequently becomes,[34] a Knowledgeable Employee;
- a company owned exclusively by Knowledgeable Employees; and
- a person who, by one or more transfers permitted under the Company Act,[35] acquired securities originally acquired by a Knowledgeable Employee.[36]

In addition, the following owners of securities of a 3(c)(1) Fund do not count against the 100-Owner Limit: (1) a Knowledgeable Employee and his or her spouse who hold the securities as a joint interest; (2) an entity jointly owned by a Knowledgeable Employee and his or her spouse; (3) a family company trust or similar estate planning vehicle for which a Knowledgeable Employee makes the investment decisions and contributes the invested assets (individually or jointly with his or her spouse); or (4) an alter ego entity of a Knowledgeable Employee (such as an IRA or self-directed retirement plan account) that is owned only by the Knowledgeable Employee (individually or jointly with his or her spouse) and for which the Knowledgeable Employee makes all investment decisions (an "Alter Ego Entity").[37]

"Knowledgeable Employee" is defined as an executive officer, director, trustee, general partner or board member of, or person serving in a similar capacity with, the 3(c)(1) Fund or 3(c)(7) Fund. It also includes persons serving in such capacities for an affiliate of the 3(c)(1) Fund or 3(c)(7) Fund that manages the investment activities of the 3(c)(1) Fund or 3(c)(7) Fund. It also includes an employee (other than an employee performing solely clerical, secretarial or administrative functions) of the 3(c)(1) Fund or 3(c)(7) Fund, its affiliates or, in certain cases, affiliates of the investment adviser to the 3(c)(1) Fund or 3(c)(7) Fund, who, in connection with his or her regular duties, participates in the investment activities[38] of the 3(c)(1) Fund or 3(c)(7) Fund or the investment activities of other Covered Companies,[39] offshore funds, banks, insurance companies or savings and loan associations, or who participates in the investment activities of such affiliates that manage assets of certain pension or profit-sharing plans, underwriters, brokers or market intermediaries. In each case, the employee must have performed those duties, or substantially similar

---

34. American Bar Association (*see* n. 23, *supra*) at Answers A.6 and A.7.
35. *See* § 3.2.2.v, *infra*.
36. Company Act Rule 3c-5, 17 C.F.R. § 270.3c-5.
37. American Bar Association (*see* n. 23, *supra*), Answers A.4 and A.8.
38. Knowledge of an appropriate entity's investment activities is insufficient unless accompanied by actual participation in those activities. American Bar Association, Answer A.1.
39. *See* § 3.2.2.i.a, *supra*.

duties on behalf of another company, for at least 12 months.[40] Marketing and investor relations professionals, attorneys, analysts, traders, or financial, compliance, operations or accounting officers are not generally Knowledgeable Employees, unless they are executives of the 3(c)(1) Fund or 3(c)(7) Fund or an investment management affiliate.[41]

v. *Transfers of Interests in 3(c)(1) Funds*

Except in the limited circumstances discussed below, each transferee who receives an interest in a 3(c)(1) Fund is counted as a beneficial owner of the 3(c)(1) Fund.

a. Permitted Transfers

Under Company Act Rule 3c-6,[42] beneficial ownership by a transferee is deemed to be beneficial ownership by the transferor, if the transferee is:

- the estate of the transferor;
- a donee (defined as a person who acquires the security or interest as a gift or bequest or pursuant to an agreement relating to a legal separation or divorce); or
- a company established by the transferor exclusively for the benefit of (or owned exclusively by) the transferor and the persons specified in the preceding clauses.

This exception applies only to the specific transfers described in Rule 3c-6, and does not cover additional securities that such a transferee acquires from the 3(c)(1) Fund.[43] In addition, the SEC has not addressed many issues related to transfers of interests in 3(c)(1) Funds, including whether securities transferred under Rule 3c-6 can be transferred again and continue to be covered by the rule.

In addition, the SEC staff has issued several no-action letters when it has considered transfers to be involuntary and outside the 3(c)(1) Fund's control. For example, if an Investing Entity is a limited partnership and the general partner dies, causing the dissolution of the partnership and distribution of the interests of the 3(c)(1) Fund to the limited partners of that Investing Entity, the former limited partners of the Investing Entity will not be counted against the 100-Owner Limit and the former Investing Entity will continue to be considered to be the sole owner of the distributed interests.[44] On the other hand, the SEC staff refused to grant no-action relief for an investment in a 3(c)(1) Fund by an employee benefit plan that was terminated and that distributed the plan's interest

---

40. Company Act Rule 3c-5, 17 C.F.R. § 270.3c-5; PPM America Special Investments CBO II, L.P., SEC No-Action Letter (Apr. 16, 1998); American Bar Association (*see* n. 23, *supra*) at Answer A.2.

41. American Bar Association (*see* n. 23, *supra*) at Answer A.1.

42. 17 C.F.R. § 270.3c-6.

43. 1997 Release (*see* n. 12, *supra*) at § III.C.

44. Boston Ventures Limited Partnership, SEC No-Action Letter (Aug. 5, 1992).

in the 3(c)(1) Fund to the plan participants, because the SEC staff viewed that termination as voluntary.[45]

b. Public Charities

If an investor in a 3(c)(1) Fund donates an interest in the 3(c)(1) Fund to one or more public charities, the SEC staff will count the charities and the donor as a single beneficial owner of the 3(c)(1) Fund. This position reflects the public policy of supporting charitable organizations.[46]

vi. General Partner's Interest

A general partner's interest in a 3(c)(1) Fund usually should not be considered to be a security, with the possible exception of a general partner that is a passive investor and that does not actively participate in managing the 3(c)(1) Fund. As long as the general partner participates in management and does not own an interest as a limited partner, the general partner is not counted as a beneficial owner for purposes of the 100-Owner Limit.[47]

vii. Non-U.S. Investors

A non-U.S. individual or entity is counted against the 100-Owner Limit if the 3(c)(1) Fund is organized in the United States.[48]

3. Integration

i. Integration of 3(c)(1) Funds

In some circumstances, two or more 3(c)(1) Funds with the same or related general partners, sponsors, promoters or investment advisers may be treated as a single 3(c)(1) Fund ("integrated") for purposes of determining whether the 100-Owner Limit is exceeded.[49]

a. The "Reasonable Investor" Test

The factors that the SEC staff considers in determining whether integration is appropriate under the Company Act include: (1) whether a reasonable investor would consider the interests in 2 or more 3(c)(1) Funds to be materially different; (2) whether the 3(c)(1) Funds share the same investment objectives, portfolio securities and portfolio risk/return characteristics; and (3) whether one or more of the following 5 factors (relevant to the question of integration under Securities Act section 4(a)(2)) exist: (a) the different offerings are part of a single plan of financing; (b) they involve the issuance of the same class of securities; (c) the

45. Trivest Special Situations Fund 1985, L.P., SEC No-Action Letter (July 13, 1989).

46. *Id.*; Commodities Corp., SEC No-Action Letter (June 7, 1991); Wm. S. Barnickel & Company, SEC No-Action Letter (Nov. 1, 1994).

47. Colony Realty Partners 1986 L.P., SEC No-Action Letter (Apr. 27, 1988); Shoreline Fund, L.P. and Condor Fund International, Inc., SEC No-Action Letter (Nov. 14, 1994).

48. *See* § 3.2.4, *infra*.

49. Monument Capital Mgmt., Inc., SEC No-Action Letter (July 12, 1990) (common investment advisers); Madison Park Investment Mgmt., Inc., SEC No-Action Letter (Apr. 4, 1986) (common sponsor); Joseph H. Moss, SEC No-Action Letter (Feb. 27, 1983) (common promoter).

offerings are made at or about the same time; (d) the same type of consideration is received; and (e) the offerings are made for the same general purpose.[50]

The first two of these factors are both difficult to distinguish from each other and subjective, affording the SEC ample latitude to challenge any arrangement that its staff disfavors. They also seem to be the most influential. In *Equitable Capital Management Corporation*,[51] for example, the SEC staff noted that three 3(c)(1) Funds trading in collateralized bond obligations had similar investment objectives, portfolio securities and risk/return characteristics. The SEC staff determined, however, that the 3(c)(1) Funds need not be integrated, because a reasonable investor would consider them materially different. The investors or underwriters had extensively negotiated the structure of each 3(c)(1) Fund, resulting in differences in the basic terms, including (1) different capital structures (different classes and relative proportions of various debt securities), (2) different projected yields and anticipated average lives of the securities, (3) different degrees of portfolio management discretion, and (4) different management fees.

In *Oppenheimer Arbitrage Partners, L.P.*,[52] the SEC staff said it would not integrate two 3(c)(1) Funds that shared a general partner. One 3(c)(1) Fund was offered to tax-exempt investors, would not engage in short sales or financial futures transactions or write uncovered options, and generally expected a low risk of loss; the other was offered to taxable investors, engaged in short sales, leveraged its assets to the maximum extent permitted, and expected a high rate of return and risk.

Two 3(c)(1) Funds also shared a general partner in *Meadow Lane Associates, L.P.*,[53] in which the SEC staff conditioned its decision not to integrate the 3(c)(1) Funds on the understanding that one invested in a wide range of growth securities while the other sought capital appreciation through arbitrage opportunities. The SEC staff noted that the risk/return characteristics of the two 3(c)(1) Funds were different, that they would be separately administered, and that no limited partner of either would, as an investor in that 3(c)(1) Fund, have the right to participate in the assets of the other.

In *Welsh, Carson, Anderson & Stowe*,[54] the SEC staff said it would not integrate three 3(c)(1) Funds that had affiliated general partners. One of the 3(c)(1) Funds was offered only to institutional clients, principally tax-exempt investors, and could not use leverage, purchase put options or sell securities short. The other two were offered solely to individuals and were allowed to use leverage, sell securities short and purchase put options. Nevertheless, these two hedge funds were not integrated because one invested only in the health

---

50. Monument Capital Mgmt., Inc., SEC No-Action Letter (July 12, 1990); Equitable Capital Mgmt. Corp., SEC No-Action Letter (Jan. 6, 1992).

51. Equitable Capital Mgmt. Corp., SEC No-Action Letter (Jan. 6, 1992).

52. Oppenheimer Arbitrage Partners, L.P./Oppenheimer Institutional Arbitrage Investors, L.P., SEC No-Action Letter (Dec. 26, 1985).

53. Meadow Lane Associates, L.P., SEC No-Action Letter (May 24, 1989).

54. Welsh, Carson, Anderson & Stowe, SEC No-Action Letter (June 18, 1993).

care industry and the other only in the information services industry, and only individuals familiar with the respective industry were allowed to invest in it.

The SEC staff has also indicated that it would not integrate an offshore hedge fund with a U.S. 3(c)(1) Fund even when the offshore hedge fund was formed to invest in the 3(c)(1) Fund, since the different tax laws and regulations of different countries would make them materially different to an investor.[55] The SEC staff similarly said it would not recommend integrating an offshore hedge fund with a U.S. 3(c)(1) Fund, even though they were to be managed virtually identically, because the different tax treatment of investments in those vehicles created materially different investments.[56] As a consequence, some investment pool managers create offshore hedge funds for non-U.S. investors and U.S. investors that are exempt from U.S. taxes and do not permit such investors to invest in the U.S. 3(c)(1) Funds that they manage.[57]

In other circumstances, the SEC staff declined to provide comfort regarding integration. In *Frontier Capital Management Company, Inc.*,[58] the SEC staff considered three separate limited partnerships with the same general partner: the "Capital Fund" would invest in a diverse portfolio consisting primarily of equity securities issued by companies with significant capital; the "Small Cap Fund" would purchase primarily corporate and equity securities of companies thought to have high growth potential; and the "Balanced Fund" would invest in a mix of common stocks and high grade fixed-income securities to balance growth, income and stability.

Refusing to take a no-action position, the SEC staff stated that it did not find the three hedge funds to be materially different to a reasonable investor qualified to purchase any of them. The SEC staff cited the similar investment objectives of the first two hedge funds and the potentially overlapping portfolios of all three hedge funds, and noted that all three hedge funds were designed, in essence, for one group of investors with similar investment profiles.

Similarly, in *Monument Capital Management, Inc.*,[59] the SEC staff took the position that a reasonable investor would not view two limited partnerships as being materially different. The two partnerships had unaffiliated general partners, but were advised by closely affiliated investment advisers and shared a common investment objective with respect to all of one partnership's capital and up to 80 percent of the other partnership's capital. The staff did not agree that simply because the two partnerships had unaffiliated general partners they should not be integrated.

In *Madison Park Investment Management*,[60] the SEC staff denied a no-action request with respect to integration for a series of trusts formed to provide high rates of return by writing covered options. The proposed trusts would have

55. Pasadena Investment Trust, SEC No-Action Letter (Jan. 22, 1993).
56. Shoreline Fund, L.P., SEC No-Action Letter (Apr. 11, 1994).
57. *See* § 4.4.1, *infra*.
58. Frontier Capital Mgmt. Co., Inc., SEC No-Action Letter (July 13, 1988).
59. Monument Capital Mgmt., Inc., SEC No-Action Letter (July 12, 1990).
60. Madison Park Investment, SEC No-Action Letter (Mar. 4, 1986).

differed only with respect to option strategy as a result of the timing of the formation of each trust.

Accordingly, to avoid integration, at least in the SEC staff's view, 3(c)(1) Funds need to be distinguished by more than different general partners, different portfolios or different expected rates of return. To support an argument that integration is not warranted, the manager should consider tailoring different 3(c)(1) Funds for distinctly different groups of investors (such as tax-exempt versus taxable investors) and avoiding overlap in the specific portfolios of the 3(c)(1) Funds or even their categories of investments.

b. Consequences of Integration

If two or more 3(c)(1) Funds are integrated, the beneficial owners are counted as if the different 3(c)(1) Funds were a single 3(c)(1) Fund. Accordingly, logic would seem to dictate that an investor in both 3(c)(1) Funds should be counted only once. The 10% Test should be calculated with respect to the assets and liabilities of the 3(c)(1) Funds on a combined basis.

In the only no-action letter specifically addressing how to calculate the number of beneficial owners when hedge funds are integrated, however, the SEC staff stated that an entity cannot use the integration doctrine to avoid the Company Act's registration requirement.[61] In that instance, the sponsor of two 3(c)(1) Funds, each with a small number of limited partners, argued that the two 3(c)(1) Funds should be integrated for purposes of determining whether a single Investing Entity held more than 10 percent of the integrated 3(c)(1) Fund's voting securities. Without addressing the factual basis for integrating the two 3(c)(1) Funds, the staff declined to assure the sponsor that the voting securities of the two 3(c)(1) Funds would be aggregated for purposes of applying the 10% Test.

ii. No Integration of 3(c)(1) and 3(c)(7) Funds

A 3(c)(1) Fund and a 3(c)(7) Fund are not integrated for purposes of determining whether the 3(c)(1) Fund's 100-Owner Limit is exceeded.[62]

iii. Integration of Hedge Funds and Separately Managed Accounts

The manager of a 3(c)(1) Fund may also manage separate client accounts outside the 3(c)(1) Fund. The SEC staff could attempt to integrate a 3(c)(1) Fund and separate accounts managed by the same investment adviser. Even if an investment adviser does not manage a 3(c)(1) Fund, in some situations the SEC may attempt to integrate the investment adviser's managed accounts and view them as forming an investment company.[63] This may occur, for example, if the investment adviser manages multiple brokerage accounts through a so-called "wrap fee" program. In a typical wrap fee program, an investment

---

61. Weiss, Peck & Greer Venture Associates II, L.P., SEC No-Action Letter (Apr. 10, 1990).

62. Company Act § 3(c)(7)(E), 15 U.S.C. § 80a-3(c)(7)(E).

63. *See* Clarke Lanzen Skalla Investment Firm, Inc., SEC administrative proceeding (June 16, 1995).

adviser employs the same investment strategy for all participants in that wrap fee program. The program participants participate through their brokerage accounts, and not by purchasing an interest in a partnership or other company (which would be subject to the 100-Owner Limit). The SEC could argue that the investment adviser effectively created an investment company for the brokerage accounts participating in the wrap fee program and apply the 100-Owner Limit.

If necessary to avoid reaching the 100-Owner Limit, an investment adviser may avoid integration of separately managed accounts with each other or with a 3(c)(1) Fund by following Company Act Rule 3a-4.[64] Rule 3a-4 provides that an investment adviser is not deemed to have created an investment company if the following conditions are satisfied:

- each client's account is managed on the basis of the client's individual needs and restrictions;
- each client can instruct the investment adviser to sell, or not to buy, particular securities that otherwise might be held or purchased;
- on opening the account and at least annually thereafter, the investment adviser determines each client's financial situation and objectives and gives the client the opportunity to impose or modify restrictions on the account;
- at least quarterly, the investment adviser gives each client an account statement and the opportunity to communicate to the investment adviser any change in the client's financial situation and to impose or modify restrictions on the account;
- appropriate employees of the investment adviser are reasonably available to each client for consultation; and
- each client maintains all indicia of ownership of the account's securities and funds, such as the right to withdraw and vote securities, and receives notification of each transaction.

4. Non-U.S. Funds

Company Act section 7(d)[65] prohibits a hedge fund organized outside the United States from using the mails or any means or instrumentality of interstate commerce (such as the telephone) to offer for sale, sell, or deliver after sale, in connection with a public offering, any security that it has issued. The SEC staff interprets Company Act section 3(c)(1)[66] in conjunction with section 7(d); a non-U.S. hedge fund may conduct a private offering of its securities in the United States in reliance on section 3(c)(1) and at the same time conduct a public offering of its securities outside the United States if it never has more than 100 beneficial holders of its securities residing in the United States and does not conduct a public offering within the United States.[67] Accordingly, a

64. 17 C.F.R. § 270.3a-4.
65. 15 U.S.C. § 80a-7(d).
66. 15 U.S.C. § 80a-3(c)(1).
67. Touche Remnant & Co., SEC No-Action Letter (Aug. 27, 1984).

non-U.S. hedge fund should appropriately restrict transfers of its securities to ensure that it does not exceed the 100-Owner Limit with respect to its U.S. beneficial owners.

5. Public Offering Prohibition

A 3(c)(1) Fund may not make or propose to make a public offering of its securities.[68] The SEC interprets the nonpublic offering condition consistently with Securities Act section 4(a)(2).[69] Section 4(a)(2) provides that the registration provisions of Securities Act section 5[70] do not apply to an issuer transaction that does not involve any public offering. To avoid engaging in a public offering, most hedge funds rely on the safe harbors provided by Rule 506(b)[71] promulgated by the SEC under Securities Act section 4(a)(2).[72] Additionally, offerings under Rule 506(c),[73] which permit advertising and general solicitation, do not constitute public offerings[74] for purposes of Company Act 3(c)(1).[75]

§ 3.3 Section 3(c)(7) Exclusion

1. General Statement of the Rule

Company Act section 3(c)(7)[76] excludes any pooled investment vehicle from the definition of "investment company" if all of the beneficial owners of its outstanding securities are "qualified purchasers," as defined under the Company Act ("Qualified Purchasers"),[77] and it does not make or propose to make a public offering of its securities.[78]

---

68. Company Act § 3(c)(1), 15 U.S.C. § 80a-3(c)(1).

69. 15 U.S.C. § 77(d)(2). *See* Arthur E. Fox, SEC No-Action Letter (Dec. 12, 1974); Underwood Neuhaus & Co., Inc., SEC No-Action Letter (Feb. 13, 1975); Glenwood Investment Corp., SEC No-Action Letter (Aug. 10, 1994). While offerings made in conformity with Rule 506 of Regulation D under the Securities Act are deemed not to involve a public offering under § 3(c)(1), offerings made in compliance with Rule 147, 504 or 505 under, or § 3(a)(11) of, the Securities Act are not necessarily nonpublic within the meaning of this section. J.Y. Barry Arbitrage Mgmt. Inc., SEC No-Action Letter (Oct. 18, 1989); C. Evans Patterson, SEC No-Action Letter (Mar. 9, 1988); San Jose Capital Corp., SEC No-Action Letter (Feb. 14, 1983).

70. 15 U.S.C. § 77e.

71. 17 C.F.R. § 230.506(b).

72. *See* § 5.3, *infra*.

73. 17 C.F.R. § 230.506(c).

74. Securities Act Release No. 9415 (July 24, 2013), 78 F.R. 44771 (July 24, 2013) at II.E.

75. 15 U.S.C. § 80a-3(c)(1).

76. 15 U.S.C. § 80a-3(c)(7).

77. Company Act § 2(a)(51), 15 U.S.C. § 80a-2(a)(51).

78. *See* § 3.2.5, *supra*. The SEC has not considered the nonpublic offering condition with respect to a 3(c)(7) Fund, but almost certainly would apply the same standards as apply to a 3(c)(1) Fund.

2. Permitted Owners of 3(c)(7) Funds

Securities of 3(c)(7) Funds may be held only by Qualified Purchasers and other persons described below in this section.

i. Qualified Purchasers

A "Qualified Purchaser" is defined as:

- an individual (including any person who holds a joint, community property or other similar shared ownership interest with that person's spouse) who holds at least $5,000,000 in Investments (as defined below);[79]
- a Family Company (defined as a legal entity or other organized group of persons that is wholly[80] owned directly or indirectly by or for two or more individuals who are related as siblings or spouses (including former spouses), or direct lineal descendants by birth or adoption, spouses (including former spouses)[81] of such persons, the estates of such persons, or foundations, charitable organizations or trusts established by or for the benefit of such persons), that owns at least $5,000,000 in Investments;[82]
- a trust that is not a Family Company as described above and that is not formed for the specific purpose of investing in the 3(c)(7) Fund and of which each trustee who makes investment decisions on behalf of the trust[83] and each contributor is a Qualified Purchaser;[84]
- a person, acting for such person's own account or the accounts of other Qualified Purchasers, who owns and invests on a discretionary basis at least $25,000,000 in Investments;[85] or
- a company (regardless of the amount of such company's Investments) beneficially owned exclusively by Qualified Purchasers[86] or by the company's Knowledgeable Employees.[87]

---

79. Company Act § 2(a)(51)(A)(i), 15 U.S.C. § 80a-2(a)(51)(A)(i); Company Act Rule 2a51-1(g)(2), 17 C.F.R. § 270.2a51-1(g)(2).

80. American Bar Association (*see* n. 23, *supra*) at Answer C.4.

81. Redwood Investment Fund, LLC, SEC No-Action Letter (Oct. 14, 1997).

82. Company Act § 2(a)(51)(A)(ii), 15 U.S.C. § 80a-2(a)(51)(A)(ii). The family relationship requirement is also satisfied if all beneficiaries of a family trust are lineal descendants of the trust's settlor and are related as aunts, uncles, nieces and nephews. Meadowbrook Real Estate Fund, SEC No-Action Letter (Aug. 26, 1998).

83. American Bar Association (*see* n. 23, *supra*) at Answer C.2.

84. Company Act § 2(a)(51)(A)(iii), 15 U.S.C. § 80a-2(a)(51)(A)(iii). A trust can be a Qualified Purchaser, notwithstanding that its settlor was not a Qualified Purchaser when he or she contributed assets to the trust, if the settlor (a) is alive, (b) is a Qualified Purchaser when the trust invests in a 3(c)(7) Fund and (c) has authority to approve the investment. Meadowbrook Real Estate Fund, SEC No-Action Letter (Aug. 26, 1998). The Qualified Purchaser status of all of a trust's beneficiaries, however, is generally insufficient to make the trust a Qualified Purchaser. American Bar Association (*see* n. 23, *supra*) at Answer C.3.

85. Company Act § 2(a)(51)(A)(iv), 15 U.S.C. § 80a-2(a)(51)(A)(iv).

86. Company Act Rule 2a51-3(b), 17 C.F.R. § 270.2a51-3(b). For purposes of this rule "company" does not include a trust. American Bar Association (*see* n. 23, *supra*) at Answer C.3.

87. Paragon Advisers, Inc., SEC No-Action Letter (Oct. 1, 1998).

For purposes of the second and fourth categories, a company will not be a Qualified Purchaser if it is formed for the specific purpose of investing in the 3(c)(7) Fund, unless each beneficial owner of the company's securities is a Qualified Purchaser.[88] The SEC staff has indicated that an employee benefit plan that permits participants to direct their investments will be disregarded and all of its participants must be Qualified Purchasers in order for the plan to be a Qualified Purchaser.[89] On the other hand, the SEC staff has stated that a 3(c)(7) Fund may look to the Qualified Purchaser status of an employee benefit plan, and not the plan's participants, if the plan is a participant-directed, defined-contribution plan whose participants could allocate their capital to generic investment options, but have no role in deciding whether assets allocated to a particular investment option will be invested in the 3(c)(7) Fund.[90]

An individual Qualified Purchaser's Alter Ego Entity, such as an IRA or self-directed retirement account, is also considered to be a Qualified Purchaser.[91]

ii. Investments

"Investments"[92] is defined to include:

- Securities of an issuer that does not have a control relationship with the prospective Qualified Purchaser that owns the securities, unless the issuer is (1) a company that files reports pursuant to Exchange Act section 13 or 15(d),[93] or that has a class of securities that are listed on a "designated offshore securities market," as defined by Regulation S[94] under the Securities Act, (2) an investment company, as defined by the Company Act, a company exempt from the definition of investment company under certain sections of the Company Act, or a commodity pool, or (3) a company with shareholders' equity of at least $50,000,000.[95]

- Real estate held for investment, not used for personal purposes, and not used as a place of business or in connection with the conduct of a trade or business by a prospective Qualified Purchaser or a family member. Real estate owned by a prospective Qualified Purchaser that is engaged primarily in the business of investing, trading or developing real estate may be deemed to be held for investment. Residential real estate will be

88. Company Act Rule 2a51-3(a), 17 C.F.R. § 270.2a51-3(a).
89. H.E. Blatt Grocery Company, SEC No-Action Letter (May 18, 2001).
90. *Id.*
91. American Bar Association (*see* n. 23, *supra*) at Answer B.2.
92. Company Act Rule 2a51-1, 17 C.F.R. § 270.2a51-1.
93. 15 U.S.C. § 78n or 78o.
94. 17 C.F.R. §§ 230.901 *et seq.*
95. Company Act Rules 2a51-1(a)(3), 2a51-1(a)(7) and 2a51-1(b)(1), 17 C.F.R. §§ 270.2a51-1(a)(3), 270.2a51-1(a)(7) and 270.2a51-1(b)(1). An equity interest in a securities-related business (such as a hedge fund) is deemed a "security" for purposes of Company Act Rule 2a51-1(b)(1), regardless of whether it would be deemed a "security" for purposes of the Securities Act. Sullivan & Cromwell, SEC No-Action Letter (Dec. 29, 1997).

deemed held for investment if deductions with respect to the property are not disallowed by Tax Code section 280A.[96]

- Commodity interests held for investment, including commodity futures contracts, options on commodity futures contracts, and options on physical commodities traded on or subject to the rules of a contract market designated for trading such instruments under the CEA or a board of trade or exchange outside the United States as contemplated by certain provisions of the CEA rules.[97]
- Physical commodities held for investment, including any commodity held in physical form with respect to which a commodity interest is traded on a market described in the preceding clause.[98]
- Certain financial contracts[99] entered into for investment purposes, such as individually negotiated swaps and repurchase agreements.[100]
- Certain unfunded capital commitments[101] from investors in a prospective Qualified Purchaser that is a Covered Company or a commodity pool.[102]
- Cash and cash equivalents (including non-U.S. currencies) held for investment, including bank deposits, certificates of deposit, bankers' acceptances and similar bank instruments, and the net cash surrender value of insurance policies.[103]
- Commodity interests, physical commodities and financial contracts will be deemed held for investment if the holder is primarily engaged in investing or trading in such instruments.[104]

---

96. Company Act Rules 2a51-1(b)(2) and 2a51-1(c)(1), 17 C.F.R. §§ 270.2a51-1(b)(2) and 270.2a51-1(c)(1).

97. Company Act Rules 2a51-1(a)(1) and 2a51-1(b)(3), 17 C.F.R. §§ 270.2a51-1(a)(1) and 270.2a51-1(b)(3).

98. Company Act Rules 2a51-1(a)(5) and 2a51-1(b)(4), 17 C.F.R. §§ 270.2a51-1(a)(5) and 2a51-1(b)(4).

99. A financial contract is any arrangement that "(a) takes the form of an individually negotiated contract, agreement, or option to buy, sell, lend, swap, or repurchase, or other similar individually negotiated transaction commonly entered into by participants in the financial markets; (b) is in respect of securities, commodities, currencies, interest or other rates, other measures of value, or any other financial or economic interest similar in purpose or function to any of the foregoing; and (c) is entered into in response to a request from a counter party for a quotation, or is otherwise entered into and structured to accommodate the objectives of the counter party to such arrangement." Company Act § 3(c)(2)(B)(ii), 15 U.S.C. § 80a-3(c)(2)(B)(ii).

100. Company Act Rule 2a51-1(b)(5), 17 C.F.R. § 270.2a51-1(b)(5).

101. A capital commitment is a firm agreement or similar binding commitment pursuant to which a person agrees to acquire an interest in, or make a capital contribution to, a prospective Qualified Purchaser. Company Act Rule 2a51-1(b)(6), 17 C.F.R. § 2a51-1(b)(6).

102. *Id.* The SEC staff also permitted a company exempted from certain provisions of the Company Act under § 6(b) to avail itself of 17 C.F.R. § 270.2a51-1(b)(6). The BSC Employee Fund, L.P., SEC No-Action Letter (Oct. 14, 1997).

103. Company Act Rule 2a51-1(b)(7), 17 C.F.R. § 270.2a51-1(b)(7).

104. Company Act Rule 2a51-1(c)(2), 17 C.F.R. § 270.2a51-1(c)(2).

iii. Valuation

The value of an Investment may be, at the option of the 3(c)(7) Fund, either the Investment's cost or its fair market value on the most recent practicable date. In the absence of recent market trading, fair market value may be determined by an appraisal by an independent third-party.[105] Commodity Interests are valued by the initial margin or portion of the premium deposited.[106]

iv. Deductions for Acquisition Debt

Any outstanding debt incurred to acquire an Investment is deducted from the value of the Investment.[107] If a prospective Qualified Purchaser is a Family Company, any outstanding debt incurred by an owner of the Family Company to acquire the Investments held by the Family Company is deducted.[108]

v. Jointly Held Investments

An individual may include in the amount of his or her Investments any Investments held jointly with the person's spouse, and Investments in which the person shares with the spouse a community property or similar shared ownership interest. If spouses make a joint investment as Qualified Purchasers, each spouse may include in the amount of its Investments any Investments owned by the other spouse, whether or not such Investments are held jointly. In determining the amount of a joint Investment, the outstanding amount of any debt incurred by either spouse to acquire the Investment is deducted.[109]

vi. Pension and Retirement Plans

An individual may include in the amount of his or her Investments any Investments held in his or her individual retirement account or similar account, such as a 401(k) plan, if he or she makes all of the investment decisions for the account.[110] This is true even if the plan's trustee or sponsor selects the range of investment options from which the individual can choose.[111]

A participant-directed, defined-contribution plan is a Qualified Purchaser only if all participants are Qualified Purchasers. A defined-benefit or other retirement plan that owns $25,000,000 of Investments and does not permit participants to decide whether or how much to invest in particular investment alternatives may be a Qualified Purchaser.[112]

---

105. Company Act Rule 2a51-1(d), 17 C.F.R. § 270.2a51-1(d); 1997 Release (*see* n. 12, *supra*) at § II.A.3.a.

106. Company Act Rule 2a51-1(d)(1), 17 C.F.R. § 270.2a51-1(d)(1).

107. Company Act Rule 2a51-1(e), 17 C.F.R. § 270.2a51-1(e).

108. Company Act Rule 2a51-1(f), 17 C.F.R. § 270.2a51-1(f).

109. Company Act Rule 2a51-1(g)(2), 17 C.F.R. § 270.2a51-1(g)(2).

110. Company Act Rule 2a51-1(g)(4), 17 C.F.R. § 270.2a51-1(g)(4).

111. 1997 Release (*see* n. 12, *supra*) at note 77.

112. 1997 Release (*see* n. 12, *supra*) at § II.A.8.

vii. Other Forms of Holding Investments

Investments held by a prospective Qualified Purchaser's Alter Ego Entity may be attributed to the prospective Qualified Purchaser.[113] For example, investments held in a prospective Qualified Purchaser's IRA are attributable to that prospective Qualified Purchaser.[114]

viii. Investments Held by Affiliated Entities

An entity it deemed to own Investments owned by (a) majority-owned subsidiaries of the entity, (b) Investments owned by a parent company (a "Parent Company") of which such entity is a majority-owned subsidiary, and (c) a majority-owned subsidiary of the Parent Company and other majority-owned subsidiaries of the Parent Company.[115]

ix. QIBs

A "qualified institutional buyer" (a "QIB"), as defined in Securities Act Rule 144A,[116] is a Qualified Purchaser if (a) it is (1) an institution that owns and invests on a discretionary basis $100,000,000 of securities of unaffiliated issuers (QIB Securities), (2) a bank that meets such $100,000,000 test and that has an audited net worth of at least $25,000,000 or (3) a registered dealer that owns and invests on a discretionary basis at least $25,000,000 of QIB Securities, and (b) it is acting for its own account, the account of another QIB or the account of a Qualified Purchaser.[117] A QIB that is a self-directed employee benefit plan, such as a 401(k) plan, will not be deemed to be acting for its own account if investment decisions with respect to the plan are made by the plan's beneficiaries, except with respect to investment decisions made solely by the fiduciary, trustee or sponsor of the plan.[118] That is, the investment decision to invest in a 3(c)(7) Fund must be made by a Qualified Purchaser.

x. Funds of Funds

A Covered Company[119] that desires to become a Qualified Purchaser (a "Purchasing Fund") must obtain the consent of its beneficial owners that acquired interests in the Purchasing Fund before May 1, 1996.[120] "Beneficial owners" in most cases means the investors in the Purchasing Fund. A Family Company or trust, however, need only obtain unanimous consent of all trustees, directors or general partners.[121] Persons that were, before May 1, 1996, beneficial owners of any Covered Company that directly or indirectly owns any of the securities of the Purchasing Fund (an "Owning Fund") must also consent to the treatment of the Purchasing Fund as a Qualified Purchaser if:

---

113. 1997 Release (*see* n. 12, *supra*) at § II.A.7.
114. *See* § 3.2.2.iii, *supra.*
115. Company Act Rule 2a51-1(g)(3), 17 C.F.R. § 270.2a51-1(g)(3).
116. 17 C.F.R. § 230.144A.
117. Company Act Rule 2a51-1(g)(1), 17 C.F.R. § 270.2a51-1(g)(1).
118. Company Act Rule 2a51-1(g)(1)(ii), 17 C.F.R. § 270.2a51-1(g)(1)(ii).
119. *See* § 3.2.2.i.a, *supra.*
120. Company Act § 2(a)(51)(C), 15 U.S.C. § 80a-2(a)(51)(C).
121. *Id.*

- the Owning Fund is an investment company or a Covered Company;
- on April 30, 1996, the Owning Fund owned 10 percent or more of the Purchasing Fund's limited partner, member or other interests;
- on April 30, 1996, the Owning Fund had more than 10 percent of its total assets invested in 3(c)(1) Funds, including the Purchasing Fund; and
- the Owning Fund controls,[122] is controlled by, or is under common control with, either the Purchasing Fund or the 3(c)(7) Fund in which the Purchasing Fund desires to invest (the "Target Fund").[123]

An Owning Fund is not deemed to own indirectly the securities of the Purchasing Fund unless there is a control relationship between the Owning Fund and either the Purchasing Fund or the Target Fund.[124] The beneficial owners of any Covered Company that owns the securities of the Owning Fund need not consent, and are deemed beneficial owners of the Purchasing Fund, unless a control relationship exists between the Owning Fund and either the Purchasing Fund or the Target Fund.[125] A Purchasing Fund can obtain a general consent with respect to most transactions in which it will be a Qualified Purchaser. A specific consent may be required in situations where a control relationship exists between the Purchasing Fund or certain of its beneficial owners and the Target Fund.[126]

xi. Reasonable Belief

Any person that a 3(c)(7) Fund or its representative reasonably believes is a Qualified Purchaser may be treated as such.[127] Neither the Company Act nor the Company Act rules prescribe the documentation required to support a reasonable belief that an investor is a Qualified Purchaser. The SEC expressly declined to prescribe such a list when promulgating the rules interpreting Company Act section 3(c)(7).[128] Nevertheless, it should be reasonable to rely on a properly completed and signed subscription agreement, at least in the absence of notice of facts that would cast doubt on the representations in the subscription agreement.

xii. When Qualified Purchaser Status Is Determined

An investor in a 3(c)(7) Fund must be determined to be a Qualified Purchaser each time the investor makes an investment in the 3(c)(7) Fund, except

---

122. For this purpose, "control" means the power to control the management or policies of a company (unless such power is solely the result of an official position in the company), or the ownership, either directly or through one or more intermediaries, of more than 25 percent of the voting securities of a company. 1997 Release, note 38.

123. Company Act § 2(a)(51)(C), 15 U.S.C. § 80a-2(a)(51)(C); Company Act Rule 2a51-1(g)(1)(ii), 17 C.F.R. 270.2a51-1(g)(1)(ii).

124. Company Act Rule 2a51-2(d), 17 C.F.R. § 270.2a51-2(d).

125. Company Act Rule 2a51-2(e), 17 C.F.R. § 270.2a51-2(e).

126. 1997 Release (*see* n. 12, *supra*) at § II.B.2.b.

127. Company Act Rule 2a51-1(h), 17 C.F.R. § 270.2a51-1(h).

128. *See* 1997 Release (*see* n. 12, *supra*) at § II.A.6.

for an additional investment pursuant to the investor's preexisting binding commitment.[129]

xiii. Knowledgeable Employees

A Knowledgeable Employee[130] is deemed not to be a beneficial owner of a 3(c)(7) Fund's securities. Accordingly, for the purpose of determining whether all of the owners of the outstanding securities of a 3(c)(7) Fund are Qualified Purchasers, Knowledgeable Employees are excluded.[131] A 3(c)(7) Fund may rely on Company Act section 3(c)(7) if Knowledgeable Employees that are not Qualified Purchasers invest in that Fund and if the Fund otherwise complies with the requirements of Company Act section 3(c)(7).

xiv. Holders of Transferred Interests in 3(c)(7) Funds

Except in the limited circumstances discussed below, each transferee who receives an interest in a 3(c)(7) Fund is counted as a beneficial owner of the 3(c)(7) Fund and, therefore, must be a Qualified Purchaser.

a. Permitted Transfers

Recipients of 3(c)(7) Fund securities from Qualified Purchasers or Grandfathered Investors (defined below)[132] by gift or bequest or under circumstances such as death, divorce, legal separation or other involuntary event are treated as Qualified Purchasers with respect to that 3(c)(7) Fund.[133] In addition, beneficial ownership by a company established by a Qualified Purchaser or Grandfathered Investor transferor exclusively for the benefit of (or owned exclusively by) the transferor and the transferees described in the preceding sentence is deemed to be beneficial ownership by the transferor.[134] These exceptions apply only to these specific transfers, however, and do not cover additional securities acquired by a transferee from the 3(c)(7) Fund.[135] In addition, the SEC has not addressed many issues related to transfers of interests in 3(c)(7) Funds, including whether securities transferred under these exceptions can be transferred again within these exceptions.

b. Public Charities

The SEC has not indicated whether, if a Qualified Purchaser or other permitted investor in a 3(c)(7) Fund donates an interest in the 3(c)(7) Fund to one or more public charities, each charity would be considered a Qualified Purchaser with respect to the 3(c)(7) Fund. An affirmative position on this issue would, however,

---

129. 1997 Release (*see* n. 12, *supra*) at § II.A.9.

130. *See* § 3.2.2.iv, *supra.*

131. Company Act Rule 3c-5(b), 17 C.F.R. § 270.3c-5(b).

132. American Bar Association (*see* n. 23, *supra*), Answer C.5(i).

133. Company Act § 3(c)(7)(A), 15 U.S.C. § 80a-3(c)(7)(A); Company Act Rule 3c-6, 17 C.F.R. § 270.3c-6.

134. Company Act Rule 3c-6(b)(3), 17 C.F.R. § 270.3c-6(b)(3).

135. 1997 Release (*see* n. 12, *supra*) at § III.C.

be consistent with SEC no-action letters regarding 3(c)(1) Funds, which reflect the public policy of supporting charitable organizations.[136]

xv. General Partner's Interest

A general partner's interest in a 3(c)(7) Fund usually should not be considered a security if the general partner actively participates in managing the 3(c)(7) Fund and does not own an interest as a limited partner. Such a general partner is deemed not to be a beneficial owner of securities of the 3(c)(7) Fund and does not need to be a Qualified Purchaser.[137]

xvi. Non-U.S. Investors

A non-U.S. individual or entity that invests in a 3(c)(7) Fund must be a Qualified Purchaser (or other permitted person) if the 3(c)(7) Fund is organized in the United States.[138]

3. Integration of Separately Managed Accounts

A 3(c)(7) Fund manager may separately manage client accounts in addition to a 3(c)(7) Fund. The SEC staff could attempt to integrate a 3(c)(7) Fund and separate accounts managed by the same investment adviser. If the SEC staff were to succeed in doing so, the 3(c)(7) Fund would not be able to rely on the exclusion provided by Company Act section 3(c)(7), unless, perhaps, the separate account holders were Qualified Purchasers whom the investment adviser did not publicly solicit. Company Act Rule 3a-4 also applies to 3(c)(7) Funds.[139]

4. Non-U.S. Funds

A hedge fund organized outside of the United States may not sell its securities to U.S. persons in connection with a public offering.[140] A non-U.S. hedge fund may conduct a private offering to U.S. persons who are Qualified Purchasers in reliance on Company Act section 3(c)(7).[141]

---

136. Trivest Special Situations Fund 1985, L.P., SEC No-Action Letter (July 13, 1989); Commodities Corp., SEC No-Action Letter (June 7, 1991); Wm. S. Barnickel & Company, SEC No-Action Letter (Nov. 1, 1994) (each allowing a 3(c)(1) Fund to count various charities to which an investor had donated securities of the 3(c)(1) Fund as a single investor for the purposes of the 100-Owner Limit).

137. *Cf.* Colony Realty Partners 1986 L.P., SEC No-Action Letter (Apr. 27, 1988); Shoreline Fund, L.P. and Condor Fund International, Inc., SEC No-Action Letter (Nov. 14, 1994) (a 3(c)(1) Fund's general partner is not counted as a beneficial owner for purposes of the 100-Owner Limit).

138. *See* § 3.3.4, *infra*, regarding offshore hedge funds.

139. *See* § 3.2.3.iii, *supra.*

140. *See* § 3.2.4, *supra.*

141. Goodwin, Proctor & Hoar, SEC No-Action Letter (Feb. 28, 1997); Goodwin, Proctor & Hoar, SEC No-Action Letter (Oct. 5, 1998). *See* § 3.2.4, *supra.*

5. Corporate Taxation

Under the Tax Code, some risk exists that a 3(c)(7) Fund with more than 100 investors could be taxed as a corporation for federal income tax purposes.[142]

6. Exchange Act Reporting Obligations

If a 3(c)(7) Fund, on the last day of its fiscal year, has at least 2,000 investors, or at least 500 investors that are not accredited investors, and total assets exceeding $10,000,000, it may be required to register[143] under the Exchange Act and file reports under Exchange Act section 13,[144] such as annual reports on Form 10-K, quarterly reports on Form 10-Q, occasional reports on Form 8-K, proxy statements under Exchange Act section 14 and other reports and statements. In that case, certain of its investors and its directors and officers would be subject to reporting requirements and restrictions with respect to their interests in the 3(c)(7) Fund.

§ 3.4 Converting 3(c)(1) Fund to 3(c)(7) Fund

1. Procedure

A 3(c)(1) Fund may be converted to a 3(c)(7) Fund if each investor in the converting hedge fund (the "Converting Fund") that first invested in the Converting Fund after September 1, 1996, is a Qualified Purchaser.[145] Before the conversion, the Converting Fund must give each beneficial owners, including beneficial owners that are Qualified Purchasers,[146] (a) notice that future investors must be Qualified Purchasers and will no longer be limited to 100 and (b) a reasonable opportunity to redeem the beneficial owner's interest in the Converting Fund for a proportionate share of the Converting Fund's net assets, even if the Converting Fund's governing documents normally would not allow such a redemption at that time.[147]

In most cases, the investors in the Converting Fund are deemed to be its beneficial owners and notice need not be provided to the constituent owners of investors that are entities (such as a fund of funds). The notice and redemption opportunity must, however, be provided to each of the security holders of any investor in the Converting Fund, if all of the following apply to the investor:

- the investor is an investment company or a Covered Company;[148]
- on October 11, 1996, the investor owned at least 10 percent of the Converting Fund's limited partner interests;

142. *See* § 16.1.2, *infra*.
143. Exchange Act § 12(g), 15 U.S.C. § 78(l)(g).
144. 15 U.S.C. § 78(n).
145. Company Act § 3(c)(7)(B)(i), 15 U.S.C. § 80a-3(c)(7)(B)(i).
146. 1997 Release (*see* n. 12, *supra*) at § II.B.1.c.i.
147. Company Act § 3(c)(7)(B)(ii), 15 U.S.C. § 80a-3(c)(7)(B)(ii).
148. *See* § 3.2.2.i.a, *supra*.

- on October 11, 1996, more than 10 percent of the investor's total assets were invested in 3(c)(1) Funds, including the Converting Fund; and
- the investor controls, is controlled by, or is under common control with, the Converting Fund.[149]

A beneficial owner's proportionate share of the Converting Fund's net assets is determined according to the Converting Fund's governing documents.[150] In many cases, the governing documents provide for a hold-back of 5 or 10 percent of the amount to be paid to a redeeming limited partner until the Converting Fund's books are audited at the end of the Converting Fund's fiscal year. The SEC has stated that such hold-backs may be permissible in the context of a redemption in connection with a 3(c)(7) conversion if they do not act as a penalty for exercising the redemption right.[151]

The redemption payment must be made in cash unless the Converting Fund elects to provide the investor with the option of receiving, and the investor agrees to receive, assets in kind. If this option is provided, disclosure concerning this opportunity must be included in the notice of conversion.[152]

The conversion rules do not override any provisions in the Converting Fund's governing documents or other agreements or applicable law that could prevent a conversion. For example, if a 3(c)(1) Fund's partnership agreement prohibits the 3(c)(1) Fund from having more than 100 investors, that agreement would need to be amended before the 3(c)(1) Fund could sell its securities to more than 100 investors, even if the 3(c)(7) conversion rules are followed.[153] The conversion rules also do not override the fiduciary duties that a 3(c)(1) Fund manager may have to its investors. For example, a manager may need to consider whether the conversion, and the concomitant increase in the Converting Fund's assets and number of investors, is in the best interests of the Converting Fund's security holders.[154]

2. Additional Investments by Grandfathered Investors

An investor that invested in a Converting Fund before September 2, 1996, and has not thereafter withdrawn from the Converting Fund, may continue to acquire securities of the Converting Fund[155], and may transfer securities of the 3(c)(7) Fund to an Alter Ego Entity,[156] whether or not such original investor is a Qualified Purchaser.

149. Company Act Rule 2a51-2(b), 17 C.F.R. § 270.2a51-2(b).
150. 1997 Release (*see* n. 12, *supra*) at § II.B.1.c.ii.
151. *Id.*
152. Company Act § 3(c)(7)(C), 15 U.S.C. § 80a-3(c)(7)(C).
153. 1997 Release (*see* n. 12, *supra*) at § II.B.1.c.ii.
154. *Id.*
155. American Bar Association (*see* n. 23, *supra*), Answers B.1 and C.5(ii).
156. American Bar Association (*see* n. 23, *supra*), Answer C.5(i).

3. Integration with New 3(c)(1) Fund

If an investment adviser manages a 3(c)(1) Fund and a 3(c)(7) Fund, even with identical investment strategies, the two hedge funds are not integrated in calculating the number of investors in the 3(c)(1) Fund.[157] An investment adviser that converts its existing 3(c)(1) Fund into a 3(c)(7) Fund and then begins a new 3(c)(1) Fund (thereby creating 100 new openings for non-Qualified Purchasers) must, however, undertake the conversion in good faith, based on the bona fide purpose of selling securities in the Converting Fund to Qualified Purchasers.[158] Whether the Converting Fund has such a bona fide purpose will be determined by the relevant facts and circumstances, including whether the Converting Fund does in fact sell its securities to Qualified Purchasers.[159]

§ 3.5 Limitations on Investments by Registered Investment Companies in Hedge Funds

Company Act sections 12(d)(1)(A) and 12(d)(1)(B)[160] prohibit a registered investment company from acquiring more than 3 percent of the voting securities of a 3(c)(1) Fund or a 3(c)(7) Fund or from acquiring securities of a 3(c)(1) Fund or 3(c)(7) Fund having a value in excess of 5 percent of the 3(c)(1) Fund or 3(c)(7) Fund. Those sections also prohibit a 3(c)(1) Fund or 3(c)(7) Fund from acquiring more than 3 percent of the voting securities of an open-end investment company.

157. Company Act § 3(c)(7)(E), 15 U.S.C. § 80a-3(c)(7)(E).
158. 1997 Release (*see* n. 12, *supra*) at § II.D.
159. *Id.*
160. 15 U.S.C. §§ 80a-12(d)(1)(A) and 12(d)(1)(B).

CHAPTER **4**

Hedge Fund Structures

§ 4.1 Introduction

An investment adviser organizing a hedge fund must bear in mind two overriding concerns:

- First, the hedge fund's structure must comply with many laws and regulations, for the primary purpose, ironically, of minimizing the scope of regulation to which the hedge fund would otherwise be subject. For example, a hedge fund for U.S. investors must comply with Company Act section 3(c)(1) or 3(c)(7)[1] to avoid being subject to the regulatory framework that applies to registered investment companies (mutual funds) and with the private offering exemption under the Securities Act[2] to avoid registering the offering of the hedge fund's securities as a public offering.[3]
- Second, the hedge fund's structure must appeal to investors. While failure to comply with regulatory requirements may discourage investors, compliance by itself will not attract investors. An investment adviser is usually well-advised to avoid innovation in structuring its hedge fund in an effort to distinguish it from other hedge funds, unless the modified structure provides pronounced and easily explained benefits. Added complexity may add documentation, accounting and other costs. From an investor's perspective, the most important distinguishing factors between one hedge fund and another are likely to be the investment adviser's skill and character and, over time, each hedge fund's performance.

---

1. *See* Chapter 3, *supra.*
2. *See* § 5.3, *infra.*
3. An offshore hedge fund should comply with Regulation S in selling shares to offshore investors. *See* § 5.4, *infra.*

§ 4.2 Pooled Investment Vehicle—Limited Partnership, Limited Liability Company or Corporation

Hedge funds typically have many common characteristics: investors have limited liability, the structure is tax-efficient, and the investment adviser has nearly complete flexibility and authority to manage the hedge fund. A U.S. hedge fund organized as a limited partnership or limited liability company ("LLC") can have these characteristics. An offshore hedge fund may exhibit these characteristics as a partnership, LLC or corporation.

Most U.S. hedge funds are organized as limited partnerships instead of LLCs, mainly because LLCs may be less familiar to investors and do not afford significant advantages over limited partnerships.[4] Accordingly, except in those few instances where we want to point out a distinctive characteristic of LLCs, we refer below only to limited partnerships, but our comments apply as well to LLCs. Similarly, where we refer to partners of a limited partnership, we are also referring to members of an LLC.

1. Limited Liability

Whether a hedge fund is organized as a limited partnership or a corporation, its investors have limited liability. Thus, an investor can lose its investment in the hedge fund and undistributed profits, but is not liable beyond that for the hedge fund's debts.[5]

2. Tax Efficiency

For a U.S. hedge fund, tax efficiency is one of the most significant advantages of the limited partnership structure. Unlike a corporation subject to tax under Subchapter C of the Tax Code,[6] a limited partnership does not itself pay U.S. income taxes and its distributions to partners are ordinarily not subject to income tax. Taxable income or loss is instead allocated to the partners, who pay the income tax on it, whether or not they receive any distributions.[7] Thus, a U.S. hedge fund structured as a limited partnership passes through to its partners

---

4. A possible advantage of an LLC is that it may afford its manager a shield from personal liability for the hedge fund's debts, and no similar shield is available to the general partner of a limited partnership. If, however, the general partner of a hedge fund is organized as a corporation or LLC, its owners should be shielded from its liabilities, including its liabilities for debts of the hedge fund.

5. *See, e.g.*, the Delaware General Corporation Law § 102(b)(6), the Delaware Revised Uniform Limited Partnership Act § 17-303 and the Delaware Limited Liability Company Act § 18-303.

6. *See* Chapter 16, *infra.* A U.S. hedge fund could be organized as a corporation and elect to be taxed as an S corporation to achieve a single level of tax, but the limitations of Subchapter S, particularly the limits on the number and types of shareholders and the requirement that an S corporation have only one class of stock, generally render it unavailable for a hedge fund.

7. *See* Chapter 16, *infra.*

all income, gains, losses and deductions, and the partners report those items directly on their own income tax returns.

Investors thus incur income tax liability for their allocable shares of the hedge fund's taxable income for each year in which hedge fund income is realized. Because hedge funds typically do not distribute any assets to their investors, the investors must either use other assets or make withdrawals from their hedge funds to pay their tax liabilities on the taxable income allocated to them. Because taxable income arises only from gains that are realized, an investor may have taxable income even in periods when the overall value of its investment in the hedge fund declines (because net unrealized losses exceed net realized gains).

When an investor makes an initial contribution to the capital of a hedge fund organized as a limited partnership, the hedge fund establishes a capital account for that investor. Each investor's capital account balance at a particular time represents the investor's pro rata interest in the net assets of the hedge fund at that time relative to the capital account balances of all of the investors and the general partner of the hedge fund.[8] An investor's capital account is increased by the investor's additional capital contributions and hedge fund profits allocated to the investor and is reduced by withdrawals by and distributions to the investor and hedge fund losses allocated to the investor. The hedge fund's assets are valued and its liabilities are determined whenever an investor makes a capital contribution or a withdrawal, the hedge fund makes a distribution, or the hedge fund allocates profits and losses. At the end of each such measurement period, the hedge fund's profits and losses are allocated to the hedge fund's investors and general partner, based on their respective capital account balances at the beginning of that measurement period.[9]

The limited partnership structure allows a hedge fund to pass through to its investors the tax characteristics of its income and loss (for example, long-term capital gain treatment). The general partner of a hedge fund ordinarily receives a special incentive or performance allocation from each investor, equal to a specified percentage of the hedge fund's realized and unrealized profits that are allocated to the investor in excess of the investor's high water mark. The special incentive or performance allocation for tax purposes comprises the same proportions of short-term and long-term capital gains and ordinary income as the profits on which it is based.[10]

The accounting for an offshore hedge fund organized as a corporation, and the consequent income tax treatment, differs markedly from a limited

---

8. A "manager" of an LLC performs the same functions as a general partner of a limited partnership. Unless the context otherwise requires, all references to a "general partner" of a limited partnership in this Chapter 4 refer also to a "manager" of an LLC.

9. Some profits and losses, however, are not always allocated in proportion to capital accounts. These include profits from new issues and special incentive or performance allocations to the general partner. *See* §§ 13.3 and 15.2, respectively, *infra*.

10. At this writing (early 2013), legislation has been proposed that would require all such profits allocated to the general partner to be treated as ordinary income. *See, e.g.*, S. 2075, 113th Cong. (2013). *See* §§ 15.2.1 and 16.3, *infra*.

partnership. A corporation does not generally pass through to its owners any income tax consequences of its business, but itself pays income tax on its income. A corporation that is organized under the laws of a non-U.S. jurisdiction and whose sole activity is trading in securities for its own account generally is not, however, subject to U.S. income tax, although it is subject to certain U.S. withholding taxes. If organized in a "tax haven" jurisdiction, its income is also not taxed by the jurisdiction in which it is organized, which enhances its appeal to non-U.S. investors. Non-U.S. investors also are potentially subject to U.S. estate tax when they invest in U.S. hedge funds.[11] Tax-exempt U.S. investors, such as ERISA plans and charitable organizations, also often prefer an offshore hedge fund to a U.S. hedge fund, particularly if the hedge fund trades on margin.[12]

3. Flexibility of Governance

Limited partnership laws do not impose significant restrictions on how a limited partnership is managed or governed. Subject to principles of fiduciary duty[13] and specific limitations in the agreement of limited partnership, the general partner completely controls the activities of a hedge fund organized as a limited partnership. Although U.S. state corporation laws typically require that shareholders be given certain protections and rights, limited partnership laws generally mandate few protections and powers for limited partners. The limited partners are free to agree to provisions that would vest control in the hedge fund's general partner. Similar flexibility can generally be built into the charter documents of an offshore hedge fund, whether it is organized as a corporation, LLC or limited partnership.

This flexibility of governance extends beyond the general partner's power to manage the business and affairs of the hedge fund. The flexibility may also extend to the economic arrangements within the hedge fund. As discussed above in section 4.2.2, the investors in a limited partnership typically share profits and losses of the hedge fund based on capital account balances. Because the general partner's special incentive or performance allocation is calculated on an investor-by-investor basis, the general partner may negotiate special incentive or performance allocation provisions that vary among the investors, subject to the general partner's fiduciary duty and disclosure obligations.[14]

---

11. *See* § 16.7.1, *infra*.

12. *See* §§ 4.3 and 16.7.6, *infra*.

13. *See, e.g.*, Advisers Act § 206, 15 U.S.C. § 80b-6; Delaware Revised Uniform Limited Partnership Act § 17-403; *see also* § 2.7, *supra*, and Chapter 11, *infra*.

14. *See* § 2.7, *supra*, and Chapter 6, *infra*.

§ 4.3 Basic Structure of a U.S. Hedge Fund—Limited Partnership

Most U.S. hedge funds are structured as limited partnerships. Diagram 1 below depicts the most common limited partnership hedge fund structure.

Diagram 1

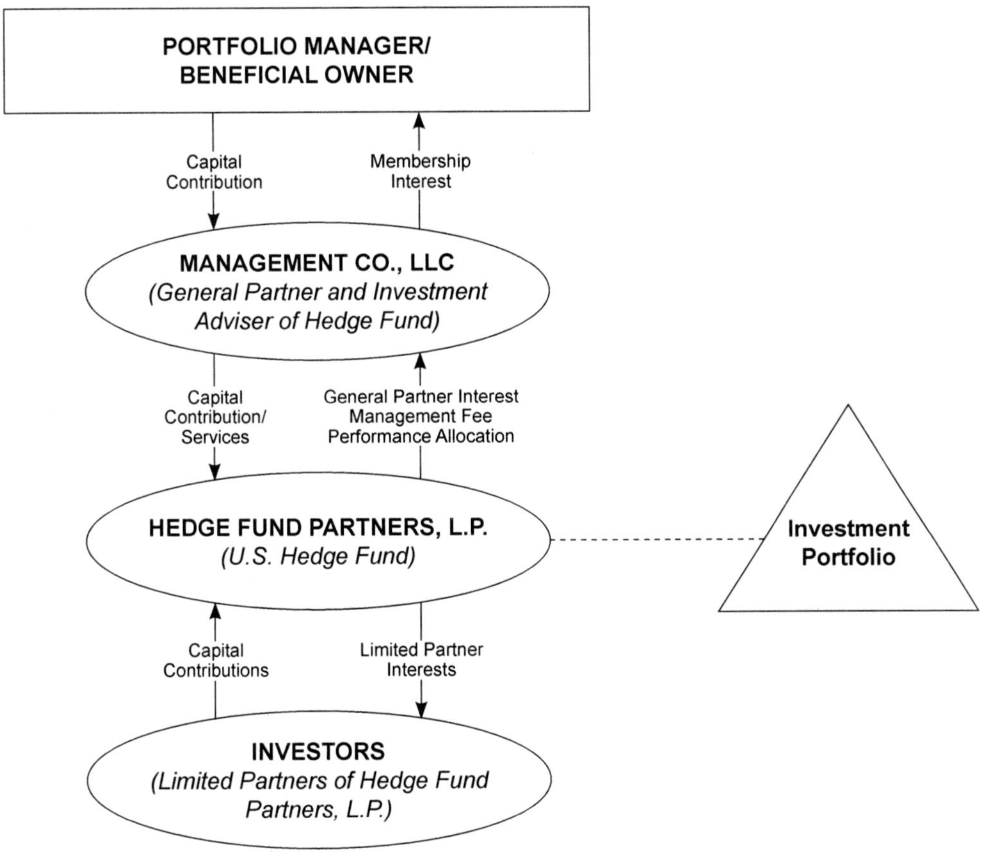

1. Parties

A hedge fund structured as a limited partnership has three main types of parties: the general partner, the investment adviser and the limited partners.

i. The General Partner

The general partner is either a natural person or, more commonly, a separate legal entity, such as an LLC or corporation. The general partner ordinarily has exclusive responsibility and authority to manage the business and affairs of the limited partnership, including managing its portfolio.[15] The general

15. If the general partner and the investment adviser of a limited partnership are not the same entity, the investment adviser manages the limited partnership's portfolio and the general partner oversees the investment adviser. *See* § 4.3.1.ii, *infra*.

partner also has unlimited liability for any of the limited partnership's debts and obligations that the limited partnership cannot satisfy. The general partner typically owes to the hedge fund's limited partners a fiduciary duty[16] and other duties specified in the hedge fund's agreement of limited partnership or similar charter documents. The general partner or its owners often invest their own money in the hedge fund, but typically have no legal or contractual duty to do so. If the general partner's owners invest directly in the hedge fund as limited partners, they are not subject to the general partner's unlimited liability with respect to their limited partner interests.[17]

Tax efficiency and limited liability are as relevant to the organization of the general partner as they are to the organization of a hedge fund. Like investors in a hedge fund, the owners of the general partner typically want pass-through tax treatment of the income and losses allocated to the general partner, both to avoid double taxation and to preserve the tax characteristics (for example, long-term capital gain) of the income or loss allocated to the general partner. The general partner's owners also want to limit their liability with respect to management of the hedge fund and their investment in the general partner. Provisions in the federal securities laws, however, impose liability for acts of controlled persons directly on their controlling persons, which owners who actively manage the general partner may not be able to avoid.[18]

Because of these concerns, the general partner is typically organized as an LLC, although the general partners of hedge funds organized before widespread enactment of state LLC statutes often were organized as corporations or limited partnerships. As discussed above, the LLC form provides the flexibility of a limited partnership in both governance and the economic arrangements among its owners, and enjoys the same tax efficiency. It also provides greater liability protection for the owners than a limited partnership. Because the general partner of a limited partnership has unlimited liability, the general partner of a hedge fund is rarely organized as a limited partnership, unless its ultimate owners are shielded by other entities.

Alternatively, a hedge fund's general partner may be organized as a corporation and elect to be taxed under Subchapter S of the Tax Code.[19] The S corporation form can provide, in appropriate circumstances, tax efficiency that is similar to that of a limited partnership. An S corporation is, however, less flexible with respect to governance and economic arrangements among the shareholders. For example, an S corporation can have only one class of stock and the shareholders must share the S corporation's income in proportion to their share ownership.[20]

---

16. *See, e.g.*, the Delaware Revised Uniform Limited Partnership Act § 17-403.

17. *See* §§ 3.2.2.iv and 3.3.2.xiii, *supra*, for a discussion about how "knowledgeable employees" of the general partner are treated for purposes of Company Act § 3(c)(1) or 3(c)(7), 15 U.S.C. § 80c-3(c)(1) or 80c-3(c)(7).

18. *See* Securities Act § 15, 15 U.S.C. § 77o; *see also* § 2.7, *supra*, and Chapter 6, *infra*.

19. Tax Code § 1361, 26 U.S.C. § 1361.

20. Tax Code § 1361(b), 26 U.S.C. § 1361(b). An S corporation may, however, pay salaries and bonuses to its owners that are not based on pro rata share ownership.

Pro rata sharing may be desirable in some instances, but it can be an impediment to other desirable economic arrangements. For example, if a general partner has four shareholders and manages two hedge funds, but three shareholders primarily manage one hedge fund and the fourth primarily manages the second hedge fund, the four principals may want to share the income and losses relating to the two hedge funds disproportionately to their ownership interests. It may be difficult or impossible to achieve that result through an S corporation. An S corporation must also observe corporate formalities and may be subject to state income tax. As a result, the general partner is rarely organized as a corporation, especially if it may have more than one or two shareholders.

The general partner of a hedge fund may also be a natural person who manages the hedge fund as a sole proprietorship. The sole proprietorship form is simple and tax-efficient, but provides no shield from liabilities of the general partner's business or the hedge fund (although a hedge fund organized as an LLC may shield its manager from its liabilities). In addition, unlike an LLC, limited partnership or S corporation, each of which can have more than one owner and add or remove owners, a sole proprietorship by definition has only one owner.

If two or more persons own the general partner, they should consider many issues relating to the day-to-day operation and management of the general partner and the relationships among themselves, including:

a. Allocation of Profits and Losses

The owners must determine how to allocate the general partner's profits and losses among themselves. The LLC form allows the owners to agree on profit and loss sharing arrangements that differ from their relative capital contributions or capital account balances. For example, an LLC may allocate in varying agreed proportions among its members its profits and losses from various sources, such as different hedge funds, different forms of compensation (management fees or performance-based compensation) and proceeds from a sale of the LLC.

b. Capital Contributions

The owners must determine how much capital, if any, each of them will contribute to the general partner. They must also determine the consequences of a default on an obligation to contribute capital.

c. Management

The owners must determine how the general partner will be managed and who makes the decisions. For each management decision, they must determine whether (a) one owner can act alone on behalf of the general partner without the consent of the other owners, (b) the consent of a majority of the owners is required, or (c) unanimous consent of the owners is required. They may also allocate responsibility and authority for various management functions to designated owners.

d. Expulsion of One or More Owners

The owners must decide whether an owner may be expelled by other owners from the general partner and if so, under what circumstances and on what terms and conditions.

e. Withdrawal of an Owner

The owners must decide on the consequences of the withdrawal by an owner, whether withdrawal would breach their agreement, and the terms and conditions of withdrawal under various foreseeable circumstances.

f. Dispute Resolution

The owners should agree on reasonable ways to resolve disputes among themselves short of arbitration or litigation, whether through buy-out options, an auction procedure or otherwise.

The general partner of a hedge fund and the general partner's management personnel have fiduciary duties to the hedge fund and its investors that arise under limited partnership laws.[21] For example, the general partner and its managers must put the investors' interests ahead of their own and conduct the business in the interests of the hedge fund and its limited partners generally.

All registered and unregistered investment advisers also have fiduciary duties under investment adviser laws to the hedge funds they manage and their investors.[22] To some extent, the nature and extent of fiduciary duties to the hedge fund and its investors can be established and limited by contract (such as the hedge fund's agreement of limited partnership). A hedge fund's agreement of limited partnership and offering circular should clearly and specifically disclose any matter that, but for an express agreement to the contrary, could constitute a breach of fiduciary duty.

Such matters include, for example, (a) the general partner's and its owners' devotion of time to the hedge fund and ability to conduct other related and unrelated activities, (b) the general partner's and its owners' ability to invest outside of the hedge fund and the related obligation to present those investment opportunities to the hedge fund, and (c) potential conflicts of interest, such as might arise from use of "soft" or commission dollars generated by brokerage commissions that the hedge fund generates.[23] Regulatory authorities, however, may determine that some types of conduct constitute breach of fiduciary duty even if permitted by the contract and fully and accurately disclosed to potential investors.[24]

ii. Investment Adviser

Typically, the general partner and the investment adviser to the hedge fund are the same entity.[25] Under some circumstances, however, it may be desirable to separate the general partner's rights and obligations in one company and the investment adviser's rights and obligations in another.

A hedge fund usually compensates the management company in two ways: (a) management fees, based on total net assets of the hedge fund from time to

21. *See, e.g.*, Delaware Revised Uniform Limited Partnership Act § 17-403.

22. *See* Advisers Act § 206, 15 U.S.C. § 80b-6; and *see* § 2.7, *supra.*

23. *See* Chapter 14, *infra.*

24. *See, e.g.*, §§ 14.2.5 and 15.5, *infra.*

25. For purposes of this discussion, we refer to an entity that serves as both the general partner and the investment adviser of a hedge fund sometimes as "general partner" and sometimes as "management company."

time, and (b) performance or incentive allocations (sometimes called a "special profit allocation"), which are a specified percentage of each limited partner's periodic hedge fund profits (typically allocated quarterly or annually).[26] The tax consequences may occasionally be preferable if the general partner and the investment adviser are separate entities, the former entitled to the special profit allocation and the latter entitled to the asset-based management fees. For example, in some jurisdictions this two-entity structure may be used to shield the special profit allocation from state or local taxes, which then apply only to the management fees.

iii. Limited Partners/Investors

The hedge fund investor base has changed significantly since the 1980s. Initially, hedge fund investors typically were wealthy individuals or families. The success and increased publicity relating to hedge funds have prompted interest from other types of investors. Institutional investors, funds of hedge funds, endowments, private foundations and pension plans (governmental and private) have increasingly invested in hedge funds. The organizer of a hedge fund business must consider not only the regulatory framework, but also its potential investor base. Among other things, the management company must determine:

- whether the hedge fund will rely on the exemption from regulation as an investment company pursuant to Company Act section 3(c)(1) or 3(c)(7);[27]
- the extent, if any, to which the hedge fund will invest in futures contracts, swaps or other commodity interests and the need for registration as a commodity pool operator or commodity trader;[28]
- the need for registration as an investment adviser with the SEC or with a state regulatory authority;[29]
- whether the hedge fund's investment strategy will generate unrelated business taxable income ("UBTI") that would have adverse tax consequences for some tax-exempt prospective investors;[30]
- whether the investor base will include employee benefit plans, pension plans or other investors that are subject to ERISA;[31] and
- whether any non-U.S. investors will invest in the hedge fund.[32]

---

26. *See* Chapter 15, *infra.*
27. *See* Chapter 3, *supra.*
28. *See* § 2.9, *supra.*
29. *See* §§ 2.1-2.4, *supra.*
30. UBTI is defined as the gross income from any trade or business unrelated to the tax-exempt business of a tax-exempt entity. *See* §§ 4.4.1.ii and 16.3.13, *infra.*
31. *See* Chapter 11, *infra.*
32. *See also* §§ 3.2.3 and 3.3.2, *supra*, and § 16.7, *infra.*

Because hedge funds rely on the private offering exemption in offering their limited partner interests, the investors should all be "accredited investors," as defined in Rule 501 of Regulation D under the Securities Act.[33]

Some investors or types of investors may expect or demand that the hedge fund have particular terms and features. In considering investment in a hedge fund, an investor may consider a variety of issues, such as:

- What is the hedge fund's investment strategy? Does it invest primarily in large-, mid-, small- or micro-cap stocks, bonds or other debt instruments, futures, or other investment products? Does it focus on a particular economic sector or a particular geographic region? Does it invest in derivative instruments? Does it invest in illiquid securities? Does it trade on margin? How risky is the investment strategy? Does it hedge against investment risks (such as through short selling or option trading)? Most investors will consider such factors in connection with their overall investment strategies, diversification and asset allocation.
- How liquid are the hedge fund's investments? How liquid is an investor's investment in the hedge fund?
- Does the hedge fund's investment strategy generate UBTI? If a hedge fund generates UBTI, it may be inappropriate for tax-exempt investors.
- What is the portfolio manager's background and performance history?
- Is the investor subject to ERISA? Are 25 percent or more of the hedge fund's assets contributed by "plan investors"?[34] If so, an ERISA investor may want certain controls in place to ensure that the hedge fund and management company comply with requirements of ERISA, such as the prohibited transaction rules and the investment adviser's bonding requirements. Similarly, the management company must be counseled about the additional responsibilities that apply to it, such as the additional fiduciary responsibilities and co-fiduciary liability.[35]

2. Basic Documents

To offer interests in a hedge fund, the general partner should prepare an offering circular, an agreement of limited partnership, and forms of a subscription agreement and an investor questionnaire.

i. Offering Circular

The offering circular serves two primary functions. First, it is a marketing document for the hedge fund. Second, it should satisfy the general partner's obligation to disclose to potential investors all facts material to a decision whether to invest in the hedge fund.[36] To fulfill both of these objectives, the

33. *See* § 5.3, *infra*. Although the hedge fund may permit up to 35 non-accredited investors to purchase securities in the hedge fund's private offering, it is inadvisable for the hedge fund to admit any non-accredited investors. *See* §§ 5.3.2.iii and 15.2.3, *infra*.

34. See § 11.1, *infra*, for definition of "plan investor."

35. *See* Chapter 11, *infra*.

36. *See* §§ 5.3.1.iii and 5.3.2.vii and Chapter 6, *infra*.

offering circular describes (a) the hedge fund's investment strategy, objectives and restrictions, (b) the general partner and portfolio manager, (c) investor suitability requirements, (d) the hedge fund's material terms (which are formally provided in the agreement of limited partnership and include matters such as limited partner withdrawal rights, compensation of the general partner and profit and loss allocations), (e) risk factors associated with investing in the hedge fund, (f) applicable regulatory and compliance requirements, (g) conflicts of interest that the general partner may face and (h) U.S. federal income tax considerations for investors.

If the hedge fund trades in futures or other commodity interests, the offering circular may also need to include disclosure required by the CFTC.[37]

ii. Agreement of Limited Partnership

The agreement of limited partnership is the main contract between the general partner and the investors in the hedge fund. The agreement of limited partnership ordinarily (a) grants plenary authority to the general partner to manage the hedge fund and its portfolio (although the general partner sometimes agrees to circumscribe its authority if it considers doing so necessary or desirable to attract investors), (b) establishes the allocation rules for the hedge fund (including any performance-based compensation to the general partner or other manager that is structured as an allocation of profits[38]), (c) provides for the management fee and its payment terms, (d) establishes the investors' withdrawal (redemption) rights and the general partner's right to expel investors, (e) specifies which expenses relating to the hedge fund will be borne by the hedge fund, (f) provides a mechanism for complying with the FINRA new issue rule,[39] and (g) establishes voting and amendment rights.

As a corollary to the general partner's comprehensive management authority, the investors usually have minimal or no rights to vote or to amend the agreement in most respects, except on matters that materially affect their economic deal with the general partner. Except for economic terms, the general partner normally has unilateral management authority, including authority to amend the agreement in many respects. An investor's primary remedy if it disagrees with an action by the general partner is to withdraw from the hedge fund.

iii. Subscription Agreement

The subscription agreement (a) provides the terms on which a prospective investor may purchase a limited partner interest in the hedge fund, (b) includes representations and warranties that are necessary for the hedge fund and the general partner to comply, or evidence their compliance, with applicable securities, anti-money laundering and other laws and regulations, and (c) appoints the general partner as attorney-in-fact for the investor to sign the agreement of limited partnership and other instruments.

---

37. *See* § 2.9, *supra*, and § 6.7, *infra*.
38. *See* § 15.2, *infra*.
39. *See* § 13.5.1, *infra*.

iv. Offering Questionnaire

The offering questionnaire elicits information about the investor, including biographical and background information, needed to establish a reasonable basis for the general partner to conclude that the investor is sufficiently sophisticated to understand the investment and has sufficient means to bear the risk of the investment. The offering questionnaire also elicits information to support the investor's representations and warranties in the investor's subscription agreement and information to aid the general partner in complying with applicable laws and regulations (such as FINRA's new issue rule, if the hedge fund may invest in new issues).

§ 4.4 Offshore Hedge Funds

1. Why Organize an Offshore Hedge Fund?

Before 1997, non-U.S. investors that invested directly in U.S. hedge funds were subject to U.S. tax on capital gains from such funds. Hedge funds organized outside of the United States, however, even if managed by U.S. investment advisers, were treated as not engaged in a U.S. trade or business, and were thus not subject to U.S. tax, if most of their administrative and shareholder activities were conducted outside of the United States.[40]

To attract non-U.S. investors, investment advisers organized offshore hedge funds as non-U.S. corporations and retained offshore administrators to conduct most of those activities. Changes to the Tax Code in 1997 eliminated the requirement that an offshore fund conduct most of such activities outside of the United States. The changes also made it possible for non-U.S. investors to invest in U.S. hedge funds without being taxed on most capital gains of those funds. This change made it more economically feasible, from the perspective of U.S. federal taxes, for a non-U.S. investor to invest in a U.S. hedge fund.[41] Notwithstanding these changes to the tax laws, and that organizing and operating an offshore hedge fund is generally more costly than organizing and operating

40. U.S. Treasury Regulations, colloquially referred to as the "ten commandments," specified 10 activities, substantially all of which were required to be performed outside of the United States for an offshore hedge fund not to be deemed to be engaged in a U.S. trade or business. These involved: (a) communicating with shareholders; (b) communicating with the general public; (c) soliciting sales of stock; (d) accepting subscriptions from prospective shareholders; (e) maintaining the fund's principal corporate records and books of account; (f) auditing books of account; (g) disbursing payments of dividends, legal fees, accounting fees and officers' and directors' salaries; (h) publishing or furnishing the offering and redemption price of shares of stock issued; (i) conducting meetings of shareholders and board of directors; and (j) redeeming stock. Treas. Reg. § 1.864-2(c)(2)(C)(iii), 26 C.F.R. § 1.864-2(c)(2)(C)(iii).

41. From the investment adviser's perspective, admitting non-U.S. investors into a U.S. hedge fund creates an additional housekeeping burden, because a U.S. hedge fund must withhold tax from a non-U.S. investor's allocable share of certain U.S. source dividend and interest income of the hedge fund, and is liable for underwithholding.

a U.S. hedge fund,[42] offshore hedge funds remain popular, primarily for the reasons outlined below.

i. Investor Confidentiality

Many non-U.S. investors are concerned about protecting their confidentiality, particularly by avoiding disclosure to U.S. tax and regulatory authorities, and prefer to deal with an offshore administrator rather than a U.S.-based investment adviser. An offshore hedge fund's administrator should be responsible for maintaining the shareholder registry and communicating with the offshore hedge fund's investors and prospective investors.

Although a U.S. partnership files income tax information returns with the IRS that identify all of the hedge fund's investors (including non-U.S. investors), the identities of non-U.S. investors in an offshore hedge fund that is treated as a corporation for U.S. tax purposes are not ordinarily reported to the IRS or other U.S. governmental agencies for tax or other purposes. The offshore hedge fund, on its own behalf and on behalf of its investment adviser and administrator, should, however, reserve its rights to disclose each investor's identity and information about the investor to cognizant U.S. or non-U.S. governmental authorities as needed to comply with U.S. and non-U.S. anti-money-laundering laws and the U.S. Foreign Account Tax Compliance Act (FATCA).[43]

ii. Taxation

Non-U.S. investors are not subject to U.S. income tax on their ownership interests in an offshore hedge fund, although the offshore hedge fund itself is subject to U.S. withholding taxes on certain types of income. Depending on the investment adviser's investment strategy, some U.S. tax-exempt investors, such as pension plans and charitable organizations, have tax reasons to prefer to invest in the investment adviser's offshore hedge fund. Because an offshore hedge fund is typically organized as a corporation instead of a partnership, which is a pass-through vehicle for U.S. tax purposes, if both a U.S. and an offshore hedge fund trade on margin, a U.S. tax-exempt investor would receive debt-financed income from the U.S. hedge fund but not from the offshore hedge fund. Debt-financed income is UBTI under Tax Code section 514, and as such is taxable to a tax-exempt investor.[44]

Except in the case of an offshore hedge fund that is structured as a partnership, the offshore hedge fund is not a pass-through vehicle for U.S. income tax purposes and the tax characteristics (as long-term or short-term capital gain or ordinary income) of its taxable income are not passed through to its investors. As a result, the investment adviser may desire to trade and invest the offshore hedge fund's portfolio differently from the investment

---

42. Offshore hedge funds typically cost more to organize and to operate because of the additional service providers that the investment adviser and the offshore hedge fund must engage, such as the directors and offshore attorneys, and because of the added cost of complying with the laws and regulations of the jurisdiction in which the offshore hedge fund is organized.

43. Pub. L. 111-147 (2010), 26 U.S.C. §§ 1471-1474, 6038D. *See* §§ 2.7.7 and 2.10, *supra*.

44. *See* § 16.7.6, *infra*.

adviser's U.S. hedge fund's portfolio. For example, the investment adviser may cause the offshore hedge fund to sell a security that the offshore hedge fund has held for less than 1 year; although this will result in short-term capital gain for the offshore hedge fund on the profits of that sale, that characteristic will not pass through to the investors in the offshore hedge fund. At the same time, the investment adviser might cause its U.S. hedge fund to hold the same security until the gain on the sale can be characterized as long-term capital gain, which will pass through to the investors in the U.S. hedge fund; any benefit to the investors in the U.S. hedge fund of selling the security simultaneously with the offshore fund's sale may be outweighed by the higher tax liability on short-term capital gain.

iii. Additional 3(c)(1) "Slots"

As discussed above,[45] many U.S. hedge funds comply with the 100 beneficial owner limit of Company Act section 3(c)(1) to be excluded from the Company Act definition of "investment company." Non-U.S. investors that are admitted to a U.S. hedge fund count toward that 100 beneficial owner limit.[46]

Additionally, if a U.S. hedge fund is managed with a similar investment strategy as an offshore hedge fund, if each hedge fund relies on Company Act section 3(c)(1), and if the offshore hedge fund admits U.S. taxable investors or the U.S. hedge fund admits non-U.S. investors, then all of the investors (U.S. and non-U.S.) in the offshore hedge fund will be integrated with the investors in the U.S. hedge fund for purposes of the 100-beneficial-owner limit under Company Act section 3(c)(1); that is, all of the offshore hedge fund's investors and all of the U.S. hedge fund's investors will count against a single 100-beneficial-owner limit for both hedge funds.[47]

If, however, the offshore hedge fund is available only to U.S. tax-exempt investors and non-U.S. investors, and the U.S. hedge fund is available only to U.S. taxable investors, the SEC staff has indicated that, for purposes of section 3(c)(1), U.S. investors in the offshore hedge fund will not necessarily be integrated with the investors in the side-by-side U.S. hedge fund.[48]

iv. Familiarity

Non-U.S. investors are typically more familiar with and comfortable investing in offshore hedge funds than in U.S. funds.

---

45. *See* § 3.2, *supra*.

46. *See* § 3.2.2.vii, *supra*.

47. Investors admitted to an offshore hedge fund that properly relies on Company Act § 3(c)(7), 15 U.S.C. § 80c-3(c)(7), will not be integrated with the U.S. hedge fund, even if U.S. taxable investors are admitted to the offshore hedge fund. *See* § 3.2.3.ii, *supra*.

48. *See* § 3.2.3.i.a, *supra*.

2. Typical Offshore Hedge Fund Structure (Side-by-Side Structure)

Unlike a U.S. hedge fund, which is typically organized as a limited partnership, an offshore hedge fund is typically organized in an offshore jurisdiction as a corporation that issues shares to its investors.[49] Alternatively an offshore hedge fund may be established as a partnership in the offshore jurisdiction and elect to be treated as a corporation for U.S. purposes.[50] Diagram 2 below depicts a common offshore hedge fund structure.

Diagram 2

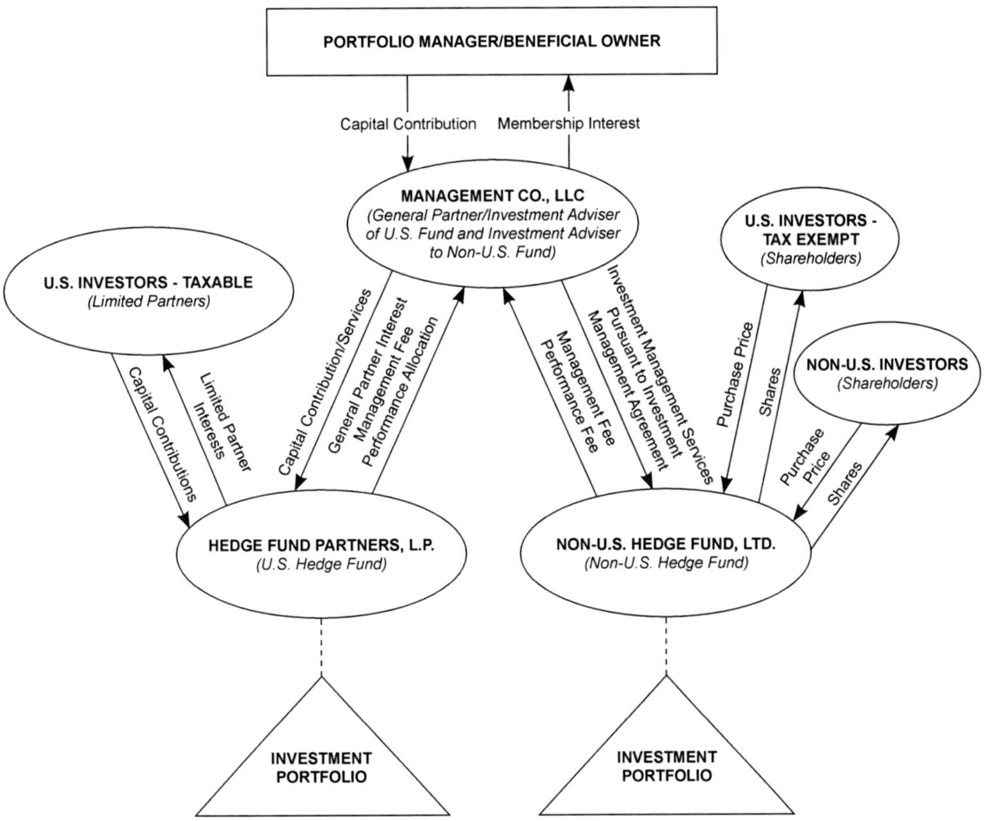

The offshore hedge fund's directors control the management of the offshore hedge fund. The directors usually delegate administrative duties (such as processing subscription and redemption requests, calculating the investment adviser's fees, and calculating the offshore hedge fund's net asset value ("NAV")) to an administrator[51] pursuant to an administration agreement. They generally delegate portfolio management duties to a U.S. investment adviser pursuant to an investment adviser agreement.

49. *See* § 4.2, *supra.*
50. *See* § 16.7.2, *infra.*
51. *See* § 4.4.5.ii, *infra.*

3. Basic Documents

i. Charter Documents

An offshore hedge fund's charter documents are analogous to a U.S. hedge fund's agreement of limited partnership,[52] in that they state most of the material terms and conditions of the relationship between the offshore hedge fund's management and the investors and the economic consequences of the investment. The charter documents establish, for example, withdrawal (redemption) rights, the expenses the offshore hedge fund must bear, and voting and amendment rights. The charter documents set forth the equity structure of the offshore hedge fund, including, for example, the different classes and series of shares and the manner of calculating the incentive fees and the high water mark.[53]

ii. Private Placement Memorandum

The private placement memorandum for an offshore hedge fund serves the same purposes as the offering circular for a U.S. hedge fund. It should disclose all material terms and risks of the offering, the terms of the shares to be issued, the offshore hedge fund's directors, regulatory matters, tax aspects, information about the administrator and the fees it charges, and information about the investment adviser and the investment adviser agreement.[54] The preparation of this disclosure document is complicated by the involvement of several parties, including lawyers, administrators and accountants (generally all in non-U.S. jurisdictions) whose expertise is required.

iii. Subscription Agreement and Offering Questionnaire

The subscription agreement and offering questionnaire serve essentially the same purposes for an offshore hedge fund as they do for a U.S. hedge fund,[55] but are drafted to reflect differences in applicable laws and regulations and the differences between U.S. and non-U.S. hedge fund structures. If an offshore hedge fund will sell shares to U.S. persons, as well as to non-U.S. persons, it will need a different form of each of the subscription agreement and the offering questionnaire for U.S. persons and non-U.S. persons, because different regulations apply with respect to each group.[56]

iv. Investment Adviser Agreement

The investment adviser agreement is a contract between the offshore hedge fund and the U.S. investment adviser, pursuant to which the offshore hedge fund's directors delegate to the investment adviser the authority to manage the offshore hedge fund's securities portfolio. The portfolio management powers delegated

52. *See* § 4.3.2.ii, *supra.*
53. *See* § 15.3, *infra.*
54. *See* § 4.3.2.i, *supra.*
55. *See* §§ 4.3.2.iii and 4.3.2.iv, *supra.*
56. *See* Chapter 5, *infra.*

to the investment adviser are typically substantially similar to the portfolio management powers granted to the general partner of a U.S. hedge fund.[57]

The investment adviser agreement also provides for the investment adviser's compensation by the offshore hedge fund. The investment adviser typically receives a management fee, which is based on the periodic NAV of the offshore hedge fund, and a performance-based fee, which is based on increases in the offshore hedge fund's NAV, including realized and unrealized gains and losses. Unlike in a U.S. hedge fund, however, the performance-based compensation from an offshore hedge fund is a fee, not a special profit allocation, unless the offshore hedge fund is organized as a partnership, or is a feeder into a master fund organized as a partnership and the performance-based compensation is an allocation at the master fund level.[58]

4. Different Capital Structures to Accommodate Performance Fees

Performance fees with respect to offshore hedge funds are occasionally based on the performance of the offshore hedge fund as a whole, rather than the performance accruing to each individual investor, as is usually the case with a U.S. hedge fund. As a result, calculating the investment adviser's performance fee can create accounting complexity for offshore hedge funds in the following circumstances:

- If an investor invests when the offshore hedge fund has sustained earlier losses that created a high water mark, the investor may enjoy a windfall, because it will enjoy appreciation in the offshore hedge fund without paying a performance fee until the prior losses related to the high water mark are recovered.
- If an investor invests during a performance fee measurement period when the offshore hedge fund has had positive performance for that measurement period, the investor may be burdened with a portion of the performance fee that is charged at the end of the measurement period on appreciation that occurred before that investor invested.

These issues are typically addressed by one of several types of adjustments, some of which impose quasi-partnership accounting methods on the corporate structure.[59]

5. Other Service Providers

i. U.S. and Offshore Attorneys

U.S. counsel may draft the offshore hedge fund's charter documents and offering documents, but parts of those documents must be drafted, or reviewed and approved, by counsel that is licensed in the jurisdiction of the offshore hedge

57. *See* § 4.3.2.ii, *supra.*
58. *See* § 15.2, *infra.*
59. *See* § 15.3, *infra.*

fund's organization. The offshore counsel also usually files all of the offshore hedge fund's organizational documents with the appropriate officials in that jurisdiction and advises on compliance with the laws of that jurisdiction on an ongoing basis.

ii. Administrator

Most offshore hedge funds engage third-party administrators to perform administrative functions. Among other things, the administrator typically calculates the NAV, maintains investor lists, accepts subscriptions, processes sales and redemptions of shares, transmits communications from the offshore hedge fund or the investment adviser to current and prospective investors, pays the offshore hedge fund's bills and performs corporate housekeeping tasks.

Offshore funds historically engaged administrators located outside of the United States. The repeal of the "ten commandments" discussed above in section 4.4.1, however, made it possible for offshore hedge funds to use administrators in the United States. U.S. hedge funds now also frequently engage third-party administrators, prompting establishment of new hedge fund administration firms in the United States, many of which market their services to offshore hedge funds. Administration firms now often have offices and affiliates located around the world and may perform services for a single fund in multiple jurisdictions. An offshore hedge fund organized in one non-U.S. jurisdiction may have an administrator located in another jurisdiction or an administrator that allocates some of its administrative duties to an office or affiliate located in another jurisdiction.

The investment adviser to an offshore hedge fund should pay attention to where the fund's administrative activities are conducted for two primary reasons. First, the jurisdiction where the administrator is located may have its own regulations that apply to hedge funds administered there. The offshore hedge fund and its investment adviser should understand those regulations and how they affect the offshore hedge fund. For example, if an offshore hedge fund organized in the British Virgin Islands has an administrator in Ireland, the Irish anti-money-laundering regulations that apply to the administrator may not be the same as the anti-money-laundering regulations of the British Virgin Islands. Second, if the administrator performs all or part of its services in a jurisdiction other than the jurisdiction in which the offshore hedge fund is organized, those activities may subject the offshore hedge fund to taxes imposed by the administrator's jurisdiction. For example, if the administrator performs services in the United States, the offshore hedge fund could be subject to U.S. state and local taxes. Some states have adopted rules similar to the U.S. federal rules for determining whether a non-U.S. entity is subject to state tax, but some have not and may regard a local office of the administrator as an office of the offshore hedge fund. In addition, if the administrator performs some or all of its services in the United States, the requirements for avoiding registration of the offshore hedge fund's offering under the Securities Act may differ from the requirements that would otherwise apply.[60]

---

60. *See* Chapter 5, *infra*.

iii. Offshore Accountant/Auditor

Before the repeal of the "ten commandments," accounting functions, like administrative functions, were performed outside the United States. Although those functions are now often performed in the United States, some offshore jurisdictions, such as the Cayman Islands, require a local audit firm to issue the audit report with respect to an offshore hedge fund organized in that jurisdiction. To facilitate compliance with these local requirements, many U.S. accounting firms that provide services to hedge funds have offices in the Cayman Islands and other offshore jurisdictions where offshore hedge funds are frequently organized.

6. Jurisdiction of Organization

When selecting a jurisdiction in which to organize an offshore hedge fund, investment advisers should focus on the following issues:

- Is the target group of prospective investors familiar and comfortable with the proposed jurisdiction?
- Does the proposed jurisdiction impose local taxes or other regulatory burdens? Most preferred offshore jurisdictions do not impose substantial local taxes on hedge funds organized there.
- Are adequate professional service firms, such as administrators, accountants and attorneys, available to provide services to offshore hedge funds in the proposed jurisdiction?
- Is the proposed jurisdiction politically stable?
- Are regulatory and service-provider costs associated with an offshore hedge fund in the proposed jurisdiction reasonable? Such costs can vary substantially.

7. Master-Feeder Structure

A management company faces inherent operating difficulties and inefficiencies when it manages one or more U.S. and offshore hedge funds side-by-side using the same investment strategy. Use of a "master-feeder" structure, in which the funds' portfolios are consolidated and managed as a single portfolio within a "master fund," may alleviate some of these inefficiencies and reduce costs and administrative burdens. For example, managing a single, consolidated "master" portfolio reduces the need to rebalance the individual funds' portfolios, helps the manager maintain similar performance across the individual funds, and may allow the manager to obtain more favorable financing, credit, brokerage and investment terms by virtue of being able to present a single, larger investing pool to third-party lenders and service providers.

In addition, funds of funds and other institutional investors sometimes cannot or will not invest in a hedge fund whose assets do not meet some minimum threshold or are unable or unwilling to hold more than a specified percentage of a hedge fund's total assets. Such investors may be more likely to invest in a hedge fund that is part of a master-feeder structure because they may apply their asset-size conditions to the master fund rather than to the individual feeders. Disadvantages of a master-feeder structure include greater regulatory complexity and the additional costs of organizing and maintaining another legal entity. Some of these advantages and disadvantages are discussed below.

A basic master-feeder structure comprises one "master" fund and two or more "feeder" funds. The feeder funds are typically one or more U.S. limited partnerships for taxable U.S. investors[61] and a non-U.S. corporations for non-U.S. investors and tax-exempt U.S. investors.[62] The feeder funds invest all of their capital in the master fund. The master fund is typically a non-U.S. entity and all of the portfolio investment activities are conducted at the master fund level. Diagram 3 below depicts this common master-feeder structure.

Diagram 3

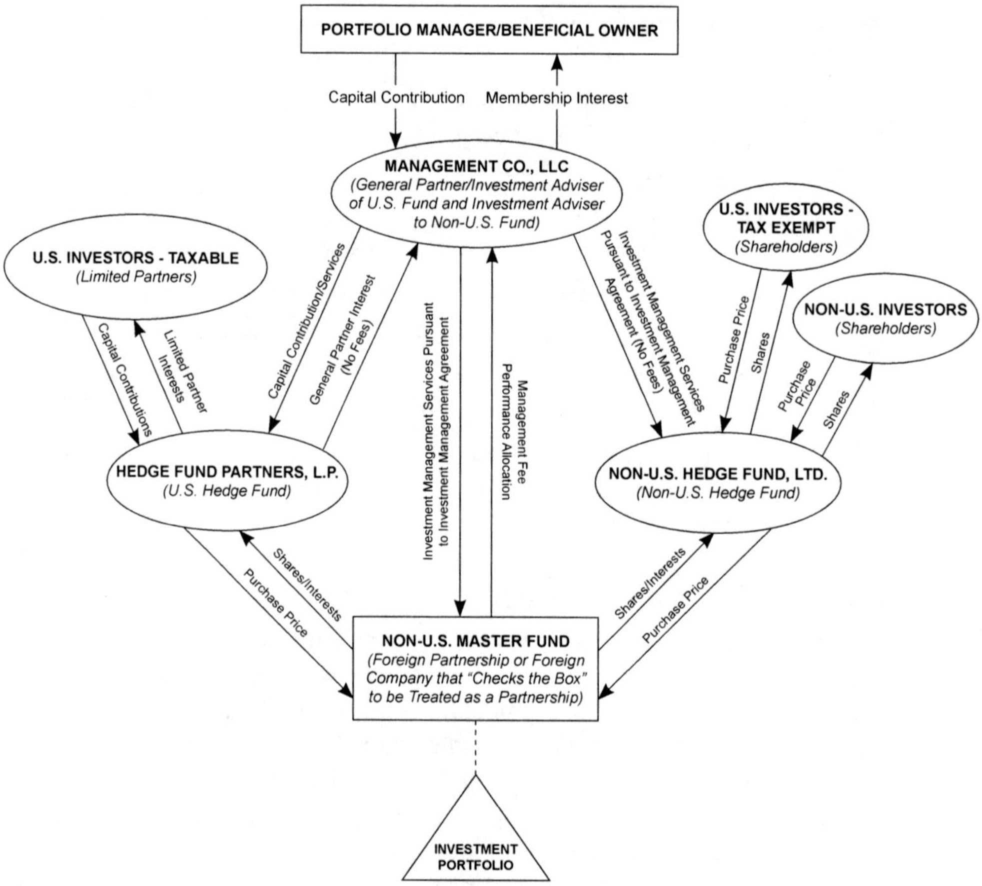

The non-U.S. master fund, whether organized as a partnership or corporation, generally can elect to be taxed as a partnership for U.S. tax purposes by making the appropriate check-the-box election on IRS Form 8832 within 75 days of the master fund's organization. If the master fund is taxed as a partnership, the

61. *See* § 4.2, *supra*.
62. *See* § 4.4.2, *supra*.

partners in the U.S. feeder fund will receive pass-through treatment for their shares of the U.S. feeder fund's income.[63]

The investment adviser for the master fund typically also serves as the investment adviser for the feeder funds. The investment adviser can receive its management fees and performance fees or performance allocations from either the master fund or the feeder funds. It may be preferable for the investment adviser to receive the management fees and performance fees or allocations from the master fund for the following reasons:

- The performance allocation from the master fund, which is typically a partnership, will be made in the form of an allocation and will give the investment adviser the tax benefits of the pass-through treatment of capital gains, which can be considerable if the master fund generates significant long-term capital gains subject to favorable rates;[64] and
- If the master fund trades frequently enough to be treated as a trader, rather than as an investor, the management fees that pass through to the limited partners in the U.S. feeder fund are generally deductible, whereas if the management fees are charged at the level of the U.S. feeder fund, the IRS might contend that those fees are investment expenses and, accordingly, that their deductibility is limited.[65]

On the other hand, charging fees at the feeder fund level gives the investment adviser flexibility to charge different fees to different feeder funds. Until 2008, another advantage of charging fees at the feeder level was that it allowed the investment adviser to defer receipt of the performance fee from the offshore feeder fund and its corresponding tax liability. Under current law, however, investment advisers generally cannot defer fees from offshore hedge funds for years after 2008.[66]

An alternative master-feeder structure, shown in Diagram 4 below, uses the U.S. hedge fund as the master fund, organized as a U.S. limited partnership with U.S. taxable investors and an offshore feeder fund.

63. *See* § 16.7.7, *infra.*

64. At this writing (early 2013), legislation has been proposed that would change the treatment of all such profits allocated to the general partner to ordinary income. *See, e.g.*, H.R. 4016, 112th Cong. (2012).

65. *See* § 16.3.10(i), *infra.*

66. *See* § 16.8.6, *infra.*

Diagram 4

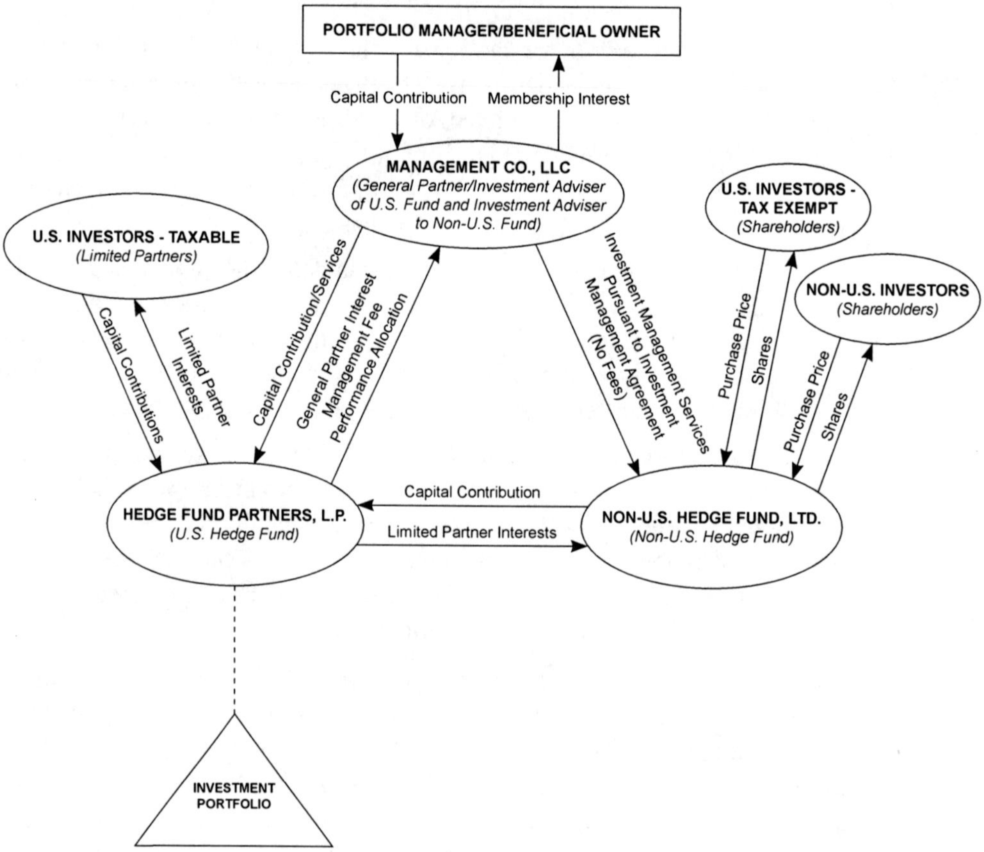

This structure allows the investment adviser to receive a performance allocation and take advantage of the tax benefits of the pass-through of capital gains. This structure is limited, however, by the constraints under the Company Act: if the master fund relies on Company Act section 3(c)(1), both the U.S. and non-U.S. investors will be counted toward the 100-beneficial-owner limit under that section; or if the master fund relies on Company Act section 3(c)(7), both the U.S. and non-U.S. investors must be Qualified Purchasers.[67]

i. Advantages

a. Portfolio Management

Traditionally, the primary reason for organizing a master-feeder structure has been the ease of portfolio management. Managing one securities portfolio rather than several has advantages. For example, the investment adviser does not need to allocate trades among its side-by-side U.S. and offshore hedge funds. It also is easier for the investment adviser to maintain uniformity of performance results. If the feeder funds are managed separately, substantial withdrawals or redemptions in one feeder fund could disproportionately affect that feeder fund; the investment adviser may be required to sell a substantial portion of the

67. *See* Chapter 3 and § 4.4.1.iii, *supra*, and § 4.4.7.iii.b, *infra*.

affected feeder fund's securities at a time or price when it is not advantageous to do so, which may result in the feeder funds no longer having similar portfolios; or it may be difficult or impractical for the investment adviser to rebalance the feeder funds' portfolios. Any of these circumstances may reduce one feeder fund's performance relative to another feeder fund.

b. Tax Efficiency for the Investment Adviser

If the master fund is organized as a pass-through vehicle for tax purposes and recognizes substantial long-term capital gains, the investment adviser may enjoy the tax benefits of taking a performance allocation rather than a performance fee.[68]

c. Additional Feeders/No Start-Up Risk

If a master-feeder structure is in place, another feeder fund, such as a private-label fund for an institution, can simply be added as an additional investor in the master fund, assuming the investment adviser continues to comply with the various applicable rules and regulations, such as, for example, Company Act section 3(c)(1) or 3(c)(7).[69] The new feeder can avoid much of the start-up risk, because it will immediately have a diversified and invested portfolio. The new feeder fund can also have a fee structure that differs from the other feeder funds (assuming fees are charged at the feeder fund level rather than at the master fund level).

ii. Disadvantages

a. More Entities, More Administration and More Cost

Creating and administering additional entities require additional effort and cost. Organizing and maintaining a master-feeder structure entail additional legal, accounting and administrative fees, in addition to the fees typically incurred at the feeder fund level.

b. Portfolio Management

While the master-feeder structure can simplify portfolio management, it also creates complexities and portfolio management challenges. For example, allocating the master fund's costs, profits and losses among the feeder funds may be complex and cumbersome because of issues such as special allocations

---

68. Alternatively, an investment adviser may achieve similar tax benefits without using a master-feeder structure by organizing its offshore hedge fund as a limited partnership in which non-U.S. investors invest directly. The principal disadvantage of this structure is that some non-U.S. investors are wary of investing in partnerships. To avoid this problem, the investment adviser can organize another version of a master-feeder structure, in which the non-U.S. investors invest directly in an offshore hedge fund organized as a corporation (the feeder fund), which is the sole limited partner of a limited partnership (the master fund). The U.S.-based investment adviser may be a co-general partner with an offshore entity that is responsible for the administration of the master fund and may receive an incentive allocation based on the master fund's appreciation. The distinction between this master-feeder structure and the other master-feeder structures is that no U.S. hedge fund feeds into this master fund. *See* §§ 15.2.1 and 16.7.7, *infra*.

69. 15 U.S.C. § 80c-3(c)(1) or 80c-3(c)(7). *See* Chapter 3, *supra*.

of profits and losses from new issues[70] and accounting adjustments relating to subscriptions and redemptions in the feeder funds (that is, for each subscription or redemption there must be a corresponding transaction between the master fund and applicable feeder fund).

In addition, tax considerations may affect how the master fund's portfolio is managed. As noted above in section 4.4.1.ii, an investment adviser may not desire to trade securities of side-by-side U.S. and offshore hedge funds in a manner that is exactly parallel, because of tax considerations. For example, the investment adviser may cause the offshore hedge fund to sell a security that the offshore hedge fund has held for less than 1 year while at the same time causing the U.S. hedge fund to hold the same security until the gain on the sale can be characterized as long-term capital gain. In a master-feeder structure, the investment adviser must consider the net results of its trades on all investors in the feeder funds and does not have the luxury of being able to trade the portfolios of the feeder funds differently to accommodate disparate tax or investment considerations of the investors in those funds.

iii. Regulatory Issues

a. Regulations D and S under the Securities Act

Sales of limited partner interests in the U.S. feeder funds and sales of shares of the non-U.S. feeder funds to U.S. investors must comply with the private placement exemption under the Securities Act (which may include compliance with Regulation D thereunder).[71] Sales of shares in the non-U.S. feeder funds to non-U.S. investors must comply with Regulation S under the Securities Act, which applies to offers and sales of securities made outside of the United States.[72]

b. Investment Company Act of 1940

In a master-feeder structure, not only must the feeder funds each comply with the Company Act, as they would otherwise do if they were side-by-side hedge funds, but the master fund must also comply with the Company Act. Thus, if the master fund relies on Company Act section 3(c)(1),[73] which limits the master fund to not more than 100 beneficial owners, the master fund must count all of the underlying beneficial owners of the feeder funds toward its 100-beneficial-owner limit.[74] Alternatively, if the master fund relies on Company Act section 3(c)(7), which is not limited in the number of its beneficial owners but requires all of the beneficial owners to be qualified purchasers, all of the underlying

70. *See* § 13.5.1, *infra.*
71. *See* § 5.3, *infra.*
72. *See* § 5.4, *infra.*
73. *See* § 3.2, *supra.*
74. The underlying beneficial owners of a feeder fund must be counted if (a) the feeder fund has been formed for the purpose of investing in the master fund, (b) the feeder fund constitutes more than 10 percent of the master fund's outstanding voting securities or (c) more than 40 percent of the assets of the feeder fund is invested in the master fund. *See* § 3.2.2, *supra.*

owners of the feeder funds must be qualified purchasers.[75] In both cases, the investor base is more limited than it would be if the hedge funds were side-by-side rather than in a master-feeder structure.

c. *ERISA*

In a master-feeder structure, the "plan assets" status of the master fund, as well as each feeder fund, must be assessed and monitored.[76] Determining the plan asset status of the master fund can be complicated; different calculation methods may apply depending on whether the feeder funds have discretion to invest part of their assets other than through the master fund.

75. *See* § 3.3.2, *supra*.
76. *See* Chapter 11, *infra*.

CHAPTER 5

Private and Regulation S Offerings[1]

§ 5.1 Application of Securities Act to Hedge Funds

The Securities Act regulates the offer and sale of securities. "Security" is broadly defined in the Securities Act, and includes instruments such as stock, notes and various derivatives.[2] Interests in limited partnerships and limited liability companies are not specifically identified in the definition, but are comprehended by the catch-all category of "investment contracts."[3] An "investment contract" for this purpose is an arrangement in which individuals are "led to invest money in a common enterprise with the expectation that they would earn a profit solely through the efforts of the promoter or of some one other than themselves."[4] Investment contracts include limited partner interests and limited liability

1. This chapter is intended as an overview of the registration requirements of the Securities Act and the exemptions therefrom, as they relate to the operation and marketing of a hedge fund. This chapter does not analyze the Securities Act registration requirements, the registration process or the exemptions from registration. For an in-depth discussion of those topics, see J. William Hicks, *Exempted Transactions Under the Securities Act of 1933* (West Group, 2009), and Harold S. Bloomenthal, *Securities Law Handbook*, 2009-2010 Ed. (West Group, 2009).

2. Securities Act §2(a)(1), 15 U.S.C. §77b(a)(1), defines a security as "any note, stock, treasury stock, security future, bond, debenture, evidence of indebtedness, certificate of interest or participation in any profit-sharing agreement, collateral-trust certificate, preorganization certificate or subscription, transferable share, investment contract, voting-trust certificate, certificate of deposit for a security, fractional undivided interest in oil, gas or other mineral rights, any put, call, straddle, option or privilege on any security, certificate of deposit, or group or index of securities (including any interest therein or based on the value thereof), or any put, call, straddle, option, or privilege entered into on a national securities exchange relating to foreign currency, or, in general, any interest or instrument commonly known as a 'security,' or any certificate of interest or participation in, temporary or interim certificate for, receipt for, guarantee of, or warrant or right to subscribe to purchase, any of the foregoing."

3. *Id.*

4. Securities & Exchange Commission v. W.J. Howey Co., 328 U.S. 293, 66 S. Ct. 1100 (1946).

company ("LLC") member interests when the limited partners or members do not have significant management authority.[5]

Most offshore hedge funds are organized as corporations that issue shares to their investors, although an increasing number are organized as limited partnerships. Most U.S. hedge funds are organized as limited partnerships or LLCs. The investors in both offshore and U.S. hedge funds typically have few managerial powers, and as a result, interests in hedge funds are generally securities.[6] Offers and sales of interests in offshore and U.S. hedge funds must therefore comply with the requirements of the Securities Act.

§ 5.2 Registration Requirements Under the Securities Act

The Securities Act prohibits the public offering or sale of securities, unless a registration statement has been filed with respect to such securities or an exemption from the registration requirement is available.[7] The Securities Act registration requirement applies to any transaction in securities that involves interstate commerce or use of the U.S. mail.[8] "Interstate commerce" includes:

> trade or commerce in securities or any transportation or communication relating thereto among the several States or between the District of Columbia or any Territory of the United States and any State or other Territory, or between any foreign country and any State, Territory or the District of Columbia, or within the District of Columbia.[9]

As a result, the Securities Act registration requirement applies to offers and sales within the United States of securities of U.S. and non-U.S. issuers. The registration requirement also applies to an offer or sale of a U.S. or non-U.S. issuer's securities to an investor outside of the United States if a jurisdictional nexus to the United States is established, such as a call or electronic mail to or from the United States in connection with the transaction. If a jurisdictional nexus exists, a U.S. or offshore hedge fund offering interests or shares to a U.S. or non-U.S. investor must either comply with the registration requirement or qualify for an available exemption from registration.

---

5. *See, e.g.*, Mayer v. Oil Field Systems Corp, et al., 721 F.2d 59 (2d Cir., 1983) (limited partner interests); McGreghar Land Co. v. Meguiar, 521 F.2d 822 (9th Cir., 1975) (limited partner interests); KFC Ventures, L.L.C. v. Metairie Medical Equipment Leasing Corp., et al., 2000 U.S. Dist. LEXIS 8294 (E.D. La., 2000) (limited liability company interests); Cogniplex, Inc., et al. v. Hubbard Ross, L.L.C., et al., 2001 U.S. Dist. LEXIS 11113 (N.D. Ill., 2001) (limited liability company interests).
6. *See* Chapter 4, *supra*, for a discussion of typical hedge fund structures.
7. Securities Act § 5(c), 15 U.S.C. § 77e(c).
8. Securities Act § 5, 15 U.S.C. § 77e.
9. Securities Act § 2(a)(7), 15 U.S.C. § 77b(a)(7).

§ 5.3 Exemptions from Registration

The Securities Act includes several exemptions from its registration requirements, and the SEC has promulgated rules providing additional exemptions. Most hedge funds rely on the exemption provided by Securities Act section 4(a)(2), which exempts from registration any securities issued in "transactions by an issuer not involving any public offering."[10] This is commonly called the "private offering" exemption. As discussed below,[11] the Securities Act does not define "public offering," and the courts typically have examined the facts and circumstances to determine when one exists. These tests involve a number of factors, with different courts giving varying weight to different factors; the factors often require subjective judgment.[12] In addition, courts construe the private offering exemption narrowly to further the purposes of the Securities Act.[13] As a result, in many instances, reliance on the exemption provided by section 4(a)(2) involves risks that are unquantifiable and to some extent unpredictable.

The SEC promulgated Regulation D[14] to provide greater certainty for an issuer seeking to rely on the private offering exemption. Regulation D Rule 506[15] establishes 2 safe harbors under Securities Act section 4(a)(2).[16] An issuer that complies with all of the requirements of either Rule 506 safe harbor is deemed not to be engaged in a transaction involving a public offering.[17] An issuer that fails to comply with the requirements of Rule 506 may nevertheless be able to rely on another exemption from registration (such as the section 4(a)(2) private offering exemption) if the issuer can establish all of the elements of that exemption. Given the subjectivity of the interpretation of the section 4(a)(2) private offering exemption, an issuer typically is well-advised to attempt to comply fully with the conditions of both the section 4(a)(2) exemption and a Regulation D safe harbor, if available. Any U.S. or offshore hedge fund that relies on the exclusion from the definition of "investment company" in section 3(c)(1) or 3(c)(7) of the Company Act[18] has a second reason (in addition to avoiding registration under the Securities Act) for complying with the section 4(a)(2) exemption or a Rule 506 safe harbor, since sections 3(c)(1) and 3(c)(7) prohibit public offerings of the hedge fund's securities.

For offshore offers and sales of securities by U.S. and non-U.S. issuers, the SEC promulgated Regulation S to clarify when the Securities Act registration

---

10. Securities Act § 4(a)(2), 15 U.S.C. § 77d(2).
11. *See* § 5.3.1, *infra.*
12. *Id.*
13. Securities & Exchange Commission v. Murphy, 626 F. 2d 633, 641 (9th Cir., 1980).
14. 17 C.F.R. §§ 230.501 *et seq.*
15. 17 C.F.R. § 230.506.
16. *See* § 5.3.2, *infra.*
17. Regulation D Rule 506(a), 17 C.F.R. § 230.506(a).
18. *See* Chapter 3, *supra,* for a description of the exclusions from the definition of investment company.

requirements apply. Regulation S also establishes safe harbors for issuances and re-sales of securities to non-U.S. investors.[19]

1. Private Offering Exemption Under Securities Act Section 4(a)(2)

Securities Act section 4(a)(2)[20] exempts from the registration requirements of Securities Act section 5[21] securities sold in a "transaction by an issuer not involving any public offering."[22] The Securities Act does not, however, define what constitutes a public offering, leaving the courts, the SEC and issuers of securities to determine whether an issuer is engaged in a transaction not involving a public offering.

In *Securities & Exchange Commission v. Ralston Purina Co.*, the U.S. Supreme Court held that a critical factor is whether the particular class of persons to whom the offering is made needs the protection of the Securities Act or whether those persons are "able to fend for themselves."[23] The purpose of the Securities Act "is to protect investors by promoting full disclosure of information thought necessary to informed investment decisions."[24] In determining whether a transaction constitutes a public offering, the focus of the courts should be on whether the offerees had access to "the same kind of information that the [Securities] Act would make available in the form of a registration statement."[25]

Since *Ralston Purina*, courts have looked to a variety of factors to determine if a transaction constitutes a public offering. These factors have varied from circuit to circuit and from case to case. For example, the First Circuit has identified a private offering as one in which "the purchasers (a) are limited in number, (b) are sophisticated, and (c) have a relationship with the issuer enabling them to command access to information that would otherwise be contained in a registration statement."[26] The Second Circuit considers (a) the number of offerees, (b) the sophistication and experience of the offerees, or the ability of the offerees to evaluate the merits of the issue, (c) the nature and kind of information provided, or to which the offerees have ready access, and (d)

---

19. *See* § 5.4, *infra*.
20. 15 U.S.C. § 77d(2).
21. 15 U.S.C. § 77e.
22. Securities Act § 4(a)(2), 15 U.S.C. § 77d(2).
23. Securities & Exchange Commission v. Ralston Purina Co., 346 U.S. 119, 125, 73 S. Ct. 981, 984 (1953).
24. *Id.* at 124, Hill York Corp., et al. v. American Int'l Franchises, Inc., et al., 448 F. 2d 680, 689 fn. 8 (5th Cir., 1971) ("the need for the protection of the [Securities] Act is greater when speculative securities in new ventures ... are offered than when a new offering of the securities of an already established firm with an available operating record is involved.")
25. Securities & Exchange Commission v. Ralston Purina Co., 346 U.S. 119, 125-126, 73 S. Ct. 981, 985 (1953).
26. Cook, et al., v. Pritchard, et. al., 573 F. 2d 685, 691 (1st Cir., 1978) (citing *Doran Petroleum Mgmt. Corp.* and *Hill York Corp.*).

the size of the offering and the precautions taken to prevent the offerees from reselling their securities.[27]

The Fifth and Sixth Circuits have considered (a) the number of offerees and their relationship to each other and the issuer, (b) the number of units offered, (c) the size of the offering, and (d) the manner of offering.[28] The Ninth Circuit has considered (a) the number of offerees, (b) the sophistication of the offerees, (c) the size and manner of the offering, and (d) the relationship of the offerees to the issuer.[29] The Tenth Circuit has considered (a) the number of offerees, (b) the sophistication of the offerees, including their access to the type of information that would be contained in a registration statement, and (c) the manner of the offering.[30]

Courts thus typically consider (a) the sophistication of the offerees, (b) the offerees' ability to assume financial risk, (c) the offerees' relationship with the issuer, (d) the offerees' access to information, (e) the size and manner of the offering, (f) the number of offerees and (g) the relationship of the offerees to each other.[31] These factors are interrelated, and courts accord them varying weight, depending on the circumstances. That one of these factors weighs heavily in favor of a private offering is not sufficient to ensure the availability of the exemption.[32] In addition, these factors are not exhaustive, but "serve as guideposts to the court in attempting to determine whether subjecting the offering to registration requirements would further the purposes of the [Securities] Act."[33]

In assessing the availability of the section 4(a)(2) exemption, courts examine the qualifications of all of the offerees; the judicial inquiry is not confined to offerees that accept an offer and in fact invest.[34] The issuer must be prepared

27. Barrett, et al. v. Triangle Mining Corp., et al., Fed. Sec. L. Rep. (CCH) ¶ 95,438, 1976 U.S. Dist. LEXIS 16883 (S.D.N.Y., 1976); Securities & Exchange Commission v. Manus, et al., Fed. Sec. L. Rep. (CCH) ¶ 98,307, 1981 U.S. Dist. LEXIS 15317 (S.D.N.Y., 1981).

28. Hill York Corp., et al. v. American Int'l Franchises, Inc., et al., 448 F. 2d 680, 687-689 (5th Cir., 1971); Mark v. FSC Securities Corp., 870 F. 2d 331, 333 (6th Cir., 1989).

29. Securities & Exchange Commission v. Murphy, 626 F. 2d 633, 646 (9th Cir., 1980).

30. U.S. v. Arutunoff, et al., 1 F. 3d 1112, 1118 (10th Cir., 1993).

31. Mark v FSC Securities Corp., 870 F. 2d 331, 333 (6th Cir., 1989); Kunz v. Securities & Exchange Commission, 2003 U.S. App. LEXIS 6011 (10th Cir., 2003); Sorrell v. Securities & Exchange Commission, 679 F.2d 1323, 1326 (9th Cir., 1982); Securities & Exchange Commission v. Ralston Purina Co., 346 U.S. 119, 73 S. Ct. 981 (1953); Barrett, et al. v. Triangle Mining Corp., et al., Fed. Sec. L. Rep. (CCH) ¶ 95,438, 1976 U.S. Dist. LEXIS 16883 (S.D.N.Y., 1976); Securities & Exchange Commission v. Manus, et al., Fed. Sec. L. Rep. (CCH) ¶ 98,307, 1981 U.S. Dist. LEXIS 15317 (S.D.N.Y., 1981).

32. Doran v. Petroleum Mgmt. Corp., et al., 545 F. 2d 893, 900 (5th Cir. 1977).

33. *Id.*

34. Barrett, et al. v. Triangle Mining Corp., et al., Fed. Sec. L. Rep. (CCH) ¶ 95,438, 1976 U.S. Dist. LEXIS 16883 (S.D.N.Y., 1976) (finding that, although the defendant had demonstrated that it had met the requirements of the § 4(a)(2) exemption with respect to the plaintiff investors, the exemption was unavailable because the defendant had not offered evidence concerning other offerees' sophistication or access to information); Securities & Exchange Commission v. Continental Tobacco Co. of South Carolina, 463 F. 2d 137, 160 (5th Cir., 1972).

to offer evidence of the offerees' qualifications. This characteristic of the judicial gloss on section 4(a)(2) provided impetus for the SEC's adoption of Regulation D, which confines the inquiry to investors.[35] Regulation D has thus substantially reduced the issuer's burden of ascertaining and documenting the qualifications of offerees even before making offers to them.

Nevertheless, to permit reliance on section 4(a)(2), a manager of a hedge fund is well advised to maintain records that establish the qualifications of each offeree. An issuer claiming the section 4(a)(2) exemption has the burden of proving that the offering meets the requirements of the exemption.[36] A court may insist that the issuer bear this burden even if an investor misrepresents to the broker selling the securities the facts on which the issuer relies to establish the section 4(a)(2) exemption.[37] An issuer that relies on the section 4(a)(2) exemption remains subject to the anti-fraud provisions of the Securities Act.[38]

i. Sophistication of Offerees

The sophistication of the offerees is generally an important factor in determining whether an offering constitutes a private offering,[39] although some courts have held that evidence of the offerees' sophistication is not always required to establish a private offering exemption under section 4(a)(2).[40] Courts consider both the offeree's expertise in the business in which the issuer will engage and the offeree's investment sophistication.[41] For an offeree to make an informed decision whether to invest, the offeree must be able to analyze, understand and evaluate the merits and risks of the investment. An offeree may be sufficiently sophisticated to analyze, understand and evaluate an offered investment in an operating company, by virtue, for example, of long-term executive experience in the industry where that company operates. If, however, an offeree is offered an investment in a hedge fund, executive experience in an operating company may not offer significant relevant sophistication. Offers to invest in a hedge fund should be confined, then, for purposes of the section 4(a)(2) exemption, to investors that are experienced and knowledgeable in financial and investment matters. An offeree's relationship to the issuer may also be relevant, as in the case, for example, of a knowledgeable employee of the investment adviser that manages the hedge fund.[42]

---

35. Securities Act Release No. 6389, 47 F.R. 11,251 (Mar. 8, 1982). *See* § 5.3.2. *infra*.

36. Securities & Exchange Commission v. Ralston Purina Co., 346 U.S. 119, 126, 73 S. Ct. 981, 985 (1953); Sorrell v. Securities & Exchange Commission, 679 F. 2d 1323, 1326 (9th Cir., 1982).

37. Woolf, et al., v. S.D. Cohn & Co., et al., 515 F.2d 591, 605 (5th Cir., 1975), *vacated and remanded*, 426 U.S. 944, 96 S. Ct. 3161, 49 L. Ed. 2d 1181 (1976).

38. Securities Act § 17(a), 15 U.S.C. § 77q(a); *see* § 6.4, *infra*.

39. *See, e.g.*, Securities & Exchange Commission v. Manus, et al., Fed. Sec. L. Rep. (CCH) ¶ 98,307, 1981 U. S. Dist. LEXIS 15317 (S.D.N.Y., 1981); Securities & Exchange Commission v. Murphy, 626 F.2d 633, 646 (9th Cir., 1980).

40. Doran v. Petroleum Mgmt. Corp., et al., 545 F. 2d 893, 902 (5th Cir. 1977).

41. Barrett, et al. v. Triangle Mining Corp., et al. Fed. Sec. L. Rep. (CCH) ¶ 95,438, 1976 U.S. Dist. LEXIS 16883 (S.D.N.Y., 1976).

42. *See* § 5.3.1.iii, *infra*.

ii. Ability to Take Risk

Courts sometimes include in the section 4(a)(2) mix consideration of whether each offeree had sufficient financial means to absorb the possible loss of the investment without undue hardship.[43] This factor, too, is addressed in context. If the amount invested is small relative to the offeree's net worth or earning capacity or if the risk of loss is slight, this factor may not be given significant weight. Conversely, a relatively large investment in a risky venture ordinarily warrants more scrutiny, not only of the offeree's ability to take risk, but also of the offeree's sophistication and access to material information.

iii. Relationship of Offerees to the Issuer and Access to Information

A critical factor in determining the availability of the section 4(a)(2) exemption is whether the offerees have access to information similar to the information that would be provided by a registration statement.[44] Even if all offerees are highly sophisticated investors, the exemption will not be available if the offerees are not provided or given access to all of the information that would be material to a decision whether to invest.[45] An offeree's sophistication avails little if the issuer does not make available adequate and accurate information about the investment so that the offeree can exercise his or her skills.[46] For example, in *Doran v. Petroleum Mgmt. Corp.*, the plaintiff sued an oil drilling limited partnership in which he had invested. The plaintiff held a degree in petroleum engineering, had a net worth in excess of $1,000,000 and held interests in approximately 26 oil and gas properties valued at $850,000. The court noted that all other offerees were similarly sophisticated,[47] but held that this alone was insufficient to establish that the offering was a private offering, absent evidence that the offerees had available the information that registration would provide. The court remanded the case for determination whether such information was available.[48]

---

43. Securities & Exchange Commission v. Manus, et al., Fed. Sec. L. Rep. (CCH) ¶ 98,307, 1981 U. S. Dist. LEXIS 15317 (S.D.N.Y., 1981).

44. *Id.*; Securities & Exchange Commission v. Ralston Purina, 346 U.S. 119, 124-126, 73 S.Ct. 981, 984-985 (1953); Doran v. Petroleum Mgmt. Corp., et al., 545 F. 2d 893, 902-903 (5th Cir. 1977); Sorrel v. Securities & Exchange Commission, 679 F.2d 1323, 1326 (9th Cir., 1982).

45. Lawler v. Gilliam, 569 F.2d 1283, 1290 (4th Cir., 1978), Doran v. Petroleum Mgmt. Corp., et al., 545 F. 2d 893, 904 (5th Cir. 1977).

46. Hill York Corp., et al. v. American Int'l Franchises, Inc., 448 F. 2d 680, 690 (5th Cir., 1971); Lawler v. Gilliam, et al., 569 F. 2d 1283, 1290 (4th Cir., 1978). *See also* Doran v. Petroleum Mgmt. Corp., et al., 545 F. 2d 893, 900 (5th Cir. 1977) (although the offering involved a "small number of units offered, relatively modest financial stakes, and an offering characterized by personal contact between the issuer and offerees free of public advertising or intermediaries," the court remanded the case for a determination concerning whether the offerees received or were provided access to information that a registration statement would have provided to a prospective investor in a public offering).

47. Doran v. Petroleum Mgmt. Corp., et al., 545 F.2d 893, 902 (5th Cir. 1977).

48. *Id.*

In *Lawler v. Gilliam*, a sophisticated businessman invested in an investment fund that later turned out to be fraudulent. The court noted that if the investor had been provided the type of information required in a registration statement, including copies of contracts, financial statements, the identity of the other partners and the specific purpose for which the funds were to be used, the investor would have been able to detect the fraud.[49] The court ruled that the businessman's sophistication and desire to participate in the program "do not supplant his lack of access to the information that a registration statement would show."[50]

An offeree may have access to information through a relationship with the issuer, such as employment or family relationships, or through contract or economic bargaining power that enables the offeree to obtain such information.[51] For example, in *Barrett, et al. v. Triangle Mining Corp., et al.*, the investors, sophisticated businessmen who were close friends of the organizer of the issuer, were encouraged to visit the issuer's mining operation before investing, were provided with "considerable information" concerning the enterprise, and were invited to audit the issuer's books and help set up proper accounts. Although the investors did not avail themselves of these opportunities, the court found that the issuer had provided them with access to substantially the same information as would have been disclosed in a registration statement.[52]

When an issuer relies on access without disclosing all material information, the issuer must demonstrate that "the offerees occupied a privileged position relative to the issuer that afforded them an opportunity for effective access to the information registration would otherwise provide."[53] "If the offerees know the issuer and have special knowledge as to its business affairs, such as high executive officers of the issuer would possess, then the offering is apt to be private."[54] The relationship must be sufficient to afford the offeree effective and complete access to all information that registration would require.[55]

Instead of merely providing access to information, the issuer may furnish directly the information that would be provided by a registration statement,[56]

---

49. Lawler v. Gilliam, et al., 569 F. 2d 1283, 1289 (4th Cir., 1978).

50. *Id.* at 1290.

51. *See* Securities & Exchange Commission v. Ralston Purina Co., 346 U.S. 119, 125-126, 73 S. Ct. 981, 985 (1953) (stating that an offering to "executive personnel who because of their position have access to the same kind of information that the [Securities] Act would make available in the form of a registration statement" may be exempt under § 4(a)(2)); Barrett, et al. v. Triangle Mining Corp., et al., Fed. Sec. L. Rep. (CCH) ¶ 95,438, 1976 U.S. Dist. LEXIS 16,883 (S.D.N.Y., 1976).

52. Barrett, et al. v. Triangle Mining Corp., et al., Fed. Sec. L. Rep. (CCH) ¶ 95,438, 1976 U.S. Dist. LEXIS 16,883 (S.D.N.Y., 1976). The court went on to find against the defendant, however, because the defendant failed to offer evidence concerning the sophistication and access to information of investors other than the plaintiffs.

53. Doran v. Petroleum Mgmt. Corp., et al., 545 F.2d 893, 906 (5th Cir. 1977).

54. Hill York Corp., et al. v. American Int'l Franchises, Inc., 448 F. 2d 680, 688 (5th Cir., 1971).

55. Doran v. Petroleum Mgmt. Corp., et al., 545 F. 2d 893, 906, fn. 18 (5th Cir. 1977).

56. *Id.* at 904 and 906.

as in a private offering memorandum that fully discloses such information. A hedge fund's private offering memorandum should contain all of the information required in a registration statement filed on Form S-1 under the Securities Act and Form N-1A under the Company Act.[57] The hedge fund should obtain a written representation from each offeree that the offeree has received and read the private offering memorandum (although such a representation by the offeree may not be sufficient by itself to establish the availability of the private offering exemption[58]).

The provision of information required by section 4(a)(2) is subject to the anti-fraud provisions of the Securities Act and the Exchange Act.[59]

iv. Size and Manner of the Offering

Courts also consider the manner in which an issuer offers and sells its securities in determining whether the transaction constitutes a private offering. "A private offering is more likely to arise when the offer is made directly to the offerees rather than through the facilities of public distribution such as investment bankers or the securities exchanges. In addition, public advertising is incompatible with the claim of private offering."[60] On the other hand, the absence of contact between an offeree and the issuer or the issuer's agents tends to indicate a public offering rather than a private offering.[61]

The fewer the number of units to be sold and the smaller the offering, the more likely the sale is private.[62] One court indicated in 1980 that a $7,500,000 offering was sufficiently large to be considered public absent a significant showing that the investors did not need the protection of the Securities Act.[63]

v. Number of Offerees

There is no maximum limitation on the number of offerees an issuer may solicit without engaging in a public offering. The Supreme Court has indicated, however, that "it may well be that offerings to a substantial number of persons would rarely be exempt" under section 4(a)(2).[64] Subsequent court decisions have held that a large number of offerees indicates that the offering is a public

---

57. *See* § 6.2.1.i, *infra.*

58. Woolf, et al., v. S.D. Cohn & Co., et al., 515 F.2d 591, 605 (5th Cir., 1975), *vacated and remanded*, 426 U.S. 944, 96 S. Ct. 3161, 49 L. Ed. 2d 1181 (1976), citing Securities & Exchange Commission v. Continental Tobacco Co., 463 F. 2d 137, 160 (5th Cir., 1972).

59. *See* Chapter 6, *infra.*

60. Hill York Corp., et al. v. American Int'l Franchises, Inc., et al., 448 F. 2d 680, 689 (5th Cir., 1971); *see* § 8.2, *infra.*

61. Woolf, et al., v. S.D. Cohn & Co., et al., 515 F. 2d 591, 614 (5th Cir., 1975), *vacated and remanded*, 426 U.S. 944, 96 S. Ct. 3161, 49 L. Ed. 2d 1181 (1976); Securities & Exchange Commission v. Murphy, 626 F. 2d 633, 646 (9th Cir., 1980).

62. Hill York Corp., et al. v. American Int'l Franchises, Inc., et al., 448 F. 2d 680, 689 (5th Cir., 1971); Securities & Exchange Commission v. Murphy, 626 F. 2d 633, 646 (9th Cir., 1980).

63. Securities & Exchange Commission v. Murphy, 626 F. 2d 633, 646 (9th Cir., 1980).

64. Securities & Exchange Commission v. Ralston Purina Co., 346 U.S. 119, 125 (1953). *See also* Lawler v. Gilliam, et al., 569 F.2d 1283, 1290 (4th Cir. 1978).

offering.[65] In addition, courts typically consider the number of offerees "in order to ascertain the magnitude of the offering and in order to determine the characteristics and knowledge of the persons thus identified."[66] The greater the number of offerees, the more difficult it may be for the issuer to establish that each offeree was of a class of investors that does not require the protection of the Securities Act. Again, the courts consider the number of offerees, not the number of purchasers, for this purpose.[67] On the other hand, an offering to only 2 offerees could be regarded as public, depending on the qualifications of the offerees, the availability of information and the manner of conducting the offering.[68]

As noted,[69] the burden of proving the availability of the private offering exemption is on the person claiming it. An issuer must be able to prove that all offerees had the necessary qualifications and had access to all of the information that would be in a registration statement. [70] An issuer that fails to keep records regarding the offerees in an offering may not be able to offer the requisite proof. One court has stated that an issuer's failure to number its private offering memoranda and keep records of the persons to whom they were delivered is evidence that the issuer failed to monitor the number of offerees.[71]

Accordingly, a hedge fund manager should maintain records of each person to whom the hedge fund offers its interests. All offers of interests in a hedge fund should be made only through a private offering memorandum.[72] The hedge fund should consecutively number each copy of the memorandum[73] and maintain records identifying the offerees and the number of the memorandum provided to each of them.

---

65. *See* Securities & Exchange Commission v. The Infinity Group Co., 993 F. Supp. 324, 327 (E.D. Penn., 1998), *affrm'd by* Securities & Exchange Commission v. The Infinity Group Co., 212 F. 3d 180 (3rd Cir. 2000) (finding a public offering where over 10,000 investors in the United States and overseas were solicited by facsimile, mailings and a website); Doran v. Petroleum Mgmt. Corp. et al., 545 F. 2d 893, 900-901 (5th Cir., 1977); Hill York Corp., et al. v. American Int'l Franchises, Inc., et al., 448 F. 2d 680, 688 (5th Cir., 1971); Securities & Exchange Commission v. Murphy, 626 F. 2d 633, 645 (9th Cir., 1980).

66. Doran v. Petroleum Mgmt. Corp., et al., 545 F. 2d 893, 900-901 (5th Cir. 1977).

67. *Id.*

68. *See* Swenson v. Engelstad, 626 F.2d 421, 427 (5th Cir., 1980).

69. Securities & Exchange Commission v. Ralston Purina Co., 346 U.S. 119, 73 S. Ct. 981 (1953); *see* notes 36-37 and accompanying text, *supra.*

70. Doran v. Petroleum Mgmt. Corp. et al., 545 F. 2d 893, 900 (5th Cir., 1977); Woolf, et al., v. S.D. Cohn & Co., et al., 515 F. 2d 591, 610 (5th Cir., 1975), *vacated and remanded,* 426 U.S. 944, 96 S. Ct. 3161, 49 L. Ed. 2d 1181 (1976); Hill York Corp., et al. v. American Int'l Franchises, Inc., et al., 448 F. 2d 680, 691 (5th Cir., 1971); Mark, et al. v. FSC Securities Corp., et al., 870 F. 2d 331, 334 (6th Cir., 1989).

71. Securities & Exchange Commission v. Murphy, 626 F. 2d 633, 645 (9th Cir., 1980).

72. *See* Chapter 6, *infra.*

73. Securities & Exchange Commission v. Murphy, 626 F. 2d 633, 645 (9th Cir., 1989) (issuer's failure to number its offering memoranda indicates that issuer failed to monitor volume of offers it made).

vi. Relationship of the Offerees to Each Other

Courts may also consider the relationship among the offerees in determining whether an offering is a public offering. If an offering is made to a diverse and unrelated group, the offering is more likely to be considered public, but if made to a select group of offerees who know each other and have similar interests and knowledge of the offering, the offering is more likely to be considered private.[74]

2. Regulation D

SEC Regulation D[75] Rules 504, 505 and 506[76] provide non-exclusive safe harbor exemptions from registration under Securities Act sections 4(a)(2)[77] and 3(b).[78]

---

74. Hill York Corp., et al. v. American Int'l Franchises, Inc., et al., 448 F. 2d 680, 688 (5th Cir. 1971).

75. 17 C.F.R. §§ 230.501 to 230.508. For a more detailed analysis of the Regulation D exemption, see J. William Hicks, *Limited Offering Exemptions: Regulation D,* 2009-2010 Ed. (West Group, 2009). On July 10, 2013, the SEC amended Regulation D in several respects, including adding Rule 506(c) and the "bad actor" provisions discussed below. At the same time, in a separate release, Securities Act Release No. 9416 (July 10, 2013), 78 F.R. 44806 (July 24, 2013), the SEC published for comment a number of proposed amendments to Regulation D, Form D and Rule 156 under the Securities Act. According to the SEC, the proposed amendments are intended to enhance the SEC's ability to evaluate the development of market practices in Rule 506 offerings and to address concerns that may arise in connection with permitting issuers to engage in general solicitation and general advertising under new Rule 506(c). Specifically, the proposed amendments to Regulation D would require the filing of a Form D in Rule 506(c) offerings before the issuer engages in general solicitation; require the filing of a closing amendment to Form D after the termination of any Rule 506 offering; require written general solicitation materials used in Rule 506(c) offerings to include certain legends and other disclosures; require the submission, on a temporary basis, of written general solicitation materials used in Rule 506(c) offerings to the SEC; and disqualify an issuer from relying on Rule 506 for 1 year for future offerings if the issuer, or any predecessor or affiliate of the issuer, did not comply, within the last 5 years, with Form D filing requirements in a Rule 506 offering. The proposed amendments to Form D would require an issuer to include additional information about offerings conducted in reliance on Regulation D. The proposed amendments to Rule 156 would extend the anti-fraud guidance in the rule to the sales literature of hedge funds and other private funds. At this writing, we cannot predict whether or when the SEC may adopt further changes to Regulation D.

76. 17 C.F.R. §§ 230.504, 230.505 and 230.506.

77. 15 U.S.C. § 77d(2).

78. Securities Act § 3(b), 15 U.S.C. § 77c(b), grants the SEC the authority to adopt rules and regulations exempting securities from the registration requirements of the Securities Act if the aggregate amount at which such securities are offered to the public does not exceed $5,000,000. Regulation D Rules 504 and 505, 17 C.F.R. §§ 230.504 and 230.505, permit an issuer to issue securities in an offering pursuant to Securities Act § 3(b), 15 U.S.C. § 77c(b), having an aggregate offering price of no more than $1,000,000 and $5,000,000, respectively, in any 12-month period. Because an offering pursuant to § 3(b) may be made to the public (*see* Chapter 3, *supra*) and because of the limits on the aggregate dollar value of such an offering, the Rule 504 and 505 safe harbors are unsuitable for a hedge fund and are not discussed in this book. For a detailed discussion of the requirements and applicability of the Rule 504 and 505 safe harbors, see J. William Hicks, *Limited Offering Exemptions: Regulation D*, 2009-2010 Ed. (West Group, 2009).

Hedge funds typically rely on a safe harbor provided by Regulation D Rule 506(b) or 506(c) under Securities Act section 4(a)(2) in offering and selling their interests. A hedge fund that relies on Rule 506(b) (prohibiting general solicitation) may also rely on the statutory section 4(a)(2) exemption, but a hedge fund that relies on Rule 506(c) (permitting general solicitation) may not also rely on section 4(a)(2). The Rule 506 safe harbors adapt some of the conditions of the section 4(a)(2) exemption, but with more specificity and objectivity, as discussed below. Regulation D is not available, however, for any issuer that, although complying with the technical requirements of Regulation D, is engaged in a plan or scheme to evade the registration requirements of the Securities Act.[79] The Rule 506 safe harbors provide exemptions from the registration requirements of the Securities Act, but not from the anti-fraud, civil liability or other provisions of the Securities Act.[80]

An issuer may not rely on Regulation D Rule 506 if the issuer or any of specified affiliates, promoters, predecessors and other related parties has been found to have engaged in specified misconduct in a securities or financial business.[81]

i. General

An issuer seeking to rely on the Regulation D Rule 506(b) safe harbor must:

- comply with the information delivery requirements of Regulation D Rule 502(b);[82]
- not employ any advertising or general solicitation in offering or selling its securities;[83]
- limit sales of its securities in an offering to not more than 35 non-accredited investors, although the number of accredited investors is not limited in an offering under Rule 506;[84]
- take steps to restrict resales of any of its securities sold in reliance on the Rule 506 safe harbor;[85] and
- file a notice on Form D[86] with the SEC for each new offering of securities no later than 15 days after the first sale of securities in the offering (or the first business day following, if the end of that period is a Saturday, Sunday or holiday) of its securities pursuant to Regulation D.[87] If an offering is continuous, as is typical of hedge funds, the notice on Form D must be amended when there is a material change in information filed

---

79. Regulation D Preliminary Note 6, 17 C.F.R. § 230.501.
80. Regulation D Preliminary Note 1, 17 C.F.R. § 230.501. *See* § 6.4, *infra.*
81. Regulation D Rule 506(d), 17 C.F.R. 230.506(d); Securities Act Release No. 9414 (July 10, 2013), __ F.R. __(________, 2013). *See* § 5.3.2.x, *infra.*
82. 17 C.F.R. § 230.502(b).
83. Regulation D Rule 502(c), 17 C.F.R. § 230.502(c); *see* §§ 5.3.2.vi and 8.2, *infra.*
84. Regulation D Rule 506(b)(2), 17 C.F.R. § 230.506(b)(2).
85. Regulation D Rule 502(d), 17 C.F.R. § 230.502(d).
86. 17 C.F.R. § 239-500.
87. Regulation D Rule 503(a), 17 C.F.R. § 230.503(a).

about the offering, when basic information previously submitted about the issuer has materially changed, and annually on or before the first anniversary of the filing of the notice or the most recent amendment to the notice.[88]

The same requirements apply to an issuer relying on Regulation D Rule 506(c), except that advertising and general solicitation are permitted if securities are sold only to accredited investors and other conditions (discussed below) are met.[89]

Regulation D Rule 507 prohibits reliance on Rule 506 if the issuer or any of its predecessors or affiliates has been enjoined for failing to comply with Regulation D Rule 503,[90] unless the SEC determines otherwise on a showing of good cause.

ii. Accredited Investors

Regulation D Rule 501 defines an "accredited investor"[91] as any person that is within, or that an issuer reasonably believes is within, one of the following categories:

- a bank as defined in Securities Act section 3(a)(2)[92] or a savings and loan association or other institution as defined in Securities Act section 3(a)(5)(A), [93] whether acting in its individual or fiduciary capacity;
- a broker or dealer registered pursuant to Exchange Act section 15;[94]
- an insurance company as defined in Securities Act section 2(13);[95]
- an investment company registered under the Company Act or a business development company as defined in Company Act section 2(a)(48);[96]
- a small business investment company licensed by the U.S. Small Business Administration under section 301(c) or (d) of the Small Business Investment Act of 1958;[97]

---

88. Securities Act Release No. 8891, 73 F.R. 10,592 (Feb. 27, 2008).

89. 17 C.F.R. § 230.506(c); *see* Securities Act Release No. 9415 (July 10, 2013), 78 F.R. 44771 (July 24, 2013).

90. Regulation D Rule 507, 17 C.F.R. § 230.507. If a hedge fund fails to comply with the notice filing requirements of Regulation D, it may be subject to an order enjoining it from relying on any of the safe harbors provided by Regulation D in the future, unless the SEC determines on a showing of good cause that it is not necessary to deny the exemption. In August 2007, the SEC proposed adding additional disqualification provisions whereby an issuer who has engaged in any of a list of specified violations, including failure to file Form D, would be disqualified from relying upon Regulation D for a period of 5 years (or 10 years for more egregious conduct). Securities Act Release No. 8828 (Aug. 3, 2007), 72 F.R. 45,116 (Aug. 10, 2007).

91. Regulation D Rule 501(a), 17 C.F.R. § 230.501(a).

92. 15 U.S.C. § 77c(a)(2).

93. 15 U.S.C. § 77c(a)(5)(A).

94. 15 U.S.C. § 78o.

95. 15 U.S.C. § 77b(a)(13).

96. 15 U.S.C. § 80a-2(a)(48).

97. 15 U.S.C. § 681.

- a plan established and maintained by a state, its political subdivisions or any agency or instrumentality of a state or its political subdivisions, for the benefit of its employees, if such plan has total assets in excess of $5,000,000;
- an employee benefit plan within the meaning of ERISA (a) if the investment decision is made by a plan fiduciary, as defined in ERISA section 3(21),[98] which is a bank, a savings and loan association, an insurance company or a registered investment adviser, or (b) if the employee benefit plan has total assets in excess of $5,000,000, or (c) if the employee benefit plan is a self-directed plan, with investment decisions made solely by persons that are accredited investors;
- a private business development company as defined in Advisers Act section 202(a)(22); [99]
- an organization described in Tax Code section 501(c)(3),[100] a corporation, Massachusetts or similar business trust, or a partnership, if such entity was not formed for the specific purpose of acquiring the securities offered and has total assets in excess of $5,000,000;
- a director, executive officer or general partner of the issuer selling the securities being offered or sold, or any director, executive officer or general partner of a general partner of the issuer;
- any natural person whose individual net worth, or joint net worth with his or her spouse, at the time of purchase exceeds $1,000,000, excluding from the net worth calculation both the fair market value of his or her primary residence and the amount of any debt secured by such residence up to its fair market value, but including in his or her liabilities the amount of any increase in the last 60 days in the debt secured by such residence (accordingly, both the portion of any debt secured by such primary residence that exceeds its fair market value and the amount of any increase in such debt in the last 60 days must be deducted, without double counting, in calculating his or her net worth); [101]
- any natural person who had an individual income in excess of $200,000 in each of the 2 most recent years or joint income with his or her spouse in excess of $300,000 in each of those years and has a reasonable expectation of reaching the same income level in the current year[102] (because an investment adviser may charge performance fees only to a U.S. investor whose net worth is more than $2,000,000,[103] these annual income tests for accredited investors ordinarily are irrelevant for a hedge fund);

---

98. 29 U.S.C. § 1002(21).
99. 15 U.S.C. § 80b-2(a)(22).
100. 26 U.S.C. § 501(c)(3).
101. The Dodd-Frank Act directed the SEC to review the accredited investor standards applicable to natural persons at 4-year intervals. Pub. L. 111-203, § 413 (July 21, 2010).
102. *Id.*
103. *See* § 15.2.3, *infra.*

- a trust, with total assets in excess of $5,000,000, not formed for the specific purpose of acquiring the securities offered, whose purchase is directed by a person who has such knowledge and experience in financial and business matters that such person is capable of evaluating the merits and risks of such investment; and
- an entity in which all of the equity owners are accredited investors.

Whether or not an investor is an accredited investor is determined at the time of investment.[104] Changes in the investor's status after investment will not result in a loss of the Rule 506 exemption, unless the investor's investment was part of a plan or scheme to evade the Securities Act registration requirements.[105]

Even an investor that is not within one of the foregoing categories may be considered an accredited investor if the issuer reasonably believed at the time of investment that the investor was within one of those categories.[106] Accordingly, before accepting investments, a hedge fund should take reasonable steps to establish that each investor is within one of the foregoing categories. If the issuer is relying on Regulation D Rule 506(b) (and therefore not engaging in any advertising or general solicitation), the issuer's reasonable belief that an investor is accredited typically is based on the investor's written representation that the investor is accredited and the investor's completed offering questionnaire identifying which of the categories applies and providing other relevant information.

If the issuer is relying on Regulation D Rule 506(c)[107] (permitting advertising and general solicitation), the issuer must take reasonable steps to verify that purchasers of its securities are accredited investors. This requirement is separate from and independent of the requirement that sales be limited to accredited investors, and must be satisfied even if all purchasers happen to be accredited investors.

According to the SEC, whether the steps taken are reasonable will be an objective determination by the issuer in the context of the particular facts and circumstances of each purchaser and transaction. Among the factors that an issuer should consider are the nature of the purchaser and the type of accredited investor that the purchaser claims to be, the amount and type of information that the issuer has about the purchaser, and the nature of the offering, such as the manner in which the purchaser was solicited to participate in the offering, and the terms of the offering, such as a minimum investment amount. The factors are interconnected and are intended to help guide an issuer in assessing the reasonable likelihood that a purchaser is an accredited investor, which would in turn affect the types of steps that would be reasonable to take to verify a purchaser's accredited investor status. After consideration of the facts and

---

104. Regulation D Rule 501(a), 17 C.F.R. § 230.501(a); Securities Act Release No. 6455, question 1, 48 F.R. 10,045 (Mar. 10, 1983).

105. Securities Act Release No. 6455, question 1, fn. 3, 48 F.R. 10,045 (Mar. 10, 1983).

106. Regulation D Rule 501(a), § 17 C.F.R. § 230.501(a).

107. 17 C.F.R. § 230.506(c); *see* Securities Act Release No. 9415 (July 10, 2013), 78 F.R. 44771 (July 24, 2013).

circumstances of the purchaser and of the transaction, the more likely it appears that the purchaser qualifies as an accredited investor, the fewer steps the issuer would be required to take to verify accredited investor status, and vice versa. For example, if the terms of the offering require a high minimum investment amount and a purchaser is able to meet those terms, the likelihood of that purchaser satisfying the definition of accredited investor may be sufficiently high that, absent any facts indicating that the purchaser is not an accredited investor, it may be reasonable for the issuer to take fewer steps to verify or, in certain cases, no additional steps to verify accredited investor status other than to confirm that the purchaser's cash investment is not being financed by a third-party.

With respect to a purchaser in a Regulation D Rule 506(c) offering who is a natural person, the issuer is deemed to take reasonable steps to verify, if it uses, at its option, one of the following non-exclusive and non-mandatory methods of verifying that the natural person is an accredited investor, so long as the issuer does not have knowledge that the person is not an accredited investor:

- if the purchaser bases accredited investor status on income, reviewing any IRS forms that report the purchaser's income for the relevant years and obtaining a written representation from the purchaser that he or she has a reasonable expectation of reaching the necessary income level for the current year (and for the purchaser to qualify based on joint income with the purchaser's spouse, the forms and representation must be provided by both spouses);
- if the purchaser bases accredited investor status on net worth, reviewing one or more of the following types of documentation dated within the prior 3 months and obtaining a written representation from the purchaser that all liabilities necessary to make a determination of net worth have been disclosed: (a) with respect to assets, bank, brokerage and other statements of securities holdings, certificates of deposit, tax assessments and appraisal reports issued by independent third parties; and (b) with respect to liabilities, a consumer report from at least one nationwide consumer reporting agency (and for the purchaser to qualify based on joint net worth with the purchaser's spouse, the documentation and representation must be provided by both spouses);
- instead of the foregoing, obtaining a written confirmation from a registered broker-dealer, an SEC-registered investment adviser, a licensed attorney or a certified public accountant that such person or entity has taken reasonable steps to verify that the purchaser is an accredited investor within the prior 3 months and has determined that the purchaser is an accredited investor.

If a purchaser of securities as an accredited investor in the issuer's Rule 506(b) offering before September 23, 2013, continues to hold such securities, for the purchaser to purchase additional securities in the issuer's subsequent Rule 506(c) offering, the issuer may continue to regard the purchaser as an accredited investor by obtaining the purchaser's certification at the time of the subsequent sale that the purchaser is an accredited investor.

The issuer is not required to use any of these methods in verifying the accredited investor status of natural persons who are purchasers in the issuers Rule 506(c) offering. These methods are examples of types of "reasonable steps to verify." According to the SEC:

> Regardless of the particular steps taken, because the issuer has the burden of demonstrating that its offering is entitled to an exemption from the registration requirements of Section 5 of the Securities Act, it will be important for issuers and their verification service providers to retain adequate records regarding the steps taken to verify that a purchaser was an accredited investor.[108]

The hedge fund should retain these documents in its records, because they may be needed to prove that the hedge fund validly relied on a Rule 506 safe harbor[109] and because the Advisers Act requires the hedge fund's investment adviser (if SEC-registered) to retain them.[110]

a. *Trusts*

As described above, a trust is an accredited investor if it has total assets in excess of $5,000,000, it is not formed for the specific purpose of acquiring the securities offered, and its decision to invest is directed by a person who has enough knowledge and experience in financial and business matters to be able to evaluate the merits and risks of such investment.[111] A trust also qualifies as an accredited investor if its trustee is a bank and the bank makes the investment decision on behalf of the trust, because a bank acting in a fiduciary capacity is an accredited investor.[112] In addition, a revocable trust qualifies as an accredited investor if all of the grantors are accredited investors and the grantors may amend or revoke the trust at any time.[113] Similarly, an individual retirement account qualifies as an accredited investor if its owner is an accredited investor. On the other hand, an irrevocable trust that does not have assets in excess of $5,000,000 and whose trustee is not a bank does not qualify as an accredited investor, even if all of its beneficiaries are accredited investors.[114]

---

108. Securities Act Release No. 9415 (July 10, 2013) at 28-29, 78 F.R. 44771 (July 24, 2013).

109. Mark v. FSC Securities Corp., 870 F. 2d 331, 336-337 (6th Cir., 1989) (holding that the burden of proving the qualification of the purchasers of an issuer's securities "could have been met by offering each of the twenty-eight purchasers' executed subscription documents into evidence ...").

110. *See* § 2.8, *supra.*

111. Regulation D Rule 501(a)(7), 17 C.F.R. § 230.507(a)(7).

112. Securities Act Release No. 6455, question 26, 48 F.R. 10,045 (Mar. 10, 1983); Regulation D Rule 501(a)(1), 17 C.F.R. § 230.501(a)(1).

113. Securities Act Release No. 6455, question 30, 48 F.R. 10,045 (Mar. 10, 1983).

114. *Id.*

b. Limited Liability Companies

Although limited liability companies are not expressly included in the definition of accredited investor, the SEC staff has opined that an LLC is an accredited investor if it was not formed for the specific purpose of acquiring the securities offered and has total assets in excess of $5,000,000.[115]

c. Directors and Executive Officers

As described above, a director, executive officer or general partner of a hedge fund or a director, executive officer or general partner of a general partner of a hedge fund is an accredited investor.[116] An executive officer is the "president, any vice president in charge of a principal business unit, division or function (such as sales, administration or finance), any other officer who performs a policy making function or any other person who performs similar policy making functions for the issuer."[117] If a person is a director or executive officer of a parent entity of the general partner of the hedge fund, such person is only an accredited investor if he or she is also a director or executive officer of the general partner.[118] An executive officer of a parent entity of the general partner will, however, be considered an executive officer of the general partner if he or she performs policy-making functions for the general partner.[119]

iii. Non-Accredited Investors

A hedge fund relying on Rule 506(b) (but not Rule 506(c)) may also sell interests to up to 35 non-accredited investors.[120] An investor that is not an accredited investor must have sufficient knowledge and experience in financial and business matters to be capable of evaluating the merits and risks of the prospective investment, or the issuer must reasonably believe immediately before making a sale to such an investor that the investor meets this requirement.[121] To meet the burden of proving that each of its investors meets the requirements of Rule 506, a hedge fund should obtain written representations from each investor, by, for example, requiring each investor to sign a subscription agreement containing representations concerning the investor's sophistication and knowledge and to complete an offering questionnaire that elicits sufficient information concerning the investor's background and experience.[122]

Determining investment sophistication is a matter of subjective judgment, and determining whether a non-accredited investor qualifies to participate in a Rule 506(b) offering is invariably uncertain. In addition, a hedge fund is required to disclose substantial information to each non-accredited investor

---

115. Wolf, Block, Schorr and Solis-Cohen, SEC No-Action Letter (Dec. 11, 1996).
116. Regulation D Rule 501(a)(4), 17 C.F.R. § 230.501(a)(4).
117. Regulation D Rule 501(f), 17 C.F.R. § 230.501(f).
118. Securities Act Release No. 6455, question 6, 48 F.R. 10,045 (Mar. 10, 1983).
119. Securities Act Release No. 6455, 48 F.R. 10,045 (Mar. 10, 1983), questions 6 and 7.
120. Regulation D Rule 506(b)(2)(i), 17 C.F.R. § 230.506(b)(2)(i).
121. Regulation D Rule 506(b)(2)(ii), 17 C.F.R. § 230.506(b)(2)(ii). *See also* § 5.3.1.i, *supra*, discussing investment sophistication for purposes of Securities Act section 4(a)(2), 15 U.S.C. § 77d(2), which is similarly used for purposes of Regulation D.
122. Mark v. FSC Securities Corp., 870 F. 2d 331, 335-338 (6th Cir., 1989).

in the hedge fund.[123] Because the net worth requirement in the performance fee rule under the Advisers Act is higher than the net worth test for individual accredited investors, a hedge fund will ordinarily be prohibited from charging a performance fee or allocation to a natural person who is not an accredited investor and is a U.S. person.[124] For these reasons, hedge funds ordinarily do not accept investments from non-accredited investors.

iv. Purchaser Representatives

A non-accredited investor may employ a purchaser representative to meet the sophistication requirement of Rule 506(b).[125] A purchaser representative is a person who assists an investor in evaluating the investment and who has, or who the issuer reasonably believes has, enough knowledge and experience in financial and business matters to be able to evaluate the merits and risks of the investment, whether alone, with the purchaser or with the purchaser's other purchaser representatives.[126] An issuer must obtain sufficient information from a purchaser representative to form a reasonable belief about the purchaser representative's qualifications; if the issuer fails to do so, it ordinarily may not rely on the purchaser representative to establish that an investor is sufficiently sophisticated under Rule 506.[127] A hedge fund should obtain sufficient written information from a purchaser representative, through the use of a questionnaire, to enable it to determine that the purchaser representative is qualified to act as such.

An affiliate, director, officer or employee of the issuer, or a beneficial owner of 10 percent or more of any class of the issuer's equity securities or of 10 percent or more of the equity interests in the issuer cannot act as a purchaser representative for an investor.[128] The "issuer" is the "person who issues or proposes to issue any security."[129] An "affiliate" is "a person that directly, or indirectly, through one or more intermediaries, controls or is controlled by, or is under common control with, the person specified."[130] This prohibition extends to officers and directors of a corporate general partner of an issuer.[131] Accordingly, none of the hedge fund, its general partner or their respective owners, directors, officers or employees can serve as a purchaser representative for an investor. If a hedge fund has a separate investment adviser, the investment adviser may not act as a purchaser representative if it controls, is controlled by or is under common control with the hedge fund or its general partner. These prohibitions

---

123. *See* § 5.3.2.vii, *infra.*
124. *See* § 15.2.3.i, *infra.*
125. Regulation D Rule 506(b)(2)(ii), 17 C.F.R. § 230.506(b)(2)(ii).
126. Regulation D Rule 501(h)(2), 17 C.F.R. § 230.501(h)(2).
127. *See, e.g.*, Western-Realco Limited Partnership, et al. v. Harrison, 791 P. 2d 1139, 1146 (Col. App. Ct., 1989).
128. Regulation D Rule 501(h)(1), 17 C.F.R. § 230.501(h)(1).
129. Securities Act § 2(a)(4), 15 U.S.C. § 77b(a)(4); Regulation D Rule 501(g), 17 C.F.R. § 230.501(g).
130. Regulation D Rule 501(b), 17 C.F.R. § 230.501(b).
131. Securities Act Release No. 6455, question 38, 48 F.R. 10,045 (Mar. 10, 1983).

do not apply, however, in certain cases when the investor and the purchaser representative are closely related or affiliated, including when the investor is:

- a relative of the purchaser representative by blood, marriage or adoption not more remote than first cousin;
- a trust or estate in which the purchaser representative and any persons related to the purchaser representative as specified in the preceding item or the following item collectively have more than 50 percent of the beneficial interest (excluding contingent interests) or of which the purchaser representative serves as trustee, executor or in any similar capacity; or
- a corporation or other organization of which the purchaser representative and any persons related to the purchaser representative as specified in either of the preceding two items collectively beneficially own more than 50 percent of the equity securities (excluding directors' qualifying shares) or equity interests.[132]

An investor employing a purchaser representative must acknowledge in writing to the issuer during the transaction that the purchaser representative is acting as the investor's purchaser representative with respect to the investment.[133] The purchaser representative must disclose to the investor in writing a reasonable time before the investment any material relationship between the purchaser representative or its affiliates and the issuer or its affiliates that exists at the time, that is mutually understood to be contemplated or that has existed at any time during the preceding 2 years.[134] Such disclosure must include the compensation received or to be received by the purchaser representative as a result of the relationship.[135] The issuer may compensate a purchaser representative for acting as such, but only if such compensation is disclosed to the investor.[136]

v. Limitations on Number of Investors

Regulation D Rule 506(b) permits sales of an unlimited amount of securities to up to 35 investors.[137] The following investors are not counted toward the 35-investor limit under Rule 506(b):

- any accredited investor;
- any relative, spouse or relative of the spouse of an investor who has the same principal residence as the investor;
- any trust or estate in which an investor or any of the persons described in the preceding item or any entity described in the following item collectively hold more than 50 percent of the beneficial interest (excluding contingent interests); and

132. Regulation D Rule 501(h)(1), 17 C.F.R. § 230.501(h)(1).
133. Regulation D Rule 501(h)(3), 17 C.F.R. § 230.501(h)(3).
134. Regulation D Rule 501(h)(4), 17 C.F.R. § 230.501(h)(4).
135. *Id.*
136. Securities Act Release No. 6455, question 39, 48 F.R. 10,045 (Mar. 10, 1983).
137. 17 C.F.R. § 230.506(b)(2).

- any corporation or other organization of which any of the persons described in either of the two preceding items collectively beneficially own more than 50 percent of the equity securities (excluding directors' qualifying shares) or equity interests.[138]

Rule 506(b) thus permits sales to an unlimited number of accredited investors and their relatives and affiliates as described above, and up to 35 non-accredited investors. Rule 506(c) similarly permits sales to an unlimited number of accredited investors, but does not permit sales to any non-accredited investors.

vi. Manner of Sale—Advertising or General Solicitation

No form of general solicitation or advertising may be used in offering or selling securities under Regulation D Rule 506(b).[139] This prohibition includes any mass mailing, any advertisement, article, notice or other communication published in any magazine, newspaper or newsletter or broadcast over television or radio, and any seminar or meeting where the attendees have been invited by any mass mailing, general solicitation or general advertising.[140] This prohibition is derived from cases interpreting the Securities Act section 4(a)(2) exemption.[141]

Regulation D Rule 506(c) permits, and does not limit, general solicitation and general advertising. As discussed above, Regulation D Rule 506(c) is conditioned on all purchasers of the securities being accredited investors and the issuer taking reasonable steps to verify that the purchasers are accredited.

vii. Information Delivery Requirements

The anti-fraud provisions of the Securities Act generally prohibit misstatements or omissions of material fact in connection with any offer or sale of securities. To comply with those provisions, an issuer must disclose material information about the offering to both accredited and non-accredited investors.[142] In a Rule 506(b) offering, the hedge fund also must give each investor, a reasonable time before the investor invests, an opportunity to ask questions and receive answers about the terms and conditions of the offering and to obtain any additional information that the hedge fund has or can acquire without unreasonable effort or expense that is necessary to verify the information furnished to the investor.[143]

In addition, a hedge fund relying on the Rule 506(b) safe harbor generally must provide to any purchaser that is not an accredited investor, a reasonable time before the sale, the same kind of information as would be required to be delivered in Part I of a registration statement filed under the Securities Act on the form that the issuer would be entitled to use.[144] A hedge fund relying on Rule 506(b) must also give the non-accredited investor a brief written description of

---

138. Regulation D Rule 501(e), 17 C.F.R. § 230.501(e).
139. Regulation D Rule 502(c), 17 C.F.R. § 230.502(c). *See* § 8.2, *infra.*
140. *Id.*
141. *See* § 5.3.1, *supra*, and § 8.2, *infra.*
142. *See* § 6.4, *infra.*
143. Regulation D Rules 502(b)(2)(v), 17 C.F.R. §§ 502(b)(2)(v).
144. Regulation D Rule 502(b), 17 C.F.R. § 230.502(b).

any material written information about the offering that the hedge fund gave to any accredited investor but did not previously give to the non-accredited investor, and, on request by the non-accredited investor, the hedge fund must give the non-accredited investor copies of that written information.[145] In any event, in light of the anti-fraud provisions of the securities laws, a hedge fund should give accredited investors the same information it gives non-accredited investors, notwithstanding that Regulation D does not require an issuer to deliver it to an accredited investor. In addition, whether relying on Rule 506(b) or Rule 506(c), a hedge fund must advise each investor, a reasonable time before the sale of interests, of the limitations on resale.[146]

viii. Restrictions on Resale

Regulation D Rule 502(d) provides that securities acquired pursuant to the Rule 506(b) or 506(c) safe harbor have the status of securities acquired in a private offering under Securities Act section 4(a)(2), and cannot be resold unless they are registered or exempt from registration under the Securities Act.[147] The registration requirements of Securities Act section 5 apply to sales of securities by any person, not only an issuer.[148] As a result, an investor that purchases an interest in a hedge fund may not resell that interest, unless either the interest is registered under the Securities Act or the investor establishes that an exemption from registration applies. Securities acquired in a Rule 506(b) or Rule 506(c) offering are "restricted securities" under Rule 144 under the Securities Act.[149] Accordingly, such securities can be resold in accordance with Rule 144 without registration under the Securities Act.[150]

Regulation D Rule 502(d) also requires issuers of securities under either Rule 506 safe harbor to exercise reasonable care to assure that the purchasers of the securities are not underwriters.[151] An "underwriter" is "any person who has purchased from an issuer with a view to, or offers or sells for an issuer in connection with, the distribution of any security, or participates or has a direct or indirect participation in any such undertaking, or participates or has a participation in the direct or indirect underwriting of any such undertaking."[152] An issuer can demonstrate that it has taken reasonable care not to sell to an underwriter by:

---

145. Regulation D Rule 502(b)(2)(iv), 17 C.F.R. § 230.502(b)(2)(iv).

146. Regulation D Rule 502(d), 17 C.F.R. § 230.502(d). *See also* § 5.3.2.viii, *infra*.

147. Regulation D Rule 502(d), 17 C.F.R. § 230.502(d).

148. Securities Act § 5, 15 U.S.C. § 77e.

149. Securities Act Rule 144(a)(3), 17 C.F.R. § 230.144(a)(3), provides that "restricted securities means: (i) securities acquired directly or indirectly from the issuer, or from an affiliate of the issuer, in a transaction or chain of transactions not involving any public offering; (ii) securities acquired from the issuer that are subject to the resale limitations of Section 230.502(d) under Regulation D...." 17 C.F.R. §§ 230.144(a)(3)(i) and (ii).

150. For a discussion of the requirements of Rule 144, see J. William Hicks, *Resales of Restricted Securities*, ch. 4, 2010 Ed. (West Group, 2010).

151. Regulation D Rule 502(d), 17 C.F.R. § 230.502(d).

152. Securities Act § 2(a)(11); 15 U.S.C. § 77b(a)(11).

- making a reasonable inquiry to determine whether the purchaser is acquiring the securities for the purchaser's own account or for other persons;
- providing written disclosure to each purchaser before sale that the securities have not been registered under the Securities Act and cannot be resold unless they are so registered or unless an exemption from registration is available; and
- placing a legend on the certificate or other document that evidences the securities stating that the securities have not been registered under the Securities Act and setting forth or referring to the restrictions on transferability and sale of the securities.[153]

This is not the only method by which an issuer can establish that it exercised reasonable care to assure that a purchaser is not an underwriter.[154] A hedge fund should attempt, however, to comply with these steps. Accordingly, the disclosures and legends identified in Rule 502(d) should be included in the subscription agreement by which an investor acquires interests in the hedge fund.

ix. Failure to Comply with Requirements of Regulation D

As discussed above, if an issuer does not comply with the requirements of Regulation D Rule 506(b), the issuer may nevertheless rely on the section 4(a)(2) private offering exemption, if it satisfies the requirements for that exemption. Because section 4(a)(2) precludes advertising and general solicitation, it is not available for an offering under Rule 506(c). An issuer that relies on either Rule 506 safe harbor and that fails to comply with a term, condition or requirement of the safe harbor may nevertheless rely on the safe harbor for an offer or sale to a particular person, if it can show that (1) the failure to comply did not pertain to a term, condition or requirement directly intended to protect that particular person, (2) the failure to comply was insignificant with respect to the offering as a whole, and (3) the issuer made a good faith and reasonable attempt to comply with all applicable terms, conditions and requirements of the relevant safe harbor.[155] Failing to comply with the limitations on the number of purchasers or the amount of securities to be sold or with the limitations on advertising and general solicitation, as applicable, is considered significant to the offering as a whole.[156] This good faith compliance rule does not, however, preclude the SEC from bringing an action against an issuer that fails to comply with any requirement of Regulation D.[157]

---

153. Regulation D Rule 502(d), 17 C.F.R. § 230.502(d).
154. *Id.*
155. Regulation D Rule 508(a), 17 C.F.R. § 230.508(a).
156. Regulation D Rule 508(a)(2), 17 C.F.R. § 230.508(a)(2).
157. Regulation D Rule 508(b), 17 C.F.R. § 230.508(b).

x. *"Bad Actor" Rule*

As mandated by the Dodd-Frank Act,[158] Regulation D Rule 506(d)[159] renders the Rule 506 safe harbor exemptions unavailable for any securities offering that involves certain "bad actors." Under Rule 506(d), the Rule 506 safe harbors are unavailable for a sale of securities if the issuer or any of its predecessors, affiliates, directors, officers, general partners, managing members, promoters or 10-percent owners, any person it paid to solicit purchasers, or any general partner, director, officer or managing member of any such solicitor:

- has been convicted within the past 10 years (or 5 years, in the case of the issuer or any of its predecessors or affiliates) of any felony or misdemeanor: (a) in connection with the purchase or sale of any security; (b) involving the making of any false filing with the SEC; or (c) arising out of the conduct of the business of an underwriter, broker, dealer, municipal securities dealer, investment adviser, or paid solicitor of purchasers of securities;
- is subject to any court order, judgment or decree entered within the past 5 years that restrains or enjoins such person from engaging in any conduct or practice: (a) in connection with the purchase or sale of any security; (b) involving the making of any false filing with the SEC; or (c) arising out of the conduct of the business of an underwriter, broker, dealer, municipal securities dealer, investment adviser, or paid solicitor of purchasers of securities;
- is subject to a final order[160] of a state securities commission (or an agency or officer of a state performing like functions), a state authority that supervises or examines banks, savings associations or credit unions, a state insurance commission (or an agency or officer of a state performing like functions), an appropriate federal banking agency, the CFTC or the National Credit Union Administration that: (a) at the time of such sale bars such person from association with an entity regulated by such commission, authority, agency or officer or from engaging in the securities, insurance or banking business or from engaging in savings association or credit union activities; or (b) constitutes a final order based on a violation of any law or regulation that prohibits fraudulent, manipulative or deceptive conduct entered within 10 years before such sale;
- is subject to an SEC order entered pursuant to Exchange Act section 15(b) or 15B(c)[161] or Advisers Act section 203(e) or (f)[162] that at

158. Pub. L. 111-203 (July 21, 2010).

159. 17 C.F.R. § 230.506(d).

160. Defined in proposed paragraph (g) of Regulation D Rule 501(c), as a written directive or declaratory statement issued by a federal or state agency described in Rule 506(d)(1)(iii) under applicable statutory authority that provides for notice and an opportunity for hearing, which constitutes a final disposition or action by such federal or state agency.

161. 15 U.S.C. § 78o(b) or 78o-4(c).

162. 15 U.S.C. § 80b-3(e) or (f).

the time of such sale: (a) suspends or revokes such person's registration as a broker, dealer, municipal securities dealer or investment adviser; (b) places limitations on the activities, functions or operations of such person; or (c) bars such person from being associated with any entity or from participating in the offering of any penny stock;

- is subject to any SEC order entered within 5 years before such sale that, at the time of such sale, orders the person to cease and desist from committing or causing a violation or future violation of: (a) any scienter-based anti-fraud provision of the federal securities laws, including Securities Act section 17(a)(1),[163] Exchange Act section 10(b),[164] Rule 10b-5 thereunder,[165] Exchange Act section 15(c)(1)[166] and Advisers Act section 206(1),[167] or any other rule or regulation thereunder; or (b) Securities Act section 5;[168]
- is suspended or expelled from membership in, or suspended or barred from association with a member of, a registered national securities exchange or a registered national or affiliated securities association for any act or omission to act constituting conduct inconsistent with just and equitable principles of trade;
- has filed (as a registrant or issuer), or was or was named as an underwriter in, any registration statement or Regulation A offering statement filed with the SEC that, within 5 years before such sale, was the subject of a refusal order, stop order or order suspending the Regulation A exemption, or is, at the time of such sale, the subject of an investigation or proceeding to determine whether a stop order or suspension order should be issued; or
- is subject to a U.S. Postal Service false representation order entered within 5 years before such sale, or is, at the time of such sale, subject to a temporary restraining order or preliminary injunction with respect to conduct alleged by the U.S. Postal Service to constitute a scheme or device for obtaining money or property through the mail by means of false representations.

The bad-actor provisions would not apply (a) with respect to any conviction, order, decree, suspension, expulsion or bar that occurred or was issued before September 23, 2013, (b) on a showing of good cause and without prejudice to any other action by the SEC, if the SEC determines that it is not necessary under the circumstances that the exemption be denied, (c) if, before the relevant sale, the court or regulatory authority that entered the relevant order, judgment or decree advises in writing (whether in the relevant judgment, order or decree or separately to the SEC or its staff) that disqualification under Rule 506(d)(1)

163. 15 U.S.C. § 77q(a)(1).
164. 15 U.S.C. § 78j(b).
165. 17 C.F.R. § 240.10b-5.
166. 15 U.S.C. § 78*o*(c)(1).
167. 15 U.S.C. § 80b-6(1).
168. 15 U.S.C. § 77e.

should not arise as a consequence of such order, judgment or decree,or (d) if the issuer establishes that it did not know, and in the exercise of reasonable care could not have known, that a disqualification existed under Rule 506(d). An issuer will not be able to establish that it has exercised reasonable care unless it has made, in light of the circumstances, factual inquiry into whether any disqualifications exist. The nature and scope of the factual inquiry will vary based on the facts and circumstances concerning, among other things, the issuer and the other offering participants. Events relating to any affiliated issuer that occurred before the affiliation arose will be not considered disqualifying if the affiliated entity is not either in control of the issuer or under common control with the issuer by a third-party that was in control of the affiliated entity at the time of such events. The issuer must furnish to each purchaser, a reasonable time before sale, a written description of any matters that would have triggered disqualification under Rule 506(d) but occurred before September 23, 2013. The failure to furnish such information timely does not prevent an issuer from relying on a Rule 506 safe harbor if the issuer establishes that it did not know and, in the exercise of reasonable care, could not have known of the existence of the undisclosed matter or matters.

§ 5.4 Regulation S

The Securities Act registration requirements apply to any transaction in securities that involves interstate commerce or use of the U.S. mail.[169] "Interstate commerce" includes "trade or commerce in securities or any transportation or communication relating thereto ... between any foreign country and any State, Territory or the District of Columbia."[170] This broad scope could encompass any transaction in securities issued by a non-U.S. company to a non-U.S. investor if a jurisdictional nexus is established, such as a call or electronic mail to or from the United States in connection with such transaction. As a result, the Securities Act registration requirements often apply to the offer and sale of shares in an offshore hedge fund. To clarify the application of the registration requirements to offshore transactions, the SEC adopted Regulation S.[171] Regulation S establishes safe harbor exemptions from the registration requirements for offers and sales of securities by issuers and distributors in offshore transactions and for resales of securities in offshore transactions.[172] A "distributor" is any "underwriter, dealer or other person who participates, pursuant to a contractual arrangement, in the distribution of the securities offered or sold in reliance on Regulation S."[173] This

169. Securities Act § 5, 15 U.S.C. § 77e.
170. Securities Act § 2(a)(7), 15 U.S.C. § 77b(a)(7).
171. Securities Act Release No. 6863 (Apr. 24, 1990), 55 F.R. 18,306 (May 2, 1990). Before the SEC adopted Regulation S, Securities Act Release No. 4708 (July 9, 1964), 29 F.R. 9,828 (July 9, 1964), which was superseded by Regulation S, provided guidance on application of Securities Act § 5 to offshore transactions.
172. Regulation S Rules 903 and 904, 17 C.F.R. §§ 230.903 and 230.904.
173. Regulation S Rule 902(d), 17 C.F.R. § 230.902(d).

section focuses on the safe harbor for offers and sales of securities by issuers and distributors and does not address offshore resales.

Regulation S provides that offers and sales that occur within the United States are subject to Securities Act section 5,[174] but offers and sales that occur outside of the United States are not.[175] For purposes of Regulation S, the United States means "the United States of America, its territories and possessions, any State of the United States, and the District of Columbia."[176] The SEC has stated that whether a transaction occurs inside or outside the United States depends on the facts and circumstances of each case.[177]

The globalization of the securities markets and the prevalence of electronic communication often make it difficult to determine where a transaction occurs. The safe harbor of Regulation S offers some certainty. A transaction that complies with Regulation S is deemed to be outside the United States and is therefore not subject to the registration requirements of Securities Act section 5.[178] Regulation S exempts offshore transactions only from the requirements of Securities Act section 5; it does not affect the anti-fraud and other provisions of the Securities Act, compliance with the requirements of the Exchange Act or any applicable state securities laws.[179]

The Regulation S safe harbor for offers of securities by issuers and distributors requires that:

- the offer be made in an offshore transaction; and
- no directed selling efforts be made in the United States by the issuer, a distributor, any affiliate of the issuer or a distributor or any person acting on behalf of any of them.[180]

Additional requirements may apply depending on the nature of the issuer and the securities being offered and sold.[181]

1. Offshore Transaction

For purposes of Regulation S Rule 903,[182] an offer or sale of securities is made in an "offshore transaction" if the offer is not made to a person in the United States and either of the following requirements is met:

- at the time the buy order is originated, the buyer is outside the United States or the seller and any person acting on its behalf reasonably believes that the buyer is outside the United States or

174. 15 U.S.C. § 77e.
175. Regulation S Rule 901, 17 C.F.R. § 230.901.
176. Regulation S Rule 902(l), 17 C.F.R. § 230.902(l).
177. Securities Act Release No. 6863 (Apr. 24, 1990), 55 F.R. 18,306 (May 2, 1990).
178. Securities Act Release No. 6863 (Apr. 24, 1990), 55 F.R. 18,306 (May 2, 1990).
179. Regulation S Preliminary Notes 1, 2 and 3, 17 C.F.R. § 230.901.
180. Regulation S Rule 903(a), 17 C.F.R. § 230.903(a).
181. *See* § 5.4.3, *infra*.
182. 17 C.F.R. § 230.903.

- the transaction is executed in, on or through a physical trading floor of an established foreign securities exchange that is located outside the United States.[183]

Offers and sales of securities specifically targeted at identifiable groups of U.S. citizens abroad, such as members of the U.S. armed forces serving overseas, are not considered to be made in offshore transactions.[184] An offer or sale to a dealer or other professional fiduciary organized, incorporated or (if an individual) resident in the United States that holds a discretionary account or similar account (other than an estate or trust) for the benefit or account of a non-U.S. person or to a nongovernmental organization of a specified type is considered to be made in an offshore transaction.[185]

2. No Directed Selling Efforts to United States

i. General

An issuer or distributor relying on the Regulation S safe harbor may not engage in any directed selling efforts to the United States. "Directed selling efforts" means any activity undertaken for the purpose of, or that could reasonably be expected to have the effect of, conditioning the market in the United States for any of the securities being offered in reliance on Regulation S.[186] The SEC identifies as directed selling efforts mailing printed material to U.S. investors, conducting promotional seminars in the United States, or placing advertisements with radio or television stations in the United States that "discuss the offering or are otherwise intended to condition, or could reasonably be expected to condition, the market for the securities purportedly being offered abroad."[187] Directed selling efforts also include placing an advertisement that refers to the offering in a publication with a general circulation in the United States. A publication has a general circulation in the United States if it is printed primarily for distribution in the United States or has had an average circulation in the United States of 15,000 or more copies per issue during the preceding 12 months.[188] If a publication has both U.S. and non-U.S. editions that would not constitute publications with general circulation in the United States, advertising only in the non-U.S. editions would not constitute directed selling efforts to the United States.[189]

---

183. Regulation S Rule 902(h)(1), 17 C.F.R. § 230.902(h)(1).
184. Regulation S Rule 902(h)(2), 17 C.F.R. § 230.902(h)(2).
185. Regulation S Rule 902(h)(3), 17 C.F.R. § 230.902(h)(3). Specifically, the nongovernmental organizations are the International Monetary Fund, the International Bank for Reconstruction and Development, the Inter-American Development Bank, the Asian Development Bank, the African Development Bank, the United Nations and their agencies, affiliates and pension plans, and any other similar international organizations, their agencies, affiliates and pension plans. Regulation S Rule 902(k)(2)(vi), 17 C.F.R. § 230.902(k)(2)(vi).
186. Regulation S Rule 902(c)(1), 17 C.F.R. § 230.902(c)(1).
187. Securities Act Release No. 6863 (Apr. 24, 1990), 55 F.R. 18,306 (May 2, 1990).
188. Regulation S Rule 902(c)(2), 17 C.F.R. § 230.902(c)(2).
189. Securities Act Release No. 6863 (Apr. 24, 1990), 55 F.R. 18,306 (May 2, 1990).

ii. Excluded Activities

Legitimate selling activities carried out in the United States in connection with an offering of securities registered under the Securities Act or exempt from registration, such as a private offering under Securities Act section 4(a)(2) or Regulation D Rule 506,[190] do not constitute directed selling efforts with respect to offers and sales under Regulation S.[191] As a result, an offshore hedge fund may sell shares to investors in the United States under Regulation D while also selling shares to investors outside the United States under Regulation S.[192] In addition, the following activities do not constitute directed selling efforts under Regulation S: [193]

- placement of an advertisement required to be published under U.S. or non-U.S. law, rules or regulations, as long as the advertisement contains no more information than legally required and includes a statement to the effect that the securities have not been registered under the Securities Act and may not be offered or sold in the United States (or, in some instances, to a U.S. person) absent registration or an applicable exemption from the registration requirements;
- contact with a dealer or other professional fiduciary organized, incorporated or (if an individual) resident in the United States that holds a discretionary account or similar account (other than an estate or trust) for the benefit or account of a non-U.S. person or with a nongovernmental organization of a specified type;
- tombstone advertisements in publications with a general circulation in the United States, if specified requirements are met;
- bona fide visits to and tours of real estate, plants or other facilities located in the United States conducted for a prospective investor by an issuer, a distributor, any affiliate of an issuer or distributor, or any person acting on behalf of any of the issuer, distributors or such affiliates;
- distribution in the United States of a non-U.S. broker's quotations by a third-party system that distributes such quotations primarily in other countries, if (a) securities transactions cannot be executed between non-U.S. brokers and persons in the United States through the system, and (b) the issuer, distributors, affiliates of the issuer and distributors, persons acting on behalf of any of the issuer, distributors or such affiliates, non-U.S. brokers and other participants in the system do not initiate contacts with any U.S. person in the United States, beyond those contacts exempted under Exchange Act Rule 15a-6;[194]
- publication of notices of an issuance of securities in accordance with Securities Act Rules 135 and 135c; [195]

190. *See* § 5.3, *supra*.
191. Securities Act Release No. 6863 (Apr. 24, 1990), 55 F.R. 18,306 (May 2, 1990).
192. *See* § 5.5, *infra*.
193. Regulation S Rule 902(c)(3), 17 C.F.R. § 230.902(c)(3).
194. 17 C.F.R. § 240.15a-6.
195. 17 C.F.R. §§ 230.135 and 230.135c.

- providing journalists with access to press conferences held outside the United States, to meetings with the issuer conducted outside the United States or to written press-related materials released outside the United States, at or in which the proposed offering of securities is discussed, in compliance with the requirements of Securities Act Rule 135e;[196] and
- publication or distribution of a research report by a broker or dealer in accordance with Securities Act Rule 138(c) or Securities Act Rule 139(b).[197]

One area of concern with respect to directed selling efforts is the use of the Internet to market securities being sold under Regulation S. According to the SEC, whether the Securities Act registration requirements apply to offers made over the Internet depends on whether Internet offers, solicitations or other communications are targeted to the United States.[198] The SEC will not "view issuers, broker-dealers, exchanges, and investment advisers that implement measures that are reasonably designed to guard against sales . . . to U.S. persons to have targeted persons in the United States with their Internet offers."[199]

Whether measures are adequate to prevent U.S. persons from participating in an offshore Internet offering depends on all of the facts and circumstances, although the SEC will typically not consider an offshore Internet offering made by a non-U.S. offeror as targeted at the United States, if:

- the website includes a prominent disclaimer making clear that the offering is directed only to countries other than the United States (for example, stating that the securities are not being offered in the United States or identifying the non-U.S. jurisdictions in which the securities are being offered); and
- the website offeror implements procedures reasonably designed to guard against sales to U.S. persons in the offshore offering (for example, ascertaining the investor's residence by obtaining his or her mailing address or telephone number).

The disclaimer included on a website must be specific and meaningful. For example, a disclaimer that "the offer is not being made in any jurisdiction in which the offer would or could be illegal" is not sufficient, because it is not meaningful, whereas a disclaimer that "this offering is intended only to be available to residents of the countries within the European Union" would be meaningful. If a U.S. person invests in the securities being offered on the Internet, notwithstanding adequate procedures reasonably designed to prevent the investment, the SEC will not for that reason alone view the offering as targeted at the United States, unless the issuer should have been on notice that the investor was a U.S. person, by virtue of such circumstances as receipt of payment

---

196. 17 C.F.R. § 230.135e.
197. 17 C.F.R. 230.138(c) and 230.139(b).
198. Securities Act Release No. 7516 (Mar. 13, 1998), 63 F.R. 14,806 (Mar. 27, 1998).
199. *Id.*

drawn on a U.S. bank, provision of a U.S. taxpayer identification number, or statements by the investor indicating that he or she is a U.S. resident.[200]

The SEC's guidelines apply to the use of Internet websites, not to the use of targeted communications, such as e-mail.[201] Targeted messages are more akin to use of the mails, and an issuer using such communications must ensure that it complies with the requirements of the Securities Act.[202]

3. Additional Requirements

Regulation S may impose additional restrictions on issuers depending on the nature of the issuer and the securities being issued. To determine whether additional requirements will be imposed, Regulation S divides securities into 3 categories.

i. Category 1

An issuer or distributor may rely on the Regulation S safe harbor for offers and sales of category 1 securities without additional requirements.[203] Securities are eligible for this category, if, among other things, (a) they are issued by a foreign issuer that reasonably believes at the commencement of the offering that no substantial U.S. market interest[204] exists in the class of equity securities to be offered or sold,[205] or no substantial U.S. market interest[206] exists in the

200. *Id.*
201. *Id.*
202. *Id.*
203. Regulation S Rule 903(b)(1), 17 C.F.R. § 230.903(b)(1).
204. *See* § 5.4.3.i, *infra.*
205. Regulation C Rule 405 defines "equity security" as "any stock or similar security, certificate of interest or participation in any profit sharing agreement, preorganization certificate or subscription, transferable share, voting trust certificate or certificate of deposit for an equity security, limited partnership interest, interest in a joint venture, or certificate of interest in a business trust; any security future on any such security; or any security convertible, with or without consideration into such a security, or carrying any warrant or right to subscribe to or purchase such a security; or any such warrant or right; or any put, call, straddle, or other option or privilege of buying such a security from or selling such a security to another without being bound to do so." 17 C.F.R. § 230.405.
206. *See* § 5.4.3.i, *infra.*

issuer's debt securities to be offered or sold;[207] or (b) they are offered and sold in an overseas directed offering.[208] Shares issued by an offshore hedge fund usually qualify as category 1 securities, because the offshore hedge fund is a foreign issuer and there is no substantial U.S. market interest in its shares, as discussed below.

a. Foreign Issuer

A corporation or other entity organized under the laws of any foreign country is a "foreign private issuer" and therefore a "foreign issuer" for purposes of

---

207. Regulation S Rule 902(a) defines "debt securities" as "any security other than an equity security as defined in Section 230.405, as well as:

(1) Non-participatory preferred stock, which is defined as non-convertible capital stock, the holders of which are entitled to a preference in payment of dividends and in distribution of assets on liquidation, dissolution, or winding up of the issuer, but are not entitled to participate in residual earnings or assets of the issuer; and

(2) Asset-backed securities, which are securities of a type that either:

(i) Represent an ownership interest in a pool of discrete assets, or certificates of interest or participation in such assets (including any rights designed to assure servicing, or the receipt or timeliness of receipt by holders of such assets, or certificates of interest or participation in such assets, of amounts payable thereunder), provided that the assets are not generated or originated between the issuer of the security and its affiliates; or

(ii) Are secured by one or more assets or certificates of interest or participation in such assets, and the securities, by their terms, provide for payments of principal and interest (if any) in relation to payments or reasonable projections of payments on assets meeting the requirements of paragraph (a)(2)(i) of this section, or certificates of interest or participations in assets meeting such requirements.

(iii) For purposes of paragraph (a)(2) of this section, the term 'assets' means securities, installment sales, accounts receivable, notes, leases or other contracts, or other assets that by their terms convert into cash over a finite period of time." Regulation S Rule 902(a), 17 C.F.R. § 230.902(a).

208. An "overseas directed offering" is:

(a) An offering of securities of a foreign issuer that is directed into a single country other than the United States to the residents thereof and that is made in accordance with the local laws and customary practices and documentation of such country; or

(b) An offering of non-convertible debt securities of a domestic issuer that is directed into a single country other than the United States to the residents thereof and that is made in accordance with the local laws and customary practices and documentation of such country, provided that the principal and interest of the securities (or par value, as applicable) are denominated in a currency other than U.S. dollars and such securities are neither convertible into U.S. dollar-denominated securities nor linked to U.S. dollars (other than through related currency or interest rate swap transactions that are commercial in nature) in a manner that in effect converts the securities to U.S. dollar-denominated securities. Regulation S Rule 903(b)(1)(ii), 17 C.F.R. § 230.903(b)(1)(ii).

Regulation S,[209] unless it meets the following conditions as of the last business day of its most recently completed second fiscal quarter:[210]

1. more than 50 percent of such issuer's outstanding voting securities are directly or indirectly owned of record by U.S. residents; and
2. any of the following:
   (i) the majority of the issuer's executive officers or directors are U.S. citizens or residents;
   (ii) more than 50 percent of the issuer's assets are located in the United States; or
   (iii) the business of the issuer is administered principally in the United States.[211]

An offshore hedge fund thus qualifies as a foreign issuer if no more than 50 percent of its outstanding voting securities are held by U.S. residents.[212] "Voting securities" are securities whose holders are entitled to vote for the election of directors.[213] In most offshore hedge funds, investors do not have the right to vote for directors. The residence of the investors in such an offshore hedge fund is irrelevant in determining whether the offshore hedge fund is a foreign issuer. If the investors in an offshore hedge fund hold shares that entitle them to vote for directors, however, then whether the offshore hedge fund is a foreign issuer depends in part on the residence of the investors.

If after reasonable inquiry an offshore hedge fund is unable to obtain information about the amount of shares owned by U.S. residents, it may assume that the owners are residents of the jurisdictions in which the investors' nominees have their principal places of business.[214] Record ownership is calculated in accordance with Exchange Act Rule 12g3-2(a),[215] except that the offshore hedge fund may limit its inquiry as to the amount of shares owned by U.S. residents to brokers, dealers, banks and other nominees in the United States, the offshore

---

209. Regulation C Rule 405, 17 C.F.R. § 230.405. Regulation S Rule 902(e), 17 C.F.R. § 230.902(e), provides that a "foreign issuer" is any issuer other than a "domestic issuer." "Domestic issuer" means any issuer other than a "foreign government" or "foreign private issuer" (both as defined in Rule 405).

210. The SEC amended Rule 405 in 2008 to permit a foreign private issuer to assess its status once a year, on the last business day of its second fiscal quarter, rather than the continuous monitoring previously required, as a means of decreasing the compliance burden of foreign private issuers and providing greater certainty to both issuers and investors as to the status of foreign issuers within a given period. Securities Act Release No. 8959 (Sep. 23, 2008), 73 F.R. 58,300 (Oct. 6, 2008).

211. Regulation C Rule 405, 17 C.F.R. § 230.405.

212. *Id.*

213. *Id.*

214. *Id.*

215. 17 C.F.R. § 240.12g3-2(a), referring to Exchange Act Rule 12g5-1, 17 C.F.R. § 240.12g5-1, which in general summary prescribes the manner of keeping the share register and rules for counting owners separately or as single owners.

hedge fund's jurisdiction of incorporation, and the jurisdiction that is the primary trading market for the offshore hedge fund's voting securities.[216]

b. Substantial U.S. Market Interest

Securities issued by an offshore hedge fund are typically equity securities.[217] "Substantial U.S. market interest" in a class of an issuer's equity securities means:

- the securities exchanges and inter-dealer quotation systems in the United States in the aggregate constituted the single largest market for such class of securities in the shorter of the issuer's prior fiscal year or the period since the issuer's incorporation, or
- 20 percent or more of all trading in such class of securities took place in, on or through the facilities of securities exchanges and inter-dealer quotation systems in the United States and less than 55 percent of such trading took place in, on or through the facilities of securities markets of a single non-U.S. country in the shorter of the issuer's prior fiscal year or the period since the issuer's incorporation.[218]

Shares of offshore hedge funds typically are not traded on securities exchanges or inter-dealer quotation systems in the United States. Accordingly, there is usually no substantial U.S. market interest in shares of an offshore hedge fund.

ii. Category 2

Category 2 securities are securities that are not eligible for category 1[219] and that are equity securities of a reporting foreign issuer or debt securities of a reporting issuer or of a nonreporting foreign issuer.[220] A "reporting issuer" is an issuer, other than an investment company registered or required to be registered under the Company Act, that has a class of securities registered pursuant to Exchange Act section 12(b) or 12(g) or is required to file reports pursuant to Exchange Act section 15(d) and has filed all the material required to be filed pursuant to Exchange Act section 13(a) or 15(d) for a period of at least 12 months preceding the offer or sale of securities pursuant to Regulation S or for such shorter period that the issuer was required to file such material.[221] This category typically will not apply to securities of an offshore hedge fund, because offshore hedge funds typically are not reporting issuers and do not issue debt securities.

iii. Category 3

Category 3 securities are any securities that are not eligible for category 1 or 2.[222] In addition to complying with the requirements that its securities be issued in an offshore transaction and that it not engage in any directed selling efforts to

216. Regulation C Rule 405, 17 C.F.R. § 230.405.
217. *See* note 215, *supra*, for the definition of "equity security."
218. Regulation S Rule 902(j)(1), 17 C.F.R. § 230.902(j)(1).
219. *See* § 5.4.3.i, *supra*.
220. Regulation S Rule 903(b)(2), 17 C.F.R. § 230.903(b)(2).
221. Regulation S Rule 902(i), 17 C.F.R. § 230.902(i).
222. Regulation S Rule 903(b)(3), 17 C.F.R. § 230.903(b)(3).

the United States, an offshore hedge fund issuing category 3 securities and any distributor offering or selling such securities must impose offering restrictions and transactional restrictions.[223] In addition, any distributor that sells securities to a distributor, dealer or person receiving a selling concession, fee or other remuneration, before the distribution compliance period[224] expires, must send a confirmation or other notice to the purchaser stating that the purchaser is subject to the same restrictions on offers and sales that apply to a distributor.[225]

As noted above, most securities of offshore hedge funds are category 1 securities. If, however, more than 50 percent of the outstanding voting securities of an offshore hedge fund are directly or indirectly owned of record by U.S. residents, and if the offshore hedge fund has another significant connection to the United States as described above in section 5.4.3.i, its securities may be category 3 securities.

a. Offering Restrictions

An offshore hedge fund issuing category 3 securities, its distributors, their affiliates and any person acting on their behalf must implement the following offering restrictions. Each distributor must agree in writing with the offshore hedge fund that all offers and sales of the securities during the "distribution compliance period" will be made only in accordance with Regulation S Rules 903 and 904, pursuant to registration of the securities under the Securities Act or pursuant to an available exemption from such registration requirements.[226]

The distribution compliance period begins when the securities are first offered to persons other than distributors in reliance on Regulation S or the date the offering closes, whichever is later. It continues with respect to equity

223. *Id.*

224. *See* § 5.4.3.iii.a, *infra.*

225. Regulation S Rule 903(b)(3)(iv), 17 C.F.R. § 230.903(b)(3)(iv).

226. Regulation S Rule 902(g)(1)(i), 17 C.F.R. § 230.902(g)(1)(i). With respect to offers and sales of equity securities of U.S. issuers, each distributor must also agree in writing not to engage in hedging transactions with respect to such securities before the distribution compliance period expires, unless in compliance with the Securities Act— Regulation S Rule 902(g)(1)(ii), 17 C.F.R. § 230.902(g)(1)(ii)—but this restriction is not ordinarily relevant to an offshore hedge fund, which is not a U.S. issuer and does not issue shares that are traded in public securities markets.

securities for a period of one year.[227] In the case of a continuous offering, which is typical of an offshore hedge fund, the distribution compliance period does not begin until the managing underwriter or person performing similar functions determines and certifies that the distribution is complete.[228] Accordingly, the offshore hedge fund's distribution compliance period will continue throughout its offering and for a year after the offering ends.

b. Transaction Restrictions

An offshore hedge fund issuing category 3 securities, its distributors, their affiliates and any person acting on their behalf, must also comply with transaction restrictions. The transaction restrictions vary depending on whether the securities are equity securities or debt securities. Offshore hedge funds typically issue only equity securities, so the restrictions on equity securities typically apply. Each of these restrictions applies with respect to any offer or sale made during the distribution compliance period.[229]

The offer or sale of equity securities, if made during the distribution compliance period, cannot be made to a U.S. person or for the account or benefit of a U.S. person (other than a distributor).[230] A "U.S. person" is:

- any natural person resident in the United States;
- any partnership or corporation organized or incorporated under the laws of the United States;
- any estate of which any executor or administrator is a U.S. person;
- any trust of which any trustee is a U.S. person;

---

227. Regulation S Rule 902(f), 17 C.F.R. § 230.902(f), provides that "'Distribution compliance period' means a period that begins when the securities were first offered to persons other than distributors in reliance upon this Regulation S (Section 230.901 through 230.905, and Preliminary Notes) or the date of closing of the offering, whichever is later and continues until the end of the period of time specified in the relevant provision of Section 230.903, except that:

(1) All offers and sales by a distributor of an unsold allotment or subscription shall be deemed to be made during the distribution compliance period;

(2) In a continuous offering, the distribution compliance period shall commence upon completion of the distribution, as determined and certified by the managing underwriter or person performing similar functions;

(3) In a continuous offering of non-convertible debt securities offered and sold in identifiable tranches, the distribution compliance period for securities in a tranche shall commence upon completion of the distribution of such tranche, as determined and certified by the managing underwriter or person performing similar functions; and

(4) That [*sic*] in a continuous offering of securities to be acquired upon the exercise of warrants, the distribution compliance period shall commence upon completion of the distribution of the warrants, as determined and certified by the managing underwriter or person performing similar functions, if requirements of Section 230.903(b)(5) are satisfied."

Regulation S Rule 903(b)(3)(iii), 17 C.F.R. § 230.903(B)(3)(iii), provides that the distribution compliance period for equity securities is one year.

228. Regulation S Rule 902(f)(2), 17 C.F.R. § 230.902(f)(2).

229. Regulation S Rule 903(b)(3)(iii), 17 C.F.R. § 230. 903(b)(3)(iii).

230. Regulation S Rule 903(b)(3)(iii)(A), 17 C.F.R. § 230.903(b)(3)(iii)(A).

- any agency or branch of a non-U.S. entity located in the United States;
- any nondiscretionary account or similar account (other than an estate or trust) held by a dealer or other fiduciary for the benefit or account of a U.S. person;
- any discretionary account or similar account (other than an estate or trust) held by a dealer or other fiduciary organized, incorporated or (if an individual) resident in the United States; or
- any partnership or corporation organized or incorporated under the laws of any non-U.S. jurisdiction that is formed by a U.S. person principally for the purpose of investing in securities not registered under the Securities Act, unless it is organized or incorporated, and owned, by accredited investors who are not natural persons, estates or trusts.[231]

A person's residence, not citizenship, determines U.S. person status. Accordingly, a non-U.S. citizen residing in the United States is a U.S. person for purposes of Regulation S.

Regulation S also excludes from the definition of "U.S." person the following:

- any discretionary account or similar account (other than an estate or trust) held for the benefit or account of a non-U.S. person by a dealer or other professional fiduciary organized, incorporated, or (if an individual) resident in the United States;
- any estate of which any professional fiduciary acting as executor or administrator is a U.S. person if an executor or administrator of the estate who is not a U.S. person has sole or shared investment discretion with respect to the assets of the estate and the estate is governed by non-U.S. law;
- any trust of which any professional fiduciary acting as trustee is a U.S. person, if a trustee who is not a U.S. person has sole or shared investment discretion with respect to the trust assets, and no beneficiary of the trust (and no settlor if the trust is revocable) is a U.S. person;
- an employee benefit plan established and administered in accordance with the law of a country other than the United States and customary practices and documentation of such country;
- any agency or branch of a U.S. person located outside the United States if the agency or branch operates for valid business reasons and the agency or branch is engaged in the business of insurance or banking and is subject to substantive insurance or banking regulation, respectively, in the jurisdiction where it is located; and

231. Regulation S Rule 902(k)(1), 17 C.F.R. § 230.902(k)(1).

- certain nongovernmental organizations.[232]

The transaction restrictions that apply to category 3 securities also require that the purchaser of the securities (other than a distributor) certify either that it is not a U.S. person and is not acquiring the securities for the account or benefit of any U.S. person or that it is a U.S. person purchasing the securities in a transaction that does not require registration under the Securities Act.[233] The purchaser also must agree (a) to resell such securities only in accordance with Regulation S, pursuant to registration under the Securities Act, or pursuant to an available exemption from registration,[234] and (b) not to engage in hedging transactions involving the securities except in compliance with the Securities Act.[235] An offshore hedge fund should include these representations in the subscription documents that it requires investors to execute.

The issuer must also, either by contract or in its bylaws, articles, charter or comparable document, refuse to register any transfer of the securities not made in accordance with Regulation S, pursuant to registration under the Securities Act, or pursuant to an available exemption from registration.[236] If, however, the securities are in bearer form or non-U.S. law prevents the issuer from refusing to register securities transfers, other reasonable procedures (such as placing a legend on the securities) may be used to prevent any transfer of the securities that does not comply with Regulation S.[237] An offshore hedge fund should include appropriate provisions in its memorandum and articles of organization or similar charter document to comply with these transfer restrictions.[238]

---

232. Regulation S Rule 902(k)(2), 17 C.F.R. § 230.902(k)(2). Specifically, the nongovernmental organizations are the International Monetary Fund, the International Bank for Reconstruction and Development, the Inter-American Development Bank, the Asian Development Bank, the African Development Bank, the United Nations and their agencies, affiliates and pension plans, and any other similar international organizations, their agencies, affiliates and pension plans.

233. Regulation S Rule 903(b)(3)(iii)(B)(*1*), 17 C.F.R. § 230.903(b)(3)(iii)(B)(*1*).

234. Regulation S Rule 903(b)(3)(iii)(B)(*2*), 17 C.F.R. § 230.903(b)(3)(iii)(B)(*2*).

235. *Id.*

236. Regulation S Rule 903(b)(3)(iii)(B)(*4*), 17 C.F.R. § 230.903(b)(3)(iii)(B)(*4*).

237. *Id.*

238. If an issuer is a U.S. issuer, the securities must bear a legend to the effect that their transfer is prohibited except in accordance with Regulation S, pursuant to registration under the Securities Act or pursuant to an available exemption from registration and that hedging transactions involving the securities may not be conducted except in compliance with the Securities Act. Regulation S Rule 903(b)(3)(iii)(B)(*3*), 17 C.F.R. § 230.903(b)(3)(iii)(B)(*3*). Offshore hedge funds ordinarily are not U.S. issuers.

§ 5.5 Concurrent Regulation D and Regulation S Offerings

A hedge fund may offer and sell its securities to investors in the United States in accordance with Regulation D Rule 506 and concurrently to investors outside the United States in accordance with Regulation S.[239] The SEC has stated that legitimate sales activities in the United States in connection with an offering of securities exempt from registration under the Securities Act do not constitute directed selling efforts under Regulation S.[240] Purchasers of securities sold pursuant to Regulation S and the proceeds of such sales are not included in determining the number of purchasers or the aggregate offering price for purposes of Regulation D.[241] Resales of securities pursuant to the safe harbor provided by Regulation S Rule 904, being exempt from registration by that rule, are not subject to the resale limitations that apply to shares sold under Regulation D.

§ 5.6 Consequences of Failure to Register

An investor may bring a claim against an issuer of securities sold in violation of the registration requirement of Securities Act section 5 to recover the consideration paid for such security, plus interest (but less any income received on the security), or for damages if the investor no longer owns the security.[242] Liability under Securities Act section 12 may be asserted against the person who "offers or sells a security" (and passes title in the security to the buyer), as well as anyone who solicits the sale.[243] Anyone who acts as an agent for the issuer in soliciting sales is subject to section 12 liability.

As a result, a plaintiff may bring an action under Securities Act section 12 against the hedge fund, its general partner, the general partner's employees who are engaged in selling efforts and any other person that sells, solicits or offers to sell interests in the hedge fund. In addition, under Securities Act section 15, any person who controls any person liable under section 12 may be jointly and severally liable with and to the same extent as the controlled person, unless the controlling person had no knowledge of or reasonable ground to believe in the existence of the facts under which the controlled person is allegedly liable.[244]

---

239. Regulation D, 17 C.F.R. § 230.501 Preliminary Note 7.

240. Securities Act Release No. 6863 (Apr. 24, 1990), 55 F.R. 18,306 (May 2, 1990).

241. *Id.*

242. Securities Act § 12(a), 15 U.S.C. § 77l(a).

243. Pinter v. Dahl, 486 U.S. 622, 644, 108 S. Ct. 2063, 2077 (1988). The Court noted, however, the lack of support for expansion of §12 liability beyond persons who pass title and persons who offer, including those who solicit offers, stating that "Congress did not intend that the section impose liability on participants collateral to the offer or sale." *Id.* at 650, 2080.

244. Securities Act §15, 15 U.S.C. §77(o).

In addition, the SEC can bring an action against the issuer for monetary penalties of up to $100,000 per violation for a natural person or $500,000 per violation for other persons.[245] The SEC may also issue cease and desist orders with respect to violations or potential violations of the Securities Act.[246]

245. Securities Act § 20(d), 15 U.S.C. § 77t(d).
246. Securities Act § 8A, 15 U.S.C. § 77h-1.

CHAPTER **6**

Disclosure Obligations

§ 6.1 Introduction

The Securities Act requires issuers offering or selling securities in registered offerings to make extensive disclosure. The Company Act imposes similar disclosure obligations on registered investment companies. Although private hedge funds are not registered under the Company Act as discussed in Chapter 3 and issue securities that are not registered under the Securities Act in reliance on the exemptions described in Chapter 5, those exemptions generally require disclosure of or access to the information that the hedge fund would be required to disclose in a registration statement under the Securities Act. In addition, the anti-fraud rules of the Securities Act and the Exchange Act, among other things, prohibit an issuer of securities from making any untrue statement of material fact or omitting to state a material fact necessary to make the statements made not misleading in light of the circumstances under which they were made.[1]

In addition to the disclosure requirements of the Securities Act, the Exchange Act and the Company Act, other federal and state laws require disclosures by hedge funds and their general partners and investment advisers. The Advisers Act and the SEC rules under it, and similar state laws and rules, impose disclosure obligations on investment advisers to hedge funds. Some hedge funds that trade commodity futures, options and swaps are subject to disclosure requirements under the CEA rules and regulations.[2] Finally, rules adopted by the SEC, the FTC and the CFTC under the GLBA[3] impose disclosure obligations on investment advisers and hedge funds with respect to their use and disclosure of nonpublic personal information of clients and investors.

---

1. *See, e.g.*, Securities Act § 17(a), 15 U.S.C. § 77q(a); Exchange Act § 10(b), 15 U.S.C. § 78j(b); and Exchange Act Rule 10b-5, 17 C.F.R. § 240.10b-5.

2. CEA Rules 4.21 and 4.31, 17 C.F.R. §§ 4.21 and 4.31.

3. GLBA, 15 U.S.C. § 6781 *et seq.*; Regulation S-P, 17 C.F.R. pt. 248; FTC Privacy Rule, 16 C.F.R. pt. 313; CFTC Privacy Rule, 17 C.F.R. pt. 160.

§ 6.2 Public Offering and Mutual Fund Disclosure Obligations

1. Securities Act

i. Disclosure Obligations in Public Offerings

As discussed in Chapter 5, an issuer may not offer or sell securities unless a registration statement is in effect with respect to those securities, or the securities or the transactions in which they are offered are exempt from registration.[4] The SEC has adopted several forms of registration statement on which an issuer may register securities. The registration statement on Form N-1A, adopted by the SEC under the Company Act, may be used by certain investment companies to register their securities under the Securities Act.[5] In addition, an issuer that does not qualify to use any other form may use Form S-1 for its registration statement.[6] If a hedge fund were to register the securities it issues under the Securities Act, it would be required to use either Form N-1A or Form S-1. The requirements of those forms are discussed in the following sections 6.2.1.ii and 6.2.1.iii.

Forms N-1A and S-1 were not, however, designed with hedge funds in mind, and some of their requirements are inappropriate in the hedge fund context. Securities Act section 4(a)(2)[7] and Regulation D[8] under the Securities Act generally contemplate that the issuer in a private offering will furnish or make available to investors the information that would be included in a registration statement on the appropriate form, to the extent that such information is material to a decision whether to invest.[9] Because no single registration form is entirely appropriate for a hedge fund, a hedge fund disclosure document should contain all of the information that would be required by either Form N-1A or Form S-1, to the extent it is material to a prospective investor.[10]

ii. Form N-1A

Form N-1A may be used by open-end management investment companies, other than separate accounts of insurance companies or companies that issue periodic payment plan certificates or that are sponsors or depositors of companies

4. Securities Act § 5(a), 15 U.S.C. § 77e(a).

5. Form N-1A General Instruction B.1(a). The text of Form N-1A does not appear in the Code of Federal Regulations, but is available on the SEC's website at http://www.sec.gov/about/forms/formn-1a.pdf. *See* 17 C.F.R. §§ 274.0-1 and 274.11A.

6. Form S-1 General Instruction I. The text of Form S-1 does not appear in the Code of Federal Regulations, but is available on the SEC's website at http://www.sec.gov/about/forms/forms-1.pdf. *See* 17 C.F.R. §§ 239.0-1 and 239.11.

7. 15 U.S.C. § 77d(2).

8. 17 C.F.R. §§ 501-508.

9. *See* §§ 5.3.1.iii and 5.3.2.vii, *supra*, and § 6.3, *infra*.

10. *But see* § 6.3.2, *infra*.

issuing such certificates.[11] An "open-end management investment company" is "a management company which is offering for sale or has outstanding any redeemable security of which it is the issuer."[12] A "redeemable security" is

> any security, other than short-term paper, under the terms of which the holder, upon its presentation to the issuer or to a person designated by the issuer, is entitled (whether absolutely or only out of surplus) to receive approximately his proportionate share of the issuer's current net assets, or the cash equivalent thereof.[13]

Most hedge funds are organized as limited partnerships or limited liability companies from which investors may withdraw capital or redeem interests periodically on request. Accordingly, hedge funds ordinarily are similar to open-end management investment companies.

Form N-1A comprises three parts: the prospectus, the statement of additional information, and other information that must be filed with the SEC. The issuer must deliver the prospectus before or concurrently with the delivery of any security sold.[14] The issuer is not required to deliver the statement of additional information but must offer to do so, on written or oral request and without charge, when the prospectus is delivered to the prospective investor.[15]

a. Prospectus

The prospectus is intended "to provide essential information about the Fund in a way that will help investors make informed decisions about whether to purchase the Fund's shares described in the prospectus."[16] The prospectus

---

11. Company Act Rule 11A, 17 C.F.R. § 274.11A.

12. Company Act § 5(a)(1), 15 U.S.C. § 80a-5(a)(1). A "management company" is an investment company that is not a face-amount certificate company or a unit investment trust. Company Act § 4(3), 15 U.S.C. § 80a-4(3). A face-amount certificate company is an investment company "which is engaged or proposes to engage in the business of issuing face-amount certificates of the installment type, or which has been engaged in such business and has any such certificate outstanding." Company Act § 4(1), 15 U.S.C. § 80a-4(1). A "face-amount certificate of the installment type" is a "certificate, investment contract, or other security which represents an obligation on the part of its issuer to pay a stated or determinable sum or sums at a fixed or determinable date or dates more than twenty-four months after the date of issuance, in consideration of the payment of periodic installments of a stated or determinable amount." Company Act § 2(a)(15), 15 U.S.C. § 80a-2(a)(15). A "unit investment trust" is "an investment company which (A) is organized under a trust indenture, contract of custodianship or agency, or similar instrument, (B) does not have a board of directors, and (C) issues only redeemable securities, each of which represents an undivided interest in a unit of specified securities, but does not include a voting trust." Company Act § 4(2), 15 U.S.C. § 80a-4(2). As discussed in Chapter 4, *supra*, hedge funds typically are not organized as either of the latter two types of entities and therefore typically are management companies.

13. Company Act § 2(a)(32), 15 U.S.C. § 80a-2(a)(32).

14. Securities Act § 5(b), 15 U.S.C. § 77e(b); Securities Act Rule 430(b), 17 C.F.R. § 230.430(b).

15. Securities Act Rule 430(b), 17 C.F.R. § 230.430(b).

16. Form N-1A General Instruction C.2(a).

"should clearly disclose the fundamental characteristics and investment risks of the Fund, using concise, straightforward, and easy to understand language" and "should emphasize the Fund's overall investment approach and strategy."[17] The principal information that a fund's prospectus must disclose under Form N-1A is summarized below.

(1) Front and Back Cover Pages

The front cover page of the prospectus must include the fund's name, the class or classes of interests being offered, the date of the prospectus and a legend to the effect that the SEC has not approved or disapproved the securities being offered or passed on the accuracy or adequacy of the disclosure in the prospectus and that any contrary representation is a criminal offense.[18] The front cover page may state the fund's investment objectives, briefly describe its operations and include other information, as long as the other information "is not incomplete, inaccurate or misleading and does not, because of its nature, quantity or manner of presentation, obscure or impede understanding of the information that is required to be included" on the front cover page.[19]

The outside back cover page of the prospectus must include disclosure, in plain English,[20] about other documents available from the fund, such as the fund's statement of additional information and its annual and semi-annual reports, a toll-free telephone number that investors can use to obtain information about the fund, and statements about whether information is incorporated by reference.[21]

(2) Risk/Return Summary

Immediately following the front cover page and the table of contents, the prospectus must include a summary of the following information in the following numerical order:[22]

1. a description of the fund's investment objectives or goals;[23]
2. a table showing the fees that may be paid by the fund's shareholders, including sales charges (on purchases, deferred loads and reinvested dividends), redemption and exchange fees, account fees, management fees and distribution or service fees, and examples of the costs that would have been incurred by an investor on a $10,000 investment in the fund over the 1-year, 3-year, 5-year and 10-year periods ending on the date of the most recently completed calendar year;[24]
3. a summary of how the fund intends to achieve its investment objectives, which identifies the fund's principal investment strategies (including the

17. Form N-1A General Instruction C.1(a); Company Act Rule 11A, 17 C.F.R. § 274.11A.
18. Form N-1A Item 1(a); Securities Act Rule 481(b)(1), 17 C.F.R. § 230.481(b)(1).
19. Form N-1A Instruction to Item 1(a) and General Instruction C.3(b).
20. *See* § 6.2.3, *infra*.
21. Form N-1A Item 1(b).
22. Form N-1A General Instruction C.3(a).
23. Form N-1A Item 2.
24. Form N-1A Item 3.

types of securities in which the fund principally invests or will invest) and any policy to concentrate in securities of issuers in a particular industry or group of industries;[25]

- a summary of the principal risks of investing in the fund, including the risks to which the fund's portfolio as a whole is subject, the circumstances reasonably likely to affect adversely the fund's net asset value ("NAV"), yield and total return, and, if the fund is nondiversified, a statement to that effect, a description of the effect of nondiversification (for example, that compared with other funds, the fund may invest a greater percentage of its assets in a particular issuer) and a summary of the risks of investing in a nondiversified fund;[26]
- a bar chart showing the fund's annual total returns for each of the preceding 10 years (or for the life of the fund, if shorter) and for the current year to date through the end of the most recent quarter, as well as the fund's highest and lowest returns for any quarter during that period;[27]
- a table showing the fund's average annual total return, average annual total return after taxes on distributions and average annual total return after taxes on distributions and redemptions, and returns of an appropriate broad-based securities market index, for the 1-year, 5-year and 10-year periods ending with the most recently completed calendar year (or for the life of the fund, if shorter);[28]

4. the name of each investment adviser of the fund, including any sub-advisers,[29] and the name, title and length of service of each person who is primarily responsible for the day-to-day management of the fund's portfolio on behalf of the investment adviser;[30]
5. the fund's minimum initial or subsequent investment amount and the procedures for redeeming fund shares;[31]
6. a statement whether the fund intends to make distributions that will be taxed as ordinary income or capital gains, or that will be tax-exempt, and a statement that a portion of the fund's distributions may be taxable (for a fund that holds itself out as investing in tax-exempt securities);[32] and

---

25. Form N-1A Item 4(a).
26. Form N-1A Item 4(b)(1).
27. Form N-1A Item 4(b)(2).
28. *Id.*
29. Form N-1A Item 5(a).
30. Form N-1A Item 5(b).
31. Form N-1A Item 6.
32. Form N-1A Item 7.

7. a statement about payments to broker-dealers and other financial intermediaries and the conflicts of interest arising from that compensation.[33]

(3) Investment Objectives, Strategies and Related Risks

The prospectus must disclose the fund's investment objectives, whether those objectives may be changed without shareholder approval,[34] and how the fund intends to achieve its investment objectives, including a description of the fund's principal investment strategies (including the particular types of securities in which the fund principally invests or will invest) and an explanation, in general terms, of how the fund's investment adviser decides which securities to buy and sell.[35] The instructions to Form N-1A provide that:

> Whether a particular strategy, including a strategy to invest in a particular type of security, is a principal investment strategy depends on the strategy's anticipated importance in achieving the Fund's investment objectives, and how the strategy affects the Fund's potential risks and returns. In determining what is a principal investment strategy, consider, among other things, the amount of the Fund's assets expected to be committed to the strategy, the amount of the Fund's assets expected to be placed at risk by the strategy, and the likelihood of the Fund's losing some or all of those assets from implementing the strategy.[36]

The prospectus should disclose "any policy to concentrate in securities of issuers in a particular industry or group of industries (*i.e.*, investing more than 25 percent of a Fund's net assets in a particular industry or group of industries)."[37] The fund should disclose whether it "may engage in active and frequent trading of portfolio securities to achieve its principal investment strategies."[38] If the fund trades actively and frequently, the prospectus should "explain the tax consequences to shareholders of increased portfolio turnover, and how the tax consequences of, or trading costs associated with, a Fund's portfolio turnover may affect the Fund's performance."[39] If applicable, the prospectus should disclose "that the Fund may, from time to time, take temporary defensive positions that are inconsistent with the Fund's principal investment strategies in attempting to respond to adverse market, economic, political or other conditions" and "the effect of taking such a temporary defensive position (*e.g.*, that the Fund may not achieve its investment objective)."[40]

---

33. Form N-1A Item 8.
34. Form N-1A Item 9(a).
35. Form N-1A Item 9(b).
36. Form N-1A Item 9(b)(1), Instruction 2.
37. Form N-1A Item 9(b)(1), Instruction 4.
38. Form N-1A Item 9(b)(1), Instruction 7.
39. *Id.*
40. Form N-1A Item 9(b)(1), Instruction 6.

The fund must "disclose the principal risks of investing in the Fund, including the risks to which the Fund's particular portfolio as a whole is expected to be subject and the circumstances reasonably likely to affect adversely the Fund's net asset value, yield or total return."[41] The risk disclosure should describe not only generic risks, but also the specific risks applicable to the fund and their potential consequences. For example, a fund that relies heavily on technology should consider disclosing the risks it faces from cyber incidents and systems vulnerability.[42] Failure to disclose a specific risk of which the fund is or should be aware can result in liability for the fund under the anti-fraud provisions of the securities laws.[43] Adequate disclosure of risks, however, can provide the fund with a defense from liability.[44]

Failure to comply with the fund's investment objectives or to follow the fund's investment strategy, as disclosed in the fund's prospectus, can give rise to a securities fraud claim against the fund and its investment advisers.[45] In *In the Matter of Fundamental Portfolio Advisors, Inc., et al.*, an investment company's investment adviser committed securities fraud by disclosing in the fund's prospectus that the fund would seek high returns with maximum safety and that the fund would limit the duration of its investments to 3 years or less, when in fact the investment adviser invested up to 30 percent of the fund's net assets in highly volatile "inverse floaters" that had durations significantly longer than 3 years.[46]

In *In re TCW/DW North American Government Income Trust Securities Litigation*, the court held that the plaintiff class of investors in an investment company could state a claim for securities fraud under the securities laws based on the fund's failure to disclose the consequences of prepayment of mortgage-backed securities.[47] On the other hand, the court in *Olkey v. Hyperion 1999 Term Trust, Inc.* dismissed fraud claims made by a class of investors in an investment company on the ground that the fund's prospectus described the effect of interest rate changes on the fund's NAV.[48]

(4) Management, Organization, Legal Proceedings and Capital Structure

The prospectus must disclose the name and address of each investment adviser to the fund. The fund must describe each investment adviser's "experience as

41. Form N-1A Item 9(c).

42. *See* SEC Division of Corporate Finance, CF Disclosure Guidance: Topic No. 2 (Oct. 13, 2011).

43. *See In re* TCW/DW North American Government Income Trust Sec. Lit., 941 F. Supp. 326 (S.D.N.Y., 1996).

44. *See* Olkey, et al. v. Hyperion 1999 Term Trust, Inc., et al., 98 F.3d 2 (2nd Cir., 1996); Sheppard v. TCW/DW Term Trust 2000, *et al.*, 938 F. Supp. 171 (S.D.N.Y., 1996).

45. *See, e.g.*, In the matter of Fundamental Portfolio Advisors, Inc., *et al.*, SEC Initial Decisions Release No. 180, 2001 SEC Lexis 156 (Jan. 29, 2001).

46. *Id.*

47. *In re* TCW/DW North American Government Income Trust Sec. Lit., 941 F. Supp. 326, 331 (S.D.N.Y, 1996).

48. Olkey, et al. v. Hyperion 1999 Term Trust, Inc., et al., 98 F.3d 2 (2nd Cir., 1996).

an investment adviser and the advisory services it provides to the Fund."[49] The prospectus must state the business experience for the preceding 5 years of each person employed by or associated with an investment adviser who is primarily responsible for the day-to-day management of the fund's portfolio and describe each such person's role if the fund is managed by more than one person.[50]

The fund also must describe the compensation of each investment adviser. If the fund has operated for a full fiscal year, it must state the aggregate fees paid to the investment adviser for the most recent fiscal year as a percentage of the fund's average net assets. If the fund has not operated for a full fiscal year, the fund must describe the investment adviser's fee as a percentage of average net assets, including any break points. If the investment adviser charges a fee, such as a performance fee, that is not based on a percentage of the fund's average net assets, the fund must describe the basis of the investment adviser's compensation.[51]

The prospectus must describe any material pending legal proceedings to which the fund or the fund's investment adviser is a party, other than ordinary routine litigation incidental to its business.[52] This disclosure must "include information about legal proceedings instituted, or known to be contemplated, by a governmental authority against any of these parties. The description should include the name of the court in which the proceedings are pending, the date instituted, the principal parties involved, a description of the factual basis alleged to underlie the proceedings and the relief sought."[53] Legal proceedings are material if they are likely to have a material adverse effect on the fund or on the investment adviser's ability to perform under its contract with the fund.[54]

The prospectus must also describe any "unique or unusual restrictions on the right freely to retain or dispose of the Fund's shares."[55] If investors may incur significant risks, material obligations or liabilities by investing in the fund (other than investment risks), the prospectus must disclose these risks, obligations or liabilities.

(5) Shareholder Information

The prospectus must describe the procedures for pricing the fund's shares, including for most funds an explanation that the price of the shares is based on the fund's NAV, "the method used to value fund shares (market price, fair value or amortized cost)" and when NAV is calculated.[56] Exchange-traded funds must explain that the price of their shares is based on market price. The prospectus must identify any holidays on which shares will not be priced. The fund may use any means that effectively communicate such holidays, such as an explanation that shares will not be priced on days on which the NYSE is closed

49. Form N-1A Item 10(a)(1)(i).
50. Form N-1A Item 10(a)(2).
51. Form N-1A Item 10(a)(1)(ii).
52. Form N-1A Item 10(a)(3).
53. *Id.*
54. Form N-1A Instruction to Item 10(a)(3).
55. Form N-1A Item 10(b).
56. Form N-1A Items 11(a)(1) and (a)(2).

for trading.[57] If the fund has securities that are listed on foreign exchanges that trade on days when the fund's shares are not priced, the fund must disclose that the value of the fund's shares will change on days when investors may not purchase or redeem shares.[58]

The prospectus must describe the procedures for purchasing the fund's shares, including any minimum investment requirements,[59] as well as the procedures for redeeming shares, including any restrictions on redemptions, any redemption charges (including how they will be collected and under what circumstances they will be waived), whether the fund has the right to redeem its shares in kind, whether a shareholder can sell his shares back to the fund and, if so, the fees that might apply to that service, the circumstances (if any) under which the fund may redeem shares automatically without action by shareholders who hold less than a certain number or value of shares, the circumstances (if any) under which the fund may delay honoring a redemption request for a certain time after a shareholder's investment and any restrictions on transferring shares held in street name.[60]

The fund must describe its policies with respect to dividends and distributions.[61] The risks of frequent purchases and sales of fund shares and the fund's policies with respect to such purchases and sales must be disclosed.[62] If the fund does not have such policies, the specific basis for the decision not to have a policy must be disclosed. If the fund has adopted restrictions to discourage frequent purchases and redemptions, the prospectus must disclose these restrictions in detail. The prospectus must describe the tax consequences to shareholders of buying, holding, exchanging and selling the fund's shares.[63]

(6) Distribution Arrangements

The fund must describe any sales commissions ("loads"), including deferred sales loads, that apply to purchases of its shares,[64] and whether sales loads are imposed on shares purchased with reinvested dividends or distributions.[65] If deferred sales loads are charged, the prospectus must describe how they are imposed and calculated.[66] The prospectus must describe any breakpoints in the sales load or other arrangements that eliminate or reduce sales loads, either generally or for specific investors.[67]

---

57. Form N-1A Item 11(a)(3) and Instruction 1 thereto.
58. Form N-1A Instruction 2 to Item 11(a)(3).
59. Form N-1A Item 11(b).
60. Form N-1A Item 11(c).
61. Form N-1A Item 11(d).
62. Form N-1A Item 11(e).
63. Form N-1A Item 11(f).
64. Form N-1A Item 12(a)(1).
65. Form N-1A Item 12(a)(1) Instruction 2.
66. Form N-1A Item 12(a)(1) Instruction 3.
67. Form N-1A Item 12(a)(2).

If the fund is part of a master-feeder fund, the main features of the structure of the fund must be described.[68] If the feeder fund can change the master fund in which it invests, the prospectus must describe the circumstances under which it can do so.[69]

(7) Financial Highlights

The prospectus also must include the following information in tabular form (with the heading "Financial Highlights") for the fund, or for the fund and its subsidiaries, audited for at least the last 5 years and consolidated as required by Regulation S-X under the Securities Act:[70]

> The financial highlights table is intended to help you understand the Fund's financial performance for the past 5 years [or, if shorter, the period of the Fund's operations]. Certain information reflects financial results for a single Fund share. The total returns in the table represent the rate that an investor would have earned [or lost] on an investment in the Fund (assuming reinvestment of all dividends and distributions). This information has been audited by ____________, whose report, along with the Fund's financial statements, are included in [the statement of additional information or annual report], which is available on request.[71]

	Year 1	Year 2	Year 3	Year 4	Year 5
Net Asset Value, Beginning of Period	$______	$______	$______	$______	$______
Income from Investment Operations					
Net Investment Income	$______	$______	$______	$______	$______
Net Gains or Losses on Securities (both realized and unrealized)	$______	$______	$______	$______	$______
Total from Investment Operations	$______	$______	$______	$______	$______
Less Distributions					
Dividends (from net investment income)	$______	$______	$______	$______	$______
Distributions (from capital gains)	$______	$______	$______	$______	$______
Returns of Capital	$______	$______	$______	$______	$______
Total Distributions	$______	$______	$______	$______	$______

68. Form N-1A Item 12(c). *See* § 4.4.7, *supra,* for a description of the master-feeder fund structure.

69. Form N-1A Item 12(c)(4).

70. Form N-1A Item 13(a); Regulation S-X, 17 C.F.R. pt. 210.

71. Form N-1A Item 13(a).

	Year 1	Year 2	Year 3	Year 4	Year 5
Net Asset Value, End of Period	$_____	$_____	$_____	$_____	$_____
Total Return					
Ratios/Supplemental Data					
Net Assets, End of Period	$_____	$_____	$_____	$_____	$_____
Ratio of Expenses to Average Net Assets	__%	__%	__%	__%	__%
Ratio of Net Income to Average Net Assets	__%	__%	__%	__%	__%
Portfolio Turnover Rate	__%	__%	__%	__%	__%

The financial highlights table should include information for the period between the end of the last fiscal year and the date of the fund's latest balance sheet or statement of assets and liabilities.[72] With respect to information for less than a year, the fund may present ratios as annualized amounts but the total returns may not be annualized. A note should be included stating whether the ratios are annualized, and stating that the total return is not annualized.[73] The narrative explanation must appear before the table, although it may be modified if it contains information comparable to that shown.[74] Form N-1A imposes specific requirements on how the information in the financial highlights table is calculated.[75]

b. Statement of Additional Information

The purpose of a statement of additional information is to "provide additional information about the Fund that the [SEC] has concluded is not necessary or appropriate in the public interest or for the protection of investors to be in the prospectus, but that some investors may find useful."[76] In a statement of additional information, a fund may "expand discussions of the matters described in the prospectus by including additional information that the Fund believes may be of interest to some investors."[77] A statement of additional information should not duplicate information that is provided in the prospectus unless it is necessary to make the statement of additional information comprehensible as an independent document.[78]

The front cover page of the statement of additional information must include specific identifying information, including the fund's name, exchange ticker symbol and the exchange on which the fund's shares trade, as applicable.[79]

72. Form N-1A Item 13(a) Instruction 1(a).
73. *Id.*, Form N-1A Item 13(a) Instruction 3(e).
74. Form N-1A Item 13(a) Instruction 1(c).
75. Form N-1A Instructions to Item 13(a).
76. Form N-1A General Instruction C(2)(b).
77. *Id.*
78. *Id.*
79. Form N-1A Item 14(a).

The front cover page must also state that the statement of additional information is not a prospectus, how the prospectus may be obtained, and whether any of the disclosure that would otherwise be in the statement of additional information is presented in the prospectus and incorporated by reference into the statement of additional information. The statement of additional information must have its own table of contents.[80]

(1) Fund History

The statement of additional information should provide the fund's date, form and jurisdiction of organization, any other names used by the fund during the preceding 5 years and the approximate date of any name change. If the fund has engaged in business other than that of an investment company during the preceding 5 years, the statement of additional information should describe the nature of the other business and give the approximate date on which the fund commenced business as an investment company.[81]

(2) Expanded Disclosure of Investments and Risks

The statement of additional information should describe any investment strategies that an investment adviser uses in managing the fund (other than the principal strategies, which are described in the prospectus) and the risks of those strategies.[82] The statement of additional information must also describe the fund's policies on issuing senior securities, borrowing money (including the purposes for which the proceeds will be used), underwriting securities of other issuers, concentrating investments in a particular industry or group of industries, purchasing or selling real estate or commodities, making loans, and any other policy that the fund deems fundamental or that may not be changed without shareholder approval.[83]

If applicable, the fund must disclose the types of investments that it may make while assuming a temporary defensive position, as described in the prospectus.[84] The fund must explain any significant variation in its portfolio turnover rates over the preceding 2 fiscal years and any anticipated variation in the future portfolio turnover rate from that reported for the last fiscal year in the financial highlights table.[85] The fund must disclose its policies and procedures for disclosing its portfolio securities to any person and any ongoing arrangements to make information about its portfolio securities available to any person or category of persons.[86]

(3) Management and Principal Shareholders

The fund must provide extensive disclosure about its board of directors and officers, and the members of its advisory board, if any, including information regarding positions and responsibilities with the fund, other occupations and

80. Form N-1A Item 14(b).
81. Form N-1A Item 15.
82. Form N-1A Item 16(b).
83. Form N-1A Item 16(c).
84. Form N-1A Item 16(d).
85. Form N-1A Item 16(e).
86. Form N-1A Item 16(f).

directorships, potential conflicts of interest and compensation.[87] For each such person who is considered an "interested person" of the fund, the fund must disclose the reason that the person is considered interested.[88] The fund must provide additional specific disclosure about the fund's board of directors, including each director's investment in the fund and the fund's related investment companies and any transactions between any director and the fund exceeding $120,000.[89] The fund must disclose the name and address of each person who controls the fund and describe the effect of such control on the voting rights of other shareholders, including the percentage of the fund's voting securities owned by the control person or any other basis for such control.[90] The fund must disclose the name, address and percentage ownership of each person who owns of record or is known by the fund to own beneficially 5 percent or more of any class of the fund's outstanding voting securities.[91]

(4) Proxy Voting Policy

The fund must disclose the policies and procedures that it uses to determine how to vote proxies relating to portfolio securities. This description must address the procedures the fund uses when a vote presents a conflict between the interests of fund shareholders and the interests of the fund's investment adviser, principal underwriter or any affiliated person of the fund or such affiliate's investment adviser or principal underwriter. The description should include the procedures that the fund's investment adviser or any other third-party uses to vote proxies on the fund's behalf.[92] These requirements may be satisfied by including copies of the policies and procedures themselves.[93]

(5) Investment Advisory and Other Services

The statement of additional information must identify any person who controls the fund's investment adviser and the basis for such person's control.[94] The fund must identify any person who is an affiliated person of both the fund and the investment adviser and list all capacities in which the person is affiliated with each entity.[95]

The fund must disclose the method of calculating the investment advisory fee payable by the fund and the total dollar amounts that the fund paid to the investment adviser under the investment advisory contract for the last 3 fiscal years.[96] The statement of additional information must describe all services performed for or on behalf of the fund that its investment adviser supplied or paid for wholly or in substantial part,[97] as well as all fees, expenses and costs

---

87. Form N-1A Item 17.
88. Form N-1A Item 17(a).
89. Form N-1A Item 17(b).
90. Form N-1A Item 18(a).
91. Form N-1A Item 18(b).
92. Form N-1A Item 17(f).
93. Form N-1A Item 17(f), Instruction 1; *see* § 2.7, *supra.*
94. Form N-1A Item 19(a)(1).
95. Form N-1A Item 19(a)(2).
96. Form N-1A Item 19(a)(3).
97. Form N-1A Item 19(c)(1).

of the fund that are to be paid by persons other than an investment adviser or the fund and identify such persons.[98]

If any person, other than a director, officer, member of an advisory board, employee or investment adviser, regularly advises the fund or its investment adviser about investing in, purchasing or selling securities or other property or has the authority to determine what securities or other property the fund should purchase or sell and receives remuneration through any formal or informal understanding, the fund must disclose the person's name, the nature of the arrangement, the advice or information provided, the remuneration paid and how and by whom the remuneration was paid.[99]

This requirement does not apply to persons who provide only statistical and other factual information, advice about economic factors and trends, or advice on occasional transactions in specific securities, without generally advising on the fund's purchase or sale of securities, or to persons who advise the investment adviser or the fund solely through uniform publications distributed to subscribers.[100]

The fund must disclose the name and principal business address of its principal underwriter (if any), custodian and independent public accountant,[101] and describe generally the services provided by its custodian and independent public accountant.[102]

The statement of additional information must summarize the substantive provisions of any other management-related service contract that may be of interest to an investor, indicating the parties to the contract, the nature of the services provided, the basis of the compensation paid, the total compensation paid for the past 3 years and who paid it.[103] The summary should include any direct or indirect relationships of the service provider with the fund, the investment adviser or the principal underwriter.[104] This requirement includes "any contract with the Fund to keep, prepare or file accounts, books, records or other documents required under federal or state law, or to provide any similar services with respect to the daily administration of the Fund . . . ."[105] It does not include investment advisory agreements, agreements for custodial, transfer agent or dividend-paying services, or contracts for personal employment or outside legal or accounting services.[106]

(6) Portfolio Managers

The statement of additional information must include additional information about each person, or portfolio manager, who is identified in the fund's prospectus as being primarily responsible for the day-to-day management of

98. Form N-1A Item 19(c)(2).
99. Form N-1A Item 19(e).
100. Form N-1A Item 19(e), Instructions (a) and (b).
101. Form N-1A Items 19(b) and 19(h)(3).
102. Form N-1A Item 19(h)(3).
103. Form N-1A Item 19(d).
104. Form N-1A Item 19(d), Instruction 3.
105. Form N-1A Item 19(d), Instruction 1.
106. *Id.*

the fund's portfolio.[107] For each such portfolio manager, the fund must disclose the total number of registered investment companies, other pooled investment vehicles, and other accounts managed by him or her and the aggregate assets under his or her management in each such category. The statement of additional information also must disclose the number of those accounts with respect to which the portfolio manager earns a performance-based advisory fee, and the total assets in those accounts.[108]

The fund must disclose any material conflicts of interest that may arise in connection with the portfolio manager's management of the fund's portfolio and such other accounts, including conflicts among investment strategies of the accounts and in allocating investment opportunities among the accounts.[109] If the portfolio manager is part of a committee, team or group that is jointly and primarily responsible for the day-to-day management of another account, information concerning that account must be included.[110] Information must be disclosed as of the end of the fund's most recently completed fiscal year, unless the statement of additional information is part of the fund's initial registration or is being updated to reflect the addition of a new portfolio manager, in which case information must be provided as of the most recent practicable date.[111]

The statement of additional information must describe the structure and method of determining the compensation to be received by each portfolio manager, including salary, bonuses, deferred compensation and pension and retirement plans.[112] The criteria on which compensation is based must be described with specificity, but the value of the compensation is not required to be disclosed.[113] For example, the statement of additional information should disclose whether compensation is fixed, is based on the fund's pre- or post-tax performance and, if so, how it is determined, or is based on the value of the fund's assets and, if so, how it is determined.[114] Information must be disclosed as of the end of the fund's most recently completed fiscal year, unless the statement of additional information is part of the fund's initial registration or is being updated to reflect the addition of a new portfolio manager, in which case information must be provided as of the most recent practicable date.[115] The fund also must disclose the dollar range of the fund's equity securities that the portfolio manager owns.[116]

---

107. Form N-1A Item 20(a). *See* § 6.2.1.ii.a(4), *supra*.
108. Form N-1A Item 20(a)(2) and (3).
109. Form N-1A Item 20(a)(4).
110. Form N-1A Item 20(a), Instruction 2.
111. Form N-1A Item 20(a), Instruction 1.
112. Form N-1A Item 20(b).
113. Form N-1A Item 20(b) and Instruction 2 thereto.
114. *Id.*
115. Form N-1A Item 20(b), Instruction 1.
116. Form N-1A Item 20(c). The dollar ranges to be identified are: "none, $1-$10,000, $10,001-$50,000, $50,001-$100,000, $100,001-$500,000, $500,001-$1,000,000, or over $1,000,000." *Id.*

(7) Brokerage Allocation and Practices[117]

The statement of additional information must disclose how "transactions in portfolio securities are effected, including a general statement about brokerage commissions, markups and markdowns on principal transactions, and the aggregate amount of any brokerage commissions paid by it during its 3 most recent fiscal years."[118] The fund should explain the reasons for any material differences between the aggregate dollar amount of brokerage commissions it paid during its most recent fiscal year and either of the 2 preceding years.[119] The fund must disclose more detailed information about commissions it paid to any broker that is an affiliated person of the fund or that has an affiliate who is also an affiliated person of the fund, the investment adviser or the principal underwriter.[120]

The statement of additional information must describe how the fund selects brokers to effect its securities transactions and how it evaluates the overall reasonableness of brokerage commissions, including the factors that it considers in making these determinations.[121] If the fund considers the receipt of research services, or products or services other than brokerage or research services, it must identify the nature of such research services and specify any such other products and services.[122]

The fund must state "whether persons acting on the Fund's behalf are authorized to pay a broker a higher brokerage commission than another broker might have charged for the same transaction in recognition of the value of brokerage or research services provided by the broker."[123] The fund must explain if any research services provided by brokers through which it effects securities transactions may be used by the fund's investment adviser in servicing all of its accounts and whether or not all of these services may be used by the investment adviser in connection with the fund.[124] The fund also must explain any other policies or practices relating to the allocation of research services provided by brokers.[125] If the fund or its investment adviser directed the fund's brokerage transactions during the last fiscal year to a broker, whether through an agreement or understanding with the broker or through an internal allocation procedure, because of research services provided by the broker, the fund must state the amount of the transactions and the related commissions.[126]

(8) Capital Stock

The statement of additional information must disclose the name of each class of securities of the fund and provide a full description of the provisions and

117. *See also* Chapter 14, *infra*.
118. Form N-1A Item 21(a).
119. *Id.*
120. Form N-1A Item 21(b).
121. Form N-1A Item 21(c).
122. Form N-1A Item 21(c), Instructions 1 and 2. *See* § 14.2, *infra*.
123. Form N-1A Item 21(c), Instruction 3.
124. Form N-1A Item 21(c), Instruction 4.
125. *Id.*
126. Form N-1A Item 21(d).

characteristics of each class, including dividend, liquidation, voting (including a description of cumulative voting if it applies) and preference rights and transfer restrictions.[127] If the rights of one class affect those of another class, the fund must explain the limitation or qualification.[128] If the prospectus does not describe how the shares of the fund are offered to the public, the statement of additional information must do so.[129] Each type of purchase plan or offering must be described, including special arrangements with particular classes of investors, and how the fund determines the offering prices of the shares.[130]

(9) Taxation of the Fund

The statement of additional information must disclose any special or unusual tax aspects of the fund, such as taxation resulting from non-U.S. investments.[131]

(10) Underwriters

For each principal underwriter distributing securities of the fund, the statement of additional information must describe the nature of the obligation to distribute such securities, whether the offering is continuous and the aggregate dollar amount of underwriting commissions, and the amount retained by the principal underwriter for each of the fund's last 3 fiscal years.[132] The fund must provide detailed information about the commissions and other compensation that each principal underwriter who is an affiliated person of the fund or an affiliated person of such affiliated person received, directly or indirectly, from the fund during the fund's most recent fiscal year.[133]

In addition, the fund must disclose the name and address of any underwriter or dealer in the fund's shares who received any payments from the fund during the fund's last fiscal year, the amount paid and basis for determining that amount, the circumstances surrounding the payments and the consideration received by the fund.[134] This last requirement does not apply to payments made through deduction from the offering price at the time of sale or payments of the purchase price or commissions on the purchase and sale of portfolio securities.[135]

(11) Financial Statements

The statement of additional information must include audited financial statements and schedules that comply with Regulation S-X.[136]

---

127. Form N-1A Item 22.
128. Form N-1A Item 22(a), Instruction 2.
129. Form N-1A Item 23.
130. *Id.*
131. Form N-1A Item 24; *see also* Chapter 16, *infra*. The fund also must disclose whether it is or intends to qualify under Subchapter M of the Tax Code, 26 U.S.C. § 851, *et seq.*, and the consequences to the fund if it does not so qualify. Hedge funds do not qualify under Subchapter M of the Tax Code.
132. Form N-1A Item 25(a).
133. Form N-1A Item 25(b).
134. Form N-1A Item 25(c).
135. Form N-1A Item 25(c)(1), (2) and (3).
136. Form N-1A Item 27(a); 17 C.F.R. pt. 210.

iii. Form S-1

If a hedge fund were to register its securities under the Securities Act and Form N-1A were unavailable, the hedge fund would be required to use Form S-1. As described above, Form S-1 is used by an issuer that is not eligible to use any other form.[137] No other registration statement form would be available for most hedge funds.[138]

Form S-1 comprises cover pages and two parts. Part I specifies the information that must be included in a prospectus that the issuer must deliver to prospective investors.[139] Delivery of the prospectus must precede or accompany the delivery of any security for sale or delivery after sale.[140] Part II specifies the information and exhibits that must be filed with the SEC but delivered to investors only on request.[141]

Part I of Form S-1 requires that the following information, among other things, be included in the prospectus:

- a brief summary, in plain English,[142] of the information contained in the prospectus where the length and complexity of the prospectus makes a summary useful;[143]
- under the heading "Risk Factors," a logically organized and concise discussion, in plain English, of the most significant factors that make the offering speculative or risky and that explains how the risks affect the issuer or its securities;[144]
- a statement of the principal purposes for which the net proceeds of the securities offering are intended to be used and the approximate amount intended to be used for each such purpose;[145]
- a description of the factors considered in determining the offering price of the securities;[146]
- a description of the plan of distribution, including the identities of any principal underwriters, material relationships between such principal underwriters and the issuer, the terms of any agreements, arrangements or understandings with any brokers or dealers that will sell the securities, a description of the basis on which any securities will be offered (other

---

137. Form S-1 General Instruction I, 17 C.F.R. § 239.11.

138. Form S-3 General Instruction I.A.2, 17 C.F.R. § 239.13; Form S-4 General Instruction A.1; Form S-6 General Instruction 1; Form S-8 General Instruction A.1; Form SB-1 General Instruction A.1; Form S-11 General Instruction A; Form S-20 General Instruction I; Form SB-2 General Instruction A.1; Regulation S-B Rule 10(a)(1), 17 C.F.R. § 228.10(a)(1) (Regulation S-B rescinded, 73 F.R. 934 (Jan. 4, 2008)); and Regulation C Rule 405, 17 C.F.R. § 230.405.

139. Form S-1 Part I.

140. Securities Act § 5(b), 15 U.S.C. § 77e(b).

141. Form S-1 Part II.

142. *See* § 6.2.3, *infra.*

143. Form S-1 Item 1; Regulation S-K Item 503(a), 17 C.F.R. § 229.503(a). *See* § 6.3 *infra.*

144. Form S-1 Item 1; Regulation S-K Item 503(c), 17 C.F.R. § 229.503(c).

145. Form S-1 Item 4; Regulation S-K Item 504, 17 C.F.R. § 229.504.

146. Form S-1 Item 5; Regulation S-K Item 505, 17 C.F.R. § 229.505.

than cash), and a description of the underwriters' compensation and the amount of discounts and commissions to be paid for each security and in total;[147]

- a description of the securities being offered;[148]
- a description of the issuer's business;[149]
- a description of the issuer's materially important physical properties;[150]
- a description of any material pending legal proceedings, other than ordinary routine litigation incidental to the issuer's business, to which the issuer is a party or its property is subject;[151]
- a description of the principal U.S. market in which each class of the issuer's common equity is traded (or a statement that there is no public trading market for a class of common equity), the approximate number of holders of each class of common equity as of the latest practicable date, information concerning the frequency and amount of cash dividends paid during the past 2 fiscal years, and information concerning compensation plans of the issuer under which equity securities of the issuer are authorized for issuance;[152]
- audited financial statements and schedules for the issuer;[153]
- selected financial information of the issuer for each of the past 5 fiscal years and any additional fiscal years necessary to keep the information from being misleading;[154]
- management's discussion and analysis of the issuer's financial condition and results of operations;[155]
- information about changes in and disagreements with accountants during the 2 most recent fiscal years;[156]
- information about the issuer's directors and executive officers, executive compensation and security ownership of certain beneficial owners and management;[157]

---

147. Form S-1 Item 8; Regulation S-K Item 508, 17 C.F.R. § 229.508.
148. Form S-1 Item 9; Regulation S-K Item 202, 17 C.F.R. § 229.202.
149. Form S-1 Item 11(a); Regulation S-K Item 101, 17 C.F.R. § 229.101.
150. Form S-1 Item 11(b); Regulation S-K Item 102, 17 C.F.R. § 229.102.
151. Form S-1 Item 11(c); Regulation S-K Item 103, 17 C.F.R. § 229.103.
152. Form S-1 Item 11(d); Regulation S-K Item 201, 17 C.F.R. § 229.201.
153. Form S-1 Item 11(e). The requirements for financial statements are set forth in Regulation S-X, 17 C.F.R. pt. 210, and are not addressed in this book.
154. Form S-1 Item 11(f); Regulation S-K Item 301, 17 C.F.R. § 229.301.
155. Form S-1 Item 11(h); Regulation S-K Item 303, 17 C.F.R. § 229.303.
156. Form S-1 Item 11(i); Regulation S-K Item 304, 17 C.F.R. § 229.304.
157. Form S-1 Items 11(k), (l) and (m); Regulation S-K Items 401, 402 and 403, 17 C.F.R. §§ 229.401, 229.402 and 229.403. *See* Securities Act Release No. 33-8814 (June 29, 2007), 72 F.R. 37, 376 (July 9, 2007), at note 40.

- information about any transaction or series of similar transactions since the beginning of the issuer's last fiscal year, or any currently proposed transaction or series of similar transactions, involving more than $60,000 and in which any director or executive officer of the issuer, any nominee for election as a director of the issuer, any person who directly or indirectly beneficially owns more than 5 percent of any class of the issuer's voting securities, or any immediate family member of any of the foregoing persons, has a direct or indirect material interest;[158] and
- a description of the indemnification provisions relating to directors, officers and controlling persons of the issuer against liability arising under the Securities Act.[159]

The description of the indemnification provision must include a statement in substantially the following form:

> Insofar as indemnification for liabilities arising under the Securities Act of 1933 may be permitted to directors, officers or persons controlling the registrant pursuant to the foregoing provisions, the registrant has been informed that in the opinion of the Securities and Exchange Commission such indemnification is against public policy as expressed in the Act and is therefore unenforceable.[160]

2. Company Act

As discussed in Chapter 3, an investment company typically must register as such under the Company Act before offering its securities to investors.[161] As under the Securities Act, the SEC has adopted several different forms that investment companies may use to register under the Company Act. The registration form that most hedge funds would use to register with the SEC, if required to register under the Company Act, is Form N-1A, which is summarized above in section 6.2.1.ii.

3. Plain English Requirements

In 1998, the SEC adopted Securities Act Rule 421,[162] which requires issuers to use the SEC's version of plain English principles in drafting specified parts of a prospectus. Rule 421 applies to prospectuses under the Securities Act and the Company Act.[163] Under Rule 421, information "in a prospectus must be presented in a clear, concise and understandable manner."[164] The issuer should:

158. Form S-1 Item 11(n); Regulation S-K Item 404, 17 C.F.R. § 229.404.
159. Form S-1 Item 12; Regulation S-K Item 510, 17 C.F.R. § 229.510.
160. *Id.*
161. Company Act § 7(a), 15 U.S.C. § 80a-7(a).
162. 17 C.F.R. § 230.421.
163. *See* Form N-1A General Instruction B.4(c).
164. Securities Act Rule 421(b), 17 C.F.R. § 230.421(b).

- present information in clear, concise sections, paragraphs and sentences and, whenever possible, use short, explanatory sentences and bullet lists;
- use descriptive headings and subheadings;
- avoid frequent reliance on glossaries or defined terms as the primary means of explaining information in the prospectus and define terms in a glossary or other section of the document only if the meaning is unclear from the context and it facilitates understanding of the disclosure; and
- avoid legal and highly technical business terminology.[165]

In addition, "to enhance the readability of the prospectus, [the issuer] must use plain English principles in the organization, language, and design of the front and back cover pages, the summary, and the risk factors section."[166] Each of these sections should be drafted so that, at a minimum, it substantially complies with the SEC's plain English writing principles by using:

- short sentences;
- definite, concrete, everyday words;
- active voice;
- tabular presentation or bullet lists for complex material, wherever possible;
- no legal jargon or highly technical business terms; and
- no multiple negatives.[167]

An issuer may include pictures, logos, charts, graphs or other design elements, as long as the design is not misleading and the required information is clear. The rule encourages the use of tables, schedules, charts and graphic illustrations of the results of operations, balance sheet and other financial data that present the information in an understandable way. Any presentation must be consistent with the financial statements and nonfinancial information in the prospectus. Graphs and charts must be drawn to scale. Any information provided must not be misleading.[168] Although the SEC's plain English rules apply only to prospectuses used in public offerings or by mutual funds, the offering documents of hedge funds should comply with Rule 421 when feasible.

165. *Id.*
166. Securities Act Rule 421(d)(1), 17 C.F.R. § 230.421(d)(1).
167. Securities Act Rule 421(d)(2), 17 C.F.R. § 230.421(d)(2).
168. Securities Act Rule 421(d)(3), 17 C.F.R. § 230.421(d)(3).

§ 6.3 Disclosure Obligations in Connection with Private Offerings and Regulation D

1. Private Offerings Under Securities Act Section 4(a)(2)

An issuer seeking to rely on the private offering exemption from registration provided by Securities Act section 4(a)(2)[169] must give offerees access to "the same kind of information that the [Securities] Act would make available in the form of a registration statement."[170] Hedge funds ordinarily should satisfy this requirement by providing each offeree with a private offering memorandum that discloses the required information.[171] The private offering memorandum should be based on Company Act Form N-1A and Securities Act Form S-1, as discussed above in section 6.2.

2. Regulation D Rule 506(b) Offerings

Regulation D specifies information that must be delivered to non-accredited investors in a Rule 506(b) offering.[172] This information must be provided a "reasonable time before the sale" of the securities to a non-accredited investor.[173] Although Regulation D does not require that the specified information be furnished to purchasers if a hedge fund sells its interests only to accredited investors, the SEC has noted that "nothing in Regulation D states that an issuer need not give disclosure to an investor."[174] In light of the potential liability under the Securities Act and Exchange Act anti-fraud provisions (discussed below in section 6.4), a hedge fund should fully disclose all facts material to a decision whether to invest.

With respect to non-accredited investors, an issuer that is not subject to the reporting requirements of Exchange Act section 13 or 15(d) (such as a hedge fund) is required to deliver the same kind of information as would be required in Part I of a registration statement filed under the Securities Act on the form that the issuer would be entitled to use.[175] A 1988 SEC staff no-action letter directed a hedge fund to use Form N-1A to determine the information that it

169. *See* Chapter 5 and § 6.2.1.i, *supra,* and § 8.2, *infra.*

170. SEC v. Ralston Purina Co., 346 U.S. 119, 125-126, 73 S. Ct. 981 (1953).

171. Doran v. Petroleum Mgmt. Corp., et al., 545 F. 2d 893, 902 (5th Cir. 1977).

172. Regulation D Rule 502(b)(1), 17 C.F.R. § 230.502(b)(1). *See* § 5.3.2, *supra.*

173. *Id.*

174. Regulation D Rule 502(b)(1), 17 C.F.R. § 230.502(b)(1); Securities Act Release No. 33-6455, 48 F.R. 10,045 (Mar. 3, 1983).

175. Regulation D Rule 502(b)(2)(i)(A), 17 C.F.R. § 230.502(b)(2)(i)(A). An issuer that is eligible to use Regulation A may deliver the information required by that Regulation, but few hedge funds are eligible to use Regulation A because it is limited to offerings of securities with an aggregate offering price of $5,000,000 or less. *See* Regulation A Rule 251(b), 17 C.F.R. § 230.251(b).

is required to deliver under Regulation D.[176] The hedge fund is only required to deliver that information "to the extent material to an understanding of the issuer, its business and the securities being offered."[177]

The issuer must also deliver to non-accredited investors the financial statements that would be required in a registration statement filed with the SEC on the form that the issuer would be entitled to use.[178] Again, the SEC staff has stated that Form N-1A is the appropriate form for guidance concerning the appropriate financial statements to include in a disclosure document for a hedge fund.[179]

Regulation D also requires the issuer to identify the contents of material exhibits required to be filed with the SEC as part of the registration statement and make them available or provide them to the purchaser on the purchaser's written request a reasonable time before the purchase.[180] Among the exhibits required to be filed with a Form N-1A registration statement are the fund's articles or certificate of incorporation and bylaws, investment adviser agreements, custodial agreements, other material agreements, and legal opinions concerning whether the securities to be issued, when sold, will be legally issued, fully paid and nonassessable, and concerning the tax consequences that are material to investors, if the filing makes representations about tax consequences.[181] The SEC has stated that a hedge fund's disclosure documents should describe the contents of these legal opinions and the hedge fund should make the legal opinions available to purchasers.[182] In addition, if the hedge fund is organized as a limited partnership or limited liability company ("LLC"), its agreement of limited partnership or LLC agreement should be described and made available to investors.

As discussed above in section 5.3.2, the SEC has proposed (but at this writing has not adopted) amendments to its rules that, if adopted, would require additional disclosure in an offering under Rule 506(c), as well as a proposal to require Rule 506(c) offering materials to be filed with the SEC.

§ 6.4 Anti-Fraud Provisions

The Exchange Act and Securities Act anti-fraud provisions apply to sales of securities pursuant to the exemptions provided by Securities Act section 4(a)(2) and Regulation D.[183] An investor in a hedge fund may bring an action for fraud

176. Robert T. Willis, Jr., P.C., SEC No-Action Letter (Jan. 18, 1988).
177. *Id.*; Regulation D Rule 502(b)(2)(i), 17 C.F.R. § 230.502(b)(2)(i).
178. Regulation D Rule 502(b)(2)(i)(B)(*3*), 17 C.F.R. § 230.502(b)(2)(i)(B)(*3*).
179. Robert T. Willis, Jr., P.C., SEC No-Action Letter (Jan. 18, 1988).
180. Regulation D Rule 502(b)(2)(iii), 17 C.F.R. § 230.502(b)(2)(iii).
181. Form N-1A Items 23(i) and (j); Regulation S-K Item 601(b)(8), 17 C.F.R. § 229.601(b)(8).
182. Securities Act Release No. 33-6455, Question 52, 48 F.R. 10,045 (Mar. 3, 1983).
183. Landreth Timber Co. v. Landreth, et al., 471 U.S. 681, 692, 105 S. Ct. 2297, 2305 (1985).

under Exchange Act section 10(b)[184] and Rule 10b-5 thereunder.[185] The SEC also may bring an action against a hedge fund under these provisions and under Securities Act section 17(a).[186]

1. Exchange Act Provisions

Exchange Act section 10(b) provides that:

> It shall be unlawful for any person, directly or indirectly, by the use of any means or instrumentality of interstate commerce or of the mails, or of any facility of any national securities exchange . . . (b) to use or employ, in connection with the purchase or sale of any security registered on a national securities exchange or any security not so registered, or any securities-based swap agreement (as defined in Section 206B of the Gramm-Leach-Bliley Act), any manipulative or deceptive device or contrivance in contravention of such rules and regulations as the commission may prescribe as necessary or appropriate in the public interest or for the protection of investors.[187]

Pursuant to Exchange Act section 10(b), the SEC adopted Rule 10b-5 on May 21, 1942.[188] Rule 10b-5 provides that:

> It shall be unlawful for any person, directly or indirectly, by the use of any means or instrumentality of interstate commerce, or of the mails, or of any facility of any national securities exchange,
>
> > (a) to employ any device, scheme, or artifice to defraud,
> >
> > (b) to make any untrue statement of a material fact or to omit to state a material fact necessary in order to make the statements made, in light of the circumstances under which they were made, not misleading, or
> >
> > (c) to engage in any act, practice, or course of business which operates or would operate as a fraud or deceit upon any person,
>
> in connection with the purchase or sale of any security.[189]

The provisions of Exchange Act section 10(b) and Rule 10b-5 "are broad and, by repeated use of the word 'any,' are obviously meant to be inclusive."[190]

---

184. 15 U.S.C. § 78j(b).
185. 17 C.F.R. § 240.10b-5.
186. 15 U.S.C. § 77q(a).
187. 15 U.S.C. § 78j(b).
188. Exchange Act Release No. 34-3230, 13 F.R. 8,177 (May 21, 1942).
189. 17 C.F.R. § 240.10b-5.
190. Affiliated Ute Citizens of Utah, et al. v. United States, et al., 406 U.S. 128, 151, 92 S. Ct. 1456, 1471 (1972).

The SEC may enforce Rule 10b-5 by, among other things, imposing a monetary penalty on the offender or seeking an injunction against the offender.[191] In addition, the Supreme Court has recognized an implied private right of action under Exchange Act section 10(b) and Rule 10b-5, pursuant to which a purchaser or seller of securities may bring an action for fraud in connection with the purchase or sale.[192] Only a person that actually buys or sells a security, or that has contracted to buy or sell a security, may bring an action under Rule 10b-5.[193] A person that decides not to buy or sell a security based on an omission or misrepresentation does not have standing to sue under Rule 10b-5.[194] In addition, the private right of action is only against the seller of the securities, and does not apply to third parties or others who do not make a misleading omission or statement.[195] Rule 10b-5 applies to both oral and written contracts to buy or sell a security.[196]

i. Omissions

Rule 10b-5 prohibits any omission of a material fact that is necessary to make statements made, in light of the circumstances under which they were made, not misleading,[197] even if the statement giving rise to such duty is not required to be made. In other words, "a duty to speak the full truth arises when a defendant undertakes a duty to say anything."[198] In addition, liability under Rule 10b-5 may arise from an omission, even absent any affirmative representation by the party that omitted the information, if that party has a duty to disclose information, such as a fiduciary duty or other relation of trust and confidence.[199]

ii. Materiality

Rule 10b-5 only applies to omissions or misrepresentations that are material. The Supreme Court has determined that, in connection with Rule 10b-5, "an omitted fact is material if there is a substantial likelihood that a reasonable

---

191. Exchange Act § 21(d), 15 U.S.C. § 78u(d).

192. *See, e.g.,* Ernst & Ernst v. Hochfelder, et al., 425 U.S. 185, 196, 96 S. Ct. 1375, 1382 (1976); Blue Chip Stamps v. Manor Drug Stores, 421 U.S. 723, 730, 95 S. Ct. 1917, 1922-1923 (1975); Affiliated Ute Citizens v. United States, 406 U.S. 128, 150-154, 92 S. Ct. 1456, 1471-1472 (1972); Superintendent of Ins. of New York v. Bankers Life & Casualty Co., *et al.*, 404 U.S. 6, 13 n. 9, 92 S. Ct. 165, 169 n. 9 (1971).

193. Blue Chip Stamps v. Manor Drug Stores, 421 U.S. 723, 749, 95 S. Ct. 1917, 1932 (1975).

194. *Id.*

195. Stoneridge Inv. Partners, LLC v. Scientific-Atlanta, Inc., 552 U.S. 148, 165, 128 S. Ct. 761 (U.S. 2008); Janus Capital Group, Inc. v. First Derivative Traders, 564 U.S. ___, 131 S. Ct. 2296 (U.S. 2011).

196. The Wharf (Holdings) Limited, et al. v. United International Holdings, Inc., 532 U.S. 588, 594-595, 121 S. Ct. 1776, 1781 (2001).

197. Exchange Act Rule 10b-5, 17 C.F.R. § 240.10b-5.

198. Rubinstein v. Collins, 20 F.3d 160, 170 (5th Cir. 1994) (quoting First Virginia Bankshares v. Benson, 559 F.2d 1307, 1317 (5th Cir. 1977)).

199. Chiarella v. U.S., 445 U.S. 222, 228, 100 S. Ct. 1108, 1114 (1980). *See also* Affiliated Ute Citizens v. United States, 406 U.S. 128, 92 S. Ct. 1456 (1972).

shareholder would consider it important" in deciding whether to buy or sell.[200] "There must be a substantial likelihood that the disclosure of the omitted fact would have been viewed by the reasonable investor as having significantly altered the 'total mix' of information made available."[201]

A plaintiff may bring an action under Rule 10b-5 based on opinions and forward-looking statements included in an offering document.[202] "[S]uch statements of 'soft information' may be actionable misrepresentations if the speaker does not genuinely and reasonably believe them."[203] An issuer will not be liable for such statements, even if they prove to be incorrect, if "1) the speaker genuinely believes the statement is accurate; 2) there is a reasonable basis for that belief; and 3) the speaker is unaware of any undisclosed facts that would tend seriously to undermine the accuracy of the statement."[204]

Cautionary statements in the offering document may diminish the materiality of statements of opinion or forward-looking statements.[205] As the court in *In re Trump Casinos Securities Litigation* stated,

> . . . when an offering document's forecasts, opinions or projections are accompanied by meaningful cautionary statements, the forward-looking statements will not form the basis for a securities fraud claim if those statements did not affect the "total mix" of information the document provided investors. In other words, cautionary language, if sufficient, renders the alleged omissions or misrepresentations immaterial as a matter of law.[206]

Boilerplate disclaimers do not, however, affect the materiality of statements in an offering document. Instead, "the cautionary statements must be substantive and tailored to the specific future projections, estimates or opinions in the prospectus which the plaintiffs challenge."[207] In addition, "the inclusion of general cautionary language regarding a prediction would not excuse the alleged failure to reveal known material, adverse facts."[208]

---

200. Basic Inc., et al. v. Levinson, et al., 485 U.S. 224, 231, 108 S. Ct. 978, 983 (1988) (quoting TSC Industries, Inc. v. Northway, Inc., 426 U.S. 438, 449, 96 S. Ct. 2126, 2132 (1976)).

201. *Id.*

202. *See In re* Donald J. Trump Casino Sec. Lit., 7 F.3d 357, 368 (3rd Cir., 1993), *cert. denied,* Gollomp v. Trump, 510 U.S. 1178, 114 S. Ct. 1219 (1994).

203. *Id.* (citations omitted).

204. Rubinstein v. Collins, 20 F.3d 160, 166 (5th Cir. 1994) (citations omitted).

205. *See, e.g.*, Olkey v. Hyperion 1999 Term Trust, Inc., 98 F.3d 2 (2nd Cir. 1996); *In re* Donald J. Trump Casino Sec. Lit., 7 F.3d 357, 371-72 (3rd Cir., 1993), *cert. denied,* Gollomp v. Trump, 510 U.S. 1178, 114 S. Ct. 1219 (1994); *In re* Worlds of Wonder Securities Litigation, 35 F.3d 1407, 1413 (9th Cir. 1994).

206. *In re* Donald J. Trump Casino Sec. Lit., 7 F.3d 357, 371-72 (3rd Cir., 1993), *cert. denied,* Gollomp v. Trump, 510 U.S. 1178, 114 S. Ct. 1219 (1994).

207. *Id.* at 368.

208. Rubinstein v. Collins, 20 F.3d 160, 171 (5th Cir. 1994).

iii. Reliance

To succeed in a claim under Rule 10b-5, a plaintiff must prove that it relied on an omission or misrepresentation.[209] The injured party can demonstrate reliance in the case of an omission, if the facts withheld are "material in the sense that a reasonable investor might have considered them important in the making of this decision."[210] Under the "bespeaks caution" doctrine discussed above in section 6.4.1.ii, a plaintiff may not be able to prove reliance where the potential risks have been adequately disclosed.[211]

iv. Scienter

A private plaintiff seeking damages under Rule 10b-5 must demonstrate that the defendants acted with scienter.[212] Scienter also is a required element in an action for injunctive relief under section 10(b) and Rule 10b-5,[213] and in any action brought by the SEC under section 10(b) or Rule 10b-5.[214] "Scienter" is a "mental state embracing intent to deceive, manipulate or defraud."[215] In determining what rises to the level of scienter, however, the courts have reached varying conclusions. Scienter has been variously held to require actual knowledge, constructive knowledge, intent to defraud or recklessness.[216]

2. Securities Act Provisions

Securities Act sections 11 and 12(a)(2) provide express private rights of actions to purchasers of securities.[217] Securities Act section 11 applies, however, only to statements in registration statements filed with the SEC.[218] Similarly, the Supreme Court has held that Securities Act section 12(a)(2) applies only to statements in prospectuses and oral communications relating to public offerings of securities.[219] Accordingly, neither of these provisions applies to the sale of securities in a hedge fund pursuant to the exemptions from registration provided by Securities Act section 4(a)(2) and Regulation D.

---

209. Basic Inc., et al. v. Levinson, et al., 485 U.S. 224, 243, 108 S. Ct. 978, 989 (1988).

210. Affiliated Ute Citizens of Utah, et al. v. U.S., et al., 406 U.S. 128, 151, 92 S. Ct. 1456, 1471 (1972) (citations omitted).

211. Rubinstein v. Collins, 20 F.3d 160, 167 (1994).

212. Ernst & Ernst v. Hochfelder, et al., 425 U.S. 185, 193, 96 S. Ct. 1375, 1381 (1976).

213. Aaron v. SEC, 446 U.S. 680, 691, 100 S. Ct. 1945, 1952-1953 (1980).

214. *Id.*

215. Ernst & Ernst v. Hochfelder, et al., 425 U.S. 185, 193 n. 12, 96 S. Ct. 1375, 1381 n. 12 (1976).

216. *See* 4 Alan R. Bromberg & Lewis D. Lowenfels, *Bromberg and Lowenfels on Securities Fraud & Commodities Fraud* (2d Ed.), § 7:125 *et seq.*, and cases cited therein.

217. Securities Act §§ 11(a) and 12(a)(2), 15 U.S.C. §§ 77k(a) and 77l(a)(2).

218. Securities Act § 11(a), 15 U.S.C. § 77k(a).

219. Gustafson, et al. v. Alloyd Co., Inc., et al., 513 U.S. 561, 584, 115 S. Ct. 1061, 1073-74 (1995).

On the other hand, Securities Act section 17(a) applies to any "offer or sale of any securities." It provides that:

> It shall be unlawful for any person in the offer or sale of any securities or any security-based swap agreement (as defined in Section 206B of the Graham-Leach-Bliley Act) by the use of any means or instruments of transportation or communication in interstate commerce or by use of the mails, directly or indirectly –
>
> (1) to employ any device, scheme or artifice to defraud, or
>
> (2) to obtain money or property by means of any untrue statement of material fact or any omission to state a material fact necessary in order to make the statements made, in light of the circumstances under which they were made, not misleading; or
>
> (3) to engage in any transaction, practice, or course of business which operates or would operate as a fraud or deceit upon the purchaser.[220]

Although this statute is similar to Exchange Act Rule 10b-5, discussed above in section 6.4.1, the two provisions have been interpreted differently. Most courts that have considered the issue have held that no private right of action can be implied under Securities Act section 17(a).[221] The Supreme Court has identified the issue in several cases, but has refused to address whether an implied cause of action exists under section 17(a).[222] Although the SEC must prove scienter under Rule 10b-5, it must only prove scienter with respect to subsection 1 of section 17(a).[223] Subsections 17(a)(2) and 17(a)(3) require a showing of only negligence by the defendant.[224] Section 17(a) applies only to fraud by a seller of securities, while Rule 10b-5 applies to fraud by either a buyer or a seller.[225]

---

220. 15 U.S.C. § 77q(a).

221. *See* Finkel, et al., v. Stratton Corp., et al., 962 F.2d 169, 175 (2nd Cir., 1992); Newcome v. Esrey, et al., 862 F.2d 1099, 1101 (4th Cir., 1988); Landry, et al., v. All American Assurance Company, et al., 688 F.2d 381, 391 (5th Cir., 1982); Schlifke v. Seafirst Corp., 866 F.2d 935, 942-943 (7th Cir., 1989); Deviries v. Prudential-Bache Securities, Inc., 805 F.2d 326, 328 (8th Cir., 1986); *In re* Washington Public Power Supply System Sec. Lit., 823 F.2d 1349, 1358 (9th Cir., 1987); Bath, et al., v. Bushkin, Gaims, Gaines and Jonas, et al., 913 F.2d 817, 819 (10th Cir., 1990), overruled on other grounds by Rotella v. Wood, et al., 528 U.S. 549, 120 S.Ct. 1075 (2000); Currie v. Cayman Resources Corp., et al., 835 F.2d 780, 784-785 (11th Cir., 1988). The Sixth Circuit recognized, however, a private cause of action under § 17(a) in Kellman v. ICS, Inc., 447 F.2d 1305, 1308-09 (6th Cir., 1971), and Craighead, et al., v. E.F. Hutton & Co., Inc., et al., 899 F. 2d 485, 492 (6th Cir., 1990).

222. *See, e.g.*, Aaron v. SEC, 446 U.S. 680, 689, 100 S. Ct. 1945, 1951-1952 (1980).

223. *See id.* at 701-702.

224. *Id.*

225. Securities Act § 17(a), 15 U.S.C. § 77q(a); Exchange Act Rule 10b-5, 17 C.F.R. § 240.10b-5.

§ 6.5 Disclosure Obligations Under the Advisers Act

1. Rule 206(4)-8: Pooled Investment Vehicles

Advisers Act Rule 206(4)-8[226] provides that it is unlawful for any registered or unregistered investment adviser that advises a pooled investment vehicle to defraud any investor or prospective investor in the pooled investment vehicle. Rule 206(4)-8(a) provides:

> It shall constitute a fraudulent, deceptive, or manipulative act, practice, or course of business within the meaning of Section 206(4) of the Act (15 U.S.C. 80b-6(4)) for any investment adviser to a pooled investment vehicle to:
>
> (1) Make any untrue statement of a material fact or to omit to state a material fact necessary to make the statements made, in the light of the circumstances under which they were made, not misleading, to any investor or prospective investor in the pooled investment vehicle; or
>
> (2) Otherwise engage in any act, practice, or course of business that is fraudulent, deceptive, or manipulative with respect to any investor or prospective investor in the pooled investment vehicle.[227]

The SEC adopted Rule 206(4)-8 to "clarify, in light of [the decision in *Goldstein v. SEC*[228]], the Commission's ability to bring enforcement actions under the [Advisers Act] against investment advisers who defraud investors or prospective investors in a hedge fund or other pooled investment vehicle."[229] The *Goldstein* court rejected the SEC's view that each investor in a hedge fund is a client of the hedge fund's investment adviser, for purposes of the private adviser exemption in Advisers Act section 203(b)(3), which was subsequently repealed by the Dodd-Frank Act. Rule 206(4)-8 clarifies that the anti-fraud protections of Advisers Act section 206(4) extend not only to clients of investment advisers (including hedge funds) but also to investors in those client funds.

"Pooled investment vehicle" includes "any company that would be an investment company under Section 3(a) of [the Company] Act but for the exclusion provided from that definition by either Section 3(c)(1) or Section 3(c)(7) of [the Company] Act."[230] Hedge funds, venture capital funds and private equity funds are all considered pooled investment vehicles. The SEC stated in the adopting release, however, that the rule does not alter the SEC's jurisdictional

---

226. 17 C.F.R. § 275.206(4)-8.

227. Advisers Act Rule 206(4)-8(a), 17 C.F.R. § 275.206(4)-8(a).

228. 451 F.3d 873 (D.C. Cir. 2006).

229. Advisers Act Release No. 2628 (Aug. 3, 2007), 72 F.R. 44756 (Aug. 9, 2007), at "Summary."

230. Advisers Act Rule 206(4)-8(b), 17 C.F.R. § 275.206(4)-8(b). *See* Chapter 3, *supra*.

authority over offshore investment advisers and their interaction with non-U.S. investors.[231]

Rule 206(4)-8 applies not only to disclosure, but also to deceptive conduct, and applies before and after the investor purchases an interest in the pooled investment vehicle.[232] According to the adopting release, Rule 206(4)-8 did not create any new fiduciary duty,[233] but it did create a new duty to take sufficient care to avoid negligent conduct that constitutes fraud.[234] Rule 206(4)-8 did not create a private right of action.[235]

The Asset Managers' Committee of the President's Working Group on Financial Markets recommends that a manager of a hedge fund "establish a disclosure framework designed to disclose material information with sufficient frequency and detail, including with respect to financial and risk information and potential conflicts of interest, so that investors are able to (i) make informed decisions regarding investments in the fund, and (ii) appropriately monitor or manage the risks associated with exposure to the fund."[236] The report includes detailed suggestions for both the hedge fund's offering materials and ongoing reporting to investors.

2. Part 2 of Form ADV—Brochure

An investment adviser registered with the SEC is required to furnish a written disclosure document (a "brochure") and one or more brochure supplements to clients and prospective clients.[237] Part 2 of Form ADV sets out the minimum disclosure that is required to be included in the brochure (Part 2A) and supplement (Part 2B).[238] Investment advisers typically prepare Parts 2A and 2B of Form ADV to use as their brochures and supplements. The brochure and supplement contain narrative descriptions of various aspects of the investment adviser's business, and must be drafted in "plain English."[239]

The investment adviser is initially required to deliver its brochure at or before the time it enters into an advisory agreement with the client.[240] The brochure must be updated annually, when the investment adviser files its annual Form ADV update, and between annual amendments if any information in the

231. Advisers Act Release No. 2628 (Aug. 3, 2007), 72 F.R. 44,756 (Aug. 9, 2007), at note 16.

232. *Id.* at Part II.C.

233. *Id.* at Part II.D.

234. *Id.*

235. *Id.* at footnote 43 and accompanying text.

236. Asset Managers' Committee Report, Jan. 15, 2009, *available at* http://www.amaicmte.org/Asset.aspx.

237. Advisers Act Rule 204-3(a) and (b), 17 C.F.R. § 275.204-3(a) and (b).

238. Advisers Act Rule 204-3(a), 17 C.F.R. § 275.204-3(a). *See* § 8.7, *infra.*

239. Form ADV General Instruction 2 for Part 2 of Form ADV. *See* § 6.2.3, *supra.*

240. Advisers Act Rule 204-3(b)(1), 17 C.F.R. § 275.204-3(b)(1). Although a limited partner of a hedge fund is not considered a "client," the SEC has indicated that an investment adviser's fiduciary duty may require it to disclose certain information to investors in a hedge fund. SEC Release No. IA-3060, 75 F.R. 49,234, 49,246 n. 192 (Jul. 28, 2010).

brochure becomes materially inaccurate.[241] Each year, if an investment adviser's brochure has changed materially since its last annual updating amendment, the investment adviser must deliver to its clients, without charge, within 120 days after its fiscal year-end, either a copy of the current brochure (which includes a summary of the material changes to it) or a summary of the material changes and an offer to provide a full copy of the current brochure.[242]

The brochure must describe the investment adviser's business and services, fees and other compensation, typical clients, and investment strategy and the associated risks.[243] The investment adviser must disclose whether it receives any performance-based compensation. If it does, and it also manages accounts that do not pay performance-based compensation, it must disclose this fact, the conflicts of interest presented by the different fees, and how it addresses those conflicts.[244]

In addition, the brochure must disclose all material facts about any "legal or disciplinary events that are material to a client's or prospective client's evaluation of [the investment adviser's] advisory business or the integrity of [its] management."[245] The SEC has established a rebuttable presumption that each of the following events involving an investment adviser or one of its management persons that is not resolved in such person's favor or subsequently reversed, suspended or vacated is material for 10 years after the date of the event:

- a criminal or civil action in a court of competent jurisdiction in which the person (a) was convicted of or pleaded guilty or no contest to (i) a felony, (ii) a misdemeanor that involved investments or an investment-related business, fraud, false statements or omissions, wrongful taking of property, bribery, perjury, forgery, counterfeiting or extortion, or (iii) a conspiracy to commit either (i) or (ii), (b) is the named subject of a pending criminal proceeding that involves any of the elements in (a)(ii), (c) was found to have been involved in a violation of an investment-related statute or regulations, or (d) was the subject of any order, judgment or decree permanently or temporarily enjoining the person from, or otherwise limiting the person from, engaging in any investment-related activity or violating any investment-related rule or order;[246]
- any administrative proceeding before the SEC or any other federal, state or foreign financial regulatory agency in which the person (a) was found to have caused an investment-related business to lose its authorization to do business or (b) was found to have been involved in a violation of any investment-related statute or regulation and was the subject of an order by such agency (i) denying, suspending or revoking the authorization of the person to act in an investment-related

241. Instruction 4 to Part 2A of Form ADV.

242. Advisers Act Rule 204-3(b)(2), 17 C.F.R. § 275.204-3(b)(2).

243. Form ADV Part 2A Items 4, 5, 7 and 8.

244. Form ADV Part 2A Item 6. Performance fees and allocations are discussed in § 15.2, *infra*.

245. Form ADV Part 2A Item 9.

246. Form ADV Part 2A Item 9.A.

business, (ii) barring or suspending the person's association with an investment-related business, (iii) otherwise significantly limiting the person's investment-related activities or (iv) imposing on the person a civil money penalty of more than $2,500;[247] or

- any self-regulatory organization proceeding in which the person (a) was found to have caused an investment-related business to lose its authorization to do business or (b) was found to have been involved in a violation of such organization's rules and was barred or suspended from membership or from association with other members or expelled from membership, fined more than $2,500, or otherwise significantly limited from investment-related activities.[248]

The date of any of these events is the date on which the final order, judgment or decree is entered, or the date on which all rights of appeal from a preliminary order, judgment or decree lapse. Even if a litigation or disciplinary event does not fall into any of the categories above or more than 10 years have passed since the event, it must be disclosed if a client may consider it material.[249]

A "management person" is a person "with power to exercise, directly or indirectly, a controlling influence over the management or policies of an adviser which is a company or to determine the general investment advice given to clients."[250] "Investment-related" means "pertaining to securities, commodities, banking, insurance, or real estate (including, but not limited to, acting as or being associated with a broker-dealer, investment company, investment adviser, government securities broker or dealer, municipal securities dealer, bank, savings and loan association, entity or person required to be registered under the [CEA] or fiduciary)."[251] A "self-regulatory organization" is "any securities or commodities exchange, registered association, or registered clearing agency."[252] "Found" means "determined or ascertained by adjudication or consent in a final [self-regulatory organization] proceeding, administrative proceeding or court action."[253] "Involved" means "acting or aiding, abetting, causing, counseling, commanding, inducing, conspiring with or failing reasonably to supervise another in doing an act."[254]

The brochure must also disclose the investment adviser's practices in selecting brokers to execute client transactions, including the use of research and soft-dollar benefits and the conflicts of interest presented by these arrangements, and aggregation of client trades.[255] It must disclose how frequently

---

247. Form ADV Part 2A Item 9.B.

248. Form ADV Part 2A Item 9.C.

249. Form ADV Part 2A Item 9. This list of events that are presumed to be material includes most but not all the events which an investment adviser must disclose in Part 1A of Form ADV. *See* § 2.4.

250. Form ADV Glossary.

251. *Id.*

252. *Id.*

253. *Id.*

254. *Id.*

255. Form ADV Part 2A Item 12.

the investment adviser reviews client accounts, and whether it compensates outside persons for client referrals.[256] An investment adviser that manages a hedge fund must disclose information about account statements that custodians send to its investors, if it relies on those account statements to comply with the custody rule.[257] The brochure must describe the investment adviser's proxy voting policies and procedures, describe how clients can obtain a copy of the policies and procedures, and disclose how clients may obtain information about the investment adviser's voting of securities on clients' behalf.[258]

The brochure must disclose any material fact about the financial condition of the investment adviser "that is reasonably likely to impair [the investment adviser's] ability to meet contractual commitments to clients."[259] This requirement applies only if the investment adviser has express or implied discretionary authority over the client's funds or securities or custody of the client's funds or securities, as typically is the case for investment advisers to hedge funds, or if the investment adviser requires the client to prepay advisory fees of more than $1,200 more than 6 months in advance.[260]

An SEC-registered investment adviser must also deliver to clients a brochure supplement for each person who has discretionary authority over a client's assets (such as a portfolio manager), and each person who formulates advice and has direct client contact (each, an "advisory person").[261] As noted above, the supplement is generally prepared on Part 2B of Form ADV. The relevant supplements must be delivered to clients before or at the time that a particular person provides advice to the client. If a team of more than 5 persons makes investment decisions, supplements are only required for the 5 advisory persons with the most significant responsibility for those investment decisions.[262] Supplements are not required to be delivered annually, but updated information must be delivered for an advisory person if certain disciplinary information must be revised in that advisory person's supplement.

The supplement must include the name of the advisory person, his or her age, education and business background, and professional qualifications.[263] It must

256. Form ADV Part 2A Items 13 and 14. Advisers Act Rule 206(4)-3 (the "solicitor's rule") does not apply to a finder who introduces investors to a hedge fund, if the investors are not also entering into a contract for advisory services. Mayer Brown LLP, SEC No-Action Letter (July 28, 2008). *See* §§ 8.8 and 10.1.3, *infra*. In the brochure, although hedge fund investors are not considered clients, an investment adviser that compensates such a finder should disclose the relationship between the hedge fund and the finder (including the compensation). The disclosure should also discuss the conflicts of interest that arise from the compensation arrangement.

257. Form ADV Part 2A Items 15 and 16. *See* § 12.1.1.iv, *infra*, regarding the account statement delivery requirements in the custody rule, Advisers Act Rule 206(4)-2, 17 C.F.R. § 275.206(4)-2.

258. Form ADV Part 2A Item 17. This disclosure is also required under Advisers Act Rules 206(4)-6(b) and 206(4)-6(c), 17 C.F.R. §§ 275.206(4)-6(b) and 275.206(4)-6(c).

259. Form ADV Part 2A Item 18.B.

260. *Id. See* § 2.5, *supra*, and Chapter 12, *infra*.

261. Advisers Act Rule 204-3(b)(3), 17 C.F.R. § 275.204-3(b)(3).

262. Form ADV Part 2B Note to Instruction 2.

263. Form ADV Part 2B Items 1 and 2.

disclose all material facts regarding any legal or disciplinary event involving the advisory person that is material to a client's or investor's evaluation of the advisory person.[264] The supplement must also disclose the advisory person's other investment-related businesses, if any, the conflicts of interest presented by those activities, certain bonus and compensation arrangements, and how the investment adviser supervises the advisory person's advisory activities.[265] Supplements must be in plain English, as described above. SEC-registered investment advisers are not required to file their supplements on the IARD or otherwise.

Most states have adopted rules similar to the SEC's brochure rule, requiring that any investment adviser registered with that state deliver Part 2 of its Form ADV, or a brochure and supplements containing similar information, to clients and prospective clients.[266] Part 2A of Form ADV requires a state-registered investment adviser to disclose additional information in its brochure, including the identity and background information of its management, any other business in which it is engaged, additional disclosures about performance-based fees and compensation, and additional disclosures about certain litigation, arbitrations and administrative proceedings.[267] A state-registered investment adviser may be required to disclose certain additional litigation and administrative proceedings in its supplements.[268]

General principles of fiduciary duty suggest that an investment adviser should comply with the Advisers Act brochure rule as if it were SEC-registered, even if it is not registered with the SEC or in a state that has a similar rule. Delivering a brochure does not, however, relieve an investment adviser of any obligations it has to disclose information to its advisory clients under any other applicable provision of the Advisers Act or any other federal or state law.[269]

3. Form PF

An investment adviser must file Form PF if it has at least $150,000,000 of regulatory assets under management attributable to private funds (including in some cases separate accounts that are managed using the same investment strategy and private funds managed by the adviser's affiliates) and is registered (or required to be registered) either with the SEC as an investment adviser or with the CFTC as a commodity pool operator or commodity trading adviser.[270]

---

264. Form ADV Part 2B Item 3. Part 1A, Item 3 of Part 2B lists civil, criminal and administrative proceedings that are deemed to be material. Part 2B, Item 3, also lists any proceeding in which the advisory person suffered the revocation or suspension of a professional attainment, designation or license because of a violation of rules relating to professional conduct, or resigned while such a proceeding was pending. Form ADV, Part 2B, Item 3.

265. Form ADV Part 2B Items 4, 5 and 6.

266. *See, e.g.*, Unif. Sec. Act Rule 203(b)-1, 1 Blue Sky Law Rptr. (CCH) ¶ 5523.20. *See* Chapter 7, *infra*.

267. Form ADV Part 2A Item 19.

268. Form ADV Part 2B, Item 7.

269. Advisers Act Rule 204-3(e), 17 C.F.R. § 275.204-3(e).

270. Advisers Act Rule 204(b)-1, 17 C.F.R. § 275.204(b)-1.

A "private fund" is a fund that would be included in the definition of investment company under the Company Act but for the exceptions under Company Act section 3(c)(1) or (7).[271]

Form PF is filed electronically through the Form PF filing system on the PFRD website (an electronic filing system similar to the IARD). Form PF is not available to the public,[272] but some investors request copies of an investment adviser's Form PF as part of their due diligence process.

The information that an investment adviser must provide on Form PF depends on the amount of its regulatory assets under management.[273] Form PF consists of 5 sections. All investment advisers that file Form PF must complete section 1. Section 2 applies only to an investment adviser that has more than $1,500,000,000 in private fund regulatory assets under management. Sections 3 and 4 apply only to large liquidity fund advisers and large private equity fund advisers, respectively. Section 5 applies only to an investment adviser that is requesting a temporary hardship exemption from filing Form PF. Sections 1 and 2 are summarized below.

i. Form PF—Section 1

Section 1a requires identifying information about the adviser and its related persons that are reporting on the Form PF with the investment adviser, including each entity's legal name and identifying numbers, if any.[274] The investment adviser must provide a breakdown of its regulatory assets under management and net assets under management for each type of fund that it manages (such as hedge, liquidity, private equity, real estate, securitized assets, venture capital and other private funds).[275]

Section 1b requires financial information for each reporting fund, including gross and net asset values, equity investments in other private funds and the values of parallel managed accounts. This information must be reported separately for each private fund, or each master-feeder set of funds or parallel funds managed by the investment adviser.[276] The information includes the amount of borrowings, with the percentage borrowed from U.S. and non-U.S. financial and nonfinancial institutions, and the aggregate value of any outstanding derivative positions. The investment adviser must categorize assets and liabilities in accordance with the Levels 1, 2 and 3 hierarchy of GAAP, based on the valuation method used for such assets and liabilities, and show monthly gross and net performance.[277]

Section 1b also requires beneficial ownership information by categories of investors.[278] The investment adviser must report the percentage that is owned

271. 15 U.S.C. 80b-2(a)(29).

272. *See* "Federal Information Law and Requirements for a Collection of Information" in Form PF: General Instructions.

273. Form PF: General Instruction 3.

274. Form PF § 1a, Items A and B.

275. *Id.*

276. Form PF, General Instruction 6.

277. Form PF § 1b, Items A, B and C.

278. Form PF § 1b, Item B, § 16.

in the aggregate by each fund's 5 largest beneficial owners and the approximate percentages that are beneficially owned by investor category (such as U.S. individuals, non-U.S. individuals, broker-dealers and insurance companies).

Section 1c applies separately to each hedge fund managed by the investment adviser. In Form PF, a "hedge fund" is generally any private fund that may use leverage over certain thresholds or sell securities short, or as to which the manager receives performance-based compensation. Section 1c requires the hedge fund's name and investment strategy or strategies, and the percentage of the hedge fund that is managed using high-frequency trading strategies.[279] The investment adviser must identify in section 1c the top 5 counterparties with whom each hedge fund has the greatest net counterparty credit exposure. Section 1c requires breakdowns of trading and clearing mechanisms used during the reporting period, including the estimated percentages of (a) securities (other than derivatives) traded on a regulated exchange versus over the counter, (b) derivatives traded on a regulated exchange or swap execution facility versus over the counter, (c) derivatives cleared by a central clearing party versus transacted bilaterally, (d) repurchase trades cleared by a central clearing party versus transacted bilaterally versus arranged as a tri-party trade, and (e) transactions not described in items (a) through (d).

ii. Form PF— Section 2

An investment adviser that, together with its related persons, had private fund regulatory assets under management of at least $1,500,000,000 as of the last day of any month in the fiscal quarter preceding its most recently completed fiscal quarter must also complete section 2 of Form PF.[280] Section 2a requires aggregate information for all of the hedge funds advised by the investment adviser, and section 2b requires information specific to each individual hedge fund that the investment adviser manages that had an NAV of at least $500,000,000 as of any month-end in the prior fiscal quarter.[281]

Section 2a requires the dollar value of long and short positions as of the last day of each month of the reporting period for a variety of asset classifications, including listed equity, unlisted equity, derivatives (on both listed and unlisted equity), corporate bonds, convertible bonds, sovereign and municipal bonds, repurchase agreements, asset-backed securities and structured products, credit derivatives, foreign exchange derivatives, interest rate derivatives, commodities (physical and derivatives), real estate, and cash and cash equivalents.

Further sub-categorization is required in most asset classes. For example, many asset classes require further identification as to the amount of those assets that were or were not issued by financial institutions. Section 2a also requires that the investment adviser provide a breakdown of the percentage of its total hedge-fund-related assets by geographical region, including the percentages invested in Africa, Asia and Pacific, Europe, Middle East, North America and South

279. Form PF § 1c, Items A and B.
280. Form PF, General Instruction 3.
281. Form PF §§ 2a and 2b.

America. Section 2a also requires a further breakdown by certain countries, including Brazil, China, India, Japan, Russia and the United States.[282]

Section 2b requires risk-related information for each hedge fund that meets the asset threshold described above, such as value-at-risk, the effect of changes in certain market factors (including equity price, risk-free interest rates, credit spreads, currency rates, commodity prices, option-implied volatilities and default rates) on the fund's long- and short-term components, and any other risk metrics the investment adviser deems important in managing the fund's risk. Section 2b also requires information about each such hedge fund's (a) unsecured and secured borrowing for each month in the reporting period, which must be further divided into categories of borrowings via prime brokers, reverse repurchase agreements and other sources and categories of U.S. and non-U.S. financial and nonfinancial institutions, and the value of certain collateral for secured borrowing, (b) derivative positions during the reporting period, including the aggregate value of such positions that were not cleared through a clearinghouse, and the collateral posted for those positions, (c) the aggregate amount of borrowings by and cash financing still available to the fund, allocated in relation to specified future time frames to show the future availability of credit to the fund, and (d) the name and amount owed to each creditor to which the fund owes more than 5 percent of its NAV.[283]

Section 2b also requires disclosure of the percentage of each such fund's assets in side pockets, indicate whether any fund assets have been placed in side pockets since the last reporting period, and information relating to withdrawal and redemption restrictions, including whether the fund uses gate or suspension provisions and the percentage of the fund's NAV that may not be withdrawn for designated periods of time.[284]

§ 6.6 Regulatory Guidance Concerning Disclosure of Side Letters

On occasion, a hedge fund investor may request or require the hedge fund or its general partner or investment adviser to enter into a "side letter," which is typically a separate, confidential agreement with the investor that gives the investor preferential rights or privileges not given to other investors in the hedge fund.[285] For example, a side letter may provide the investor access to more information than is provided to other investors in the hedge fund, or may give the investor the right to withdraw funds or redeem its interest on shorter notice or without regard to limitations or conditions that would otherwise apply, or may

282. Form PF § 2a.
283. Form PF § 2b.
284. Form PF § 2b, Item E.
285. The legal issues arising from a side letter with one hedge fund investor and related disclosure are discussed in Umbach v. Carrington Investment Partners, 2009 U.S. Dist. LEXIS 11952 (D. Conn. 2009).

give assurances about the hedge fund's or its general partner's or investment adviser's status under ERISA.

Apart from the disclosure requirements discussed generally above in sections 6.3, 6.4 and 6.5, U.S. law provides little specific guidance about whether the existence or terms of a side letter must be disclosed to other investors or whether the general partner or investment adviser of the hedge fund breaches a fiduciary or other duty to the other investors by granting special rights to selected investors.[286] Two private sector committees established by the President's Working Group on Financial Markets released a report of best practices by hedge funds, which states that investment advisers should disclose the material terms of side letters that may affect other fund investors adversely.[287] In addition to being a best practice, such disclosure may be required by law in many circumstances.

The U.K. Financial Services Authority (FSA) issued a discussion paper[288] in 2005 and a feedback statement[289] in 2006 concerning the market risks and regulatory environment for hedge funds and their managers in the United Kingdom. The discussion paper and the feedback statement suggested that hedge funds and their managers had made insufficient disclosures concerning side letters in some cases. The Alternative Investment Management Association (AIMA) subsequently published a U.K. industry guidance note to inform its members and the industry about meetings between AIMA and the FSA and their conclusions about side letters.[290] The FSA, in exercising its regulatory functions, will require hedge funds to "disclose the existence of side letters which contain 'material terms'...." Other side letters do not need to be disclosed. According to AIMA, a material term is:

> Any term the effect of which might reasonably be expected to be to provide an investor with more favourable treatment than other holders of the same class of share or interest which enhances that investor's ability either (i) to redeem shares or interests of that class or (ii) to make a determination as to whether to redeem shares or interests of that class, and which in either case might, therefore, reasonably be expected to put

286. Testimony by Susan Ferris Wyderko Concerning Hedge Funds Before the Subcommittee on Securities and Investment of the U.S. Senate Committee on Banking, Housing, and Urban Affairs (May 16, 2006), *available at* http://www.sec.gov/news/testimony/ts051606sfw.htm. *See also* § 2.7, *supra*.

287. Asset Managers' Committee Report, Jan. 15, 2009, *available at* http://www.amaicmte.org/Asset.aspx.

288. Hedge funds: A Discussion of Risk and Regulatory Engagement, FSA Discussion Paper 05/04 (June 2005).

289. Hedge funds: A Discussion of Risk and Regulatory Engagement, FSA Feedback Statement 06/02 (Mar. 2006).

290. AIMA's Industry Guidance Note on Side Letters (Sep. 2006), *available at* http://www.aima.org/download.cfm/docid/5520727E-1DBF-4979-84C80FC279339312. In view of the paucity of guidance from U.S. securities regulatory authorities regarding disclosure of side letters, the general partner or investment adviser of a U.S. hedge fund may want to consider the FSA and AIMA guidance.

> other holders of shares or interests of that class who are in the same position at a material disadvantage in connection with the exercise of their redemption rights.[291]

Absent specific guidance from the SEC and other U.S. securities regulatory authorities, the general partner or investment adviser of a hedge fund should consider the disclosure obligations discussed above, with respect to both existing and prospective investors.[292] In compliance examinations, the SEC Office of Compliance Inspections and Examinations routinely asks SEC-registered investment advisers to provide copies of side letters.[293] The SEC staff may also request side letters from investment advisers (whether registered or unregistered) in connection with regulatory sweeps affecting hedge funds. The SEC's former Director of the Office of Investor Education and Assistance stated in testimony before Congress in 2006 that the SEC is less troubled by side letters that give the investor "the ability to make additional investments, receive treatment as favorable as other investors or limit management fees and incentives," than side letters that might harm the interests of other investors, such as letters that "give certain investors liquidity preferences or provide them with more access to portfolio information."[294]

According to AIMA, even if the general partner or investment adviser of a hedge fund is not required to disclose the number of side letters or the dates of and parties to specific side letters, it should disclose the side letters' material terms. If the investors who are parties to side letters own a material amount of the hedge fund, that fact also should be disclosed.[295]

§ 6.7 Disclosure Obligations Under the CEA

The general partner or investment adviser of a hedge fund that trades in commodity interests, including certain swaps, may be required to register as a commodity pool operator (a "CPO") or a commodity trading adviser (a "CTA"), or both, under the CEA.[296] An investment entity, such as a hedge fund, that invests in commodity futures and other commodity interests is referred to as a "commodity pool" in the CEA. The CEA imposes disclosure and reporting obligations on CPOs and CTAs. Many general partners and investment advisers of hedge funds are exempt from registration as CPOs and CTAs.

---

291. *Id.*

292. *See* §§ 6.3, 6.4 and 6.5, *supra.*

293. *See* "CCOutreach National Seminar, Common Examination Areas: Documents and Information Examiners Request and How Advisers Can Use This Information to Enhance Their Compliance Programs" (Nov. 14, 2006), *available at* http://www.sec.gov/info/cco/ccons2006examareas.pdf.

294. Testimony by Susan Ferris Wyderko Concerning Hedge Funds Before the Subcommittee on Securities and Investment of the U.S. Senate Committee on Banking, Housing, and Urban Affairs (May 16, 2006), *available at* http://www.sec.gov/news/testimony/ts051606sfw.htm.

295. AIMA's Industry Guidance Note on Side Letters (Sep. 2006), *supra*, note 290, at 2.

296. *See* § 2.9, *supra.*

Some widely used exemptions require, however, that specific disclosure be furnished to investors, which is typically included in the hedge fund's disclosure document.[297]

1. Disclosure Requirements for Registered CPOs and CTAs

The CEA generally requires registered CPOs and CTAs to make specific disclosures to current and prospective investors and clients. As discussed below in section 6.7.4, some CPOs and CTAs may qualify for exemptions from certain disclosure requirements with respect to some funds and accounts they manage. A registered CPO that does not qualify for relief from the CEA's disclosure requirements must deliver a disclosure document to each prospective investor in a commodity pool no later than the time that it delivers a subscription agreement to the prospective investor.[298] A registered CTA that does not qualify for relief from the CEA's disclosure requirements must deliver a disclosure document to a prospective client before entering into an advisory agreement with the client.[299] An investment adviser that is registered as both a CTA and a CPO is required to furnish only its CPO disclosure document, and not its CTA disclosure document, to persons who are clients solely by virtue of their participation in a pool operated by the CPO. Before a CPO or CTA that is required to provide a disclosure document may accept funds from a prospective investor or client, it must receive a signed acknowledgment of receipt of the disclosure document from the investor or client.[300]

CEA regulations specify many types of disclosure that must be included in CPO and CTA disclosure documents, including detailed disclosure of the past performance of the CPO's pool and the CTA's client accounts and, in some cases, the past performance of the CPO's or CTA's principals.[301] The entire CPO or CTA disclosure document must comply with the SEC's plain English rule.[302]

The CEA regulations generally require that a disclosure document be submitted to the NFA for review before it is used.[303] A CPO or CTA must generally file all CEA-required disclosure documents with the NFA at least 21 days before delivering them to any prospective investor.[304]

If interests in a pool are offered and sold solely to accredited investors in an offering exempt from the registration requirements of the Securities Act pursuant

---

297. *See* CEA Rule 4.13(a)(3), 17 C.F.R. § 4.13(a)(3), and § 6.7.4, *infra*.

298. CEA Rule 4.21(a), 17 C.F.R. § 4.21(a).

299. CEA Rules 4.21 and 4.31, 17 C.F.R. §§ 4.21 and 4.31.

300. CEA Rule 4.21(b), 17 C.F.R. § 4.21(b); CEA Rule 4.31(b), 17 C.F.R. § 4.31(b).

301. The required content of a CPO's disclosure document is set forth in CEA Rules 4.24 and 4.25, 17 C.F.R. §§ 4.24 and 4.25. The required content of a CTA's disclosure document is set forth in CEA Rules 4.34 and 4.35, 17 C.F.R. §§ 4.34 and 4.35.

302. NFA Compliance Rule 2-35(a)(1), *available at* http://www.nfa.futures.org/nfamanual/NFAManual.aspx?Rule ID=RULE 2-35&Section=4. *See* § 6.2.3, *supra*, regarding the plain English rule.

303. CEA Rule 4.26(d); 17 C.F.R. § 4.26(d). CEA Rule 4.36(d); 17 C.F.R. § 4.36(d).

304. *Id.*

to Rule 505 or 506 of Regulation D,[305] the 21-day advance filing requirement does not apply, and a registered CPO may solicit, accept and receive funds and other property from prospective participants on filing the disclosure document with the NFA and providing it to such participants.[306] A CPO may decide, however, not to take advantage of this relief, because the NFA may require changes to the CPO's disclosure document and require the CPO to redistribute the revised document to all prospective investors who received the original version and to offer rescission of any investment made on the basis of the original version.

A CPO or CTA that continually solicits investors must update any CEA-mandated disclosure document at least every 9 months, because no CPO or CTA may use such a document dated more than 9 months preceding its use.[307]

If a CPO disclosure document becomes inaccurate or incomplete, the CPO must furnish a corrected document to existing clients and file it with the NFA within 21 days after the CPO has reason to know of the deficiency.[308] The CPO may not accept funds from a prospective investor until the prospective investor has received the corrected disclosure document.[309]

2. Required Reports to Clients and Pool Participants

A CPO receives confirmations and month-end account statements for a hedge fund from the hedge fund's futures commission merchant, which is a broker for commodity interests.[310] The futures commission merchant is required to send the confirmations only to the CPO, not to investors in the CPO's pool.[311]

A registered CPO that does not qualify for any of various exemptions from the CEA's reporting requirements described below must provide investors with account statements that include financial statements prepared in accordance with GAAP and any previously undisclosed material business dealings between the pool and its CPO, CTA, futures commission merchant or any of their respective principals.[312] These statements must be provided within 30 days of the end of each month, although in some cases such statements are required only quarterly, and for certain qualifying pools the reports may be less detailed.[313] In addition, the CPO must provide investors with annual reports, within 90 days after the end of each fiscal year of the pool, that include performance data and financial statements prepared in accordance with GAAP and audited by an independent

305. *See* § 5.3.2, *supra*.

306. CEA Rule 4.8, 17 C.F.R. § 4.8. CEA Rule 4.12(b), 17 C.F.R. § 4.12(b), described at § 6.7.4.i, *infra*, provides similar relief from the 21-day requirement for certain 4.12(b) Pools.

307. CEA Rule 4.26(a)(2), 17 C.F.R. § 4.26(a)(2); CEA Rule 4.36(a)(2), 17 C.F.R. § 4.36(a)(2).

308. CEA Rules 4.26(c) and 4.26(d)(2), 17 C.F.R. §§ 4.26(c) and 4.26(d)(2).

309. CEA Rule 4.26(c); 17 C.F.R. § 4.26(c).

310. CEA Rule 1.33, 17 C.F.R. § 1.33.

311. CEA Rule 1.33(b)(4), 17 C.F.R. § 1.33(b)(4).

312. CEA Rule 4.22(a), 17 C.F.R. § 4.22(a).

313. *Id.*

public accountant.[314] CEA Rule 4.22 identifies the information that must be disclosed in the account statements and annual reports.[315] A copy of each annual report must be filed electronically with the NFA.[316]

If the annual report is sent to pool participants within 45 days of the end of the pool's fiscal year, the CPO is not required to deliver an account statement for the final month of that fiscal year.[317] If a CPO cannot distribute the report within 90 days from the end of the pool's fiscal year, the CPO may request an extension from the NFA.[318]

3. Position Limits and Reports of Substantial Market Positions

Registered CPOs must report to the CFTC positions in commodity interests and futures contracts that exceed thresholds set forth in the CEA regulations and must maintain books and records detailing the CPO's positions and transactions in such commodity interests.[319] CEA regulations also limit a CPO's speculative trading and the size of the positions that any CPO may hold.[320]

4. Exemptions from Certain Disclosure and Reporting Requirements

CEA regulations afford registered CPOs and CTAs relief from some of the CFTC disclosure, record-keeping and reporting requirements. This relief applies only with respect to specific qualifying pools and accounts, not to the CPO or CTA generally, and the CPO or CTA must file a notice with the NFA to claim the relief.

i. Rule 4.12(b) Pools

Under CEA Rule 4.12(b), a CPO to a qualifying commodity pool (a "4.12(b) Pool") is exempt from some disclosure, reporting and record-keeping requirements that generally apply to CPOs.[321] To qualify as a 4.12(b) Pool, a pool must:

- be offered and sold in accordance with the registration provisions of the Securities Act or an exemption therefrom;
- generally and routinely engage in buying and selling securities and securities- derived instruments;
- not enter into commodity future and commodity options contracts for which the aggregate initial margin and premiums, and the required

314. CEA Rule 4.22(c) and 4.22(d), 17 C.F.R. §§ 4.22(c) and 4.22(d).
315. 17 C.F.R. § 4.22.
316. CEA Rule 4.22(c), 17 C.F.R. § 4.22(c); NFA Compliance Rule 2-13(c), *available at* http://www.nfa.futures.org/nfamanual/NFAManual.aspx?Rule ID=RULE 2-13&Section=4.
317. CEA Rule 4.22(b), 17 C.F.R. § 4.22(b)
318. CEA Rule 4.22(f), 17 C.F.R. § 4.22(f); NFA Compliance Rule 2-13(c).
319. CEA Rules 15.01 and Part 18, 17 C.F.R. § 15.01 and pt. 18.
320. CEA Rules Part 150, 17 C.F.R. pt. 150.
321. 17 C.F.R. § 4.12.

minimum security deposit for retail foreign exchange transactions, exceed 10 percent of the fair market value of the pool's assets (measured on an ongoing basis), after taking into account unrealized profits and unrealized losses on such contracts to which the pool is already a party, but excluding the in-the-money amount of options that are in-the-money at the time of purchase;[322]

- trade commodity interests in a manner solely incidental to its securities trading activities; and
- disclose to investors and prospective investors the foregoing restrictions before the pool starts trading commodity interests.[323]

To claim this exemption, a CPO must file a notice with the NFA before the 4.12(b) Pool enters into its first transaction in commodity interests and include specified additional legends in the 4.12(b) Pool's disclosure document.[324]

The disclosure document for a 4.12(b) Pool is not required to include most of the cautionary legends or any of the past performance disclosure that is required in disclosure documents of other commodity pools.[325] This rule, however, does not relieve a CPO from the obligation to disclose all material information.[326] In addition, the disclosure document must be prepared in accordance with the Securities Act and Company Act or the exemptions from the registration requirements of those Acts on which the pool relies.[327] If the CPO of a 4.12(b) Pool chooses to provide performance data to prospective investors, that performance disclosure must comply with the applicable CEA regulations.

The CPO of a 4.12(b) Pool may solicit, accept and receive funds and other property from prospective investors (even investors that are not accredited investors under Securities Act Regulation D) immediately after filing the pool's disclosure document with the NFA and providing it to the prospective investors.[328] The utility of this exemption may be limited, however, if the NFA requires changes to the disclosure document, because the CPO may be required to provide the revised document to all prospective investors who received the original version and to offer rescission of any investment made on the basis of the original version.

---

322. CEA Rule 4.12(b)(1)(i)(C), 17 C.F.R. § 4.12(b)(i)(C). The "in-the-money amount" of an option is defined as "(1) with respect to a call option, the amount by which the value of the physical commodity or the contract for sale of a commodity for future delivery which is the subject of the option exceeds the strike price of the option; and (2) with respect to a put option, the amount by which the value of the physical commodity or the contract for sale of a commodity for future delivery which is the subject of the option is exceeded by the strike price of the option." CEA Rule 190.01(x), 17 C.F.R. § 190.01(x).

323. CEA Rule 4.12, 17 C.F.R. § 4.12.

324. CEA Rules 4.12(b)(3) and 4.12(b)(5), 17 C.F.R. §§ 4.12(b)(3) and 4.12(b)(5).

325. CEA Rule 4.12(b)(2), 17 C.F.R. § 4.12(b)(2).

326. CEA Rules 4.12(b)(2)(i)(C) and 4.24(w), 17 C.F.R. §§ 4.12(b)(2)(i)(C) and 4.24(w).

327. *See* §§ 6.2 and 6.3, *supra*.

328. CEA Rule 4.8(b), 17 C.F.R. § 4.8(b).

The NFA generally does not review even the initial disclosure document of a fund-of-funds that is a 4.12(b) Pool and that invests in commodity interests only through other 4.12(b) Pools.[329]

CPOs of 4.12(b) Pools also are relieved from some of the CEA's reporting and record-keeping requirements. For example, CPOs are required to send reports only quarterly, rather than monthly, to participants in their 4.12(b) Pools, and the reports need not be as detailed as reports to participants in other commodity pools.[330]

ii. Offshore Pools

A registered CPO that operates an offshore pool is exempt from all disclosure and reporting and some record-keeping requirements of the CEA regulations with respect to that pool, if:

- the pool is organized and will remain and be operated outside the United States;
- the pool does not hold pool owner meetings or conduct administrative activities within the United States;
- no pool owner is a U.S. person (as described below);
- the pool does not contain any capital directly or indirectly contributed from sources within the United States; and
- the CPO, the pool and persons affiliated with them will not solicit participation in the pool by U.S. persons.[331]

For purposes of this exemption, the following persons are not considered to be U.S. persons:

- a natural person who is not a resident of the United States;
- a partnership, corporation or other entity (other than an entity organized principally for passive investment) organized under the laws of a non-U.S. jurisdiction and which has its principal place of business in a non-U.S. jurisdiction;
- an estate or trust, the income of which is not subject to U.S. income tax, regardless of source;
- any entity organized principally for passive investment, such as a pool, investment company or similar entity, if units of participation in the entity held by U.S. persons represent in the aggregate less than 10 percent of the beneficial interest in the entity, and if the entity was not formed principally for the purpose of facilitating investment by U.S. persons in a pool with respect to which the operator is exempt from specified requirements of Part 4 of the CFTC's regulations by virtue of its participants being non-U.S. persons; and

---

329. CFTC Advisory 95-44, 1999 CFTC Ltr. LEXIS 41 (Apr. 20, 1995).

330. CEA Rule 4.12(b)(2)(ii), 17 C.F.R. § 4.12(b)(2)(ii).

331. CFTC Advisory 18-96, [1994-1996 Transfer Binder] Comm. Fut. L. Rep (CCH) ¶ 26,659, 1996 CFTC Ltr. LEXIS 24 (Apr. 11, 1996).

- a pension plan for the employees, officers or principals of an entity organized and with its principal place of business outside the United States.[332]

To claim this exemption, a CPO must file a notice with the NFA before beginning to operate the offshore pool.[333]

iii. QEP Pools

Under CEA Rule 4.7(a), a registered CPO is not required to provide any disclosure document and is granted significant relief from periodic reporting and record-keeping requirements with respect to a pool (a "QEP Pool"), the interests of which are offered and sold only to "qualified eligible persons" in an offering that is exempt from registration under the Securities Act pursuant to Securities Act section 4(a)(2) or Regulation S.[334] As discussed in sections 6.7.4.iii.a and b, below, the two categories of qualified eligible persons are those who are required to meet certain portfolio holdings requirements and those who are not.

To claim the relief available to a QEP Pool, the CPO must file a notice with the NFA.[335] Although the CEA and CEA regulations do not require the CPO of a QEP Pool to provide a disclosure document to prospective investors, the Securities Act, the Company Act and SEC rules thereunder require complete and adequate disclosure, and accordingly most QEP Pools have disclosure documents.[336] The disclosure document, however, is not subject to review by the NFA and need not include any CFTC-mandated disclosure, except for a legend required by the CEA regulations.[337]

a. Qualified Eligible Persons Not Required to Meet Portfolio Requirements

A qualified eligible person is any person that the CPO reasonably believes, at the time the person purchases a pool participation or opens an account, is:

- a futures commission merchant, retail foreign exchange dealer or swap dealer registered under the CEA;
- a securities broker or dealer registered under the Exchange Act;
- a CPO or CTA that has been registered and active as such for 2 years or advises pools or accounts, as the case may be, that have total assets in excess of $5,000,000 or a principal of such a CPO or CTA;
- an investment adviser registered under the Advisers Act, or any state law, that has been so registered and active for 2 years or provides securities investment advice to accounts having total assets in excess of $5,000,000;

332. *Id*, n. 7.
333. *Id.*
334. CEA Rule 4.7(b), 17 C.F.R. § 4.7(b).
335. CEA Rule 4.7(d), 17 C.F.R. § 4.7(d).
336. *See* §§ 6.2 and 6.3, *supra.*
337. CEA Rule 4.7(b), 17 C.F.R. § 4.7(b).

- a qualified purchaser, as defined in Company Act section 2(a)(51);[338]
- a knowledgeable employee, as defined in Company Act Rule 3c-5;[339]
- the CPO, CTA or investment adviser of the QEP pool, any of their affiliates, any principal of the pool or any of the foregoing, certain employees of the pool or any of the foregoing, certain family members of any such principal or employee (provided the investment is made at the direction of such principal or employee), persons who acquired an interest in the pool through gift, bequest or divorce from such principal or employee, and any company established by any of the foregoing;
- a trust not formed for the specific purpose of investing in the QEP Pool, if the trustee or other person authorized to make the investment decisions for the trust and each settlor of the trust are qualified eligible persons;
- certain charitable organizations if the trustee or other person authorized to make the investment decisions for the trust and the persons who established the organization are qualified eligible persons;
- any Non-U.S. person;[340]
- any entity in which all of the owners or participants are qualified eligible persons;
- a QEP Pool; and
- an account described in CEA Rule 4.5 in which all owners or participants are qualified eligible persons.[341]

b. Qualified Eligible Persons Required to Meet Portfolio Requirements

A person may also be a qualified eligible person if the CPO of the QEP Pool reasonably believes, at the time that such person invests in the QEP Pool, that the person satisfies one of the portfolio requirements listed below and is:

- an investment company registered under the Company Act or a business development company as defined in Company Act section 2(a)(48)[342] not formed for the specific purpose of investing in the QEP Pool;
- a bank as defined in Securities Act section 3(a)(2)[343] or a savings and loan association or other institution as defined in Securities Act

338. *See* § 3.3.2.i, *supra.*

339. *See* § 3.2.2.iv, *supra.*

340. A "Non-U.S. Person" is a person who is not resident in the United States; an entity that is not organized principally for passive investment and that is organized under the laws of a non-U.S. jurisdiction and has its principal place of business in a non-U.S. jurisdiction; a pension plan for the employees, officers or principals of such an entity; an estate or trust whose income is not subject to U.S. taxation; and an entity organized principally for passive investment if fewer than 10 percent of its beneficial interests are owned by persons who are not QEPs or Non-U.S. Persons and the entity was not formed principally to facilitate investment by persons other than Non-U.S. Persons. CEA Rule 4.7(a)(1)(iv), 17 C.F.R. § 4.7(a)(1)(iv).

341. CEA Rule 4.7(a)(2), 17 C.F.R. § 4.7(a)(2).

342. 15 U.S.C. § 80a-2(a)(48).

343. 15 U.S.C. § 77c(a)(2)(C)(iii).

section 3(a)(5)(A),[344] whether acting for its own account or the account of a qualified eligible person;

- an insurance company as defined in Securities Act section 2(13)[345] acting for its own account or the account of a qualified eligible person;
- a plan established and maintained by a state, its political subdivisions, or any agency or instrumentality of a state or its political subdivisions, for the benefit of its employees, if such plan has total assets in excess of $5,000,000;
- an employee benefit plan within the meaning of ERISA (a) if the investment decision is made by a plan fiduciary, as defined in ERISA section 3(21),[346] which is a bank, a savings and loan association, an insurance company or a registered investment adviser, or (b) if the employee benefit plan has total assets in excess of $5,000,000, or (c) if the employee benefit plan is a self-directed plan and the investment decisions are made solely by persons that are qualified eligible persons;
- a private business development company as defined in Advisers Act section 202(a)(22);[347]
- an organization described in Tax Code section 501(c)(3),[348] with total assets in excess of $5,000,000;
- a corporation, Massachusetts or similar business trust, or partnership, LLC or similar business venture, other than a commodity pool, not formed for the specific purpose of participating in the QEP Pool, with total assets in excess of $5,000,000;
- a natural person who qualifies as an "accredited investor" under Rule 501(a)(5) under the Securities Act by virtue of his or her individual net worth or joint net worth with his or her spouse;
- a pool, trust, insurance company separate account or bank collective trust, with total assets in excess of $5,000,000, not formed for the specific purpose of acquiring the securities offered, whose purchase is directed by a qualified eligible person; or
- except as provided for the governmental entities described above, if otherwise authorized by law to engage in such transactions, a governmental entity (including the United States, a state, or a non-U.S. government) or political subdivision thereof, or a multinational or supranational entity or an instrumentality, agency or department of any of the foregoing.[349]

---

344. 15 U.S.C. § 77c(a)(5)(A).
345. 15 U.S.C. § 77b(a)(13).
346. 29 U.S.C. § 1002(21).
347. 15 U.S.C. § 80b-2(a)(22).
348. 26 U.S.C. § 501(c)(3).
349. CEA Rule 4.7(a)(3), 17 C.F.R. § 4.7(a)(3).

The CPO of the QEP Pool must also, however, reasonably believe, at the time that the person invests in the QEP Pool, that the person meets one of the following portfolio requirements:

- owns securities of issuers not affiliated with the person (including pool participations) and other investments with an aggregate market value of at least $2,000,000;
- has had on deposit with a futures commission merchant, for the person's own account at any time during the 6-month period preceding the date of sale to the person of a participation in a QEP Pool, at least $200,000 in commodity exchange-specified initial margin and option premiums for commodity interest transactions, together with required minimum security deposit for retail forex transactions; or
- owns a portfolio comprising a combination of the funds or properties described in the two preceding clauses in which the sum of the funds or property includable under the first clause, expressed as a percentage of the minimum amount required thereunder, and the amount of futures margin and option premiums includable under the second clause, expressed as a percentage of the minimum amount required thereunder, equals at least 100 percent (for example, a composite portfolio consisting of $1,000,000 in securities and other investments and $100,000 in exchange-specified initial margin and option premiums on commodity interests would satisfy this requirement).[350]

iv. QEP Accounts

CEA Rule 4.7(b) grants CTAs relief from certain disclosure, reporting and record-keeping requirements with respect to accounts of clients that are QEPs and have agreed to be treated as such. The relief is similar to that provided under CEA Rule 4.7(a) for QEP Pools, as described above.[351]

5. Anti-Fraud Provisions

CTAs and CPOs are subject to broad anti-fraud provisions under the CEA. See Chapter 2, section 2.9.12, and sections 6.4, 6.5 and 6.6 above.

§ 6.8 Privacy Notifications

Pursuant to the GLBA,[352] the, CFTC, FTC and SEC adopted regulations concerning the disclosure of nonpublic personal information by financial institutions. For this purpose, "financial institutions" include investment advisers, CPOs, CTAs and hedge funds. The SEC regulation, Regulation S-P,[353]

350. CEA Rule 4.7(a)(1)(v), 17 C.F.R. § 4.7(a)(1)(v).
351. CEA Rule § 4.7(b).
352. 15 U.S.C. §§ 6801 *et seq.*
353. 17 C.F.R. pt. 248.

applies to SEC-registered investment advisers; the FTC regulation[354] applies to SEC-Exempt Advisers and exempt investment companies (including hedge funds); and the CFTC regulation[355] applies to CPOs and CTAs. The 3 sets of regulations impose substantially similar disclosure obligations on investment advisers, CPOs, CTAs and hedge funds.[356]

These FTC, SEC and CFTC regulations require each investment adviser, CPO, CTA or hedge fund to deliver to each new customer an initial notice describing in detail:[357]

- the categories of nonpublic personal information that the investment adviser, CPO, CTA or hedge fund collects;
- the categories of such information that the investment adviser, CPO, CTA or hedge fund may disclose to affiliates and nonaffiliated third parties;
- the categories of affiliates and third parties to whom the investment adviser, hedge fund or CPO might disclose the information;
- the policies and practices of the investment adviser, CPO, CTA or hedge fund with respect to protecting confidential information;[358]
- if the investment adviser, CPO, CTA or hedge fund discloses nonpublic personal information about former customers, the categories of such information that the investment adviser, CPO, CTA or hedge fund discloses and the categories of affiliates and third parties to whom the investment adviser, CPO, CTA or hedge fund might disclose that information; and
- if the investment adviser, CPO, CTA or hedge fund discloses nonpublic personal information about its customers to nonaffiliated third parties, additional information about the disclosures and an election for the consumer to "opt-out" of the disclosure (some exceptions to this additional disclosure and opt-out requirement apply, as discussed below).[359]

---

354. 16 C.F.R. pt. 313.

355. 17 C.F.R. pt. 160.

356. *See* § 2.7.8, *supra.*

357. Regulation S-P Rule 248.4, 17 C.F.R. § 248.4; FTC Privacy Rule 313.4, 16 C.F.R. § 313.4; CFTC Privacy Rule 160.4, 17 C.F.R. § 160.4. These notices may be delivered electronically under certain circumstances as discussed at §9.3.2.

358. *See* § 2.7.8, *supra.*

359. Regulation S-P Rule 248.6, 17 C.F.R. § 248.6; FTC Privacy Rule 313.6, 16 C.F.R. § 313.6; CFTC Privacy Rule 160.6, 17 C.F.R. § 160.6. In addition, an investment adviser or hedge fund may not use nonpublic personal information about a customer's "eligibility" for products or services that the investment adviser or hedge fund has received from an affiliate unless the customer has received notification of the right to opt out of that sharing of his or her eligibility information and has not elected to opt out of that disclosure. Regulation S-AM Rule § 121, 17 C.F.R. § 248.121 (effective July 1, 2010); FTC Affiliate Marketing Rule 680.21, 16 C.F.R. § 680.21.

A "customer" of an investment adviser, CPO, CTA or hedge fund is a consumer with whom the investment adviser, CPO, CTA or hedge fund enters into a relationship or agreement to provide financial services, including investment advisory services.[360] A "consumer" is an individual who applies for financial services, including investment advisory services, from an investment adviser, CPO, CTA or hedge fund.[361]

Thereafter, the investment adviser, CPO, CTA or hedge fund must deliver a notice containing the same disclosure items to each existing customer at least once during each 12-month period.[362] The investment adviser, CPO, CTA or hedge fund may define the 12-month period, but must apply it consistently.[363] After providing a notice to a customer, the investment adviser, CPO, CTA or hedge fund may not disclose any nonpublic personal information of that customer to an affiliate or a third-party other than as described in the notice, unless a new notice describing the proposed disclosure is given to the customer.[364] The notice thus establishes the boundaries of disclosure by the investment adviser, CPO, CTA or hedge fund and the persons to whom the investment adviser, CPO, CTA or hedge fund may disclose it.

An investment adviser, CPO, CTA or hedge fund that does not disclose nonpublic personal information to affiliates or third parties (except as discussed in the following paragraph) may use a fairly simple form of notice to comply with the privacy regulations. The SEC, the FTC and the CFTC have adopted model privacy forms: one for a situation where the opt-out described above is not required, and other model forms for various situations in which an opt-out is required.[365] The model form must be in the exact form that the agencies specified. It must be on two pages, or the front and back of one sheet of paper, and it has a standardized page layout, content, format, style, pagination and shading. It may be part of another document, but it must be clear and conspicuous, and it must be intact so that the customer can save it.[366]

An investment adviser, CPO, CTA or hedge fund is not required to notify consumers about certain disclosures of their personal financial information. First, sharing information as necessary to effect, administer or enforce a

360. Regulation S-P Rule 248.3(g), (j) and (k), 17 C.F.R. §§ 248.3(g), (j) and (k); FTC Privacy Rule 313.3(e), (h) and (i), 16 C.F.R. §§ 313(e), (h) and (i); CFTC Privacy Rule 160.3(h), (k) and (l), 17 C.F.R. § 160.3(h), (k) and (l).

361. Regulation S-P Rule 248.3(g), 17 C.F.R. § 248.3(g); FTC Privacy Rule 313(e), 16 C.F.R. § 313(e); CFTC Privacy Rule 160.3(h), 17 C.F.R. § 160.3(h).

362. Regulation S-P Rule 248.5, 17 C.F.R. § 248.5; FTC Privacy Rule 313.5, 16 C.F.R. § 313.5; CFTC Privacy Rule 160.5, 17 C.F.R. § 160.5.

363. *Id.*

364. Regulation S-P Rule 248.10(a)(1)(i), 17 C.F.R. § 248.10(a)(1)(i); FTC Privacy Rule 313.10(a)(1)(i), 16 C.F.R. § 313.10(a)(1)(i); CFTC Privacy Rule 160.10(a)(1)(i), 17 C.F.R. § 160.10(a)(1)(i).

365. Advisers Act Release No. 2950 (Nov. 15, 2009), 74 F.R. 62,890 (Dec. 1, 2009); Federal Trade Commission RIN 3084-AA94 Project No. 034815 (Nov. 15, 2009), 74 F.R. 62,890 (Dec. 1, 2009); Commodities Futures Trading Commission RIN 3038-AC04 (Nov. 15, 2009), 74 F.R. 62,890 (Dec. 1, 2009).

366. *Id.* at Appendix A, General Instruction B.

transaction that a consumer requests or authorizes is not considered disclosing the information.[367] Second, releasing information to various parties involved in the business of the investment adviser, hedge fund or CPO is specifically permitted and is not subject to the notice requirements.[368] This includes disclosures to the attorneys, accountants and auditors of the investment adviser, hedge fund or CPO. In addition, disclosures required by law, such as disclosures to regulatory agencies, are permitted.[369] Finally, disclosures expressly requested by the customer (such as to a mortgage banker in connection with a loan application) are not subject to the notice requirements.[370] An investment adviser, CPO, CTA or hedge fund that releases nonpublic personal information about its customers only within the foregoing exceptions may state in its initial and annual notices to customers that it does not release nonpublic personal information except for everyday business purposes or as permitted by law.[371]

If an investment adviser, CPO, CTA or hedge fund intends either to disclose to nonaffiliated third parties nonpublic personal information about customers outside of the above exceptions or to share certain information with affiliates for marketing purposes, it must deliver more complicated disclosure notices to its customers and provide a reasonable means for the customer to opt out of having personal information disclosed.[372] For example, if a former employee of an investment adviser brings nonpublic personal information to his or her new employer, a specific disclosure must be included in the notice and the opt-out election.[373] In addition, the laws of some states require investment advisers, CPOs, CTAs or hedge funds to get a customer's affirmative permission before sharing information with nonaffiliates.[374]

Notices must also be provided to consumers who have given nonpublic personal information to, but have not established a customer relationship with, the investment adviser, CPO, CTA or hedge fund, if the investment adviser, CPO, CTA or hedge fund will disclose to nonaffiliated third parties nonpublic personal information about those consumers, other than the excepted disclosures

---

367. Regulation S-P Rule 248.14, 17 C.F.R. § 248.14; FTC Privacy Rule 313.14, 16 C.F.R. § 313.14; CFTC Privacy Rule 160.14, 17 C.F.R. § 160.14.

368. Regulation S-P Rule 248.15(a)(3), 17 C.F.R. § 248.15(a)(3); FTC Privacy Rule 313.15(a)(3), 16 C.F.R. § 313.15(a)(3); CFTC Privacy Rule 160.15(a)(3), 17 C.F.R. § 160.15(a)(3).

369. Regulation S-P Rule 248.15(a)(7), 17 C.F.R. § 248.15(a)(7); FTC Privacy Rule 313.15(a)(7), 16 C.F.R. § 313.15(a)(7); CFTC Privacy Rule 160.15(a)(7), 17 C.F.R. § 160.15(a)(7).

370. Regulation S-P Rule 248.15(a)(1), 17 C.F.R. § 248.15(a)(1); FTC Privacy Rule 313.15(a)(1), 16 C.F.R. § 313.15(a)(1); CFTC Privacy Rule 160.15(a)(1), 17 C.F.R. § 160.15(a)(1).

371. Regulation S-P Rule 248.6(c)(5), 17 C.F.R. § 248.6(c)(5); FTC Privacy Rule 313.6(c)(5), 16 C.F.R. § 313.6(c)(5); CFTC Privacy Rule 160.6(c)(5), 17 C.F.R. § 160.6(c)(5).

372. Regulation S-P Rules 248.7 and 248.10(a), 17 C.F.R. §§ 248.7 and 248.10(a); FTC Privacy Rules 313.7 and 313.10(a), 16 C.F.R. §§ 313.7 and 313.10(a); CFTC Privacy Rules 160.7 and 160.10(a), 17 C.F.R. §§ 160.7 and 160.10(a).

373. *See, e.g.*, In the Matter of NEXT Financial Group, Inc., Exchange Act Rel. No. 56316 (Aug. 24, 2006). The SEC has proposed, but not yet adopted, a limited exception for this disclosure. Advisers Act Rel. No. 2712 (Mar. 4, 2008); 73 F.R. 13,692 (Mar. 13, 2008).

374. *See, e.g.*, Cal. Fin. Code §§ 4050 to 4060.

described above.[375] These notices must be provided before the nonpublic personal information is disclosed to the third-party and must permit the consumer to opt out.[376]

The opt-out requirements do not apply when an investment adviser, hedge fund or CPO shares nonpublic personal information about customers or consumers with a nonaffiliated third-party who performs services for the investment adviser, hedge fund or CPO or functions on its behalf, such as an outside consultant, solicitor or marketer, if (a) the investment adviser, hedge fund or CPO discloses in its initial and annual notices that it makes such disclosures (detailing categories of personal information disclosed as well as the types of third parties that receive the information), and (b) the agreement with the third-party prohibits the third-party from disclosing the information.[377]

If an investment adviser is affiliated with another entity or has associated persons who are affiliated with another entity, such as a broker that is a FINRA member, the investment adviser may share information with that affiliate, pursuant to either legal requirements or business arrangements. For example, if a person associated with the investment adviser is a registered representative of a broker, FINRA rules require the broker to supervise the activities of that person.[378] The notices provided by an investment adviser that is affiliated with another entity may need to include additional disclosure about the sharing of information with the affiliate and may need to include an opt-out election.

375. Regulation S-P Rule 248.4, 17 C.F.R. § 248.4; FTC Privacy Rule 313.4, 16 C.F.R. § 313.4; CFTC Privacy Rule 160.4, 17 C.F.R. § 160.4.

376. Regulation S-P Rules 248.4(a)(2) and 248.10(a)(1), 17 C.F.R. §§ 248.4(a)(2) and 248.10(a)(1); FTC Privacy Rules 313.4(a)(2) and 313.10(a)(1), 16 C.F.R. §§ 313.4(a)(2) and 313.10(a)(1); CFTC Privacy Rules 160.4(a)(2) and 160.10(a)(1), 17 C.F.R. §§ 160.4(a)(2) and 160.10(a)(1).

377. Regulation S-P Rule 248.13, 17 C.F.R. § 248.13; FTC Privacy Rule 313.13, 16 C.F.R. § 313.13; CFTC Privacy Rule 160.13, 17 C.F.R. § 160.13.

378. FINRA Conduct Rule 3010.

CHAPTER 7

State Blue Sky Regulation

§ 7.1 Introduction

Sales of securities, including limited partner or member interests in a hedge fund, are regulated by state securities laws, often called "Blue Sky" laws, in addition to the Securities Act and the SEC rules thereunder.[1] A state's securities laws apply to offers and sales of securities within the state, and may require the registration of the persons who make those offers and sales, such as brokers and agents.

Before the National Securities Markets Improvement Act of 1996 ("NSMIA")[2] was enacted, state securities laws typically required a hedge fund to register or qualify its securities with a state securities regulatory authority before the securities could be offered or sold in that state. Most states provided exemptions from registration or qualification similar to those available under the Securities Act and Exchange Act.[3] If a hedge fund failed to comply with the requirements of such an exemption in a state, however, every purchaser of interests in that state could have a right of rescission against the hedge fund and its general partner and other controlling persons.

In enacting NSMIA, Congress intended to create uniformity among the various state Blue Sky laws and the Securities Act.[4] NSMIA preempts state laws that regulate the offer and sale of certain types of securities and securities sold in certain types of transactions. Most importantly for hedge funds, NSMIA prohibits states from requiring the registration or qualification of securities that are exempt from registration under the Securities Act pursuant to any rule under Securities Act section 4(a)(2), including Rule 506 of Regulation D.[5] States may, however, require issuers to make filings concerning the securities they sell.[6] NSMIA does not preempt state registration of brokers and other persons who

1. *See* Chapter 5, *supra*.

2. Pub. L. 104-290, Oct. 11, 1996, 110 Stat. 3416 (codified in scattered sections of 15 U.S.C.).

3. *See* Chapter 5, *supra*, and Chapter 10, *infra*.

4. Conference Report on the Nat'l Securities Markets Improvement Act of 1996, H.R. Rep. No. 104-864 at 39 (Sep. 28, 1996).

5. Securities Act § 18(b)(4)(D), 15 U.S.C. § 77r(b)(4)(D). *See* § 5.3.2, *supra*, regarding Rule 506 of Regulation D.

6. Securities Act § 18(c)(2), 15 U.S.C. § 77r(c)(2).

sell securities; accordingly, hedge funds still must comply with Blue Sky laws that require registration of those persons.

Efforts to create consistency among the states' Blue Sky laws have met only limited success. On August 25, 1956, the National Conference of Commissioners on Uniform State Laws ("NCCUSL") adopted the Uniform Securities Act (the "1956 Uniform Securities Act") "to promote, insofar as may be practicable, uniformity in legislation having for its purpose the regulation of commerce of securities or the suppression of fraud therein, and the procedure thereunder."[7] The 1956 Uniform Securities Act has been adopted or substantially adopted (with modifications) in the following jurisdictions:[8]

Alabama	Alaska	Arkansas	Colorado
Connecticut	Delaware	District of Columbia	Guam
Kentucky	Maryland	Massachusetts	Montana
Nebraska	Nevada	New Hampshire	New Jersey
New Mexico	North Carolina	Oregon	Pennsylvania
Puerto Rico	Rhode Island	Utah	Virginia
Washington	West Virginia	Wyoming	

In 2002, the National Conference of Commissioners on Uniform State Laws adopted a second, new uniform securities act, the Uniform Securities Act (2002) (the "2002 Uniform Securities Act").[9] The 2002 Uniform Securities Act is intended principally to reconcile federal and state securities laws in view of NSMIA.[10] The 2002 Uniform Securities Act has been adopted in the U.S. Virgin Islands and the following states:

Georgia	Hawaii	Idaho	Indiana
Iowa	Kansas	Maine	Michigan
Minnesota	Mississippi	Missouri	New Mexico
Oklahoma	South Carolina	South Dakota	Vermont
Wisconsin			

7. Official Comment to the 1956 Uniform Securities Act, 1 Blue Sky Law Rptr. (CCH) ¶ 5501.02.
8. 1 Blue Sky Law Rptr. (CCH) ¶ 5500.
9. 1 Blue Sky Law Rptr. (CCH) ¶ 6431.
10. 1 Blue Sky Law Rptr. (CCH) ¶ 5600.

Several states, including California, Florida, Illinois, New York, Ohio and Texas, have not adopted either version of the Uniform Securities Act, but instead continue to rely on the securities laws they have developed.[11]

This chapter does not review separately the laws of each state. Instead, it discusses the 1956 Uniform Securities Act, the 2002 Uniform Securities Act and the securities laws of California[12] and New York.[13]

§ 7.2 Pre-NSMIA State Blue Sky Regulation

1. 1956 Uniform Securities Act

The 1956 Uniform Securities Act requires securities offered and sold in a state to be registered with that state's securities regulatory authority.[14] It also requires registration of persons that offer and sell such securities within that state.[15]

i. Offers and Sales of Securities within a State

The 1956 Uniform Securities Act registration requirements, both for securities and for brokers, apply only if there is an offer or sale of a security within the state.[16] An "offer" includes every attempt to offer to dispose of, or solicitation of an offer to buy, a security or an interest in a security for value.[17] A "sale" includes every contract of sale of, contract to sell, or disposition of a security or interest in a security for value.[18] These definitions are substantially the same as the definitions of offer and sale in the Securities Act.[19] The 1956 Uniform Securities Act definition of "security" is also substantially the same as the definition of that term in the Securities Act.[20]

The securities and broker registration requirements of the 1956 Uniform Securities Act apply when an offer to sell is made in the state or an offer to buy is made and accepted in the state.[21] An offer to sell a security is made in a state, whether or not either party is present in the state at the time of the offer, if the offer originates from that state or is directed by the offeror to that state and is received at the place to which it is directed (or at any post office in that

---

11. *See* 1 Blue Sky Law Rptr. (CCH) ¶¶ 5500 and 6431 for jurisdictions adopting 1956 and 2002 Uniform Securities Act, respectively.

12. Cal. Corp. Code §§ 25000 *et seq.*

13. N.Y. Gen. Bus. Law §§ 352 *et seq.*

14. 1956 Uniform Securities Act § 301, 1 Blue Sky Law Rptr. (CCH) ¶ 5531.

15. 1956 Uniform Securities Act § 201(a), 1 Blue Sky Law Rptr. (CCH) ¶ 5521.

16. 1956 Uniform Securities Act §§ 301 and 401(c), 1 Blue Sky Law Rptr. (CCH) ¶¶ 5531 and 5541.

17. 1956 Uniform Securities Act § 401(j)(2), 1 Blue Sky Law Rptr. (CCH) ¶ 5541.

18. 1956 Uniform Securities Act § 401(j)(1), 1 Blue Sky Law Rptr. (CCH) ¶ 5541.

19. *See* Securities Act § 2(a)(3), 15 U.S.C. § 77b(2)(a)(3).

20. *See* § 5.1, note 2, *supra*. *Compare* 1956 Uniform Securities Act § 401(i), 1 Blue Sky Law Rptr. (CCH) ¶ 5541, *with* Securities Act § 2(a)(1), 15 U.S.C. § 77b(2)(a)(1).

21. 1956 Uniform Securities Act § 414(a), 1 Blue Sky Law Rptr. (CCH) ¶ 5554.

state if the offer is made by mail).[22] An offer to sell is accepted in a state if acceptance is communicated to the offeror in that state and has not previously been communicated to the offeror, orally or in writing, outside that state.[23]

In addition, acceptance is communicated to an offeror in a state, whether or not either party is present in that state at the time of the communication, if the offeree directs it to the offeror in that state reasonably believing that the offeror is in that state and it is received at the place to which it is directed (or at any post office in that state in the case of a mailed acceptance).[24] The state in which an individual is a resident and the state in which an entity is formed or organized are not relevant under these definitions for determining which state securities laws apply.[25]

ii. Securities Registration under the 1956 Uniform Securities Act

a. Securities Registration Requirements

The 1956 Uniform Securities Act requires that the offer and sale of any security in a state be registered in that state.[26] Under the 1956 Uniform Securities Act, registration may be accomplished in one of three ways: by coordination, by notification or by qualification.[27] Registration by coordination is available only if the issuer has filed a registration statement under the Securities Act in connection with the same offering.[28] Registration by notification is only available for issuers that have been in continuous operation for at least 5 years and meet certain net earnings tests.[29] Registration by coordination is not available for use by a hedge fund, because hedge funds are prohibited from making public offerings.[30] Registration by notification is typically not practical even for hedge funds that have operated for at least 5 years, because of the difficulty of applying the earnings test in the partnership context.[31]

Registration by qualification is available for any issuer to register any security.[32] Accordingly, if a hedge fund is required to register with a state securities regulatory authority, it ordinarily would register by qualification. To register by qualification, the issuer must file a registration statement.[33] The registration

22. 1956 Uniform Securities Act § 414(c), 1 Blue Sky Law Rptr. (CCH) ¶ 5554.
23. 1956 Uniform Securities Act § 414(d), 1 Blue Sky Law Rptr. (CCH) ¶ 5554.
24. *Id.*
25. 1956 Uniform Securities Act § 414, 1 Blue Sky Law Rptr. (CCH) ¶ 5554.
26. 1956 Uniform Securities Act § 301, 1 Blue Sky Law Rptr. (CCH) ¶ 5531.
27. 1956 Uniform Securities Act §§ 302, 303 and 304, 1 Blue Sky Law Rptr. (CCH) ¶¶ 5532, 5533 and 5534.
28. 1956 Uniform Securities Act § 303(a), 1 Blue Sky Law Rptr. (CCH) ¶ 5533.
29. 1956 Uniform Securities Act § 302(a), 1 Blue Sky Law Rptr. (CCH) ¶ 5532.
30. *See* §§ 3.2.5 and 3.3.1, *supra.*
31. 1956 Uniform Securities Act § 302(a), 1 Blue Sky Law Rptr. (CCH) ¶ 5532.
32. 1956 Uniform Securities Act § 304(a), 1 Blue Sky Law Rptr. (CCH) ¶ 5534.
33. 1956 Uniform Securities Act § 304(b), 1 Blue Sky Law Rptr. (CCH) ¶ 5534.

statement must include detailed disclosure similar to that required in a Form S-1 registration statement filed with the SEC,[34] including:[35]

- with respect to the issuer and its subsidiaries, identifying information including name, address, form and jurisdiction of organization, date of organization, general character and location of its business, a description of its physical properties and equipment, and a statement of the general competitive conditions in the industry in which it is or will be engaged;
- with respect to every director and officer of the issuer (or person occupying a similar status or performing similar duties), his or her name, address, principal occupation for the prior 5 years, the amount of securities of the issuer held by him or her as of a date within 30 days of filing the registration statement, the amount of the securities covered by the registration statement for which he or she has indicated he or she intends to subscribe, a description of any material interest in any material transaction with the issuer or any of its significant subsidiaries that is proposed or that was effected within the past 3 years, and the remuneration paid during the prior 12 months and estimated to be paid during the next 12 months (directly or indirectly) to all such persons in the aggregate;
- with respect to any person who beneficially owns 10 percent or more of the outstanding shares of any class of the issuer's securities, his or her name, address, the amount of securities of the issuer held by him or her as of a date within 30 days of filing the registration statement, the amount of the securities covered by the registration statement for which he or she has indicated he or she intends to subscribe, and a description of any material interest in any material transaction with the issuer or any of its significant subsidiaries that is proposed or that was effected within the past 3 years;
- with respect to any promoter of the issuer (if the issuer was organized in the past 3 years), his or her name, address, principal occupation for the prior 5 years, the amount of securities of the issuer held by him or her as of a date within 30 days of filing the registration statement, the amount of the securities covered by the registration statement for which he or she has indicated he or she intends to subscribe, a description of any material interest in any material transaction with the issuer or any of its significant subsidiaries that is proposed or that was effected within the past 3 years, and any amount paid, or intended to be paid, to him or her including the consideration for any such payment;
- with respect to any person on whose behalf any part of the offering is to be made in a nonissuer distribution, his or her name, address, the amount of securities of the issuer held by him or her as of the date of

---

34. *See* § 6.2.1.iii, *supra.*
35. 1956 Uniform Securities Act § 304(b), 1 Blue Sky Law Rptr. (CCH) ¶ 5534.

the filing of the registration statement, a description of any material interest in any material transaction with the issuer or any of its significant subsidiaries that is proposed or that was effected within the past 3 years, and a statement of his or her reasons for making the offering;

- the capitalization and long-term debt (on both a current and a pro forma basis) of the issuer and any significant subsidiary, including a description of each security outstanding or being registered or otherwise offered, and a statement of the amount and kind of consideration for which the issuer or any subsidiary has issued any of its securities within the past 2 years or is obligated to issue any of its securities;
- the kind and amount of securities to be offered, the proposed offering price or the method by which it is to be computed, any variation therefrom at which any proportion of the offering is to be made to any person or class of persons other than the underwriters (specifying any such person or class), the basis on which the offering is to be made if other than for cash, the estimated aggregate underwriting and selling discounts or commissions and finders' fees (including securities, contracts or anything else of value to accrue to the underwriters or finders in connection with the offering), the estimated amounts of other selling expenses, including legal and accounting charges, the name and address of every underwriter and every recipient of a finder's fee, a copy of any underwriting or selling group agreement pursuant to which the distribution is to be made (or the proposed form of any such agreement whose terms have not been determined), and a description of the plan of distribution of any securities that are to be offered other than through an underwriter;
- the estimated cash proceeds to be received by the issuer from the offering, the purposes for which the proceeds are to be used by the issuer, the amount to be used for each purpose, the order or priority in which the proceeds will be used for the purposes stated, the sources of any such funds, and if any part of the proceeds is to be used to acquire any property other than in the ordinary course of business, the names and addresses of the vendors, the purchase price, the names of any persons who have received commissions, and any other expense in connection with the acquisition (including the cost of borrowing money to finance the acquisition);
- a description of any stock options or other security options outstanding or to be created in connection with the offering;
- the dates of, parties to, and general effect of every management or other material contract made or to be made other than in the ordinary course of business if it is to be performed as a whole or in part at or after the filing of the registration statement or if it was made within the past 2 years, together with a copy of every such contract;
- a description of any pending litigation or proceeding to which the issuer is a party and that materially affects its business or assets (including

any such litigation or proceeding known to be contemplated by governmental authorities);

- a copy of any prospectus, pamphlet, circular, form letter, advertisement or other sales literature intended as of the effective date to be used in connection with the offering;
- a specimen or copy of the security being registered, a copy of the issuer's articles of incorporation and bylaws or their substantial equivalents, and a copy of any indenture or other instrument covering the security to be registered;
- a signed or conformed copy of an opinion of counsel as to the legality of the security being registered, stating whether the security when sold will be legally issued, fully paid and nonassessable and, if it is a debt security, whether it will be a binding obligation of the issuer;
- the written consent of any accountant, appraiser or other person whose profession gives authority to a statement made by him or her, if any such person is named as having prepared or certified a report or valuation (other than a public and official document or statement) that is used in connection with the registration statement;
- a balance sheet of the issuer as of a date within 4 months before the filing of the registration statement, a profit and loss statement and analysis of surplus for each of the 3 fiscal years preceding the date of the balance sheet and for any period between the close of the last fiscal year and the date of the balance sheet (or for the period of the issuer's and any predecessor's existence if less than 3 years), and if any part of the proceeds of the offering is to be applied to the purchase of any business, the same financial statements as would be required if that business were the registrant; and
- such additional information as the relevant state regulatory authority requires by rule or order.

b. Limited Offering Exemption from Securities Registration Requirements

Similar to the Securities Act, the 1956 Uniform Securities Act includes several exemptions from its securities registration requirements.[36] Before NSMIA was adopted, the exemption under the 1956 Uniform Securities Act on which a hedge fund typically would rely is the exemption provided by 1956 Uniform Securities Act section 402(b)(9), which exempts:

> any transaction pursuant to an offer directed by the offeror to not more than ten persons (other than those designated in paragraph 8) in this state during any period of twelve consecutive months, whether or not the offeror or any of the offerees is then present in this state, if (A) the seller reasonably believes that all the buyers in this state (other than those

36. *See* 1956 Uniform Securities Act § 402, 1 Blue Sky Law Rptr. (CCH) ¶ 5542.

> designated in paragraph 8) are purchasing for investment, and (B) no commission or other remuneration is paid or given directly or indirectly for soliciting any prospective buyer in this state (other than those designated in paragraph 8); but the [cognizant state regulatory authority] may by rule or order, as to any security or transaction or any type of security or transaction, withdraw or further condition this exemption, or increase or decrease the number of offerees permitted, or waive the conditions in Clauses (A) and (B) with or without the substitution of a limitation on remuneration.[37]

Paragraph 8 of 1956 Uniform Securities Act section 402(b) exempts any offer or sale of securities to "a bank, savings institution, trust company, insurance company, investment company as defined in the [Company Act], pension or profit sharing trust, or other financial institution or institutional buyer, or to a broker-dealer, whether the purchaser is acting for itself or in some fiduciary capacity."[38] Accordingly, a U.S. or offshore hedge fund offering its securities under the exemption provided by 1956 Uniform Securities Act section 402(b)(9) is not required to include such entities when determining the number of investors to which it has offered securities in a particular state.

The Official Code Comments on the 1956 Uniform Securities Act state that, although a written representation concerning an investor's investment intent is not required, "it would be prudent on the part of the seller to obtain something in writing."[39] An investor who acquires an interest in a U.S. or offshore hedge fund can later change his or her mind and resell the interest without violating section 402(b)(9).[40] The shorter the interval between purchase and sale, however, the more difficult it will be for the investor to prove a bona fide intent to invest at the time of investment.[41]

Some states have modified section 402(b)(9) to include an express prohibition on advertising and general solicitation, similar to that in Rule 506(b) of Regulation D under the Securities Act.[42] In addition, some states have increased the number of offerees to which an issuer may offer securities in an exempt offering.[43]

---

37. 1956 Uniform Securities Act § 402(b)(9), 1 Blue Sky Law Rptr. (CCH) ¶ 5542.

38. 1956 Uniform Securities Act § 402(b)(8), 1 Blue Sky Law Rptr. (CCH) ¶ 5542.

39. Official Comment to 1956 Uniform Securities Act § 402(b)(9), 1 Blue Sky Law Rptr. (CCH) ¶ 5542.01.

40. *Id.*

41. *Id.*

42. *See, e.g.*, Ala. Code § 8-6-11(a)(9)(c); Ga. Code Ann. § 10-5-11(14)(B); Haw. Rev. Stat. § 485A-202(13)(D); Neb. Rev. Stat. § 8-1111(9)(d); Nev. Rev. Stat. § 90.530(11)(b). *See also* § 5.3.2, *supra*.

43. *See, e.g.*, Ark. Code Ann. § 23-42-504(a)(9)(A) (35 offerees); Fla. Stat. § 517.061(11)(a)(1) (35 offerees); Ga. Code Ann. § 10-5-11(14)(A) (fifteen offerees); Haw. Rev. Stat. § 485A-202(13)(A) (25 offerees); Neb. Rev. Stat. § 8-1111(9) (15 offerees); Nev. Rev. Stat. § 90.530(11)(a) (25 offerees); N.C. Gen. Stat. § 78A-17(9) (25 offerees).

iii. Broker-Dealer and Agent Registration under the 1956 Uniform Securities Act

The 1956 Uniform Securities Act prohibits a person from transacting business in a state as a broker-dealer or an agent unless the person is registered as such under the 1956 Uniform Securities Act.[44] In addition, the 1956 Uniform Securities Act prohibits an issuer or a broker-dealer from employing an agent unless the agent is registered.[45]

a. Definitions of Broker-Dealer, Issuer and Agent

A "broker-dealer" under the 1956 Uniform Securities Act is "any person engaged in the business of effecting transactions in securities for the account of others or for his own account."[46] The definition of "broker-dealer" excludes:

> (1) an agent, (2) an issuer, (3) a bank, savings institution, or trust company, or (4) a person who has no place of business in this state if (A) he effects transactions in this state exclusively with or through (i) the issuers of the securities involved in the transactions, (ii) other broker-dealers, or (iii) banks, savings institutions, trust companies, insurance companies, investment companies as defined in the [Company Act], pension or profit-sharing trusts, or other financial institutions or institutional buyers, whether acting for themselves or as trustees, or (B) during any period of twelve consecutive months he does not direct more than fifteen offers to sell or buy into this state in any manner to persons other than those specified in clause (A), whether or not the offeror or any of the offerees is then present in this state.[47]

An "issuer" is "any person who issues or proposes to issue any security ...."[48] U.S. and offshore hedge funds are issuers because they issue limited partner interests, limited liability company ("LLC") interests or shares, depending on whether they are organized as partnerships, LLCs or corporations. A few exceptions from the definition of "issuer" are included in 1956 Uniform Securities Act section 401(g), but none applies to a U.S. or offshore hedge fund.[49] A U.S. or offshore hedge fund is thus an issuer and therefore is not an agent.

An "agent" under the 1956 Uniform Securities Act is "any individual other than a broker-dealer who represents a broker-dealer or issuer in effecting or attempting to effect purchases or sales of securities."[50] The definition of "agent" excludes an individual representing an issuer effecting a transaction exempted under 1956 Uniform Securities Act section 402(b), which includes

44. 1956 Uniform Securities Act § 201(a), 1 Blue Sky Law Rptr. (CCH) ¶ 5521.
45. 1956 Uniform Securities Act § 201(b), 1 Blue Sky Law Rptr. (CCH) ¶ 5521.
46. 1956 Uniform Securities Act § 401(c), 1 Blue Sky Law Rptr. (CCH) ¶ 5541.
47. *Id.*
48. 1956 Uniform Securities Act § 401(g), 1 Blue Sky Law Rptr. (CCH) ¶ 5541.
49. *Id.*
50. 1956 Uniform Securities Act § 401(b), 1 Blue Sky Law Rptr. (CCH) ¶ 5541.

the limited offering exemption described above,[51] but not all states have adopted this exemption. In addition, "a partner, officer, or director of a broker-dealer or issuer, or a person occupying a similar status or performing similar functions, is an agent only if he otherwise comes within the definition."[52] Such persons are not required to register as agents, and information about them is included in a broker-dealer's application for registration.[53] Accordingly, the officers of a general partner of a hedge fund typically are exempt from agent registration, unless they receive compensation directly tied to their solicitation activities.

b. Broker-Dealer and Agent Registration Process

Under the 1956 Uniform Securities Act, a broker-dealer or an agent must register by filing an application and a consent to service of process with the cognizant state regulatory authority.[54] The application must contain any information that the state regulatory authority requires concerning such matters as:

- the applicant's form and place of organization;
- the applicant's proposed method of doing business;
- the qualifications and business history of the applicant and any of its partners, officers or directors, any person occupying a similar status or performing similar functions, or any person directly or indirectly controlling the broker-dealer;
- any injunction or administrative order or conviction of a misdemeanor involving a security or any aspect of the securities business and any conviction of a felony; and
- the applicant's financial condition and history.[55]

The cognizant state regulatory authority also may require the broker-dealer to publish an announcement of its application for registration in one or more specified newspapers.[56] The registration typically becomes effective 30 days after an application is filed, unless a denial order is in effect or a proceeding for a denial order has commenced.[57] The applicant also must pay a filing fee specified by the state.[58]

The 1956 Uniform Securities Act authorizes the cognizant state regulatory authority to establish minimum capital requirements for broker-dealers or to require registered broker-dealers (other than broker-dealers whose net capital exceeds $25,000) to post surety bonds of up to $10,000.[59]

Because a broker-dealer's registration application must include information about its partners, officers, directors and similarly situated persons, such

51. *Id. See* § 7.2.1.ii.b, *supra.*
52. 1956 Uniform Securities Act § 401(b), 1 Blue Sky Law Rptr. (CCH) ¶ 5541.
53. *See* § 7.2.1.iii.b, *infra.*
54. 1956 Uniform Securities Act § 202(a), 1 Blue Sky Law Rptr. (CCH) ¶ 5522.
55. *Id.*
56. *Id.*
57. *Id.*
58. 1956 Uniform Securities Act § 202(b), 1 Blue Sky Law Rptr. (CCH) ¶ 5522.
59. 1956 Uniform Securities Act § 202(d) and (e), 1 Blue Sky Law Rptr. (CCH) ¶ 5522.

persons need not register as agents.[60] Instead, the broker-dealer's registration "automatically constitutes registration of any agent who is a partner, officer or director."[61] Consequently, the state regulatory authority may "institute a proceeding to deny or revoke the registration of a particular partner, officer or director without disturbing the status of the firm. At the same time, the disqualification of a director, officer or partner, as distinct from an ordinary agent, is also a basis for proceeding against the firm's registration if the [state securities administrator] finds it in the public interest to do so."[62]

c. Post-Registration Requirements

Under the 1956 Uniform Securities Act, a registered broker-dealer must make and keep "such accounts, correspondence, memoranda, papers, books, and other records as the [Administrator] by rule prescribes" for at least 3 years, unless the state regulatory authority otherwise prescribes.[63] The model rules proposed under the 1956 Uniform Securities Act require that a broker-dealer registered or required to be registered under the 1956 Uniform Securities Act make, maintain and preserve books and records in compliance with SEC rules 17a-3, 17a-4, 15c2-6 and 15c2-11.[64]

In addition, a registered broker-dealer must file such financial reports as the state regulatory authority may require by rule.[65] A registered broker-dealer also must amend any document filed with the state regulatory authority promptly after it becomes inaccurate or incomplete in any material respect.[66] The state regulatory authority has the right to conduct periodic, special or other examinations of the books and records required to be maintained by a registered broker-dealer.[67]

d. Denial, Revocation or Suspension of Registration

Under the 1956 Uniform Securities Act, a state regulatory authority may deny a broker-dealer's application for registration or suspend or revoke such a registration if it finds that doing so is in the public interest and that the applicant or registrant, any partner, officer, director or person occupying a similar position or performing a similar function for the applicant or registrant, or any person directly or indirectly controlling the applicant or registrant:

- has filed a registration application that, as of its effective date, was incomplete in any material respect or contained any statement that was, in light of the circumstances under which it was made, false or misleading with respect to any material fact;

---

60. *See* § 7.2.1.iii.a, *supra*.

61. Official Code Comment to 1956 Uniform Securities Act § 202(a), 1 Blue Sky Law Rptr. (CCH) ¶ 5522.01.

62. *Id.*

63. 1956 Uniform Securities Act § 203(a), 1 Blue Sky Law Rptr. (CCH) ¶ 5523.

64. 1998 NASAA Amended Rules under the Uniform Securities Act, rule 203(a)-1(a), 1 Blue Sky Law Rptr. (CCH) ¶ 5523.60, referring to 17 C.F.R. §§ 240.17a-3, 240.17a-4, 240.15c2-6 and 240.15c2-11.

65. 1956 Uniform Securities Act § 203(b), 1 Blue Sky Law Rptr. (CCH) ¶ 5523.

66. 1956 Uniform Securities Act § 203(c), 1 Blue Sky Law Rptr. (CCH) ¶ 5523.

67. 1956 Uniform Securities Act § 203(d), 1 Blue Sky Law Rptr. (CCH) ¶ 5523.

- has willfully violated or willfully failed to comply with any provision of the 1956 Uniform Securities Act or a predecessor act or any order under the 1956 Uniform Securities Act or a predecessor act;
- has been convicted, within the past 10 years, of any misdemeanor involving a security or any aspect of the securities business or any felony;
- is permanently or temporarily enjoined by any court of competent jurisdiction from engaging in or continuing any conduct or practice involving any aspect of the securities business;
- is the subject of an order of the state regulatory authority denying, suspending or revoking registration as a broker-dealer, agent or investment adviser;
- was within the past 5 years determined by a securities or commodities agency or administrator of another state or a court to have violated the Securities Act, the Exchange Act, the Company Act, the Advisers Act, the CEA, or the securities or commodities law of any other state;
- has engaged in dishonest or unethical practices in the securities business;
- is insolvent, either in the sense that liabilities exceed assets or in the sense that obligations cannot be met as they mature;
- is not qualified on the basis of such factors as training, experience and knowledge of the securities business, except that the state regulatory authority (i) may not deny, suspend or revoke a natural person's registration based on any other person's lack of qualification, (ii) may not enter an order solely on the basis of lack of experience if the applicant or registrant is qualified by training or knowledge or both, (iii) must consider that an agent who will work under the supervision of a registered broker-dealer need not have the same qualifications as a broker-dealer, and (iv) may require that an applicant pass an examination;[68]
- has failed reasonably to supervise its agents; or
- has failed to pay the proper filing fee, but the state regulatory authority must vacate any such order when the deficiency is corrected.[69]

iv. Consequences of Failure to Register Under the 1956 Uniform Securities Act

a. Regulatory Action

Under the 1956 Uniform Securities Act, the cognizant state regulatory authority may issue a cease and desist order (with or without a prior hearing) or bring an action in an applicable state court for an injunction or to enforce compliance

68. 1956 Uniform Securities Act § 204(b), 1 Blue Sky Law Rptr. (CCH) ¶ 5524.
69. 1956 Uniform Securities Act § 204(a)(k), 1 Blue Sky Law Rptr. (CCH) ¶ 5524.

with the Act, if it appears that a person has engaged or is about to engage in any act or practice that violates the Act.[70] On a proper showing by such regulatory authority, a court may also enter an order of rescission, restitution or disgorgement directed to any person who has violated any provision of the 1956 Uniform Securities Act or any rule or order under that Act.[71]

b. Criminal Actions

Any person who violates any provision of the 1956 Uniform Securities Act or any rule or order under the 1956 Uniform Securities Act is subject to a fine of up to $5,000 or imprisonment for up to 3 years or both.[72] A person who proves he or she had no knowledge of a rule or order may not, however, be imprisoned for violating it.[73]

c. Private Actions

A person who offers or sells a security in violation of the broker-dealer or agent registration requirements of the 1956 Uniform Securities Act is liable to the person buying the security for damages or for the consideration paid for the security, plus interest, costs and reasonable attorneys' fees, less the amount of any income received on the security.[74] A purchaser of securities may also recover from the seller of the securities under the 1956 Uniform Securities Act if the seller offered or sold the security "by means of any untrue statement of a material fact or any omission to state a material fact necessary in order to make the statements made, in light of the circumstances under which they are made, not misleading (the buyer not knowing of the untruth or omission)" and if the seller does not prove that he did not know and reasonably could not have known the untruth or omission.[75] In addition,

> every person who directly or indirectly controls a seller liable [for such a violation], every partner, officer, or director of such a seller, every person occupying a similar status or performing similar functions, every employee of such a seller who materially aids in the sale, and every broker-dealer or agent who materially aids in the sale are also liable jointly and severally with and to the same extent as the seller, unless the non-seller who is so liable sustains the burden of proof that he did not know, and in the exercise of reasonable care could not have known, of the existence of the facts by reason of which the liability is alleged to exist.[76]

---

70. 1956 Uniform Securities Act § 408, 1 Blue Sky Law Rptr. (CCH) ¶ 5548.
71. *Id.*
72. 1956 Uniform Securities Act § 409, 1 Blue Sky Law Rptr. (CCH) ¶ 5549.
73. *Id.*
74. 1956 Uniform Securities Act § 410(a)(2), 1 Blue Sky Law Rptr. (CCH) ¶ 5550.
75. 1956 Uniform Securities Act § 410(a)(2), 1 Blue Sky Law Rptr. (CCH) ¶ 5550. *See also* § 6.4, *supra,* regarding the anti-fraud provisions of the Securities Act and the Exchange Act.
76. 1956 Uniform Securities Act § 410(b), 1 Blue Sky Law Rptr. (CCH) ¶ 5550.

Under these provisions, not only a hedge fund, but also its investment adviser or general partner and their officers, may be liable to the hedge fund's limited partners for failure to comply with the requirements of the 1956 Uniform Securities Act.

Any private action brought under the 1956 Uniform Securities Act must be brought within 2 years after the contract of sale.[77] A buyer may not bring a private action under the 1956 Uniform Securities Act,

> (1) if the buyer received a written offer, before suit and at a time when he owned the security, to refund the consideration paid together with interest at 6 percent per year from the date of payment, less the amount of any income received on the security, and he failed to accept the offer within 30 days of its receipt, or (2) if the buyer received such an offer before suit and at a time when he did not own the security, unless he rejected the offer in writing within 30 days of its receipt.[78]

Any provision in a contract for sale of securities purporting to waive the buyer's right to bring any such action is void.[79]

2. Other State Securities Laws

As noted, not all states have adopted the 1956 Uniform Securities Act. The laws of two of those states, California and New York, are reviewed below.

i. California

a. Registration of Securities

Under the California Corporate Securities Law of 1968, it is unlawful to offer or sell in California any security in an issuer transaction unless the sale has been qualified or the security or transaction is exempted or not subject to qualification.[80] "Offer" has the same meaning under the California Securities Law as under the 1956 Uniform Securities Act.[81] "Sell" and "sale" generally have the same meanings under the California Securities Law as under the 1956 Uniform Securities Act, except that under the California Securities Law, they expressly include "any exchange of securities and any change in the rights, preferences, privileges, or restrictions of or on outstanding securities."[82] "Security" generally has the same meaning under the California Securities

---

77. 1956 Uniform Securities Act § 410(e), 1 Blue Sky Law Rptr. (CCH) ¶ 5550.

78. *Id.*

79. 1956 Uniform Securities Act § 410(g), 1 Blue Sky Law Rptr. (CCH) ¶ 5550.

80. Cal. Corp. Code § 25110.

81. *Compare* Cal. Corp. Code § 25017 *with* 1956 Uniform Securities Act § 401(k)(1) and (2), 1 Blue Sky Law Rptr. (CCH) ¶ 5541. *See* § 7.2.1.i, *supra*.

82. *Id.*

Law as under the 1956 Uniform Securities Act, except that under the California Securities Law, it expressly includes a nonmanagement interest in an LLC.[83]

"Issuer transaction" is not defined under the California Securities Law, but a "non-issuer transaction" is any transaction not directly or indirectly for the benefit of the issuer,[84] which implies that an issuer transaction is a transaction directly or indirectly for the benefit of the issuer. A transaction is indirectly for the benefit of the issuer if "any portion of the purchase price of any securities involved in the transaction will be received indirectly by the issuer."[85] This section addresses the qualification requirements only for issuer transactions, including securities issuances by a U.S. or offshore hedge fund.

As under the 1956 Uniform Securities Act, the California Securities Law provides for qualification by coordination with respect to securities for which a registration statement has been filed under the Securities Act in connection with the same offering.[86] In addition, the California Securities Law permits an issuer that has any class of shares registered under Exchange Act section 12 or that is registered as an investment company under the Company Act to qualify additional securities by notification.[87] Neither of these methods of qualification is available for a U.S. or offshore hedge fund engaged in a private offering of securities.[88]

Securities issued by a hedge fund must be qualified by permit.[89] To qualify by permit, an issuer must file an application in the form specified by

---

83. Cal. Corp. Code § 25019. Under this section, "security means any note; stock; treasury stock; membership in an incorporated or unincorporated association; bond; debenture; evidence of indebtedness; certificate of interest or participation in any profit-sharing agreement; collateral trust certificate; preorganization certificate or subscription; transferable share; investment contract; viatical settlement contract or a fractionalized or pooled interest therein; voting trust certificate; certificate of deposit for a security; interest in a limited liability company and any class or series of those interests (including any fractional or other interest in that interest), except a membership interest in a limited liability company in which the person claiming this exception can prove that all of the members are actively engaged in the management of the limited liability company; provided that evidence that members vote or have the right to vote, or the right to information concerning the business and affairs of the limited liability company, or the right to participate in management, shall not establish, without more, that all members are actively engaged in the management of the limited liability company; certificate of interest or participation in an oil, gas or mining title or lease or in payments out of production under that title or lease; put, call, straddle, option or privilege on any security, certificate of deposit, or group or index of securities (including any interest therein or based on the value thereof); or any put, call, straddle, option or privilege entered into on a national securities exchange relating to foreign currency; any beneficial interest or other security issued in connection with a funded employees' pension, profit sharing, stock bonus, or similar benefit plan; or, in general, any interest or instrument commonly known as a 'security'; or any certificate of interest or participation in, temporary or interim certificate for, receipt for, guarantee of, or warrant or right to subscribe to or purchase, any of the foregoing."

84. Cal. Corp. Code § 25011.

85. *Id.*

86. Cal. Corp. Code § 25111(a).

87. Cal. Corp. Code § 25112(a).

88. *See* § 7.2.1.ii.a, *supra.*

89. Cal. Corp. Code § 25113.

the California Commissioner of Corporations.[90] As with the 1956 Uniform Securities Act, this application requires extensive disclosure somewhat similar to that required by Form S-1 under the Securities Act.[91]

b. Exemptions from Securities Registration Requirements

The California Securities Law provides several exemptions from its qualification requirements.[92] As under the 1956 Uniform Securities Act, a U.S. or offshore hedge fund typically relies on a form of limited offering exemption.[93] The California Securities Law limited offering exemption is similar to Rule 506 of Regulation D[94] and is available if:

- sales of securities are made to no more than 35 persons, including persons not in California,[95] but excluding certain types of purchasers as discussed below;
- all purchasers either have a preexisting personal or business relationship with the offeror or any of its partners, officers, directors, controlling persons or managers (as appointed or elected by the members) if the offeror is an LLC, or by reason of their business or financial experience or the business or financial experience of their professional advisers who are unaffiliated with and who are not compensated by the issuer or any affiliate or selling agent of the issuer, directly or indirectly, could be reasonably assumed to have the capacity to protect their own interests in connection with the transaction;[96]
- each purchaser represents that the purchaser is purchasing for the purchaser's own account (or a trust account if the purchaser is a trustee) and not with a view to or for sale in connection with any distribution of the security;[97] and
- the offering and sale of the security are not accomplished by the publication of any advertisement.[98]

A notice of transaction must be filed with the California Commissioner of Corporations on a form prescribed by the Commissioner, but failure to file the notice does not affect the availability of the exemption.[99] In determining the number of purchasers, an issuer may exclude purchasers that are accredited investors under Rule 501(a) of Regulation D.[100] An issuer may also count a

90. *See* 10 Cal. Code Reg. §§ 260.110 and 260.113.
91. *Id. See* § 6.2.1.iii, *supra*.
92. *See* Cal. Corp. Code §§ 25101 and 25102.
93. Cal. Corp. Code § 25102(f).
94. *Compare* Cal. Corp. Code § 25102(f) and 10 Cal. Code Reg. §§ 260.102.12–260.102.14 *with* 17 C.F.R. §§ 230.501-230.503 and 230.506-230.508. *See also* § 5.3.2, *supra*.
95. Cal. Corp. Code § 25102(f)(1).
96. Cal. Corp. Code § 25102(f)(2).
97. Cal. Corp. Code § 25102(f)(3).
98. Cal. Corp. Code § 25102(f)(4).
99. Cal. Corp. Code § 25102(f) and Cal. Code Reg. § 260.102.14.
100. 10 Cal. Code Reg. § 260.102.13(g); 17 C.F.R. § 230.501(a). *See* § 5.3.2.ii, *supra*.

husband and wife, or a custodian or trustee acting for the accounts of his or her minor children, as one purchaser.[101] The issuer is not required to count any of its officers, directors, affiliates, managers, trustees, general partners (or officers, directors or general partners of a general partner) or any person who occupies a position with the issuer or a general partner of the issuer with duties similar to those of an executive officer of a corporation.[102]

Also excluded from the number of purchasers are any bank, savings and loan association, trust company, insurance company, investment company registered under the Company Act, pension or profit-sharing trust (other than a pension or profit-sharing trust of the issuer, a self-employed individual retirement plan or an individual retirement account) or other institutional investor designated by rule, whether the purchaser is acting for itself or as trustee.[103] The California Commissioner of Corporations also has excluded the following categories of persons from the 35 purchaser limit:

- any relative, spouse or relative of the spouse of a purchaser who has the same principal residence as the purchaser;[104]
- any trust or estate in which a purchaser and any of the persons related to such purchaser as specified in the preceding clause or the following clause collectively have more than 50 percent of the beneficial interest (excluding contingent interests);[105]
- any corporation or other organization of which a purchaser and any of the persons related to the purchaser as specified in the two preceding clauses beneficially own more than 50 percent of the equity securities (excluding directors' qualifying shares) or equity interests;[106]
- any individual who is a promoter of the issuer (that is, a person who, acting alone or in conjunction with others, takes the initiative in founding and organizing the business or enterprise of the issuer);[107]
- any person who purchases $150,000 or more of the securities offered in the transaction, provided that the issuer reasonably believes that either such purchaser has the capacity to protect such person's own interest in connection with the transaction or the investment (including mandatory assessments) does not exceed 10 percent of such person's net worth or joint net worth with his or her spouse;[108] and
- any entity in which all of the equity owners are accredited investors or persons described above.[109]

---

101. Cal. Corp. Code § 25102(f)(4).
102. Cal. Corp. Code § 25102(f); Cal. Code Reg. §§ 260.102.13(a) and (b).
103. Cal. Corp. Code §§ 25102(f) and (i); Cal. Code Reg. § 260.102.10.
104. 10 Cal. Code Reg. § 260.102.13(c)(1).
105. 10 Cal. Code Reg. § 260.102.13(c)(2).
106. 10 Cal. Code Reg. § 260.102.13(c)(3).
107. 10 Cal. Code. Reg. §§ 260.102.13(d) and 260.102.12(f).
108. 10 Cal. Code Reg. § 260.102.13(e).
109. 10 Cal. Code Reg. § 260.102.13(h).

c. Registration of Broker-Dealers and Agents

The California Securities Law provides that "no broker-dealer shall effect any transaction in, or induce or attempt to induce the purchase or sale of, any security in this state unless the broker-dealer has first applied for and secured from the commissioner a certificate, then in effect, authorizing that person to act in that capacity."[110] In addition, "no person shall, on behalf of a broker-dealer licensed pursuant to Section 25211, or on behalf of an issuer, effect any transaction in or induce or attempt to induce the purchase or sale of, any security in this state unless that broker-dealer and agent have complied with any rule as the commissioner may adopt for the qualification and employment of those agents."[111]

Under the California Securities Law, a "broker-dealer" is "any person engaged in the business of effecting transactions in securities in this state for the account of others or for his own account."[112] The definition of "broker-dealer" expressly excludes an issuer (other than a person engaged in the regular business of issuing or guaranteeing options with regard to securities not issued by him) and an agent, when an employee of a broker-dealer or issuer.[113] Accordingly, in issuing its own securities, a U.S. or offshore hedge fund is not a broker-dealer.

An "agent" is "any individual, other than a broker-dealer or a partner of a licensed broker-dealer, who represents a broker-dealer or who for compensation represents an issuer in effecting or attempting to effect purchases or sales of securities in this state."[114] An officer or director of a broker-dealer or issuer, or an individual occupying a similar status or performing similar functions, is an agent only if he or she otherwise comes within the definition of an agent and receives compensation specifically related to purchases or sales of securities.[115] Accordingly, the general partner of a U.S. hedge fund and its officers, and the directors of an offshore hedge fund, are only agents if they receive compensation specifically related to their sales of securities.

An application for a certificate as a broker-dealer must be accompanied by a consent to service of process and include information required by rules of the California Commissioner of Corporations.[116] The Commissioner may deny, suspend or revoke a broker-dealer certificate for reasons similar to those under the 1956 Uniform Securities Act.[117]

---

110. Cal. Corp. Code § 25210(a).
111. Cal. Corp. Code § 25210(b).
112. Cal. Corp. Code § 25004(a).
113. Cal. Corp. Code §§ 25004(a) and (b).
114. Cal. Corp. Code § 25003(a).
115. Cal. Corp. Code § 25003(d).
116. Cal. Corp. Code § 25211(a).
117. Cal. Corp. Code § 25212. *See* § 7.2.1.iii.d, *supra.*

d. Consequences of Failure to Register under the California Securities Law

(1) Administrative Actions

If the California Commissioner of Corporations determines that any person has engaged or is about to engage in any act or practice that violates the California Securities Law or any rule or order under the California Securities Law, the Commissioner may bring an action to enjoin such act or practice or to enforce compliance with the California Securities Law.[118] The Commissioner also may include an action for ancillary relief, including a claim for restitution or disgorgement or damages on behalf of the persons injured by the act or practice.[119]

If in the opinion of the California Commissioner of Corporations the sale of a security is subject to qualification or a notice filing under the California Securities Law and the security is being offered or sold without being qualified, the Commissioner may order the issuer to desist and refrain from further offers or sales of the security until the security is qualified or the notice filing is made.[120] Similarly, if in the opinion of the Commissioner a person has been or is acting as a broker-dealer in violation of the registration requirements under the California Securities Law, the Commissioner may order that person to desist and refrain from such activity until the person is appropriately licensed or has filed the appropriate notices.[121] A person subject to such an order may request a hearing. Failure to file a written request for a hearing within 30 days after being served with the order will result in the order being deemed final.[122]

(2) Criminal and Civil Penalties

Any person who willfully violates any provision of the California Securities Law or any rule or order under it is subject to a fine of up to $1,000,000, up to a year in prison or both.[123] Any person who violates the California Securities Law or any rule or order under it also may be liable for a civil penalty of up to $25,000 for each violation.[124] Any action to enforce such a civil penalty must be brought within 4 years after the act or transaction constituting the violation.[125]

(3) Private Actions

Any person who violates the securities qualification requirements of the California Securities Law is liable to any person who acquired the securities from the violator for the consideration paid for the securities, with interest at the legal rate, less the amount of any income the purchaser received therefrom, on tender of the securities to the issuer.[126] If the purchaser no longer owns

---

118. Cal. Corp. Code § 25530(a).
119. Cal. Corp. Code § 25530(b).
120. Cal. Corp. Code § 25532(a).
121. Cal. Corp. Code § 25532(b).
122. Cal. Corp. Code § 25532(d).
123. Cal. Corp. Code § 25540(a).
124. Cal. Corp. Code § 25535(a).
125. Cal. Corp. Code § 25535(c).
126. Cal. Corp. Code § 25503.

the securities or if the consideration for the securities is not capable of being returned, the purchaser may sue for damages equal to the purchaser's purchase price plus interest at the legal rate from the date of purchase, less the total value of the securities when sold by the plaintiff and any income received by the purchaser from the securities.[127]

In addition, every person who directly or indirectly controls a person liable under these provisions, every partner in a firm so liable, every principal executive officer or director of a corporation so liable, every person occupying a similar status or performing similar functions, and every employee of a person so liable who materially aids in the act or transaction constituting the violation is liable jointly and severally with and to the same extent as such person, unless he or she had no knowledge of or reasonable grounds to believe the existence of the facts by reason of which the liability is alleged to exist.[128] Any person who materially assists in any such violation also is jointly and severally liable with any other person so liable.[129]

Such a private action must be brought within 2 years after the violation on which it is based or 1 year after the purchaser discovers the facts constituting the violation, whichever period ends earlier.[130] No purchaser can commence such an action if, before the suit is commenced, the purchaser receives a written offer approved in form by the California Commissioner of Corporations stating the respect in which such liability may have arisen, offering to repurchase the security for a cash price payable on delivery of the security, offering to pay the purchaser an amount in cash equal to the amount recoverable by the purchaser, or offering to rescind the transaction by putting the parties back in the same position as before the transaction, providing that such offer may be accepted by the purchaser at any time within a specified period of at least 30 days after receipt of the offer, setting forth the provisions of California Corporate Securities Law section 25507(b) and containing such other information as the California Commissioner of Corporations may require, and the purchaser fails to accept such offer in writing within the specified period.[131]

ii. New York

The issuance of securities and registration of brokers in New York is governed by the New York Fraudulent Practices Act, or "Martin Act."[132] The securities and broker registration requirements of the Martin Act are closely intertwined[133] and are addressed together in this section.

---

127. *Id.*
128. Cal. Corp. Code § 25504.
129. Cal. Corp. Code § 25504.1.
130. Cal. Corp. Code § 25507(a).
131. Cal. Corp. Code § 25507(b).
132. *See* N.Y. Gen. Bus. Law §§ 352 *et seq.*
133. *See* N.Y. Gen. Bus. Law § 359-e.

a. Definitions

A "dealer" under the Martin Act is

> any person, firm, association or corporation engaged in the business of buying and selling securities from or to the public within or from this state for his or its own account, through a broker or otherwise ..., but does not include any person, firm, association or corporation in so far as he or it buys or sells securities for his or its bona fide investment account, either individually or in some fiduciary capacity.[134]

Under the Martin Act, a "person, firm, association or corporation selling or offering for sale from or to the public within or from [New York] securities issued by it"[135] is also a dealer.

"Dealer" does not include a person selling or offering for sale any security or securities as part of a private placement of securities, if the sales and offers are made only to banks, corporations, savings institutions, trust companies, insurance companies, investment companies (as defined under the Company Act), pension or profit-sharing trusts or other financial institutions or institutional buyers.[136] A hedge fund that offers interests to individual investors, as well as institutional investors, cannot rely on this exemption.

Whether a hedge fund that offers interests to anyone in New York is a dealer under the Martin Act thus depends on whether the hedge fund is selling securities "to the public" in New York. A hedge fund's offering that is exempt under Securities Act section 4(a)(2) and Rule 506 of Regulation D[137] is not made to the public for purposes of the Securities Act. The Committee on Securities Regulation of the New York State Bar Association has expressed the view that all such nonpublic offerings are excluded from the Martin Act's dealer registration requirements.[138] Under this view, a hedge fund would not be a dealer for purposes of the Martin Act. Nevertheless, the New York State Attorney General has consistently taken the strained view of the Martin Act that a sale to even one person in New York is a sale to the public in New York.[139] Regardless of the merits of this decades-long controversy, many hedge funds are disinclined to

---

134. N.Y. Gen. Bus. Law § 359-e(1)(a).

135. *Id.*

136. *Id.*

137. *See* Chapter 5, *supra.*

138. Comm. on Sec. Reg. of the N.Y. State Bar Ass'n, *Private Offering Exemptions and Exclusions Under the New York State Martin Act and Section 18 of the Securities Act of 1933* (Aug. 2002), citing People v. Landes, 84 N.Y.2d 655 (1994); People v. Glenn Realty Corp., 106 Misc. 2d 46 (Sup. Ct. Spec. Term, N.Y. County 1980); Puro v. Zimmerman, N.Y.L.J. at 14, col. 3, Apr. 18, 1977 (Sup. Ct.), *aff'd* 61 A.D.2d 772 (1st Dep't 1978); and N.Y. Attorney General Interpretive Opinion, 2A Blue Sky L. Rep. (CCH) ¶ 42,584 (Dec. 6, 1994).

139. An issuer, however, is not a dealer under the Martin Act solely because it offers its securities through a broker or dealer. In fact, the Committee on Securities Regulation of the New York State Bar Association has expressed the view that an issuer selling its securities through a New York-registered broker-dealer in a best-efforts offering (even a public offering) is not a dealer that is itself subject to the filing requirements of N.Y. Gen. Bus. Law § 359-e.

risk the expense of defending a claim by the New York Attorney General and elect to comply with the Martin Act as if they were dealers.

A "broker" is "any person, firm, association or corporation, other than a dealer, engaged in the business of effecting transactions in securities for the account of others within or from this state."[140] Hedge funds ordinarily are not brokers under this definition because, in general, they are dealers (in the view of the New York State Attorney General) and also because they effect transactions in securities for their own accounts, not the accounts of others.

A "salesman" is a person employed by a broker or dealer "for the purpose of representing such broker or dealer in the sale or purchase of securities to or from the public within or from this state."[141] A "principal" is "every person or firm directly or indirectly controlling any broker or dealer."[142] Under these definitions, the general partner of a U. S. hedge fund, and its officers, directors, managers and other controlling persons, and the directors of an offshore hedge fund, are all principals of the hedge fund. They generally are not, however, salesmen of the hedge fund, unless they are employed for the purpose of representing the hedge fund in the purchase or sale of securities.

b. Registration Requirements

If an issuer is a dealer under the Martin Act (or, as discussed above, does not want to risk defending a claim by the New York State Attorney General that it is a dealer), then before it may offer its securities in New York, the Martin Act requires it to file a registration statement for each broker, dealer or salesman engaged in the offering, a state notice and a further state notice.[143]

(1) Registration Statement for Brokers and Dealers

No dealer or broker may sell, purchase or offer to sell or purchase any security to or from the public within or from New York unless the dealer, broker or salesman has filed a registration statement.[144] The registration statement for brokers and dealers is called the "broker-dealer statement" and must include "such information pertaining to the business history for the last preceding 5 years, criminal record, and educational background of the applicant and his or its partners, officers, directors or other principals thereof deemed pertinent by the attorney-general."[145] Registration as a broker or dealer must be renewed every 4 years, within 60 days before expiration of the current 4-year period.[146]

Generally, to register as a dealer or broker, an issuer of securities must file a Form M-11.[147] After NSMIA was adopted, however, the New York Department of Law, Bureau of Investor Protection and Securities, adopted the Form 99

140. N.Y. Gen. Bus. Law § 359-e(1)(b).
141. N.Y. Gen. Bus. Law § 359-e(1)(c).
142. N.Y. Gen. Bus. Law § 359-e(1)(d).
143. N.Y. Gen. Bus. Law §§ 359-e(2), (3) and (8).
144. N.Y. Gen. Bus. Law § 359-e(3).
145. N.Y. Gen. Bus. Law § 359-e(3)(a).
146. N.Y. Gen. Bus. Law § 359-e(3)(c).
147. N.Y. Comp. Codes R. & Regs. tit. 13, § 10.1.

Notification Filing Pursuant to NSMIA.[148] An issuer relying on Rule 506 of Regulation D may file a Form 99 instead of a Form M-11.[149] Accordingly, a hedge fund may file a Form 99 broker-dealer statement. An issuer filing a Form 99 also must file:

- a consent to services of process;
- copies of its offering documents;
- a copy of its Form D, as filed with the SEC; and
- filing fees that range from $300 to $1,200, depending on the size of the offering in New York.[150]

(2) Registration Statement for Salesmen

No salesman may sell, purchase or offer to sell or purchase any security to or from the public within or from New York unless the salesman has filed a registration statement.[151] Furthermore, no broker or dealer may employ a salesman unless the salesman is registered.[152] The registration statement for a salesman is called the salesman's statement and requires the same information as is required by the broker-dealer statement described above.[153] A salesman also must pass the Series 63 or Series 66 examination as administered by the North American Securities Administrators Association ("NASSAA") before applying for registration as a salesman.[154]

A partner, officer, director or principal of a broker or dealer who is named as such in the broker's or dealer's registration statement is not required to register as a salesman of the broker or dealer.[155] As discussed above, neither the general partner of a U.S. hedge fund, nor its officers, directors, managers and other controlling persons, nor the directors of an offshore hedge fund, are likely to be considered salesmen of the hedge fund. Even if they were, however, as long as they are identified in the Form 99, they are not required to register as salesmen under the foregoing exception.

The Martin Act also generally requires all persons regularly employed in New York by a broker or dealer required to register under the Martin Act to file their fingerprints with the New York Attorney General.[156] This requirement does not apply, however, to employees of dealers required to register under the Martin Act solely because the dealers are "engaged in selling or offering securities issued by themselves."[157] Accordingly, the fingerprinting requirements ordinarily do not apply to principals or employees of a hedge fund.

---

148. Form 99 – Notification Filing Pursuant to Nat'l Securities Market Improvement Act of 1996, 2A Blue Sky Law Rptr. ¶ 42,587.

149. *Id.*

150. *Id.*

151. N.Y. Gen. Bus. Law § 359-e(3).

152. N.Y. Gen. Bus. Law § 359-e(11).

153. N.Y. Gen. Bus. Law § 359-e(3)(b).

154. *Id.*

155. N.Y. Gen. Bus. Law § 359-e(4).

156. N.Y. Gen. Bus. Law § 359-e(12).

157. *Id.*

(3) State Notice

No dealer or broker may sell, purchase or offer to sell or purchase to or from the public within or from New York, as a principal or a broker, any securities until it files a "state notice" with the New York Department of State.[158] A hedge fund that is a dealer (or, as discussed above, does not want to risk defending a claim by the New York State Attorney General that it is a dealer) must file a state notice. The state notice must include:

- the name and business or post office address of the dealer or broker;
- if the dealer or broker is a corporation, the state or country of incorporation; and
- if the dealer or broker is a partnership, the names of its partners.[159]

State notices are published in the New York State bulletin.[160]

(4) Further State Notice

A dealer may not sell or offer for sale to the public in New York, as a principal or an agent, any securities unless the dealer files a "further state notice."[161] The further state notice must contain the same information as the state notice described above, except that the names of partners of a dealer organized as a partnership do not need to be included.[162] The further state notice also must include the name of the security or securities and the name, post office address, and state or country of incorporation or organization of the corporation, association, common law trust or similar organization issuing the securities.[163] If 2 or more dealers are engaged in the offering, they may file a joint further state notice and must identify the syndicate manager or managers.[164]

Several categories of securities are exempt from the requirement to file a further state notice, but none of these exclusions applies to a hedge fund.[165] Accordingly, if a hedge fund is a dealer (or, as discussed above, does not want to risk defending a claim by the New York State Attorney General that it is a dealer), it ordinarily must file a further state notice.

§ 7.3 NSMIA

1. State Securities Registration Under NSMIA

In 1996, Congress enacted NSMIA "to eliminate duplicative and unnecessary regulatory burdens while preserving important investor protections by

158. N.Y. Gen. Bus. Law § 359-e(2).
159. *Id.*
160. N.Y. Gen. Bus. Law § 359-c.
161. N.Y. Gen. Bus. Law § 359-e(8).
162. *Id.*
163. *Id.*
164. *Id.*
165. *See* N.Y. Gen. Bus. Law § 359-f.

reallocating responsibility over the regulation of the nation's securities markets in a more logical fashion between the Federal government and the states."[166] NSMIA provides, among other things, that

> no law, rule, regulation, or order, or other administrative action of any State or any political subdivision thereof (1) requiring, or with respect to, registration or qualification of securities, or registration or qualification of securities transactions, shall directly or indirectly apply to a security that (A) is a covered security; or (B) will be a covered security upon completion of the transaction.[167]

The definition of "covered security" under NSMIA includes several categories of securities.[168] Only one is relevant to U.S. and offshore hedge funds.[169] Securities Act section 18(b)(4)(D) provides that

> A security is a covered security with respect to a transaction that is exempt from registration under [the Securities Act] pursuant to...(D) Commission rules or regulations issued under [Securities Act] Section 4[(a)](2), except that this subparagraph does not prohibit a State from imposing notice filing requirements that are substantially similar to those required by rule or regulation under Section 4[(a)](2) that are in effect on September 1, 1996.[170]

Rule 506 of Regulation D was promulgated by the SEC under Securities Act section 4(a)(2).[171] Accordingly, securities sold by a U.S. or offshore hedge fund in a transaction that is exempt under Rule 506 of Regulation D are covered securities under NSMIA. NSMIA preempts the states from requiring registration of such securities. As a result, states can no longer pursue civil or criminal remedies against, or grant rescission rights to investors in, a U.S. or offshore hedge fund that fails to register its securities with the state, if the hedge fund complies with the requirements of Rule 506 of Regulation D.

NSMIA expressly provides, however, that the states retain jurisdiction "to investigate and bring enforcement actions with respect to fraud or deceit, or unlawful conduct by a broker or dealer, in connection with securities or securities transactions."[172] In addition, NSMIA permits the states to continue to collect filing or registration fees with respect to securities or securities transactions.[173] NSMIA also permits the states to require issuers of covered securities to file

---

166. Conference Report on the Nat'l Securities Markets Improvement Act of 1996, H.R. Rep. No. 104-864 at 39 (Sep. 28, 1996).
167. Securities Act § 18(a)(1), 15 U.S.C. § 77r(a).
168. *See* Securities Act § 18(b), 15 U.S.C. § 77r(b).
169. *See* §§ 3.2.5 and 3.3.1, *supra*.
170. Securities Act § 18(b)(4)(D), 15 U.S.C. § 77r(b)(4)(D).
171. *See* § 5.3.2, *supra*.
172. Securities Act § 18(c)(1), 15 U.S.C. § 77r(c)(1).
173. Securities Act § 18(c)(2)(B)(i), 15 U.S.C. § 77r(c)(2)(B)(i).

notices with the cognizant state regulatory authority.[174] If an issuer fails to make a notice filing with a state or pay to a state a fee permitted under NSMIA, the state may suspend the offer or sale of securities within the state.[175]

Accordingly, although a U.S. or offshore hedge fund issuing securities in a state pursuant to Rule 506 of Regulation D is not required to register such securities under that state's securities laws, the hedge fund may be required to file a notice with and pay a fee to the cognizant state regulatory authority. A 1997 amendment to the 1956 Uniform Securities Act permits the state regulatory authority to require an issuer to file a notice no later than 15 days after the first sale of a federally covered security in the state.[176] Most states require an issuer relying on Rule 506 of Regulation D to file a notice within 15 days after the first sale of securities in that state.[177]

The required filing consists of a copy of the Form D filed with the SEC under Regulation D, a consent to service of process and a fee established by state law or regulation.[178] A possible exception is New York, which, as discussed above, in addition to a Form D, consent to service of process and filing fee, may require the filing of a Form 99, Notification Filing Pursuant to National Securities Markets Improvement Act of 1996, a State Notice and a Further State Notice.[179] New York also may require a filing before the first sale of securities in New York.[180]

Some states require the filing only with the first sale of securities. A few states require filings periodically. For example, Illinois law provides that a filing is only good for a year and must be renewed if securities will be sold in Illinois more than a year after the last filing in Illinois.[181] Similarly, the notice filing in New York must be renewed every 4 years.[182]

---

174. Securities Act § 18(b)(4)(D) and 18(c)(2)(A), 15 U.S.C. § 77r(b)(4)(D) and (c)(2)(A).

175. Securities Act § 18(c)(3), 15 U.S.C. § 77r(c)(3).

176. 1956 Uniform Securities Act § 307 and Rule 307(b)-1, 1 Blue Sky Law Rptr. (CCH) ¶¶ 5536.10 and 5536.15.

177. The following states require filing of SEC documents no later than 15 days after the first sale in the state: Alabama, Alaska, Arizona, Arkansas, California, Colorado, Connecticut, Delaware, the District of Columbia, Georgia, Hawaii, Idaho, Illinois, Indiana, Iowa, Kansas, Kentucky, Louisiana, Maine, Maryland, Massachusetts, Michigan, Minnesota, Mississippi, Missouri, Montana, Nebraska, Nevada, New Hampshire, New Jersey, New Mexico, North Carolina, North Dakota, Ohio, Oklahoma, Oregon, Pennsylvania, Rhode Island, South Carolina, South Dakota, Tennessee, Texas, Utah, Vermont, Virginia, Washington, West Virginia, Wisconsin and Wyoming. *See* 1 Blue Sky Law Rptr. (CCH) ¶ 6251 (listing state filing requirements).

178. *Id.* and 1956 Uniform Securities Act § 307(b) and Rule 307(b)-1, 1 Blue Sky Law Rptr. (CCH) ¶¶ 5536.10 and 5536.15.

179. *See* N.Y. Gen. Law § 359-e; New York Form 99, Notification Filing Pursuant to Nat'l Securities Markets Improvement Act of 1996, 2A Blue Sky Law Rptr. (CCH) ¶ 42,587. *See* § 7.2.2.ii, *supra.*

180. *See* New York Form 99, Notification Filing Pursuant to Nat'l Securities Markets Improvement Act of 1996, 2A Blue Sky Law Rptr. (CCH) ¶ 42,587.

181. 815 Ill. Comp. Stat. § 5/2a.

182. N.Y. Gen. Law § 359-e(3)(c). *See* § 7.2.2.ii, *supra.*

2. NSMIA and Broker-Dealer and Agent Registration

Although NSMIA preempts state securities registration requirements that otherwise would apply to sales of limited partner interests in U.S. hedge funds and shares of offshore hedge funds, it does not preempt the broker-dealer registration requirements under state securities laws.[183] Accordingly, even after the adoption of NSMIA, investment advisers that serve as the general partners of hedge funds or as the investment advisers to offshore hedge funds may be required to comply with such registration requirements.[184]

3. Amendments to the 1956 Uniform Securities Act following NSMIA

After NSMIA was adopted, the NASAA amended the 1956 Uniform Securities Act to exclude federal covered securities from the registration requirements of 1956 Uniform Securities Act section 301.[185] A "federal covered security" under this Act is

> any security that is a covered security under Section 18(b) of the [Securities Act] or rules or regulations promulgated thereunder, except, up through October 10, 1999, or such other date as may be legally permissible, a federal covered security for which a fee has not been paid and promptly remedied following written notification from the [state securities administrator] to the issuer of the nonpayment or underpayment of such fees, as required by this Act, shall not be a federal covered security.[186]

The amendment also gives the state regulatory authority the authority to require the issuer of a federal covered security described in Securities Act section 18(b)(4)(D), such as a security issued pursuant to Rule 506 of Regulation D, to file a Form D, a consent to service of process and a filing fee with the state regulatory authority within 15 days of the date on which the first sale of securities occurs in the state.[187]

The NASAA amendments exclude from the definition of "agent" an individual who represents an issuer in "effecting transactions in a covered security as described in Section 18(b)(3) and 18(b)(4)(D) of the [Securities Act]."[188] An individual representing a U.S. or offshore hedge fund in selling its securities in a transaction under Rule 506 of Regulation D is therefore not an agent and is not required to register as such.

---

183. *See* Conference Report on the Nat'l Securities Markets Improvement Act of 1996, H.R. Rep. No. 104-864 at 39 (Sep. 28, 1996).

184. *See* § 7.2.1.iii, *supra.*

185. 1 Blue Sky Law Rptr. (CCH) ¶ 5531.05.

186. 1956 Uniform Securities Act § 401(c)(2), 1 Blue Sky Law Rptr. (CCH) ¶ 5541.30.

187. 1956 Uniform Securities Act § 307, 1 Blue Sky Law Rptr. (CCH) ¶ 5536.10. *See also* the NASAA rule that implements this section, Rule 307(b)-1, at 1 Blue Sky Law Rptr. (CCH) ¶ 5536.25.

188. 1956 Uniform Securities Act § 401(b)(1)(C), 1 Blue Sky Law Rptr. (CCH) ¶ 5541.30.

§ 7.4 2002 Uniform Securities Act

In 2002, the NCCUSL proposed the 2002 Uniform Securities Act. The stated goals of this Act are to achieve greater uniformity among state securities laws, to achieve consistency with NSMIA, and to facilitate electronic records, signatures and filings.[189] The 2002 Uniform Securities Act has been adopted by several states that had previously adopted the 1956 Uniform Securities Act, and by some states that did not adopt the 1956 Uniform Securities Act. The 2002 Uniform Securities Act has been adopted in Georgia, Hawaii, Idaho, Indiana, Iowa, Kansas, Maine, Michigan, Minnesota, Mississippi, Missouri, New Mexico, Oklahoma, South Carolina, South Dakota, the U.S. Virgin Islands, Vermont and Wisconsin.[190]

1. Offers and Sales of Securities within a State

As with the 1956 Uniform Securities Act, the 2002 Uniform Securities Act registration requirements, both for securities and for brokers, apply only if there is an offer or sale of a security within the state.[191] "Offer" and "sale" have substantially the same definitions under the 1956 Uniform Securities Act and the 2002 Uniform Securities Act.[192] The 2002 Uniform Securities Act definition of "security" has been updated to reflect, among other things, amendments to the Securities Act definition and "to amplify the definition of investment contract so that it can expressly reach interests in limited partnerships, limited liability companies, or viatical settlement agreements, among other contracts, when they satisfy the definition of investment contract."[193] To this end, a "security" under the 2002 Uniform Securities Act:

> (D) includes as an "investment contract," among other contracts, an investment in a common enterprise with the expectation of profits to be derived primarily from the efforts of a person other than the investor and a "common enterprise" means an enterprise in which the fortunes of the investor are interwoven with those of either the person offering the investment, a third-party, or other investors, and (E) includes as an "investment contract," among other contracts, an interest in a limited partnership and a limited liability company and an investment in a viatical settlement or similar agreement.[194]

189. 1 Blue Sky Law Rptr. (CCH) ¶ 5600.

190. *See* "A Few Facts About the Uniform Securities Act (2002)," *supra*, n. 11.

191. 2002 Uniform Securities Act §§ 301 and 401(a), 1 Blue Sky Law Rptr. (CCH) ¶¶ 5610 and 5617.

192. *Compare* 2002 Uniform Securities Act § 102(26), 1 Blue Sky Law Rptr. ¶ 5602, *with* 1956 Uniform Securities Act § 401(j), 1 Blue Sky Law Rptr. 5541.

193. Prefatory Note to the 2002 Uniform Securities Act, 1 Blue Sky Law Rptr. ¶ 5600.

194. 2002 Uniform Securities Act § 102(28), 1 Blue Sky Law Rptr. (CCH) ¶ 5602.

2. Securities Registration Under the 2002 Uniform Securities Act

Under the 2002 Uniform Securities Act, no person may offer or sell a security in a state unless the security is a federal covered security, the security, transaction or offer is exempt from registration, or the security is registered under the 2002 Uniform Securities Act.[195] Under this Act, a "federal covered security" is "a security that is, or upon completion of a transaction will be, a covered security under Section 18(b) of the [Securities Act] or rules or regulations adopted pursuant to that provision."[196] Under the 2002 Uniform Securities Act, the cognizant state regulatory authority may require that an issuer of a federal covered security under Securities Act section 18(b)(4)(D),[197] which includes a security issued pursuant to Rule 506 of Regulation D,[198] file a Form D, file a consent to service of process and pay a filing fee.[199] Generally, under the 2002 Uniform Securities Act, a hedge fund that complies with Rule 506 of Regulation D is required only to make such notice filings and is not required to register its securities with the state.

If a hedge fund is required to register its securities with a state, the 2002 Uniform Securities Act registration requirements are substantially the same as the registration requirements of the 1956 Uniform Securities Act.[200]

3. Broker-Dealer and Agent Registration Under 2002 Uniform Securities Act

Like the 1956 Uniform Securities Act, the 2002 Uniform Securities Act provides that a person may not transact business in a state as a broker-dealer or as an agent, unless the person is registered as such under the 2002 Uniform Securities Act.[201] The 2002 Uniform Securities Act also forbids an issuer or a broker-dealer to employ an agent, unless the agent is registered.[202]

i. Definitions of Broker-Dealer, Issuer and Agent

Under the 2002 Uniform Securities Act, a "broker-dealer" is "any person engaged in the business of effecting transactions in securities for the account of others or for his own account."[203] The definition of "broker-dealer" excludes, among others, agents and issuers.[204]

195. 2002 Uniform Securities Act § 301, 1 Blue Sky Law Rptr. (CCH) ¶ 5610.
196. 2002 Uniform Securities Act § 102(7), 1 Blue Sky Law Rptr. (CCH) ¶ 5602.
197. 15 U.S.C. § 77r(b)(4)(D).
198. *See* §§ 5.3.2 and 7.3.1, *supra.*
199. 2002 Uniform Securities Act § 302(c), 1 Blue Sky Law Rptr. (CCH) ¶ 5611.
200. *See* §§ 7.2.1.ii.a and 7.2.1.ii.b, *supra.*
201. 2002 Uniform Securities Act §§ 401(a) (broker-dealer registration) and 402(a) (agent registration), 1 Blue Sky Law Rptr. (CCH) ¶¶ 5617 and 5618.
202. 2002 Uniform Securities Act § 402(b), 1 Blue Sky Law Rptr. (CCH) ¶ 5618.
203. 2002 Uniform Securities Act § 102(4), 1 Blue Sky Law Rptr. (CCH) ¶ 5602.
204. *Id.*

An "issuer" is "any person who issues or proposes to issue any security."[205] U.S. and offshore hedge funds are issuers of their limited partner interests or shares. As an issuer, a U.S. or offshore hedge fund is thus not a broker-dealer.

An "agent" is "any individual other than a broker-dealer who represents a broker-dealer or issuer in effecting or attempting to effect purchases or sales of securities."[206] A "partner, officer, or director of a broker-dealer or issuer, or an individual having a similar status or performing similar functions, is an agent only if the individual otherwise falls within the definition."[207] An individual is exempt from the agent registration requirements of the 2002 Uniform Securities Act if he or she represents an issuer in transactions solely in federal covered securities and, for federal covered securities described in Securities Act section 18(b)(4)(D), if he or she is not compensated by the payment of commissions or other remuneration based, directly or indirectly, on transactions in those securities.[208]

ii. Broker-Dealer and Agent Registration Process

Under the 2002 Uniform Securities Act, a broker-dealer or an agent must register by filing an application and a consent to service of process with the cognizant state regulatory authority and paying the appropriate filing fee.[209] The application must contain the information required for filing a uniform application and any other financial or other information or records that the state regulatory authority may request.[210] Registration as a broker-dealer or agent remains effective until December 31 of the year of the application and then may be automatically renewed each year by filing such records as are required by rule or order of the state regulatory authority.[211]

The 2002 Uniform Securities Act authorizes the cognizant state regulatory authority to establish minimum capital requirements for broker-dealers, to require broker-dealers to file financial reports and to require broker-dealers to maintain books and records specified by the regulatory authority.[212]

iii. Denial, Revocation or Suspension of Registration

Under the 2002 Uniform Securities Act, a state regulatory authority may deny a broker-dealer's application for registration or suspend or revoke such a registration on substantially the same grounds as those identified in the 1956 Uniform Securities Act.[213]

---

205. 2002 Uniform Securities Act § 102(17), 1 Blue Sky Law Rptr. (CCH) ¶ 5602.
206. 2002 Uniform Securities Act § 102(2), 1 Blue Sky Law Rptr. (CCH) ¶ 5602.
207. *Id.*
208. 2002 Uniform Securities Act § 402(b)(5), 1 Blue Sky Law Rptr. (CCH) ¶ 5618.
209. 2002 Uniform Securities Act § 406(a), 1 Blue Sky Law Rptr. (CCH) ¶ 5622.
210. *Id.*
211. 2002 Uniform Securities Act § 406(d), 1 Blue Sky Law Rptr. (CCH) ¶ 5622.
212. 2002 Uniform Securities Act § 411, 1 Blue Sky Law Rptr. (CCH) ¶ 5627.
213. 2002 Uniform Securities Act § 412, 1 Blue Sky Law Rptr. (CCH) ¶ 5628; *see* § 7.2.1.iii.d, *supra.*

4. Consequences of Failure to Register Under 2002 Uniform Securities Act

i. Regulatory Action

The 2002 Uniform Securities Act provides that the cognizant state regulatory agency may issue a cease and desist order (with or without a prior hearing) or bring an action in an appropriate state court for an injunction or to enforce compliance with the 2002 Uniform Securities Act if it appears to that agency that a person has engaged or is about to engage in any act or practice constituting a violation of the 2002 Uniform Securities Act.[214] On a proper showing by such regulatory agency, a court may also enter an order of rescission, restitution or disgorgement directed to any person who has violated any provision of the 2002 Uniform Securities Act or any rule or order under it.[215]

ii. Criminal Actions

Any person who willfully violates any provision of the 2002 Uniform Securities Act or any rule or order under the Act, except for the notice filing requirement for federal covered securities, is subject to a fine or imprisonment or both.[216] An individual so convicted of violating a rule or order may be fined but not imprisoned, if the individual did not know of the rule or order.[217]

iii. Private Actions

A person who offers or sells a security in violation of the broker-dealer, agent or securities registration requirements of the 2002 Uniform Securities Act is liable for damages to the person buying the security.[218] Similarly, a person is liable for damages to the purchaser of a security if the person offered or sold the security

> by means of any untrue statement of a material fact or any omission to state a material fact necessary in order to make the statements made, in light of the circumstances under which they are made, not misleading, the purchaser not knowing of the untruth or omission and the seller not sustaining the burden of proof that the seller did not know and, in the exercise of reasonable care, could not have known the untruth or omission.[219]

Any such private action must be brought within 1 year after the violation occurs.[220] Any provision in a contract for sale of securities that purports to waive the purchaser's right to bring such an action is void under the 2002 Uniform

214. 2002 Uniform Securities Act § 603(a), 1 Blue Sky Law Rptr. (CCH) ¶ 5641.
215. 2002 Uniform Securities Act § 603(b), 1 Blue Sky Law Rptr. (CCH) ¶ 5641.
216. 2002 Uniform Securities Act § 508(a), 1 Blue Sky Law Rptr. (CCH) ¶ 5636.
217. *Id.*
218. 2002 Uniform Securities Act § 509(b) and (d), 1 Blue Sky Law Rptr. (CCH) ¶ 5637.
219. 2002 Uniform Securities Act § 509(b), 1 Blue Sky Law Rptr. (CCH) ¶ 5637.
220. 2002 Uniform Securities Act § 509(j)(1), 1 Blue Sky Law Rptr. (CCH) ¶ 5637.

Securities Act.[221] Like the 1956 Uniform Securities Act, the 2002 Uniform Securities Act prohibits a purchaser from recovering if the issuer or broker-dealer makes a rescission offer that complies with it.[222]

221. 2002 Uniform Securities Act § 509(l), 1 Blue Sky Law Rptr. (CCH) ¶ 5637.
222. 2002 Uniform Securities Act § 510, 1 Blue Sky Law Rptr. (CCH) ¶ 5638.

CHAPTER **8**

Marketing Activities

§ 8.1 Introduction

As discussed in Chapter 5, in offering and selling its interests to investors in the United States, a hedge fund (whether domestic or offshore) relies on the private offering exemption from registration under the Securities Act. Hedge funds that offer and sell interests outside of the United States generally rely on the exemption provided by Regulation S under the Securities Act. The Advisers Act regulates advertising by investment advisers. These rules narrowly circumscribe how a hedge fund manager may market interests in a hedge fund.

§ 8.2 Private Offering Exemption

1. Limitation on Manner of Offering and Qualification of Persons Solicited

Securities Act section 4(a)(2)[1] and its progeny, including Rule 502(c) of Regulation D, proscribe the offer or sale of securities in a private offering by any form of general solicitation or general advertising (except in an offering that complies with Rule 506(c) of Regulation D).[2] Rule 502(c) defines "general solicitation and general advertising" to include any advertisement, article, notice or other communication published in any newspaper, magazine or similar medium or broadcast over television or radio, and any seminar or meeting whose attendees have been invited by any general solicitation or general advertising.[3] Communications through electronic mail and the Internet (although invented after Regulation D was adopted in 1982 and not mentioned in Rule 502(c)) may also constitute general solicitation or general advertising if access to them is not

1. 15 U.S.C. § 77d(2); *see* Chapter 5, *supra.*

2. 17 C.F.R. § 230.502(c); *see* § 5.3.2, *supra. See generally*, Louis Loss and Joel Seligman, *Securities Regulation*, Aspen Law & Business (4th Ed. 2009), at 266-368; Carl Schneider, *The Statutory Law of Private Placements*, 14 Rev. Sec. Reg. 869 (1981).

3. Regulation D Rule 502(c), 17 C.F.R. § 230.502(c).

sufficiently restricted.[4] Rule 506(c) of Regulation D permits general solicitation in certain offerings.[5]

The private offering requirements apart from Rule 506(c) of Regulation D implicate the medium, the message and the audience. The issuer in a non-Rule 506(c) offering may not communicate anything about its offering using media available to the general public. As discussed in Chapter 6, regardless of the medium, in all cases the message must satisfy the issuer's obligation to make complete and accurate disclosure. As discussed in Chapter 5, the audience in a non-Rule 506(c) offering should include only persons who the issuer reasonably believes are sufficiently sophisticated in business and financial matters to be able to understand the merits and risks of the investment and who are able to bear the financial risk of the investment.[6] Such a belief may be based on a preexisting substantive relationship between the issuer or its promoters and the offeree or may be formed by other means, and such relationships can help show the absence of a general solicitation.

Whether a general solicitation occurs depends on the facts and circumstances of the particular case.[7] The SEC staff has stated that the Rule 502(c) analysis can be divided into two separate inquiries:

> First, is the communication in question a general solicitation or general advertisement? Second, if it is, is it being used by the issuer or by someone on the issuer's behalf to offer or sell the securities? If either question can be answered in the negative, then the issuer will not be in violation of Rule 502(c). Questions under Rule 502(c) typically present issues of fact and circumstances that the staff is not in a position to resolve.[8]

Without being particularly helpful, SEC staff interpretations of Rule 502(c) (discussed below) suggest that the following factors should be considered in determining whether a solicitation or advertisement violates Rule 502(c):

- the relationship, if any, between the issuer and the person making the communication;
- the relationship, if any, between the issuer and the person receiving the communication;
- the timing of the communication; and
- the subject matter of the communication.

Determining whether or not a solicitation is general often involves subjective judgment. In the hedge fund context, the stakes are considerable, because miscalculation could be the basis for claims that the hedge fund and its manager

---

4. *See also* § 9.2, *infra*.
5. *See* § 5.3.2, *supra*.
6. *See, e.g.*, Mineral Lands Research and Marketing Corp., SEC No-Action Letter (Dec. 4, 1985).
7. Securities Act Release No. 6825, 54 F.R. 11,369 (Mar. 20, 1989).
8. Securities Act Release No. 6455, 48 F.R. 10,045 (Mar. 10, 1983).

have violated not only the registration requirement of the Securities Act,[9] but also the requirement for registration as a mutual fund under the Company Act.[10] These risks do not, however, arise in a hedge fund offering that complies with Rule 506(c) of Regulation D, which permits general solicitation.[11] The discussion in this section 8.2 addresses private offerings that rely on Rule 506(b) of Regulation D or Securities Act section 4(a)(2), and not on Rule 506(c) of Regulation D.

2. Relationship between Hedge Fund and Person Making Communication

When a hedge fund or its representative arranges or is otherwise responsible for a general solicitation or general advertisement about the hedge fund or its offering, the private offering exemption is not available, unless the offering complies with Rule 506(c).[12] If, however, an unrelated third-party makes a general solicitation or advertisement without involving the hedge fund or its representatives, the Rule 502(c) prohibition should not be violated.

i. Advertisements by Affiliates

Press releases or other communications by an affiliate of a hedge fund may be deemed to be general advertisements or solicitations on behalf of the hedge fund for purposes of Rule 502(c) if that person "expect[s] to exercise direct and active management control over any substantial part of the activities, business dealings or administration" of the hedge fund.[13] In *In re Robert Testa*, an affiliate of a corporation that had formed a limited partnership to raise funds to develop the corporation's intellectual property rights assisted a selling agent by drafting a solicitation letter and obtaining a large mailing list. The SEC found that the affiliate had participated in a proscribed general solicitation on behalf of the issuer.[14]

ii. Advertisements by Nonaffiliates

When a hedge fund or its affiliate arranges for a third-party to publish an advertisement or a solicitation, the third-party will be deemed to be acting on the hedge fund's behalf, even if the third-party independently decides which information about the hedge fund to include in the communication or is solely

9. *See* Chapter 5, *supra.*

10. *See* Chapter 3, *supra.* The SEC staff has observed that, if an offer is public for purposes of the Securities Act, it would also ordinarily be public for purposes of the Company Act. *See, e.g.,* Gerard Rizzuti, SEC No-Action Letter (June 7, 1983); Lamp Technologies, Inc., SEC No-Action Letter (May 29, 1998).

11. 17 C.F.R. § 230.506(c); Securities Act Release No. 9415 (July 10, 2013), 78 F.R. 44771 (July 24, 2013). *See* § 5.3.2, *supra.*

12. *Id.*

13. American Bar Association proposal to the SEC Division of Corporation Finance on behalf of the Subcommittees on Partnerships, Trusts and Unincorporated Associations and Registration Statements—Securities Act (June 1984).

14. *In re* Robert Testa, Securities Act Release No. 7018 (Sep. 29, 1993). *See also In re* EMX Corp. & EMF Assocs., L.P., Securities Act Release No. 7019 (Sep. 29, 1993).

responsible for deciding whether to publish a particular newsletter, trade journal or other publication containing the hedge fund's solicitation. In *J.D. Manning, Inc.*, the SEC staff determined that a publisher's proposed newsletter containing a list and description of closely held businesses that were expected to raise capital in future private placements would constitute a general solicitation on behalf of the participating businesses.[15] In the *Lamp Technologies, Inc.* no-action letters,[16] the SEC provided the conditions under which a third-party website could post information about a hedge fund, when the hedge fund arranges or consents to the disclosure.

A hedge fund should not, however, be viewed as conducting a general solicitation by virtue of a communication by a person who is not an affiliate of the hedge fund, is otherwise independent from any offering of the hedge fund's interests, and does not look to the hedge fund or its affiliates for assistance or compensation with respect to the materials communicated, even if that communication might constitute a general advertisement or solicitation if it were made by the hedge fund or its affiliate.[17] In such circumstances, the hedge fund would be allowed to retain any benefits flowing from the communication. If, however, a publication were to contain analyses and recommendations or feature forward-looking information from persons likely to participate in a future hedge fund offering, the SEC staff has stated that it would likely withhold no-action relief,[18] presumably on the grounds that the publication could be deemed a general solicitation or advertisement by the hedge fund.

iii. Matching Services

The SEC staff has allowed computer matching and listing services to link issuers with potential investors in limited circumstances. In *Texas Capital Network, Inc.*, the SEC staff allowed a nonprofit corporation ("TCN") to develop a computer database of subscribers consisting of investors and entrepreneurs to be matched, each of whom paid an annual membership fee. In deciding that the activities did not involve a general solicitation, the SEC focused on the following facts as evidence that TCN was not acting on any issuer's behalf:

- TCN had no affiliation or association with any participating entrepreneur;
- in soliciting investors to participate in its network, TCN used generic advertisements and never mentioned specific entrepreneurs;
- TCN undertook no investigation of the information entrepreneurs provided to it;
- TCN's service was limited to matching, and TCN did not assist in developing the terms of any investment opportunity;

---

15. J.D. Manning, Inc., SEC No-Action Letter (Jan. 21, 1986).

16. Lamp Technologies, Inc., SEC No-Action Letters (May 29, 1997, and May 25, 1998); *see* § 9.2.2, *infra*.

17. Richard Daniels, SEC No-Action Letter (Dec. 19, 1984); Nancy H. Blasberg, SEC No-Action Letter (July 12, 1986).

18. Securities Act Release No. 6455, at 2637-13, 48 F.R. 10,045 (Mar. 10, 1983).

- TCN did not receive compensation from any participant except for nominal administrative expenses; and
- persons associated with TCN were prohibited from participating in the matching network.[19]

The SEC staff has also stated that, if a matching service engages in a general solicitation, an issuer using the service may also be engaging in the general solicitation.[20]

3. Relationship between Person Making Communication and Offeree

The SEC and its staff have underscored the importance of the existence and substance of a preexisting relationship between an issuer and those being solicited in determining what would not constitute a general solicitation.[21] The nature of the preexisting relationship has, however, been described differently in different cases and SEC no-action letters. The relationship should be either one of significant substance or duration, or extensive enough to enable the hedge fund or someone acting on its behalf to be aware of the financial circumstances and investment sophistication of the person solicited. In general, an offer should be personally directed to the offeree; the SEC staff has viewed impersonal communications as general solicitations.[22]

i. Preexisting Relationship

A substantive relationship is established when an issuer or its agent has sufficient information to evaluate the prospective offeree's sophistication and

19. Texas Capital Network, Inc., SEC No-Action Letter (Feb. 23, 1994). In The Colorado Capital Alliance, Inc., SEC No-Action Letter (May 4, 1995), the SEC staff stated that persons associated with such a matching service could participate as investors, as long as their treatment is the same as any other investor. Other SEC no-action letters concerning listing and matching services are Venture Listing Services, Inc., SEC No-Action Letter (June 15, 1994); Investex Investment Exchange, Inc., SEC No-Action Letter (Apr. 9, 1990); Petroleum Information Corp., SEC No-Action Letter (Nov. 28, 1989); Tri-State Livestock Credit Corp., SEC No-Action Letter (Oct. 18, 1989); CNB Corp., SEC No-Action Letter (June 9, 1989); Real Estate Financing Partnership, SEC No-Action Letter (Apr. 4, 1989); Venture Capital Network, Inc. SEC No-Action Letter (May 7, 1984); Venture Capitol Exchange, Inc. SEC No-Action Letter (Apr. 23, 1986); Venture Capital Network of New York, Inc., SEC No-Action Letter (Nov. 10, 1986).

20. The Colorado Capital Alliance, Inc., SEC No-Action Letter (May 4, 1995).

21. In the Matter of Kenman Corp. and Kenman Securities Corp., Admin. Proc. File No. 3-6505 (Apr. 19, 1985). *See also* Woodtrails-Seattle, Ltd., SEC No-Action Letter (July 8, 1992).

22. *See, e.g.*, In the Matter of EMX Corp. and EMF Assocs., L.P., Admin. Proc. File No. 3-8185 (Sept. 29, 1993); In the Matter of Kenman Corp. and Kenman Securities Corp., Admin. Proc. File No. 3-6505; Pennsylvania Securities Commission, SEC No-Action Letter (Jan. 16, 1990); Webster Mgmt. Assured Return Equity Mgmt. Group Trust, SEC No-Action Letter (Feb. 7, 1987); Aspen Grove, SEC No-Action Letter (Dec. 8, 1982); Trust Mortgage and Loan Svcs., Inc., SEC No-Action Letter (Dec. 27, 1979); A.A. Ajax Co., Inc., SEC No-Action Letter (Jan. 15, 1979); and Thoroughbred Racing Stable, SEC No-Action Letter (Jan. 5, 1976).

financial circumstances. Substantive relationships can also be established through business dealings or questionnaires. Even when a hedge fund solicits previous investors, however, it must believe that "each of the proposed offerees currently has such knowledge and experience in financial and business matters that he or she is capable of evaluating the merits and risks of the proposed investments."[23]

In *Royce Exchange Fund, Quest Advisory Corp.*,[24] the SEC staff permitted a registered investment adviser setting up a new fund to solicit the past and present directors and officers of portfolio companies, the immediate family members of such directors and officers, clients of various investment advisers that were significantly involved in the investment adviser's financial network, and parties related to the portfolio companies who were referred by a placement agent who believed that the parties met the fund's suitability criteria. The SEC staff noted the nature and extent of preexisting relationships between the investment adviser and portfolio companies whose officers and directors were to be solicited, between the investment adviser and other registered investment advisers whose clients were to be solicited, and between such clients and their investment advisers.

ii. Questionnaires

A substantive relationship may also be established through the use of an investor questionnaire, if sufficient time passes between receipt of the completed questionnaire and the time when an offering is first contemplated.[25] How much time is sufficient is unclear. Such a questionnaire must provide sufficient information for the hedge fund to evaluate a prospective offeree's sophistication and financial circumstances.

iii. Brokers

The SEC staff has generally taken the view that traditional relationships between brokers and their customers, which require brokers to deal fairly with and make suitable recommendations to the customers, are "substantive" in the private offering context.[26] Accordingly, the SEC staff has held that a broker's program of contacting prospective investors will not constitute a general solicitation or advertisement, if the proposed solicitation is generic and does not refer to any specific investment that the broker is then offering or contemplating offering, and the broker implements procedures to ensure that persons solicited are not offered any securities that were offered or contemplated for offering at the time of the solicitation.[27]

A broker's generic recruitment of prospective investors must be followed, however, by the development of a more substantive relationship before any

23. Woodtrails-Seattle, Ltd., SEC No-Action Letter (Aug. 9, 1982).

24. SEC No-Action Letter (Aug. 28, 1996).

25. E.F. Hutton, SEC No-Action Letter (Dec. 3, 1985); H.B. Shaine & Co., SEC No-Action Letter (May 1, 1987).

26. Securities Act Release No. 7856 ("Use of Electronic Media") (Apr. 28, 2000), 65 F.R. 25,843 (May 4, 2000).

27. Bateman, Eichler, Hill Richards, Inc., SEC No-Action Letter (Dec. 3, 1985).

offer is made. The SEC staff has stated that a subsequent offer to a person who responds to a broker's generic recruitment efforts will be deemed made by general solicitation as a result of the initial contact, unless the broker or the issuer establishes a substantive relationship with the offeree between the initial solicitation and the later offer. Again, before making an offer, the broker or the issuer must obtain sufficient information to evaluate the prospective offeree's sophistication and financial circumstances.[28]

4. Timing

When a general solicitation or general advertisement coincides with the timing of an offer and sale of hedge fund interests, the advertisement or other communication will likely be deemed to have been used in connection with the offer or sale of hedge fund interests.[29] Even a public relations or marketing campaign that promotes a hedge fund but that does not invite prospective investors to contact the hedge fund directly may be deemed a general solicitation if it "conditions the market." The SEC staff has noted:

> Rule 502(c) does not specifically prohibit advertising or other activities intended to promote or market an issuer's products or services. Rather, it prohibits the use of general solicitation or general advertising in connection with the offer or sale of the issuer's securities in reliance on Regulation D. Whether or not an issuer's product promotion can also be deemed general solicitation or general advertising for the offer or sale of its securities under Regulation D is a question of fact that the Division [of Corporation Finance] generally will not be in a position to resolve. The question requires an evaluation not only of the content of the specific advertising but also of the actual use of each advertisement in relation to the offering of securities.[30]

5. Subject Matter of Communication

The offeror must ensure that each offeree understands that the hedge fund offers interests only by way of its disclosure documents and only to persons that the hedge fund's general partner believes are qualified for purposes of the private offering exemption.[31]

6. Number of Persons Solicited

The number of persons solicited is not necessarily a critical factor in determining whether or not a solicitation is general. In interpretations of Rule 502(c), for example, the SEC focuses primarily on the nature of persons solicited. When

---

28. *Id.*
29. J.D. Manning, Inc., SEC No-Action Letter (Jan. 21, 1986).
30. Printing Enterprise Mgmt. Science, Inc., SEC No-Action Letter (Apr. 25, 1983).
31. E. F. Hutton & Co., SEC No-Action Letter (Dec. 3, 1985); *see also* Chapters 5 and 6, *supra.*

the SEC staff has found the nature of the persons solicited acceptable, it has not objected to solicitations to hundreds of persons. *In Woodtrails-Seattle, Ltd.*, a solicitation of more than 300 former investors was acceptable.[32] In *Mineral-Lands Research and Marketing Corporation*, the acceptable class of offerees included 600 persons who were existing clients of an officer who was also an insurance broker.[33]

The focus on a preexisting relationship between an offeror and offeree requires that the offeror be in a position to evaluate all of the prospective offerees, no matter how few or how numerous they are, to determine whether each of them is sophisticated in business and financial matters.[34] If the issuer cannot demonstrate preexisting relationships with its offerees, it may not be able to bear its burden of proof that its solicitation was private and not general.

7. Sophistication of Offerees

That an offeree is financially sophisticated or wealthy does not by itself enable a hedge fund to solicit that offeree without having any prior contact or relationship. In *Kenman Corporation and Kenman Securities Corporation*, the SEC sued an SEC-registered broker and its associated person for mailing information relating to interests in a land development limited partnership to an unknown number of persons identified on lists of executive officers of Fortune 500 companies, persons who had previously invested $10,000 or more in real estate offerings by other issuers, physicians in California, managerial engineers employed by aircraft companies, and presidents of companies listed in the Morris County, New Jersey, Industrial Directory.[35] In *EMX Corporation and EMF Associates, L.P.*, the SEC sued a company that had mailed solicitation materials to between 80,000 and 90,000 physicians throughout the United States.[36] There, the SEC noted, "[a]lthough the make-up of the lists may indicate that the persons themselves have some degree of sophistication or financial well-being, utilization of lists of thousands of persons with no pre-existing relationship to the offeror clearly does not comply with the limitations of Rule 502(c) on the manner of solicitation."[37]

8. Disclosure Requirements

Regulation D does not require that any particular information be furnished to purchasers if a hedge fund sells interests only to accredited investors. The SEC staff directs an unregistered hedge fund to use Form N-1A as a guide in

32. Woodtrails-Seattle, Ltd., SEC No-Action Letter (July 8, 1982).

33. Mineral Lands Research & Marketing Corp., SEC No-Action (Dec. 4, 1985).

34. Woodtrails-Seattle, Ltd., SEC No-Action Letter (July 8, 1982); E.F. Hutton & Co., SEC No-Action Letter (Dec. 3, 1985).

35. In the Matter of Kenman Corp. and Kenman Securities Corp., Admin. Proc. File No. 3-6505 (Apr. 19, 1985).

36. In the Matter of EMX Corp. and EMF Associates, L.P., Admin. Proc. File No. 3-8185 (Sep. 29, 1993).

37. *Id.*

preparing its Regulation D disclosure documents.[38] If, however, a sale is made to any non-accredited investor, the hedge fund must furnish the more extensive information specified in Rule 502(b)(2) a "reasonable time before the sale."[39] A hedge fund may choose to furnish to potential investors a short-form offering memorandum in anticipation of actual selling activities, so long as it follows with delivery of an expanded disclosure document such that "all the information is delivered prior to sale."[40]

§ 8.3 Marketing Activities Outside of the United States

1. Regulation S; Directed Selling

The SEC adopted Regulation S[41] in 1990 to clarify its position that securities offered and sold outside of the United States do not need to be registered under the Securities Act, if specified conditions are met. Regulation S provides a safe harbor exemption from the registration requirements of the Securities Act. Under Regulation S, no directed selling efforts may be made in the United States in connection with an offer, sale or resale.[42] "Directed selling efforts" include mailing printed materials to U.S. investors; conducting promotional seminars in the United States; placing advertisements in publications with general circulation in, or with radio or television stations broadcasting into, the United States; and making offers directed at identifiable groups of U.S. citizens in another country.[43]

The following activities are specifically excluded from the definition of directed selling efforts:

- advertising that is required under law or regulations;
- communicating with persons excluded from the definition of "United States person";
- advertising in the form of tombstones in publications with less than 20 percent of their circulation in the United States;
- prospective investors making bona fide visits to real estate facilities;

38. *Regulation D Rule 502(b)(2)(i)(A), 17 C.F.R. § 230.502(b)(2)(i)(A)*; Robert T. Willis, Jr., P.C., SEC No-Action Letter (Jan. 18, 1988). *But see* Chapter 6, *supra.*

39. Robert T. Willis, Jr., P.C., SEC No-Action Letter (Jan. 18, 1988). *See* § 5.3.2 and Chapter 6, *supra.*

40. Securities Act Release No. 6455, Question (4), at 2637-8, 48 F.R. 10,045, Question 4 (Mar. 10, 1983); *see* Chapter 6, *supra.*

41. Regulation S Rules 901 through 904, 17 C.F.R. §§ 230.901-904. *See* § 5.4, *supra.*

42. Regulation S Adopting Release, Release No. 6863, Fed. Sec. L. Rep. (CCH) ¶ 84,524, at 80,666 (Apr. 24, 1990), 55 F.R. 18,306 (May 2, 1990).

43. Regulation S Rule 902(c)(2), 17 C.F.R. § 230.902(c)(2).

- distributing quotations of a non-U.S. broker using a third-party system in non-U.S. countries, as long as the system does not allow any security transaction to be executed between the non-U.S. broker and any person in the United States and no contact with U.S. persons is initiated;
- giving proper notice under Rule 135 under the Securities Act that an issuer intends to make a registered public offering of its securities;
- providing journalists with access to issuer meetings held outside of the United States;
- having isolated and limited contact;
- placing routine advertisements unrelated to selling efforts; and
- conducting customary and legal activities outside of the United States.[44]

2. Private Offering; Marketing to Non-U.S. Investors

A hedge fund may offer and sell its interests in the United States without registration in reliance on the private offering exemption, including Rule 506 of Regulation D, while simultaneously making an offering to non-U.S. investors without registration in reliance on either or both of the private offering exemption and Regulation S. Alternatively, a hedge fund may rely solely on the private offering exemption in offering its interests to both U.S. and non-U.S. persons, as long as the offering meets all of the requirements of Regulation D.[45]

In *Jack B. Straus*,[46] a non-U.S. investment adviser sought to conduct a public solicitation through non-U.S. media to attract non-U.S. investors while offering and selling the same securities in the United States pursuant to Rule 505 of Regulation D. He proposed to solicit investors in his country through advertisements in non-U.S. magazines and newspapers that were published and distributed in his country and then follow up leads from those advertisements.

The SEC staff noted that since the investment adviser was considering advertising the offering in French newspapers of general circulation, there could be no assurance that such newspapers would not ultimately be distributed in the United States. Accordingly, the SEC staff concluded that, although the investment adviser's intent may have been to use the advertisements to solicit only investors who were outside of the United States, the effect may have been to solicit U.S. citizens or residents in violation of Rule 502(c). *Jack B. Straus* predated the adoption of Rule 506(c) of Regulation D, which permits general solicitation.[47] Presumably, the SEC staff would reach a different conclusion with respect to an offering that complies with Rule 506(c) in soliciting in the United States and complies with Regulation S in soliciting elsewhere.

---

44. Rule 902(c)(3); 17 C.F.R. § 230.902(c)(3).
45. Intron, Ltd., SEC No-Action Letter (Dec. 10, 1984).
46. Jack B. Straus, SEC No-Action Letter (Aug. 20, 1985).
47. *See* § 5.3.2, *supra*

3. Non-U.S. Exchange Listing

Offshore hedge funds sometimes list their interests on recognized non-U.S. exchanges. One reason for doing so is that some non-U.S. investors are prohibited from investing, or reluctant to invest, in unregistered securities that are not listed on a recognized or regulated exchange. An offshore hedge fund seeking to expand its marketing reach may list its shares on the Irish Stock Exchange, the Hong Kong Stock Exchange, the Bermuda Stock Exchange, the Cayman Islands Stock Exchange or another appropriate exchange—various jurisdictions recognize different exchanges for these purposes. These stock exchanges typically impose requirements such as an application with a prospectus, investment guidelines and limitations, periodic audited financial statements and ongoing duties to update disclosures. These requirements are usually less onerous than the listing requirements of U.S. exchanges. Local counsel may be engaged to coordinate the listing process and oversee maintenance procedures.

4. Marketing within the European Union

An investment adviser that offers interests in a hedge fund in a country other than the United States must comply with that country's securities laws that apply to private offerings. Those laws vary from country to country, and ascertaining and complying with them can be cumbersome and expensive for an investment adviser that markets hedge funds outside of the United States. In 2011, the European Union (the "EU") adopted the Alternative Investment Fund Managers Directive (the "AIFMD"),[48] in an effort to harmonize across EU member states the regulations governing the marketing of hedge funds in the EU.[49] The AIFMD will become effective in stages, which are expected to begin in 2013, 2015 and 2018; over that period, the existing private placement regimes of the EU member states are expected to be phased out and replaced with a single, unified regulatory scheme. The discussion below is preliminary at this writing, as the AIFMD has not been implemented and may be altered before it becomes fully effective.

A U.S. investment adviser will generally be subject to the AIFMD if it markets any non-EU domiciled fund (whether U.S. or offshore) in the EU. The AIFMD defines "marketing" broadly as covering any direct or indirect offering, at the investment adviser's initiative or on its behalf, of interests in a hedge fund to investors that are domiciled in the EU or have an office there. If, however, an EU-domiciled investor approaches an investment adviser on its own initiative concerning an investment in a hedge fund (a "reverse solicitation"), the issuance of an interest in the hedge fund to that investor is not subject to

48. Directive 2011/61/EU of the European Parliament and of the Council of 8 June 2011 on Alternative Investment Managers and amending Directives 2003/41/EC and 2009/65/EC and Regulations (EC) No 1060/2009 and (EU) No 1095/2010, published in the Official Journal of the European Union, July 1, 2011.

49. It is expected that the AIFMD will be implemented in the broader European Economic Area, which also includes Iceland, Liechtenstein and Norway.

the AIFMD. The AIFMD provides little guidance about the scope and limits of reverse solicitation, but its parameters may become clearer as the AIFMD is implemented. Another, more limited, exemption is available for investment advisers whose assets under management do not exceed certain thresholds, but such investment advisers are nevertheless subject to many of the AIFMD reporting requirements.

A U.S. investment adviser that markets a hedge fund in the EU after July 22, 2013, and is not exempt from the AIFMD, must continue to comply with the private placement laws in each EU member state where marketing occurs.[50] In addition, it must provide reports and disclosures mandated by the AIFMD, including, among other things, specific pre-investment disclosures to potential investors (which should be included in the hedge fund's offering documents), annual reports to investors and member state regulators, additional reports to member state regulators regarding trading instruments, trading market participation and diversification, and periodic disclosures regarding side pockets, arrangements for managing liquidity, risk profile and risk management systems, and changes to maximum leverage levels. The investment adviser may market a hedge fund only in member states whose regulatory authorities have signed cooperation agreements with the investment adviser's regulatory authority (such as the SEC) and the hedge fund.

The AIFMD establishes a "passport regime," intended ultimately to allow investment advisers to market throughout the EU without complying with the separate private placement laws in each member state (although they will be required to comply with the AIFMD's extensive reporting and disclosure requirements). It is expected that, beginning in September 2015, a U.S. investment adviser that is subject to the AIFMD will be able to choose whether to continue to comply with the private placement laws of each member state in which it markets it hedge fund, or to comply with the passport regime. The passport regime will require the investment adviser to adopt a single EU member state as its "state of reference" and obtain that state's authorization to market its hedge fund in the EU. The investment adviser will also be required to comply with the full panoply of AIFMD reporting, disclosure and operational requirements, which are much more extensive than those described above. Beginning in September 2018, the EU country-specific private placement laws are expected to be repealed, and all investment advisers marketing in the EU will be required to rely on the passport regime.

---

50. EU member states are currently revising their private placement laws in response to the AIFMD, and some are expected to adopt rules that will impose stricter limits on marketing of funds.

§ 8.4 Advisers Act Regulation of Content

Advertisements relating to hedge funds are subject to the prohibitions of false and misleading advertisements in Advisers Act section 206(4)[51] and Advisers Act Rules 206(4)-1 and 206(4)-8[52] and to the general anti-fraud prohibitions of Advisers Act sections 206(1) and (2).[53] The Advisers Act and the rules under it impose these requirements on all investment advisers, whether or not registered with the SEC as investment advisers. Rule 206(4)-1(b) provides, in part, that:

> For purposes of this rule the term "advertisement" shall include any notice, circular, letter or other written communication addressed to more than one person, or any notice or other announcement in any publication or by radio or television, which offers (1) any analysis, report, or publication concerning securities, or which is to be used in making any determination as to when to buy or sell any security, or which security to buy or sell, or (2) any graph, chart, formula or other device to be used in making any determination as to when to buy or sell any security, or which security to buy or sell, or (3) any other investment advisory service with regard to securities.

Most hedge fund offering circulars are or contain advertisements under this definition, even though they are distributed only to the limited extent permitted by the private offering exemption.

1. Fraudulent, Deceptive or Manipulative Advertising

Rule 206(4)-1 defines the following practices in any advertisement as fraudulent, deceptive or manipulative:

- publishing or distributing testimonials of any kind concerning the investment adviser or concerning any advice, analysis, report or other services rendered by that investment adviser (see below);
- referring to past specific recommendations of the investment adviser that were or would have been profitable to any persons, unless the advertisement sets out or offers to furnish a list of all recommendations made by the investment adviser within the preceding year and contains a legend that states: "It should not be assumed that recommendations made in the future will be profitable or will equal the performance of the securities in this list";[54]

51. 15 U.S.C. § 80b-6(4).
52. 17 C.F.R. §§ 275-206(4)-1 and 275.206(4)-8. *See also* § 6.5.1, *supra*.
53. 15 U.S.C. §§ 80b-6(1) and 80b-6(2).
54. *See* § 8.5.3, *infra*.

- representing that any graph, chart, formula or other device offered in the advertisement (1) can, in and of itself, be used to determine which securities to buy or sell or when to buy and sell securities or (2) will assist any person in making investment decisions, without prominently disclosing the limitations of such graph, chart, formula or other device used;
- falsely promising to furnish reports or analyses free of charge to investors; and
- containing any untrue statement of a material fact or otherwise being false or misleading.[55]

i. Testimonials

The prohibition of Rule 206(4)-1 on testimonials reflects the SEC's view that statements of a customer's experience or endorsement are likely to give rise to a fraudulent or deceptive implication or mistaken inference that the positive experience of the person providing the testimonial is typical of the experience of all of the investment adviser's clients. The SEC has stated that advertisements containing testimonials are inherently misleading, as they inevitably emphasize favorable reactions while ignoring unfavorable ones.[56]

The SEC staff has interpreted the term "testimonial" to include any explicit or implicit "statement of a client's experience with, or endorsement of, an adviser,"[57] including statements about an investment adviser's character, religious affiliation, diligence, attention to detail, prudence or knowledge of investing.[58] The SEC staff has stated that even a statement that a mutual acquaintance would be willing to act as a reference and discuss with an investment adviser's potential client his investment experience with that investment adviser is a testimonial.[59] In *Investor Intelligence*, the SEC staff viewed a proposed statement that an investment adviser was a "recognized powerful psychic medium" as a prohibited indirect testimonial to that person's capabilities.[60] The SEC staff has stated that an article by an unbiased third-party concerning an investment adviser's performance is not a testimonial, unless it includes a statement of a client's experience with, or endorsement of, the investment adviser.[61]

A third-party rating is a testimonial if it is an implicit statement of one or more clients' experience with an investment adviser or if it relies primarily on client evaluations of the investment adviser. A third-party rating is not a testimonial if the responses by clients of the investment adviser are an insignificant factor, relative to other criteria, in formulating the rating.[62]

---

55. Advisers Act Rule 206(4)-1(a), 17 C.F.R. § 275.206(4)-1.
56. Advisers Act Release No. 121 (Nov. 2, 1961); 26 F.R. 10,549 (Nov. 9, 1961).
57. Cambiar Investors, Inc., SEC No-Action Letter (Aug. 28, 1997).
58. Letters to the Editor, *Journal of Financial Planning*, from Jack W. Murphy, SEC Associate Director and Chief Counsel (publicly available Feb. 2, 1996).
59. Analytic Inv. Mgmt., Inc., SEC No-Action Letter (Mar. 22, 1971).
60. Investor Intelligence (John Anthony), SEC No-Action Letter (Apr. 18, 1975).
61. Richard Silverman, SEC No-Action Letter (Feb. 25, 1985).
62. Investment Adviser Association, SEC No-Action Letter (Dec. 2, 2005).

ii. Favorable Press

The SEC staff has stated that the reprint of an article or publication by an unbiased third-party that refers to an investment adviser's performance is not a testimonial, unless the article includes a quote from a client. An article that contains favorable quotes only from nonclients is not considered to be a testimonial.[63] Even if a reprint is not a testimonial, however, its distribution is subject to the anti-fraud provisions of the Advisers Act. If the reprint implies something about, or is likely to cause an unwarranted inference to be drawn about, the experience of advisory clients, the possibility of other clients enjoying an investment experience similar to that of prior clients, or the investment adviser's competence, its use could be a fraudulent, deceptive or manipulative practice prohibited by Rule 206(4)-1.[64]

iii. Use of Client Lists

An investment adviser may use an advertisement that includes a list of representative clients if (a) the investment adviser uses objective criteria (such as account size, geographic location or client classification) to determine which clients to include in the list, and the criteria do not include the performance of clients' accounts; (b) each client list includes a statement disclosing the objective criteria used to determine which clients to include in the list; and (c) each client list includes a disclaimer stating that "it is not known whether the listed clients approve or disapprove of [name of investment adviser] or the advisory service provided."[65] In addition, state rules sometimes require that an investment adviser obtain the consent of a client before it discloses the identity, affairs or investments of that client to any third-party (unless such disclosure is required by law).[66]

iv. Ratings

The SEC staff will likely allow the dissemination of numerical ratings of an investment adviser prepared by an independent company based on client surveys when the following conditions are met:

- all participating investment advisers have had to meet specified eligibility criteria and the advertisement discloses the criteria on which the rating is based;
- the rating firm is not affiliated with any participating investment adviser or representative and the advertisement discloses prominently who created and conducted the survey;
- the rating firm surveys all or a statistically valid sample of the investment adviser's clients and does not emphasize favorable client responses or include favorable ratings without disclosing unfavorable ratings;

---

63. Stalker Advisory Services, SEC No-Action Letter (Jan. 18, 1994).
64. *Id.*; Kurtz Capital Mgmt., SEC No-Action Letter (Jan. 18, 1988).
65. Denver Investment Advisors, Inc., SEC No-Action Letter (July 30, 1993); and Cambiar Investors, Inc., SEC No-Action Letter (Aug. 28, 1997).
66. *See, e.g.*, 10 Cal. Code of Reg., § 260.238(m).

- the investment adviser discloses any facts it knows that would call into question the validity of any favorable rating or the appropriateness of advertising the rating (for example, if the investment adviser has been the subject of numerous client complaints relating to the rating category or in areas not included in the survey);
- if the advertisement states or implies that the investment adviser is the top-rated investment adviser in a category, the investment adviser must be rated first in that category;
- the advertisement clearly and prominently discloses the category for which the rating is calculated or determined, the number of investment advisers surveyed in that category, and the percentage of investment advisers that receive the same rating as the investment adviser that is the subject of the advertisement;
- the advertisement discloses that the rating may not be representative of any one client's experience because the rating reflects an average of all, or a sample of all, of the experiences of the investment adviser's clients;
- the advertisement discloses that the rating is not indicative of the investment adviser's future performance;
- the advertisement discloses, if true, that all participating investment advisers are charged a fee by the rating firm;
- the rating firm issues only ratings that are statistically valid; and
- if the advertisement publishes the results of a survey, it identifies the percentage of investment advisers that received each rating.[67]

An advertisement that meets the foregoing criteria may nonetheless be a prohibited testimonial.[68] To determine whether the rating is a testimonial, the investment adviser should review the criteria used by the third-party that formulated the rating and the significance of client evaluations in formulating the rating. If client evaluations of the investment adviser are more than an insignificant factor in the rating, relative to other criteria, the rating is a testimonial and is prohibited. An investment adviser may contact the third-party to obtain the information necessary to make this determination.[69]

Advertisements that use ratings information that satisfies the foregoing conditions and is not a testimonial are nonetheless prohibited under Advisers Act section 206(4)[70] if they are false or misleading.

v. Misleading Implications

Advertisements must disclose all material facts about the information conveyed that are necessary to avoid any misleading implications. If the overall impression

67. DALBAR, Inc., SEC No-Action Letter (Mar. 24, 1998), as described in Investment Adviser Ass'n, SEC No-Action Letter (Dec. 2, 2005).

68. *See* § 8.4.1.i, *supra.*

69. Investment Adviser Ass'n, SEC No-Action Letter (Dec. 2, 2005).

70. 15 U.S.C. § 80b-6(4).

conveyed by an advertisement is misleading or deceptive, the advertisement is prohibited, even if no individual statement in it is untrue and it does not violate any of the other specific prohibitions discussed above.[71] Whether an advertisement is false or misleading depends on the facts and circumstances, including: the form and content of the advertisement; the investment adviser's ability to perform what it has advertised; the implications arising out of the advertisement in its total context; and the sophistication of the prospective client[72] (although the SEC staff has stated that advertisements must be evaluated "from the viewpoint of a person unskilled and unsophisticated in investment matters").[73] The SEC may also deem an advertisement to be misleading, and take enforcement action against the investment adviser, if it includes even a single particular statement that is specifically prohibited.[74]

vi. Information Relating to Third Parties

If an investment adviser to a hedge fund advises investors in the hedge fund about the services of third parties, the investment adviser should not distribute misleading marketing materials regarding those third parties.[75]

vii. Information Provided to Consultants or Publications

The SEC also applies its standards for investment adviser advertisements to a variety of communications from an investment adviser to an intermediary who may be expected to relay that information to investors who may invest in a hedge fund managed by the investment adviser. Accordingly, the anti-fraud rules apply to information that an investment adviser distributes to consultants[76] and reporting services,[77] press releases,[78] interviews with advisory publications,[79] and other materials provided by investment advisers to newspapers and other periodicals.[80]

71. SEC v. C.R. Richmond & Co., 565 F.2d 1101, 1106-07 (9th Cir. 1977).

72. Triad Asset Mgmt., Inc., SEC No-Action Letter (Apr. 22, 1993); Anametrics Inv. Mgmt., SEC No-Action Letter (May 5, 1977).

73. *In re* Spear & Staff, Inc., Advisers Act Release No. 188 (Mar. 25, 1965). *See also* SEC v. C.R. Richmond & Co., 565 F.2d 1101, 1104 (9th Cir. 1977); Marketlines, Inc. v. SEC, 384 F.2d 264, 266 (2d Cir. 1967).

74. 1 James E. Anderson et al., *Investment Advisers: Law & Compliance* (Rev Ed.), § 7.05.

75. *In re* Performance Analytics, Inc., Advisers Act Release No. 1978 (Sep. 27, 2001).

76. Advisers Act Rule 206(4)-1, 17 C.F.R. § 275.206(4)-1.

77. *In re* Oxford Capital Mgmt., Inc., Advisers Act Release No. 2061 (Sep. 23, 2002); *In re* Engebretson Capital Mgmt., Inc., Advisers Act Release No. 1825 (Sep. 13, 1999); *In re* Boston Inv. Counsel. Inc., Advisers Act Release No. 1801 (June 10, 1999); *In re* Profitek, Inc., Advisers Act Release No. 1764 (Sep. 29, 1998); Investment Company Institute, SEC No-Action Letter (Sep. 23, 1988).

78. *In re* Finarc, LLC, Advisers Act Release No. 1763 (Sep. 29, 1998).

79. *In re* C&G Asset Mgmt., Inc., Advisers Act Release No. 1536 (Nov. 9, 1995).

80. *In re* Profitek, Inc., Advisers Act Release No. 1764 (Sep. 29, 1998).

viii. Communications Not Deemed "Advertisements"

To constitute an advertisement, a communication must offer advisory services. Periodic reports to existing clients (such as monthly or quarterly statements or narrative reports) are not considered advertisements, if they include all material disclosures.[81] Communications intended to induce existing clients to renew advisory services, however, are treated as advertisements.[82]

2. General Anti-Fraud Provisions

Even if a communication is not an advertisement under Rule 206(4)-1,[83] it may nevertheless be subject to the anti-fraud provisions of Advisers Act sections 206(1), (2) and (4)[84] and Rule 206(4)-8.[85] Section 206(1) prohibits an investment adviser from using the mails or any means or instrumentality of interstate commerce to employ any device, scheme or artifice to defraud any current or prospective client. In an enforcement action under Advisers Act section 206(1) (unlike Rule 206(4)-8), the SEC must prove that an investment adviser acted with scienter (that is, a knowing or reckless disregard for the truth).[86] A principal may, however, be deemed to have scienter and liable as an aider and abettor of an entity's primary violation of Advisers Act section 206(1).[87]

Advisers Act section 206(2) prohibits an investment adviser from engaging in any transaction, practice or course of business that operates as a fraud or deceit on any current or prospective client, and section 206(4) prohibits "any act, practice, or course of business which is fraudulent, deceptive, or manipulative." Rule 206(4)-8(a)[88] provides that current and prospective investors in a hedge fund managed by an investment adviser are protected by these general anti-fraud rules. In an enforcement action under Advisers Act section 206(2) or 206(4) or Rule 206(4)-8, the SEC must prove only negligence.[89] Sections 206(2) and 206(4) and Rule 206(4)-8 prohibit an investment adviser from omitting to state material information, and an individual may be liable as an aider and abettor of another's violation.[90]

---

81. Investment Counsel Ass'n of America, Inc., SEC No-Action Letter (Mar. 1, 2004); Askin Capital Mgmt., L.P., Advisers Act Release No. 1492 (May 23, 1995).

82. *In re* Spear & Staff, Advisers Act Release No. 188 (Mar. 25, 1965).

83. 17 C.F.R. § 275.206(4)-1.

84. 15 U.S.C. §§ 80b-6(1), 80b-6(2) and 80b-6(4).

85. 17 C.F.R. § 275.206(4)-8. *See* § 6.5.1, *supra.*

86. SEC v. Steadman, 967 F.2d 636 (D.C. Cir. 1992).

87. SEC v. Washington Investment Network, 475 F.3d 392 (D.C. Cir. 2007).

88. 17 C.F.R. § 275.206(4)-8(a).

89. SEC v. Steadman, 967 F.2d 636 (D.C. Cir. 1992); Advisers Act Release No. 2628 (Sep. 10, 2007), at Part II.D.

90. SEC v. Capital Gains Research Bureau, Inc., 375 U.S. 180, 84 S. Ct. 275, 11 L. Ed. 237 (1963); *see also* SEC v. Washington Investment Network, 475 F.3d 392 (D.C. Cir 2007).

§ 8.5 Performance Advertising

If the past performance information of a hedge fund or its investment adviser is material to a decision whether to invest in the hedge fund, that information must be disclosed in the hedge fund's offering circular or private placement memorandum.[91] A hedge fund may, but is not required to, disclose past performance information that is not material (although investors often consider past performance information relevant). The SEC focuses considerable attention on performance advertising and conducts vigorous enforcement actions when it perceives misleading or inappropriate advertising practices.[92]

SEC staff no-action letters relating to performance advertising are promulgated under the anti-fraud provisions discussed in the preceding section and apply to all investment advisers, whether or not registered with the SEC.[93] These anti-fraud provisions also specifically apply to advertising directed to investors and prospective investors in hedge funds.[94] The SEC imposes the following limitations on the use of actual or model performance results:[95]

- The effect of material market or economic conditions on the results portrayed must be disclosed (that is, results must be compared to market performance for the same period).
- The results must reflect the deduction of advisory fees, brokerage or other commissions, and other expenses that a client paid or, in the case of a model portfolio, would have paid, with limited exceptions.[96]
- The advertisement must state whether and to what extent the results portrayed include the reinvestment of dividends and other earnings.
- An advertisement that suggests or makes claims about the potential for profit must also disclose the possibility of loss.
- Any comparison of model or actual results to an index must be to a closely comparable index and must disclose all material facts relevant to the comparison (such as differences in security selection, volatility and diversification).
- Material conditions, objectives or investment strategies used to obtain the performance advertised must be disclosed.

---

91. *See* Chapter 6, *supra.*

92. *See, e.g.*, In the Matter of Warwick Capital Mgmt., Inc., et al., Advisers Act Release No. 2694 (Jan. 16, 2008); In the Matter of Weiss Research, Inc., et al., Exchange Act Release No. 2525 (June 22, 2006); In the Matter of Groh Asset Mgmt., Inc., et al., Advisers Act Release No. 2308 (Sep. 30, 2004); *In re* Van Kampen Investment Advisory Corp., et al., Advisers Act Release No. 1819 (Sep. 8, 1999); *In re* Leeb Investment Advisors; Advisers Act Release No. 1545 (Jan. 16, 1996); *In re* Wall Street Money Mgmt. Group, Inc., Advisers Act Release No. 1464 (Jan. 30, 1995); *In re* Seaboard Investment Advisers, Inc., Advisers Act Release No. 1431 (Aug. 3, 1994). *See also* Chapter 6, *supra*, and Chapter 9, *infra.*

93. Advisers Act Release No. 121 (Nov. 2, 1961), 26 F.R. 10,549 (Nov. 9, 1961).

94. Advisers Act Rule 206(4)-8; 17 C.F.R. § 275.206(4)-8; *see* § 6.5.1, *supra.*

95. Clover Capital Mgmt., Inc., SEC No-Action Letter (Oct. 28, 1986) (hereinafter, *Clover*). *See also* CFA Institute, Global Investment Performance Standards (GIPS®), revised Jan. 2010, *available at* http://www.gipsstandards.org/ (hereinafter "GIPS standards").

96. *See also* § 8.5.2, *infra.*

These disclosures must be made clearly and prominently; disclaimers in small type or obscure font are not sufficient to dispel an advertisement's potential to mislead investors. If past performance is shown only for a selected group of clients, the investment adviser must also disclose the basis on which the selection was made and the effect of this practice on the results portrayed, if material.[97] If including the performance of other accounts that the investment adviser manages would materially affect the performance data shown, the investment adviser should explain why those accounts were excluded (for example, because they use different investment strategies).

1. Inclusion of Advisory Fees

In some instances, the SEC has relaxed the general requirement that performance results be shown net of all actual fees and expenses. For example, the SEC staff stated that it would not recommend enforcement action against an investment adviser that proposed to advertise the composite performance of all accounts for which it would use a particular investment strategy, deducting only a model fee equal to the highest fee charged to any account using that strategy during the period of the performance.[98] In addition, the SEC staff has stated that performance data need not reflect the deduction of custodian fees paid to a bank or other institution for safekeeping client funds and securities.[99]

The SEC staff has also permitted written performance material that shows performance on a gross basis, if it is used only in one-on-one presentations made to sophisticated persons[100] in a private and confidential manner and not made available to the public. The SEC staff based this position on a belief that an investment adviser's fees are frequently negotiable in one-on-one meetings with sophisticated clients.[101] The SEC staff requires in such circumstances that the investment adviser provide the following in writing:[102]

- disclosure that the performance figures do not reflect the deduction of advisory fees;
- disclosure that the client's return will be reduced by the advisory fees and other expenses the client may incur;
- a statement that the investment adviser's fees are described in Part 2 of the investment adviser's Form ADV or an equivalent disclosure document; and
- a representative example showing the effect the advisory fees would have on the total value of the client's portfolio, compounded over a period of years.

---

97. *Clover* (*see* n. 92, *supra*).

98. J.P. Morgan Investment Mgmt., Inc., SEC No-Action Letter (May 7, 1996).

99. Investment Company Institute, SEC No-Action Letter (Aug. 24, 1987).

100. In this context, wealthy individuals, pension funds, universities and other institutions may be sophisticated. Investment Company Institute, SEC No-Action Letter (Sep. 23, 1988).

101. *Id. See also* J.P. Morgan Investment Mgmt., Inc., SEC No-Action Letter (May 7, 1996).

102. *Clover* (*see* n. 92, *supra*).

If the presentation is made to a consultant who will use it in presentations to potential clients, the investment adviser must instruct the consultant to provide the gross performance data and the additional information described above only to similarly sophisticated prospective advisory clients, and only in one-on-one presentations.[103]

2. Model Results

Model results are results for hypothetical or model portfolios that do not reflect the performance of actual accounts. A manager of a new hedge fund that has not yet generated actual performance over a significant period sometimes includes in marketing materials model results that reflect the performance of its investment model, particularly if the model is based on a software program, or on an objective, technical system, rather than fundamental analysis, and the program or system, when fed the relevant factual data for a given period, can be applied to generate hypothetical portfolios for that period. Even well-established investment advisers may use model results to market new investment strategies that are based on software programs or technical systems and that have not yet been used to manage actual accounts. The SEC staff has warned that the use of hypothetical portfolios in marketing materials can raise various fraud problems. The SEC requires the following additional disclosures when an investment adviser advertises model results:[104]

- a description of the limitations inherent in model results, in particular that model results do not represent actual trading and may not reflect the effects that material economic and market factors would have on the investment adviser's decision-making if the investment adviser were actually managing clients' assets;
- if applicable, the description of material changes in the conditions, objectives or investment strategies of the model portfolio during the period shown and the effects of those changes;
- if applicable, a statement that some of the securities or strategies reflected in the model portfolio do not relate, or relate only partially, to the services that the investment adviser currently offers; and
- if applicable, a statement that the investment adviser's clients actually had investment results that were materially different from those shown in the model.

If the results are generated by the retroactive application of a model (such as back-testing), the investment adviser should consider including additional disclosures, such as disclosure about the methodology used to create the model and the statistical validity of the results.

The SEC has sanctioned a number of investment advisers that advertised misleading model performance results, finding that they violated Advisers Act

103. Investment Company Institute, SEC No-Action Letter (Sep. 23, 1988).

104. *See* Scientific Market Analysis, SEC No-Action Letter (Mar. 21, 1976); *Clover* (*see* n. 92, *supra*).

section 206(4)[105] and Rule 206(4)-1[106] by failing to disclose in advertisements that the advertised performance was developed by retroactive or inappropriate application of a model,[107] lack of actual trading,[108] deduction of various fees that would have been incurred,[109] market conditions that may have affected client accounts,[110] and the potential for losses.[111] The above list of limitations on model performance advertising is not exhaustive and does not define a safe harbor. Whether model performance results are misleading depends on the facts and circumstances and may also depend in part on the nature and sophistication of the intended recipients.[112]

3. Specific Recommendations

Advisers Act Rule 206(4)-1[113] applies to advertisements by an investment adviser that is required to be registered with the SEC. It prohibits any advertisement that refers, directly or indirectly, to any past specific recommendations of the investment adviser, unless the advertisement contains or offers to furnish information about all recommendations the investment adviser made during at least the past year.[114] This rule is grounded in a concern that investment advisers could publish selective lists of only their most successful investment recommendations. The SEC has stated that

> material of this nature, which may refer only to recommendations which were or would have been profitable and ignore those which were or would have been unprofitable, is inherently misleading and deceptive, and consequently the rule prohibits this type of advertising unless all recommendations for a minimum specified period are included.[115]

---

105. 15 U.S.C. § 80b-6(4).

106. 17 C.F.R. § 275.206(4)-1.

107. *In re* Patricia Owen-Michel, Advisers Act Release No. 1584 (Sep. 27, 1996); *In re* Profitek, Inc. and Edward G. Smith, SEC Administrative Proceeding, File No. 3-9743 (Sep. 29, 1998); *In re* LBS Capital Mgmt., Inc., Advisers Act Release No. 1644 (July 18, 1997).

108. *In re* Engebretson Capital Mgmt., Inc. and Lester W. Engebretson, SEC Administrative Proceeding File No. 3-10010 (Sep. 13, 1999); *In re* Profitek, Inc. and Edward G. Smith, SEC Administrative Proceeding, File No. 3-9743 (Sep. 29, 1998).

109. *In re* Engebretson Capital Mgmt., Inc. and Lester W. Engebretson, SEC Administrative Proceeding File No. 3-10010 (Sep. 13, 1999); *In re* Meridian Investment Mgmt. Corp., SEC Administrative Proceeding File No. 3-9796 (Dec. 28, 1998); *In re* Patricia Owen-Michel, Advisers Act Release No. 1584 (Sep. 27, 1996).

110. *In re* Patricia Owen-Michel, Advisers Act Release No. 1584 (Sep. 27, 1996).

111. *Id.*

112. *In re* LBS Capital Mgmt., Inc., Advisers Act Release No. 1644 (July 18, 1997).

113. 17 C.F.R. § 275.206(4)-1.

114. Advisers Act Rule 206(4)-1(a)(2), 17 C.F.R. § 275.206(4)-1(a)(2). *See also* Sutro & Co., Inc., SEC No-Action Letter (June 22, 1977); E.F. Hutton & Co., Inc., SEC No-Action Letter (Feb. 2, 1979).

115. All investment advisers, whether or not registered, are subject to the Advisers Act anti-fraud provisions. Advisers Act Release No. 121 (Nov. 2, 1961), 26 F.R. 10,549 (Nov. 9, 1961). *See* § 8.4, *supra*.

i. Permitted Uses of Selected Past Specific Recommendations

The SEC staff views most reports that discuss past specific recommendations as advertisements. An investment adviser may, however, include past recommendations in marketing materials in the circumstances discussed below. In addition, reports only to existing clients that contain past specific recommendations are not advertisements if such reports are part of the investment adviser's services and are not intended to offer additional advisory services to such clients.

Notwithstanding the general prohibition in Rule 206(4)-1,[116] an investment adviser to a hedge fund may in limited circumstances prepare and distribute a list of selected past specific recommendations. In *Franklin Management, Inc.*,[117] the SEC allowed an investment adviser to send to clients with separately managed accounts quarterly reports containing information about some, but not all, specific portfolio management decisions made during the preceding quarter. The investment adviser proposed to use a report that would identify some securities that were bought, sold or held for accounts that the investment adviser managed using a particular investment strategy, some of the reasons for the portfolio management decisions, and a brief analysis of each issuer. The SEC staff indicated that such a report must meet the following conditions:

- The investment adviser must use objective, non-performance-based criteria to select the specific securities it lists.
- The investment adviser must use the same selection criteria for each report of each particular investment category.
- The report may not discuss, directly or indirectly, the amount of profits or losses, realized or unrealized, of any of the specific securities.
- The investment adviser must maintain, and make available to the SEC for inspection on request, records that show (a) the complete list of all securities the investment adviser recommended in the last year for the specific category covered by each report, (b) the information regarding each recommendation described above and (c) the criteria used to select the specific securities listed in each report.

The SEC staff concluded in a subsequent no-action letter[118] that a written communication by an investment adviser that does no more than respond to an "unsolicited" request by a client, prospective client or consultant for specific information about the investment adviser's past specific recommendations is not an advertisement for purposes of Advisers Act Rule 206(4)-1(b).[119] Thus, past recommendations provided in response to such unsolicited requests need not comply with the conditions listed above. A "solicited" request would be the result of, for example, an affirmative effort by the investment adviser that

116. 17 C.F.R. § 275.206(4)-1.
117. Franklin Mgmt., Inc., SEC No-Action Letter (Dec. 10, 1998).
118. Investment Counsel Ass'n. of America, Inc., SEC No-Action Letter (Mar. 1, 2004).
119. 17 C.F.R. § 275.206(4)-1(b).

is intended or designed to induce a client, prospective client or consultant to request that the investment adviser provide past specific recommendations, or an advertisement stating that the investment adviser will provide past specific recommendations on request.

Moreover, the SEC staff continued, an investment adviser that provides a list of past recommendations to one consultant who requests the information for several clients or to several consultants is not engaged in advertising—and thus not subject to the requirements listed above—as long as the investment adviser provides the information in response to a specific, unsolicited request for information about the investment adviser's past specific recommendations. The SEC staff added that a written communication by an investment adviser only to its existing clients discussing past specific recommendations about securities held or recently held in those clients' accounts would generally not be regarded as an advertisement, because such communications are typically part of an investment adviser's services, unless the context suggests that the purpose of the communication is to offer advisory services.

The SEC staff has also permitted an investment adviser to distribute charts showing at least 5 holdings that contributed most positively to a representative account's performance and an equal number of holdings that contributed most negatively, to prospective and current clients not invested in the investment strategy related to the charts, including prospective and current clients and consultants who did not make specific, unsolicited requests for such information.[120] The SEC staff stated that any such chart must satisfy the following conditions:

- The calculation used to compute each holding's contribution to performance must take into account, consistently for each measurement period, the weighting of each such holding and the chart must reflect consistently the results of such calculation.
- The information and number of holdings presented must be consistent from measurement period to measurement period.
- Each chart must disclose how to obtain the methodology for calculating each holding's contribution to performance and list the contribution of every holding in the account to the account's overall performance.
- Each chart must include all information necessary to make it not misleading, including presenting the best- and worst-performing holdings on the same page with equal prominence, close to disclosures that such holdings do not represent all securities purchased, sold or recommended for advisory clients and that past performance does not guarantee future results.
- The investment adviser must maintain and make available to the staff on request records showing the criteria used to select the holdings listed in each chart, a list showing the contribution of each holding in the account to the account's overall performance during the measurement

120. The TCW Group, Inc., SEC No-Action Letter (Nov. 11, 2008).

period, and all data necessary to demonstrate the calculation of each holding's contribution to performance and the appropriateness of the holdings included in each chart.

ii. Required Disclosures

Each advertisement or report subject to Advisers Act Rule 206(4)-1[121] that includes a list of all recommendations that an investment adviser made during the past year must include the following information with respect to each recommendation:[122]

- the name of each security recommended;
- the date and nature of each recommendation (that is, whether to buy or sell);
- the market price at that time;
- the price at which the recommendation was to be acted on; and
- the market price of each security as of the most recent practicable date.

Any separately provided list must also contain the following legend in type at least as large as the largest print used in the text: "It should not be assumed that recommendations made in the future will be profitable or will equal the performance of the securities on this list."[123] Any list proffered pursuant to Rule 206(4)-1 must be provided free of charge.[124]

Any advertisement that includes past specific recommendations of a security by an investment adviser should offer to provide the list and include the legend described in the preceding paragraph, even if the advertisement complies with no-action letters or other SEC staff interpretations permitting the use of such past recommendations.

iii. Portfolio Holdings and Other Current Recommendations

The investment adviser to a hedge fund may want to include lists of representative current portfolio holdings—as opposed to past recommendations—in its marketing materials. The SEC staff has indicated informally that it would not object to such a list, if it is truly representative of current holdings and is a nonmanipulated sample (such as a list of top 10 holdings or all holdings above a de minimis level) rather than a cherry-picked sample. Similarly, the SEC staff has indicated that a list of current recommendations is not subject to Rule 206(4)-1(a)(2).[125] Whether a list consists of current or past recommendations, however, depends on exactly what information is presented and how it is presented. For example, a list would involve past recommendations and thus

121. 17 C.F.R. § 275.206(4)-1.

122. Advisers Act Rule 206(4)-1(a)(2)(A), 17 C.F.R. § 275.206(4)-1(a)(2)(A).

123. Advisers Act Rule 206(4)-1(a)(2)(B), 17 C.F.R. § 275.206(4)-1(a)(2)(B).

124. Scientific Market Analysis, SEC No-Action Letter (Mar. 24, 1976).

125. 17 C.F.R. § 275.206(4)-1(a)(2). Franklin Mgmt., Inc., SEC No-Action Letter (Dec. 10, 1998).

be subject to the rule if it includes some securities that the investment adviser no longer recommends or if it indicates that any of the securities listed were recommended in the past.[126] In any event, all such advertisements are subject to the general prohibition of false or misleading advertising of Rule 206(4)-1(a)(5).[127] An investment adviser may also breach its fiduciary duty by making this information available only to selected investors in its hedge fund.

4. CFA Institute Global Investment Performance Standards

The CFA Institute (CFAI), an industry trade group, has published Global Investment Performance Standards (GIPS®), which differ from the SEC guidelines described above. For example, GIPS standards recommend presentation of performance data gross of fees.[128] To satisfy both SEC guidelines and GIPS standards, an investment adviser may present two sets of performance data, one gross and one net of fees, as long as they are presented with equal prominence and in a format designed to facilitate ease of comparison, and as long as the accompanying disclosure is sufficient to ensure that the material presented is not misleading.[129] Key requirements of GIPS standards for an investment adviser claiming GIPS compliance include the following:

- The investment adviser must adhere to GIPS standards on a firmwide basis and should also adhere to GIPS best practices recommendations in calculating and presenting performance.
- The investment adviser must include all actual, discretionary, fee-paying portfolios in at least one composite.
- The investment adviser must adhere to certain calculation methodologies in computing performance, including valuing portfolios in accordance with GIPS valuation principals, and include specific disclosures with performance, such as the investment adviser's assets under management, the composite's creation date and investment strategy, the asset classes it includes and the extent to which the composite uses derivatives, leverage, short-selling or hedging.
- The investment adviser must comply with all requirements of GIPS standards, including any updates, Guidance Statements, interpretations, Questions & Answers, and clarifications published by CFAI and the GIPS Executive Committee, which are available on the GIPS website (www.gipsstandards.org).

---

126. *Id.*

127. 17 C.F.R. § 275.206(4)-1(a)(5).

128. GIPS standards (*see* n. 92, *supra*).

129. The Ass'n. for Investment Mgmt. and Research, SEC No-Action Letter (Dec. 18, 1996). Nevertheless, where applicable law or regulation conflicts with GIPS standards (*see* n. 92, *supra*), GIPS standards require investment advisers to comply with the law or regulation and disclose the conflict.

- The investment adviser must document its policies and procedures for complying with GIPS standards and apply such policies and procedures consistently.

CFAI strongly encourages each investment adviser claiming compliance with GIPS standards to perform periodic internal compliance checks. In addition, the GIPS Executive Committee strongly recommends that such an investment adviser have an independent third-party verification that tests the construction of its composites and its policies and procedures as they relate to compliance with GIPS standards. Verification is a best practice under GIPS standards. An investment adviser that is claiming GIPS compliance must state in its compliance statement whether it has been verified.

GIPS standards also require an investment adviser claiming GIPS compliance to show at least 5 years (or since inception, if less than 5 years) of GIPS-compliant annual investment performance. Thereafter, the investment adviser must present an additional year of performance each year, building up to at least 10 years of GIPS-compliant performance. In addition, the investment adviser must show 1-, 3-, and 5-year annualized composite returns and returns through the most recent period. If the composite is less than 5 years old, the investment adviser must also present the annualized returns since the composite inception date. (For example, if a composite is 4 years old, the investment adviser must present 1-, 3-, and 4-year annualized returns through the most recent period). Returns for periods of less than 1 year may not be annualized.

An investment adviser is not required to comply with GIPS unless it is a member of CFAI, but some investors may expect that their investment advisers will comply. An investment adviser's representation that its performance presentations comply with GIPS standards would violate Advisers Act anti-fraud rules,[130] if that representation is not true.

5. FINRA Rules Governing Hedge Fund Sales Literature

Two FINRA interpretive letters to the Securities Industry Association under FINRA Rule 2210 together state that a broker may not publish or distribute sales materials for a Company Act section 3(c)(1) hedge fund that present "related performance information," even if the sales materials (other than offering circulars, according to FINRA's informal comments) were prepared by the hedge fund or its investment adviser rather than the broker.[131] Related performance information includes information about performance of predecessor funds, clone funds and comparable managed accounts, extracts, hypothetical and composite records and the like.

If a hedge fund manager manages a U.S. hedge fund and opens a non-U.S. hedge fund that will use the same investment strategy, FINRA's interpretation of Rule 2210 could prevent a broker from showing potential investors in the

---

130. *See* § 8.4, *supra*.

131. FINRA Interpretive Letter (Oct. 2, 2003), as revised in part by FINRA Interpretive Letter (Dec. 30, 2003).

non-U.S. hedge fund the performance of the U.S. hedge fund.[132] FINRA sanctioned a member firm for using marketing materials regarding hedge funds and funds of funds that "listed a targeted rate of return without providing a sound basis for evaluating the target, improperly used hypothetical returns in charts or graphs and/or failed to include inadequate [*sic*] risk disclosure."[133]

The FINRA staff does not object if a member-broker includes related performance information in sales materials for a Company Act section 3(c)(7) hedge fund, if the member ensures that all recipients of such materials are "qualified purchasers" under Company Act section 2(a)(51).[134] The FINRA staff has, however, declined to allow a FINRA member to distribute sales material containing related performance information to "qualified institutional buyers" (who would be eligible to invest in a Company Act section 3(c)(7) hedge fund) in connection with marketing a section 3(c)(1) hedge fund.[135]

6. Funds That Trade Commodity Interests

As discussed in section 6.7 above, a manager of a hedge fund that trades commodity interests (including many types of swaps) may be subject to CFTC and NFA rules regarding performance advertising.

7. Portability of Performance

An investment adviser who was previously employed by another firm may want to advertise the performance he or she achieved in the prior position. In general, the investment adviser may not advertise such prior performance unless the investment adviser was solely responsible[136] for achieving the results represented and the prior account was sufficiently similar to the hedge fund the investment adviser is currently managing or proposes to manage to make the comparison meaningful and relevant to a potential investor.[137]

i. Performance Results from Previous Advisory Firms

The SEC staff will generally allow an investment adviser to advertise the performance of accounts that the investment adviser managed at a prior firm, if the investment adviser meets the following conditions:

---

132. *See* Thomas P. Lemke & Gerald T. Lins, *Regulation of Investments Advisers*, § 2:88, West (2013).

133. "NASD Fines Citigroup Global Markets, Inc. $250,000 in Largest Hedge Fund Sales Sanction to Date," FINRA Notice to Members, Disciplinary Actions, Nov. 2004, at D15-D16.

134. FINRA Interpretive Letter (Dec. 30, 2003).

135. FINRA Interpretive Letter (Sep. 14, 2004).

136. Where an investment adviser selected portfolio securities by committee, a "substantial identity" of personnel is needed for a successor fund to use the predecessor's performance. Great Lakes Advisors, Inc., SEC No-Action Letter (Apr. 3, 1992). If an investment adviser leaves one hedge fund to start another, he may advertise the performance of the first hedge fund in marketing materials for the second hedge fund only if he was actually responsible for making the investment decisions at the first hedge fund and will be responsible for doing so at the second hedge fund. Horizon Asset Mgmt., LLC, SEC No-Action Letter (Sep. 13, 1996).

137. Growth Stock Outlook, SEC No-Action Letter (Apr. 7, 1988).

- The person or persons who manage the accounts currently were also responsible for achieving the prior performance results.
- The accounts managed at the old firm were so similar to those currently managed that their performance would be relevant to prospective clients of the new firm.
- The advertisements are consistent in all other respects with all other relevant rules and SEC staff interpretations relating to performance advertising.
- The advertisements include disclosure that the performance results shown were of accounts managed at another firm.[138]
- The advertisements disclose all other material factors.[139]

A successor investment adviser, portfolio manager or hedge fund seeking to use a predecessor's performance data must also keep all records necessary to form the basis for or calculate the performance data.

In the mutual fund context, the SEC staff has stated that when a portfolio manager joins a new investment adviser, the prospectus for the mutual fund managed by the portfolio manager may include the performance of the mutual fund that the individual previously managed, if the following conditions are met:[140]

- The current and previously managed funds have substantially similar investment objectives, policies and strategies.
- The portfolio manager managed no other comparable registered funds or private accounts while managing the prior fund.
- No other person played a significant part in achieving the prior fund's performance.
- The performance of the prior fund is not presented in a misleading way.

The performance of the prior fund should be presented separately from and given no greater prominence than the current fund's performance.

ii. GIPS Standards

GIPS standards take the position that performance is generally the record of the firm, not of an individual. GIPS standards require, however, that performance of a past firm or affiliation be linked to or used to represent the historical record of a new affiliation if:

- substantially all the investment decision makers are employed by the new firm (such as research department, portfolio managers and other relevant staff),
- the staff and decision-making process remain intact and independent within the new firm, and

138. Horizon Asset Mgmt., LLC, SEC No-Action Letter (Sep. 13, 1996).
139. Great Lakes Advisors, Inc., SEC No-Action Letter (Apr. 3, 1992).
140. Bramwell Growth Fund, SEC No-Action Letter (Aug. 7, 1996).

- the new firm has records that document and support the reported performance.

The new firm must disclose that the performance results from the past firm are linked to the performance record of the new firm.[141]

§ 8.6 Government Investors ("Pay-to-Play")

The SEC and many states have adopted "pay-to-play" rules that prohibit or limit arrangements by which campaign contributions or other payments are made by, or on behalf of, investment advisers to government officials or candidates who can influence the selection of investment advisers to manage state and local government entities' accounts. The SEC's rule applies to all investment advisers that are or are required to be registered with the SEC, exempt reporting advisers and foreign private advisers.[142]

The SEC's pay-to-play rule generally restricts an investment adviser from providing advisory services (either directly or through a hedge fund) for compensation to a government account, such as a government pension plan, if the investment adviser or any of its "covered associates" (as defined below) has made a contribution within the preceding 2 years to any government official or any person who was a candidate for election to a government position having influence to select, directly or indirectly, an investment adviser to manage that government account.[143] "Covered associate" includes (1) an investment adviser's general partner, managing member, executive officer or other person with a similar status or performing similar functions, (2) an investment adviser's employee who solicits government accounts for the investment adviser and any person who directly, or indirectly, supervises the employee and (3) any political action committee controlled by an investment adviser or any person in category (1) or (2) above. Even a contribution that a covered associate made before being hired by the investment adviser will trigger the 2-year freeze if made within 2 years before being hired.

Limited relief from this broad restriction on election contributions exists. First, a *de minimis* exception allows a covered associate to make aggregate contributions of up to $350 in a single election to a candidate for whom the covered associate is entitled to vote, or $150 to a candidate for whom the covered associate is not entitled to vote. Second, a covered associate's contribution that would otherwise trigger the 2-year freeze will not do so if (i) the contribution was made to an official or candidate for whom the covered associate could not vote, (ii) the investment adviser discovers the contribution within 4 months of the date it was made, (iii) the contribution did not exceed $350, and (iv) the contribution is returned to the covered associate within 60 days after discovery by the investment adviser. The rule sets specific limits on how frequently this

141. GIPS standards (*see* n. 92, *supra*).
142. Advisers Act Rule 206(4)-5, 17 C.F.R. § 275.206(4)-5.
143. Advisers Act Rule 206(4)-5(a)(1), 17 C.F.R. § 275.206(4)-5(a)(1).

exception may be used. Third, regarding contributions a covered associate made before being hired, if the covered associate does not solicit clients for the investment adviser, the restriction looks back for only 6 months before the date of hire, instead of 2 years.[144]

The SEC's pay-to-play rule also regulates the use of a third-party (such as a solicitor or placement agent) to solicit a government account. Neither an investment adviser nor any covered associate may pay or agree to pay such a solicitation agent unless such agent is either an SEC-registered investment adviser or a broker-dealer that is a member of a national securities association, such as FINRA, that has pay-to-play rules that are substantially as restrictive as the SEC's pay-to-play rule.[145]

Lobbying restrictions or special placement agent registration requirements are also imposed by the laws of many states. For example, California law generally requires an individual, including an employee or outside consultant of an investment adviser, to register as a placement agent if the person's duties include offering the investment adviser's services to state or local pension plans.[146] New York City's lobbying law similarly requires placement agents for the city's pension plans to register as lobbyists.[147]

§ 8.7 "Brochure Rule"

Advisers Act Rule 204-3 (the "brochure rule") requires an SEC-registered investment adviser to provide Part 2 of its Form ADV, or a comparable document providing at least the same information, to prospective clients before or at the time an investor enters into an advisory contract with that client.[148] The investment adviser also must deliver certain annual and additional updates or summaries of material changes.[149] The brochure rule does not require an investment adviser to a hedge fund to deliver the brochure to prospective investors in the hedge fund, but the SEC has stated that it believes such an investment adviser must provide such information to hedge fund investors in keeping with its duty to disclose all material facts to investors under Advisers Act Rule 206(4)-8.[150]

144. Advisers Act Rule 206(4)-5(b), 17 C.F.R. § 275.206(4)-5(b).
145. Advisers Act Rule 206(4)-5(a)(2), 17 C.F.R. § 275.206(4)-5(a)(2)
146. CA Gov. Code §§ 7513.8, 7513.86, 7513.87, 82025.3 and 82039.
147. 3 NYC Admin Code, §§ 3-211-233.
148. Advisers Act Rule 204-3, 17 C.F.R. § 275.204-3. *See* § 6.5.2, *supra.*
149. *Id.*
150. *See* § 6.5.1. Advisers Act Release No. 3060, 75 F.R. 49,234, 49,246 n. 192 (July 28, 2010).

§ 8.8 Solicitation Disclosures

Advisers Act Rule 206(4)-3[151] (the "solicitors rule") establishes conditions under which an SEC-registered investment adviser may pay a cash fee, directly or indirectly, to a person who solicits clients for the investment adviser. The solicitors rule does not apply to solicitation of investment in a hedge fund, unless the investor is also entering into an advisory contract with the investment adviser to the hedge fund.[152] In any event, if a solicitor is to be compensated by a hedge fund or its investment adviser, any conflicts of interest that arise from such compensation must be disclosed to prospective investors in the hedge fund.[153] In addition, whether or not the safe harbor of the solicitors rule is available, an investment adviser to a hedge fund should make at least the disclosures required by the solicitors rule to any potential investor solicited by a paid solicitor.[154]

If an independent contractor is assisting an investment adviser in marketing hedge fund interests or an employee of an investment adviser does not have substantial duties other than marketing such interests, the independent contractor or employee ordinarily also will be required to register as a broker.[155]

The SEC has stated that an investment adviser that is not registered with the SEC in reliance on the private adviser exemption (which was repealed by the Dodd-Frank Act) may not rely on the solicitors rule, because an investment adviser that engages a solicitor is holding itself out to the public as an investment adviser.[156] The SEC's analysis would also apply to the foreign private adviser exemption discussed in section 2.1.2 above. The SEC has instituted a number of enforcement actions alleging violations of the solicitors rule by investment advisers and solicitors.[157]

§ 8.9 Broker Requirements

Exchange Act section 15[158] makes it unlawful for a person to sell securities unless that person is registered with the SEC as a broker.[159] A general partner of a hedge fund or any employee, officer, director or partner of the general partner of the hedge fund, however, may be exempt from registration under Exchange Act Rule 3a4-1,[160] which provides a safe harbor exemption from the broker

---

151. 17 C.F.R. § 275.206(4)-3. *See* § 10.1.3, *infra.*
152. Mayer Brown LLP, SEC No-Action Letter (July 28, 2008).
153. *Id. See* Chapter 6, *supra.*
154. Advisers Act Rule 206(4)-3(b), 17 C.F.R. § 275.206(4)-3(b).
155. Advisers Act Rule 206(4)-3, 17 C.F.R. § 275.206(4)-3. *See* § 8.9 and Chapter 10, *infra.*
156. Advisers Act Release No. 688 (July 12, 1979), 44 F.R. 42,130 (July 18, 1979).
157. *See, e.g.,* Advisers Act Release No. 1409 (Apr. 6, 1994); Advisers Act Release No. 1500 (June 16, 1995); and Advisers Act Release No. 2514 (May 9, 2006).
158. 15 U.S.C. § 78o.
159. *See* § 10.1, *infra.*
160. 17 C.F.R. § 240.3a4-1.

registration requirement for any person who is considered to be an "associated person of an issuer" if such person meets specified conditions.[161]

§ 8.10 Foreign Private Advisers

An investment adviser that has no place of business in the United States and only a limited number of clients or investors in the United States may be exempt from registration under the Advisers Act if it does not hold itself out generally to the public in the United States as an investment adviser.[162] Although no bright-line rules define holding oneself out to the public as an investment adviser, the SEC staff interpreted the concept broadly in the context of the now-repealed "private adviser exemption"[163] to include: advertising related to investment advisory activities; maintaining a listing as an investment adviser in a telephone or building directory;[164] letting it be known through word of mouth or other channels that the investment adviser is accepting new clients;[165] participating in a "mini-account" or similar investment advisory program;[166] using the label "investment adviser" on business cards or stationery;[167] and using an Internet website to provide information about its services.[168]

The SEC staff did not view the foreign manager of a hedge fund that participates in a nonpublic offering of interests in the hedge fund as "holding itself out generally to the public in the United States" for purposes of the private advisor exemption in Advisers Act section 203(b)(3),[169] which was repealed by the Dodd-Frank Act. Again in the context of the now-repealed private adviser exemption, the SEC staff has deemed certain password-protected online services

161. *Id.*

162. Advisers Act §§ 202(a)(30) and 203(b)(3); 15 U.S.C. §§ 80b-2(a)(30) and 80b-3(b)(3).

163. Advisers Act § 203(b)(3) was amended by the Dodd-Frank Act, Pub. L. 11-203, to replace the former private adviser exemption with the foreign private adviser exemption. The exclusion from the definition of investment adviser for a family office also depends in part on the adviser not holding itself out generally to the public as an investment adviser. Advisers Act § 202(a)(11)(G), 15 U.S.C. § 80b-2(a)(11)(G); Advisers Act Rule 202(a)(11)(G)-1(b)(3), 17 C.F.R. § 275.202(a)(11)(G)-1(b)(3).

164. Dale M. Mueller, SEC No-Action Letter (Feb. 20, 1984).

165. Peter H. Jacobs, SEC No-Action Letter (Feb. 7, 1979).

166. Company Act Release No. 21260 n. 8 (July 27, 1995), 60 F.R. 39,574 (Aug. 2, 1995); Resource Bank and Trust, SEC No-Action Letter (Mar. 29, 1991).

167. Richard W. Blanz, SEC No-Action Letter (Jan. 28, 1985).

168. Securities Act Release No. 7288 (May 9, 1996), 61 F. R. 24,644 (May 15, 1996). If sufficient procedures exist to limit access to selected accredited investors, the SEC staff has permitted website providers to post hedge fund information on Internet websites, without causing the investment advisers to the hedge funds to be deemed to be holding themselves out to the public within the meaning of former Advisers Act § 203(b)(3). *See* Lamp Technologies, Inc., SEC No-Action Letter (May 29, 1997). *See* Chapter 9, *infra.*

169. Advisers Act Rule 202(a)(30)-1(d) 17 C.F.R. § 275.202(a)(30)(d); *see also* Resource Bank and Trust, SEC No-Action Letter (Mar. 29, 1991); Weiss, Barton Asset Mgmt., SEC No-Action Letter (Mar. 12, 1981).

that offer targeted groups biographical and contact information about hedge fund managers (such as names, phone numbers, biographical information about the managers, data about the firms and their assets under management and the like) not to violate the "holding out" prohibition.[170]

In *Thomson Financial Inc.*, Thomson proposed to provide investment professionals with data, analyses and information tools on the equity and bond holdings of mutual funds, pension plans, insurance companies and variable annuity products, as well as biographical information about these companies' investment managers that had been derived from nonpublic sources (the fund managers themselves). The SEC staff granted no-action relief, based particularly on Thomson's representations that (a) it would make its services available exclusively to institutional sales and trading desks of registered brokers to streamline their communications with institutional investors and to fund managers to allow them to monitor the portfolio holdings of competing funds with similar investment strategies and (b) it had implemented procedures to prevent persons seeking investment advisory services from gaining access to its services.[171]

When dealing with U.S. media to discuss analyses, current holdings or past recommendations, an investment adviser that is relying on the foreign private adviser exemption should not describe its advisory services in ways that could be construed as advertising those services.[172]

§ 8.11 Record Retention

Under the Advisers Act, an SEC-registered investment adviser to a hedge fund must keep the following marketing records:[173]

- each notice, circular, advertisement, newspaper article, investment letter, bulletin or other communication that the investment adviser circulates or distributes, directly or indirectly, to 10 or more persons (other than persons connected with the investment adviser), and if the communication recommends the purchase or sale of a specific security, but the communication does not state the reasons for a recommendation, a memorandum by the investment adviser indicating the investment adviser's reasons for the recommendation;[174]
- a copy of each Part 2 of Form ADV and amendment or revision given to any person and a record of the dates and persons to whom such statements were given or offered to be given;[175]

170. Thomson Financial Inc., SEC No-Action Letter (July 10, 2002).
171. *Id. See* § 9.2, *infra.*
172. *See* § 2.1.2.v, *supra.*
173. *See also* § 2.8, *supra.*
174. Advisers Act Rule 204-2(a)(11), 17 C.F.R. § 275.204-2(a)(11).
175. Advisers Act Rule 204-2(a)(14), 17 C.F.R. § 275.204-2(a)(14). *See* § 6.5, *supra.*

- all accounts, books, internal working papers and any other records or documents that are necessary to form the basis for or demonstrate the calculation of the performance or rate of return of any or all managed accounts or securities recommendations in any marketing material, except that, with respect to the performance of managed accounts, this requirement is satisfied by the retention of all account statements, if they reflect all debits, credits and other transactions in a client's account for the period of the statement, and the retention of all worksheets necessary to demonstrate the calculation of the performance or rate of return of all managed accounts;[176] and
- originals of all written communications received and copies of all written communications sent by the investment adviser relating to recommendations or advice given or proposed; receipt, disbursement or delivery of funds or securities; or the placing or execution of securities transaction orders. When sending correspondence to a client, the investment adviser should either retain a copy of the correspondence or retain a form of the correspondence sent to all or a group of clients with a list of the clients to whom such correspondence is sent.[177]

An investment adviser must also maintain complete records relating to its compliance with the private offering exemption,[178] so that it will be able to demonstrate the availability of the exemption should the need arise. Those records include, among other things, copies of the hedge fund's offering circular and other offering documents, the names of all offerees and a log showing that offering circulars were sent to them, records evidencing the investment sophistication and financial capacity of the offerees, and records showing the investment adviser's preexisting relationships with them. If the investment adviser uses a broker or finder, it should obtain and keep copies of all similar records collected by the broker or finder, as well as its written agreement with the broker or finder.

As discussed in section 8.5 above, if an investment adviser advertises its performance, it must maintain all records necessary to substantiate the performance information. The investment adviser must retain for 5 years from the end of the fiscal year in which the advertisement is last published or otherwise disseminated all worksheets and account statements necessary to demonstrate

176. Advisers Act Rule 204-2(a)(16), 17 C.F.R. § 275.204-2(a)(16). *See* Jennison Associates LLC, SEC No-Action Letter (July 6, 2000).

177. Advisers Act Rule 204-2(a)(7), 17 C.F.R. § 275.204-2(a)(7); *see* § 2.8, *supra.* Under the Advisers Act, an investment adviser is not required to keep any unsolicited market letters and other similar communications of general public distribution not prepared by or for the investment adviser, and if the investment adviser sends any notice, circular or other advertisement offering any report, analysis, publication or other investment advisory service to more than 10 persons, the investment adviser is not required to keep a record of the names and addresses of the persons to whom it was sent, except that, if such notice, circular or advertisement is distributed to persons named on any list, the investment adviser must retain with the copy of such notice, circular or advertisement a memorandum describing the list and its source.

178. *See* §§ 5.3 and 8.2, *supra.*

the accuracy of the advertisement.[179] The investment adviser must keep records that cover the entire period for which performance is advertised. These record retention requirements also apply to performance achieved at a predecessor or prior investment adviser, if the investment adviser continues to use it in its own marketing materials.[180] If an investment adviser does not retain the required records, it may be precluded from advertising the unsubstantiated historical performance. Independent audit or review of performance information, however, is not required by law.

The pay-to-play rule discussed above at section 8.6 requires an investment adviser to maintain detailed records of its and its covered associates' campaign and other political contributions, and the identity of all its covered associates.[181]

179. Advisers Act Rules 204-2(a)(16) and 204-2(e)(3), 17 C.F.R. §§ 275.204-2(a)(16) and 275.204-2(e)(3). *See also* § 2.8, *supra.*

180. Horizon Asset Mgmt., LLC, SEC No-Action Letter (Sep. 13, 1996); Great Lakes Advisors, Inc., SEC No-Action Letter (Apr. 3, 1992).

181. Advisers Act Rule 204-2(a)(18), 17 CFR § 275.204-2(a)(18).

CHAPTER **9**

Websites and Social Media

§ 9.1 Introduction

Websites and other forms of electronic communication such as blogs and social media are increasingly important tools for hedge funds and investment advisers in building and maintaining relationships with investors, gauging investor suitability and marketing hedge funds. The prohibition of general solicitation and advertising in certain private offerings[1] applies equally to online communications. The anti-fraud rules of the Securities Act and the Exchange Act, discussed above in section 6.4, apply to anything on or linked to the investment adviser's or the hedge fund's website that is (or might be deemed to be) part of the hedge fund's offering materials.

The general partner of a hedge fund must exercise great care in using the Internet, to preserve both the hedge fund's private offering exemption under the Securities Act and its exception from the definition of "investment company" under the Company Act.[2] Interpretive issues also arise when a hedge fund's or investment adviser's website hyperlinks to third-party information. Websites must also comply with state and other regulatory regimes, and websites that offer interests in hedge funds to non-U.S. investors must comply with the additional requirements of Regulation S.[3]

§ 9.2 Preserving the Private Offering Exemption

In general, the general partner of a hedge fund should not offer or sell interests in the hedge fund by using the Internet. When the SEC first considered whether a private offering could be conducted over the Internet, it concluded that an offering made through an unrestricted and publicly available website would violate the prohibition of general solicitation or advertising that applied to the

1. *See* Chapters 5 and 8, *supra.*
2. *See* Chapter 3, *supra.*
3. *See* §§ 5.4 and 8.3, *supra.*

offering.[4] Accordingly, access to a hedge fund's website should be strictly controlled to ensure that neither unsophisticated nor non-accredited investors can gain access, unless the hedge fund's offering complies with Rule 506(c) of Regulation D.[5]

The SEC interpretations discussed below for the most part address private offerings made in reliance on Regulation D. It is unclear whether those interpretations would also apply to a private offering made in reliance on Securities Act section 4(a)(2) apart from Regulation D, but the tenor of the pre-Regulation D case law suggests that they would not.

1. Online Marketing by Broker Affiliates

In *IPONET*,[6] the SEC staff gave no-action relief to a registered broker and its affiliate ("IPONET") that planned to invite prospective investors who had previously registered as members of IPONET to complete a questionnaire posted on IPONET's Internet website "as a means of building a customer base and database of accredited and sophisticated investors." The registered broker affiliated with IPONET would determine whether a prospective investor who completed IPONET's Internet questionnaire was "accredited" or "sophisticated" within the meaning of Rule 506 of Regulation D.

Prospective investors who were determined to be so qualified would be given access to a password-protected website that displayed offering materials of private placement offerings that commenced after the investor was determined to be qualified. The SEC staff allowed such use of the website, in part because the questionnaire would be generic in nature and would not refer to any specific transactions posted or to be posted on the password-protected page of IPONET.[7] The SEC staff concluded that a general solicitation would not occur when a preexisting, substantive relationship exists between offerees and an issuer or its broker.[8]

2. Third-Party Websites

In the *Lamp Technologies, Inc.* no-action letters,[9] the SEC staff allowed Lamp Technologies, Inc. ("Lamp") to establish and administer a website displaying hedge funds' offering memoranda, performance information and other

---

4. Securities Act Release No. 7233 (Oct. 6, 1995), 60 F.R. 53,458 (Oct. 6, 1995); *see* Chapters 5 and 8, *supra*. If an offer is public for purposes of the Securities Act, it is also public for purposes of Company Act §§ 3(c)(1) and 3(c)(7). *See, e.g.*, Gerard Rizzuti, SEC No-Action Letter (June 7, 1983); Lamp Technologies, Inc., SEC No-Action Letter (May 29, 1998). In offerings that comply with Rule 506(c) of Regulation D, 17 C.F.R. 230.506(c), general solicitation is now permitted; *see* § 5.3.2, *supra*.

5. *See* § 5.3 and Chapter 8, *supra*. *In re* PriorityAccess, Inc., Endpoint Technologies, Inc. and Roger Shearer, SEC Administrative Proceeding File 3-10621 (Oct. 3, 2001); *In re* CGI Capital, Inc., SEC Administrative Proceeding File No. 3-10331 (Sep. 29, 2000).

6. IPONET, SEC No-Action Letter (July 26, 1996).

7. *Id.*

8. *See* §§ 5.3.1.iii and 8.2.3, *supra*.

9. Lamp Technologies, Inc., SEC No-Action Letters (May 29, 1997, and May 29, 1998).

information. The hedge funds were excepted from Company Act registration under section 3(c)(1) or 3(c)(7) and privately offered their securities under Regulation D. The SEC staff agreed that posting such information on the website would not (a) involve any form of general solicitation or general advertising within the meaning of Rule 502(c) of Regulation D, or (b) constitute a public offering of securities for purposes of Company Act sections 3(c)(1) and 3(c)(7).[10] The SEC staff emphasized that posting private offering materials on an Internet website requires procedures that limit access to accredited investors and impose a waiting period.[11]

Lamp represented in its request for no-action relief that it would use procedures designed to limit access to website information to a select group of accredited investors and require that managers of the private hedge funds listed on the website post only information related to those hedge funds and not offer other services or products on the website. Neither Lamp nor any of its affiliates would operate or provide investment advisory services to any of the hedge funds listed on the website. Lamp was not a broker or affiliated with a broker; no employee of Lamp was a registered representative of a broker; and Lamp, its affiliates and their employees would not effect transactions in securities for the participating hedge funds or assist them in negotiating such transactions.

To gain access to the hedge fund information, a subscriber would be required to complete a questionnaire designed to allow Lamp to "form a reasonable basis for determining" that the subscriber was an accredited investor, within the meaning of Rule 501(a) of Regulation D. Such subscribers would then receive passwords giving them access to the hedge fund information posted on the website. Lamp would require subscribers to agree not to invest in any posted hedge fund (other than a hedge fund in which the subscriber was then already invested or considering investment or for which the subscriber had already been solicited) for 30 days following qualification.[12] Lamp maintained that this waiting period and the fact that most hedge funds were available for subscription on a quarterly or annual basis would ensure that subscribers would not join the website specifically to invest in any particular hedge fund and that Lamp's qualification of a subscriber would not be deemed a solicitation for any particular hedge fund.

3. Self-Qualification

Some third-party service providers that are neither registered brokers nor affiliates of registered brokers establish websites inviting prospective investors to qualify themselves as accredited or sophisticated. These services raise significant concerns under both the Exchange Act and the Securities Act. The SEC staff has

10. *Id.*

11. Lamp Technologies, Inc., SEC No-Action Letter (May 29, 1997). Presumably, the limitations addressed in this No-Action Letter would not be relevant to an offering that complies with Rule 506(c) of Regulation D; *see* § 5.3.2, *supra*.

12. Lamp also required subscribers to agree not to deliver hedge fund information posted on the website to anyone other than their authorized personnel and professional advisers. For SEC staff treatment of other matching or listing services, *see* § 8.2.2(iii), *supra*.

stated that these third-party service providers that participate "at key points in the chain of distribution" in securities offerings must register as brokers under the Exchange Act, even when the securities are exempt from registration under the Securities Act.[13] The SEC staff has also stated that offerees who learn of an offering on a website operated by a third-party that is neither a broker nor an affiliate of a broker may not have preexisting, substantive relationships with the issuer. In such case, the issuer would not have a basis for reasonably believing that such offerees who purchase its securities are qualified, and the issuer could therefore be precluded from relying on some Securities Act exemptions.[14]

§ 9.3 Advisers Act Rules

1. Advertising Rules; Anti-Fraud Requirements

The SEC advertising rules[15] apply to websites of all investment advisers, whether or not they are registered with the SEC. As investment advisers increasingly use customized websites as marketing tools and to provide investor services, the SEC staff is focusing more scrutiny on the access to and content of such websites. Hedge fund websites are subject to the general anti-fraud rules of the Advisers Act, and any description on a website of a hedge fund's investment strategy and other characteristics must be consistent with information in the hedge fund's offering circular.

Investment advisers must use particular caution using interactive websites or other social media such as LinkedIn. In 2012, the SEC's Office of Inspections and Examinations issued a National Examination Risk Alert on the use of social media and interactive networking websites by registered investment advisers and their advisory personnel, following a sweep examination relating to social media.[16] The SEC reminded investment advisers that a website that permits postings by other users may be considered testimonial advertising, which the SEC prohibits.[17] The risk alert noted that registered investment advisers that use social media must adopt robust policies and procedures that guide the content of communications, the approval of postings, supervision and training, and record retention.

---

13. Progressive Technology Inc., SEC No-Action Letter (Oct. 11, 2000), quoting from Massachusetts Financial Services, Inc. v. Securities Investor Protection Corp., 411 F. Supp. 411, 415 (D. Mass.), aff'd 545 F.2d 754 (1st Cir. 1976), cert denied, 431 U.S. 904 (1977).

14. Securities Act Release No. 7856, 65 F.R. 25,843, at § II.C.2 ("Use of Electronic Media") (Apr. 28, 2000).

15. *See* §§ 8.4 and 8.5, *supra.*

16. National Examination Risk Alert on Investment Adviser Use of Social Media (SEC Office of Compliance Inspections and Examinations, Jan. 4, 2012); Jessica Toonkel, "Advisers' fear factor spikes amid SEC social-media sweep" *Investment News* (Feb. 16, 2011) (www.investmentnews.com/article/20110216/FREE/110219946).

17. *See* § 8.4.1.i, *supra.*

Investment advisers should limit the use of charts and graphs on their websites. Advisers Act Rule 206(4)-1(a)(3)[18] proscribes representing that investors can use charts, graphs, formulas or other devices included in marketing materials to determine which securities they should buy, sell or hold, unless the investment adviser discloses prominently the limitations or difficulties of using the charts, graphs, formulas or other devices. This rule may be implicated when an investment adviser's website offers tools (such as interactive questionnaires) designed to assist an investor in deciding whether to invest in a particular hedge fund. These pages should include appropriate disclaimers and explanations about the limitations of the tools or assumptions in the model (such as imputed rates of return).

Historical information, including investor letters, explanations and data, needs to be dated so that a website user knows the dates to which it relates. For greater clarity, older dated information may be archived to a different location from more recent data, with an appropriate explanation, so that it is clear to users that the information has not been updated.

An investment adviser with no place of business in the United States that relies on the "foreign private adviser" exemption from investment adviser registration[19] must strictly control access to its website, so that the website does not hold the investment adviser out to the public in the United States as an investment adviser.[20] Some state securities regulatory agencies take the position that if a website offers and promotes an investment adviser's services and is accessible by residents of that state, the investment adviser is offering its advisory services in that state and must either register or notice file as an investment adviser in that state, unless the website contains appropriate disclaimers.[21]

2. Electronic Delivery of Required Disclosures

SEC-registered investment advisers may use electronic communications or websites to deliver required disclosures, such as privacy notices, performance reports and Form ADV, Part 2, if they follow the SEC's requirements for such communications.[22] For example, electronic delivery of Form ADV, Part 2, satisfies an investment adviser's delivery obligation only if the recipient has affirmatively consented to receive communications electronically.[23] For annual privacy notices, an investment adviser may rely on electronic delivery only if the recipient accesses the investment adviser's financial products and services electronically and has agreed to receive the notices at the investment adviser's

---

18. 17 C.F.R. § 275.206(4)-1(a)(3).
19. Advisers Act 203(b)(3); 15 U.S.C. 80b-3(b)(3). *See* §§ 2.1.2.v and 8.10, *supra.*
20. *See* § 8.10, *supra.*
21. *See* § 9.5.2, *infra.*
22. Advisers Act Release No. 1562, 61 F.R. 24,644, at § III.B (May 15, 1996) ("Electronic Media Release").
23. Advisers Act Release No. 3060, 75 F.R. 49,234, at § II.A.3.a (Aug. 12, 2010) (citing the Electronic Media Release at note 196).

website.[24] Hedge funds organized as partnerships may deliver K-1s to their partners electronically if they comply with disclosure, consent and delivery procedures established by the IRS.[25]

More generally, the Electronic Signatures in Global and National Commerce Act[26] permits parties to agree to contract electronically and give required disclosures electronically, if the requirements of that Act are satisfied. For example, if an investment adviser provides services electronically and delivers required notices electronically, it must:

- inform the consumer of (i) the consumer's right to have an electronic record made available in nonelectronic (paper) form, (ii) the consumer's right to withdraw consent to have the record provided in an electronic form, and (iii) any conditions, consequences (such as termination of the parties' relationship), or fees if the consumer's consent is withdrawn;[27]
- inform the consumer whether his or her consent applies only to the specific transaction that gave rise to the obligation to provide the record or also to identified categories that may be provided over the course of the parties' relationship;[28]
- describe the procedures the consumer is required to use to withdraw consent and to update information needed to contact the consumer electronically;[29]
- inform the consumer of how, after consenting to the electronic record, the consumer may obtain a paper copy of the electronic record on request, and the fee, if any, to be charged for such copy;[30]
- provide the consumer (before the consumer consents) with a description of the hardware and software requirements for access to and retention of the electronic records;[31] and
- if the software or hardware requirements necessary to gain access to the electronic record change, inform the consumer of the new hardware and software requirements and the consumer's right to withdraw consent without the imposition of any fees or any condition or consequence not previously disclosed.[32]

---

24. Regulation S-P Rules 248.9(b)(1)(iii), (c)(1) and (e)(2)(iii), 17 C.F.R. §§ 248.9(b)(1)(iii), (c)(1) and (e)(2)(iii); FTC Privacy Rules 313.9(b)(1)(iii), (c)(1) and (e)(2)(iii), 16 C.F.R. §§ 313(b)(1)(iii), (c)(1) and (e)(2)(iii); CFTC Privacy Rules 160.9(b)(1)(iii), (c)(1) and (e)(2)(iii), 17 C.F.R. §§ 160(b)(1)(iii), (c)(1) and (e)(2)(iii).
25. Revenue Procedure 2012-17, Feb. 13, 2012.
26. 15 U.S.C. §§ 7001-7031.
27. 15 U.S.C. § 7001(c)(1)(B)(i).
28. 15 U.S.C. § 7001(c)(1)(B)(ii).
29. 15 U.S.C. § 7001(c)(1)(B(iii).
30. 15 U.S.C. § 7001(c)(1)(B)(iv).
31. 15 U.S.C. § 7001(c)(1)(C)(i).
32. 15 U.S.C. § 7001(c)(1)(D)(i).

§ 9.4 Hyperlinks

Hyperlinked information on an investment adviser's website or in other electronic communications may give rise to liability under the securities laws for fraud, misrepresentation, unregistered public offerings or other violations. According to the SEC, liability for hyperlinked information may arise if a hedge fund or investment adviser has adopted the hyperlinked content, which may occur if it has "involved itself in the preparation of the information, or explicitly or implicitly endorsed or approved" the information.[33] Investment advisers that use hyperlinks or post content prepared by others on websites, blogs or social media should follow the principles that govern the use of reprints in advertising materials; for example, such materials may not be testimonial in nature and their use may not be false or misleading.[34]

1. Adoption of Another's Content

The SEC considers the following factors in determining whether a hedge fund or investment adviser has adopted the hyperlinked information, for purposes of attributing liability:

- Context—A reference on the hedge fund's or the investment adviser's website to linked information on a different website as "authoritative" may imply that the hedge fund or investment adviser has adopted it.
- Risk of Confusion—Hyperlinks that operate in ways that do not clearly distinguish the hyperlinked website from the hedge fund's or the investment adviser's website may imply that the hedge fund or the investment adviser has adopted the hyperlinked material. A "jump page" that indicates that the viewer is leaving the hedge fund's or the investment adviser's website to move to another website may reduce the likelihood that an investor would be confused about the source of linked information. The SEC has indicated that the presence of a disclaimer alone will not shield against liability.[35]
- Presentation—Hyperlinking selectively to specific information, rather than to a third-party's website generally, may imply that the hedge fund or the investment adviser has adopted that particular material. An investment adviser may violate the anti-fraud rules of the Advisers Act by singling out, in analyses or other communications, hyperlinks that falsely or misleadingly advantage it or are otherwise false or misleading.[36]

33. Securities Act Release No. 7856 (Apr. 28, 2000), 65 F.R. 25,843 (May 4, 2000).

34. *See* §§ 8.4 and 8.5, *supra*, and "Web Compliance Revisited," *IA Week*, May 22, 2000.

35. Securities Act Release No. 7856 (Apr. 28, 2000), 65 F.R. 25,843 (May 4, 2000), at § II.B.1. Factors the SEC considers are whether the investment adviser was involved in preparing the hyperlinked information, what the investment adviser says about the hyperlinked information, the risk of confusion and the manner in which the website presents the link.

36. *Id. See also* "Web Compliance Revisited," *IA Week*, May 22, 2000.

2. Guidelines

If an investment adviser or a hedge fund hyperlinks to third-party information from its website, it should follow the following guidelines:

- Hyperlinks should only go to the home pages of third-party websites, rather than to specific pages in those websites.
- Investment advisers and hedge funds should not download content from other websites to their own without express written consent. "Deep linking" (that is, connecting directly to the desired feature in another person's website while skipping the home page and other pages where solicitations and advertisements are placed) may infringe copyrights.
- Investment advisers should not use the logos or trademark designs of any other business without the approval of the business that owns them.
- Investment advisers should carefully review hyperlinked third-party websites to ensure that nothing in those websites, especially the referenced information, might be misleading. The linked website also should comply with any applicable advertising restrictions that apply to investment advisers. For example, testimonials are not permitted.[37]
- If any information about a hedge fund is hosted by a solicitor's website, the investment adviser should make clear that the host website is not recommending or endorsing the hedge fund, ensure that the presentation looks like a conventional marketing document in print media, and ensure that the host website does not use framing technology so that a potential investor that follows a link will properly leave the host website to go to the hedge fund or investment adviser website before being offered any interest in the hedge fund.[38]

§ 9.5 Other Regulations

1. FINRA Guidance

Concerned about the pace of change in communication technology, FINRA issued a Notice to Members in 2007 addressing members' supervisory and regulatory responsibilities and duties to customers with respect to the use of electronic communication, including electronic mail, instant messaging, blogging and message boards, by themselves or associated persons. The Notice to Members also specified procedures for risk-based reviews of electronic communication.[39]

FINRA issued additional guidance in 2010 on the use of social media websites, such as Facebook, Twitter and LinkedIn, by associated persons of

37. *See* §§ 8.4 and 8.5, *supra*.
38. *See* "Web Compliance Revisited," *IA Week*, May 22, 2000.
39. FINRA Notice to Members 07-59 (Dec. 2007).

FINRA members.[40] The 2010 guidelines generally require FINRA members to supervise their associated persons' use of social media, including interactive postings, and to require prior approval for static postings.[41] FINRA issued further guidance on FINRA members' record-keeping and supervisory responsibilities in 2011.[42] Although investment advisers that are not also FINRA members are not subject to FINRA's guidance, the FINRA approach is instructive.[43]

2. State Laws

Laws of some states require investment advisers with websites to make specified disclosures to avoid state licensure or certification requirements. For example, some states have issued specific guidance stating that an investment adviser located outside of the state will not be deemed to be transacting business in the state if its website and electronic communications include legends prescribed by the state's regulatory authority and meet certain other requirements.[44] Other state laws require an investment adviser with no place of business in the state to register there if it directs communications to more than 5 prospective clients in the state, which may include websites and other electronic communications.[45] Massachusetts issued its own guidance on social media use in early 2012, following the SEC's guidance noted above.[46]

Some states have privacy and other disclosure requirements that apply to investment advisers' websites.[47] For example, an investment adviser that operates in Massachusetts or has clients or investors in Massachusetts must adopt a comprehensive information security program if its clients can access personal information on its website.[48]

---

40. FINRA Notice to Members 10-06 (Jan. 2010).

41. *Id.*

42. FINRA Notice to Members 11-39 (Aug. 2011).

43. Investment advisers reviewing the FINRA guidance should be aware that FINRA's advertising rules are different from the SEC's advertising restrictions governing investment advisers. For example, FINRA requires all advertising to be filed with FINRA before its use, and FINRA permits testimonials subject to specific requirements. FINRA Rules 2210(d)(1)(E) and (d)(2)(A).

44. *See, e.g.,* CA Corp. Sec. Rel. No. 107-C, Use of the Internet by Broker-Dealers and Investment Advisers for the Dissemination of Information on Products and Services (Aug. 19, 1997), http://www.corp.ca.gov/Commissioner/Releases/107-C.asp; and Maryland Administrative Order, In the Matter of: Broker-Dealers, Investment Advisers, Broker-Dealer Agents, and Investment Adviser Representatives Using the Internet for General Dissemination of Information on Products and Services (St. of Md. Office of Attorney General, Sec. Div.), Mar. 18, 1998, 1998 Md. Sec. No-Act. LEXIS 1.

45. *See, for example*, Nev. Revised Statutes § 90.340.1(a)(3).

46. Guidance on the Use of Social Media by Investment Advisers (Massachusetts Securities Division, Jan. 18, 2012) (*available at* http://www.sec.state.ma.us/sct/sctpdf/The-Use-of-Social-Media-by-Investment-Advisers.pdf). *See* § 9.3.1, *supra.*

47. For example, CA Bus. and Prof. Code §§ 22575-22579 require the operator of a website that collects information about individuals who reside in California to include a privacy statement on the website.

48. 201 Massachusetts Reg. 17.00. *See* § 2.7.6, *supra.*

Apart from investment adviser licensing requirements, making hedge fund offering materials available on a website or through other electronic means may constitute an offer of securities to residents of a state, subject to the state's securities registration requirements.[49]

§ 9.6 Offshore Offerings via the Internet

The SEC has outlined procedures that a hedge fund must use in soliciting non-U.S. investors over the Internet to ensure compliance with the restrictions of Regulation S:[50]

- The website should contain a prominent, meaningful disclaimer on an initial screen stating that the offer is directed only to countries other than the United States and should include measures to prevent users from distributing information from the website.[51] If applicable, the disclaimer should make clear that the offering is not open to U.S. investors.
- The hedge fund should implement procedures reasonably designed to prevent actual sales of its interests in the United States or, where applicable, to U.S. investors.[52]
- The hedge fund should confirm that that there are no indirect indications (such as payments drawn on U.S. banks) that investors solicited over the Internet are in the United States or are U.S. persons.
- The hedge fund should ensure that the content of the solicitation does not appear to be targeted to persons in the United States or, where applicable, to U.S. persons. The SEC cites selling materials that discuss avoiding U.S. income taxes as one example of a solicitation that targets U.S. persons.[53]
- The hedge fund should limit access to the posted materials to persons or entities that provide residence information to confirm their non-U.S. addresses and, where applicable, their status as non-U.S. persons.[54]

---

49. Bulldog Investors Gen. Partnership v. Secretary of the Commonwealth, 457 Mass. 210 (Mass. 2010).

50. Securities Act Release No. 7516 (Mar. 23, 1998), 63 F.R. 14,806 (Mar. 27, 1998). *See also* §§ 5.4 and 8.3, supra.

51. Perfect Information, SEC No-Action Letter (Dec. 22, 2000); Europrospectus.com Limited, SEC No-Action Letter (Apr. 28, 2004).

52. Securities Act Release No. 7516 at § III.A (Mar. 23, 1998), 63 F.R. 14,806 (Mar. 27, 1998).

53. *Id.*

54. *Id.* at § IV.A.2.

CHAPTER **10**

Avoiding Broker Registration

§ 10.1 Exchange Act

The Exchange Act generally defines a "broker" as a person engaged in the business of effecting transactions in securities for the accounts of others[1] and generally defines a "dealer" as a person engaged in the business of buying and selling securities for that person's own account, through a broker or otherwise.[2] The general partner of a hedge fund may be required to register as a broker or dealer by virtue of the role it plays in offering and selling interests in and buying and selling securities on behalf of the hedge fund.

1. Rule 3a4-1 Safe Harbor Exemption from Broker Registration

Exchange Act section 15[3] provides generally that it is unlawful for any broker to use the mails or any means or instrumentality of interstate commerce to effect any transactions in, or to induce or attempt to induce the purchase or sale of, any security, unless that broker is registered as such with the SEC. Rule 3a4-1[4] under the Exchange Act provides a safe harbor exemption from the broker registration requirements for any associated person of an issuer if that person meets conditions specified in the rule. "Associated person of an issuer," as defined in Rule 3a4-1, includes any natural person who is an employee, officer, director or partner of (a) the issuer, (b) a corporate general partner of a limited partnership that is the issuer or (c) a company or partnership that controls, is controlled by or is under common control with the issuer. Presumably, although no definitive authority has been published, natural persons who are managers of a limited liability company that is the general partner of an issuer are also associated persons of the issuer.

---

1. Exchange Act § 3(a)(4), 15 U.S.C. § 78c(a)(4).
2. Exchange Act § 3(a)(5), 15 U.S.C. § 78c(a)(5).
3. 15 U.S.C. § 78o.
4. 17 C.F.R. § 240.3a4-1.

An investment adviser[5] that is the general partner of a hedge fund, and its managers and employees who solicit investors for the hedge fund, may qualify for the Rule 3a4-1 exemption from broker registration if they (a) are not subject to a statutory disqualification, as that term is defined in Exchange Act section 3(a)(39),[6] (b) do not receive any compensation related to the amount of hedge fund interests sold (whether by commission or otherwise), (c) primarily perform or intend primarily to perform at the end of the offering substantial duties (other than in connection with the offering) for or on behalf of the hedge fund, (d) are not associated with a broker or dealer, (e) were not employed by a broker or dealer within the preceding 12 months, and (f) do not participate in an offering of securities (other than in certain limited circumstances) more than once every 12 months. A person is subject to a "statutory disqualification" if such person:

> (a) has been and is expelled or suspended from membership or participation in, or barred or suspended from being associated with (1) a member of, any self-regulatory organization or non-U.S. equivalent, (2) any non-U.S. or international securities exchange, (3) any contract market designated pursuant to CEA section 5[7] or any substantially equivalent non-U.S. statute or regulation, (4) any futures association registered under CEA section 17[8] or any substantially non-U.S. statute or regulation, or has been and is denied trading privileges on any such contract market or non-U.S. equivalent;
>
> (b) is subject to:
>
> (1) an order of the SEC, other appropriate regulatory agency or non-U.S. financial regulatory authority
>
> (i) denying, suspending for a period not exceeding 12 months, or revoking his registration as a broker, dealer, municipal securities dealer, government securities broker or government securities dealer or limiting his activities as a non-U.S. person performing a function substantially equivalent to any of the above; or
>
> (ii) barring or suspending for a period not exceeding 12 months his being associated with a broker,

5. The adopting release for Rule 3a4-1 also clarifies that if the employees of a corporate general partner sell securities of an issuer-limited partnership in compliance with Rule 3a4-1, neither the employees nor the corporate general partner would be required to register as a broker, even though the general partner is not a natural person. A corporate general partner that sells issuer-limited partnership securities through its employees and pays the employees a sales commission would, however, be acting as a broker and must register as such, and the employees would be associated persons of a broker. Exchange Act Release No. (22172 (June 27, 1985), 50 F.R. 27,940 (July 9, 1985).

6. 15 U.S.C. § 78c(a)(39).

7. 7 U.S.C. § 7.

8. 7 U.S.C. § 21.

dealer, municipal securities dealer, government securities broker or government securities dealer, or non-U.S. person performing a function substantially equivalent to any of the above;

(2) an order of the CFTC denying, suspending or revoking his registration under the CEA;[9] or

(3) an order by a non-U.S. financial regulatory authority denying, suspending or revoking the person's authority to engage in transactions in contracts of sale of a commodity for future delivery or other instruments traded on or subject to the rules of a contract market, board of trade or non-U.S. equivalent thereof;

(c) by his conduct while associated with a broker, dealer, municipal securities dealer, government securities broker or government securities dealer, or while associated with an entity or person required to be registered under the CEA,[10] has been found to be a cause of any effective suspension, expulsion or order of the character described in clause (a) or (b) above, and in entering such a suspension, expulsion or order, the SEC or an appropriate regulatory agency or self-regulatory organization has jurisdiction to find whether or not any person was a cause thereof;

(d) by his conduct while associated with any broker, dealer, municipal securities dealer, government securities broker, government securities dealer or other entity engaged in transactions in securities, or while associated with an entity engaged in transactions in contracts of sale of a commodity for future delivery or other instruments traded on or subject to the rules of a contract market, board of trade or non-U.S. equivalent thereof, has been found to be a cause of any effective suspension, expulsion or order by a non-U.S. or international securities exchange or non-U.S. financial regulatory authority empowered by a non-U.S. government to administer or enforce its laws relating to financial transactions as described in clause (a) or (b) above;

(e) has associated with him any person whom he knows, or in the exercise of reasonable care should know, to be a person described by clause (a), (b), (c) or (d) above; or

(f) (1) has committed or omitted any act, or is subject to an order or finding, enumerated in subparagraph (D), (E), (H) or (G) of paragraph (4) of Exchange Act section 15(b),[11] (2) has

9. 7 U.S.C. §§ 1 *et seq.*
10. *Id.*
11. 15 U.S.C. § 78o(b)(4).

> been convicted of any offense specified in subparagraph (B) of such paragraph (4) or any other felony within 10 years of the date of filing an application for membership or participation in, or to become associated with a member of, such self-regulatory organization, (3) is enjoined from any action, conduct or practice specified in subparagraph (C) of such paragraph (4), (4) has willfully made or caused to be made in any application for membership or participation in, or to become associated with a member of, a self-regulatory organization, report required to be filed with a self-regulatory organization, or proceeding before a self-regulatory organization, any statement which was at the time, and in the light of circumstances under which it was made, false or misleading with respect to any material fact, or (5) has omitted to state in any such application, report or proceeding any material fact required to be stated therein.

2. Non-Safe-Harbor Cases

Even if the general partner of a hedge fund or its managers or employees do not satisfy the safe harbor conditions, they might not be required to register as brokers on the grounds that they are not in the business of selling securities. Whether a person is in the business of selling securities depends on whether the person sells securities as part of a regular business.[12] For this purpose, the SEC may examine a number of factors, including the type of and basis for any compensation received, the extent to which the person holds funds or securities for others, the extent of contact with the public, and whether the person is "engaged in the business" of effecting transactions in securities.[13] Even if a person's securities activities are only a small part of the person's business activities, or the income from them is only a small part of the person's total business income, if the person engages in such activities often enough to support the inference that those activities are part of his business, the person will be deemed to be engaged in the business.[14]

The SEC views receipt of compensation related to sales of securities as an important factor in determining whether a person is acting as a broker. This factor (which is also an element of the Rule 3a4-1 safe harbor exemption) can be frustrating for investment advisers who desire to pay employees based in part on the amount of capital they raise for a hedge fund. Most such incentive-based compensation models are not available to hedge fund marketers who are not registered as brokers or employed as registered representatives of registered brokers. The SEC staff declined to take a no-action position when a registered

12. *See, e.g.*, Boston Advisory Group, SEC No-Action Letter (Oct. 21, 1980); InTouch Global, SEC No-Action Letter (Nov. 14, 1995).

13. InTouch Global, SEC No-Action Letter (Nov. 14, 1995).

14. *Id.* Such activity need not, however, be a person's principal business or principal source of income. *See, e.g.*, SEC v. United Financial Group, Inc., 474 F.2d 354, 356-57 (9th Cir. 1973).

investment adviser proposed to assist a broker or dealer with solicitation and to receive transaction-related compensation.[15] In that no-action letter, an investment adviser proposed to assist a brokerage firm in presenting and explaining section 8 housing limited partnerships and other real estate partnerships or oil and gas partnerships to interested persons. For the investment adviser's services, the brokerage firm proposed to pay the investment adviser a consulting fee based on sales of partnership units to customers. The SEC staff concluded that the proposed activities would require the investment adviser to register as a broker or dealer, or as an associated person of a registered broker or dealer.

Even a person who is not paid any commissions or other transaction-related fees may be required to register as a broker if the person proposes to locate issuers, solicit new clients and act as a customers' agent in structuring or negotiating transactions. In one SEC no-action letter,[16] an investment adviser requested relief from registering as a broker where it proposed to locate prospective real estate investment trust (REIT) issuers and negotiate the terms of private placements by the REITs. The investment adviser would then attempt to interest its clients in purchasing those REIT securities. No registered broker or dealer would be involved in effecting these transactions. Even though the investment adviser was to be compensated by an annual fee based on the percentage of its assets under management, rather than on a transaction-specific basis, the SEC staff declined to provide no-action relief.

In another no-action letter,[17] an investment adviser proposed to engage in 3 activities: (a) advising both U.S. and non-U.S. clients as to the value of U.S. securities, U.S. mutual funds and American Depositary Receipts; (b) publishing a newsletter, available for a flat subscription fee, containing business and economic information on India, including closing stock prices for Indian stocks and buy/sell/hold recommendations for Indian stocks; and (c) acting as a purchaser's representative by buying and selling securities on behalf of clients. The SEC warned the investment adviser that it might be required to register as a broker or dealer under the Exchange Act.

In a 2013 enforcement action, the SEC filed and settled charges against a hedge fund manager, one of its senior executives and an external marketing consultant.[18] The SEC alleged that the consultant had acted as an unregistered broker in violation of Exchange Act section 15(a)[19] when he marketed and received placement fees for the sale of interests in two real estate funds managed by the hedge fund manager. Unlike most earlier cases brought for failure to register as a broker or dealer, this case did not allege fraud. In addition to charging the consultant for failing to register as a broker, the SEC charged the hedge fund manager for causing the consultant's violations and charged the hedge fund manager's senior executive with aiding and abetting the violation.

---

15. Boston Advisory Group, SEC No-Action Letter (Oct. 21, 1980).
16. PRA Securities, L.P., SEC No-Action Letter (Mar. 3, 1993).
17. InTouch Global, SEC No-Action Letter (Nov. 14, 1995).
18. In the Matter of Ranieri Partners LLC and Donald W. Phillips, Exchange Act Release No. 69091 (Mar. 3, 2013).
19. 15 U.S.C. § 78o(a).

Remarks by David Blass, the Chief Counsel of the SEC's Division of Trading and Markets, further illustrate the SEC's increased attention in this area.[20] Mr. Blass suggested that private fund managers think through how they go about obtaining new investors. Although transaction-based compensation has long been viewed as a hallmark of being a broker, Mr. Blass noted that a dedicated sales force of employees working within a marketing department may strongly indicate that they are in the business of effecting transactions in the private fund, regardless of how the personnel are compensated. Also relevant would be whether these employees have other responsibilities or if their primary functions consist of soliciting investors, and how the personnel who solicit investors are compensated (for example, with bonus or other compensation linked to successful investments).

Mr. Blass further considered the argument that a general partner of a hedge fund (not its investment adviser) that receives what may be considered a transaction-based fee is not a broker because it is not acting for the account of others (because the general partner and the fund are effectively one and the same). Mr. Blass rejected this argument, saying that the fund and the general partner are distinct entities with distinct interests.

Individuals and firms in the business of marketing hedge funds sometimes take the position that they are not required to register as brokers because they are "finders" who merely introduce prospective investors to hedge funds, rather than participating in selling them interests in those hedge funds. The SEC staff generally views with suspicion an arrangement under which a person claims to be soliciting investors as no more than a finder. In rare cases,[21] however, the SEC staff has not objected to a finder's participation in private offerings, if the putative finder does no more than introduce investors to the issuers or their promoters, even if the finder is paid a commission on the amount of securities sold to introduced investors. The SEC staff would not agree that a solicitor is a finder, rather than a broker, if the solicitor assists in any other way in selling securities or negotiating or documenting the securities transaction.

Except for the Rule 3a4-1 safe harbor for associated persons and the limited exception for finders, a person or firm that assists in offering interests in a hedge fund must be registered with the SEC as a broker. The general partner should enter into a written agreement with any finder or broker it engages to assist it in the offering. The agreement should reflect the applicable requirements of the private offering exemption, the Exchange Act, the Advisers Act and state law.

---

20. David W. Blass, Chief Counsel, SEC Division of Trading and Markets, "A Few Observations in the Private Fund Space" (Apr. 5, 2013).

21. *See, e.g.*, Paul Anka, SEC No-Action Letter (July 24, 1991) (Paul Anka will provide names of potential investors but will not contact them, solicit them, make any recommendations to them, participate in any negotiations with them or contact them concerning the issuer); John W. Loofbourrow Associates, Inc, SEC No-Action Letter (June 29, 2006) (Eagle One Mortgage Solutions, Inc. not required to register as a broker or dealer, notwithstanding commission-like arrangement tied to amount of securities offered, where role is limited to introducing parties).

The hedge fund's offering circular should disclose the nature and terms of any such relationship or arrangement.[22]

3. Solicitors

The Advisers Act generally prohibits an investment adviser required to be registered under the Advisers Act from paying cash fees directly or indirectly with respect to solicitation of clients, except under arrangements that comply with Advisers Act Rule 206(4)-3 (the "solicitors rule").[23] Historically, the SEC took the position that the solicitors rule applied to the solicitation of investors for hedge funds.[24] More recently, however, the SEC staff stated explicitly in a no-action letter that the solicitors rule does not apply to cash payments by a registered investment adviser to a person solely as compensation for soliciting investors for an investment pool managed by the investment adviser.[25] Nevertheless, the general anti-fraud provisions of the Advisers Act apply to all of an investment adviser's marketing and solicitation activities, and complying with the solicitors rule may promote adequate disclosure.

To comply with the solicitors rule, an investment adviser must have a written agreement with the solicitor. The agreement must require the solicitor to give each prospective client written disclosure about the solicitor's relationship with the investment adviser, including the compensation arrangement. The client must acknowledge in writing having received the written disclosure, and the investment adviser must retain copies of this disclosure and acknowledgement.[26] The investment adviser must make a bona fide effort to ascertain whether the solicitor has complied with the agreement and have a reasonable basis for believing that the solicitor has complied.

No such disclosure, however, is required if the solicitor solicits only prospective clients for impersonal advisory services, such as an advisory newsletter.[27] Although partners, officers, directors and employees of an investment adviser are subject to the solicitors rule and must be compensated pursuant to written agreements and disclose their affiliation with the investment adviser, they need not disclose their compensation for solicitation activities or obtain acknowledgments from prospective clients that they solicit.[28]

The written disclosure document provided to each prospective client must include the names of the solicitor and the investment adviser, the nature of the relationship (including any affiliation) between the solicitor and the investment adviser, and a statement that the investment adviser will compensate the solicitor for his or her services. The solicitor's compensation must also be described. If the client will be charged any extra amount over the advisory fee because of the solicitor's involvement, that must be disclosed, as well as any difference in

22. *See* §§ 6.2.1.ii and 6.2.1.iii, *supra*.
23. 17 C.F.R. § 275.206(4)-3.
24. Dana Point Investment Advisors, Inc. SEC No-Action Letter (Oct. 12, 1994).
25. Mayer Brown LLP, SEC No-Action Letter (July 28, 2008).
26. Advisers Act Rule 206(4)-3(b), 17 C.F.R. § 275.206(4)-3(b). *See also* § 8.8, *supra*.
27. Advisers Act Rule 206(4)-3(a)(2)(i), 17 C.F.R. § 275.206(4)-3(a)(2)(i).
28. Advisers Act Rule 206(4)-3(a)(2)(ii), 17 C.F.R. § 275.206(4)-3(a)(2)(ii).

the fees the investment adviser charges different clients that are attributable to the investment adviser's arrangement with the solicitor.

The solicitors rule prohibits an SEC-registered investment adviser from paying fees to a solicitor (whether or not an employee and whether or not the solicitation is for impersonal advisory services) who has been convicted within the past 10 years of certain felonies or misdemeanors, has violated the federal securities laws, is subject to an SEC order or decree, or is permanently or temporarily enjoined by order, judgment or decree of any court of competent jurisdiction from acting as, or as an affiliated person or employee of, an investment adviser, underwriter, broker, dealer, transfer agent or certain other occupations relating to the purchase or sale of securities.[29] This part of the solicitors rule effectively prevents an SEC-registered investment adviser from engaging as a solicitor a person whom the investment adviser would not be permitted to hire as an employee because of other provisions in the Advisers Act, and thus it prevents the investment adviser from doing indirectly what it cannot do directly.[30]

The solicitors rule is primarily a disclosure rule that reflects the SEC's concern about the potential for prospective clients to be misled or unduly influenced by a solicitor whose arrangement with the investment adviser is not fully disclosed. It is not a safe harbor from any broker registration requirements. Thus, a solicitor who helps an investment adviser market interests in a hedge fund in full compliance with the solicitors rule is nevertheless likely required to register as a broker.

The SEC has stated that investment advisers not registered with the SEC may not rely on the solicitors rule.[31] In addition, the solicitors rule authorizes the payment of only cash referral fees to solicitors. Although no formal SEC statement prohibits the payment of noncash referral fees to solicitors, the solicitors rule is not relevant to such arrangements, and the SEC might question the propriety of such payments, particularly absent full disclosure about the arrangement.[32] Any investment adviser, whether or not registered with the SEC, should make at least the disclosures required by the solicitors rule to any potential client that a paid solicitor solicits. The SEC has instituted several enforcement actions alleging violations of the solicitors rule and the broker registration requirements by investment advisers and solicitors.[33]

4. Dealer Registration

Because a hedge fund buys and sells securities for its own account, it arguably might be deemed a "dealer." The SEC staff has, however, recognized a

29. Advisers Act Rule 206(4)-3(a)(1)(ii), 17 C.F.R. § 275.206(4)-3(a)(1)(ii).

30. Advisers Act Release No. 688 (July 12, 1979), 44 F.R. 42,126 (July 18, 1979).

31. *Id.*

32. *See* § 14.2, *infra.*

33. *See, e.g.*, Advisers Act Release No. 1409 (Apr. 6, 1994); Advisers Act Release No. 1500 (June 16, 1995); Advisers Act Release No. 2514 (May 9, 2006).

distinction between "dealers" and "traders."[34] Even if a person buys securities for its own account, it may not be a dealer if it is not engaged in the business of buying and selling securities for its own account as part of a regular business. The SEC staff has said:

> As developed over the years, the dealer/trader distinction recognizes that dealers normally have a regular clientele, hold themselves out as buying or selling securities at a regular place of business, have a regular turnover of business (or participate in the distribution of new issues), and generally transact a substantial portion of their business with investors (or, in the case of dealers who are market makers, principally trade with other professionals) . . . . In contrast, traders have a less regular volume, do not handle others' money or securities, do not make a market, and do not furnish dealer-type services such as rendering investment advice, extending or arranging for credit, or lending securities.
>
> A person generally may satisfy the definition, and therefore, be acting as a dealer in the securities markets by conducting various activities: (1) underwriting; (2) acting as a market maker or specialist on an organized exchange or trading system; (3) acting as a de facto market maker whereby market professionals or the public look to the firm for liquidity; or (4) buying and selling directly to securities customers together with conducting any of an assortment of professional market activities such as providing investment advice, extending credit and lending securities in connection with transactions in securities, and carrying a securities account.[35]

On other occasions, in assessing whether a person is a dealer, the SEC has also considered whether the person runs a book of repurchase and reverse repurchase agreements, uses an interdealer broker for securities transactions, issues or originates any securities, or guarantees contract performance or indemnifies

---

34. Exchange Act Release No. 46745 (Oct. 30, 2002), 67 F.R. 67,496 (Nov. 5, 2002); Exchange Act Release No. 47369 (Feb. 13, 2003), 68 F.R. 8,686 (Feb. 24, 2003); Guide to Broker-Dealer Registration (SEC, Apr. 2008), *available at* www.sec.gov/divisions/marketreg/bdguide.htm. (Last visited May 11, 2013.)

35. Davenport Mgmt., Inc., SEC No-Action Letter (Apr. 13, 1993). The SEC staff also provided relief from broker registration for the investment partnership's general partner, based on the requester's assertion that all investments and other decisions of the partnership were controlled by the general partner and the general partner's activities making decisions on behalf of the partnership to buy or sell securities were not the activities of a broker, but rather activities necessary to carry out the business of the partnership. *See also* Int'l Investment Group, Inc., SEC No-Action Letter (July 23, 1987); Acqua Wellington North American Equities Fund, Ltd., SEC No-Action Letter (Oct. 11, 2001).

the parties for any loss or liability from the failure of the transaction to be successfully consummated.[36]

Apart from issuing or originating securities (the interests in the hedge fund), the typical hedge fund does not engage in any of the above activities. It does not even render investment advice, because the investment adviser, rather than the hedge fund itself, provides investment advice to the hedge fund. As a result, a hedge fund should be considered a trader and not a dealer.

No authority provides guidance on whether the general partner of a hedge fund should be considered a dealer. The lack of reported judicial opinions and SEC staff no-action letters, in the face of such a common structure, suggests that the general partner should not be regarded as a dealer. That may be because the general partner engages in securities transactions for the account of the hedge fund, rather than for its own account (disregarding that it may have itself invested in the hedge fund), or because the general partner does not provide investment advice about investing in the hedge fund or engage in any of the other activities described above that characterize dealers.[37]

§ 10.2 Avoiding State Registration

1. Generally

Definitions of "broker" and "dealer" in many state laws are similar to those in the Exchange Act, and many state laws provide similar exemptions from those definitions.[38] A general partner that offers and sells hedge fund interests in a particular state and does not qualify for an exemption from broker or dealer registration under that state's laws would be required either to register as a broker or dealer, or to rely on the position that it is not in the business of selling securities, notwithstanding its activities in offering and selling hedge fund interests. As noted above, although managers of private investment funds frequently maintain this position, it is subject to challenge by securities regulatory authorities or a private plaintiff. For example, California law defines "broker-dealer" as any person engaged in the business of effecting transactions in

---

36. Acqua Wellington North American Equities Fund, Ltd., SEC No-Action Letter (Oct. 11, 2001).

37. Notwithstanding the foregoing, the SEC is rumored to be developing rules that would require hedge fund firms to register as dealers. "SEC May Tag Some Funds as Broker-Dealers," *Hedge Fund Alert* (Nov. 9, 2011). The registration requirement would apparently apply to high-frequency-trading firms and other fund operators that effectively function as market makers, even if that is not their intention. The SEC staff raised the question in a concept release, Advisers Act Release No. 34-61358, 75 F.R. 3594 (Jan. 21, 2010). In addressing a range of market issues, including risks posed by high-frequency traders, the SEC staff asked, "Should, for example, all proprietary firms be required to register as broker-dealers and become members of FINRA to help assure that their operations are subject to full regulatory oversight?" At this writing, however, the SEC has not issued any such rule proposal.

38. *See, e.g.*, Cal. Corp. Code § 25004. *See* Chapter 7, *supra*.

securities for the accounts of others or his own account[39] and explicitly excludes an issuer and its agents from the registration requirements. Nevertheless, the California Commissioner of Corporations has indicated that an investment adviser and the hedge fund that it manages, if located in California, might be required to register as broker-dealers because they may be deemed to be in the business of effecting transactions in securities.[40]

2. Employees as Agents

Employees of a hedge fund's general partner may be required to register as agents or salespersons under state law. Many states, however, exclude from their definitions of agent any individual who represents the issuer in selling federally covered securities if no remuneration is paid specifically for selling the securities.[41]

3. New York

Unlike most states' laws, New York law does not exclude issuers from the definition of broker or dealer. Accordingly, before offering or selling interests in a hedge fund in New York, the general partner may be required (at least in the view of the New York State Attorney General) to file, among other things, a "broker-dealer statement."[42] This statement generally requires information regarding business history for the last 5 years, criminal record and educational background of the general partner and its partners, officers, directors or other principals. The broker-dealer statement is effective for 4 years from the date of filing. A general partner that fails to file the broker-dealer statement before offering hedge fund interests in New York could be subject to penalties and other disciplinary action assessed or prosecuted by the New York Attorney General.

---

39. *Id.*
40. Cal. Blue Sky Letter (Sep. 21, 1998).
41. *See, e.g.*, Cal. Corp. Code §§ 25003(c) and 25003(d); Utah Uniform Securities Act § 61-1-13(b)(ii). *See* Chapter 7, *supra.*
42. N.Y. GBL § 359-e. *See* § 7.2.2.ii, *supra.*

CHAPTER **11**

ERISA Considerations

§ 11.1 Introduction

If an employee benefit plan or individual retirement account ("IRA") invests in a hedge fund, the hedge fund makes collective investments of assets that include funds of the employee benefit plan or IRA. Domestic employee benefit plans established by private-sector employers for their employees or by unions for their members (including, for example, pension plans and health plans, disability and life insurance plans, and severance pay plans) are generally subject to Title I of the Employee Retirement Income Security Act of 1974, as amended ("ERISA"), to some parallel requirements in the Tax Code, and to oversight by the U.S. Department of Labor ("DOL") and the Internal Revenue Service ("IRS"). Plans that cover only the owners of the businesses that sponsor them ("owner-only" or "Keogh" plans) and IRAs generally are not subject to ERISA or DOL oversight, but they are subject to many of the Tax Code provisions that apply to ERISA plans, as well as to IRS oversight.[1]

At any time that ERISA plans, IRAs, owner-only plans (collectively, "Plan Investors") and other benefit plan investors (as defined in section 11.2.2 below) own at least 25 percent in value of any class of a hedge fund's equity interests (excluding interests held by the general partner, paid investment advisers and affiliates of either) of a hedge fund, the general partner, the investment adviser and the hedge fund generally will be subject to ERISA's requirements and prohibitions. These include fiduciary conduct standards, prohibitions against engaging in certain transactions, bonding requirements, and special requirements as to investment in foreign securities, indemnification and reporting. The penalties for noncompliance can be severe. Many hedge funds adopt policies to prevent the 25-percent level from being reached.

Depending on how their hedge funds are structured and the investments are made, however, some hedge fund managers find the advantages of being able to admit more investors outweigh the burdens and risks of being subject to ERISA and the Tax Code, and of DOL and IRS oversight. Moreover, employee benefit plans and IRAs have shown more interest in adding nontraditional investments, such as hedge funds, to their portfolios.

1. Some defined benefit pension plans are also subject to oversight by the Pension Benefit Guaranty Corporation (PBGC) under Title IV of ERISA. Owner-only defined benefit plans and IRAs are exempt from Title IV and PBGC oversight.

§ 11.2 Plan Asset Regulations—Look-Through Rule

ERISA and the DOL's final regulation relating to the definition of plan assets (the "Plan Asset Regulations")[2] generally provide that when a Plan Investor holds an equity interest in a fund, such as a hedge fund, that is neither a publicly offered security nor a security issued by an investment company registered under the Company Act, the Plan Investor's assets include both the equity interest and an undivided interest in each of the fund's underlying assets, unless (a) equity participation in the hedge fund by benefit plan investors is not significant, (b) the hedge fund is an operating company, or (c) the hedge fund satisfies the special "grandfather" rule.[3] If the Plan Investor is deemed to have an interest in the underlying assets of a hedge fund, the hedge fund's assets will then be treated as "plan assets" for purposes of ERISA and the prohibited transaction provisions of the Tax Code. In that event, the hedge fund's general partner and investment adviser will be treated as managing the Plan Investor's assets and be subject to the requirements and prohibitions imposed by ERISA and the Tax Code that apply to management of those assets. In addition, assets of an ERISA plan generally must be held in trust;[4] the trust requirement is satisfied with respect to the hedge fund if the indicia of ownership of the plan's interest in the hedge fund are held in trust.[5]

1. Definition of "Equity Interest"

The Plan Asset Regulations define an "equity interest" as "any interest in any entity other than an instrument that is treated as indebtedness under applicable local law and which has no substantial equity feature." Under the Plan Asset Regulations, a "profit interest in a partnership, an undivided interest in property, and a beneficial interest in a trust" are all equity interests.[6] Thus, an investor's interest in a hedge fund is an equity interest.

2. 25-Percent Test

Participation in a hedge fund by benefit plan investors is "significant" at times that such investors hold, in the aggregate, 25 percent or more of the value of any class of the hedge fund's equity interests. A "benefit plan investor" is any Plan Investor or any entity, such as a fund of funds, whose underlying assets are plan assets of their Plan Investors by virtue of the 25-percent look-through

2. ERISA § 3(42), 29 U.S.C. § 1002(42); DOL Reg. § 2510.3-101, 29 C.F.R. § 2510.3-101.
3. DOL Reg. § 2510.3-101(k), 29 C.F.R. § 2510.3-101(k).
4. ERISA § 403(a), 29 U.S.C. § 1103(a).
5. DOL Reg. § 2550.403a-1(b)(3), 29 C.F.R. § 2550.403a-1(b)(3).
6. DOL Reg. § 2510.3-101(b)(1), 29 C.F.R. § 2510.3-101(b)(1).

rule.[7] Classes of hedge fund interests should be treated as distinct classes for this purpose if they have different substantive rights. For purposes of determining the percentage, the equity interests held by certain parties related to the hedge fund, such as the general partner, investment adviser and their affiliates, are disregarded (although their plan and IRA investments are taken into account). The 25-percent test is applied each time an investor acquires (or redeems) any equity interest in the hedge fund.[8] Accordingly, determining the percentage of a hedge fund's equity interests held by benefit plan investors under the Plan Asset Regulations requires continuous monitoring, and careful attention to hedge fund contributions and withdrawals.

3. Operating Company Exception

A Plan Investor generally will not be deemed to have an interest in the underlying assets of a fund if the fund is an operating company. The Plan Asset Regulations define "operating company" as (1) an "entity that is primarily engaged, directly or through a majority-owned subsidiary or subsidiaries, in the production or sale of a product or service other than the investment of capital," (2) a venture capital operating company or (3) a real estate operating company.[9] Hedge funds generally do not satisfy the conditions of the operating company exception.

4. Grandfather Rule

Generally, a hedge fund qualifies for the grandfather exception from the Plan Asset Regulations if it existed on March 13, 1987, and no plan has acquired any equity interests in the hedge fund since that date.[10]

---

7. ERISA § 3(42), 29 U.S.C. § 1002(42). For purposes of the 25-percent calculation, the entity will be deemed to hold plan assets in the hedge fund only to the extent of the percentage of the entity owned by its benefit plan investors. Thus, for example, if a fund of funds holds a $15,000,000 interest in a hedge fund, and benefit plan investors own 30 percent of the fund of funds, $4,500,000 of the $15,000,000 investment is deemed owned by benefit plan investors for purposes of the hedge fund's 25-percent calculation. DOL Reg. § 2510.3-101, 29 C.F.R. § 2510.3-101.

8. DOL Reg. § 2510.3-101(f)(1), 29 C.F.R. § 2510.3-10(f)(1). DOL Advisory Opinion 89-05A (Apr. 5, 1989) indicated that a redemption of an equity interest in the hedge fund should also be treated as an acquisition for this purpose, because such redemption results in an increase in the interests of the remaining partners.

9. DOL Reg. § 2510.3-101(c), 29 C.F.R. § 2510.3-101(c). A "venture capital operating company" is an entity that, within specified time periods, has at least 50 percent of its long-term investments in "venture capital investments" or "derivative investments" and, in the ordinary course of business, exercises "management rights" with respect to one or more of its portfolio companies. DOL Reg. § 2510.3-101(d), 29 C.F.R. § 2510.3-101(d). A "real estate operating company" is an entity that, within specified time periods, has at least 50 percent of its long-term investments in real estate that is managed or developed and with respect to which it has the right to substantially participate directly in the management or development activities, and that, in the ordinary course of business, engages directly in such activities. DOL Reg. § 2510.3-101(e), 29 C.F.R. § 2510.3-101(e).

10. DOL Reg. § 2510.3-101(k), 29 C.F.R. § 2510.3-101(k).

§ 11.3 ERISA Fiduciary Duties

At times that the assets of a hedge fund are plan assets of an investor that is an ERISA plan, the fund's general partner and investment adviser are ERISA fiduciaries of such plan with respect to all of such plan's assets invested in the fund. As fiduciaries, they must comply with the fiduciary responsibility provisions of ERISA.[11] Under ERISA, fiduciary status is determined with reference to a person's activities with respect to a plan; it does not depend on any formal undertaking or agreement.[12] A "fiduciary" is any person who (a) exercises discretionary authority or discretionary control in the management of a plan, or authority or control in the management or disposition of its assets, (b) provides investment advice to a plan for a fee or other compensation, directly or indirectly, with respect to any moneys or other property of such plan, or (c) has discretionary authority or discretionary responsibility in the administration of such plan.[13]

In general, the trustee of an ERISA plan has exclusive authority and discretion to manage and control the assets of the plan. Under ERISA section 402(c)(3),[14] however, a named fiduciary of a plan may appoint an investment manager to manage, acquire or dispose of assets of the plan, if the plan so provides. When an ERISA plan invests in a hedge fund whose assets are plan assets, a fiduciary of such plan usually appoints the hedge fund's investment adviser as an investment manager for the plan. ERISA provides that if the plan fiduciary chooses and retains the investment manager prudently, the investment manager is registered under the Advisers Act or under a state securities law,[15] and the investment manager acknowledges in writing that it is acting as a fiduciary,[16] neither the plan trustee nor the appointing plan fiduciary will be liable for the acts or omissions of the investment manager. The plan fiduciary remains responsible, however, for monitoring the investment manager's performance.[17]

1. Exclusive Purpose; Plan Documents

An ERISA fiduciary must act for the exclusive purpose of providing benefits to plan participants and their beneficiaries and defraying the reasonable expenses of administering the plan.[18] The fiduciary must also act in accordance with the documents and instruments governing the plan, insofar as those documents and

11. *See* ERISA§§ 3(21) and 401 *et seq.*, 29 U.S.C. §§ 1002(21) and 1101 *et seq.*
12. *See* H.R. Rep. No. 1280, 93d Cong., 2d Sess., 323 (1974).
13. ERISA § 3(21)(A), 29 U.S.C. § 1002(21)(A).
14. 29 U.S.C. § 1102(c)(3).
15. *See* §§ 2.2 and 2.3, *supra.*
16. ERISA §§ 3(38) and 405(d), 29 U.S.C. §§ 1002(38) and 1105(d). DOL Reg. 2510.3-38, 29 C.F.R. § 2510.3-38 also requires state-registered investment advisers seeking this investment manager-adviser status to register electronically through the Investment Advisers Registration Depository ("IARD"). *See* § 2.4, *supra.*
17. ERISA §§ 405(c)(2) and 405(d)(1), 29 U.S.C. §§ 1105(c)(2) and (d)(1); DOL Reg. § 2509.75-8, Q&A FR-17, 29 C.F.R. § 2509.75-8, Q&A FR-17.
18. ERISA § 404(a)(1)(A), 29 U.S.C. § 1104(a)(1)(A).

instruments are consistent with ERISA.[19] A fiduciary of an investing ERISA plan should review the plan's governing documents to make sure that investments in or by a particular hedge fund are not prohibited by the plan and should satisfy itself that the plan provisions comply with ERISA.

An investment adviser that is an ERISA fiduciary must not favor any other accounts over a plan assets fund when it allocates trades among that plan assets fund and other accounts that it manages. An investment adviser that serves multiple clients should maintain a policy for allocating investment opportunities fairly among them.

2. Standard of Prudence

An ERISA fiduciary must act with the care, skill, prudence and diligence that a prudent person acting in a like capacity and familiar with such matters would use under the circumstances in the conduct of an enterprise of a like character with like aims.[20] The prudence standard also applies to a fiduciary's appointment of another fiduciary with investment discretion. Under the prudence standard, fiduciaries must take into account the "special nature and purpose" of employee benefit plans.[21] The prudence rule applies to the total performance of a plan's entire portfolio, rather than the actual performance of any particular investment. Accordingly, in determining whether any investment is imprudent, the investment must be analyzed in the context of the overall portfolio. Evidence of due diligence and analysis performed by the fiduciary is useful to show that the fiduciary has met this standard of care.[22]

A plan's trustee or other fiduciary responsible for the plan's investment decisions should determine whether an investment in a particular hedge fund is appropriate and prudent by comparing the plan's risk tolerance and objectives to the hedge fund's investment strategy. A hedge fund's investment adviser generally manages plan assets that are invested in the hedge fund on an aggregate basis with other invested funds and thus does not examine each investing plan's objectives, risk tolerance, diversification strategies or other individualized needs. Accordingly, subscription documents for a hedge fund that accepts ERISA plans as investors should expressly allocate responsibility for diversification, market-risk testing, liquidity, consistency with the plan documents and with ERISA, and other considerations relating to the plan's overall portfolio to the plan trustee or other plan fiduciary that has chosen to invest in the hedge fund, rather than to the hedge fund's general partner or investment adviser.

3. Diversification

A plan fiduciary must diversify the investments of the ERISA plan to minimize the risk of large losses, unless under the circumstances it is clearly prudent not

19. ERISA § 404(a)(1)(D), 29 U.S.C. § 1104(a)(1)(D).
20. ERISA § 404(a)(1)(B), 29 U.S.C. § 1104(a)(1)(B).
21. H.R. Rep. No. 93-1280, at 302 (1974)(Conf. Rep.).
22. *See, e.g.*, *In re* Unisys Sav. Plan Litigation, 74 F.3d 420 (3rd Cir. 1996); Glennie v. Abitibi-Price Corp., 912 F. Supp. 993 (W.D. Mich. 1996).

to do so.[23] Diversification analysis may entail examining and monitoring the plan's entire portfolio. The DOL has concluded that derivatives sometimes used by hedge funds (such as futures, options, options on futures, forward contracts, swaps, structured notes and collateralized mortgage obligations) may be useful tools for managing risk and for broadening a plan's portfolio investments. The DOL has also taken the position, however, that investments in certain derivatives characterized by high price volatility or leverage or illiquidity (such as structured notes and collateralized mortgage obligations) may require the hedge fund's investment adviser to have a higher degree of sophistication and understanding than for other investments.[24]

4. Proxy Voting

The fiduciary act of managing plan assets that are shares of corporate stock includes the voting of proxies appurtenant to the stock. The responsibility for voting proxies lies exclusively with an ERISA plan's trustee except to the extent that either (a) the trustee is subject to the directions of a named fiduciary pursuant to ERISA section 403(a)(1),[25] or (b) pursuant to ERISA section 403(a)(2),[26] a named fiduciary has delegated the power to manage, acquire or dispose of the relevant assets to one or more investment managers pursuant to ERISA section 402(c)(3)[27] as discussed above (for example, by investing in a "plan assets" hedge fund).

If the authority to manage plan assets has been delegated, no person other than the investment manager has authority to vote proxies appurtenant to such plan assets except to the extent that the named fiduciary has reserved to itself (or to another named fiduciary so authorized by the plan document) the right to direct a plan trustee regarding the voting of proxies. A named fiduciary, in delegating investment management authority to an investment manager, could reserve to itself the right to direct a trustee with respect to the voting of all proxies or reserve to itself the right to direct a trustee in the voting of only those proxies relating to specified assets or issues. If the plan document or investment management agreement provides that the investment manager is not required to vote proxies but does not expressly preclude the investment manager from doing so, the investment manager is deemed to have exclusive responsibility for voting proxies.[28]

If a hedge fund's investment adviser has responsibility for voting proxies, it must act prudently and solely in the ERISA plan participants' and beneficiaries' interest in the economic value of the hedge fund's assets.[29] Such an investment adviser is not relieved of its fiduciary responsibility in proxy voting by following

23. ERISA § 404(a)(1)(C), 29 U.S.C. § 1104(a)(1)(C).

24. Letter from Olena Berg, Assistant Secretary, Pension and Welfare Benefits Administration, DOL, to Eugene A. Ludwig, Comptroller of the Currency (Mar. 21, 1996).

25. 29 U.S.C. § 1103(a)(1).

26. 29 U.S.C. § 1103(a)(2).

27. 29 U.S.C. § 1102(c)(3).

28. DOL Reg. § 2509.08-2, 29 C.F.R. § 2509.08-2.

29. *Id.*

the directions of some other person or by delegating its proxy voting duty to another person.[30] A hedge fund's investment adviser that has the authority to vote proxies has an obligation under ERISA to take reasonable steps under the particular circumstances to ensure that the proxies for which it is responsible are received and to keep accurate records of its voting of proxies. According to the DOL, ERISA plan fiduciaries must treat proxy voting rights essentially as ERISA plan assets.

If a hedge fund in which multiple ERISA plans invest is subject to those plans' conflicting proxy voting policies, an investment adviser that has responsibility for voting proxies may either (1) not comply with any such policies if doing so would be imprudent or not solely in the economic interest of plan participants or would otherwise violate ERISA, (2) vote the proxies in proportion to each plan's interest in the hedge fund, if each policy is consistent with ERISA, or (3) require each plan, as a condition of investing in the hedge fund, to accept the investment adviser's own proxy voting policy. The investment adviser must take into account costs, such as those of developing proxy resolutions, proxy voting services, and analysis of the likely net effect of a particular issue on the economic value of the ERISA plan's investment, in deciding whether and how to exercise voting and other shareholder rights.

If the investment adviser reasonably determines that the cost of voting is likely to exceed its expected economic benefits to the plan, or that voting would result in the imposition of unwarranted trade or other restrictions, the investment adviser must refrain from voting. Prospectively, when deciding whether to invest in shares of a foreign corporation, the investment adviser should consider whether the additional difficulty and expense in voting those shares is reflected in its market price. The investment adviser must maintain records of proxy voting decisions, which must include, where appropriate, cost-benefit analyses.[31]

ERISA does not require a hedge fund's investment adviser that has responsibility for voting plan proxies automatically to tender shares to capture any premium over the market price in takeover situations. Rather, the investment adviser must weigh the terms of any offer against the underlying intrinsic value of the company and the likelihood that such value will be realized by current management or by another offer.[32]

5. Penalties and Co-Fiduciary Liability

ERISA provides that any fiduciary that breaches its responsibilities, obligations or duties is personally liable to the plan for any losses that result, as well as any profits that the fiduciary has obtained through use of the plan's assets. Courts may also fashion equitable relief, such as removal of the plan fiduciary.[33] The DOL has authority to impose a civil penalty for a breach of fiduciary

30. Avon Products, Inc., DOL Letter (Feb. 23, 1988).
31. DOL Reg. § 2509.08-2, 29 C.F.R. § 2509.08-2.
32. Joint Department of Labor/Department of Treasury Statement on Pension Investments (Jan. 31, 1989).
33. ERISA § 409, 29 U.S.C. § 1109.

responsibility. The penalty is generally 20 percent of the "applicable recovery amount" and is payable by the fiduciary or any other person who knowingly participates in the breach.[34]

A hedge fund's investment adviser may also be liable under ERISA for another fiduciary's breach by knowingly participating in or concealing such breach, if the investment adviser's failure to comply with fiduciary obligations enables the second fiduciary's breach, or if the investment adviser knows of the other fiduciary's breach and does not take reasonable actions to remedy it.[35]

§ 11.4 Prohibited Transactions

The fiduciary responsibility provisions of ERISA also include prohibited transaction rules that restrict an ERISA plan fiduciary's dealings with the assets of that plan.[36] In general, an ERISA fiduciary may not use the assets of a plan for which it acts as a fiduciary to engage in transactions with parties in interest to that plan or other plans for which the fiduciary is acting.[37] The Tax Code complements the prohibited transaction provisions of ERISA by imposing an excise tax on disqualified persons who engage in prohibited transactions.[38] The Tax Code excise tax provisions apply also to transactions involving owner-only plans and IRAs.

A "party in interest" of an employee benefit plan includes a fiduciary; a service provider; a contributing employer; an employee organization whose members are covered by the plan; an owner of 50 percent or more of such employer or employee organization; a spouse, ancestor, lineal descendant or spouse of a lineal descendent of any such person; a corporation, partnership, trust or estate 50 percent or more of which is owned directly or indirectly by such persons; an employee, officer, director or 10 percent or more shareholder of any such entity; and a 10 percent or more partner of any such entity.[39] "Disqualified person," as defined in the Tax Code, has essentially the same meaning as "party in interest" as defined in ERISA. For simplicity, we use the term "party in interest" to include a disqualified person in the remainder of this section 11.4.

1. Specific Transactions Prohibited

ERISA and the Tax Code specifically enumerate, as prohibited transactions, any direct or indirect:

- selling, exchanging or leasing of property, including securities or swap contracts, between the plan (including an IRA under the Tax Code provisions) and a party in interest;

34. ERISA § 502(l), 29 U.S.C. § 1132(l).
35. ERISA § 405(a), 29 U.S.C. § 1105(a).
36. *See* ERISA § 406, 29 U.S.C. § 1106.
37. DOL Reg. § 2510.3-101, 29 C.F.R. § 2510.3-101.
38. *See* Tax Code § 4975, 26 U.S.C. § 4975.
39. ERISA § 3(14), 29 U.S.C. § 1002(14); Tax Code § 4975(e)(2), 26 U.S.C. § 4975(e)(2).

- lending of money or other extension of credit between the plan and a party in interest;
- furnishing of goods, services or facilities (other than the specific services for which the party in interest is engaged) between the plan and a party in interest;
- transfer to, or use by or for the benefit of, a party in interest of any assets of the plan (other than reasonable compensation for the services rendered to the plan); or
- acquiring or holding by the plan of any employer security or employer real property, in violation of specified limits.[40]

2. Fiduciary Self-Dealing

In addition, a fiduciary is prohibited from:

- dealing with the assets of the plan in the fiduciary's own interest or for the fiduciary's own account; and
- receiving any consideration for the fiduciary's personal account from any party dealing with the plan, in connection with a transaction involving the plan.[41]

ERISA, but not the Tax Code, provides that a fiduciary's acting in any transaction involving the plan, on behalf of a party whose interests are adverse to the interests of the plan or its participants, is also a prohibited transaction.[42] The DOL has also taken the position[43] that a fiduciary's receipt of soft dollars, in a form other than brokerage and research services falling within the safe harbor of Exchange Act section 28(e),[44] is a prohibited transaction.

3. Prohibited Transaction Exemptions

ERISA and the Tax Code provide statutory exemptions for certain transactions deemed necessary for the operation of plans and authorize the DOL to grant individual or class exemptions.[45] Some prohibited transaction exemptions that may apply to hedge fund structures or transactions are discussed below.

i. Services

ERISA and the Tax Code allow a plan to make reasonable arrangements with a party in interest for office space or legal, accounting or other services necessary for establishing or operating the plan, if no more than reasonable compensation

---

40. ERISA §§ 406(a)(1)(A)-(E) and 406(a)(2), 29 U.S.C. §§ 1106(a)(1)(A)-(E) and 1106(a)(2); Tax Code § 4795(c)(1)(A)-(D), 26 U.S.C. § 4975(c)(1)(A)-(D).

41. ERISA § 406(b)(1) and (3), 29 U.S.C. § 1106(b)(1) and (3); Tax Code §§ 4975(c)(1)(E)-(F), 26 U.S.C. §§ 4975(c)(1)(E)-(F).

42. ERISA § 406(b)(2), 29 U.S.C. § 1106(b)(2).

43. ERISA Technical Release 86-1, Statement on Policies Concerning Soft Dollar and Directed Commission Arrangements (May 22, 1986). *See* § 14.2.5.ii, *infra*.

44. 15 U.S.C. § 78bb(e).

45. ERISA § 408, 29 U.S.C. § 1108.

is paid.[46] A fiduciary may receive reasonable compensation (such as reasonable investment management fees) for services rendered or for reimbursement of expenses incurred in the performance of the fiduciary's duties to the plan, unless the fiduciary is receiving full-time pay from an employer or employer association whose members are participants in the plan, in which case the fiduciary may only receive reimbursement for expenses.[47] As a condition for this exemption, the fiduciary must provide the plan with specified written disclosures regarding the services it will provide, its status as a fiduciary, whether it will be providing services directly to the plan as an adviser under the Advisers Act or state law, and all direct or indirect compensation it will receive for its services.[48]

The exemption for payment of fees for necessary services does not apply to a payment to the fiduciary that results from fiduciary conduct in violation of the fiduciary self-dealing prohibitions.[49]

ii. Transactions with Service Providers

Sales, purchases, loans, leases, transfers and similar transactions between a plan and a person who is a party in interest solely by virtue of providing services to the plan (or by virtue of a relationship to a service provider) are exempted from the prohibited transaction rules if:

- the party in interest is not the investment adviser or other fiduciary (or an affiliate) that has or exercises any discretionary authority or control over investment of the assets involved in the transaction; and
- the plan receives no less, and pays no more, than "adequate consideration," as defined in the exemption.[50]

iii. Securities Transactions

A DOL administrative exemption allows plans to engage, subject to certain conditions, in some commonplace securities transactions that would otherwise be prohibited transactions, including:

- principal transactions when the party in interest is a registered broker or reporting dealer in government securities that customarily trades for its own account;
- purchases of securities from a member of an underwriting syndicate of which the fiduciary is a member, if the purchase is not from the fiduciary;
- purchases or sales of securities from a fiduciary that is a market-maker for those securities; and

---

46. ERISA § 408(b)(2), 29 U.S.C. § 1108(b)(2); Tax Code § 4975(d)(2), 26 U.S.C. § 4975(d)(2).

47. ERISA § 408(c)(2), 29 U.S.C. § 1108(c)(2); Tax Code § 4975(d)(10), 26 U.S.C. § 4975(d)(10).

48. DOL Reg. § 2550.408b-2(c); 29 C.F.R. § 2550.408b-2(c).

49. DOL Reg. § 2550.408b-2, 29 C.F.R. § 2550.408b-2; Treas. Reg. § 54.4975-6(a)(5); 26 C.F.R. § 54.4975-6(a)(5).

50. ERISA § 408(b)(17), 29 U.S.C. § 1108(b)(17); Tax Code § 4975(d)(20), 26 U.S.C. § 4975(d)(20).

- extensions of credit to a plan by a broker in connection with settlements, short sales and option contracts, if no interest is received by a broker that is a fiduciary or an affiliate of a fiduciary.[51]

iv. Use of Affiliated Broker

An investment adviser that is an ERISA fiduciary would be engaging in a prohibited transaction if the investment adviser-fiduciary were to direct the hedge fund's brokerage business to an affiliated broker. Such transactions, however, are common. In recognition of this industry practice, the DOL issued Prohibited Transaction Class Exemption ("PTE") 86-128. This exemption permits a hedge fund's investment adviser to direct the hedge fund's brokerage transactions to an affiliated broker if, under the circumstances, the transactions are not excessive in amount or frequency, and the following additional conditions are met:

- the investment adviser must not be an administrator of the plan and must not employ any employees covered by the plan;
- if the investment adviser is a discretionary trustee of the plan, then either the plan must have at least $50,000,000 in net assets, or at least 50 percent of the hedge fund's beneficial interests must be owned by plans having total net assets of at least $50,000,000;
- the brokerage services must be provided under a written authorization executed in advance by a plan fiduciary (typically the plan's trustee) that is independent of the investment adviser and the broker;
- the independent fiduciary's authorization must be terminable at will by the plan on the investment adviser's receipt of written notice of termination, and the broker must annually provide this termination form to the independent fiduciary; and
- the investment adviser must furnish the independent fiduciary with various reports described in PTE 86-128 relating to the brokerage services rendered to the plan, such as the total of all transaction-related charges during the period, the amount of such charges retained by the fiduciary and paid to others and the portfolio turnover rate.[52]

These additional conditions do not need to be met for the exemption to apply to IRAs and owner-only plans.

v. Dual Fees

A hedge fund that includes plan assets may not impose a dual fee. A "dual fee" is an investment management fee payable to the hedge fund's investment adviser in addition to another such fee charged by the investment adviser, such as for managing a mutual fund or other fund in which the hedge fund invests.[53]

---

51. DOL Prohibited Transaction Exemption 75-1. 40 F.R. 50,845 (Oct. 31, 1975), amended by 71 F.R. 5,883 (Feb. 3, 2006).

52. DOL Prohibited Transaction Exemption 86-128, 51 F.R. 41,686 (Nov. 5, 1986), amended by 67 F.R. 64,137 (Oct. 17, 2002).

53. DOL Prohibited Transaction Exemption 77-4, 42 F.R. 18,732 (Mar. 31, 1977).

A plan adviser or fiduciary may, however, cause plan assets to be invested in a mutual fund it advises under the following conditions:

- the plan does not pay a mutual fund advisory fee (this condition would be satisfied if the plan pays an investment advisory fee based on total plan assets, from which a credit is subtracted representing the plan's pro rata share of the mutual fund advisory fee);
- the plan does not pay a sales commission when purchasing or selling mutual fund shares;
- the plan does not pay any redemption fee, unless (1) the fee is paid only to the mutual fund and (2) the fee is disclosed in the mutual fund's prospectus that is effective at the time of both the purchase and the redemption of the mutual fund shares;
- a second plan fiduciary that is independent of the investment adviser receives a current mutual fund prospectus and written disclosure of the fees to be paid by the plan, the reasons why the investment adviser may consider a purchase of mutual fund shares appropriate for the plan, and any restrictions on the investment adviser regarding which plan assets may be invested in mutual fund shares;
- the second fiduciary approves the mutual fund share purchases as consistent with the ERISA fiduciary obligations; and
- the second fiduciary approves in writing any change in the fees to be paid by the plan.[54]

The DOL has not extended PTE 77-4 to investments of plan assets in hedge funds. Thus, a plan assets fund of funds may not rely on PTE 77-4 with respect to fees charged by hedge funds in which it invests that are managed by the investment adviser of the fund of funds.[55]

vi. Cross Trades

Cross trades between a plan assets hedge fund and another fund or account served by the same investment adviser can raise prohibited transaction concerns because of the potential conflicts inherent in the investment adviser's acting for both seller and buyer. A statutory exemption permits cross trades to be made directly (that is, not through a public exchange) between a plan assets hedge fund and another fund or account served by the same investment adviser under the following conditions:

- the transaction is a purchase or sale for no consideration other than cash payment for prompt delivery of a security for which market quotations are readily available;
- the transaction is executed at the security's independent market price;
- no brokerage commission, fee or other remuneration (other than customary transfer fees, if disclosed) is paid in connection with the transaction;

---

54. *Id.*
55. *Id.*

- a fiduciary (other than the fund manager or investment adviser) for each plan participating in the transaction provides the investment adviser with advance authorization to engage in discretionary cross trades after the investment adviser has fully disclosed the conditions under which the investment adviser may effect cross trades, if the authorization and the disclosures are in written documents that are separate from any other written agreement or disclosure;
- each plan (or master trust for plans of employers within the same controlled group) participating in the transaction has assets of at least \$100,000,000;
- the investment adviser reports to the authorizing plan fiduciary all cross trades in which the plan participates during each quarter;
- the investment adviser's fees are not affected by the plan's consent to cross trading, and no other service (other than the investment opportunities or cost savings available through cross trades) is conditioned on the plan's consent to cross trading;
- cross trades are implemented according to written policies and procedures that are fair and equitable to all participating accounts; and
- compliance with those policies and procedures is periodically reviewed by an individual designated by the investment adviser, and the designated individual issues an annual compliance report, signed under penalty of perjury, to the authorizing plan fiduciary.[56]

A cross trade that does not meet the conditions for the statutory exemption may nevertheless be exempt under PTE 86-128. PTE 86-128 allows an authorized person to effect or execute certain agency cross transactions on behalf of a plan assets hedge fund as long as the plan fiduciary does not have discretion for or provide investment advice to both the buyer and the seller in the transaction.[57] PTE 86-128 requires that a person engaging in a covered transaction receive written authorization, executed in advance, from an independent fiduciary. Thereafter, the authorized person must notify the plan at least annually that the plan may terminate the authorization at will and without penalty. Such notice must include both a statement that failure to terminate the authorization will result in its continuation and a form on which to effect such a termination. The exemption applies only if the person engaging in the covered transaction is not a trustee or an administrator of the plan, or an employer whose employees are covered by the plan, and the following conditions are satisfied:[58]

---

56. ERISA § 408(b)(19), 29 U.S.C. § 1108(b)(19); Tax Code § 4975(d)(22), 26 U.S.C. § 4975(d)(22). DOL Reg. § 2550.408b-19, 29 C.F.R. § 2550.408b-19.

57. DOL Prohibited Transaction Exemption 86-128, 51 F.R. 41,686 (Nov. 18, 1986), amended by 67 F.R. 64,137 (Oct. 17, 2002). An agency cross transaction is a transaction in which securities are transferred by the seller to the buyer, both using the same broker. *See* §§ 13.9.3-13.9.5, *infra*.

58. *Id.*

- the investment adviser must disclose the potential for conflicts of interest in connection with agency cross transactions;
- the investment adviser must provide an annual summary that includes a statement identifying the total number of agency cross transactions and the total amount of all commissions or other remuneration received by the broker (or any of its affiliates) in connection with the transactions;
- each transaction must be a purchase or sale for no consideration other than a cash payment against prompt delivery of a security, and the security must be one for which market quotations are readily available; and
- each agency cross trade must be effected at a price that is at or between the independent bid price and independent asked price for the security prevailing at the time of the transaction.

vii. Qualified Professional Asset Manager

The DOL has granted a class exemption[59] for certain prohibited transactions if the decision to engage in them is made by a qualified professional asset manager ("QPAM") that is unrelated to the party in interest involved in the transaction. In general, the QPAM exemption permits a plan assets hedge fund to engage in a transaction with a party in interest, other than one that has the power to appoint or terminate the QPAM (or an affiliate of that party) with respect to the transaction. The QPAM exemption does not, however, generally permit principal transactions between the QPAM (or any of its related persons) and the plan assets hedge fund, and it does not exempt securities lending transactions, although the DOL permits some such transactions if specified requirements are satisfied.[60] The QPAM exemption also does not allow an investment adviser to engage in conflict-of-interest transactions.

A QPAM includes, among other institutions, an SEC-registered investment adviser that has total nonproprietary client assets under its management in excess of $85,000,000 and shareholders' or partners' equity in excess of $1,000,000. The equity requirement may be met by a guaranty of payment of all liabilities of the investment adviser by certain affiliates (such as a registered broker), shareholders or partners of the investment adviser, as long as such affiliates, shareholders or partners, together with the investment adviser, meet the $1,000,000 equity requirement. A QPAM must acknowledge in the advisory contract that it is a fiduciary with respect to the plan that retains it. An investment adviser cannot be a QPAM with respect to a plan if the assets of the plan managed by the investment adviser (together with the assets of other plans of the same plan sponsor managed by the investment adviser) are more than 20 percent of all the assets managed by the investment adviser or if the investment adviser or

59. DOL Prohibited Transaction Exemption 84-14, 49 F.R. 9,494 (Mar. 13, 1984), amended by 50 F.R. 41,430 (Oct. 10, 1985), 70 F.R. 49,305 (Aug. 23, 2005) and 75 F.R. 38,837 (July 6, 2010).

60. DOL Prohibited Transaction Exemption 81-6, 46 F.R. 7,527 (Jan. 23, 1981), amended by 52 F.R. 18,754 (May 19, 1987).

any owner of 5 percent or more of the investment adviser has been convicted of specified felonies within 10 years.[61]

viii. Block Trades

Sales of securities (or other property, as may be determined by the DOL) between plans and nonfiduciary parties in interest will be permitted if:

- the transaction involves a block trade, of at least 10,000 shares with a market value of at least $200,000 to be allocated among 2 or more unrelated client accounts;
- at the time of the transaction, the interests of the plan (together with the interests of other plans of the same plan sponsor) do not exceed 10 percent of the block trade;
- the price and other terms are at least as favorable to the plan as in an arm's length transaction; and
- the compensation associated with the transaction is no more than that in an arm's length transaction with an unrelated party.[62]

ix. Correction Period

Some inadvertent prohibited transactions will be exempted from adverse consequences if they are corrected within 14 days of the date they were or reasonably should have been discovered. The transaction must have been one in connection with the acquisition, holding or disposition of a security or commodity, other than one between a plan and its sponsor (or any affiliate) involving the acquisition or sale of an employer security, or the acquisition, sale or lease of employer real property. The exemption is not available if, at the time of the transaction, its prohibited nature was known or reasonably should have been known. A transaction is "corrected" if it is undone to the extent possible and the plan or affected account is reimbursed its losses or paid its profits from the prohibited use of its assets.[63]

x. Foreign Exchange Transactions

Foreign exchange transactions between a plan and a party in interest that is a bank or broker (or affiliate of either) are exempted, if:

- the transaction is in connection with the purchase, holding or sale of securities or other assets (other than a foreign exchange transaction unrelated to any other investment in securities or investment assets);
- at the time of the foreign exchange transaction, its terms are no less favorable to the plan than those under comparable arm's length transactions between or involving unrelated parties;

61. *Id.*

62. ERISA § 408(b)(15), 29 U.S.C. § 1108(b)(15); Tax Code § 4975(d)(18), 26 U.S.C. § 4975(d)(18).

63. ERISA § 408(b)(20), 29 U.S.C. § 1108(b)(20); Tax Code § 4975(d)(23), 26 U.S.C. § 4975(d)(23).

- the exchange rate used does not deviate by more than 3 percent from the interbank bid and ask rates for comparable transactions as displayed by an independent exchange rate reporting service; and
- the bank or broker (or affiliate) neither has investment discretion nor provides investment advice with respect to the transaction.[64]

Foreign exchange transactions between ERISA plans and parties in interest that do not satisfy these requirements may nevertheless be exempted if they satisfy the conditions in PTE 94-20[65] or PTE 98-54.[66] Under these PTEs, a principal foreign exchange transaction, including one pursuant to standing instructions, between a plan and a party in interest that is a bank or broker-dealer is exempt if directed by an independent fiduciary. These PTEs are not available to transactions involving assets of owner-only plans or IRAs.

xi. Electronic Communication Networks

Purchases and sales of securities (or other property, as may be determined by the DOL) between a plan and a party in interest that are executed through an electronic communication network, alternative trading system, or execution system or trading venue that is subject to regulation and oversight by an applicable federal or foreign entity, are exempt under the following conditions:

- either (1) the transaction is effected through rules designed to match purchases and sales at the best price available through the system in accordance with applicable rules of the SEC or other relevant government authority, or (2) neither the system nor the parties to the transaction take into account the identity of the parties;
- the price and compensation associated with the transaction are no more than in an arm's length transaction with an unrelated party;
- if the party in interest has an ownership interest in the system, the system has been authorized by the plan sponsor or other independent fiduciary; and
- a plan fiduciary is provided with at least 30 days' written or electronic notice of the first system transaction for the plan.[67]

4. Performance-Based Fees

A fee or a special profit allocation calculated on the basis of portfolio performance may constitute a prohibited transaction for an investment adviser that is an ERISA fiduciary if the investment adviser can manipulate the formula or mechanism for calculating it. The plan (or a participant) might assert that the investment adviser is using the assets for the investment adviser's benefit

---

64. ERISA § 408(b)(18), 29 U.S.C. § 1108(b)(18); Tax Code § 4975(d)(21), 26 U.S.C. § 4975(d)(21).

65. DOL Prohibited Transaction Exemption 94-20, 59 F.R. 8,022 (Feb. 17, 1994).

66. DOL Prohibited Transaction Exemption 98-54, 63 F.R. 63,503 (Nov. 13, 1998).

67. ERISA § 408(b)(16), 29 U.S.C. § 1108(b)(16); Tax Code § 4975(d)(19), 26 U.S.C. § 4975(d)(19).

or that the investment adviser (who is a fiduciary) is dealing with the assets of the plan in the investment adviser's own interest, either of which would be a prohibited transaction.

The DOL has issued limited guidance, in a few Advisory Opinions, permitting ERISA fiduciaries to receive performance fees in some circumstances. *BDN Investment Advisers, Inc.* involved a fee consisting of a base fee and an incentive fee based on a percentage of net capital appreciation in the plan's account.[68] *Batterymarch Financial Management* involved a fulcrum fee, under which the investment adviser's fee varied in accordance with the account's performance relative to a recognized index.[69] *Alliance Capital Management Corporation* involved 3 different fee structures, with each client plan selecting one of the fee structures: (1) a percentage of appreciation fee (similar to the fee structure in *BDN*); (2) a base-plus fee; and (3) a fulcrum fee (similar to the fee structure in *Batterymarch*).[70] *Mount Lucas Management Corporation* involved the investment of plan assets in commodity futures and forward contracts, and in options on commodities and commodity future contracts.[71] Under *Mount Lucas*, for certain plans, permitted fees included an annual performance fee equal to a specified percentage (established through arm's length negotiations) of the amount by which the cumulative profits of a plan client's account at the end of a performance period exceeded the highest level of cumulative profits for that account as of the end of any prior performance period, and in some cases exceeded a pre-established hurdle rate.[72]

Although the DOL did not articulate the specific factors on which it based its decisions allowing performance fees, the following features were common to all 4 arrangements:

- investments generally were limited to securities with readily available market quotations, and the small number of investments in securities without readily available market quotations were valued by third parties independent of the investment advisers;
- the compensation formula took into account both realized and unrealized gains and losses and income during pre-established valuation periods and the measurement period generally was at least 12 months;
- the investment advisers were registered under the Advisers Act;
- the arrangements complied with Advisers Act Rule 205-3 (the "performance fee rule");

68. DOL Advisory Opinion 86-20A, BDN Investment Advisers, Inc. (Aug. 29, 1986) (hereinafter "*BDN*").

69. DOL Advisory Opinion 86-21A, Batterymarch Financial Mgmt. (Aug. 29, 1986) (hereinafter "*Batterymarch*").

70. DOL Advisory Opinion 89-28A, Alliance Capital Mmgt. Corp. (Oct. 11, 1989) (hereinafter "*Alliance*").

71. DOL Advisory Opinion 99-16A, Mount Lucas Mgmt. Corp. (Dec. 9, 1999) (hereinafter "*Mount Lucas*").

72. *Id.*

- the plans were substantial in size (each had aggregate assets of at least $50,000,000); and
- not more than 10 percent of any plan's assets were managed by the investment adviser.

The DOL has indicated that performance-based compensation arrangements can nevertheless give rise to prohibited transactions, that performance fees should be structured to avoid conflicts of interest, and that each arrangement must be evaluated on its own facts and circumstances.[73] The $50,000,000 in assets standard probably suggests financial sophistication to the DOL and the 10-percent limit probably indicates diversification. The DOL has not indicated, however, whether or not these amounts are absolute thresholds or bright-line tests.

5. Directed Brokerage in Exchange for Referrals

As noted above, the DOL has opined that an ERISA fiduciary's receipt of soft dollars in the form of goods or services outside the safe harbor of Exchange Act section 28(e) is a prohibited transaction. The safe harbor of Exchange Act section 28(e) is not available for directed brokerage transactions.[74] Accordingly, a hedge fund investment adviser's decision to direct brokerage transactions with respect to plan assets must be made prudently and solely in the best interest of the plan participants and beneficiaries.[75] The investment adviser is not permitted to consider other factors, such as relationships with the broker or its employees outside of the plan context, in directing brokerage.[76] An investment adviser that refers a plan's brokerage business to a broker in exchange for the broker's referring advisory business to the investment adviser would be engaging in a prohibited transaction, because the investment adviser would be using the plan's assets for the investment adviser's own benefit and receiving consideration from a party dealing with the plan.

6. Participant-Controlled Accounts

ERISA provides that, if ERISA plan participants or beneficiaries exercise investment control over the assets in individual plan accounts, the participants or beneficiaries are not treated as fiduciaries, but others who are plan fiduciaries are not liable for any losses or any breaches resulting from the participants' or beneficiaries' exercise of investment control.[77] An investment adviser engaged by an individual participant or beneficiary to provide investment advice or manage the account may, however, be liable for losses resulting from the investment adviser's breaches.[78]

73. *See, e.g.*, *BDN* (*see* n. 68, *supra*), *Alliance* (*see* n. 70, *supra*) and *Mount Lucas* (*see* n. 71, *supra*).

74. DOL Information Letter, Capital Institutional Services, Inc. (Oct. 16, 1986).

75. *Id.* A failure to fulfill this requirement would violate the prudence requirements of ERISA § 404(a)(1)(B), 29 U.S.C. § 1104(a)(1)(B).

76. *Id.*

77. ERISA § 404(c), 29 U.S.C. § 1104(c); DOL Reg. § 2550.404c-1(b)(2), 29 C.F.R. § 2550.404c-1(b)(2).

78. DOL Advisory Opinion 2005-23A (Dec. 7, 2005).

7. Caution

The prohibited transaction rules may appear straightforward on their face, but can be extraordinarily complex in their application. Prohibited transactions can arise when an investment adviser inadvertently engages in a transaction with a plan, such as a transaction with a company or partnership or involving an asset (such as real estate) that is partially or wholly owned by a plan. For example, if an investment adviser to a plan rents an office in a building that is partly owned by the plan, the plan and the investment adviser may, depending on the circumstances, be engaging in a prohibited transaction.

Prohibited transactions may also arise when an investment adviser causes a plan to engage in a transaction with an affiliate of the investment adviser, another service provider of the plan (such as another investment adviser or the hedge fund's administrator) or an affiliate of such other service provider, unless an exemption applies. For these reasons, potential derivative counterparties or service providers may be hesitant or unwilling to deal with a plan assets hedge fund. A general partner or investment adviser to a plan assets hedge fund should keep records of the parties in interest and monitor any circumstances that might be or might cause a prohibited transaction.

8. Consequences of Prohibited Transactions

An ERISA fiduciary that causes a plan to engage in a transaction that it knows or should know is a prohibited transaction has breached its fiduciary duties and is subject to the liabilities and penalties under ERISA that are described in section 11.3.5 above. Nonfiduciaries that participate in the prohibited transaction may be obligated to provide restitution or other equitable relief to the plan.[79]

The Tax Code imposes an excise tax of 15 percent of the amount involved in the prohibited transaction for the year in which it occurs and each following year until it is rescinded or otherwise corrected. The excise tax applies to prohibited transactions involving ERISA plans, owner-only plans and IRAs. The tax must by paid by any disqualified person (other than a fiduciary acting solely in that capacity) who participates in the transaction.[80] If the transaction is not rescinded or otherwise corrected within the taxable period, a tax may be assessed equal to the full amount involved in the prohibited transaction.[81] The excise tax will reduce the amount of the 20 percent civil penalty that the DOL may impose with respect to the same transaction.[82]

79. Harris Trust and Sav. Bank v. Salomon Smith Barney Inc., 530 U.S 238 (2000).
80. Tax Code § 4975(a), 26 U.S.C. § 4975(a).
81. Tax Code § 4975(b), 26 U.S.C. § 4975(b).
82. ERISA § 502(l)(4), 29 U.S.C. § 1132(l)(4).

§ 11.5 Other ERISA Rules Applicable to Hedge Funds

1. Bonding Requirements

ERISA imposes bonding requirements on certain fiduciaries and other persons who handle funds or other property of ERISA plans.[83] "Handle" means have physical contact with, have power to transfer or disburse, or have or exercise discretionary control over the investment of plan assets. Thus, the ERISA bonding requirements apply to the general partner and investment adviser of a hedge fund when its assets are plan assets of an ERISA plan. The amount of the bond is determined on a per-plan basis (rather than a per-hedge-fund basis), at 10 percent of the plan assets handled by the investment adviser, with a minimum of $1,000 and a maximum of $500,000 per plan ($1,000,000 if the plan's assets include securities of an employer sponsoring the plan).[84] No bonding is required for an investment adviser that renders investment advice for a fee but does not handle plan assets. SEC-registered broker-dealers subject to the requirements of a self-regulatory organization are exempt from ERISA's bonding requirements.[85]

2. Foreign Custody Rules

Except in limited circumstances, the fiduciary of an ERISA plan may not maintain indicia of ownership of any assets of the plan outside the jurisdiction of the U.S. district courts.[86] The requirement to maintain the indicia of ownership of a hedge fund's assets within U.S. jurisdiction does not, however, strictly prohibit or restrict non-U.S. investments. Rather, "indicia of ownership" refers to the evidence of ownership of the hedge fund's assets (such as stock certificates). If the hedge fund has a U.S. custodian, assets maintained by that custodian (even in accounts outside of the United States) are within the jurisdiction of U.S. district courts.

The DOL has promulgated custody regulations that provide exceptions to this general prohibition.[87] An exception permits a foreign security (such as a security issued by a corporation that is not organized under U.S. law and that does not have its principal place of business in the United States) to be held outside U.S. jurisdiction under the "asset manager alternative." This alternative requires that the custodian be a hedge fund investment adviser (that is, a fiduciary) that is a substantial U.S. bank, an insurance company or an SEC-registered investment adviser whose assets under management and shareholder or partner equity exceed specified minimums.[88]

83. ERISA § 412(a), 29 U.S.C. § 1112(a).
84. *Id.*
85. *Id.*
86. ERISA § 404(b), 29 U.S.C § 1104(b); DOL Reg. § 2550.404b-1, 29 C.F.R. § 2550.404b-1.
87. DOL Reg. § 2550.404b-1, 29 C.F.R. § 2550.404b-1.
88. DOL Reg. § 2550.404b-1(a)(2)(i), 29 C.F.R. § 2550.404b-1(a)(2)(i).

3. Exculpatory Provisions; Indemnification

Under ERISA, any agreement that purports to relieve a fiduciary from liability for an ERISA fiduciary breach is void as against public policy.[89] An agreement under which an ERISA plan is obligated to indemnify the fiduciary for such a breach is also void.[90] The use of plan assets to indemnify a fiduciary, whether or not on account of a breach of an ERISA fiduciary duty, may constitute a prohibited transaction. Thus, a hedge fund agreement provision that obligates the hedge fund to indemnify the general partner or investment adviser of the hedge fund could not be enforced if the hedge fund assets are plan assets and the general partner or investment adviser is an ERISA fiduciary of a plan. ERISA does not, however, prohibit third-parties from indemnifying fiduciaries or prohibit fiduciaries from obtaining insurance to protect themselves against losses. Insurance and proper indemnification can be important tools for investment advisers to limit some of the risks related to ERISA plans.

4. Reporting Requirements

When a hedge fund holds plan assets of an ERISA plan, the plan will also hold an interest in the underlying assets of the hedge fund. Consequently, when the plan makes its required annual reports to the DOL and IRS on Form 5500, it must report its interests in both the hedge fund and its underlying assets. The hedge fund is obligated to provide this information to the plans. As an alternative, the hedge fund itself may report its underlying assets directly to the government, and each investing plan could then report only its interest in the hedge fund.[91]

89. ERISA § 410, 29 U.S.C. § 1110.
90. DOL Reg. § 2509.75-4, 29 C.F.R. § 2509.75-4.
91. DOL Reg. § 2520.103-12, 29 C.F.R. § 2520.103-12.

CHAPTER **12**

Custody

§ 12.1 SEC-Registered Investment Advisers

1. General Rule

An SEC-registered investment adviser that has or is deemed to have custody of client funds or securities must comply with conditions in Rule 206(4)-2(a) under the Advisers Act (the "custody rule"). The custody rule establishes detailed requirements related to engaging a qualified custodian, notifying clients, providing account statements to clients and obtaining independent verification of client funds and securities.[1] An investment adviser that manages a hedge fund, however, may take advantage of alternative and less onerous procedures in the custody rule with respect to notices to clients, account statements and verification of client assets, discussed below in section 12.1.1.vi.

i. Definition of Custody

An SEC-registered investment adviser that holds (or whose related person holds), directly or indirectly, client funds or securities, or has any authority to obtain possession of client funds or securities, is deemed to have custody of those funds or securities under the SEC's custody rule.[2] An SEC-registered investment adviser that is authorized to deduct fees from its clients' accounts has custody of the assets of those accounts (although such investment adviser is not required to obtain independent verification of client funds and securities if that is the only reason the investment adviser has custody).[3] An SEC-registered investment adviser that serves as the general partner of an investment limited partnership has custody of the partnership's assets.[4]

An SEC-registered investment adviser can avoid being deemed to have custody of client assets that it receives inadvertently if it returns the assets to

1. Advisers Act Rule 206(4)-2(a), 17 C.F.R. § 275.206(4)-2(a).

2. Advisers Act Rule 206(4)-2(d)(2), 17 C.F.R. § 275.206(4)-2(d)(2). The custody rule, Advisers Act Rule 206(4)-2, 17 C.F.R. § 275.206(4)-2, applies to any investment adviser that is registered or required to be registered with the SEC under the Advisers Act. For convenience, we refer to all such investment advisers as "SEC-registered investment advisers."

3. Advisers Act Rules 206(4)-2(b)(3) and (d)(2)(ii), 17 C.F.R. § 275.206(4)-2(b)(3) and (d)(2)(ii). *See* § 12.1.1.vi, *infra*.

4. Advisers Act Rule 206(4)-2(d)(2)(iii), 17 C.F.R. § 275.206(4)-2(d)(2)(iii).

the sender within 3 business days.[5] The SEC has indicated that an investment adviser may forward certain client assets directly to the intended recipient without being deemed to have had custody of them, if it does so promptly (no more than 5 days) after receiving the assets and adopts and implements certain written policies and procedures.

These policies and procedures must be reasonably designed to ensure that the investment adviser (a) promptly identifies client assets that it inadvertently receives; (b) promptly identifies the client or former client to whom such assets are attributable; (c) either forwards client assets to the client or former client, or to the client's qualified custodian, within 5 business days after receipt, or returns them to the appropriate third-party within 5 business days; and (d) maintains and preserves appropriate records of all client assets inadvertently received, including written explanations of whether and, if so, when the assets were forwarded or returned to the third-party.[6]

ii. Qualified Custodian

An SEC-registered investment adviser with custody of client assets must maintain those assets with one or more qualified custodians.[7] "Qualified custodians" are banks, registered broker-dealers, futures commission merchants and certain non-U.S. financial accounts that customarily hold assets for their clients and segregate those assets from their proprietary assets.[8] In addition, an SEC-registered investment adviser that trades mutual fund shares may use the mutual fund transfer agents as qualified custodians for the limited purpose of holding those shares.[9] An SEC-registered investment adviser that allocates investments within a stock life insurance company's variable annuity contracts may rely on the insurance company to act as a qualified custodian, if the insurance company performs the functions traditionally performed by a mutual fund transfer agent.[10]

An exception from the qualified custodian requirement applies to privately offered uncertificated securities, if they are transferable only with the consent of the issuer or its security holders. Such securities need not be held by a qualified custodian; in such case, however, if the securities are held for the account of a limited partnership or other pooled investment vehicle, the financial

---

5. *Id.* Possession of checks drawn by clients and made payable to third parties, however, would not cause an investment adviser to have custody. Advisers Act Rule 206(4)-2(d)(2)(i), 17 C.F.R. § 275.206(4)-2(d)(2)(i).

6. *Investment Adviser Association*, SEC No-Action Letter (Sep. 20, 2007) and *Staff Responses to Questions About the Custody Rule*, *available at* http://www.sec.gov/divisions/investment/custody_faq_030510.htm (updated Mar. 5, 2010). The no-action letter was limited to tax refunds, settlement proceeds from class action lawsuits and stock certificates or dividend checks.

7. Advisers Act Rule 206(4)-2(a)(1), 17 C.F.R. § 275.206(4)-2(a)(1).

8. Advisers Act Rule 206(4)-2(d)(6), 17 C.F.R. § 275.206(4)-2(d)(6).

9. Advisers Act Rule 206(4)-2(b)(1), 17 C.F.R. § 275.206(4)-2(b)(1).

10. American Skandia Life Assurance Corp., SEC No-Action Letter (May 16, 2005).

statements of that vehicle must be audited and distributed in accordance with the custody rule.[11]

An investment adviser or its related person that is a qualified custodian may serve as the qualified custodian of the investment adviser's client assets. For example, if the investment adviser is also registered as a broker-dealer or is affiliated with a registered broker-dealer, it may maintain client assets in accounts at such broker-dealer. In such case, the investment adviser must obtain (or receive from its related person) annually an internal control report that includes an opinion from an independent public accountant regarding the suitability and effectiveness of the investment adviser's (or its related person's) controls relating to custody of client assets.[12] The independent public accountant must be registered with, and subject to inspection by, the Public Company Accounting Oversight Board ("PCAOB") and must verify that client funds and securities are reconciled to a custodian other than the investment adviser or its related person.

iii. Notice to Clients

When an SEC-registered investment adviser with custody opens an account in the client's name or in the investment adviser's name as agent, it must promptly notify the client in writing of the qualified custodian's name and address and the manner in which the funds or securities are held. Thereafter, it must promptly notify the client if any of that information changes.[13] Clients who do not want to receive such notices may appoint an independent representative to receive the notices on their behalf.[14] An "independent representative" for this purpose is a person who:

- acts as agent for the clients, including, in the case of a hedge fund, for limited partners of the hedge fund,
- by law or contract is obligated to act in the best interest of the represented clients or limited partners,
- does not control, is not controlled by, and is not under common control with the investment adviser, and
- does not have, and has not had within the preceding 2 years, a material business relationship with the investment adviser.[15]

The same independent representative may receive notices on behalf of any number of clients or hedge fund limited partners.

An exception to the notice requirement for hedge funds is discussed below in section 12.1.1.vi.

11. Advisers Act Rule 206(4)-2(b)(2), 17 C.F.R. § 275.206(4)-2(b)(2).
12. Advisers Act Rule 206(4)-2(a)(6), 17 C.F.R. § 275.206(4)-2(a)(6).
13. Advisers Act Rule 206(4)-2(a)(2), 17 C.F.R. § 275.206(4)-2(a)(2).
14. Advisers Act Rule 206(4)-2(a)(7), 17 C.F.R. § 275.206(4)-2(a)(7).
15. Advisers Act Rule 206(4)-2(d)(4), 17 C.F.R. § 275.206(4)-2(d)(4).

iv. Account Statement Delivery Requirement

The reporting requirements of the custody rule generally require an SEC-registered investment adviser with custody to have a qualified custodian deliver account statements at least quarterly directly to the client (rather than through the investment adviser).[16] If the investment adviser is the general partner or manager of a hedge fund, the qualified custodian must send the account statement to each limited partner, member or other beneficial owner of the hedge fund. The statements must show the amount of funds and each security in the account at the end of the quarter and each transaction in the account during the quarter.[17]

The investment adviser must have a reasonable basis, after due inquiry, for believing that the qualified custodian is sending such statements. Account statements may be delivered to an independent representative of any one or more of the designated recipients.[18] Account statements may be delivered electronically if the client has consented and can effectively access the information and if the custodian receives evidence that the client received the information.[19] Providing a hedge fund's quarterly account statements to investors or their independent representatives is intended to help deter improper payments to the hedge fund's general partner and its affiliates.[20] An exception to the account statement delivery requirement for hedge funds is discussed below in section 12.1.1.vi.

v. Surprise Examination Requirement

Before the SEC custody rule was amended in 2003, an SEC-registered investment adviser with custody of client assets was required to undergo an annual surprise examination and file its audited balance sheet with Part 2 of its Form ADV. A series of SEC no-action letters commonly called the *PIMS/Bennett* letters set forth procedures that investment advisers that were the general partners of hedge funds could follow to avoid being deemed to have custody of the hedge funds' assets (and thus avoid being subject to the surprise examination requirement).[21] Under those letters, the investment adviser was not deemed to have custody if it entered into an arrangement with the hedge fund's prime broker that required an independent representative to authorize all payments by the hedge fund to the investment adviser or its affiliates. The SEC formally withdrew the *PIMS/Bennett* letters when it amended the custody rule in 2003, although some states

16. Advisers Act Rule 206(4)-2(a)(3), 17 C.F.R. § 275.206(4)-2(a)(3). The 2010 amendments to the custody rule eliminated the option for an investment adviser to send account statements to clients itself if subject to an annual surprise audit by an independent public accountant. *See* Advisers Act Release No. 2968 (Dec. 30, 2009), 75 F.R. 1,456 (Jan. 11, 2010).

17. Advisers Act Rules 206(4)-2(a)(3) and 206(4)-2(a)(5), 17 C.F.R. § 275.206(4)-2(a)(3) and § 275.206(4)-2(a)(5).

18. *See* n. 14 and 15, *supra*, and accompanying text.

19. Securities Act Release No. 7288 (May 9, 1996), 61 F.R. 24,644 (May 15, 1996), and *Staff Responses to Questions About the Custody Rule*, *available at* http://www.sec.gov/divisions/investment/custody_faq_030510.htm (last visited May 13, 2013).

20. Advisers Act Release No. 2176 (Sep. 30, 2003), 68 F.R. 56,692 (Oct. 1, 2003).

21. Bennett Mgmt. Co., SEC No-Action Letter (Feb. 26, 1990); PIMS, Inc., SEC No-Action Letter (Oct. 21, 1991).

still allow investment advisers to rely on the *PIMS/Bennett* procedures to avoid being deemed to have custody.

Under the current custody rule, subject to certain exceptions, investment advisers with custody must engage an independent public accountant to conduct annually a surprise examination of client assets.[22] An investment adviser subject to the surprise examination requirement must enter into a written agreement with an independent public accountant to conduct the examination. The agreement must require that:

- the accountant conduct the first examination within 6 months from the time that the investment adviser becomes subject to this requirement and annually thereafter, at irregular times chosen by the accountant without prior notice to the investment adviser;
- the accountant notify the SEC, by facsimile or electronic mail and followed by first class mail, within 1 business day of finding any material discrepancy during the course of an examination;
- the accountant submit a Form ADV-E to the SEC within 120 days of each surprise examination; and
- if the accountant resigns or if its engagement is terminated or not renewed, the accountant file within 4 business days Form ADV-E and a statement of the date of the resignation, termination or nonrenewal, the accountant's contact information, and an explanation of any problems relating to examination scope or procedure that contributed to the resignation, termination or nonrenewal.

The custody rule provides limited exceptions to the surprise examination requirement. First, as discussed below in section 12.1.1.vi, investment advisers to hedge funds (and other pooled investment vehicles) whose financial statements are audited annually by an independent public accountant are deemed to satisfy the surprise audit requirement if the financial statements are prepared in accordance with GAAP and distributed to investors within 120 days (or 180 days, for funds of funds) after the end of the hedge fund's fiscal year.[23] Second, an investment adviser that is deemed to have custody solely because a related person holds client assets in connection with the investment adviser's advisory services is exempt from the surprise examination requirement if the investment adviser is "operationally independent" from the related person.[24] A related person is presumed not to be operationally independent except in certain enumerated circumstances.[25] An investment adviser that overcomes the presumption is not required to have the surprise examinations, but must continue to meet the custody rule's other requirements and must keep a memorandum describing its

22. Advisers Act Rule 206(4)-2(a)(4), 17 C.F.R. § 275.206(4)-2(a)(4).
23. Advisers Act Rule 206(4)-2(b)(4), 17 C.F.R. § 275.206(4)-2(b)(4).
24. Advisers Act Rule 206(4)-2(b)(6), 17 C.F.R. § 275.206(4)-2(b)(6).
25. Advisers Act Rule 206(4)-2(d)(5), 17 C.F.R. § 275.206(4)-2(d)(5).

relationship with the related person and explaining its determination that the related person is operationally independent.[26]

vi. Exceptions and Alternative Procedures for Hedge Funds

An SEC-registered investment adviser that is the general partner of a hedge fund is not subject to the surprise examination if the investment adviser has custody solely as a consequence of having authority to make withdrawals from client accounts to pay its advisory fee.[27]

An SEC-registered investment adviser that is the general partner of a hedge fund is not required to notify clients of the qualified custodian information, have the qualified custodian deliver quarterly account statements to clients or investors, or submit to surprise examinations, if the investment adviser sends the hedge fund's audited annual financial statements to each investor within 120 days (or, for a fund of funds,[28] 180 days) after the end of the hedge fund's fiscal year.[29] The financial statements must be prepared in accordance with GAAP and must be audited by an independent public accountant registered with, and subject to inspection by, the PCAOB.[30]

Most hedge funds have their annual financial statements audited, but some common hedge fund practices might not comply with GAAP. For example, a hedge fund may amortize organizational costs over several years or may decline to attach to the audited financial statements a list of the hedge fund's holdings, either of which may not accord with GAAP. A hedge fund that has financial statements that span a period longer than 1 year (for example, from the hedge fund's inception late in its first fiscal year to the end of the following fiscal year) may not take advantage of this alternative procedure for that period, even if its financial statements accord with GAAP and are audited.

The accountant performing the audit must be independent in accordance with SEC rules.[31] In a no-action letter to Deloitte & Touche LLP before the 2010 amendment,[32] however, the SEC staff stated that it would not recommend enforcement action under the rule against a newly registered investment adviser to a hedge fund that has the hedge fund's financial statements audited by an accountant that has performed services for the hedge fund or the auditor in the past, if certain conditions are met. First, the accountant must have performed

26. Advisers Act Rule 206(4)-2(a)(6)(ii), 17 C.F.R. § 275.206(4)-2(a)(6)(ii).

27. Advisers Act Rule 206(4)-2(b)(3), 17 C.F.R. § 275.206(4)-2(b)(3).

28. American Bar Association, SEC No-Action Letter (Aug. 10, 2006). A fund of funds is defined as "a limited partnership (or limited liability company, or another type of pooled investment vehicle) that invests 10 percent or more of its total assets in other pooled investment vehicles that are not, and are not advised by, a related person (as defined in Form ADV), of the limited partnership, its general partner or its adviser." Advisers Act Rule 206(4)-2(b)(4), 17 C.F.R. § 275.206(4)-2(b)(4); Advisers Act Release No. 2968 (Dec. 30, 2009), 75 F.R. 1,456 (Jan. 11, 2010).

29. Advisers Act Rule 206(4)-2(b)(4), 17 C.F.R. § 275.206(4)-2(b)(4).

30. *Id.*

31. *Id*; Regulation S-X Rule 1-02(d), 17 C.F.R. 210.1-02(d).

32. Deloitte & Touche LLP, SEC No-Action Letter (Aug. 28, 2006).

certain nonaudit services for, or had certain relationships with, the hedge fund or its affiliates, including the investment adviser, before the investment adviser became registered, that did not impair the accountant's independence under independence standards applicable to a hedge fund audit, and any services or relationships prohibited by the SEC's independence rules must have ended by June 30, 2007. Second, the investment adviser must cause the hedge fund to disclose in the financial statement footnotes (a) that, under independence standards applicable to a hedge fund audit, the accountant was independent before the investment adviser's registration but not independent under SEC independence rules, (b) the general reasons why the accountant was not independent, and (c) a brief description of the relief and duration of the relief granted by the SEC staff.

The SEC staff has said that it would not recommend enforcement against an investment adviser that relies on the alternative procedure for hedge funds and that does not distribute its audited financial statements within 120 days after the end of its fiscal year, if the investment adviser reasonably believed that the pool's audited financial statements would be distributed within the deadline but failed to do so because of unforeseeable circumstances.[33]

2. Guidance on Custody Policies and Procedures

SEC-registered investment advisers are required to adopt written policies and procedures reasonably designed to prevent violations of the Advisers Act and the SEC rules under it.[34] In the adopting release for the 2010 amendments, the SEC provided guidance regarding the types of custody policies and procedures that investment advisers should consider incorporating into their compliance programs, including (1) conducting background and credit checks on employees, (2) requiring more than one employee to authorize movements of assets, (3) limiting the number of employees permitted to interact with custodians, and (4) if the investment adviser serves as qualified custodian, segregating the duties of its advisory personnel from those of custodial personnel.[35] The SEC also recommended that an investment adviser consider adopting procedures to test the effectiveness of the investment adviser's controls over the safekeeping of client assets. At the same time, the SEC issued interpretive guidance for independent public accountants that conduct surprise examinations and report on internal controls.[36]

---

33. *Staff Responses to Questions About the Custody Rule, available at* http://www.sec.gov/divisions/investment/custody_faq_030510.htm (last visited May 13, 2013).

34. Advisers Act Rule 206(4)-7, 17 C.F.R. § 275.206(4)-7.

35. Advisers Act Release No. 2968 (Dec. 30, 2009), 75 F.R. 1,456 (Jan. 11, 2010).

36. *Id.*

§ 12.2 State-Registered Investment Advisers

The SEC custody rule, Advisers Act Rule 206(4)-2,[37] applies only to SEC-registered investment advisers. Many states have rules that specify procedures that an investment adviser registered in those states must follow if it has custody of client assets.[38] The SEC's custody rule does not affect those states' custody rules. Some states allow investment advisers to hedge funds to follow the *PIMS/Bennett* disbursement procedures to avoid being deemed to have custody. Under the *PIMS/Bennett* interpretations, if an investment adviser that is the general partner of a hedge fund wants to avoid having custody, it must adopt and implement the following procedures restricting its access to the hedge fund's assets, including its own capital and its fees and expense reimbursements:

- one or more independent banks or brokerage firms must hold the hedge fund's funds and securities in the name of the hedge fund;
- investors in the hedge fund must deposit subscription funds directly with the custodian;
- the hedge fund must retain an independent representative (a lawyer or certified public accountant)[39] to review and authorize transfers to the general partner or manager;
- each time the general partner or manager requests a payment, withdrawal or distribution, it must send simultaneously to the independent representative and the custodian a statement showing (a) the amount of the payment or withdrawal, (b) if a fee payment, the value of the hedge fund's assets on which the fee is based and the manner in which the payment is calculated, (c) if the withdrawal is by the general partner or manager, the amount in the general partner's or manager's capital account before and after the withdrawal, and (d) the aggregate amount in all partners' or members' capital accounts before and after the withdrawal;
- the custodian may transfer funds from the hedge fund's account to the general partner or manager only with the written authorization of the independent representative and only if the custodian receives a copy of the written request from the general partner or manager; and

---

37. 17 C.F.R. § 275.206(4)-2.

38. *See, e.g.*, 10 Cal. Code of Reg. § 260.237 (2010). California proposed amendments to § 260.237 (*available at* http://www.dbo.ca.gov/Licensees/default.asp) that largely mirror the SEC custody rule as in effect from 2003 to 2010. The current status of these proposed amendments is unclear.

39. The requirements relating to this "independent representative" of a hedge fund have not been clearly delineated, unlike the requirements relating to the independent representative of limited partners of a hedge fund discussed in §§ 12.1.1.iii and 12.1.1.iv, *supra*.

- the custodian must provide quarterly statements to the hedge fund and the independent representative.[40]

These procedures should be set forth in an appropriate written agreement between the investment adviser and the custodian. If the general partner intends to follow these procedures, it should direct all other brokers and dealers that hold any of the hedge fund's assets to remit such assets only to the hedge fund's custodian for the hedge fund's account.

The North American Securities Administrators Association ("NASAA") has adopted a model rule for states to consider that combines certain aspects of the SEC custody rule with the *PIMS/Bennett* disbursement procedures.[41] Under the model rule, it is unlawful for an investment adviser that is registered or required to be registered to have custody of client funds or securities unless:

- the investment adviser notifies the state regulatory authority promptly via its Form ADV that the investment adviser has or may have custody;
- a qualified custodian (including any of certain independent institutions (such as a bank or a broker) that is not affiliated with the investment adviser by any direct or indirect control relationship and has not had a material business relationship with the investment adviser in the preceding 2 years) maintains the funds and securities in a separate account under the client's name or in accounts that contain only the investment adviser's clients' funds and securities under the investment adviser's name as agent or trustee for the clients;
- the investment adviser notifies its clients of the qualified custodian's name and address and the manner in which the funds or securities are maintained promptly when the account is opened and when that information changes;
- either (1) a qualified custodian sends account statements at least quarterly to each client (if the client is a hedge fund, to each investor) for which the investment adviser maintains funds or securities, identifying the amount of funds and securities in the account at the end of the period and setting forth all transactions in the account during that period; or (2) (a) the investment adviser sends such account statements, (b) an independent certified public accountant verifies all client funds and securities by surprise examination at least annually and files a copy of the auditor's report and financial statements with the state regulatory authority within 30 days after completion of the examination, along with a letter stating that it examined the funds and securities and describing the nature and extent of the examination, and (c) the accountant notifies the state regulatory authority within 1 business day of finding any material discrepancy;

---

40. Bennett Mgmt. Co., SEC No-Action Letter (Feb. 26, 1990); and PIMS, Inc., SEC No-Action Letter (Oct. 21, 1991).

41. NASAA Custody Requirements for Investment Advisers, Model Rule 102(e)(1)-1, adopted Apr. 3, 2000, amended Apr. 18, 2004, and Sep. 11, 2005, *available at* http://www.nasaa.org/1325/adopted-model-rules/ (last visited July 2, 2013).

- if the investment adviser has fees directly deducted from client accounts, the investment adviser obtains written authorization from the client, provides notice of the fee deduction to the client and provides notice of the safeguards described above to clients through its Form ADV; and
- if the investment adviser has custody because it is the general partner or manager of a hedge fund and it is not subject to an annual audit, the investment adviser engages an independent party to review all fees, expenses and capital withdrawals from the hedge fund.

As under the SEC custody rule, an investment adviser may use a mutual fund's transfer agent in lieu of a qualified custodian. In addition, investment advisers are not required to comply with the above requirements with respect to certain privately offered securities. A hedge fund subject to an annual audit is not required to comply with the quarterly account statement requirement if it distributes its financial statements to each beneficial owner within 120 days of the end of its fiscal year and notifies the state regulatory authority, via its Form ADV, that it intends to use the safeguards described above. Registered investment companies and certain beneficial trusts are also not required to comply with the above requirements. An investment adviser that intends to have custody but is not able to use a qualified custodian must first obtain approval from the state regulatory authority and comply with all applicable safekeeping provisions of the rule.

§ 12.3 Unregistered Investment Advisers

An investment adviser that is not registered or required to be registered with the SEC or any state is generally not subject to the custody rules described above. Nevertheless, such an investment adviser would be well-advised to adopt and implement custody procedures that comply at least with the laws of its state.

CHAPTER **13**

Trading Activities and Reporting

§ 13.1 Consequences of Large Shareholdings

1. Exchange Act Section 13(d) Filing Requirements

Exchange Act section 13(d)[1] requires any person or group that acquires beneficial ownership of more than 5 percent of any class of equity securities registered under the Exchange Act to report that person's or group's beneficial ownership in filings with the SEC. Section 13(d) filing requirements apply regardless of a lack of intent to acquire over 5 percent of a class of securities; for example, they apply if a person acquires over 5 percent inadvertently or as a result of a trade error.[2]

i. Persons Subject to Filing Requirement

a. Beneficial Ownership

A person "beneficially owns" a security if the person has or shares the power to vote or dispose of the security.[3] One who has all of the economic rights in a security may not beneficially own it; one who has none of the economic rights in a security may be its only beneficial owner. The investment adviser to a hedge fund typically has discretionary authority to purchase, sell and vote the securities held by the hedge fund and, therefore, the investment adviser and its control persons beneficially own the securities held by the hedge fund. A person also beneficially owns any securities that the person has the right to acquire (such as on exercise of an option), if the right is exercisable within 60 days or was acquired with the purpose or effect of changing or influencing control of the issuer.[4] Thus, a hedge fund that retains the right to terminate its

---

1. 15 U.S.C. § 78m(d).

2. Exchange Act §§ 13(d) and 13(g) and Regulation 13D-G Beneficial Ownership Reporting Compliance and Disclosure Interpretations (Nov. 16, 2009), Question 101.06, *available at* http://www.sec.gov/divisions/corpfin/guidance/reg13d-interp.htm (hereinafter "C&DIs").

3. Exchange Act Rule 13d-3(a), 17 C.F.R. § 240.13d-3(a).

4. Exchange Act Rule 13d-3(d)(1), 17 C.F.R. § 240.13d-3(d)(1).

investment management agreement with an investment adviser within 60 days also beneficially owns the securities in its account.[5]

A hedge fund for which the investment adviser also is the general partner or manager, however, usually does not have the ability to terminate the advisory relationship within 60 days. Thus hedge funds organized as partnerships or limited liability companies (LLCs) usually do not beneficially own the securities they hold.[6] An investor in a hedge fund does not beneficially own the securities held by the hedge fund, unless that investor has the power to require the hedge fund to distribute to it specific securities (as opposed to securities selected by the general partner or cash) within 60 days. The governing documents of hedge funds ordinarily do not give investors such rights.

b. Convertible Securities

As discussed above, a person who has the right to acquire securities through the exercise or conversion of a convertible security is deemed to beneficially own the underlying securities if the right is exercisable within 60 days. Convertible securities are often issued, however, in private offerings that contemplate the registration of the underlying shares. A hedge fund that, without the purpose or effect of changing or influencing control of the issuer, receives a right to acquire more than 5 percent of a class of Exchange Act-registered securities that is exercisable within 60 days and that is conditioned on the effectiveness of a related registration statement is not required to file a Schedule 13D or Schedule 13G until the condition is removed.[7]

The terms of convertible securities also often limit their conversion rights to an amount of underlying shares that limit the holder's beneficial ownership to less than 5 percent. Binding and valid conversion provisions that so limit a holder's beneficial ownership of a class of underlying securities effectively negate the holder's right to acquire those shares and relieve it of the section 13(d) reporting obligation. Provisions that are binding and valid include those that are nonwaivable, are enforceable, are established in the issuer's governing documents and apply to affiliates and assigns.[8]

c. Swaps

The owner of a derivative instrument, such as the long party to a total return swap, typically does not beneficially own the reference equity securities. Although such swaps may provide the same economic benefit as owning shares outright, they typically do not provide voting rights. In addition, they typically are subject to "cash settlement," meaning that the long party to the swap never actually receives the shares when the swap is unwound. The Dodd-Frank Act amended the Exchange Act to provide that a person is deemed to beneficially

---

5. *Id.*

6. *See also* Washington Bancorporation v. Washington, CCH Fed. Sec. L. Rep. ¶ 94,893 (D.D.C. 1989) (a partnership that has ceded all voting and investment power to its general partner is not a beneficial owner under Exchange Act § 13(d) of the securities held by the partnership and therefore may not be a member of a § 13(d) group).

7. *See* C&DIs, *supra* n. 2, Question 105.02.

8. *Id.*, Question 105.03.

own an equity security based on the purchase or sale of a security-based swap only to the extent that the SEC so provides by rule.[9]

In response, the SEC readopted without change Exchange Act Rule 13d-3 relating to beneficial ownership, purportedly to ensure that its then-current definition of beneficial ownership would continue to apply to persons who purchase or sell security-based swaps.[10] In readopting Rule 13d-3, the SEC stated that it was not addressing whether a security-based swap would be treated as a purchase or sale of the underlying securities for the purposes of the federal securities laws, but stated that under those rules as they existed before readoption, a security-based swap may involve beneficial ownership for purposes of Exchange Act section 13, as follows:

- Anyone who has or shares voting or investment power over securities based on the purchase or sale of a security-based swap is a beneficial owner of the underlying security.[11]
- Anyone who uses a security-based swap as part of a plan or scheme to evade beneficial ownership reporting requirements is a beneficial owner of the underlying security.[12]
- Anyone who has the right through a security-based swap to acquire beneficial ownership of a security within 60 days, or at any time if the right is held for the purpose of changing or influencing control, is a beneficial owner of the underlying security.[13]

Before the Dodd-Frank Act, in *CSX Corp. v. Children's Investment Fund Management*,[14] a federal court challenged hedge funds' use of swaps to circumvent the Exchange Act's beneficial ownership reporting requirements. In that case, 2 hedge funds sought changes to the board of directors of CSX Corp. The hedge funds initially acquired total return swaps with several banks and carefully distributed the swaps so that they never exceeded 5 percent of CSX ownership at any one institution, intending to avoid section 13(d) reporting. When the CSX board dismissed their demands, the hedge funds consolidated their derivatives and purchased stock. They accumulated the economic equivalent of over 14 percent of CSX, almost all of which was held through swaps. After filing a Schedule 13D and proxy statement, the hedge funds prepared to wage a proxy fight to replace 2 members of the CSX board. CSX sued to enjoin the hedge funds from voting the shares that they had acquired between the time they allegedly should have filed under section 13(d) and the

---

9. 15 U.S.C. § 78m(o).

10. Exchange Act Rule 13d-3, 17 C.F.R. § 240.13d-3, and Exchange Act Release No. 64628 (June 8, 2011), 76 F.R. 34,579 (June 14, 2011).

11. Exchange Act Rule 13d-3(a), 17 C.F.R. § 240.13d-3(a).

12. Exchange Act Rule 13d-3(b), 17 C.F.R. § 240.13d-3(b).

13. Exchange Act Rule 13d-3(d)(1), 17 C.F.R. § 240.13d-3(d)(1).

14. CSX Corp. v. Children's Inv. Fund Mgmt. (UK) LLP, 562 F. Supp. 2d 511 (S.D.N.Y. 2008), *affirmed without opinion by* CSX Corp. v. Children's Inv. Fund Mgmt. (UK) LLP, 292 Fed. Appx. 133 (2d Cir. 2008).

time they actually filed, arguing that the hedge funds' derivative interest in CSX stock constituted beneficial ownership.

The Court held that because the hedge funds had purposefully designed their investment strategy to avoid section 13(d) reporting, they had engaged in a plan or scheme to evade Schedule 13D reporting, in violation of Exchange Act Rule 13d-3(b),[15] and beneficially owned the underlying shares. The Court did not, however, enjoin the hedge funds from voting their shares. On appeal, the U.S. Court of Appeals for the Second Circuit declined to resolve the beneficial ownership issue and found that an injunction prohibiting the voting of shares acquired while in violation of section 13(d) reporting requirements is not an available remedy if the required disclosure is made in sufficient time for informed action by stockholders.[16] This case indicates that an activist hedge fund that uses total return swaps but does not report its holdings under section 13(d) may be deemed by a court or regulatory authority to be engaging in a plan or scheme to evade section 13(d) reporting apart from any rules that the SEC might enact.

d. Short Sales, Pledges and Writing Call Options

Selling securities short, pledging securities and writing call options normally will not change a person's beneficial ownership, because such transactions typically do not change the amount of shares over which the person has voting or investment power.[17] Short sales may, however, require amendment of a previously filed Schedule 13D, if they materially change or reflect a material change to the data reported. For example, a short sale may reflect a material change in the beneficial owner's previously reported plans or proposals regarding the securities.[18] In the case of securities pledged to secure a loan, if the pledge agreement grants the pledgee voting or investment power over more than 5 percent of the class on default by the pledgor, the pledgee will be deemed to have acquired beneficial ownership of the securities on the date of default and must report its beneficial ownership on Schedule 13D or Schedule 13G, as appropriate.[19] This is true whether or not the pledgee has taken all formal steps necessary to declare a default or perfect its rights.[20]

e. "Group" Status

When 2 or more persons act in concert "for the purpose of acquiring, holding, voting or disposing of equity securities," the group formed thereby is considered to beneficially own all the equity securities owned by each member of the

---

15. Exchange Act Rule 13d-3(b), 17 C.F.R. § 240.13d-3(b), provides in substance that any person who, directly or indirectly, creates or uses a trust, proxy, power of attorney, pooling arrangement or any other contract, arrangement or device with the purpose or effect of divesting that person of beneficial ownership of a security as part of a plan or scheme to avoid beneficial ownership of that security is deemed to have beneficial ownership of that security.

16. CSX v. The Children's Inv. Fund Mgmt. (UK) LLP, 654 F. 3d 276 (2d Cir. 2011).

17. *See* C&DIs, *supra* n. 2, Question 104.01.

18. *Id.*

19. *See* § 13.1.1.ii, *infra*.

20. *See* C&DIs, *supra* n. 2, Question 105.01.

group.[21] Persons can be members of a group for this purpose without any formal agreement among them. The SEC or a court may infer from circumstantial evidence that 2 or more persons have a formal or informal understanding and are acting in furtherance of a common objective and thus constitute a group.[22]

A mere relationship among persons or entities, however, whether family, personal or business, is insufficient to create a group under Exchange Act section 13(d).[23] Thus, partnerships and other entities, including hedge funds, generally are not considered to be members of a group with one another solely because they are under common control, such as by having a common general partner or investment adviser. Where such entities have a history of engaging in similar investment patterns, however, such as regularly investing in the same issuers at the same times, courts have been willing to infer the existence of a group.[24] In any event, the investment adviser to those hedge funds and separate accounts must file reports under Exchange Act section 13(d) for itself if the

---

21. Exchange Act Rule 13d-5(b)(1), 17 C.F.R. § 240.13d-5(b)(1).

22. Wellman v. Dickinson, 682 F.2d 355, 362-64 (2nd Cir. 1982).

23. Transcon Lines v. A. G. Becker, Inc., 470 F. Supp. 356, 375 (S.D.N.Y. 1979), quoting Texasgulf, Inc. v. Canada Development Corp., 366 F. Supp. 374, 403 (S.D. Tex. 1973). *See also* Mgmt. Assistance, Inc. v. Edelman, 584 F. Supp. 1016, 1019 (S.D.N.Y. 1984) (principal of corporation who was a limited partner in a limited partnership that was a member of § 13(d) group was deemed not to be a member of that group); Polaroid Corp. v. Disney, 698 F. Supp. 1169, 1180 (D. Del. 1988) (limited partners in a partnership that hold shares directly and indirectly, through the partnership, do not necessarily form a group with the partnership).

24. Goldstein v. QVT Associates GP LLC, Fed. Sec. L. Rep. (CCH) ¶ 95,937 (S.D.N.Y. Oct. 15, 2010) (the court could reasonably infer that U.S. and Cayman Islands hedge funds with the same investment adviser and similar but not identical trading patterns were a group); Strauss v. American Holdings, Inc., 902 F. Supp. 475, 479 (S.D.N.Y. 1995) (where a corporation and a partnership both traded in an issuer's shares and the same individual was responsible for the trading activities of both, it could be inferred that the entities were a group); and Schaffer v. Soros, 1994 WL 381442 (S.D.N.Y. July 20, 1994) (an investment adviser, investment advisory firm under the investment adviser's control, the director of the firm and 2 investment companies whose investments were under the control of the investment advisers all deemed to be members of a § 13(d) group). *See also* C&DIs, *supra* n. 2, Question 107.01 ("group" formed by arrangement whereby major shareholders of an issuer contemplating a rights offering retained an investment adviser to persuade the issuer to revise or drop the offer). *But see* Wellman v. Dickinson, 682 F.2d 355, 362-64 (2nd Cir. 1982) (mutual fund clients of an investment adviser that was a member of a § 13(d) group were not named as defendants or as members of the § 13(d) group); Bath Industries, Inc. v. Blot, 427 F.2d 97, 103, 112 (7th Cir. 1970) (investment firm that exercised continuous voting control over its clients' securities deemed to have beneficial ownership of the securities and to be a member of the § 13(d) group, but no indication that clients of that firm were members of the group); Champion Parts Rebuilders, Inc. v. Cormier Corp., 661 F. Supp. 825, 834 (N.D. Ill. 1987) (investment adviser and several stockholders deemed to be members of § 13(d) group, but clients of investment adviser not listed as defendants or referred to in Court's opinion); Jacobs v. Pabst Brewing Co., 549 F. Supp. 1050, 1065-1066 (D. Del. 1982) (§ 13(d) group does not exist where investment adviser and its clients have not agreed to act together); and Nat'l Home Products, Inc. v. Gray, 416 F. Supp. 1293, 1323-24 (D. Del. 1976) (stockholder who sought investment advice from member of § 13(d) group not a member of the group in absence of evidence of agreement to act in concert).

discretionary accounts it manages collectively exceed the 5 percent threshold, even if some or all of its clients are not considered part of a group.

ii. Filing Requirements

Under Exchange Act section 13(d), a person or group that acquires beneficial ownership of more than 5 percent of any class of equity securities registered under the Exchange Act (a "5 Percent Owner") must report its holdings on Schedule 13D or 13G.[25] Schedule 13G requires less information and must be amended less frequently than Schedule 13D.[26]

a. Schedule 13D

A 5 Percent Owner must report its holdings on a Schedule 13D within 10 days after the date on which its beneficial ownership exceeds 5 percent, unless it is eligible to file a Schedule 13G.[27] A report on Schedule 13D must be amended "promptly" (which can mean "immediately" in some circumstances) if the information disclosed in the Schedule changes materially. Any acquisition or disposition of 1 percent or more of the class of securities is deemed material for this purpose. Acquisitions and dispositions of less than 1 percent may or may not be material, depending on the circumstances.[28]

b. Schedule 13G Exceptions for Certain Filers

A 5 Percent Owner may file a Schedule 13G instead of a Schedule 13D to report the 5 Percent Owner's holdings if the 5 Percent Owner acquired the securities in the ordinary course of business and without the purpose or effect of changing or influencing the control of the issuer. A Schedule 13G may be filed under either of 2 Exchange Act rules, and the 2 types of Schedule 13G have slightly different filing and amendment requirements. If the 5 Percent Owner is among the types of persons and entities listed in Exchange Act Rule 13d-1(b), including a registered investment adviser (state or federal), it may file a Schedule 13G under that rule (the "Investment Adviser Rule").[29] A 5 Percent Owner that does not qualify to file a Schedule 13G under the Investment Adviser Rule, because it is not a type of person or entity on such list, may nevertheless file on Schedule 13G under Exchange Act Rule 13d-1(c), if it is a passive holder as described above and owns, directly or indirectly, less than 20 percent of the outstanding securities of the applicable class (the "Passive Owner Rule").[30]

If a 5 Percent Owner initially files on Schedule 13G in reliance on the Investment Adviser Rule or the Passive Owner Rule and subsequently develops

---

25. The holder of a security-based swap may beneficially own equity securities underlying the swap; *see* § 13.1.1.i.c, *supra*.

26. Exchange Act Rules 13d-1(b) and 13d-1(c), 17 C.F.R. §§ 240.13d-1(b) and 240.13d-1(c).

27. Exchange Act Rule 13d-1(a), 17 C.F.R. § 240.13d-1(a). The Dodd-Frank Act authorizes the SEC to fix by rule an earlier filing deadline. Dodd-Frank Act, Pub. L. No. 111-203, § 929R(a)(1), 124 Stat. 1376 (2010). At this writing, the SEC has not done so.

28. Exchange Act Rule 13d-2(a), 17 C.F.R. § 240.13d-2(a).

29. Exchange Act Rule 13d-1(b), 17 C.F.R. § 240.13d-1(b).

30. Exchange Act Rule 13d-1(c), 17 C.F.R. § 240.13d-1(c).

the purpose or effect of changing or influencing the control of the issuer (in the case of a 5 Percent Owner relying on the Investment Adviser Rule or the Passive Owner Rule) or exceeds the 20 percent threshold (in the case of a 5 Percent Owner relying on the Passive Owner Rule), it must file a Schedule 13D within 10 days after that change occurs.[31] From the date of the triggering event until the expiration of the tenth day from the date that it files a Schedule 13D, a 5 Percent Owner may not vote the securities or acquire any additional equity securities of the issuer.[32]

A 5 Percent Owner that first files on Schedule 13G and switches to reporting on Schedule 13D may switch back if it again becomes eligible to report on Schedule 13G. In this case, the second Schedule 13G amends the Schedule 13D and no separate Schedule 13D filing is required. A 5 Percent Owner that was not originally eligible to file a Schedule 13G, but instead filed a Schedule 13D and later filed a final amendment on Schedule 13D to report that its beneficial ownership fell to 5 percent or less, may thereafter qualify to file a Schedule 13G if its beneficial ownership again increases to over 5 percent.[33]

A 5 Percent Owner relying on the Investment Adviser Rule is generally not required to file its initial Schedule 13G until 45 days after the end of the year in which it becomes a 5 Percent Owner, and must file only if it is a 5 Percent Owner on the last day of the year. If, however, such 5 Percent Owner's beneficial ownership exceeds 10 percent on the last day of any month before the end of that year, it must file its initial Schedule 13G within 10 days after the end of that month. A 5 Percent Owner relying on the Passive Owner Rule must file an initial Schedule 13G within 10 days after becoming a 5 Percent Owner and is subject to more stringent amendment requirements than a filer relying on the Investment Adviser Rule.[34]

An investment adviser is not eligible for the relaxed filing requirements of the Investment Adviser Rule if any hedge fund that it manages beneficially owns more than 5 percent of a security, because a hedge fund is not among the types of persons or entities listed in the Investment Adviser Rule.[35] To take advantage of the Investment Adviser Rule, an investment adviser could disclaim ownership in a group with the hedge fund and cause the hedge fund to file its own separate Schedule 13G (assuming the hedge fund is eligible to rely on the Passive Owner Rule). In most cases, however, this approach will not reduce the investment adviser's administrative burden and filing costs, because the investment adviser, as the general partner or manager of the hedge fund, is responsible for filing the Schedule 13G on behalf of the hedge fund.

---

31. Exchange Act Rules 13d-1(e)(1) and 13d-1(f)(1), 17 C.F.R. §§ 240.13d-1(e)(1) and 240.13d-1(f)(1).

32. Exchange Act Rules 13d-1(e)(2) and 13d-1(f)(2), 17 C.F.R. §§ 240.13d-1(e)(2) and 240.13d-1(f)(2).

33. *See* C&DIs, *supra* n. 2, Question 103.07.

34. Exchange Act Rules 13d-1(c), 13d-1(f)(1) and 13d-2(d), 17 C.F.R. §§ 240.13d-1(c), 240.13d-1(f)(1) and 240.13d-2(d).

35. *See also* C&DIs, *supra* n. 2, Question 101.03.

A 5 Percent Owner may not rely on the Investment Adviser Rule if its parent holding company or control person (such as the manager of the investment adviser) holds more than 1 percent of the class of securities.[36] A parent holding company's or control person's interest includes both securities owned directly and securities owned indirectly. A hedge fund investor is deemed to own indirectly the portion of the securities held by the hedge fund equal to the person's proportionate interest in the hedge fund. The control person of an investment adviser seeking to rely on the Investment Adviser Rule must aggregate all of his or her indirect holdings—for example, indirect holdings through the investment adviser's ownership interest in hedge funds as a result of his or her ownership interest in the investment adviser—in calculating whether he or she exceeds the 1 percent limit.

All 5 Percent Owners must amend their reports on Schedule 13G within 45 days after the end of each calendar year to reflect any changes in the information in the preceding report, unless the change results solely from a change in the aggregate number of outstanding securities in the class.[37] If a 5 Percent Owner purchases or sells securities of the class after filing on Schedule 13G, a change in the percentage of the class beneficially owned by that 5 Percent Owner is not deemed to result solely from a change in the aggregate number of outstanding securities, even if the percentage change would not have occurred but for the change in the number of outstanding securities.

A 5 Percent Owner relying on the Investment Adviser Rule must also amend its Schedule 13G within 10 days after the end of the first month in which its beneficial ownership as of the last day of that month exceeds 10 percent, and thereafter, within 10 days of the end of the first month in which its beneficial ownership as of the last day of that month changes by more than 5 percent. A 5 Percent Owner relying on the Passive Owner Rule must amend its Schedule 13G promptly when its beneficial ownership exceeds 10 percent and, thereafter, promptly when its beneficial ownership changes by more than 5 percent.

iii. Delivery Requirements

Each Schedule 13D or 13G and each amendment to it must be filed with the SEC through its Electronic Data Gathering, Analysis, and Retrieval ("EDGAR") system.[38] Under the Dodd-Frank Act, Schedules 13D and 13G and their amendments need not be filed with any stock exchange and copies of filed Schedules 13D and 13G and their amendments need not be sent to the issuer of the securities.[39] Under an SEC rule that precedes the Dodd-Frank Act, however, a copy of each Schedule 13D and its amendments must be sent to the issuer of the securities and to each national securities exchange on which the securities are traded.[40] Under that rule, a copy of each Schedule 13G and its amendments must be sent to the issuer of the securities.[41] At this writing, the SEC has not amended the rule and, therefore, these requirements are still applicable.

---

36. Exchange Act Rule 13d-1(b)(1)(ii)(G), 17 C.F.R. § 240.13d-1(b)(1)(ii)(G).
37. Exchange Act Rule 13d-2(b), 17 C.F.R. § 240.13d-2(b).
38. Regulation S-T, Rule 101(a)(1)(iii), 17 C.F.R. § 232.101(a)(1)(iii).
39. Dodd-Frank Act, Pub. L. No. 111-203, § 939(a), 24 Stat. 1376 (2010).
40. Exchange Act Rule 13d-7, 17 C.F.R. § 140 13d-7.
41. *Id.*

iv. Noncompliance

a. SEC Penalties

The SEC may require an investment adviser and hedge funds to file the reports required under section 13(d), if they do not do so of their own accord. The SEC may also levy fines or recommend criminal prosecution for violations of section 13(d).[42]

b. Private Right of Action

Neither section 13(d) nor the rules thereunder expressly provide for private enforcement of the filing requirements. Courts have implied private causes of action for issuers to require necessary filings, but no reported federal decision has allowed an issuer a cause of action for damages.[43] The Delaware Chancery Court has held, however, that a misleading Schedule 13D may give rise to a damages claim under state law. That case arose out of the failed attempt by NACCO Industries, Inc. ("NACCO") to acquire Applica Inc. ("Applica").[44] NACCO alleged that, while it and Applica were negotiating a merger agreement in 2006, Applica insiders provided information to the Harbinger hedge funds. Harbinger acquired a substantial stake in Applica (which ultimately reached 40 percent) but reported only an investment purpose on its Schedules 13D, disclaiming any intent to control Applica. After NACCO agreed to the merger, communications between Harbinger and Applica continued. Eventually, Harbinger amended its Schedule 13D and made a topping bid for Applica, which then terminated the NACCO merger agreement. After a bidding contest with NACCO, Harbinger succeeded in acquiring Applica.

NACCO brought claims against Applica for, among other things, common law fraud based on the alleged inaccuracy of Harbinger's Schedule 13D disclosures. The Court upheld the fraud claims and dismissed Harbinger's contention that all claims related to Schedules 13D belong in federal court. The Court held instead that, when a Delaware entity engages in fraud, even in an SEC filing required by the Exchange Act, it should expect that it can be held to account in the Delaware courts. The Court rejected the argument that one need not disclose any intent other than an investment intent until one actually makes a bid.

---

42. Exchange Act § 21(d)(1), 15 U.S.C. § 78u(d)(1).

43. Hallwood Realty Partners, L.P. v. Gotham Partners, L.P., 286 F.3d 613, 620 (2d Cir. 2001) (holding, in a case of first impression for that circuit, that there is no private right of action for damages to issuers under § 13(d)). *Also see* Dan River, Inc. v. Unitex Ltd., 624 F.2d 1216, 1224 (4th Cir. 1980) (issuer can require filer of an incorrect Schedule 13D to amend such filing until it is accurate); Ind. Nat'l Corp. v. Rich, 712 F.2d 1180, 1184, 1186 (7th Cir. 1983) (issuer has right to injunctive relief); Gearhart Indus., Inc. v. Smith Int'l. Inc., 741 F.2d 707, 714, 717 (5th Cir. 1984) (issuer must demonstrate likelihood of irreparable harm to apply for injunctive relief); and Chevron Corp. v. Pennzoil Co., 974 F.2d 1156, 1158 (9th Cir. 1992).

44. NACCO Industries, Inc. v. Applica Inc., CA No. 2541-VCL (Del. Ch. Dec. 22, 2009) 2009 Del.Ch. Lexis 217.

2. Exchange Act Section 16(a) Filing Requirements

Exchange Act section 16[45] requires any person who directly or indirectly beneficially owns (discussed below) more than 10 percent of any class of equity securities registered under the Exchange Act, or who is an officer or director of an issuer with a class so registered (each, an "insider"), to report that person's beneficial ownership of and transactions in such securities.

Investment advisers and hedge funds usually are more concerned about the 10 percent beneficial ownership test than the "officer" or "director" definitions, because most do not serve as officers or directors of portfolio companies. Beneficial ownership under Exchange Act section 16 is determined using a 2-part test. The first beneficial ownership test is applied to determine if a person owns more than 10 percent of any class of equity securities registered under the Exchange Act (a "10 percent holder"). Because of the extent of their stock holdings, 10 percent holders are deemed to have the potential to gain nonpublic information about an issuer. Accordingly, 10 percent holders are subject to the filing and short-swing profit recapture requirements of section 16. The second beneficial ownership test, the "pecuniary interest" test, is applied to a 10 percent holder to identify the profit potential of the holder's securities holdings, which holdings and transactions the holder must report, and which such transactions give rise to short-swing profit liability.

i. Beneficial Ownership

The first beneficial ownership test under section 16 generally applies the same analysis, relating to the possession of voting or dispositive power, used under Exchange Act section 13(d).[46] A person that has or shares the power to vote or dispose of a security beneficially owns that security for purposes of this test. The SEC has stated that the purchase or sale of a security-based swap can provide incidents of ownership comparable to direct ownership of the underlying equity security. The SEC also stated that a person who has the right to acquire securities that would cause the person to own more than 10 percent of a class of equity securities through a security-based swap that confers a right to receive equity at settlement or otherwise would be subject to section 16.[47]

A federal or state registered investment adviser may, however, exclude from its beneficial ownership any shares held in a customer or fiduciary account in the ordinary course of business, if and so long as the securities were acquired and are held without the purpose or effect of changing or influencing control of the issuer. A control person and parent holding company of such an investment adviser may also rely on this exclusion from beneficial ownership if such person or company owns, directly and indirectly, no more than 1 percent of that class of securities.[48]

---

45. 15 U.S.C. § 78p(a).
46. *See* § 13.1.1.i, *supra.*
47. Exchange Act Release No. 64628 (June 8, 2011), 76 F.R. 34579 (June 14, 2011).
48. Exchange Act Rule 16a-1(a)(1)(vii), 17 C.F.R. § 240.16a-1(a)(1)(vii).

ii. Pecuniary Interest

Under the pecuniary interest test, a beneficial owner is "any person who, directly or indirectly, through any contract, arrangement, understanding, relationship or otherwise, has or shares a direct or indirect pecuniary interest in the equity securities."[49] A "direct pecuniary interest" is defined as "the opportunity, directly or indirectly, to profit or share in any profit derived from a transaction in the subject securities."[50] The investment adviser to a hedge fund may be deemed to have an "indirect pecuniary interest" with respect to, among other things:

- if the investment adviser is also the general partner of the hedge fund, its proportionate interest in the portfolio securities held by the hedge fund, which is the greater of its share of the hedge fund's profits or its capital account in the hedge fund;[51] some commentators have suggested that if a partnership agreement specifies different profits participations for different types of income, the appropriate percentage would be that related to capital gains;[52]
- securities held by immediate family members of the investment adviser sharing the same household; and
- all of the securities in a hedge fund, if the investment adviser receives a performance fee or performance allocation and either (1) the performance fee or allocation is calculated over a period of less than 1 year or (2) equity securities of the issuer in question account for more than 10 percent of the hedge fund's market value.[53] Thus, an investment adviser that receives quarterly performance allocations must include all of the hedge fund's securities in computing its own pecuniary interest. An investment adviser also will need to be especially vigilant with respect to this test, if the hedge fund's investment strategy involves taking large positions in a few issuers, or if the hedge fund also has significant other assets managed by other investment advisers that use the same strategy.

A 10 percent holder is also deemed to have an indirect pecuniary interest in securities that it has a right to acquire through the exercise of any derivative security (such as a put or call), whether or not that security is presently exercisable.[54] The SEC has stated that the holder of fixed-price derivative securities can have an indirect pecuniary interest in the underlying securities. The SEC believes that, because an insider's opportunity to profit through a security-based swap is not different from the opportunity to profit through any other fixed-price derivative, holdings and transactions in security-based swaps

49. Exchange Act Rule 16a-1(a)(2), 17 C.F.R. § 240.16a-1(a)(2).
50. Exchange Act Rule 16a-1(a)(2)(i), 17 C.F.R. § 240.16a-1(a)(2)(i).
51. Exchange Act Rule 16a-1(a)(2)(ii)(B), 17 C.F.R. § 240.16a-1(a)(2)(ii)(B).
52. *See, e.g.*, Arnold S. Jacobs, *Section 16 of the Securities Exchange Act,* § 2:9 (West 2013).
53. Exchange Act Rule 16a-1(a)(2)(ii)(C), 17 C.F.R. § 240.16a-1(a)(2)(ii)(C).
54. Exchange Act Rule 16a-1(a)(2)(ii)(F), 17 C.F.R. § 240.16a-1(a)(2)(ii)(F).

that are fixed-price derivative securities can provide incidents of ownership comparable to direct ownership of the underlying equity security.[55]

A typical investor in a hedge fund does not need to make any section 16 filings and does not have short-swing profit liability for securities held by the hedge fund. An investor in a hedge fund is not deemed to have a pecuniary interest in the hedge fund's portfolio securities if the investor is not a controlling shareholder of the hedge fund and does not have or share investment control over the hedge fund's portfolio.[56] A "controlling shareholder" is an investor that has the power to exercise control over the hedge fund by virtue of its interest in the hedge fund.[57] Most hedge funds grant plenary management authority to the hedge fund's general partner or manager. The investors in the hedge fund typically have no authority to remove the general partner or manager, and thus have no ability to exercise control over the hedge fund.

Because of the two prongs of the test for beneficial ownership under section 16, a hedge fund manager may be considered a 10 percent holder under the first test but not have any pecuniary interest in securities that are subject to the reporting or short-swing profit recapture provisions of section 16 under the second test. For example, a hedge fund manager ordinarily has the power to vote and dispose of securities acquired by the hedge fund (and may be unable to exclude them from the 10 percent calculation because it fails to meet the conditions described above), thereby satisfying the first test; but it may not have a pecuniary interest in such securities if it only receives an asset-based fee or a conforming performance allocation, or both, from the hedge fund (thereby failing the second test). In such case, the investment adviser must file a beneficial ownership report on Form 3, because all insiders must file a Form 3, but the report may either state that no securities are beneficially owned, or report the securities but disclaim beneficial ownership of them. Such an investment adviser would not be required to file Forms 4 or 5 to report changes in its beneficial ownership if it has no pecuniary interest in the securities, because only changes to beneficial ownership that reflect changes in the insider's pecuniary interest are required to be reported on Forms 4 and 5.

iii. Filing Requirements and Deadlines

a. Initial Report: Form 3

A person who becomes an insider generally must file an initial ownership report on Form 3 within 10 days after becoming an insider.[58] The report must disclose all equity securities of the issuer in which the insider has a pecuniary

55. Exchange Act Release No. 64628 (June 8, 2011), 76 F.R. 114 (June 14, 2011).

56. Exchange Act Rule 16a-1(a)(2)(iii), 17 C.F.R. § 240.16a-1(a)(2)(iii); Widett, Slater & Goldman, P.C., SEC No-Action Letter (Mar. 25, 1992).

57. Exchange Act Rule 16a-1(a)(2)(iii), 17 C.F.R. § 240.16a-1(a)(2)(iii).

58. Exchange Act Rule 16a-3, 17 C.F.R. § 240.16a-3; Securities Act Release No. 8230 (May 7, 2003), 68 F.R. 25,788 (May 13, 2003). The Dodd-Frank Act authorizes the SEC to fix by rule an earlier filing deadline. Dodd-Frank Act, Pub. L. No. 111-203, § 929R(b)(2), 124 Stat. 1376 (2010). At this writing, the SEC has not done so.

interest, whether or not those securities are of a class that is registered under the Exchange Act.[59]

b. Subsequent Reports: Form 4

When an insider's pecuniary interest in the securities changes, or if the insider has purchased or sold any security-based swap agreements or security-based swaps with respect to such securities, the insider must file a report on Form 4 with the SEC before the end of the second business day following the day on which the transaction resulting in such change or involving any such security-based swap agreement or security-based swap is executed.[60]

c. Annual Report: Form 5

Every person who was an insider of an issuer at any time during the issuer's fiscal year must file an annual report on Form 5 within 45 days after the end of that fiscal year, to report (a) previously unreported transactions for the fiscal year that were required to have been reported but were not, (b) transactions exempt from short-swing profit recapture under Exchange Act section 16(b) (other than, among other things, exempt exercises and conversions of derivative securities) and not reported voluntarily on Form 4, and (c) any small acquisitions or series of acquisitions in a 6-month period during the issuer's fiscal year that in the aggregate do not exceed $10,000 market value.[61] An insider with no transactions reportable on Form 5 for a fiscal year is not required to file a report on Form 5 for that year.[62]

iv. Delivery Requirements

Forms 3, 4 and 5 must be filed with the SEC through its EDGAR system.[63] Copies of the reports filed with the SEC must also be sent to the issuer but are not required to be filed with any exchange.[64]

v. Noncompliance

a. SEC Penalties

The SEC may require an investment adviser and hedge fund to file the reports required under section 16(a), if they do not do so of their own accord. The SEC may also levy fines or recommend criminal prosecution for violations of section 16(a).[65]

---

59. Exchange Act § 16(a)(3)(A), 15 U.S.C. § 78p(a)(3)(A); Exchange Act Rule 16a-2, 17 C.F.R. § 240.16a-2.

60. Exchange Act § 16(a)(2)(C), 15 U.S.C. § 78p(a)(2)(C); Exchange Act Rule 16a-3(g)(1), 17 C.F.R. § 240.16a-3(g)(1); Securities Act Release No. 8230 (May 7, 2003), 68 F.R. 25,788 (May 13, 2003).

61. Exchange Act Rule 16a-3(f)(1), 17 C.F.R. § 240.16a-3(f)(1).

62. Exchange Act Rule 16a-3(f)(2), 17 C.F.R. § 240.16a-3(f)(2).

63. Regulation S-T, Rule 101(a)(iii), 17 C.F.R. § 232.101(a)(iii).

64. Dodd-Frank Act § 929(b)(1), 124 Stat. 1376 (2010).

65. Exchange Act § 21(d)(1), 15 U.S.C. § 78u(d)(1).

b. No Private Right of Action

The courts have not sustained any claim of a private right of action, whether for injunction relief or damages, for an investment adviser's or hedge fund's failure to file the required reports under section 16(a).[66]

3. Exchange Act Section 16(b) Short-Swing Profits

Insiders are subject to liability for "short-swing" trades that produce profits. Under Exchange Act section 16(b),[67] an insider (including a 10 percent holder) may be required to disgorge to the issuer any profits it realized or is deemed to have realized from its purchases and sales or sales and purchases of the issuer's securities, or any security-based swap agreement involving any such security, within any 6-month period.[68] Each 10 percent holder[69] is subject to the short-swing profit rule to the extent of that person's pecuniary interest in the securities.[70]

The transaction that results in a person becoming a 10 percent beneficial owner is not subject to the short-swing profit recapture rules, unless the person is already otherwise subject to Exchange Act section 16 with respect to the same issuer (for example, the person is an officer or director of the issuer).[71] Complex and technical issues are involved in computing profits received, matching purchases and sales of securities within a 6-month period, determining which types of transactions constitute purchases and sales, and determining which transactions are exempt from Exchange Act sections 16(a) and 16(b). Those issues are not addressed in this book.[72]

Issuers and shareholders (derivatively, if the issuer fails to bring a suit) are the only persons authorized to bring actions pursuant to section 16(b). The SEC has no authority to sue for disgorgement, to impose a penalty or to seek a penalty from any court.[73] Typically, actions brought against hedge funds and their managers for disgorgement of short-swing profits are the result of the efforts of plaintiffs' attorneys who file such actions nominally on behalf of a shareholder to obtain a fee from the issuer if such efforts actually result in recovering short-swing profits.[74]

---

66. Arnold S. Jacobs, *§ 16 of the Securities Exchange Act*, § 2:1 (West 2013).
67. 15 U.S.C. § 78p(b).
68. *Id.*
69. *See* § 13.1.2, *supra*.
70. CBI Industries, Inc. v. Horton, 682 F.2d 643, 646 (7th Cir. 1982).
71. Exchange Act Rule 16a-2(c), 17 C.F.R. § 240.16a-2(c).
72. *See generally*, Arnold S. Jacobs, *Section 16 of the Securities Exchange Act* (West 2013); and Peter J. Romeo & Alan L. Dye, *The Section 16 Deskbook* (E.P. Executive Press, Inc. Winter 2012).
73. Exchange Act § 16(b), 15 U.S.C. § 78p(b).
74. *See generally*, Peter J. Romeo & Alan L. Dye, *The Section 16 Deskbook*, E.P. Executive Press, Inc. (Winter 2012).

4. Exchange Act Section 16(c) Short Sale Prohibition

An issuer's insiders generally are prohibited from effecting short sales (except for certain short sales against the box) in the issuer's equity securities.[75]

5. Exchange Act Section 13(f) Filing Requirements

i. General Reporting Requirements

Any investment adviser, including a hedge fund manager, or a hedge fund that, on the last trading day of any month of a calendar year, exercises investment discretion over or owns section 13(f) securities with an aggregate value of at least $100,000,000 is deemed an "institutional investment manager" under Exchange Act section 13(f) and as such is required to report to the SEC on Form 13F[76] its holdings as of December 31 of that year.[77] Section 13(f) securities are generally equity securities traded on U.S. stock exchanges (and certain security-based swaps that cause the filer to be deemed to own such securities). The initial report is due by February 14 of the following year. Thereafter, a Form 13F filing is required within 45 days after the end of each calendar quarter. The last Form 13F filing required is with respect to the third quarter of the calendar year after the calendar year in which the investment adviser does not have investment discretion over, or the hedge fund does not own, at least $100,000,000 invested in section 13(f) securities on the last trading day of any month.[78]

An institutional investment manager is deemed to exercise investment discretion over all accounts over which any person under its control exercises investment discretion.[79] Therefore, an investment adviser may be required to include personal securities portfolios over which its employees and other persons under its control exercise investment discretion.[80] Filed Forms 13F are publicly available unless the investment adviser applies to the SEC for and is granted confidential treatment. Confidential treatment is rarely granted.[81]

---

75. *See* § 13.6.4, *infra.*
76. Exchange Act Release No. 40934 (Jan. 12, 1999), 64 F.R. 2,843 (Jan. 19, 1999).
77. Exchange Act Rule 13f-1(a)(1), 17 C.F.R. § 240.13f-1(a)(1).
78. *Id.*
79. Exchange Act Rule 13f-1(b), 17 C.F.R. § 240.13f-1(b).
80. *But see* Division of Investment Management: Frequently Asked Questions About Form 13F, Question 3 (August 2013), *available at* http://www.sec.gov/divisions/investment/13ffaq.htm, which states that a natural person who exercises investment discretion over his or her own account is not an institutional investment manager.
81. In October 2006, a hedge fund manager requested confidential treatment of all of its hedge fund's positions on the grounds that the required disclosure would constitute a "taking" of property (that is, intellectual property regarding the hedge fund's positions) without just compensation in violation of the Fifth Amendment of the U.S. Constitution. The U.S. Court of Appeals for the D.C. Circuit dismissed the constitutional challenge to the regulations as unripe and denied the challenges to the disclosure of information to the SEC as compelled speech and as a regulatory taking. Full Value Advisors, LLC v. SEC, 633 F.3d 1101 (D.C. Cir. 2011), *cert. denied*, Full Value Advisors, LLC v. SEC, 131 S.Ct. 3003 (2011).

ii. Proxy Voting Reporting Requirements for 13F Filers

Exchange Act section 14A(d), added by the Dodd-Frank Act, requires an investment adviser that is required to file a Form 13F to report at least annually how it voted on all executive-compensation-related shareholder votes required by Exchange Act sections 14A(a) and (b) (each, a "Section 14A Vote").[82] Section 14A Votes relate to the approval of executive compensation, the frequency of executive compensation approval and the approval of executive compensation that relates to an acquisition, merger, consolidation, or proposed sale or other disposition of all or substantially all of an issuer's assets.

To implement section 14(A)(d), the SEC has proposed rule and form amendments that, if adopted, would require such investment advisers to file records of their Section 14A Votes with the SEC via EDGAR on Form N-PX by August 31 of each year for the preceding 12-month period ended June 30.[83] An investment adviser would not be required to file a report for the 12-month period ending June 30 of the calendar year in which the investment adviser's initial Form 13F is due.[84] An investment adviser would be required to report a Section 14A Vote for each security that the investment adviser has or shares the power to vote or direct the vote, directly or indirectly.[85] The first reports on Form N-PX were to cover Section 14A Votes at meetings that occurred on or after January 21, 2011 (and thus the first reports would have been required to be filed by August 31, 2011). At this writing, however, the SEC has not adopted these rules.

iii. Potential Short-Sale Reporting Requirements for 13F Filers

Exchange Act section 13(f)(2) requires the SEC to promulgate rules for the public disclosure of short sales on a monthly basis, including "the name of the issuer and the title, class, CUSIP number, aggregate amount of the number [*sic*] of short sales of each security, and any additional information" that the SEC determines.[86] The SEC appears to have the authority to apply the short-sale reporting requirements to all short sellers, although it may limit the reporting requirements to some subset of short sellers, such as short sellers that are institutional investment managers required to file Forms 13F. At this writing, the SEC has not proposed those rules.

6. State Anti-Takeover Statutes

State anti-takeover laws may affect a hedge fund's rights as a large shareholder. For example, some state statutes require approval of an issuer's board of directors or shareholders before a shareholder (or affiliated shareholders collectively) may acquire stock representing more than a specified percentage interest in

---

82. 15 U.S.C. § 78N-1(d).
83. *See* Exchange Act Release No. 63123 (Oct. 18, 2010), 75 F.R. 66,622 (Oct. 28, 2010).
84. *Id.* (to be codified at 17 C.F.R. § 240.14Ad-1(b)).
85. *Id.* (to be codified at 17 C.F.R. § 240.14Ad-1(a)).
86. 17 U.S.C. § 78m(f)(2).

the issuer. Such a state statute typically applies with respect to issuers that are incorporated in that state. If an investment adviser's hedge fund and other clients collectively exceed the prescribed percentage, any such hedge fund or client may lose its right to vote its shares, or the transaction that caused the hedge fund and clients to exceed the percentage may be voided.[87] Some states empower the issuer in such cases to redeem the controlling shareholder's shares at the shareholder's average purchase price.[88]

Statutes of other states, such as Delaware and New York, target tender offers instead of merely large shareholdings.[89] Those statutes generally prohibit specified business combinations between large shareholders and issuers. For many hedge fund managers, these statutes are less worrisome because, as passive investors, the managers do not plan to acquire or engage in other transactions with the companies in which they invest. The definitions of the business combinations that are subject to these statutes, however, typically are written broadly, so investment advisers should review them carefully before assuming that their passive investments will not cause complications under these statutes.

Some of these state statutes allow an issuer to opt out of the anti-takeover provisions by amending its charter documents. An investment adviser should review the issuer's charter documents in considering whether those state statutes apply.

7. Issuer's Takeover Defenses

Before taking a substantial position in an issuer's securities, an investment adviser should investigate whether the issuer has adopted takeover defenses that may affect any large shareholding, even if the investment adviser does not intend to attempt a takeover or to influence management. Some such mechanisms may be in the issuer's charter documents or a contract, and all should be available from the SEC.

8. Hart-Scott-Rodino Filings

Under the Hart-Scott-Rodino Antitrust Improvements Act of 1976 (the "HSR Act"), an investment adviser (or one or more of the hedge funds or other clients whose securities portfolios it manages) may be required to file a confidential notice with the the Federal Trade Commission (the "FTC") and the Department of Justice (the "DOJ") before acquiring a substantial amount of voting securities or assets of an issuer (whether the issuer's securities are publicly traded or

87. *See, e.g.,* Ohio Gen. Corp. L. § 1701.831, Ohio Rev. Code Anno. § 1701.831 (Lexis Nexis 2010).

88. *See, e.g.,* Nevada Gen. Corp. L. § 78-3792, Nev. Rev. Stat. Ann. § 78-3792 (Lexis Nexis 2010).

89. *See, e.g.,* Delaware Gen. Corp. L. § 203, 8 Del. C. § 203; N.Y.L. 1985 Ch. 915 Bus. Corp. L. § 513(e), NYCLS Bus. Corp. § 513(e).

privately held).[90] After the notice is filed, the FTC and DOJ are afforded a statutory period for review of the competitive effects of the transaction.

Various ownership thresholds trigger a filing requirement under the HSR Act, and the computation of each threshold depends on the facts and circumstances. Generally, an investment adviser should review whether an HSR filing is required if the investment adviser, its affiliates, and the hedge funds and the other accounts they manage acquire (a) more than the amount specified by the FTC (the FTC adjusts this amount annually) of an issuer's voting securities or (b) more than 50 percent of an issuer's voting securities.

Investment advisers routinely rely on two provisions of the HSR Act that limit the scope of the filing requirement. First, an acquisition of voting securities is exempt from the HSR Act filing requirements if it is made "solely for the purpose of investment" and if, as a result of such acquisition, the securities acquired or held do not exceed 10 percent of the issuer's outstanding voting securities. Securities are acquired solely for investment purposes if the person acquiring the securities has no intention of participating in the formulation, determination or direction of the issuer's basic business decisions. Many investment advisers to hedge funds are passive investors for which this exemption may be useful, but so-called activist investment advisers may not be able to rely on this exemption.

Second, an investment adviser need not aggregate positions in a hedge fund that it manages with another fund or account for purposes of the HSR Act calculation, if (1) with respect to any such fund that is organized as a corporation (for example, an offshore corporation), the investment adviser and its affiliates do not hold 50 percent or more of the outstanding voting securities of such fund[91] and do not have the power to designate the directors of such fund,[92] and (2) with respect to any such fund that is organized as a limited partnership or limited liability company, the investment adviser and its affiliates do not have the right to 50 percent or more of such fund's profits or, on dissolution, 50 percent or more of such fund's assets.[93]

9. Speculative Position Limits and Reporting Obligations

The CFTC, the SEC and various futures exchanges establish maximum position limits on commodities, futures and swaps.

The CFTC also establishes reportable position thresholds for various futures contracts. Traders (including hedge funds) that hold contracts at or above the specified threshold amounts ("reportable positions") are required to make

---

90. *See* U.S.A. v. James D. Dondero (Complaint for Civil Penalties for Failure to Comply with the Premerger Reporting Requirements of the Hart-Scott-Rodino Act), for an example of an action against a hedge fund manager that did not make the required filings, *available at* http://www.ftc.gov/os/caselist/0510184/complaint.pdf (last visited May 14, 2013).

91. HSR Rule 801.1(b)(1), 16 C.F.R. § 801.1(b)(1).

92. HSR Rule 801.1 (b), 16 C.F.R. § 801.1(b).

93. HSR Rule 801.1(b)(2), 16 C.F.R. § 801.1(b)(2).

specified reports and keep specified records.[94] If a trader has a reportable position and receives a special call from the CFTC, it must file a Statement of Reporting Trader on CFTC Form 40 with the CFTC, at the time and place specified in the call.[95] In the Statement of Reporting Trader, various information about the trader and controlling persons must be disclosed, such as the trader's name, address and principal business; whether trades are made for a commodity pool or for personal use; the type of trader; the trader's registration status with the CFTC; and the name, address and telephone number of each person who controls the trader's trading.[96] A trader with reportable positions must maintain books and records that log details about all positions and transactions in the commodity, as well as all cash commodities, their products and by-products and all commercial activities that the trader hedges in the futures contract in which the trader has reportable positions.[97] Information from these records must be available to the CFTC on request.[98]

To determine whether a trader has exceeded a position limit or has a reportable position, positions in multiple accounts that the trader (whether by power of attorney or otherwise) directly or indirectly controls generally must be aggregated.[99] The CFTC and the various futures exchanges have enforcement authority over the respective maximum position limits that each sets, and the CFTC also has authority to enforce violations of exchange-set position limits.[100]

The SEC is similarly authorized to establish reportable position thresholds for security-based swaps, and to require traders that hold contracts at or above the specified threshold amounts to make specified reports and keep specified records, although it has not done so as of this writing.[101]

10. Form SLT

The U.S. Department of the Treasury implemented Form SLT (Aggregate Holdings of Long-Term Securities by U.S. and Foreign Residents) to gather monthly information about long-term foreign securities held by certain U.S. residents and long-term U.S. securities held by foreign residents (Reportable Securities), including hedge funds and their managers.[102] Only entities file Form SLT.[103] Natural persons do not file.

In general, 2 categories of persons required to file Form SLT are relevant to a hedge fund manager. The first are U.S. investors (such as a domestic hedge fund managed by the hedge fund manager) that own certain types of

94. CEA Rules 15.01-15.03, 17 C.F.R. §§ 15.01-15.03.
95. CEA Rule 18, 17 C.F.R. § 18.
96. CEA Rule 18.04(a), 17 C.F.R. § 18.04(a).
97. CEA Rule 18.05, 17 C.F.R. § 18.05.
98. *Id.*
99. CEA Rules 150.4(b) and 150.5(g), 17 C.F.R. §§ 150.4(b) and 150.5(g).
100. CEA Rule 150.5, 17 C.F.R. §150.5.
101. Exchange Act § 10B, 15 U.S.C. § 78j-2.
102. 76 F.R. 37403 (June 27, 2011).
103. Form SLT, General Instructions, Part II.A.

non-U.S. securities (for example, stock of a non-U.S. issuer or interests in a non-U.S. hedge fund). The second are U.S. issuers (again, such as the same domestic hedge fund) whose securities are held by non-U.S. investors (such as a non-U.S. hedge fund). As a result, a hedge fund manager may be required to file Form SLT if the hedge funds that it manages and their subsidiaries hold Reportable Securities having an aggregate fair market value of $1,000,000,000 or more.[104]

i. "Reportable Security"

A security must meet all 4 of the following tests to be a Reportable Security:[105]

- The security must not be held by a U.S. custodian. Any security maintained in a brokerage account in the United States is not a Reportable Security. Accordingly, Reportable Securities generally will be securities held in non-U.S. brokerage accounts or securities that are not represented by a certificate (such as an interest in a limited liability company).
- The security must be a long-term security. All equity securities (including interests in a limited liability company) are "long-term securities." Other securities are long-term securities if they either have no maturity or have maturity dates of more than 1 year.
- The security must either be (a) a security issued by a non-U.S. issuer and held by a U.S. investor, or (b) a security issued by a U.S. issuer and held by a non-U.S. investor.
- The security must not be a direct investment. A "direct investment" generally is an investment in which the investor owns at least 10 percent of the issuer's voting securities or equivalent interests. Limited partner interests generally are not direct investments, even if the investor owns 10 percent or more of the issuer.[106]

ii. Persons Required to File

For a hedge fund manager that is required to file, Reportable Securities typically include:

- interests in U.S. master funds held by foreign feeder funds;
- interests in foreign master funds held by U.S. feeder funds;
- interests held by third-party foreign investors in a U.S. fund of which the investment adviser is the general partner; and
- portfolio securities held by U.S. funds that are issued by foreign issuers and are not held by a U.S. custodian.[107]

A hedge fund manager must file a consolidated report for all U.S. entities in its organization and all U.S. hedge funds that it manages if the aggregate

104. Form SLT, General Instructions, Part II.C.
105. 76 F.R. 37404 (June 27, 2011); Form SLT, General Instructions, Part II.F.
106. Form SLT, General Instructions, Part VI, Glossary.
107. *See* Form SLT, General Instructions, Part II.B.

fair value of Reportable Securities in all such accounts is $1,000,000,000 or more.[108]

iii. Information Reported

If a hedge fund manager is required to file Form SLT, the hedge fund manager should complete Part B of Form SLT. Part A of Form SLT is completed by U.S. custodians. If Reportable Securities are held in custody with a U.S. prime broker, such as a hedge fund's portfolio securities, the custodian is responsible for reporting those securities. [109] They are not reported by the hedge fund manager or the hedge fund (although an investment adviser should not rely on a custodian to determine the investment adviser's filing obligation).

iv. Time and Manner of Filing

Form SLT must be filed monthly and must include the required information as of the last business day of each calendar month. The Form for any month is due on the 23rd of the next month or the first business day thereafter if the 23rd is a Saturday, Sunday or holiday. If an entity's Reportable Securities on the last business day of any month exceed the $1,000,000,000 threshold, then the entity must begin filing Form SLT as of that month and must continue to file for each remaining month in that calendar year whether or not its Reportable Securities continue to meet the reporting threshold. Investment advisers must file Form SLT with the Federal Reserve Bank of New York.[110]

v. Confidentiality of Information Reported

The Department of the Treasury has stated that it, the Board of Governors of the Federal Reserve System and the Federal Reserve Banks will keep the information reported by individual respondents on Form SLT confidential. Aggregate data derived from Forms SLT may be published or publicly disclosed only in a manner that will not reveal the amounts reported by any individual respondent.[111]

vi. Penalty for Failing to File

Filing Form SLT is required by law.[112] Failure to report can result in a civil penalty of from $2,500 to $25,000. Willful failure to report can result in criminal prosecution and on conviction a fine of up to $10,000 and imprisonment of up to 1 year, or both. Any officer, director, employee or agent of any corporation who knowingly participates in such violation may, on conviction, be punished by a similar fine, imprisonment or both.[113]

108. Form SLT, General Instructions, Part II.C.
109. Form SLT, General Instructions, Part III.
110. Form SLT, General Instructions, Part II.H.
111. Form SLT, Instructions, Introduction, Part I.C.
112. 22 U.S.C. §§ 286f and 3103; 31 C.F.R. § 128.1(a).
113. 22 U.S.C. §§ 3105(a), (b) and (c); 31 C.F.R. §§ 128.4(a), (b) and (c).

§ 13.2 Form PF

In October 2011, the SEC and the CFTC adopted rules[114] requiring investment advisers to larger private funds to file Form PF. Form PF elicits substantial nonpublic information about investment advisers and private funds to assist the SEC and CFTC in monitoring potential systemic risk.

An investment adviser must file Form PF if it has at least $150,000,000 of regulatory assets under management ("AUM") attributable to private funds and is registered (or required to be registered) either with the SEC as an investment adviser or with the CFTC as a commodity pool operator or commodity trading adviser (each, a "Private Fund Adviser").[115] "Regulatory AUM" is calculated in the same way that it is for purposes of Form ADV.[116] A "private fund" is a fund that would be an investment company under the ICA, but for the exemption under ICA section 3(c)(1) or 3(c)(7).[117]

Form PF is filed with the SEC, and may be made available to the CFTC, the Financial Stability Oversight Council, other federal agencies and self-regulatory organizations.[118] The SEC and CFTC are required to keep all Form PF information confidential and cannot be compelled to disclose it pursuant to the Freedom of Information Act, but may use it for inspection and enforcement purposes.

Most of the guidance for completing Form PF is in the Instructions to Form PF. To determine whether it meets the $150,000,000 reporting threshold, a Private Fund Adviser must aggregate the regulatory AUM of all –

- private funds it advises (without double-counting funds that are part of the same master-feeder structure),[119]
- parallel managed accounts it advises, excluding accounts that individually or in the aggregate exceed the size of the parallel private funds with which they are managed, and
- private funds and parallel managed accounts managed by the adviser's related persons.

"Parallel managed accounts" are accounts that pursue substantially the same investment objective and strategy as one or more of the Private Fund Adviser's private funds and that invest side by side in substantially the same positions. "Related persons" are advisory affiliates of the Private Fund Adviser and persons under common control with the Private Fund Adviser.

---

114. Advisers Act Release No. 3308 (Oct. 31, 2011), 76 F.R. 71128 (Nov. 16, 2011). Form PF itself is at http://www.sec.gov/rules/final/2011/ia-3308-formpf.pdf. The SEC adopted Advisers Act Rule 204(b)-1, 17 C.F.R. 275.204(b)(1). The CFTC adopted CEA Rule 4.27, 17 C.F.R. § 4.27. While both the SEC and CFTC adopted Form PF, only the SEC adopted §§ 3 and 4 of Form PF.

115. Advisers Act Rule 204(b)-1, 17 C.F.R. § 275.204(b)-1.

116. *See* §§ 2.2 and 2.4, *supra*.

117. Advisers Act § 202(a)(29), 15 U.S.C. § 80b-2(a)(29). *See* Chapter 3, *supra*.

118. Advisers Act §§ 204(b)(1), (9) and (10), 15 U.S.C. § 80b-4(b)(1), (9) and (10).

119. Form PF, General Instructions 5 and 6.

An investment adviser may disregard a private fund's equity investments in other private funds for both reporting thresholds and responding to questions on Form PF as long as it does so consistently,[120] although the investment adviser does not need to exclude those investments when reporting the private fund's performance.[121] A Private Fund Adviser that aggregates parallel managed accounts with a fund for determining whether it crosses a reporting threshold should disregard those accounts for reporting purposes. A registered investment adviser that sub-advises a fund for which the principal investment adviser is filing reports need not report the sub-advised funds.

A Private Fund Adviser that advises particular types of private funds and reaches specified levels of AUM is further identified as a "large hedge fund adviser," a "large liquidity fund adviser" or a "large private equity fund adviser," each of which is a "large private fund adviser." For example, a large hedge fund adviser (a "Large Hedge Fund Adviser" or "LHFA") is a Private Fund Adviser that, together with its related persons, had at least $1,500,000,000 in regulatory AUM attributable to hedge funds as of the last day of any month in the fiscal quarter preceding its most recently completed fiscal quarter, excluding any regulatory AUM that is "separately operated" (this exclusion is discussed below). While all Private Fund Advisers must file Form PF, the timing requirements for filing and the information required on Form PF depend on the Private Fund Adviser's classification, as described below. This book addresses only the requirements applicable to Large Hedge Fund Advisers and Private Fund Advisers that are not large.

The timing requirements for filing Form PF depend on the Private Fund Adviser's classification and AUM, as shown in the following table for Private Fund Advisers and Large Hedge Fund Advisers.[122]

Private Fund Adviser	Filing Obligations
Private Fund Advisers that are not large	Within 120 days after each fiscal year end.
LHFAs (by total hedge fund regulatory AUM)	
$1,500,000,000 to $5,000,000,000	Within 60 days after each calendar quarter.
Over $5,000,000,000	Within 60 days after each calendar quarter.

120. Form PF, General Instruction 5.
121. Form PF, General Instruction 7.
122. Advisers Act Release No. 3308 (Oct. 31, 2011), 76 F.R. 71128, 71157 (Nov. 16, 2011).

The information that a Private Fund Adviser must provide on Form PF depends on its AUM. A Large Hedge Fund Adviser must provide more information than a Private Fund Adviser that is not large. Form PF comprises 5 sections.[123] Every Private Fund Adviser must complete section 1. Section 2 applies only to Large Hedge Fund Advisers. Sections 3 and 4 apply only to large liquidity fund advisers and large private equity fund advisers, respectively. Section 5 applies only to Private Fund Advisers that are requesting a temporary hardship exemption from filing.

Section 1(a) requires identifying information about the Private Fund Adviser and its related persons that are reporting on the Form PF with the Private Fund Adviser, including each entity's legal name and identifying numbers, if any. The Private Fund Adviser must provide a breakdown of its regulatory AUM and net AUM for each type of fund that it manages (such as hedge, liquidity, private equity, real estate, securitized assets, venture capital and other private funds).

The Private Fund Adviser must complete a separate section 1(b) for each private fund that it manages, or each master-feeder or parallel fund structure. Section 1(b) requires each fund's legal name and identifying numbers, if any, but the Private Fund Adviser may use an internally created code instead of the actual private fund name if it wants to maintain the confidentiality of a particular fund. If the Private Fund Adviser chooses to cover a master-feeder or parallel fund on an aggregated basis, information is reported for the master fund or the largest fund in the parallel fund structure. If section 1(b) covers parallel funds on an aggregated basis, it must include identifying information for any such parallel fund.

Section 1(b) requires financial information for each reporting fund, including gross and net asset values, equity investments in other private funds and the values of parallel managed accounts. Section 1(b) also requires beneficial ownership information for each reporting fund by categories of investors.

A Private Fund Adviser that advises one or more hedge funds must complete a separate section 1(c) for each hedge fund. Because a hedge fund is a private fund, the Private Fund Adviser will complete separate sections 1(b) and 1(c) for each hedge fund. If the Private Fund Adviser aggregated a hedge fund as part of a master-feeder or parallel fund structure in section 1(b), however, it must remain consistent and provide aggregated information in section 1(c). "Hedge funds" for purposes of Form PF are private funds (other than "securitized asset funds," which are private funds whose primary purpose is to issue asset-backed securities and whose investors are primarily debt holders) with regard to which:[124]

- one or more investment advisers (or related persons of investment advisers) may be paid a performance fee or allocation calculated by taking into account unrealized gains (other than a fee or allocation that may be calculated by taking into account unrealized gains solely for the purpose of reducing such fee or allocation to reflect net unrealized losses);

123. The CFTC did not adopt §§ 3 and 4 of Form PF.

124. Form PF, Glossary of Terms.

- the private fund may borrow an amount in excess of one-half of its net asset value (NAV) or may have gross notional exposure in excess of twice its NAV (in either case, including any committed capital); or
- the private fund may sell securities or other assets short or enter into similar transactions (other than for the purpose of hedging currency exposure or managing duration).

For purposes of defining a hedge fund, an investment adviser should not net long and short positions and should include any borrowings or notional exposure of another person that are guaranteed by the private fund or that the private fund is otherwise obligated to satisfy. A commodity pool is categorized as a hedge fund for purposes of Form PF.

Section 1(c) requires the private fund's name and identification number, as well as information regarding each private fund's investment strategy, performance information, counterparties with whom the private fund has the significant credit exposure and breakdowns of trading and clearing mechanisms.

Only Large Hedge Fund Advisers must complete section 2, which has 2 parts. Section 2(a) requires aggregate information for all of the hedge funds advised by the Large Hedge Fund Adviser, including the dollar value of long and short positions as of the last day of each month of the reporting period for a variety of asset classifications and a breakdown of the percentage of its total hedge fund related NAV by geographical region and specified countries. In section 2(b), the Large Hedge Fund Adviser must provide, for each of its qualifying hedge funds, the hedge fund's name and identification number and the same information required in section 2(a) as it relates to that particular hedge fund. A "qualifying hedge fund" is a hedge fund with NAV greater than $500,000,000 as of the last day of any month in the fiscal quarter preceding the Large Hedge Fund Adviser's most recently completed fiscal quarter.[125] The calculation must include the value of any feeder funds, parallel funds and parallel managed accounts. Section 2(b) requires risk-related information for each hedge fund, information about each hedge fund's financing for each month in the reporting period and information about hedge fund provisions specific to its investors.

§ 13.3 Large Trader Registration

Exchange Act Rule 13h-1[126] requires any person designated as a large trader to file Form 13H electronically with the SEC and receive a large trader identification number, or LTID. A large trader must provide its LTID to each registered broker with which it has an account and the accounts with the broker to which

125. Form PF, Glossary of Terms.
126. 17 C.F.R. § 240.13h-1.

the LTID applies.[127] Large traders' registered brokers also must record trading information and disclose it to the SEC on request.[128]

1. Large Trader

A "large trader" is any person that:

- directly or indirectly, including through other persons controlled by such person, exercises investment discretion over one or more accounts and purchases or sells any national market system ("NMS") security for or on behalf of such accounts, by or through one or more registered brokers, in an aggregate amount equal to or greater than the identifying activity level; or
- voluntarily registers as a large trader by filing Form 13H.[129]

This definition focuses on the ultimate parent companies behind trading activities rather than subordinate persons or account owners, unless the latter independently qualify as large traders.[130] Thus, in determining whether it is a large trader, a hedge fund manager must aggregate the trades of all of the hedge funds and other client accounts for which it or its securities affiliates have investment discretion, whether or not any securities affiliate would independently meet the large trader threshold.[131] Alternatively, one or more of a parent's securities affiliates that is a large trader may elect to file Form 13H and comply with the requirements independently or may file on the parent's behalf if the securities affiliate can comply with all of the parent's filing obligations and the parent's obligation to report required LTIDs to brokers on the parent's behalf. Consequently, if a parent and its securities affiliates collectively engage in trading above the large trader threshold:

- the parent may file for itself and its securities affiliates;
- the parent and any securities affiliates may file separately; or
- one or more of the parent's securities affiliates may file on the parent's behalf if such securities affiliate or affiliates can collectively comply with all of the Form 13H filing and broker disclosure requirements on the parent's behalf.[132]

The SEC encourages (but does not require) large traders to identify subordinate persons (such as hedge funds or other client accounts) with "LTID suffixes" to facilitate information gathering.[133]

---

127. Exchange Act Rule 13h-1(b), 17 C.F.R. § 240.13h-1(b).

128. Exchange Act Rules 13h-1(d) and 13h-1(e), 17 C.F.R. §§ 240.13h-1(d) and 240.13h-1(e).

129. Exchange Act Rule 13h-1(a)(1), 17 C.F.R. § 240.13h-1(a)(1).

130. Exchange Act Release No. 64976 (July 27, 2011), 76 F.R. 46,960 (Aug. 3, 2011) (hereinafter, "LT Adopting Release").

131. Exchange Act Rules 13h-1(a)(1), 13h-1(b) and 13h-1(c), 17 C.F.R. §§ 240.13h-1(a)(1), 240.13h-1(b) and 240.13h-1(c).

132. Exchange Act Rule 13h-1(b)(3), 17 C.F.R. § 240.13h-1(b)(3).

133. LT Adopting Release, *supra,* n. 131.

2. Other Key Terms

i. Securities Affiliate

A "Securities Affiliate" is an affiliate of a large trader that exercises investment discretion over NMS securities.[134]

ii. Control

"Control" means possessing, directly or indirectly, the power to direct or cause the direction of the management and policies of a person, whether through security ownership, by contract or otherwise. A person is presumed to control an entity if the person directly or indirectly has the right to vote or direct the vote, or to sell or direct the sale, of at least 25 percent of a class of voting securities of such entity. In the case of a partnership, a person is presumed to control the partnership if the person has contributed, or has the right to receive on dissolution, 25 percent or more of the partnership's capital.[135]

iii. Investment Discretion

"Investment discretion" is the authority to make trading decisions for an account. Employees who make such decisions within the scope of their employment are deemed to do so on behalf of their employer.[136]

iv. Identifying Activity Level

"Identifying activity level" means aggregate transactions in NMS securities of at least:

- 2,000,000 shares or shares with a fair market value of $20,000,000 in a day; or
- 20,000,000 shares or shares with a fair market value of $200,000,000 in a calendar month.[137]

All transactions in NMS securities are counted, except for exercises or assignments of option contracts and certain other transactions that are not typical market trades.[138]

v. NMS Securities

"NMS security" is any security for which transaction reports are collected, processed and made available pursuant to an effective transaction reporting plan, or an effective national market system plan for reporting transactions in listed options. Thus, any equity security, exchange-traded fund or option listed on a

---

134. Instructions to Form 13H.

135. Exchange Act Rule 13h-1(a)(3), 17 C.F.R. § 240.13h-1(a)(3).

136. Exchange Act § 3(a)(35), 15 U.S.C. § 78c(3)(a)(35); LT Adopting Release, *supra,* n. 131.

137. Exchange Act Rules 13h-1(a)(1) and 13h-1(a)(7), 17 C.F.R. §§ 240.13h-1(a)(1) and 240.13h-1(a)(7).

138. Exchange Act Rule 13h-1(a)(6), 17 C.F.R. § 240.13h-1(a)(6).

U.S. securities or option exchange is an NMS security.[139] Rule 13h-1 applies to trading NMS securities through any facility, including any exchange, foreign or domestic over-the-counter market or after-hours system.[140]

3. Time of Filing

A hedge fund manager must file an initial Form 13H promptly after it first meets the definition of large trader, that is, after it first effects aggregate transactions in NMS securities that equal or exceed the identifying activity level,[141] unless its controlling person or controlled persons separately comply with the information and disclosure requirements that would otherwise apply to the hedge fund manager. The SEC has indicated that "promptly" normally means within 10 days.[142] On receiving the Form 13H, the SEC will issue an LTID to the large trader.[143] Thereafter, the large trader must file Form 13H promptly (within 10 days) after the end of any calendar quarter during which information in its last filed Form 13H becomes inaccurate and annually not later than February 14.[144]

A hedge fund manager that expects to cross the large-trader threshold at some point but has not done so may make voluntary filings to avoid the need for ongoing monitoring of its status. Any hedge fund manager that elects to file voluntarily will be treated as a large trader, and will be subject to all of the obligations of a large trader, notwithstanding that the hedge fund manager did not meet the definition of large trader at the time it registered.[145]

A large trader whose aggregate transactions at all times during the preceding calendar year were less than the identifying activity level becomes "inactive" on filing a Form 13H so stating. Thereafter, the inactive large trader is not required to file Form 13H or disclose its large-trader status unless its transactions again reach the identifying activity level (at which time it must promptly file a Form 13H).[146]

---

139. Exchange Act Regulation NMS, Rule 600, 17 C.F.R. § 242.600. Rule 600 generally provides that an NMS security is any security or class of securities for which transaction reports are collected, processed and made available pursuant to an effective transaction reporting plan, or an effective national market system plan for reporting transactions in listed options. The effective transaction reporting plans referred to in Rule 600 are the Consolidated Tape Association (CTA) Plan and the Nasdaq UTP Plan. *See* Exchange Act Release No. 51808 (June 9, 2005), 70 F.R. 37,496 (June 29, 2005). The CTA Plan includes securities quoted and traded on the New York Stock Exchange and NYSE Arca, NYSE Amex and other regional exchanges. The Nasdaq UTP Plan includes Nasdaq-listed securities and its participants generally are all of the national securities exchanges.

140. Exchange Act Release No. 61908 (Apr. 14, 2010), 75 F.R. 21,456 (Apr. 23, 2010).

141. Exchange Act Rule 13h-1(b)(1)(i), 17 C.F.R. § 240.13h-1(b)(1)(i).

142. LT Adopting Release, *supra,* n. 131.

143. *Id.*

144. Exchange Act Rule 13h-1(b), 17 C.F.R. § 240.13h-1(b).

145. LT Adopting Release, *supra,* n. 131; Instructions to Form 13H.

146. Exchange Act Rule 13h-1(b)(3)(iii), 17 C.F.R. § 240.13h-1(b)(3)(iii).

4. Confidentiality of Information Reported

Form 13H elicits information regarding a large trader's business, SEC filings, CFTC filings, organization, governance, and brokers, but that information is not publicly available. Information gathered on Form 13H is not subject to the Freedom of Information Act and, as such, is generally not subject to compelled disclosure. The SEC has stated that it is committed to protecting the confidentiality of information gathered under Rule 13h-1 to the fullest extent permitted under the law.[147]

5. Broker Reporting and Recordkeeping—Unidentified Large Traders

Rule 13h-1 imposes various monitoring, recordkeeping and reporting requirements on a registered broker that effects transactions in an account for a large trader or an unidentified large trader, whether such account is carried internally or by a nonbroker.[148] On the SEC's request, a broker must report to the SEC via the Electronic Blue Sheets system transactions in a single account that involve at least 100 shares of NMS securities.[149] Generally, the requested information must be made available on the morning of the day following the request (including Saturdays and holidays).[150]

If a registered broker knows or has reason to know that a person is not in compliance with the filing and disclosure requirements, the person is considered an "unidentified large trader."[151] In determining whether a registered broker has reason to know that a person is a large trader, the broker need take into account only transactions in NMS securities effected by or through the broker.[152] Brokers are permitted to engage in client relationships with unidentified large traders, but their reporting and recordkeeping obligations also apply to unidentified large traders. Because an unidentified large trader will not have identified itself to its brokers, they may be expected to maintain broad monitoring mechanisms to identify clients as unidentified large traders and to record and maintain the requisite information.

§ 13.4 Trading Restricted Securities and Control Securities

A hedge fund that has purchased unregistered securities in a private offering ("Restricted Securities") directly from an issuer or an affiliate of the issuer, or that holds securities that constitute a controlling interest in an issuer, whether

147. LT Adopting Release, *supra,* n. 131.
148. Exchange Act Rule 13h-1(d), 17 C.F.R. § 240.13h-1(d).
149. Exchange Act Rule 13h-1(e), 17 C.F.R. § 240.13h-1(e).
150. Exchange Act Rule 13h-1(d)(5), 17 C.F.R. § 240.13h-1(d)(5).
151. Exchange Act Rule 13h-1(a)(9), 17 C.F.R. § 240.13h-1(a)(9).
152. *Id.*

or not those securities are registered ("Control Securities"), may not resell those securities unless either the resale is registered under Securities Act section 5[153] or an exemption from the registration requirements of section 5 is available.

Securities Act section 4(a)(1)[154] exempts from the registration requirements of Securities Act section 5 transactions by any person other than an issuer, underwriter or dealer. An "issuer" is any "person who issues or proposes to issue any security."[155] A "dealer" is any "person who engages either for all or part of his time, directly or indirectly, as agent, broker, or principal, in the business of offering, buying, selling, or otherwise dealing or trading in securities issued by another person."[156] Hedge funds generally rely on the common law "trader" exception from the definition of "dealer."[157] Except in unusual circumstances, a hedge fund that desires to resell securities under Securities Act section 4(a)(1) is neither an issuer nor a dealer.

The definition of "underwriter" is framed in terms of the purchaser's mental state and therefore is subjectively applied. An "underwriter" is "any person who has purchased from an issuer with a view to, or offers or sells for an issuer in connection with, the distribution of any security, or participates or has a direct or indirect participation in any such undertaking . . . ."[158] The SEC has adopted Securities Act Rule 144[159] and has acquiesced in an informal exemption commonly called "Section 4(1 1/2)" that exempts private resales of Restricted Securities and Control Securities by deeming the resellers of those securities not to be underwriters within the meaning of Securities Act section 4(a)(1). Rule 144 applies to any type of resale of Restricted Securities and resales of Control Securities through brokers on securities exchanges or over-the-counter markets.[160]

1. Securities Act Rule 144

Rule 144[161] allows a holder of Restricted Securities or Control Securities to resell those shares without being deemed to be an underwriter and, therefore, without registering those shares pursuant to Securities Act section 5, if the reseller and the resale satisfy the conditions of Rule 144. Those conditions are summarized below.

---

153. 15 U.S.C. § 77(e).

154. 15 U.S.C. § 77(d)(1).

155. Securities Act § 2(a)(4), 15 U.S.C. § 77b(a)(4).

156. Securities Act § 2(a)(12), 15 U.S.C. § 77b(a)(12).

157. Norman S. Poser, *Broker-Dealer Law and Regulation*, § 14.01[A], at 14-8.1 (3rd ed. Supp. 2004). *See* Chapter 10, *supra*.

158. Securities Act § 2(a)(11), 15 U.S.C. § 77b(a)(11).

159. 17 C.F.R. § 230.144.

160. Securities Act Release No. 8813 (June 22, 2007), 72 F.R. 36,822 (July 5, 2007).

161. 17 C.F.R. § 230.144.

i. Control Securities

If a hedge fund is an affiliate of the issuer, the securities of the issuer that it owns are Control Securities (whether or not they are also Restricted Securities). Rule 144(a) defines an "affiliate" of an issuer as a person that directly, or indirectly through one or more intermediaries, controls, or is controlled by, or is under common control with, an issuer.[162] "Control" means "the possession, direct or indirect, of the power to direct or cause the direction of the management and policies of a person, whether through the ownership of voting securities, by contract, or otherwise."[163] Percentage ownership does not determine control, but the SEC staff has attempted to establish some ad hoc standards. To avoid controversy, a hedge fund may assume that it is an affiliate of the issuer if it owns 10 percent or more of the voting power of the issuer.[164] Control, however, is ultimately a question of fact and a more aggressive position may be justified in some circumstances.

ii. Holding Period

A hedge fund that acquires Control Securities in the public market is not subject to any holding period requirement under Rule 144. A hedge fund that acquires Control Securities in some other manner or that acquires Restricted Securities may sell those securities under Rule 144 after a 6-month holding period if the issuer of the security is subject to the reporting requirements of Exchange Act section 13 or 15(d), or after a 12-month holding period if the issuer is not subject to those reporting requirements. The holding period begins when the hedge fund pays the full purchase price or other consideration. A holder of Restricted Securities or Control Securities may sell short securities of the same class to hedge its position without tolling the holding period under Rule 144.[165]

A hedge fund may sell Restricted Securities of a reporting issuer under Rule 144 without limitation after the 6-month holding period, if current public information is available about the issuer. After 12 months, a hedge fund can make unlimited resales of Restricted Securities under Rule 144.

A hedge fund may sell Control Securities under Rule 144 after the requisite holding period (if any) and subject to all of the other Rule 144 requirements discussed below, including the requirements regarding current public information, volume limitations, manner of sale (for equity securities only) and Form 144 notice filing. These requirements apply whether or not the hedge fund purchased the securities in the public market.

---

162. 17 C.F.R. § 230.144(a).

163. Securities Act Regulation C, Rule 405, 17 C.F.R. § 230.405.

164. *See, e.g.,* Servo Sys., Inc., SEC No-Action Letter (Sep. 10, 1979) (owner of a 14 percent interest in the issuer deemed an affiliate); Torr Laboratories, Inc., SEC No-Action Letter (May 16, 1975) (owner of approximately 10 percent interest in the issuer deemed an affiliate); and Dataproducts Corp., SEC No-Action Letter (June 30, 1976) (owner of 2 percent of the common stock of issuer that was also represented on the issuer's board of directors deemed an affiliate).

165. Jesse M. Brill, SEC No-Action Letter (June 8, 1990).

a. Tacking (Nonaffiliates)

In calculating the holding period, a hedge fund may add or "tack" to its own holding period the holding period of prior holders of Restricted Securities, provided in general that the prior holders were not affiliates of the issuer (see exception below).[166] If, however, the shares are reacquired by an affiliate of the issuer within the holding period (thus converting the Restricted Securities into Control Securities), the affiliate may not tack the holding period of any prior holder. In that case, any subsequent resale of those Control Securities by the affiliate to a nonaffiliate purchaser will begin a new holding period for the nonaffiliate.[167]

b. Tacking (Affiliates)

A subsequent holder may tack the holding period of an affiliate of the issuer only if there is an identity of interest between the transferor and transferee.[168] For example, if a donee acquires Control Securities from an affiliate of the issuer as a gift, the donee is deemed to have acquired them when the donor-affiliate acquired them.[169]

iii. Current Public Information

Any "current public information" requirement that applies to a particular sale of Restricted Securities or Control Securities is satisfied if the issuer (a) has securities registered pursuant to Exchange Act section 12,[170] (b) has been subject to the reporting requirements of Exchange Act section 13[171] for at least 90 days preceding the sale, and (c) has filed all reports required to be filed under Exchange Act section 13 during the 12 months preceding the sale.[172] Alternatively, this requirement is satisfied if the issuer (a) has securities registered pursuant to the Securities Act, (b) has been subject to the reporting requirements of Exchange Act section 15(d)[173] for at least 90 days preceding the sale, and (c) has filed all reports required by Exchange Act section 15(d) during the 12 months preceding the sale.

iv. Volume Limits

For Control Securities that are equity securities, the maximum number of shares that a holder may sell in any 3-month period is generally the greatest of:

- 1 percent of the shares or other units of the class outstanding;
- the average weekly reported volume of trading in such securities on all national securities exchanges or reported through the automated quotation system of a registered securities association during the 4

166. Securities Act Rule 144(d)(1), 17 C.F.R. § 230.144(d)(1).
167. *Id.*
168. Securities Act Rule 144(d)(3), 17 C.F.R. § 230.144(d)(3).
169. Securities Act Rule 144(d)(3)(v), 17 C.F.R. § 230.144(d)(3)(v).
170. 15 U.S.C. § 78l.
171. 15 U.S.C. § 78m.
172. Securities Act Rule 144(c), 17 C.F.R. § 230.144(c).
173. 15 U.S.C. § 78o(d).

calendar weeks preceding the filing of the notice of sale on Form 144, or if no such notice is required, the receipt of the order to execute the transaction by the broker or the date of execution of the transaction directly with a market maker; and

- the average weekly volume of trading in such securities reported through the consolidated transaction reporting system.

For Control Securities that are debt securities, the maximum that a holder may sell in any 3-month period is generally 10 percent of a tranche (or class when the securities are nonparticipatory preferred stock). For purposes of Rule 144, debt securities include, but are not limited to, nonparticipatory preferred stock and asset-backed securities.

The volume limits apply to all such Control Securities that a hedge fund holds (that is, all securities, whether registered or unregistered, of an issuer held by a hedge fund that is an affiliate of the issuer). If the hedge fund is not an affiliate of the issuer, the volume limits apply only to the Restricted Securities held by the hedge fund.

In some circumstances, a hedge fund's sales must be aggregated with those of another person for purposes of the volume limits. For example, when 2 or more affiliates or other persons agree to act in concert for the purposes of selling securities of an issuer, all securities of the same class sold for the account of all such persons must be aggregated for the purpose of determining compliance with the volume limitation.[174] If an investment adviser manages 2 hedge funds *pari passu,* the hedge funds may be subject to this aggregation rule.[175]

v. Manner of Sale

Under Rule 144(f),[176] Control Securities (other than debt securities) may be sold only:

- in a brokers' transaction, which is a brokers' transaction executed on a customer's order on any exchange or in the over-the-counter market (but not the solicitation of such order),[177] and includes, for purposes of Rule 144, a transaction directly with a market maker,[178] in any case subject to Rule 144(g) (summarized below),[179] or

174. Securities Act Rule 144(e)(3)(vi), 17 C.F.R. § 230.144(e)(3)(vi).

175. Securities Act Release No. 6099 (Aug. 2, 1979), 44 F.R. 46,752 (Aug. 8, 1979), at n. 7 (if a fiduciary administers various trusts and estates in a manner that results in their acting in concert, they would be treated as 1 person).

176. 17 C.F.R. § 230.144(f).

177. Securities Act Rule 144(f)(1)(i), 17 C.F.R. § 230.144(f)(1)(i); Securities Act § 4(4), 15 U.S.C. § 77d(4).

178. Securities Act Rule 144(f)(ii), 17 C.F.R. § 230.144(f)(ii), which refers to Exchange Act § 3(a)(38), 15 U.S.C. § 78c(a)(88), defining "market maker" as "any specialist permitted to act as a dealer, any dealer acting in the capacity of block positioner, and any dealer who, with respect to a security, holds himself out (by entering quotations in an inter-dealer communications system or otherwise) as being willing to buy or sell such security for his own account on a regular or continuous basis."

179. Securities Act Rule 144(g), 17 C.F.R. § 230.144(g).

- in a riskless principal transaction where the offsetting trades must be executed at the same price (exclusive of an explicitly disclosed mark-up or mark-down, commission equivalent or other fee), the transaction is permitted to be reported as riskless under the rules of a self-regulatory organization, and the last 3 requirements of Rule 144(g) (summarized below) are met.[180]

The seller may not (a) solicit or arrange for the solicitation of orders to buy the shares in anticipation of or in connection with the Rule 144 transaction, or (b) make any payment in connection with the offer or sale of the shares to any person other than the broker who executes the order to sell the shares.[181] For purposes of Rule 144, "broker's transaction" includes any transaction by a broker in which such broker:

- does no more than execute the order to sell the securities as agent for the seller,
- receives no more than the usual and customary broker's commission,
- neither solicits nor arranges for the solicitation of customers' orders to buy the securities in anticipation of or in connection with the transaction, although this does not preclude the broker from making inquiries of specified persons who have expressed interest in buying the securities within specified times or the broker's publication of specified quotations, and
- after reasonable inquiry is not aware of circumstances indicating that the seller is an underwriter with respect to the securities or that the transaction is part of a distribution of securities of the issuer (the broker being deemed to be aware of the information in the seller's Form 144 notice, discussed below). Rule 144(g) also lists matters about which the broker should inquire, which relate mainly to the seller's eligibility to sell the securities under Rule 144.[182]

vi. Form 144—Notice of Proposed Sale

If the number of Control Securities to be sold during any 3-month period exceeds 5,000 shares or other units or if the aggregate sale price is greater than $50,000, a Form 144 notice must be filed with the SEC. The notice must be signed by the stockholder and sent to the SEC not later than the time that the sell order is placed with a broker or executed by a market maker. If the shares are admitted to trading on any national securities exchange, 1 copy of the notice must also be submitted to the principal exchange on which the shares are admitted.

---

180. Securities Act Rule 144(f)(iii), 17 C.F.R. § 230.144(f)(iii); Securities Act Rule 144(g), 17 C.F.R. § 230.144(g).

181. Securities Act Rule 144(f)(2), 17 C.F.R. § 230.144(f)(2).

182. Securities Act Rule 144(g), 17 C.F.R. § 230.144(g).

vii. Summary Table

The final conditions applicable to the resale under Rule 144 of Restricted Securities and Control Securities can be summarized as follows:[183]

	Affiliate or Person Selling on behalf of an Affiliate (that is, "Control Securities")	**Nonaffiliate (and Has Not Been an Affiliate during the Prior 3 Months)**
Restricted Securities of Reporting Issuers	**During 6-month holding period**— no resales under Rule 144 permitted. **After 6-month holding period**— may resell in accordance with all Rule 144 requirements including: • Current public information, • Volume limitations, • Manner of sale requirements for equity securities, and • Filing of Form 144.	**During 6-month holding period**—no resales under Rule 144 permitted. **After 6-month holding period but before 1 year**—unlimited public resales under Rule 144 except that the current public information requirement still applies. **After 1-year holding period**—unlimited public resales under Rule 144; need not comply with any other Rule 144 requirements.
Restricted Securities of Nonreporting Issuers	**During 1-year holding period**—no resales under Rule 144 permitted. After 1-year holding period—may resell in accordance with all Rule 144 requirements, including: • Current public information, • Volume limitations, • Manner of sale requirements for equity securities, and • Filing of Form 144.	**During 1-year holding period**—no resales under Rule 144 permitted. **After 1-year holding period**—unlimited public resales under Rule 144; need not comply with any other Rule 144 requirements.

2. Section 4(1-1/2)

Resales under Rule 144 are permitted only after the expiration of the applicable holding period and, with respect to Control Securities, subject to the other requirements described above. In contrast, the informal "Section 4(1-1/2)" exemption exempts private resales of Restricted Securities (whether or not they are also Control Securities) that meet the requirements described below.

183. Securities Act Release No. 8869 (Dec. 6, 2007), 72 F.R. 71,546 (Dec. 17, 2007), at § II.B.2.

Technically, Section 4(1-1/2) is an exemption from the registration requirements of Securities Act section 5[184] under Securities Act section 4(a)(1)[185] for transactions by any person other than an issuer, underwriter or dealer. Section 4(1-1/2) derives its nickname from the importation into section 4(a)(1) of the private offering standards of Securities Act section 4(a)(2).[186] Whether the reseller of Restricted Securities is an underwriter for purposes of section 4(a)(1) depends on whether the resale "in all other respects comport[s] fully with the requirements of bona fide [Securities Act section] 4[(a)](2) transactions."[187] The Supreme Court described these criteria in, among other cases, *SEC v. Ralston Purina Co.*[188]

To avoid being deemed an underwriter, a nonaffiliate that desires to resell Restricted Securities acquired from an issuer must be able to show that it did not purchase the Restricted Securities with a view to distributing those securities. The following criteria are typically used to determine whether a reseller purchased Restricted Securities from an issuer with no view to distributing those securities and is not reselling them for the issuer, and thus, is not an underwriter for purposes of section 4(a)(1).[189]

i. Investment Intent

The reseller should have purchased the Restricted Securities with the intent to hold those securities for an indefinite time, and not with a view to selling or distributing any of those securities in any public or private sale or other disposition. The reseller must conduct some due diligence to satisfy itself that the buyer intends to hold the securities for an indefinite period of time and does not intend to distribute the shares to others; relying on representations made by the buyer in a purchase agreement may not be sufficient.[190] The reseller should also inquire into the buyer's record with respect to holding Restricted Securities for long-term investment.[191] The certificates evidencing the shares should bear a legend stating that the shares have not been registered and are subject to restrictions on disposition.[192]

The SEC and courts have also stated that a stop-transfer order that requires an opinion of counsel as to the legality of the resale is an effective device to avoid

---

184. 15 U.S.C. § 77(e).

185. 15 U.S.C. § 77(d)(1).

186. *See* § 5.3.1, *supra*.

187. H.R. Rep. No. 96-1341, 96th Cong., 2d Sess. 40 n. 7 (1980).

188. 346 U.S. 119, 125 (1953).

189. SEC v. Cavanaugh, 1 F. Supp. 2d 337, 368 (S.D.N.Y. 1998); *see also The Section "4(1-1/2)" Phenomenon: Private Resales of "Restricted" Securities*, A Report to the ABA Comm. on Fed. Reg. of Sec. from the Study Group on Section 4(1-1/2) of the Subcomm. on the 1933 Act, 34 Bus. Law 1961 (1979).

190. SEC v. Cavanaugh, *id.* at 369.

191. SEC v. Cavanaugh, *id.* at 370; Louis Loss & Joel Seligman, *Securities Regulation*, pp. 421-423 (4th ed. 1989).

192. SEC v. Cavanaugh, *id.* at 369*; see also* Securities Act Rule 502(d)(3), 17 C.F.R. § 230.502(d)(3).

illegal resales.[193] Thus, resellers taking advantage of Section 4(1-1/2) typically obtain an opinion of counsel that the transaction is exempt from registration based on representations of the seller and the buyer designed to assure that neither party is an underwriter or an affiliate of the issuer.[194]

ii. Offeree Qualification

The reseller should inquire into the buyer's financial condition to assess whether the buyer can reasonably assume the financial risk of the investment and hold the securities for an indefinite time. The reseller should ascertain that the buyer:

- is able to bear the economic risk of the purchase;
- has sufficient knowledge and experience in financial and business matters to be capable of evaluating the risks and merits of the investment; and
- has the capacity to protect the buyer's own interests in connection with the transaction.[195]

iii. Information

The buyer should be furnished with, or at least have access to, all financial and other information about the investment and the business and proposed business of the issuer that the buyer considers necessary in connection with the investment.[196]

iv. Manner of Offering

The seller should communicate the offer directly to the buyer. No form of general advertising or general solicitation may be used. The number of offerees should also be limited.[197]

§ 13.5 Purchasing Shares in Public Offerings

1. FINRA New Issue Rules

FINRA Rule 5130, "Restrictions on the Purchase and Sale of Initial Equity Public Offerings" and Rule 5131, "New Issue Allocations and Distributions" (the "New Issue Rules") regulate the purchase of shares in initial public offerings. The New Issue Rules apply only to initial public offerings of equity securities ("New Issues"). They do not apply to subsequent offerings, private placements, offerings of securities in commodity pools, rights offerings, exchange offers, offerings in mergers or acquisitions, offerings of investment grade asset-backed

193. *See Use of Legends and Stop-Transfer Instructions as Evidence of Non-Public Offerings*, Securities Act Release No. 5121 (Dec. 30, 1970), 36 F.R. 1525 (Feb. 2, 1971); *see also* SEC v. Cavanaugh, 1 F. Supp. 2d 237 (S.D.N.Y. 1998).

194. Louis Loss & Joel Seligman, *Securities Regulation*, pp. 421-423, (4th ed. 1989).

195. *Id. See also* § 5.3.1, *supra*.

196. *Id.*

197. *Id.*

securities, offerings of convertible securities, offerings of preferred securities, offerings of registered investment companies, and offerings of securities with preexisting markets outside the United States.[198]

i. Rule 5130

Rule 5130 purportedly is designed to protect the integrity of the public offering process by ensuring that (a) FINRA members make bona fide New Issue offerings at the offering price; (b) FINRA members do not withhold New Issues for their own benefit or use such securities to reward persons (such as hedge funds and their investment advisers) who are in a position to direct future business to members; and (c) industry insiders, including FINRA members and their associated persons, do not take advantage of their "insider" positions to purchase New Issues for their own benefit at the expense of the public.[199]

In furtherance of these objectives, Rule 5130 prohibits a FINRA member from selling a New Issue to any account in which a restricted person has a beneficial interest, with certain exceptions.[200] The FINRA member also must meet specified preconditions for sale before selling a New Issue to any account.[201]

Rule 5130 prohibits hedge funds from allocating their profits (and losses) from New Issues to restricted persons, except as described below. Rule 5130 does not, however, require a hedge fund to sell the New Issue before restricted persons can be allocated subsequent profits and losses from the New Issue. Thus, a hedge fund may begin to allocate profits and losses from a New Issue to restricted persons when the New Issue no longer is traded at the initial public offering price and instead is traded at secondary market prices.[202]

a. Restricted Persons

"Restricted persons" include:

- brokers or dealers and their personnel,[203] other than limited business brokers or dealers whose authorization to engage in the securities business is limited solely to the purchase and sale of investment company/variable contracts securities and direct participation program securities;[204]
- finders and any person acting in a fiduciary capacity to the managing underwriter, including, but not limited to, attorneys, accountants and financial consultants;[205]
- portfolio managers, defined to include any person who has the authority to buy or sell securities for a bank, savings and loan institution, insurance company, investment company, investment adviser, hedge

---

198. FINRA Manual – FINRA Rule 5130(i)(9). *See also*, FINRA Rule 5131(e)(7).
199. NASD Notice to Members, Notice 03-79 (Dec. 2003), p. 832.
200. FINRA Manual – FINRA Rule 5130(a)(1). *See* §§ 13.5.1.i(c) and 13.5.1.i(d), *infra*.
201. FINRA Manual – FINRA Rule 5130(b) and 5131(e)(7).
202. NASD Notice to Members, Notice 03-79 (Dec. 2003), p. 842.
203. FINRA Manual – FINRA Rule 5130(i)(10)(A) and (i)(10)(B).
204. FINRA Manual – FINRA Rule 5130 (i)(7) and (i)(10)(B).
205. FINRA Manual – FINRA Rule 5130 (i)(10)(C).

fund, investment partnership, investment corporation or other collective investment vehicle, but a person with authority to buy or sell securities for an investment club or family investment vehicle is not a portfolio manager for this purpose;[206]

- owners of brokers or dealers;[207]
- affiliates of brokers or dealers;[208] and
- immediate family members of restricted persons.[209] "Immediate family" means a person's parents, parents-in-law, spouse, siblings, brothers-in-law, sisters-in-law, sons-in-law, daughters-in-law, children, and any individuals to whom the person provides material support.[210] Providing "material support" means directly or indirectly having provided more than 25 percent of the supported person's income in the preceding calendar year. Members of an immediate family living in the same household are deemed to provide material support to each other.[211]

b. Beneficial Interest

"Beneficial interest" means any economic interest, excluding receipt of a management fee or performance-based fee for operating a hedge fund.[212] Members of the FINRA staff (when it was the NASD staff) indicated informally that receiving management or performance-based fees by persons other than the investment adviser would cause such persons to have beneficial interests in a hedge fund's profits and losses from New Issues, but any such payments or allocations by a hedge fund to affiliated parties of the investment adviser who are involved in the investment adviser's portfolio management for the hedge fund would not cause such persons to have beneficial interests in the New Issue profits and losses of the hedge fund.[213] Thus, a restricted person other than a hedge fund's investment adviser and its affiliates who are involved in portfolio management (such as a broker or finder entitled to referral fees) who receives a portion of a management or performance fee based in part on proceeds from New Issues may only receive that portion to the extent that it is within the *de minimis* exemption, which reduces the amount available to investors in the hedge fund who are restricted.

In addition, if fees are deferred, the accumulation of such amounts, if subsequently invested in the hedge fund (as a deferred fee arrangement or

---

206. FINRA Manual – FINRA Rule 5130 (i)(10)(D).
207. FINRA Manual – FINRA Rule 5130 (i)(10)(E).
208. *Id.*
209. FINRA Manual – FINRA Rule 5130(i)(10)(E)(vi).
210. FINRA Manual – FINRA Rule 5130(i)(5).
211. FINRA Manual – FINRA Rule 5130(i)(8).
212. FINRA Manual – FINRA Rule 5130(i)(1) and 5131(e)(2).
213. Telephone conversation with Gary Goldsholle, Esq. and Afshin Atabaki, Esq., NASD, Feb. 10, 2004.

otherwise), constitutes a beneficial ownership interest in the hedge fund's account under the New Issue Rules.[214]

c. De Minimis Exemption

An account (such as a hedge fund) in which restricted persons are allocated no more than 10 percent of the New Issue profits and losses is exempt from the prohibition of Rule 5130.[215] To comply with the *de minimis* exemption, some hedge funds may establish separate brokerage accounts that purchase only New Issues and allocate to restricted persons 10 percent or less of the profits or losses from purchases and sales of New Issues through those accounts. A hedge fund may also purchase New Issues through a general brokerage account, but adjust the profit and loss allocations to remove or reduce allocations to restricted persons of gains (or losses) attributable to New Issues as needed to comply with Rule 5130.[216]

d. Other Exemptions

The following are not restricted persons, even if they might otherwise be within the definition of "restricted person" in Rule 5130:

- a person with authority to buy or sell securities for a family investment vehicle, defined as a legal entity beneficially owned solely by immediate family members;
- a registered investment company (mutual fund);
- a common trust fund or similar fund, as described in Securities Act section 3(a)(12)(A),[217] that has investments from 1,000 or more accounts and that does not limit beneficial interests principally to trust accounts of restricted persons;
- an insurance company general, separate or investment account funded by premiums from 1,000 or more policyholders, or an insurance company general account, if the insurance company has 1,000 or more policyholders and does not limit participation principally to restricted persons;
- a publicly traded entity (other than a broker or dealer or an affiliate of a broker or dealer where such broker or dealer is authorized to engage in the public offering of New Issues either as a selling group member or underwriter) whose securities are listed on an exchange or the Nasdaq Stock Market, or that is a foreign issuer who meets the criteria for listing on an exchange or the Nasdaq Stock Market;
- a non-U.S. investment company listed on a non-U.S. exchange or authorized for sale to the public by a non-U.S. regulatory authority in which no person owning more than 5 percent is a restricted person;

214. NASD Notice to Members, Notice 03-79 (Dec. 2003), p. 841. *See also* FINRA Rule 5131(e)(2).

215. FINRA Manual – FINRA Rule 5130(c)(4).

216. NASD Notice to Members, Notice 03-79 (Dec. 2003), p. 836.

217. 15 U.S.C. § 78c(a)(12)(A).

- an ERISA plan that is not sponsored solely by a broker or dealer;
- a state or municipal government benefits plan subject to state or municipal regulation;
- a tax-exempt charitable organization under Tax Code section 501(c)(3);[218]
- a church plan under Tax Code section 414(e);[219] and
- specified issuer-directed securities.[220]

ii. FINRA Rule 5131

FINRA Rule 5131 generally prohibits a FINRA member from allocating shares of any New Issue to any account (including a hedge fund) in which an executive officer or director or person materially supported by an executive officer or director of a particular public company or covered nonpublic company (defined below) in the following categories has a beneficial interest of 25 percent or more:

- a company that is currently an investment banking client of the member, or a company from which the member has received compensation for investment banking services in the last 12 months;
- a company that the person responsible for making the New Issue allocation decision on behalf of the broker knows, or has reason to know, that the broker intends to provide, or expects to be retained by that company to provide, investment banking services within the next 3 months; or
- a company with which there is an express or implied understanding that the executive officer or director, on behalf of that company, will retain the broker to perform investment banking services in the future. [221]

"Covered nonpublic company" is defined as any nonpublic company that: (1) had income of at least $1,000,000 in the last fiscal year or in 2 of the last 3 fiscal years and has shareholders' equity of at least $15,000,000, (2) has shareholders' equity of at least $30,000,000 and a 2-year operating history or (3) had total assets and total revenue of at least $75,000,000 in the latest fiscal year or in 2 of the last 3 fiscal years.[222]

iii. Application to Hedge Funds

Before selling a New Issue to a hedge fund, a FINRA member must, in good faith, obtain a representation from the hedge fund or its investment adviser that the hedge fund's purchases of New Issues comply with the New Issue Rules. The FINRA member must receive the representation during the 12 months

218. 26 U.S.C. § 501(c)(3).
219. 26 U.S.C. § 414(e); FINRA Manual – FINRA Rule 5130(c).
220. FINRA Manual – FINRA Rule 5130(d).
221. FINRA Manual – FINRA Rule 5131(b).
222. FINRA Manual – FINRA Rule 5131(e)(3).

before the sale.[223] The initial representation must positively affirm the hedge fund's nonrestricted status. Thereafter, the FINRA member must annually verify the hedge fund's status. Annual verification may be effected by negative confirmation, such as a letter to the hedge fund that recites the hedge fund's New Issue status and asks the hedge fund to respond only if any such status has changed.[224]

To enable the hedge fund to make an accurate representation, the hedge fund's subscription documents should require each investor to make an initial representation as to its New Issue status. Thereafter, the hedge fund manager annually may follow the negative confirmation procedure described above by sending a letter to each investor confirming the investor's New Issue status and asking the investor to respond only if the investor's status has changed. Following these procedures will enable the hedge fund manager to respond appropriately to requests from brokers concerning the hedge fund's ability to purchase New Issues.

To make an accurate representation to a broker regarding its New Issue status, a hedge fund in which another fund (a fund of funds) has invested must ascertain the New Issue status of the investors in the fund of funds. If a hedge fund is unable to ascertain the status of investors in a fund of funds, the hedge fund should deem that entire fund of funds to be ineligible to participate in New Issues. A hedge fund may rely on information received from a fund of funds within the preceding 12 months. To determine the ownership level of restricted persons in a hedge fund, the interests of restricted persons in each fund of funds should be attributed to the hedge fund in an amount equal to restricted persons' beneficial interests in the fund of funds multiplied by the fund of funds' interest in the hedge fund. For example, if 50 percent of a fund of funds is beneficially owned by restricted persons and the fund of funds beneficially owns 10 percent of the hedge fund, under Rule 5130 the resulting ownership level of restricted persons in the hedge fund attributable to the fund of funds would be 5 percent.

A hedge fund must "look through" to the investors in any fund of funds investor in this manner to determine whether the hedge fund complies with the *de minimis* exemption of Rule 5130 or the 25 percent exemption of Rule 5131. A hedge fund cannot treat a fund of funds that itself meets the *de minimis* exemption as wholly unrestricted for purposes of determining whether the hedge fund meets the *de minimis* exemption. Instead, the hedge fund must count the percentage of restricted investors in the fund of funds (multiplied by the fund of funds' percentage interest in the hedge fund) toward the hedge fund's own percentage of restricted investors.[225]

---

223. FINRA Manual – FINRA Rule 5130(b) and FINRA Rule 5131, Supplementary Material: .02 Annual Representation.

224. FINRA Notice to Members, Notice 03-79 (Dec. 2003), pp. 834-835 and FINRA Regulatory Notice 10-60 (Nov. 2010), p. 3.

225. Telephone call with Gary Goldsholle, Esq. and Afshin Atabaki, Esq., NASD, Feb. 10, 2004.

iv. Provision in Hedge Fund Agreement

To assure that restricted persons are allocated only the appropriate portion of profits and losses from New Issues, a hedge fund's governing agreement should provide that the hedge fund will allocate profits and losses from New Issues in accordance with the New Issue Rules, but otherwise consistently with the general allocation provisions in the agreement.

v. Fiduciary Duty to Allocate New Issues

An investment adviser that manages more than one hedge fund or other client accounts has a fiduciary duty to consider the appropriateness of each New Issue for each eligible hedge fund or other client account, and adequately to disclose its policy for allocating New Issues among its eligible clients. The SEC staff insists that investment advisers have written policies and procedures for allocating shares of initial public offerings among their accounts.[226]

2. Regulation M

The SEC rules that apply to short sellers of securities immediately before a public offering are discussed below in section 13.6.5.

§ 13.6 Short Selling Rules and Reporting Requirements

Hedge funds often sell securities short. A short sale is a sale of securities that the seller does not own (whether or not the seller owns other securities of the same class). The seller borrows the securities sold short, usually from a broker, for delivery to the buyer, posting cash or securities as collateral for the loan. The short seller typically buys a like number of the securities in the market at a later time for delivery to the lending broker to discharge the debt. Short selling is subject to extensive regulation, mostly under the Exchange Act.[227]

1. "Net Long" or "Net Short" Determination

Under SEC and self-regulatory organization short sale and position reporting rules, it is necessary to determine whether a sale is a short sale. For example, Regulation SHO's "circuit-breaker" provision (if triggered) restricts the prices at which securities may be sold short; Regulation SHO regulates naked short sales; Regulation M[228] prohibits certain short sales in connection with a public offering; Exchange Act Rules 17a-3 and 17a-4[229] require accurate recordkeeping of orders by brokers; and margin rules, such as Regulations T, U and X under

226. *See* § 13.13, *infra*.
227. 15 U.S.C. § 77j(a)(1).
228. 17 C.F.R. §§ 242.100-105.
229. 17 C.F.R. §§ 240.17a-3 and 240.17a-4.

the Exchange Act, apply particular margin requirements in connection with borrowing for, among other things, short sales.[230]

A seller is generally deemed to own securities (and thus cannot be deemed to be engaged in short selling with respect to those securities) to the extent that the seller is net long in those securities.[231] Conversely, a seller who is not net long the stock is short the stock; thus a hedge fund with a perfectly "boxed" position—equal long and short positions—is treated as being short that security. All sales of securities must be designated "long," "short" or "short exempt."[232] The short exempt category relates solely to the circuit-breaker provisions of Rule 201 of Regulation SHO.[233] A broker may mark a sell order "long" only if the hedge fund's account with the broker owns or is deemed to own the security involved and the security either is in the physical possession or control of the broker or is reasonably expected to be so by the time the transaction settles.[234] The broker must generally aggregate the number of those securities that the seller owns in all accounts held by the broker to determine whether and the extent to which the seller is net long in the security. If, however, the broker qualifies for "independent trading unit aggregation," each independent trading unit, rather than the entire brokerage firm, may aggregate its positions in a security to determine its net position. Independent trading unit aggregation is available if the brokerage firm's written organizational plan identifies and describes each independent trading unit and its trading objective and supports its independent identity, and traders in each unit pursue only that unit's trading objective without coordinating with other units.[235]

Regulation SHO Rule 200(b)[236] provides generally that a seller is deemed to own a security if the seller or its agent has title to it. A person also owns a security for these purposes if such person (a) owns a security convertible into or exchangeable for the security and has tendered such security for conversion or exchange, (b) has an option, warrant or right to purchase or acquire the security and has exercised the option, warrant or right, (c) has purchased the security or entered into an unconditional contract, binding on both parties, to purchase the security, but has not yet received it, or (d) holds a security futures contract to purchase the security, has received notice that the position will be physically settled, and is bound to receive the underlying security.[237] Long positions in convertible securities, rights, warrants or call options are not considered long

230. *See* § 13.8, *infra*, regarding the margin rules of the Federal Reserve Board, Regulations T, U and X, 12 C.F.R. §§ 220 through 224.

231. Regulation SHO Rule 200(c), 17 C.F.R. § 242.200(c). Regulation SHO provides limited exceptions to this rule by deeming a seller to own securities even if it is not "net long" if it acquired them while acting as a block positioner and has entered into offsetting arbitrage or hedge transactions, and in connection with unwinding certain index arbitrage positions. Regulation SHO Rules 200(d) and 200(e), 17 C.F.R. §§ 242.200(d) and 200(e).

232. Regulation SHO Rule 200(g), 17 C.F.R. § 242.200(g).

233. Regulation SHO Rule 201, 17 C.F.R. § 242.201; *see* § 13.6.2, *infra*.

234. *Id.*

235. Regulation SHO Rule 200(f), 17 C.F.R. § 242.200(f).

236. 17 C.F.R. § 242.200(b).

237. *Id.*

positions in the underlying securities, unless they have been converted or exercised.

A broker does not count Restricted Securities in determining whether a customer is net long in a stock, because Restricted Securities are not "in good deliverable form." Thus, a person placing an order to sell a security will not be deemed to be net long (and the sale will be a short sale) even if the person owns an equal or greater number of shares of the same class that are Restricted Securities. Moreover, because the SEC staff has asserted that the shares underlying a short sale are deemed to be sold at the time of the short sale, covering a short sale with Restricted Securities could violate Securities Act section 5, because the cover of the short sale would be deemed a sale of unregistered securities.[238] The SEC staff's position has been rejected twice by federal district courts.[239]

2. Regulation SHO Circuit Breaker

The Regulation SHO "circuit-breaker provision" (the "Circuit-Breaker Rule") limits the prices at which a security may be sold short if its value declines by a certain amount.[240] The Circuit-Breaker Rule is intended to prevent short selling, including potentially manipulative or abusive short selling, from driving down the price of a security that has already experienced a significant intraday price decline.

Under the Circuit-Breaker Rule, if the price of a "covered security" (defined as a security, other than an option, that is listed on the New York, American or Nasdaq Stock Exchange[241]) declines by 10 percent or more from the closing price on the listing market of the security on the preceding day, each trading center must prevent the execution or display of a short sale order for that security at a price that is less than or equal to the current national best bid.[242] The trading center must impose these restrictions for the remainder of that day and the next trading day when a national best bid for the security is calculated and disseminated on a current and continuing basis by a plan processor pursuant to an effective national market system plan.[243] Thus, the short sale restrictions apply at different hours depending on the plan that disseminates bids for a particular security. In the adopting release for the Circuit-Breaker Rule, the SEC stated that it may reconsider whether the Circuit-Breaker Rule should apply at other times based on information regarding short selling during those times.[244]

---

238. *See* § 13.6.5, *infra*.

239. SEC v. Lyon; F. Supp. 2d 444 (S.D.N.Y. 2008); SEC v. John M. Mangan, Jr., Transcript of Proceedings before the Honorable Graham C. Mullen, Oct. 24, 2007, at p. 44 (*available at* http://online.wsj.com/public/resources/documents/mangan.pdf); *but see* note 279, *infra*.

240. Regulation SHO Rule 201, 17 C.F.R. § 242.201; Exchange Act Release No. 63247 (Nov. 4, 2010); 75 F.R. 68,702 (Nov. 9, 2010).

241. Thus, the Circuit-Breaker Rule does not apply to, among other things, securities quoted on the OTC Bulletin Board or elsewhere in the OTC market.

242. Regulation SHO Rule 201(b)(1)(i), 17 C.F.R. § 242.201(b)(1)(i).

243. Regulation SHO Rule 201(b)(1)(ii), 17 C.F.R. § 242.201(b)(1)(ii).

244. Exchange Act Release No. 61595 (Feb. 26, 2010), 75 F.R. 11,232 (Mar. 10, 2010), at § III.A.5.

According to SEC staff, the Circuit-Breaker Rule applies to short sales effected using U.S. jurisdictional means, regardless of the jurisdiction in which the short sale is executed. For example, the Circuit-Breaker Rule applies to a U.S. investment adviser's order placed with a U.S. broker that routes the trade to the broker's foreign affiliate.[245] The adopting release is unclear whether the Circuit-Breaker Rule applies to a U.S. investment adviser's order placed with a non-U.S. broker on a bona fide foreign exchange.

The Circuit-Breaker Rule provides that a broker may mark a short sale order as "short exempt."[246] The listing market on which the security is traded may display or execute a short exempt order whether or not the price is below the national best bid price.[247] The Circuit-Breaker Rule lists the situations in which a broker may mark a short sale order as "short exempt."[248] A few of these situations likely to be relevant to investment advisers are:

- Delivery delays: The broker has a reasonable basis to believe that the short sale order is made by a person that owns the security and will deliver the security as soon as any restrictions on the delivery are removed.[249]
- Domestic and international arbitrage transactions: The short sale is submitted to profit from the difference between its price and either (a) the price of a security that is convertible into securities of the same class as the securities sold if the seller is or will be entitled to convert the convertible security or (b) the price of the same security on a foreign exchange if the seller has placed an offer to buy the security on the foreign exchange.[250]
- Transactions at VWAP: It is a short sale at the volume-weighted average price.251

3. Naked Short Sales

"Naked short sale" is not defined in the federal securities laws, but generally refers to a sale of securities to a buyer without owning or borrowing the securities at the time of the sale to make delivery to the buyer. As discussed below, only abusive naked short sales may be illegal. Nonabusive naked short sales are not illegal, but because of their perceived negative effects on the market, Regulation SHO Rule 203[252] establishes a uniform standard specifying procedures for all short sellers to locate securities for borrowing. Regulation SHO Rule 203 (b)(1)[253] prohibits a broker from accepting a short sale order from another

245. *Id.* at § VI.
246. Regulation SHO Rule 200(g), 17 C.F.R. § 242.200(g).
247. Regulation SHO Rule 201(b)(1)(iii)(B), 17 C.F.R. § 242.200(b)(1)(iii)(B).
248. Regulation SHO Rule 200(d), 17 C.F.R. § 242.200(d).
249. Regulation SHO Rule 201(d)(1), 17 C.F.R. § 242.201(d)(1).
250. Regulation SHO Rules 201(d)(3) and (4), 17 C.F.R. §§ 242.201(d)(3) and (4).
251. Regulation SHO Rule 201(d)(7), 17 C.F.R. § 242.201(d)(7).
252. 17 C.F.R. § 242.203.
253. Regulation SHO Rule 203(b)(1), 17 C.F.R. § 242.203(b)(1).

person or executing a short sale order for its own account unless the broker (a) has borrowed the securities or entered into a bona fide arrangement to borrow the securities, or (b) has reasonable grounds to believe that the securities can be borrowed and delivered by the settlement date. The SEC allows a broker to rely on the assurance of its customer that the customer has identified its own source of borrowable securities if it is reasonable for the broker to do so. Rule 203 provides certain exceptions from this locate requirement relating to orders received from introducing brokers, orders executed by market makers, and certain sales where delivery of the securities is delayed.

Abusive naked short sales as part of a manipulative scheme are illegal under the general anti-fraud provisions of the federal securities laws, including Rule 10b-5[254] under the Exchange Act. Due to the SEC's concern that some short sellers deliberately misrepresent to their brokers that they have located borrowable securities, and thus engage in abusive naked short selling, the SEC adopted Exchange Act Rule 10b-21,[255] which imposes liability directly on short sellers who deceive their brokers about their ownership of or ability to borrow shares to comply with Regulation SHO's locate requirement. Short sellers who rely on their brokers to locate the borrow, or who rely in good faith on their broker's "easy to borrow" list, will generally not be liable under Rule 10b-21.[256] The SEC staff believes that it would be reasonable for a short seller to make a representation that it can deliver shares on the settlement date if the shares are held in a margin account but the broker has lent them out pursuant to a margin agreement.[257]

A short seller is potentially liable under Rule 10b-21 only if it represents falsely to the broker that it will deliver the securities, and then fails to do so. The SEC staff believes that a private plaintiff that proves the elements of a violation of Rule 10b-21 would be able to assert a claim under Exchange Act section 10(b)[258] and Rule 10b-5 thereunder.[259] A hedge fund that falsely represents to a broker that it has located the securities to borrow also could be deemed to violate Securities Act section 17(a)(2).[260]

Regulation SHO Rule 204[261] penalizes a broker for executing a short sale and then failing to deliver the securities sold short by the settlement date. Rule 204 requires that for long and short sales in equity securities, a clearing broker generally must either deliver the securities for clearance and settlement by the settlement date or close out the fail-to-deliver position by borrowing or

254. 17 C.F.R. § 240.10b-5.

255. 17 C.F.R. § 240.10b-21.

256. Exchange Act Release No. 58774 (Oct. 14, 2008), 73 F.R. 61,666 (Oct. 17, 2008), at § III.B.

257. *Id.* at § III.D.

258. 15 U.S.C. § 78j(b).

259. Exchange Act Release No. 58774 (Oct. 14, 2008), 73 F.R. 61,666 (Oct. 17, 2008), at § III.E.

260. Securities Act § 17(a)(2), 15 U.S.C. § 77q(a)(2); *see In re* Sandell Asset Mgmt. Corp., et al., Advisers Act Release No. 2670 (Oct. 10, 2007) (investment adviser's personnel reported to a broker that they had located stock to borrow when in fact they had not).

261. Regulation SHO Rule 204, 17 C.F.R. § 242.204.

buying the securities by the beginning of regular trading hours on the day after the settlement date.[262] A broker has more time to close out a fail-to-deliver position that results from a long sale, Rule 144 securities and bona fide market making.[263] If the clearing broker does not close out a fail-to-deliver position by the applicable deadline, it and its introducing brokers (including market makers) may not accept any short sale orders in the same equity security from any customer, or make short sales in the security for their own accounts, without first borrowing the security or entering into a bona fide arrangement to borrow the security, until the clearing broker closes out the fail-to deliver-position.[264]

Because Regulation SHO Rule 204 applies to brokers, not hedge funds, it does not impose operational restrictions on hedge funds or their managers. It does, however, affect the way brokers conduct business by limiting their ability to execute short sales in stocks where they have fail-to-deliver positions that are not closed out by the applicable deadline. As a result, hedge fund managers may have difficulty selling short securities that are not easily borrowed.

State laws also may apply to naked short sales. For example, in 2007, a California court refused to dismiss lawsuits by 2 issuers against numerous prime brokerage firms based on state law claims of market manipulation, unfair business practices, conversion and trespass to chattels.[265]

4. Exchange Act Section 16(c) Short Sale Prohibition

Exchange Act section 16(c) prohibits any sale by an insider of an issuer of any equity security of the issuer if the insider (a) does not own the security or (b) if owning the security, does not deliver it within 20 days after selling it or does not, within 5 days after the sale, deposit the security in the mail.[266] Although section 16(c) thus permits insiders to engage in short sales against the box, an insider cannot borrow shares to meet its delivery obligation.[267]

5. Covering Short Sales from Publicly Offered Stock

Under Exchange Act Rule 105,[268] a hedge fund (or any other person) may not purchase equity securities in a public offering conducted on a firm commitment basis from a participating underwriter or broker if it makes a short sale of the security during the 5 business days before the offering is priced. The rule applies whether or not shares purchased in the offering are used to cover the

262. Regulation SHO Rule 204(a), 17 C.F.R. § 242.204(a).

263. Regulation SHO Rules 204(a)(1)-204(a)(3), 17 C.F.R. §§ 242.204(a)(1)-204(a)(3).

264. Regulation SHO Rule 204(b), 17 C.F.R. § 242.204(b).

265. Overstock.com v. Morgan, Stanley & Co., Inc. (Cal. Sup. Ct. 2007) (No. CGC-07-460147); Avenius v. Banc of America Securities LLC (Cal. Sup. Ct. 2006) (No. CGC-06-453422).

266. Exchange Act § 16(c), 15 U.S.C. § 78p(c).

267. *See* Willkie Farr & Gallagher, SEC No-Action Letter (Mar. 26, 1980).

268. 17 C.F.R. § 240.105.

short position. The 5-day period may be shortened to the period beginning with the initial filing of the registration statement or notification on Form 1-A and ending with the pricing. The rule does not apply if the hedge fund that has sold securities short during the restricted period purchases an equal number of shares before the offering.[269] The rule includes exemptions for separate accounts of a particular person if decisions regarding those accounts are made separately and without coordination and for trades by a mutual fund if other trades are made by separate series of that mutual fund or an affiliated mutual fund.[270]

This rule is intended to limit the ability of short sellers to put pressure on the price of a public offering, lowering the offering price and yielding reduced proceeds for the issuer. A hedge fund that takes a short position cannot have a pre-arrangement to purchase shares to cover the short position from someone who buys in the public offering, but it may purchase shares in the public market to cover the short position. If the hedge fund buys shares in the public market to cover the short position, and sells shares it was allocated in the public offering, it should wait a substantial period between these trades.

The rule applies to shorting of the same security as that purchased in the offering. Thus, the rule does not prohibit a hedge fund from shorting an equity security and purchasing a security convertible into the shorted security in the offering.[271] Similarly, the rule does not apply to derivatives (such as options and over-the-counter instruments). Thus, a hedge fund may close an option position with stock allocated to it in a public offering. The SEC has warned that it will monitor the use of derivatives to ensure that they are not used simply as a functional substitute for equity trading prohibited by the rule.[272] The SEC has cautioned that manipulative short sales involving derivatives are nevertheless addressed by the general anti-manipulation provisions, including Exchange Act section 9(a)(2)[273] and Exchange Act Rule 10b-5.[274] The rule also does not apply to debt offerings. The SEC believes that an extension of the prohibitions of this rule to debt offerings would be inconsistent with the approach of Regulation M, which is to focus on those securities having the greatest manipulative potential.[275]

---

269. Exchange Act Rule 105(b)(1), 17 C.F.R. § 240.105(b)(1).

270. Exchange Act Rules 105(b)(2) and 105(b)(3), 17 C.F.R. §§ 240.105(b)(2) and 240.105(b)(3).

271. Exchange Act Release No. 56206 (Aug. 6, 2007), 72 F.R. 45,094 (Aug. 10, 2007), at § II.C.

272. *Id.* at § III.

273. 15 U.S.C. § 78i(a)(2).

274. 17 C.F.R. § 240.10b-5.

275. Exchange Act Release No. 56206 (Aug. 6, 2007), 72 F.R. 45,094 (Aug. 10, 2007) at § II.C.

6. Covering Short Sales with Restricted Securities

Securities Act section 5[276] generally prohibits the sale of unregistered securities in the public market. The SEC staff has in the past asserted that it is a violation of section 5 to use Restricted Securities (such as securities purchased in a private investment in public securities ("PIPES") transaction) to cover a short position, either before or after the registration statement for the Restricted Securities becomes effective. The SEC staff's rationale is based on its position that a short sale is deemed to occur when the short sale is executed and not when it is covered.[277] Thus, according to the SEC staff, the Restricted Securities are unregistered (and perhaps not even in existence) at the time the short sale is executed and cannot be legally sold to the public when the short sale is executed, without complying with the registration requirements of Securities Act section 5.

That those shares are subsequently registered is irrelevant, because the critical date is the trade date of the short sale and the subsequent registration cannot be applied retroactively. For the same reasons, the person cannot wait until the expiration of the Rule 144 holding period to cover a short sale with Restricted Securities and claim that he or she was allowed to sell without restriction under Securities Act Rule 144.[278]

Two federal district courts have disagreed with the SEC staff's position and it is unclear whether the SEC will continue to assert it.[279] Those courts did not, however, dismiss the SEC's insider trading claims in those cases, which were based on the general theory that the existence of the issuers' upcoming secondary offerings were material nonpublic information and that the defendants in the 2 actions improperly used that information by engaging in short sales of those issuers' securities before the offerings.[280]

One technique that has been suggested to hedge a restricted position is to (a) sell short securities of a similar issuer to hedge the risk of owning the Restricted Securities for the Rule 144 holding period, (b) sell the Restricted Securities under Rule 144 after the Rule 144 holding period is satisfied and (c) use the sale proceeds to buy shares in the market to close out the short position. This 3-step approach involves some cost, including 2 extra brokerage commissions for the 3 transactions; the spread in closing out the position resulting from selling the

---

276. 15 U.S.C. § 77e.

277. Securities Act Release No. 6099, question 80 (Aug. 2, 1979), 44 F.R. 46,752, question 80 (Aug. 8, 1979); SEC v. Hilary V. Shane, Litigation Release No. 19227 (May 18, 2005); SEC v. Edwin Buchanan Lyon, et al., Litigation Release No. 19942 (Dec. 12, 2006); SEC v. John F. Mangan, Jr., Litigation Release No. 19955 (Dec. 28, 2006); SEC v. Robert A. Berlacher, et al., Litigation Release No. 20278 (Sep. 13, 2007); SEC v. TCMP3 Partners, L.P., et al., Litigation Release No. 20356 (Nov. 5, 2007).

278. *See* § 13.4.1, *supra*.

279. SEC v. Lyon; F. Supp. 2d 444 (S.D.N.Y. 2008); SEC v. John M. Mangan, Jr., Transcript of Proceedings before the Honorable Graham C. Mullen, Oct. 24, 2007, at p. 44 (*available at* http://online.wsj.com/public/resources/documents/mangan.pdf); *but see* Zacharias v. SEC, No. 08-1134, slip op. (D.C. Cir., June 23, 2009 (§ 5 liability may arise from an aggravated series of related transactions even if individual transactions appear to be technically compliant)).

280. *Id.*

Restricted Securities at the bid price and buying (to cover the short) at the asked price; and the margin costs involved in keeping the short position open.[281]

7. Short Sale Reporting

Exchange Act section 13(f)(2) requires the SEC to promulgate rules for the public disclosure of short sales.[282] At this writing, the SEC has not proposed those rules. Separately, Dodd-Frank Act section 417(a)(2) requires the SEC staff to conduct studies regarding the feasibility, benefits and costs of (a) requiring reporting in real time, publicly, or, in the alternative, only to the SEC and the FINRA, short sale positions in publicly listed securities, and (2) conducting a voluntary pilot program in which public companies could agree to have their shares marked "long," "short" or "market maker short," and purchases of their shares marked "buy" or "buy-to-cover," and reported as such in real time through the Consolidated Tape.[283] On May 4, 2011, the SEC published a request for public comment on the existing uses of short selling in securities markets and the adequacy or inadequacy of the information regarding short sales currently available.[284] At this writing, the SEC has not taken further action with respect to real-time reporting of short sales.

§ 13.7 Swaps

The Dodd-Frank Act significantly restructured the regulatory framework for derivative instruments.[285] Formerly, many of these instruments were not regulated. The Dodd-Frank Act subjects "security-based swaps"[286] to regulation by the SEC, "swaps"[287] (all derivative products other than security-based swaps) to regulation by the CFTC, and "mixed swaps"[288] to regulation by the SEC and CFTC jointly. The definitions of these terms are complex and are discussed in Chapter 2.

An investment adviser that enters into swap transactions must determine whether they are of a type regulated by the CFTC and if so, determine whether the investment adviser is a commodity pool operator or a commodity trading adviser required to register with the CFTC or claim an exemption from registration. The CFTC registration requirements are discussed in Chapter 2.

---

281. *See The Corporate Counsel*, Vol. XXV, No. 3 (May-June 2000). *See also The Corporate Counsel*, Vol. XVII, No. 2, at p. 5 (Mar.-Apr. 1992); *The Corporate Counsel*, Vol. XXII, No. 1, at p. 1 (Jan.-Feb. 1997); and *The Corporate Counsel*, Vol. XXIII, No. 5, at p. 2 (Sep.-Oct. 1998).

282. *See* § 13.1.5.iii, *supra*.

283. Dodd-Frank Act, Pub. L. No. 111-203, §§ 417(a)(2), 124 Stat. 1376, 1579 (2010).

284. Exchange Act Release No. 64383 (May 4, 2011), 76 F.R. 26,787 (May 9, 2011).

285. Dodd-Frank Act, Pub. L. No. 111-203, §§ 701-774, 124 Stat. 1376, 1641-1802 (2010). *See* §§ 2.9 and 13.1.1.i, *supra*.

286. Defined in Exchange Act § 3(a)(68), 15 U.S.C. 78c(a)(68).

287. Defined in CEA § 1a(47), 7 U.S.C. 1a(47).

288. Defined in CEA § 1(a)(47)(D), 7 U.S.C. 1a(47)(D), and Exchange Act § 3(a)(68)(D), 15 U.S.C. 78c(a)(68)(D).

The Dodd-Frank Act imposed new clearing, reporting and recordkeeping requirements on participants in all types of swaps, whether regulated by the CFTC or the SEC. Most of these have not yet been fully implemented at this writing. A detailed discussion of those requirements as they apply to investment advisers to hedge funds is beyond the scope of this book. Generally, most relatively standardized swap transactions will be subject to mandatory clearing through clearinghouses and traded on exchanges.[289] Thus, a hedge fund that engages in those transactions will be subject to the clearinghouse's credit risk and collateral requirements instead of those of the swap counterparty. The mandatory clearing requirement does not apply to swaps that are not accepted by any clearinghouse for trading; those swap transactions will continue to be traded over-the-counter rather than through a clearinghouse and entered into bilaterally using standard swap documentation. Parties to noncleared swaps will be subject to increased margin and capital reserve requirements based on the exposure of the parties.

One of the main goals of the Dodd-Frank Act was to increase transparency in the derivatives markets and, accordingly, it imposed substantial new reporting obligations on swap participants. Swap data must be reported electronically to "swap data repositories," and certain pricing, volume and transaction data relating to "publicly reportable swap transactions" must be reported publicly in real time.[290] Most of the new reporting obligations, however, are imposed on the swap clearing organizations, exchanges and institutional counterparties that enter into swap transactions with hedge funds, rather than on those funds or their investment advisers.

§ 13.8 Federal Reserve Regulations T, U and X, and Portfolio Margining

U.S. brokers and dealers are subject to the margin regulations of Regulation T[291] of the Board of Governors of the Federal Reserve System as well as stock exchange margin rules. Regulation T's margin limits generally are a fixed percentage or amount for positions in specified categories (such as 50 percent for most long equities and 150 percent for most short equities).[292] Other U.S. entities (such as banks or other lenders that are not brokers or dealers) are subject to Regulation U, which imposes limits similar to those in Regulation T on loans for the purpose of buying or holding securities.[293] A hedge fund therefore is limited in the amount that it can borrow from firms that are subject to Regulations T and U.

289. CEA § 2(h)(1)(A), 7 U.S.C. § 2(h)(1)(A); Exchange Act § 3C(a)(1), 15 U.S.C. 78c-3C(a)(1).

290. CEA § 2(a)(13)(C), 7 U.S.C. § 2(a)(13)(C); Exchange Act § 13(m)(1)(C), 15 U.S.C. § 78m(m)(1)(C).

291. Regulation T Rule 220, 12 C.F.R. § 220.

292. Regulation T Rule 220.12, 12 C.F.R. § 220.12.

293. Regulation U, 12 C.F.R. § 221 *et seq.*

Regulation X applies directly to U.S.-based hedge funds and to non-U.S. persons controlled by U.S. persons.[294] Regulation X generally applies the loan limits of Regulation U (that is, 50 percent) to borrowing by such parties from anyone other than a U.S. broker or dealer (or foreign branch of a U.S. broker or dealer) to purchase U.S. securities.[295] A non-U.S. hedge fund (such as an offshore corporation or partnership) is deemed to be controlled by U.S. persons if U.S. investors directly or indirectly have more than a 50 percent beneficial interest in the non-U.S. hedge fund. For example, if a "master fund" formed as a Cayman Islands partnership or corporation has a U.S.-based feeder fund and a Cayman Islands feeder fund, the master fund must combine the U.S. feeder fund and any U.S. beneficial owners in the Cayman Islands feeder fund to determine whether U.S. persons have more than 50 percent of the beneficial interests in the master fund.[296]

The borrowing limits do not apply to a suitable account established with a U.S. broker or dealer that employs portfolio margin systems approved by the SEC.[297] The NYSE and Chicago Board Options Exchange ("CBOE") have received such approval for portfolio margining by their member brokerage firms.[298] Portfolio margin systems permit the broker or dealer to calculate a hedge fund's margin requirement based on an assessment of the aggregate net risk of eligible types of securities in the hedge fund's account, instead of the position-by-position calculations required by Regulation T.

§ 13.9 Related Party Trades Involving Investment Adviser and Its Other Clients or Its Affiliated Broker

An investment adviser's fiduciary duty to its clients includes the duty to put its clients' interests ahead of its own. Neither an investment adviser nor any of its affiliates may act as principal or broker in buying securities from or selling securities to a client of the investment adviser (such as a hedge fund), unless the investment adviser provides written disclosure to the hedge fund of the investment adviser's capacity in the transaction and obtains the client's consent.[299] This rule applies to every investment adviser, whether SEC-

294. Regulation X Rule 224.2, 12 C.F.R. § 224.2.

295. Regulation X Rule 724.3(a), 12 C.F.R. § 224.3(a).

296. Federal Reserve Board Interpretation Letter to Steven Fredman, Esq. (Oct. 22, 1999), *available at* http://www.federalreserve.gov/boarddocs/legalint/MarginRequirements/1999/19991022/.

297. Regulation T Rule 220.1(b)(3)(i), 12 C.F.R. § 220.1(b)(3)(i).

298. Exchange Act Releases Nos. 54918 and 54919, 71 F.R. 75,790 (Dec. 18, 2006) and 71 F.R. 75,781 (Dec. 18, 2006); *see also* FINRA Manual-Conduct Rule 2520(g) and NYSE Rule 431(g).

299. Advisers Act § 206(3), 15 U.S.C. § 80b-6(3); *see also* Cal. Corp. Code § 25235(c); *see* In the Matter of Credit Suisse Asset Mgmt. Inc., Advisers Act Release No. 1452 (Nov. 16, 1994).

registered, state registered or unregistered. For this purpose, each investor in the hedge fund should be regarded as a client, even if for other purposes the hedge fund is considered the investment adviser's client. Otherwise, an investment adviser that is also the general partner or manager of a hedge fund could approve such transactions itself on behalf of the hedge fund, without notice to or the consent of the investors.[300] Advisers Act section 206(3)[301] requires that this disclosure be provided "before the completion of the transaction." The timing and content of the disclosure depends on the circumstances and may include the nature and extent of the investment adviser's position in the securities sold and the availability of information about the transaction before and after execution.

According to the SEC staff, Advisers Act section 206(3) would apply to transactions between an investment adviser's client account and an account of which the investment adviser and its controlling persons, in aggregate, own greater than 25 percent but would not apply if such persons own 25 percent or less.[302]

1. Broker Transactions

An investment adviser may also be registered as a broker or dealer or affiliated with a broker or dealer (for example, as its parent, subsidiary or sister corporation), or a registered representative of a broker or dealer may be a principal or employee of an investment adviser or registered as an investment adviser ("RR/IA") (in all 3 situations, we refer to the affiliated broker or dealer as an "IA/BD"). If an IA/BD executes client transactions as a broker or dealer, the IA/BD must inform its clients (a) that they may request that their transactions be executed through brokers other than the IA/BD, (b) that the clients may be able to obtain a better price elsewhere if the brokerage commissions plus advisory fees are higher than otherwise obtainable and (c) of the nature and extent of the investment adviser's interest in the transaction, including the compensation the IA/BD will receive.[303]

2. Principal Transactions

If an IA/BD effects any principal transaction with a client (for example, out of the inventory of the broker or dealer or in an over-the-counter transaction), the investment adviser typically must disclose in writing to the client the IA/BD's

---

300. *But see* Merrill Lynch Asset Mgmt., SEC No-Action Letter (Apr. 28, 1997) (allowing mutual fund's portfolio manager who is also an officer or authorized signatory of a mutual fund to execute such transactions without providing such notice to itself or to mutual fund's investors).

301. 15 U.S.C. § 80b-6(3).

302. Gardner Russo & Gardner, SEC No-Action Letter (June 7, 2006).

303. United Missouri Bank of Kansas City, SEC No-Action Letter (May 11, 1990); *see also* 10 Cal. Code of Reg., § 260.238(k).

capacity in the transaction and obtain the client's consent before the transaction is completed.[304]

An investment adviser to a separate account client that causes the client to invest in a hedge fund affiliated with the investment adviser could be deemed to be engaging in an indirect principal transaction because the hedge fund, as an entity controlled by the investment adviser, sold the securities to the client. An investment adviser might be able to avoid the need to make the disclosures otherwise required under Advisers Act section 206(3) in this case by (a) waiving duplicative fees or providing value to the client separately from the value that the investment adviser provides to the hedge fund (for example, if the investment in the hedge fund is made in connection with asset allocation services), (b) fully disclosing any conflicts and obtaining the informed consent of the separate account client before any such transaction with the client, (c) selling or redeeming interests of the hedge fund only at their net asset value, and (d) forgoing any transaction-based compensation for the investment adviser or its affiliates.[305]

3. Agency Cross Transactions

An "agency cross transaction" is a transaction in which an IA/BD acts as a broker both for its advisory client and for its brokerage client on the other side of the transaction. An open market transaction through an IA/BD is not an agency cross transaction. An investment adviser to a hedge fund must receive the prior written consent of each investor in the hedge fund to execute agency cross transactions involving the hedge fund. Unlike principal transactions, however, the investors may provide advance blanket written consents authorizing all agency cross transactions, if the IA/BD has fully disclosed the capacities in which it will act and the potentially conflicting division of loyalties and responsibilities regarding both parties to such transactions.

The IA/BD must also provide to each investor a confirmation of each agency cross transaction and an annual summary of all agency cross transactions (including the number of agency cross transactions, the commissions generated for the IA/BD and the commissions generated for the RR/IA). A blanket consent is insufficient, however, if the IA/BD recommends the transaction to both the

---

304. *In re* Gruntal & Co., Inc., Advisers Act Release No. 1560 (Apr. 9, 1996) (IA/BD violated Advisers Act § 206(3) by failing to get client consent to principal transactions before each such transaction); *In re* Feldman Inv. Group, Inc., Advisers Act Release No. 1538 (Nov. 27, 1995) (IA/BD failed to obtain client consent before executing riskless principal transaction); *In re* Concord Inv. Co., Advisers Act Release No. 1585 (Sep. 27, 1996); *In re* Calamos Asset Mgmt., Advisers Act Release No. 1594 (Oct. 16, 1996); *In re* Rothschild Inv. Corp., Advisers Act Release No. 1714 (Apr. 13, 1998) (IA/BD failed to obtain client consent before executing riskless principal transaction).

305. *Q&A: Principal Trades for Hedge Fund IAs*, Compliance Reporter, Jan. 26, 2004, relying in part on Merrill Lynch Trust Co., SEC No-Action Letter (July 6, 2000) (allowing an investment adviser to place clients in affiliated mutual funds without the disclosure and client consent otherwise required by Advisers Act § 206(3)).

seller and the purchaser or acts as the placement agent for the issuer or seller.[306] All statements to investors must disclose that the investor may terminate the agency cross transaction authority at any time by written notice to the IA/BD.[307] The governing documents of a hedge fund may allow the hedge fund to expel any investor that terminates such authority.

4. Cross Transactions

An investment adviser to a hedge fund may cross-trade between or among accounts that it manages to maintain a *pari passu* investment strategy. An investment adviser that arranges a cross trade between client accounts is not subject to the disclosure and consent requirements of Advisers Act section 206(3)[308] if (a) it does not "act as a broker" by receiving compensation for effecting the cross trade and (b) it and its controlling persons own 25 percent or less of any such account.[309] The investment adviser's management fee is not deemed compensation for this purpose. The relatively lenient treatment accorded to cross trades is based on the SEC's reasoning that the primary conflict of interest involved with agency cross transactions (that is, the IA/BD's incentive to earn additional commissions) is not present in cross trades.[310]

Cross trading, however, can implicate an investment adviser's fiduciary duties under Advisers Act sections 206(1) and (2).[311] For example, SEC enforcement actions have focused on the quality of the execution of those transactions.[312] An investment adviser may accomplish a cross trade simply by journaling a position from one hedge fund or client to another, which could provide an opportunity for pricing irregularities. The basis for the price in such a journal cross trade should be the market price at that time and should be well-documented. To satisfy the anti-fraud rules of Advisers Act sections 206(1) and (2), an investment adviser should disclose to its clients and hedge fund investors that it engages in cross trades, and should consider providing specific information regarding those trades.[313]

---

306. Additional procedures are required if the IA/BD acts as the placement agent.

307. Advisers Act Rule 206(3)-2, 17 C.F.R. § 275.206(3)-2; *see also* applicable state laws, *e.g.*, 10 Cal. Code Reg., § 260.235.3.

308. 15 U.S.C. § 80b-6.

309. Gardner Russo & Gardner, SEC No-Action Letter (June 7, 2006).

310. Advisers Act Release No. 1732 (July 17, 1998), 63 F.R. 39,505 (July 23, 1998).

311. 15 U.S.C. §§ 80b-6(1) and 80b-6(2).

312. *In re* Michael L. Smirlock, Advisers Act Release No. 1393 (Nov. 29, 1993) (officer of investment adviser aided and abetted violations of Advisers Act § 206(2) by setting price of agency cross transactions without asking broker for an independent evaluation of price and failing to follow investment adviser's procedure of obtaining price information from more than one broker); *In re* Renberg Capital Mgmt. Inc., Advisers Act Release No. 2064 (Oct. 1, 2002) (investment adviser violated Advisers Act § 206(2) by cross trading between two sets of client accounts at slightly higher prices than the prices at which the first set of accounts purchased the shares when slightly lower price was available in the market).

313. Advisers Act Release No. 1732 (July 17, 1998), 63 F.R. 39,505 (July 23, 1998).

5. ERISA Prohibition of Cross Transactions

An investment adviser that is an ERISA plan fiduciary because the hedge fund it manages has at least 25 percent plan assets may be prohibited from effecting cross trades involving ERISA plans.[314]

6. FINRA Rules on Registered Representative/ Investment Adviser

FINRA Conduct Rule 3040 requires that any associated person of a FINRA member who participates in a private securities transaction, beyond the mere provision of recommendations, must, before such participation, provide written notice to the FINRA member describing the proposed transaction, the associated person's role[315] and any selling compensation that the associated person will receive. "Selling compensation" is broadly defined as any compensation paid directly or indirectly, from whatever source, in connection with or as a result of the purchase or sale of a security, including, but not limited to, commissions, finder's fees, securities or rights to acquire securities, profit participation rights, tax benefits, dissolution proceeds, asset-based advisory fees, and expense reimbursements. Thus, if an investment adviser manages a hedge fund and is affiliated with (or is) a FINRA member, it or its principals and employees may be subject to Rule 3040.

In a transaction in which an associated person has received or may receive selling compensation, the FINRA member must advise the associated person in writing whether the FINRA member approves or disapproves of the associated person's participation in the proposed transaction. If the FINRA member approves the associated person's participation, the FINRA member must record the transaction on its books and records and supervise the associated person's participation in the transaction, as if the transaction were executed on behalf of the FINRA member. To comply with Rule 3040, an RR/IA must report to the affiliated brokerage firm all securities transactions in the RR/IA's hedge fund and other discretionary advisory accounts. The brokerage firm must supervise the RR/IA in these transactions and record them on its books and records. The record-keeping and supervisory system must be adequate to ensure that full and complete transaction information is captured and to detect and prevent misconduct that could violate the federal securities laws or FINRA Rules.

If the FINRA member disapproves of an associated person's participation, the associated person may not participate in the transaction in any manner, directly or indirectly. In a transaction or a series of related transactions in which an associated person has not and will not receive any selling compensation, the FINRA member must promptly acknowledge in writing the associated person's notice describing his or her participation, and the FINRA member may, in its discretion, require the associated person to adhere to specified conditions in connection with the associated person's participation.

---

314. *See* § 11.4.3.vi, *supra*.

315. NASD Notice to Members, Notice 96-33 (May 1996), pp. 237-241.

7. Other Considerations

Exchange Act section 11(a)[316] may restrict an IA/BD from effecting transactions of hedge funds and other discretionary accounts on a securities exchange of which the IA/BD is a member, unless an exception applies.[317]

§ 13.10 Personal Trading

The personal trading of investment advisers, portfolio managers and other investment professionals has provided a fertile source of cases for the SEC's Division of Enforcement.[318] As interpreted by courts, Advisers Act sections 206(1) and 206(2) impose on an investment adviser, as a fiduciary, affirmative duties of utmost good faith and full disclosure of material facts, including conflicts of interest, to its advisory clients.[319] When questionable trading practices are not adequately disclosed to clients, suits and enforcement actions are also brought under the anti-fraud provisions of Exchange Act section 10(b)[320] and Rule 10b-5[321] thereunder. These enforcement actions may be brought for

316. 15 U.S.C. § 78k(a).

317. Jerry W. Markham & Thomas Lee Hazen, *Broker Dealer Operations Under Securities and Commodities Law*, § 9:8 (West 2009).

318. *See, e.g., In re* Embry, Advisers Act Release No. 1382 (Sep. 16, 1993) and SEC v. Embry, Lit. Release No. 13777 (Sep. 9, 1993) (investment adviser and portfolio manager violated Advisers Act §§ 206(1) and 206(2), Exchange Act § 10(b) and Exchange Act Rule 10b-5 by, in part, failing to disclose availability and by purchasing common stock that functioned as an equity "kicker" to help sell high-yield securities purchased on behalf of clients); *In re* Strong/Corneliuson Cap. Mgmt., Inc., Advisers Act Release No. 1425 (July 12, 1994) (investment adviser violated Advisers Act §§ 206(1) and 206(2) by failing to disclose that it invested in securities recommended to clients and that it recommended securities of an investment fund to clients in which the investment adviser had an interest); *In re* Conan, Advisers Act Release No. 1446 (Sep. 30, 1994) (portfolio manager violated Advisers Act §§ 206(1) and 206(2) by purchasing stock warrants from an issuer for her personal account when, if she had allowed her clients to purchase such warrants, they would have enhanced the value of notes of the same issuer that were held by those advisory clients; the portfolio manager failed to (a) preclear the purchase with the investment adviser, (b) report the purchase to the investment adviser or the advisory clients and (c) purchase the warrants for the advisory clients); *In re* Chancellor Cap. Mgmt., Inc., Advisers Act Release No. 1447 (Oct. 18, 1994) (citing the need for disclosure of conflicts when a portfolio manager directs client purchases of securities issued in 2 public offerings while personally holding securities of the same companies that he had purchased privately more than a year earlier at nominal prices); and *In re* Honour, Advisers Act Release No. 1527 (Sep. 29, 1995) (finding violations by a portfolio manager who bought and sold securities for his personal account at about the same time as purchases and sales made for client accounts without getting advance approval from the investment adviser, without reporting the trades as required by Advisers Act Rule 204-2(a)(12) and without disclosing the conflicts of interest to the advisory clients).

319. 15 U.S.C. §§ 80b-6(1) and (2); SEC v. Capital Gains Research Bureau, Inc., 375 U.S. 180, 194 (1963).

320. 15 U.S.C. § 78j(b).

321. 17 C.F.R. § 240.10b-5.

failing to report personal trades as required by the Advisers Act,[322] failing to avoid conflicts of interest, failing to disclose potential conflicts of interest to the clients,[323] failing to disclose conflicts of interest on the Form ADV,[324] or failing to establish or consistently enforce adequate procedures to prevent the misuse of material nonpublic information[325] and to detect unauthorized trading.[326]

To avoid violations of the Advisers Act and SEC rules regarding personal trading, investment advisers and their employees should (a) establish procedures to bring to light and to avoid situations in which the investment adviser's or its employees' investing conflicts with the interests of its advisory clients; (b) if such a conflict cannot be avoided, provide notice to clients and obtain written client consent to the transaction before the transaction; (c) adopt a written policy for reporting personal securities transactions and take reasonable measures to assure that employees read, understand and comply with the policy; (d) disclose all potential conflicts of interest in the investment adviser's Form ADV; and (e) implement procedures to prevent the misuse of material nonpublic information.[327]

1. Report Personal Trades

An investment adviser must maintain records of all personal securities transactions by its advisory representatives.[328] "Advisory representatives" are generally all persons in a position to have advance information about the investment adviser's recommendations on behalf of the hedge fund and its other accounts.[329] An advisory representative must disclose any trades involving securities in which he or she has beneficial ownership.[330] For this purpose, the test for beneficial ownership is the same as in the rules under Exchange Act section 16.[331] For example, trades by an advisory representative's spouse and

---

322. Advisers Act Rule 204-2(a)(12), 17 C.F.R. § 275.204-2(a)(12); *In re* Honour, Advisers Act Release No. 1527 (Sep. 29, 1995).

323. Advisers Act §§ 206(1) and (2), 15 U.S.C. §§ 80b-6(1) and (2); *In re* Conan, Advisers Act Release No. 1446 (Sep. 30, 1994).

324. *In re* Chancellor Cap. Mgmt., Inc., Advisers Act Release No. 1447 (Oct. 18, 1996); Advisers Act § 207, 15 U.S.C. § 80b-7.

325. *In re* Gabelli & Co., Inc., Advisers Act Release No. 1457 (Dec. 8, 1994); *In re* Alliance Cap. Mgmt., L.P., Advisers Act Release No. 1630 (Apr. 28, 1997); Advisers Act § 204(A), 15 U.S.C. § 80b-4(a).

326. *In re* First Capital Strategists, Advisers Act Release No. 1648 (Aug. 13, 1997); *In re* Nicholas Applegate Cap. Mgmt., Advisers Act Release No. 1741 (Aug. 12, 1998); *In re* Rhumbline Advisers, Advisers Act Release No. 1765 (Sep. 29, 1998); *In re* Scudder Kemper Inv., Inc., Advisers Act Release No. 1848 (Dec. 22, 1999).

327. *See also* Report of the Advisory Group on Personal Investing, Investment Company Institute, May 9, 1994, *available at* http://www.ici.org/pdf/rpt_personal_investing.pdf (last visited May 16, 2013).

328. Advisers Act Rules 204-2(a)(12)(i) and 204-2(a)(13)(i), 17 C.F.R. §§ 275.204-2(a)(12)(i) and 275.204-2(a)(13)(i).

329. Advisers Act Rule 204-2(a)(12)(ii)(A), 17 C.F.R. § 275.204-2(a)(12)(ii)(A).

330. Advisers Act Rule 204-2(a)(12)(iii)(B), 17 C.F.R. § 275.204-2(a)(12)(iii)(B).

331. *See* § 13.1.2, *supra*.

other immediate family members must be reported. Disclosure of employees' trades can highlight insider trading and front-running (trading ahead of the investment adviser's recommendations to its clients) and facilitate preventive or remedial action.

2. Written Policy

Advisers Act Rule 206(4)-7 requires an SEC-registered investment adviser to adopt and implement written policies and procedures reasonably designed to prevent violation by the investment adviser and its supervised persons of the Advisers Act and the rules thereunder. Advisers Act Rule 204A-1 requires an SEC-registered investment adviser to adopt, maintain and enforce a written code of ethics, which must include (among other things) provisions requiring all "access persons" to report, and the investment adviser to review, their personal securities transactions and holdings.[332]

3. Investment Company Act Section 17(j)

A hedge fund investment adviser that is also affiliated with an investment company regulated by the Company Act must also comply with Company Act section 17(j)[333] and Rule 17j-1[334] thereunder. Rule 17j-1 requires that an investment adviser affiliated with an investment company (a) adopt a code of ethics and procedures to detect and prevent improper personal trading, (b) file quarterly reports concerning personal securities transactions and initial and annual reports concerning personal securities holdings, and (c) maintain records regarding personal trading, including a copy of the code of ethics and a list of violations thereof, copies of all reports made by all persons required to submit such reports and a list of all such persons.[335]

§ 13.11 Policies and Procedures Regarding Insider Trading

An investment adviser may receive material, nonpublic information from its industry sources or in connection with serving on the boards of directors of issuers or other relationships. To ensure that investment advisers do not tip or trade on material, nonpublic information, Advisers Act section 204A[336] requires all investment advisers (whether SEC-registered, state-registered or unregistered) to establish, maintain and enforce written policies and procedures designed to prevent insider trading. The SEC is particularly concerned about

332. Advisers Act Rules 206(4)-7 and 204A-1, 17 C.F.R. §§ 270.206(4)-7 and 270.204A-1; *see* § 2.7, *supra*.

333. 15 U.S.C. § 80a-17(j).

334. 17 C.F.R. § 270.17j-1.

335. Thomas P. Lemke, Gerald T. Lins & A. Thomas Smith III, *Regulation of Investment Companies*, § 8.05 (Matthew Bender & Co., Inc. 2009).

336. 15 U.S. § 80b-4a.

"expert networks" that connect institutional investors such as hedge funds to industry experts who may be current or former employees of issuers of securities. Some expert network firms purport to be in the business of providing legitimate research about publicly traded companies, but actually provide nonpublic information obtained from sources inside such companies. The SEC has brought enforcement proceedings against such firms and their employees and in certain cases, the hedge funds that used their services.[337] An investment adviser to a hedge fund that uses the services of an expert network firm or other third-party research provider should have insider trading policies and procedures that specifically address the use of such firms.

1. Insider Trading

Exchange Act section 10(b)[338] and Exchange Act Rule 10b-5[339] are frequently the bases for SEC investigations and prosecutions. Section 10(b) prohibits any "manipulative or deceptive device in connection with the purchase or sale of any security." Among other things, Rule 10b-5, as interpreted by courts, prohibits insider trading, which has been given high priority in SEC enforcement efforts. While the law concerning insider trading is evolving, it is generally understood that the law prohibits:

- Trading in securities by an insider while in possession of material, nonpublic information.[340] This includes "temporary insiders," such as attorneys, accountants, consultants and others who temporarily become fiduciaries of the corporation.[341] Trading on such information by any such insider is a "deceptive" device under Exchange Act section 10(b) and a device to defraud under Exchange Act Rule 10b-5, because the insider breaches his or her relationship of trust and confidence with the shareholders of a corporation by using for his or her own benefit information obtained by reason of his or her position with the corporation.
- Trading in securities by a noninsider while in possession of material, nonpublic information, where the information either was disclosed to the noninsider in violation of an insider's duty to keep it confidential, or was misappropriated.[342] Instead of basing liability on a fiduciary relationship between the company insider and the purchaser or seller of the company's stock, the misappropriation theory bases liability on

337. SEC v. Longoria, et al., 2012 SEC LEXIS 1448 (S.D.N.Y. 2012); SEC v. Kinnucan, 2012 SEC LEXIS 545 (S.D.N.Y. 2012)

338. 15 U.S.C. § 78j(b).

339. 17 C.F.R. § 240.10b-5.

340. Dirks v. SEC, 463 U.S. 646, 655, n. 14 (1983).

341. Chiarella v. U.S., 445 U.S. 222, 228 (1980); Dirks v. U.S., 463 U.S. 646, 655, n. 14 (1983).

342. U.S. v O'Hagan, 521 U.S. 642 (1997) (partner in law firm misappropriated information from his law firm and law firm's clients by trading in securities of company regarding which law firm's client was preparing a tender offer, in breach of his fiduciary duty owed to the law firm and the client).

a fiduciary-turned-trader's deception of those who entrusted him or her with confidential information.[343]

- Communicating material, nonpublic information to others, or recommending a securities transaction to others while in possession of material, nonpublic information about the security or the company in question (commonly called tipping).

i. Material Nonpublic Information

Trading while in possession of nonpublic information may be illegal if the information is material. Information about a company or its securities is "material" if it is of such importance that it has a substantial likelihood of altering the "total mix of information" regarding the company.[344] "Material information" is information that, if generally known, would affect the market price of the security.[345] Material information can relate to current events or to possible future events. When information relates to a possible future event, materiality is determined by balancing the probability that the event will occur and the anticipated magnitude of the event in light of the totality of the company's activities.[346] The more likely it is that an event will occur, the less significant the event needs to be for the information to be deemed material; the more significant the event, the less likely the probability of its occurrence needs to be for the information to be deemed material. Whether a particular item of information is material may depend on how specific it is, the extent to which it differs from public information, and its reliability in light of its source, its nature and the circumstances under which it is received.

Information that an investment adviser's personnel should consider material includes, among other things, information about earnings estimates; changes in previously released earnings estimates; manufacturing problems; changes in control or management; mergers; acquisitions; tender offers; joint ventures; changes in assets; major litigation; liquidity problems; significant new products, discoveries, services or contracts; cancellation or loss of significant orders, products, services or contracts; change in auditors or auditor notification that the issuer may no longer rely on an auditor's audit report; events regarding the issuer's securities; defaults on senior securities; calls of securities for redemption; repurchase plans; stock splits or changes in dividends; changes to rights of security holders; public or private sales of additional securities; and bankruptcies or receiverships.[347]

---

343. *Id.* at 652.

344. TSC Industries v. Northway, Inc., 426 U.S. 438, 449 (1976); Harkavy v. Apparel Industries, Inc., 571 F.2d 737, 741 (2d Cir. 1978) (applying *TSC Industries* to insider trading cases).

345. Elkind v. Liggett & Myers, Inc., F.2d 156, 166 (2d Cir. 1980).

346. SEC v. Texas Gulf Sulphur Co., 401 F.2d 833, 849 (2d Cir. 1968).

347. *See, e.g.,* SEC v. Howard, SEC Litigation Release No. 13965 (Feb. 10, 1994) (new product); Elkind v. Ligget & Myers, Inc., 635 F.2d 156 (2d Cir. 1980) (change in earnings estimates); and Securities Act Release No. 7881 (Aug. 15, 2000), 65 F.R. 51,716 (Aug. 24, 2000) (SEC's list of various matters that may be considered material).

Material information can also relate to events or circumstances affecting the market for a company's securities. For example, a reporter for *The Wall Street Journal* was criminally liable for disclosing to others the dates that articles about various companies would be published in *The Wall Street Journal* and whether those reports would or would not be favorable.[348]

"Nonpublic" information is information that has not been disseminated in a manner that makes it available to public investors generally. If information is being disseminated to traders generally by brokers and institutional analysts, it would be considered public unless there is a reasonable basis to believe that such information is confidential and came from an insider.[349] Information that has been selectively disclosed to a few analysts or investors is not public. Public information is information that has been effectively disclosed in a manner sufficient to ensure that it is available to the investing public, such as by disclosure in a report filed with the SEC or publication in the Dow Jones broad tape, Reuters Economic Services, the Associated Press or United Press International wire services, newspapers of general circulation in New York City, or, if the subject company's operations or stockholders are geographically localized, in local news media, or the electronic media. Even after information becomes public, persons who were aware of the information when it was nonpublic must wait to trade until the market absorbs the information.[350]

ii. Insiders

"Insiders" of a company are generally its officers, directors, employees and controlling shareholders. Thus, an investment adviser that has a large position in an issuer and has frequent conversations with management may be deemed an insider, as would an investment adviser whose employee or representative serves on the board of an issuer. In addition, persons outside a company who gain inside information in the course of dealings with that company may be considered "temporary insiders" of the company and thus be bound by the same legal restrictions as traditional insiders. For example, investment advisers, investment bankers, lawyers or accountants retained to represent or assist the company on an ongoing basis or in major corporate transactions may be insiders for purposes of insider trading laws.

Under this analysis, an investment adviser and its employees could be deemed temporary insiders of a company if the investment adviser advises or performs other services for the company. Thus, an investment adviser's policies and procedures should warn its personnel that if they receive material, nonpublic information regarding a company that might have originated directly or indirectly from any insider (temporary or traditional), they should not trade in that company's securities for a hedge fund or other client, and should not discuss the information with any other person, without first consulting the appropriate persons.

---

348. Carpenter v. U.S., 484 U.S. 19 (1987).
349. Elkind v. Liggett & Myers, Inc., 635 F.2d 156, 168 (2d Cir. 1980).
350. U.S. v. Libera, 989 F.2d 596, 601 (2d Cir. 1993).

iii. Misappropriation

"Misappropriation" is a basis for insider trading liability that is established when trading occurs based on material, nonpublic information that was misappropriated from another person. This theory has been used to reach a variety of individuals who are not traditional or temporary insiders. *The Wall Street Journal* reporter mentioned above was found by the U.S. Supreme Court to have defrauded the newspaper when he misappropriated information about upcoming articles from the newspaper and used the information for trading in the securities markets.[351] Similarly, a partner in a law firm was held to have used a "deceptive device" in violation of Exchange Act section 10(b) by misappropriating information from his law firm and the law firm's client, in breach of his fiduciary duty owed to this law firm and the client, and using it in trading in securities of a company regarding which the client was preparing a tender offer.[352]

iv. Tipping

"Tipping" is the disclosure of material, nonpublic information about a company or its securities to a third-party, when such disclosure is not made strictly for corporate purposes. The disclosure may be made by an insider of the company, by one who has misappropriated the information from the company in question or from another person or company, or by anyone who received information traceable to an insider or one who has misappropriated the information.[353] Those who disclose the information are called "tippers"; those who receive the information are called "tippees." Criminal and civil liability for trading on the basis of tipped information may attach even where the information is received second- or third-hand, or more remotely, if the other requirements for finding liability are present.[354] The same legal standards apply to remote tippees. In addition, the tipper may be liable for any profits gained or losses avoided by a tippee, even if the tipper did not trade.[355] Thus, an investment adviser's policies and procedures should forbid its personnel from disclosing to anyone any information someone has tipped to him or her. The individual and the investment adviser may be liable if anyone trades on material, nonpublic information received from or through that person.

2. Penalties for Insider Trading

Penalties for trading on or tipping material, nonpublic information are severe. They may include a civil injunction, disgorgement of the profit gained or the loss

351. Carpenter v. U.S., 484 U.S. 19 (1987).

352. U.S. v O'Hagan, 521 U.S. 642 (1997).

353. Dirks v. SEC, 463 U.S. 646 (1983). In *Dirks*, an investment analyst received information from a former insider regarding massive fraud at a company. The analyst discussed his findings with the contacts and investors, some of whom traded on the information. The court held that the analyst was not a "tippee" and thus had no duty to refrain from communicating the information to others because the insiders had not acted for profit and had not breached a duty to the company.

354. U.S. v. Chestman, 903 F.2d 75 (2d. Cir.1990).

355. SEC v. Texas Gulf Sulphur Co., 446 F.2d 1301, 1308 (2d Cir. 1971).

avoided, a civil penalty of up to 3 times the profit gained or the loss avoided, a criminal fine of up to $5,000,000 for an individual or $25,000,000 for an entity (in addition to civil penalties based on the profit gained or the loss avoided) and jail time of up to 20 years.[356]

Even if an investment adviser and any managerial and supervisory personnel or other controlling persons (collectively, Controlling Persons) do not engage in insider trading, a Controlling Person may be civilly liable in an amount up to the greater of $1,000,000 and 3 times the profit realized or loss avoided by the person who made the illegal trades, if (a) the Controlling Person knew or recklessly disregarded the fact that the person was likely to engage in insider trading and failed to take appropriate steps to prevent the violation, or (b) the Controlling Person knowingly or recklessly failed to establish, maintain or enforce the policies and procedures required by Advisers Act section 204A.[357] In addition, contemporaneous traders in the market may bring private suits for damages against insider trading violators and their Controlling Persons.[358]

§ 13.12 Order Aggregation

1. In General

An investment adviser (whether SEC-registered, state-registered or unregistered) to multiple hedge funds or other clients has a fiduciary duty not to prefer one account over another and to treat each account fairly.[359] For example, an investment adviser that manages a hedge fund and separate accounts should treat those accounts fairly when it aggregates those clients' trades.

2. Aggregation of Trades for Clients and Investment Adviser Personnel

In a 1995 no-action letter,[360] the SEC staff stated that it would not recommend enforcement action under Company Act section 17(d),[361] Company Act Rule 17d-1[362] or Advisers Act section 206,[363] if an SEC-registered investment adviser aggregates trades of nonaffiliated clients and clients in which persons associated

356. Exchange Act §§ 21A (civil penalties) and 32(a) (criminal penalties), 15 U.S.C. §§ 78u-1 and 78ff(a).

357. Exchange Act § 21A(b)(1), 15 U.S.C. § 78u-1(b)(1).

358. Exchange Act § 20A(a), 15 U.S.C. § 78t-1(a).

359. *In re* Acct. Mgmt. Corp., Advisers Act Release No. 1529 (Sep. 29, 1995) (investment adviser breached its fiduciary duty by consistently allocating short-term trading opportunities in "hot IPOs" to a limited group of accounts); *In re* Monetta Fin. Serv., Inc., et al., Advisers Act Release No. 1702 (Feb. 28, 1998).

360. SMC Capital, Inc., SEC No-Action Letter (Sep. 5, 1995).

361. 15 U.S.C. § 80b-17(d).

362. 17 C.F.R. § 270.17d-1.

363. 15 U.S.C. § 80b-6.

with the investment adviser have invested, as long as the investment adviser implements the following policies:

- Aggregation of transactions is fully disclosed in the investment adviser's Form ADV and separately to the investment adviser's existing clients and the brokers through which such orders are placed, and the policies for aggregation are submitted to and approved by the board of directors of any registered investment company for which transactions are aggregated.
- The investment adviser does not aggregate transactions unless it believes that aggregation is consistent with its duty to seek best execution for its clients and is consistent with the investment adviser's investment advisory agreement with each client for which trades are aggregated.
- No advisory client is favored over any other client, and each client that participates in an aggregated order participates at the average share price for all of the investment adviser's transactions in that security on a given business day, with transaction costs shared pro rata based on each client's participation.
- The investment adviser prepares, before entering an aggregated order, a written allocation statement specifying the participating client accounts and how it intends to allocate the order among those clients, and such statements, as well as any record of deviation therefrom, are maintained in the investment adviser's records for at least 5 years (the first 2 years in the investment adviser's office) and are easily accessible.[364]
- If the aggregated order is filled in its entirety, it is allocated among clients in accordance with the allocation statement, and if the order is partially filled, it is allocated pro rata based on the allocation statement.
- The order may be allocated on a basis different from that specified in the allocation statement, if all client accounts receive fair and equitable treatment and if the reason for the different allocation is explained in writing and is approved in writing by the investment adviser's compliance officer no later than an hour after the opening of the markets on the trading day following the day the order is executed.
- The investment adviser's books and records separately reflect, for each client account the orders of which are aggregated, the securities held by or bought or sold for that account.
- Funds and securities of clients whose orders are aggregated are deposited with one or more banks or brokers, and neither the clients' cash nor their securities are held collectively any longer than is necessary to settle the purchase or sale in question on a delivery versus payment basis and cash or securities held collectively for clients are delivered to the custodian bank or broker as soon as practicable following settlement.

---

364. *See* § 2.8, *supra*.

- The investment adviser receives no additional compensation or remuneration of any kind as a result of the proposed aggregation.
- Individual investment advice and treatment are accorded to each advisory client.
- The investment adviser annually reviews its aggregation procedures to ensure that they are adequate to prevent any account from being systematically disadvantaged as a result of the aggregation of orders.
- No separate employee accounts are included in the aggregation (unless those employee accounts are also client accounts).

§ 13.13 Other Trade Allocation Issues

An investment adviser (whether SEC-registered, state-registered or unregistered) may breach its fiduciary duty to its clients in violation of Advisers Act sections 206(1) and 206(2)[365] and, in some cases, state law, by unfairly favoring one account over another or not allocating securities and advisory recommendations among its clients on an equitable basis.[366] The SEC staff typically demands that an investment adviser adopt and implement a formula or program for allocating securities and recommendations among its clients (for example, a pro rata allocation based on the amount of assets each client has under the investment adviser's management or the suitability of each client for an investment). The SEC has sanctioned investment advisers under both the Advisers Act[367] and the Company Act[368] for failing to allocate trades promptly or fairly among client accounts.

Investment advisers should be particularly careful when allocating securities that are difficult to obtain or in short supply, such as hot initial public offerings, and when allocating profitable securities to hedge funds for which they receive performance allocations and other accounts for which they charge performance fees. The SEC has brought several enforcement actions regarding delayed

365. 15 U.S.C. §§ 80b-6(1) and (2).

366. SEC Inspection Manual (1980), p. 29; *In re* Acct. Mgmt. Corp., Advisers Act Release No. 1529 (Sep. 29, 1995) (investment adviser breached fiduciary duty by consistently allocating short-term trading opportunities in "hot IPOs" to a limited group of accounts); *In re* Monetta Fin. Serv., Inc., et al., Advisers Act Release No. 1702 (Feb. 28, 1998).

367. *In re* Smirlock, Advisers Act Release No. 1393 (Nov. 29, 1993) (investment adviser sanctioned for executing purchase transactions in securities in which it failed to allocate to particular client accounts for periods of 2 to 9 days).

368. *In re* Kemper Fin. Servs., Inc., Advisers Act Release No. 1387 (Oct. 20, 1993) (investment adviser sanctioned for delaying the designation of futures trades and later allocating such trades to mutual funds).

allocations,[369] discrimination among clients[370] and misappropriation of client opportunities.[371] Other forms of favoritism that an investment adviser should avoid are allocating profitable trades to accounts for which it receives a higher management fee and making a disproportionate number of trades on behalf of a hedge fund that has authorized the investment adviser to use soft dollars for its own benefit.

§ 13.14 Trade Errors

An investment adviser is obligated to place orders correctly for its advisory accounts. Investment advisers should have trade error policies and procedures in place, and consistently implement them. The SEC has not dictated any particular policies or procedures and has not published guidance on what

---

369. *Id.* (involving portfolio manager of funds who time-stamped securities transactions after the time of order entry); *In re* Smirlock, Advisers Act Release No. 1393 (Nov. 29, 1993) (involving failure to allocate to particular client accounts for periods of 2 to 9 days); *In re* Richards, Advisers Act Release No. 1495 (June 6, 1995) (involving portfolio manager who delayed designation of the account for which securities trades were being placed until after the trades were effected); *In re* Burstein, Advisers Act Release No. 1511 (July 28, 1995) (involving intra-day prearranged purchases in which an investment manager did not identify purchaser at the time of such transactions and subsequently allocated any profits therefrom to a bank with which he was affiliated); *In re* Zion Cap. Mgmt., LLC, Advisers Act Release No. 2200A (Dec. 11, 2003) (investment adviser allocated profitable trades to account in which it had a proprietary interest instead of other accounts, contrary to representations that conflicts of interest would be resolved fairly); *In re* Gerson Asset Mgmt., Inc., Advisers Act Release No. 2457 (Dec. 2, 2005) (investment adviser allocated profitable trades to its own account and unfavorable trades to client accounts by delaying allocations until later in the day).

370. *In re* Acct. Mgmt. Corp., Advisers Act Release No. 1529 (Sep. 29, 1995) (investment adviser consistently allocated short-term trading opportunities in hot IPOs to a limited group of accounts); *In re* McKenzie Walker Inv. Mgmt., Inc., Advisers Act Release No. 1571 (July 16, 1996) (discrimination between performance-based fee accounts and asset-based fee accounts in the allocation of equity trades and hot IPOs); *In re* The Dreyfus Corp., Advisers Act Release No. 1870 (May 10, 2000) (allocation of securities purchased in IPOs favored one fund over 3 other of investment adviser's funds); *In re* F.W. Thompson Co., Inc., Advisers Act Release No. 1895 (Sep. 7, 2000) (allocations of securities purchased in IPOs were made solely to 15 of investment adviser's 29 accounts eligible to purchase such securities); *In re* Nevis Cap. Mgmt., LLC, Advisers Act Release No. 2214 (Feb. 9, 2004) (investment adviser allocated IPOs solely to mutual funds and hedge funds instead of other IPO-eligible accounts, contrary to disclosures on Form ADV).

371. *In re* Conan, Advisers Act Release No. 1446 (Sep. 30, 1994) (portfolio manager misappropriated client opportunity by purchasing for her personal account profitable warrants without first offering to her clients eligible to purchase such warrants the opportunity to purchase them); Kemper Fin. Serv., Inc., et al., Advisers Act Release No. 1476 (Mar. 2, 1995) (firm fraudulently diverted client investment opportunities to a private investment fund for the benefit of the firm's employees); *In re* Speaker, Advisers Act Release No. 1605 (Jan. 13, 1997) (portfolio manager breached his fiduciary duty to a mutual fund by personally purchasing debentures without disclosing such opportunity to and first obtaining prior consent of the mutual fund).

constitutes an error. The following examples are typically cited as investment adviser trade errors:

- buying or selling a stock that results in the account being managed outside of its written investment guidelines or contrary to client instructions (for example, buying a stock that is on the client's restricted list, or buying or selling a stock that causes the account to be improperly concentrated in a particular industry or asset class);372
- executing a discretionary trade in a nondiscretionary account;
- entering an order as a sell rather than a buy or vice versa;[373]
- buying or selling the incorrect amount of shares (for example, 1,000 instead of 10,000 shares);
- buying or selling the wrong stock (for example, buying ticker symbol ZYX instead of XYZ);
- buying or selling the right stock in the right amount, but for the wrong account;
- allocating a transaction incorrectly among accounts;
- incorrectly noting the price executed; and
- sending the trade to the wrong broker.

A clerical error may not always rise to the level of a trade error. For example, a trade may be properly executed and entered into a client's account, but an incorrect notation entered on the order ticket. In that case, the proper action may be to correct the order ticket and add a notation explaining why the correction was made. An investment adviser should be careful, however, when excluding categories of errors from its error correction policies. Several of the most typical trade errors, such as over- and under-purchases, or purchases of the wrong stock are, in essence, clerical errors.

If an investment adviser makes an error in placing a trade for an account, the SEC believes that the investment adviser, whether SEC-registered, state-registered or unregistered, has a fiduciary duty to bear the cost of correcting the error.[374] Many practitioners believe that an investment adviser may cause client accounts to bear the costs of trade errors if the investment adviser adequately discloses its trade error policy to its clients. The U.K. Financial Services

---

372. *In re* Pirrie, Advisers Act Release No. 1284 (July 29, 1991) (investment adviser made trade error by purchasing stock in contravention of the client's investment guideline prohibiting purchases and sales of securities of companies doing business in South Africa); *In re* Balatsos, Advisers Act Release No. 1324 (Aug. 18, 1992) (investment adviser's portfolio summaries erroneously reported that client acquired bonds in a single transaction when such bonds were actually acquired in 2 transactions).

373. *In re* M & I Inv. Mgmt. Corp., Advisers Act Release No. 1318 (June 30, 1992) (investment adviser's trader erroneously directed broker to sell certain stock with respect to which investment adviser had placed a buy order).

374. *See* Charles Lerner, SEC No-Action Letter (Oct. 25, 1988) (investment adviser that makes trade error for an account must bear costs of correcting).

Authority has, for example, stated that an advisory agreement may provide that a trade error is borne by the client,[375] but the SEC has not provided guidance on this issue.

Trade errors should be corrected as quickly as possible after detection. By promptly resolving errors, investment advisers can limit their potential market exposure and liability to clients. Moreover, the Advisers Act and rules thereunder require that certain records be kept accurate and current.[376] An undetected or uncorrected error may result in a firm's records not being accurate and current and therefore lead to a recordkeeping violation.[377] An investment adviser should not delay correction in the hope that a favorable market or offsetting transaction will allow the error to be corrected with no loss to the client or cost to the investment adviser.

The cost of errors includes both direct costs, such as market losses and commission charges to reverse the error, as well as indirect costs, such as the opportunity costs of not being able to invest the erroneously invested assets. An investment adviser may compensate a client for missed investment opportunities due to an error by paying a fixed rate of interest or a rate based on the performance of the remainder of the account. In general, the longer an erroneous trade remains undetected and uncorrected, the greater the difficulty of determining the cost of the error.

The SEC staff has stated that an investment adviser's use of client assets to correct trade errors without disclosing the corrective action to the client and obtaining the consent of the client is a breach of the investment adviser's fiduciary duty and a violation of the anti-fraud provisions of the Advisers Act.[378] In addition, an investment adviser violates its fiduciary duties to treat each client fairly if it disadvantages one client to make another client whole. Soft dollars should not be used to cover an investment adviser's errors. Error correction through the use of a soft-dollar arrangement with a broker is not within the safe harbor of Exchange Act section 28(e),[379] because error correction is not a

---

375. FSA Feedback Statement 06/2: Hedge funds: A discussion of risk and regulatory engagement; § 3.43 (Mar. 2006).

376. *See* Advisers Act Rule 204-2(a), 17 C.F.R. § 275.204-2(a); *see* § 2.8, *supra.*

377. *In re* Smirlock, Advisers Act Release No. 1393 (Nov. 29, 1993) (failure to write trade tickets promptly after trades caused investment adviser's records to fail to reflect accurate date of entry, resulting in violation of record- keeping provisions of Advisers Act Rule 204(c)(1)-(2)).

378. *In re* M & I Inv. Mgmt. Corp., Advisers Act Release No. 1318 (June 30, 1992) (by failing to have a procedure for disclosing trade errors, investment adviser violated Advisers Act § 206(1)-(3)); *In re* Balatsos, Advisers Act Release No. 1324 (Aug. 18, 1992) (failure to disclose erroneous portfolio summaries was a factor in SEC finding that investment adviser violated Advisers Act § 206(3)); Company Act Release No. 1270 (Jan. 31, 1991) (alleging that investment adviser violated Advisers Act §§ 206(1) and (2) because its president did not disclose to client the investment adviser's conflict of interest in not realizing the loss created by investment adviser's error).

379. 15 U.S.C. § 78bb(e); *see* § 14.2.5.i, *infra.*

brokerage or research service.[380] This issue may arise when a broker with whom an investment adviser has a longstanding relationship offers to bear all or part of the loss involved in an error. If an investment adviser accepts such an offer, it should make clear that such acceptance does not create any express or implied commitment to direct brokerage, or any other benefit, to that broker.

380. *In re* Pirrie, Advisers Act Release 1284 (July 29, 1991) (investment adviser violated Advisers Act §§ 206(1) and (2) by failing to disclose that investment adviser used soft-dollar arrangements to offset loss that resulted from investment adviser's trade error); Charles Lerner, SEC No-Action Letter (Oct. 25, 1988) (investment management firm and broker using soft-dollar arrangements to correct orders would not be able to rely on the safe-harbor of Exchange Act § 28(e)).

CHAPTER **14**

Brokerage Allocation Practices

The fiduciary duties regarding brokerage allocation practices apply to every investment adviser, whether or not registered with the SEC. In recent years, the SEC, and especially the SEC inspection staff, have increased their focus on brokerage allocation issues, such as best execution and soft-dollar transactions.

§ 14.1 Best Execution

The SEC has indicated repeatedly that all investment advisers (whether or not registered or required to be registered with the SEC) have a fiduciary duty to clients to obtain "best execution," that is, to execute securities transactions for their clients so that the clients' total costs or proceeds in each transaction are the most favorable under the circumstances.[1] Best execution is not merely a matter of paying the lowest possible commissions. The brokerage transaction must represent the best qualitative execution for the client, taking into account a variety of factors, such as the efficiency of execution, the timing of the transaction, the price of the security purchased or sold, the commission rate, the financial responsibility of the broker and the broker's responsiveness to the investment adviser.

The SEC inspection staff requires investment advisers periodically and systematically to evaluate the quality and cost of services received from brokers with whom they place client orders. Since 2004, Rule 206(4)-7[2] under the Advisers Act has required investment advisers to adopt written policies and procedures to evaluate execution, but even before 2004 the SEC inspection staff urged investment advisers to conduct formal periodic evaluations of

---

1. Exchange Act Release No. 23170 (Apr. 23, 1986), 51 F.R. 16,004 (Apr. 30, 1986); In the Matter of Synovus Securities, Advisers Act Release No. 1423 (July 5, 1994) (willful failure to obtain best execution and nondisclosure of brokerage practices violates Exchange Act § 10(b), Exchange Act Rule 10b-5, and Advisers Act §§ 206(1) and 206(2)); In the Matter of Portfolio Management Consultants, Advisers Act Release No. 1568 (June 27, 1996) (willful failure to obtain best execution violates Advisers Act § 206(2)); In the Matter of Fleet Investment Advisors, Advisers Act Release No. 1821 (Sep. 9, 1999) (failure to seek best available price violates Advisers Act §§ 206(1) and 206(2)); In the Matter of Fidelity Mgmt. & Research Co., Advisers Act Release No. 2713 (March 5, 2008) (adviser willfully violated Advisers Act § 206(2) by allowing employees' receipt of travel, entertainment and gifts to affect the selection of brokers).

2. 17 C.F.R. § 275-206(4)-7.

execution and the brokerage and research services provided by brokers, to determine whether the investment advisers were achieving best execution in client transactions. Under Advisers Act Rule 206(4)-7, investment advisers' policies and procedures relating to execution must be formalized in writing and made available to the SEC on request.[3]

The SEC inspection staff has indicated that in evaluating execution, an investment adviser should consider possible execution alternatives such as electronic communication networks (ECNs), alternative brokers, market makers and market centers.[4] The investment adviser should also analyze conflicts of interest that result from receiving services from brokers, such as client referrals and soft-dollar payments for research and other services, in exchange for directing transactions to brokers, and adopt policies to manage such conflicts.[5] The SEC inspection staff has indicated that appropriate documentation of the periodic evaluations might comprehend minutes of meetings, including the conclusions reached and decisions made, copies of information received and evaluated, and a determination that execution practices are consistent with disclosures in the investment adviser's Form ADV. The execution practices should also be consistent with the disclosures in the offering materials of hedge funds that an investment adviser manages.

§ 14.2 Soft-Dollar Arrangements

1. Definition

In a soft-dollar arrangement, an investment adviser receives from a broker goods or services other than client trade executions, in exchange for directing client brokerage transactions to the broker.[6]

2. Disclosure Duty in General

An investment adviser has a fiduciary duty to disclose all soft-dollar arrangements and describe all associated potential and actual conflicts of interest to its clients.[7] If an SEC-registered or state-registered investment adviser has the discretion to select, or even to suggest, a broker to a client and the value of products, research or services that the broker provides to the investment adviser could affect the investment adviser's choice or suggestion, the investment adviser must describe its brokerage practices and the conflicts of interest they create in Part 2 of its

3. *Id.*

4. Exchange Act Release No. 23170 (Apr. 23, 1986), 51 F.R. 16,004 (Apr. 30, 1986).

5. Lori A. Richards, Director, Office of Compliance Inspections and Examinations, SEC, Speech at 2001 Mutual Fund Compliance Conference of the Investment Company Institute, June 14, 2001, (*available at* http://www.sec.gov/news/speech/spch499.htm).

6. Inspection Report on the Soft Dollar Practices of Broker-Dealers, Investment Advisers and Mutual Funds, Office of Compliance, Inspections and Examinations, SEC (Sep. 22, 1998), *available at* www.sec.gov/news/studies/softdolr.htm (last visited May 17, 2013)

7. SEC v. Capital Gains Research, 375 U.S. 180, 191-192 (1963).

Form ADV, including (among other things) the products, research and services obtained, whether clients may pay commissions higher than those charged by other brokers in return for those products and services, whether and how the research, products and services so obtained are allocated among the investment adviser's accounts, and any procedures the investment adviser used during the last fiscal year to direct client transactions to a particular broker in return for products and research services.[8]

3. Section 28(e) Safe Harbor

As a fiduciary to its clients, an investment adviser has a duty to deal fairly with them in all respects.[9] In response to investment advisers' concerns that an investment adviser that receives anything from brokers other than the lowest possible commissions for its clients could be deemed to have breached its fiduciary duty, Congress enacted Exchange Act section 28(e).[10] Section 28(e) provides a safe harbor from a breach of fiduciary duty claim under state or federal law if the investment adviser causes a client to pay a broker a higher commission than another broker would have charged for the same transaction, if the investment adviser determines in good faith that the amount of the commission is reasonable in relation to the value of the brokerage and research services provided.[11]

Section 28(e) does not, however, provide any exception or exemption from an investment adviser's fiduciary duty to obtain best execution for its clients. Thus, an investment adviser that determines in good faith that the value of the research and brokerage services it generates is reasonable in relation to the commissions charged could nevertheless violate its duty of best execution if those commissions are in fact higher than the most favorable under the circumstances.[12]

i. Brokerage and Research Services

Exchange Act section 28(e)(3) states that a person provides "brokerage and research services" if that person:

(A) furnishes advice, either directly or through publications or writings, as to the value of securities, the advisability of investing in, purchasing or selling securities, and the availability of securities or purchasers or sellers of securities;

---

8. Form ADV, Part 2, Item 12.A (*available at* http://www.sec.gov/about/forms/formadv-part2.pdf). *See* § 14.2.4, *infra*, regarding disclosure required for soft-dollar arrangements outside the safe harbor.

9. SEC v. Capital Gains Research, 375 U.S. 180, 191-192 (1963); Exchange Act Release No. 23170 (Apr. 23, 1986), 51 F.R. 16,004 (Apr. 30, 1986); In the Matter of Kidder, Peabody, Advisers Act Release No. 232 (Oct. 16, 1968).

10. 15 U.S.C. § 78bb(e).

11. *Id.*

12. Exchange Act Release No. 23170 (Apr. 23, 1986), fn. 30., 51 F.R. 16,004, fn. 30 (Apr. 30, 1986).

(B) furnishes analyses and reports concerning issuers, industries, securities, economic factors and trends, portfolio strategy and the performance of accounts; or

(C) effects securities transactions and performs functions incidental thereto (such as clearance, settlement and custody) or required in connection therewith by rules of the [SEC] or a self-regulatory organization of which such person is a member or person associated with a member or in which such person is a participant.

In a 2006 Interpretive Release,[13] the SEC interpreted "brokerage" products and services to mean products and services that the investment adviser uses from the point at which the investment adviser communicates with a broker to execute an order through the point at which the funds or securities are delivered or credited to the client's account. Communication services related to execution, clearing and settlement, such as dedicated lines between the broker and the investment adviser or the investment adviser's order management system, and message services used to transmit orders, are eligible for the section 28(e) safe harbor as brokerage services. Trading software used to route orders to market centers, software that provides algorithmic trading strategies and software that transmits orders to direct market access systems are also eligible brokerage products. Order management systems that include such trading software or provide connectivity to such software may also be permitted brokerage services under section 28(e).

Items that are not permitted brokerage products or services under the section 28(e) safe harbor include:

- software used for record-keeping or administrative purposes, including software used to manage portfolios and quantitative analytical software used to test "what if" scenarios (including such functionality provided by order management system and trade analytic software);
- hardware, such as telephones and computer terminals;
- products or services that an investment adviser uses to meet a client's specific investment parameters or for internal compliance, including analysis of best execution, portfolio turnover rate or performance of similarly managed accounts, creation of trade parameters and portfolio stress-testing; and
- capital introduction services, margin services and error-correction trades or related services related to trade-error correction.

Trade financing, such as stock lending fees, and long-term custody costs are excluded from "brokerage" because clients are responsible for payment of such items themselves, and thus the section 28(e) safe harbor is not implicated.

In the 2006 Release,[14] the SEC provided additional guidance about the meaning of "research," defining it as specialized advice, analyses and reports that reflect the expression of reasoning or knowledge. The 2006 Release lists several examples of permissible research, including:

13. Exchange Act Release No. 54165 (July 18, 2006), 71 F.R. 41,978 (July 24, 2006).
14. *Id.*

- traditional research reports;
- discussions with analysts and meetings with corporate executives to obtain reports about a company's performance;
- data services, such as those that provide market data, company financial data and economic data;
- research related to the market for securities (such as pre-trade and post-trade analytics, software and other products that depend on market information to generate market research, research on optimal execution venues and trading strategies, and advice from brokers on order execution, execution strategies, market color and the availability of buyers and sellers);
- tuition for research-related seminars and conferences (excluding associated travel and related expenses, such as meals and entertainment);
- software that provides analyses of the performance of securities portfolios, unless the software is used for marketing purposes; and
- corporate governance research and rating services, if such reports and ratings are used to make investment decisions. If a proxy voting service incorporates corporate governance services in its overall product, only the portion of the proxy voting service that investment advisers use to make investment decisions (as opposed to voting decisions) is considered research.

A portion of the expense of an order management system or trade analytical software that provides permissible research may also be treated as research under the section 28(e) safe harbor.

Items outside of the section 28(e) safe harbor include:

- mass-marketed publications (low-cost publications that are intended for and marketed to a broad, public audience, rather than intended to serve the specialized interests of a small readership);
- inherently tangible products and services (such as telephone lines and office furniture) and other operational overhead expenses;[15] and
- computer hardware (whether or not dedicated to delivery of particular research products) and the peripherals and delivery mechanisms associated with computer hardware or associated with the oral delivery of research (such as telecommunication lines).

---

15. *Id.* The 2006 Release lists a number of such expenses, including expenses for travel, entertainment and meals associated with attending seminars; travel and related expenses associated with arranging trips to meet corporate executives, analysts or other individuals who may provide eligible research; office equipment; office furniture; business supplies; salaries (including research staff); rent; accounting fees and software; website design; electronic mail software; Internet service; legal expenses; personnel management; marketing; utilities; membership dues; professional licensing fees; and software to assist with administrative functions, such as managing back-office functions, operating systems, word processing, and equipment maintenance and repair services.

ii. Mixed-Use Products and Services

Investment advisers that use client commissions to pay for products and services that are only partly used for permissible brokerage and research must reasonably allocate the expense of those items between eligible and ineligible uses and keep adequate books and records concerning those allocations. The percentage used to assist the investment adviser in investment decision-making may be paid in commission, or "soft," dollars and the remaining percentage must be paid from the investment adviser's own funds or "hard" dollars.

The 2006 Release gives examples of the factors on which an investment adviser may base its allocation decision, such as the amount of time a product or service is used for eligible and ineligible purposes, an objective measure of the usefulness of the eligible and ineligible uses, and the extent to which the product or service is redundant with other products or services that the firm uses for the same purpose. The 2006 Release states that investment advisers should disclose to their clients the conflicts of interest inherent in their allocation determinations.

Mixed-use products may include:

- order management systems, which are broadly defined as systems that integrate trading and execution, on the one hand, and accounting, record-keeping and other administrative matters, on the other hand;
- trade analysis and portfolio performance software;
- proxy voting services; and
- quotation equipment that serves a research function in pricing securities and keeping the investment adviser informed of market developments, but also performs nonresearch functions, such as client reporting.

Proxy voting services may be mixed-use services if they provide information that investment advisers use to make investment decisions, such as corporate governance reports and ratings, because such information is research within the section 28(e) safe harbor. Research that investment advisers use to decide how to vote proxies, and services related to the mechanical aspects of voting (such as casting, counting, recording and reporting votes), however, are not permitted research within the section 28(e) safe harbor.

iii. Lawful and Appropriate Assistance

To be within the section 28(e) safe harbor, the research or brokerage expense must provide lawful and appropriate assistance to the investment adviser in the performance of its investment decision-making responsibilities. For example, the use of a research product, such as portfolio performance analytics, for marketing purposes would be outside the section 28(e) safe harbor.[16]

iv. Good Faith Determination of Reasonableness

An investment adviser relying on the section 28(e) safe harbor must determine in good faith that the commission paid is reasonable in relation to the goods and services the broker provides. For example, if a broker simply copies or

16. *Id.*

aggregates a research product, an investment adviser should analyze whether or not paying additional commissions for that item is warranted. An investment adviser should not use commissions to pay for research that is overpriced or barely useful, as a means of compensating a broker for another product or service that does not meet the section 28(e) safe harbor. An investment adviser should consider the unbundled price (when that price is available) that a broker charges for research when making its good faith determination about the reasonableness of a commission.[17]

v. *Third-Party Research and Other Commission-Sharing Arrangements*

The section 28(e) safe harbor is only available to an investment adviser that pays a broker for "effecting" a securities transaction if the commission charged by the broker is reasonable in relation to the value of the services "provided by" the broker. Thus, an investment adviser that enters into any of these arrangements with a broker should ascertain that the broker actually effects the trade and provides the services.

An investment adviser may execute trades with one broker and use a portion of the commissions generated to obtain research and other services from another source. An investment adviser also may send trades to an introducing broker with the understanding that another broker will execute, clear and settle the transactions. To give investment advisers greater flexibility to obtain best execution by using multiple sources of execution, research and other services, the 2006 Release relaxed some of the SEC's prior guidance regarding the level of involvement an introducing broker must have in a securities trade to be deemed to effect the transaction. Pursuant to the 2006 Release, a broker "effects" a transaction if it executes, clears or settles a trade, or if it meets at least 1 of the following 4 criteria: the broker is financially responsible to the clearing broker for all customer trades until the clearing broker receives payment or securities; the broker keeps required records relating to its customer trades; the broker monitors and responds to customer comments concerning the trading process; or the broker generally monitors trades and settlements.[18]

According to the 2006 Release, a broker "provides" research and brokerage services within the section 28(e) safe harbor if the broker is legally obligated to pay for those goods or services. In addition, a broker can be deemed to provide research and brokerage under the section 28(e) safe harbor, even when it is not legally obligated to pay for the goods and services, if it (1) pays the research preparer directly, (2) reviews the descriptions of the services for red flags that indicate that the services are not within the section 28(e) safe harbor and agrees with the investment adviser to pay only for items that reasonably are within

17. *Id.*
18. *Id.*

the section 28(e) safe harbor[19] and (3) develops and maintains procedures for properly documenting and paying for research.

vi. Principal Transactions

The section 28(e) safe harbor is available only for soft dollars paid out of commissions. The SEC views commissions as being paid both in transactions in which the broker acts as agent and in eligible riskless principal transactions. Eligible riskless principal transactions are transactions in which a broker purchases and sells a security in a principal capacity at the same price and the investment adviser receives full disclosure of the mark-up, mark-down, fee or commission-equivalent paid to the broker and the transaction price.[20] Underlying this extension of the section 28(e) safe harbor to certain principal transactions is the assumption that the investment adviser has sufficient price transparency to determine whether the transaction costs are in fact reasonable in relation to the brokerage and research services that the broker provides.[21]

Section 28(e) is not available for mark-ups or mark-downs on principal transactions other than eligible riskless principal transactions. Thus, soft dollars generated in transactions in the over-the-counter market executed on a principal basis are not protected by the safe harbor of section 28(e). In addition, a broker that fills a customer order using securities from its own inventory is acting as a principal, and the safe harbor is unavailable.[22]

4. Soft-Dollar Arrangements Outside of Section 28(e)

An investment adviser does not necessarily breach its fiduciary duty by engaging in soft-dollar practices outside the section 28(e) safe harbor. Such transactions are risky, however, even if the commission rates the clients pay are not higher than those charged by other brokers. The SEC insists on specific and extensive disclosure of any soft-dollar arrangement outside the safe harbor, including the

19. In 2008, FINRA announced that it had fined a broker-dealer, SMH Capital Inc., for failing to implement policies and procedures to ensure that its soft-dollar payments on behalf of its hedge fund clients were made in compliance with § 28(e) and, if not, whether the hedge fund's investment adviser had disclosed to its clients that it was operating outside the § 28(e) safe harbor. FINRA News Release (Jan. 9, 2008), *available at* http://www.finra.org/Newsroom/NewsReleases/2008/P037758 (last visited May 17, 2013).

20. Exchange Act Release No. 45194 (Dec. 27, 2001), 67 F.R. 6 (Jan. 2, 2002).

21. *Id.*

22. Letter to Charles Lerner, Director of Enforcement, Pension and Welfare Benefits Administration, from Richard Ketchum, Director, SEC Division of Market Regulation (July 25, 1990); Ronald H. Hoenig, SEC No-Action Letter (Oct. 15, 1990).

conflicts of interest inherent in such a relationship.[23] The SEC has typically focused on the lack of adequate disclosure by the investment adviser and not on the soft-dollar arrangement itself as the basis for enforcement under the Advisers Act.[24]

In 1996 and 1997, the SEC staff examined the soft-dollar practices and disclosures of 280 investment advisers and investment companies. The SEC staff's report[25] the following year noted, among other things, that many investment advisers failed to provide sufficient disclosure to their clients or potential clients to enable the clients to understand the investment advisers' soft-dollar practices and the conflicts of interest those practices present. The SEC staff characterized most investment advisers' descriptions of their soft-dollar practices as simply "boilerplate," even while acknowledging that similarly situated investment advisers with similar soft-dollar practices might be expected to make similar disclosures.

The SEC staff also observed that many investment advisers used soft dollars to pay for products and services they did not use in making investment decisions (that is, not protected by the section 28(e) safe harbor) and did so without providing detailed disclosures of these products and services. The SEC continues to focus on investment advisers' soft-dollar practices and related breaches of fiduciary duty.

An investment adviser that uses soft dollars generated by a hedge fund's trades to pay expenses that are not within the section 28(e) safe harbor and that are typically paid by the investment adviser rather than the hedge fund (such as office rent, employee salaries, employee benefits, office equipment, telephone charges and other overhead expenses) should disclose those soft-dollar arrangements to clients in specific detail. The disclosure should include the name of the broker to whom the hedge fund's brokerage transactions are directed,

---

23. *See* Exchange Act Release No. 23170 (Apr. 23, 1986), 51 F.R. 16,004 (Apr. 30, 1986); SEC v. Capital Gains Research, 375 U.S. 180, 190-92 (1963); In the Matter of Kingsley, Jennison, McNulty & Morse, SEC Administrative Proceeding 3-7446 (Nov. 14, 1991); SEC v. Galleon Capital Mgmt., Litigation Release No. 14315 (Nov. 1, 1994); In the Matter of Sheer Asset Mgmt., Advisers Act Release No. 1459 (Jan. 3, 1995); In the Matter of Acevedo, Advisers Act Release No. 1496 (June 6, 1995); SEC v. Tandem Mgmt., Litigation Release No. 14670 (Oct. 2, 1995); In the Matter of S Squared Technology, Advisers Act Release No. 1575 (Aug. 7, 1996); In the Matter of Oakwood Counselors, Advisers Act Release No. 1614 (Feb. 11, 1997); In the Matter of Parnassus Investments, Advisers Act Release No. 1634 (May 28, 1997); In the Matter of Fleet Investment Advisors, Advisers Act Release No. 1821 (Sep. 9, 1999); In the Matter of Marvin & Palmer Associates, Advisers Act Release No. 1841 (Sep. 30, 1999).

24. *See, e.g.,* In the Matter of Kingsley, Jennison, McNulty & Morse, SEC Administrative Proceeding 3-7446, note 8 (Nov. 14, 1991) (investment adviser violated Advisers Act by not adequately disclosing use of soft dollars for its own marketing and training purposes, even though the investment adviser paid no more in brokerage commissions than it would otherwise have paid and the soft dollars used for nonresearch purposes represented a miniscule fraction of the total commissions).

25. Inspection Report on the Soft Dollar Practices of Broker-Dealers, Investment Advisers and Mutual Funds, Office of Compliance, Inspections and Examinations, SEC (Sep. 22, 1998), *available at* www.sec.gov/news/studies/softdolr.htm (last visited May 17, 2013).

the brokerage commissions charged, the transaction volume, the amount that would be paid to an ECN for the same transactions, and the nature, provider and value of the goods and services provided.

i. Payment of Expenses of the Hedge Fund

Soft-dollar arrangements are those by which the investment adviser uses soft-dollar credits to pay expenses for which the investment adviser is responsible. Brokerage credits generated by hedge fund trades are not soft dollars if they are used to pay expenses for which the hedge fund is responsible under the terms of the hedge fund's governing documents. Using a hedge fund's brokerage credits to pay the hedge fund's own expenses may nevertheless violate the hedge fund manager's fiduciary duty to the hedge fund, even if only the amount by which the hedge fund arguably "pays up" is used to pay the hedge fund's expenses. This practice could artificially lower the hedge fund's expense ratio if the hedge fund only includes in the expense ratio expenses that it pays with hard dollars and effectively hides the additional expenses as brokerage commissions. Again, however, such a potential breach of fiduciary duty can be avoided by complete and adequate disclosure.

Investment advisers to one or more hedge funds and other clients sometimes use soft-dollar credits generated by one hedge fund or client to benefit another hedge fund or client or pay for another hedge fund's or client's expenses. For example, the investment adviser may use research purchased through brokerage generated by one hedge fund to benefit another hedge fund's portfolio. This is practically unavoidable when several client accounts are managed using similar strategies and trades for them are placed on an aggregated basis, because any resulting soft dollars are also generated in the aggregate across all accounts that participate in the trades.

Although it may be possible to disaggregate the soft dollars and allocate them separately to each client account, it may be logistically difficult and time-consuming to do so. Using soft dollars from one client to benefit other clients should be permissible if disclosed in advance to each hedge fund's investors and to each other client. This type of arrangement, however, is subject to abuse, if, for example, a hedge fund uses all of the soft-dollar credits it generates to pay for its own nonresearch expenses, and receives its research at no cost from the brokerage credits generated by the investment adviser's other hedge funds and clients.

ii. Client Referrals

Directing brokerage transactions to brokers that refer hedge fund investors to an investment adviser is not sheltered by the section 28(e) safe harbor, because referring clients is not providing research or brokerage services. Depending on the circumstances, this practice may violate the anti-fraud provisions of the Advisers Act if the investment adviser does not disclose it adequately and completely to its clients.[26] As always in determining how to allocate brokerage, the investment adviser has a fiduciary duty to achieve best execution for its client. Thus, an investment adviser that agrees to direct brokerage to a particular broker in exchange for client referrals or other solicitation services should provide in any agreement with such solicitor or broker that any commitment to direct client trades to that person is subject to the investment adviser's fiduciary duty of best execution and other fiduciary duties to its clients. Promising to direct a specific trading volume or specific amount of commission dollars to a broker in exchange for client referrals may breach an investment adviser's fiduciary duty. The investment adviser must in all events fully disclose any referral arrangement to its clients that may be affected by it.

iii. Futures Transactions

Section 28(e) is not available for transactions with futures commission merchants. First, section 28(e) applies only to securities transactions, and futures (other than security futures) and other commodity interests are not "securities" under Exchange Act section 3(a)(10).[27] Second, section 28(e)(4)[28] specifically states that the section 28(e) safe harbor does not apply to security futures products (which include security futures and derivatives thereof, such as single-stock futures and futures on narrow-based security indices).[29] Soft dollars generated by securities transactions may, however, be used to obtain research regarding futures and other commodity interests.[30]

5. Prohibited Soft-Dollar Arrangements

i. Trade Error Correction

A hedge fund's investment adviser should not use soft dollars to pay any expense related to correcting a trade error if it has not disclosed such potential use to the hedge fund's investors. Even if the investment adviser does disclose that possibility, it is unclear whether such disclosure is sufficient to insulate

26. In the Matter of Fleet Investment Advisors, Advisers Act Release No. 1821 (Sep. 9, 1999); In the Matter of Michalski, Advisers Act Release No. 1822 (Sep. 9, 1999); In the Matter of Capital Markets Research, Advisers Act Release No. 1834 (Sep. 27, 1999); In the Matter of Lieberman, Advisers Act Release No. 1835 (Sep. 27, 1999); In the Matter of Marvin & Palmer Associates, Advisers Act Release No. 1841 (Sep. 30, 1999).
27. 15 U.S.C. § 78c(a)(10).
28. 15 U.S.C. § 78bb(e)(4).
29. Exchange Act §§ 3(a)(55) and (56); 15 U.S.C. §§ 78c(a)(55) and (56).
30. Department of Labor, SEC No-Action Letter (Nov. 25, 1990), note 4.

the investment adviser from liability.[31] Some commentators have suggested, however, that a hedge fund's investment adviser may use soft dollars to pay expenses relating to trade errors if the hedge fund's governing documents specify that trade errors are the hedge fund's responsibility or liability.[32] If a broker offers to bear some of the financial loss resulting from a trade error, the investment adviser should make clear that the broker cannot use the investment adviser's soft dollars to offset any portion of that loss and that the investment adviser will not direct future transactions to that broker to compensate it for having borne the loss.[33]

ii. ERISA Considerations

An investment adviser may not engage in soft-dollar practices outside the section 28(e) safe harbor with respect to any hedge fund whose assets are 25 percent or more "plan assets."[34] An investment adviser that manages both such a plan assets hedge fund and accounts that are not subject to ERISA (whether other hedge funds or separate accounts) may violate its fiduciary duties if it causes the plan assets hedge fund to pay more than its share of research or other section 28(e)-eligible expenses that benefit all of the accounts. For example, using soft-dollar credits generated by the other accounts to pay those accounts' nonresearch expenses and using a disproportionate amount of soft-dollar credits generated by the plan assets hedge fund to pay research expenses that benefit all of the accounts would breach the investment adviser's fiduciary duty.

§ 14.3 Reciprocal Brokerage

Reciprocal brokerage is the direction of a hedge fund's trades to a broker in exchange for the broker's assistance in selling interests in the hedge fund. Such assistance may include inviting the investment adviser to speak at conferences organized by the broker, and the broker's conducting its own solicitation activities on behalf of the hedge fund.

---

31. In the Matter of Pirrie, Advisers Act Release No. 1284 (July 29, 1991) (investment adviser used soft-dollar credits to pay for trade errors without disclosing such use to clients); Charles Lerner, Esq., SEC No-Action Letter (Oct. 25, 1988). *See also* Uhlenhop and Sammares, "Best Execution and Soft Dollar Arrangements," National Association of Compliance Professionals, 258, 264 (Oct. 6-9, 1993), quoted in Thomas P. Lemke and Gerald T. Lins, *Soft Dollars and other Brokerage Arrangements*, § 4:11, 2009-2010 (the only safe course of conduct for an investment adviser is to obtain specific consent to using future brokerage to settle an error or, alternatively, be certain that the future business given to the broker-dealer will be executed at best price and commission).

32. Thomas P. Lemke and Gerald T. Lins, *Soft Dollars and other Brokerage Arrangements*, § 4:11, 2009-2010 Ed.

33. Charles Lerner, Esq., SEC No-Action Letter (Oct. 25, 1988); *see also* § 13.14, *supra.*

34. *See* § 11.4.2, *supra.*

In the context of investment companies, the SEC has acknowledged and seems grudgingly to permit reciprocal brokerage practices.[35] The practice must be disclosed in the investment company's prospectus and approved by its board of directors. The SEC has censured an investment company's investment adviser that engaged in reciprocal brokerage allocation practices on an undisclosed basis.[36] In permitting reciprocal brokerage allocation practices by investment companies, the SEC reasoned that an open-end investment company was permitted to bear the distribution expenses of selling its shares and that reciprocal brokerage was another form of distribution expense. The SEC has not extended this principle to hedge funds, but by analogy, the SEC might permit reciprocal brokerage by a hedge fund that is obligated to pay the distribution expenses for offering and selling hedge fund interests, if the practice is fully disclosed to investors.[37]

---

35. FINRA Manual - NASD Conduct Rule 2830(k)(7)(B); In the Matter of NASD, Exchange Act Release No. 17599 (Mar. 4, 1981).

36. In the Matter of Stein, Roe & Farnham, Advisers Act Release No. 1217 (Jan. 22, 1990).

37. The SEC has broadened the scope of Company Act § 17(e)(1), 15 U.S.C. § 80a-17(e)(1), by maintaining that disclosure of soft-dollar practices outside the safe harbor of Exchange Act § 28(e) does not cure a Company Act § 17(e)(1) violation. An SEC administrative law judge has held that § 17(e)(1) is violated even if the investment company actually benefits from the investment adviser's receipt of such soft-dollar services and even if such soft-dollar practices are fully disclosed. In finding that the investment adviser and its founder/president violated § 17(e)(1), the judge reasoned that an investment adviser's receipt of nonresearch soft-dollar services constituted "compensation in connection with the purchase or sale of property to or from the investment company," the "essence of a violation of [s]ection 17(e)(1)." The judge further reasoned that prior disclosures, if made with specificity and accuracy, would have been an ineffectual defense, consistent with Congress's determination that "disclosure alone is not adequate protection in the investment company field." *See* In the Matter of Parnassus Investments, Jerome L. Dodson, Marilyn M. Chou and David L. Gibson, Administrative Proceeding 3-9317 (Sep. 3, 1998); Exchange Act Release No. 23170 (Apr. 23, 1986), 51 F.R. 16,004 (Apr. 30, 1986); In the Matter of Portfolio Mgmt. Consultants, Advisers Act Release No. 1821 (Sep. 9, 1999).

CHAPTER **15**

Fees and Special Profit Allocations

Except for performance-based compensation and excessive fees discussed below, the Advisers Act does not specifically address the types or amounts of advisory fees an investment adviser may charge a hedge fund. The Advisers Act requires, however, that the investment adviser, as a fiduciary, make full and fair disclosure to its clients about the fees it charges. An investment adviser to a hedge fund should disclose its fees and special profit allocations in the hedge fund's offering materials and (if the investment adviser is registered) in Part 2 of the investment adviser's Form ADV.

§ 15.1 Management Fee

Investment advisers to hedge funds typically charge management fees at annual rates of 1 to 2 percent of managed assets, although a few investment advisers charge up to 4 percent. Management fees typically are paid quarterly or monthly. For U.S. hedge funds, the expense of the management fee is typically charged to the capital account of each investor that pays the fee. For an offshore hedge fund that is structured as a corporation, the fee is typically charged to the hedge fund itself, and the hedge fund's governing documents allocate the fee as appropriate among its shares.

An investment adviser may charge different management fees to different groups of investors; for example, an investor may be charged a lower management fee if the investor invests more than a specified amount in the hedge fund, or agrees to pay performance-based compensation at a higher rate, or agrees to a longer lock-up. The investment adviser does not pay management fees with respect to its own investment in the hedge fund, and investment advisers frequently waive fees for their affiliates, employees and family members.

Management fees may be charged in advance or arrears. Typically, an investment adviser that charges fees in advance does not return the unearned portion of the fee to an investor that withdraws from a hedge fund before the end of the period for which the management fee is charged. In the SEC staff's view, an investment adviser should refund prepaid but unearned advisory fees to a client when the client terminates the investment advisory relationship.[1]

1. Robert D. Brown Investment Counsel, Inc., SEC No Action Letter (July 19, 1984).

Otherwise, in the staff's view, the investment adviser would be requiring its client to forfeit the entire prepayment as a penalty for termination, which would violate the investment adviser's fiduciary duty to its clients.[2]

This staff position should not require a hedge fund's investment adviser to refund prepaid management fees to a withdrawing investor, however, because the hedge fund, rather than the withdrawing investor, is regarded as the client.[3] The refund issue does not arise, of course, if withdrawals or redemptions are permitted only at the end of the monthly or quarterly fee period or if the fees are charged in arrears.

§ 15.2 Performance Fees and Allocations

Performance-based compensation is a defining characteristic of a hedge fund. An investment adviser to a hedge fund typically receives a performance fee, if the hedge fund is organized as a corporation (as are many offshore hedge funds), or a performance allocation, if the hedge fund is organized as a limited liability company ("LLC") or a limited partnership (as are most U.S. hedge funds) and the investment adviser is a member or partner of the hedge fund (as is typical). The performance fee or allocation is most commonly 20 percent of the profits generated during each given measurement period, subject to a "high-water mark" as described below.

Some investment advisers charge lower or higher performance fees or allocations, ranging up to 50 percent; higher fees are more common in hedge funds managed by investment advisers with extensive and highly successful track records. For regulatory reasons, investment advisers to other investment funds, such as mutual funds and registered hedge funds, are generally unable to charge similar performance fees or allocations.

1. Implications of Performance Fee Versus Allocation

i. Implications for Investment Adviser

If the investment adviser is a partner or member of the hedge fund and the hedge fund is a partnership or LLC,[4] the investment adviser's performance-based compensation may consist of a special, disproportionate allocation of the hedge fund's periodic profits that would otherwise have been allocated to its investors (other than the investment adviser). This special profit allocation is made directly to the investment adviser's capital account and thus reduces the amount of profit that would otherwise be allocated to the investors. As an allocation, rather than a fee, the special profit allocation retains the tax characteristics of the underlying profits on which it is based.

2. *Id.*
3. Goldstein v. SEC, 451 F.3d 873 (2006).
4. *See* § 4.2, *supra.*

This provides two advantages to the investment adviser: depending on the tax character of the hedge fund's profits, all or part of the income may be characterized as long-term capital gain, rather than ordinary income; and tax on the special profit allocation is deferred until the gains are realized. For example, if 25 percent of the hedge fund's profits are unrealized and 15 percent are realized gains subject to long-term capital gain tax rates, 25 percent of the investment adviser's special profit allocation will not be taxed currently and 15 percent will be taxed as long-term capital gain.[5]

At this writing (early 2013), bills are pending in Congress that would require performance-based special profit allocations to hedge funds' investment advisers to be taxed as ordinary income, on the theory that such compensation is another form of fee income.[6]

ii. Implications for Investors in the Hedge Fund

A performance fee is treated as a miscellaneous itemized deduction for income tax purposes. Thus it is charged as an expense to the investor but often is not deductible. A special profit allocation, by comparison, has more favorable tax consequences for a hedge fund's investors because, by reducing the amount of profits that would otherwise be allocated to their capital accounts, it creates a corresponding reduction in their taxable income from the hedge fund.[7]

2. Features

i. High-Water Mark

Traditionally, an investment adviser's performance fee or allocation is charged only against profits that exceed the previous highest value of each account, either on initiation of the account or at the most recent date when a performance fee or allocation was paid. This is colloquially called a "high-water mark." Because investors may invest at different times, each investor typically begins with a unique high-water mark. A standard high-water mark provides that a hedge fund investor's capital account or shares will not be charged a performance allocation or fee until prior losses are fully recouped, after adjusting for additions to and withdrawals from the account. Thus, for example, if an investor contributes $500,000 on January 1, which depreciates to $400,000 on December 31, but appreciates to $505,000 on the following December 31, a performance fee or allocation would be payable only for the second year and would be based on only the $5,000 of overall profits above the high-water mark. The high-water mark almost never looks forward, however, and the investor in this example that was charged a performance fee or allocation for the second year would not receive a refund if the hedge fund loses money in its third year.

The high-water mark ordinarily is adjusted for partial withdrawals. The high-water mark is reduced in the proportion that the capital account balance immediately after the withdrawal bears to the capital account balance immediately before the withdrawal.

---

5. *See* § 16.8, *infra*.
6. *See, e.g.*, S.B. 2075, 113th Cong. (2013).
7. *See* §§ 4.2.2, *supra*, and 16.3.2 and 16.3.10.i, *infra*.

Multiple investments in a hedge fund by a single investor may or may not be tracked separately with their own high-water marks. For example, assume that an investor contributes $500,000 on January 1, which depreciates to $400,000 the following December 31, and the investor contributes another $500,000 on the second January 1. Assume further that the hedge fund appreciates by 10 percent in the second year, so that the first investment is worth $440,000 and the second is worth $550,000. If the high-water marks for both investments are aggregated, the investment adviser would not be entitled to a performance fee or allocation for the second year, because only $90,000 of the total $100,000 loss would have been recouped. If, however, the high-water marks are not aggregated and the two contributions are viewed as separate investments, the investment adviser would not be entitled to a performance fee or allocation with respect to the first investment, because it would have appreciated in the second year only from $400,000 to $440,000 (still $60,000 below its high-water mark), but would be entitled to a performance fee or allocation with respect to the second investment, based on the $50,000 gain (from $500,000 to $550,000).[8]

With the decline of the stock markets from 2000 to 2003 and from 2007 to 2009, many hedge funds experienced unprecedented depreciation in value, rendering it unlikely that losses would be recouped any time soon and vividly illustrating for some investment advisers a weakness in the traditional high-water-mark provision. As a result, a few investment advisers restructured their high-water marks to mitigate the consequences to them of extraordinary market declines. For example, some limited their high-water marks to look back only a year or two, establishing a new high-water mark every year or two and disregarding prior losses. The asserted rationale for such changes was the need to provide incentive to the investment adviser and its most skilled portfolio managers (in the form of a realistic possibility of earning a performance fee or allocation), without which the investment adviser might be inclined to liquidate and dissolve its hedge fund and form a new hedge fund with new investors (and any investors from the old hedge fund willing to forego their high-water marks). A limited look-back also decreases an investment adviser's incentive to take greater risk to recoup prior losses.

Other investment advisers diluted the high-water mark concept and began charging a reduced performance fee or allocation on profits that recoup prior losses. To make such arrangements palatable to investors, such an investment adviser typically continues to charge a reduced performance fee or allocation on some specified amount of profits in excess of the high-water mark, thus giving investors an added incentive to remain in the hedge fund after the prior losses are recouped. For example, a performance fee or allocation of 10 percent instead of 20 percent might be charged on profits that recoup prior losses, as well as on subsequent profits equal to 50 to 100 percent of the prior losses. This high-water-mark structure allows the investment adviser to compensate employees while recouping losses, but affords the investors the benefit of a reduced performance fee or allocation on some of the profits in excess of those

8. This discussion relates primarily to U.S. hedge funds. *See* § 15.3, *infra*, for more on performance fee computation methods for offshore hedge funds.

losses. High-water-mark provisions will likely continue to evolve in response to market conditions and investor expectations.

ii. Hurdle Rates

Some hedge funds employ a hurdle, basing the investment adviser's performance fee or allocation on only the amount by which the hedge fund's performance exceeds a specified index, benchmark or rate of return. Some other hedge funds pay a full performance fee or allocation on the entire return, but only if it exceeds the hurdle. Thus, for example, an investment adviser to a hedge fund with a $1,000,000 gain on a $10,000,000 account that is subject to a 20 percent performance allocation with a 5 percent hurdle rate would receive $100,000 under the former method and $200,000 under the latter. The latter method can produce anomalous results if the appreciation is only slightly above the hurdle rate, because it can result in a performance allocation for the investment adviser that lowers the net return for the investor to a rate below the hurdle.

3. Rules

i. The Performance Fee Rule

An SEC-registered investment adviser that receives a performance fee or allocation from a hedge fund must comply with Advisers Act Rule 205-3 (the "Performance Fee Rule"),[9] which provides an exception to the general prohibition in Advisers Act section 205(a)(1)[10] of compensation based on the capital appreciation of a client's account. The Performance Fee Rule reflects the SEC's belief that fees and allocations of profits calculated as a portion of an account's performance are potentially abusive, but that wealthy investors can fend for themselves against such abuses.[11]

The Performance Fee Rule provides that an investment adviser may charge an investor[12] in a hedge fund that relies on Company Act section 3(c)(1)[13] a performance-based fee only if the investor is a "qualified client," defined for this purpose in Rule 205-3(d)(1)[14] as:

- a natural person who, or a company[15] that, immediately after entering into the contract to invest in the hedge fund has at least $1,000,000 under the management of the investment adviser,[16]

---

9. 17 C.F.R. § 275.205-3.
10. 15 U.S.C. § 80b-5(a)(1).
11. Advisers Act Release No. 996 (Nov. 14, 1985), 50 F.R. 48,556 (Nov. 26, 1985).
12. Rule 205-3(b), 17 C.F.R. § 275.205-3(b).
13. 15 U.S.C. § 80a-3(c)(1); *see also* § 3.2, *supra.*
14. 17 C.F.R. § 275.205-3(d)(1).
15. Defined as a corporation, a partnership, an association, a joint-stock company, a trust or any organized group of persons, whether incorporated or not, or any receiver, trustee in a case under Title 11 of the U.S. Code, or similar official, or any liquidating agent for any of the foregoing, in his or her capacity as such; 17 C.F.R. § 275.205-3(d)(2).
16. Rule 205-3(e), 17 C.F.R. § 275.205-3(e), provides for the SEC to adjust the $1,000,000 amount for inflation every 5 years, starting in 2016, as required by Advisers Act § 205(e), 15 U.S.C. § 80b-5(e).

- a natural person who, or a company[17] that, the investment adviser (and any person acting on its behalf) reasonably believes, immediately before entering into the contract for the investor to invest in the hedge fund, either has a net worth in excess of $2,000,000 (for a natural person, excluding from the net worth calculation both the fair market value of his or her primary residence and the amount of any debt secured by such residence up to its fair market value, but including in his or her liabilities the amount of any increase in the last 60 days in the debt secured by such residence (accordingly, both the portion of any debt secured by such primary residence that exceeds its fair market value and the amount of any increase in such debt in the last 60 days must be deducted, without double counting, in calculating his or her net worth)),[18]
- a "qualified purchaser," as defined in Company Act section 2(a)(51)(A)[19] at the time of entering into the contract to invest in the hedge fund, or
- a natural person who immediately before entering into the contract to invest in the hedge fund is either (a) an executive officer, director, trustee, general partner or person serving in a similar capacity of the investment adviser, or (b) an employee of the investment adviser (other than one performing solely clerical, secretarial or administrative functions) who, in connection with his or her regular functions or duties, participates in the investment activities of the investment adviser, if the employee has been performing such functions and duties for or on behalf of the investment adviser, or substantially similar functions or duties for or on behalf of another company, for at least 12 months.

Rule 205-3(c) provides transition rules generally permitting an investment adviser to continue to charge performance fees and allocations to investors in a hedge fund that are not qualified clients, if they were qualified clients under a prior version of the Performance Fee Rule that was in effect when they initially invested, or if the investment adviser was not registered with the SEC when they invested.[20]

The prohibition in Advisers Act section 205 does not apply to an advisory contract with a non-U.S. person (including an offshore hedge fund) or a hedge fund that relies on Company Act section 3(c)(7).[21] An investment adviser may not, however, charge a performance fee to U.S. investors in an offshore hedge fund that relies on Company Act section 3(c)(1),[22] except in compliance

---

17. Defined, *supra*, n. 15.

18. Rule 205-3(e), 17 C.F.R. § 275.205-3(e), provides for the SEC to adjust the $2,000,000 amount for inflation every 5 years, starting in 2016, as required by Advisers Act § 205(e), 15 U.S.C. § 80b-5(e).

19. 15 U.S.C. § 80a-2(a)(51)(A); *see also* Advisers Act Release No. 1731 (July 15, 1998), 63 F.R. 39,027 (July 28, 1998). *See* § 3.3.2, *supra*, regarding qualified purchasers.

20. 17 C.F.R. § 275.205-3(c).

21. Advisers Act § 205(b)(5), 15 U.S.C. § 80b-5(b)(5).Non-U.S. persons are persons who are not residents of the United States.

22. *See* Rosenberg Institutional Equity Mgmt., SEC No Action Letter (Mar. 14, 1990); Advisers Act § 205(b)(5), 15 U.S.C. § 80b-5(b)(5).

with the Performance Fee Rule. If a hedge fund that relies on Company Act section 3(c)(1) or a registered investment company (such as a mutual fund or registered hedge fund) invests in another hedge fund that relies on Company Act section 3(c)(1), each investor in the investing fund must meet the test of the Performance Fee Rule if the investing fund is charged a performance fee or allocation with respect to its investment in the hedge fund.

Some states have similar rules that apply to state-registered investment advisers. For example, California follows the Performance Fee Rule, but, as discussed below, also expressly requires that the investment adviser fully disclose all material information about the proposed compensation arrangement.[23] Some other states have not amended their performance fee rules to reflect amendments to the Performance Fee Rule since 1998. Thus, those states require the investment adviser to calculate the performance fee or special profit allocation over a 1-year period and impose other obligations that were previously part of the Performance Fee Rule.[24]

If an investment adviser admits to its hedge fund an investor that is not a "qualified client", the investment adviser is not permitted to charge performance fees or allocations to that investor. If the hedge fund's charter documents so provide, the investment adviser may instead charge a higher asset-based management fee to that investor, while at the same time charging performance fees or allocations to investors in the hedge fund who are qualified clients. Such alternative fee arrangements should be disclosed to all prospective investors in the hedge fund.[25]

Although the Performance Fee Rule does not explicitly require any particular disclosure, an investment adviser has an obligation as a fiduciary to deal fairly with its clients and make full and fair disclosure of its compensation arrangements.[26] The investment adviser must fully disclose all material information about a performance fee or allocation arrangement and any material conflicts that arrangement creates.[27] Accordingly, any investment adviser that charges performance-based compensation should disclose, among other things:

- that the fee or allocation arrangement may create an incentive for the investment adviser to make investments that are riskier or more speculative than it would make absent performance-based compensation;
- if true, that the investment adviser may receive increased compensation with regard to unrealized appreciation as well as realized gains in the client's account;
- the periods that will be used to measure investment performance throughout the contract and their significance in computing the fee or allocation;

---

23. 10 Cal. Code of Reg, § 260.234(b)(3); Cal. Corp. Code § 25234(a)(1).

24. *See, e.g.*, 21 Code of Vt. Rules (CVR 21-030-002) § 3.10(d).

25. *See* Chapter 6, *supra*. *See also* Advisers Act Rule 206(4)-8, 17 C.F.R. § 275.206(4)-8.

26. *Id.;* Advisers Act Release No. 1731 (July 15, 1998), 63 F.R. 39,022 (July 21, 1998).

27. Advisers Act §§ 206 and 207, 15 U.S.C. § 80b-6 and 80b-7. *See* Advisers Act Release No. 1731 (July 15, 1998), 63 F.R. 39,022 (July 21, 1998).

- the nature of any index that will be used as a comparative measure of investment performance, the significance of the index and the reason the investment adviser believes the index is appropriate; and
- if the compensation is based in part on the unrealized appreciation of securities for which market quotations are not readily available, how the securities will be valued and the extent to which the valuation will be independently determined.

ii. When the Performance Fee Rule Does Not Apply

The prohibition of performance fees in Advisers Act section 205(a) does not apply to an SEC-Exempt Adviser.[28] Even though an SEC-Exempt Adviser is not subject to the Performance Fee Rule, it may be subject to a different performance fee rule under state law. Whether or not the Performance Fee Rule or a comparable state rule applies, an investment adviser must comply with its fiduciary duties under federal and state law to the hedge fund's investors. In addition to making complete and accurate disclosure, even an unregistered investment adviser should conform its performance-based fees or allocations to otherwise applicable state and federal standards.[29]

iii. ERISA Limits

ERISA may prohibit an investment adviser that is deemed a plan fiduciary from charging performance fees or allocations to certain ERISA plan investors in the hedge fund.[30] Investment advisers to U.S. hedge funds can usually waive performance fees or allocations that would otherwise be due from ERISA plan investors, because such fees and allocations are typically calculated and charged separately for each investor. An investment adviser to an offshore hedge fund, however, should consider providing a separate class of shares for investors that will not be charged performance fees, so that the hedge fund can maintain a single net asset value ("NAV") for each series and class of its shares.[31]

§ 15.3 Performance Fee Computation Methods for Offshore Hedge Funds

Performance fee computations are often more complicated for offshore hedge funds than for U.S. hedge funds, because offshore hedge funds are typically structured as corporations. The corporate structure requires a single NAV for each class and series of shares, unlike a partnership or LLC with a separate capital account for each investor. A performance fee charged to a corporation is an expense that affects the NAV of each share in the same way. Without some adjustment, an investor that purchases shares in an offshore hedge fund on a date other than the first day of the period over which the performance fee is calculated

28. Advisers Act § 205(a), 15 U.S.C. § 80b-5(a); *see* § 2.1.2, *supra*.
29. *See also* § 15.5, *infra*.
30. *See* § 11.4.4, *supra*.
31. *See* Chapter 11, *supra*, and § 15.3, *infra*.

would suffer the same per-share decrease in NAV on payment of the performance fee at the end of the period as investors that held shares from the beginning of the period, even if the new investor's shares enjoyed less appreciation.

Similarly, an investor that purchases shares on other than the first day of the performance fee calculation period at a time when the NAV of the shares is less than its value at the beginning of the period will not be charged a performance fee at the end of the period if the NAV has then increased back to its value at the beginning of the period, even though that investor's shares will have appreciated. Thus, equitable problems arise in charging performance fees to an offshore hedge fund, because investors may invest at different times during the year, when the offshore hedge fund has accrued differing performance fees or high-water marks.[32] Several ways of addressing these problems are described below.

1. Classes and Series

The most common method uses multiple series of shares. The offshore hedge fund either creates a new "series" of a class of shares on each date that investors purchase shares of that class, or creates a new series of shares for each investor. The performance fee is calculated and charged separately for each series, in essence imposing partnership accounting on the corporation.

This method creates different NAVs for the various series of shares. This method, however, is widely used and accepted by investors, and relatively easy to administer. Some investors may be troubled by the different NAVs. An investor that invests on multiple dates and is issued shares of a different series for each investment will be charged performance fees that are calculated separately with respect to each such series, rather than on its aggregate holdings. This may result in its paying performance fees with respect to periods in which the aggregate value of its shares has declined or remained the same, if shares of some series have appreciated while shares of other series (purchased on different dates) have depreciated. If a new series is created on each subscription date, the offshore hedge fund may limit the proliferation of series by converting, at the end of each year, all shares in series that are charged a performance fee into the original "benchmark series" of the same class. Shares of a series that have an unrecouped loss and are below their high-water mark are not converted, however, and remain in that series until the NAV of that series appreciates to its high-water mark. At that time, the shares of that series are converted into the benchmark series.

2. Monthly Accrual

Under this method, the performance fee is computed and paid monthly. Monthly payment of the performance fee eliminates the performance fee computation problems as long as the offshore hedge fund appreciates, because (assuming monthly openings) each new investor purchases shares at a NAV that reflects the performance fee accrued to date. Adjustments are appropriate, however, if an investor purchases shares when other shareholders are below their high-

32. *See* § 4.4.4, *supra*.

water mark. This method was less common in the past when redemptions were often permitted only quarterly and NAV was accordingly not calculated monthly. Improvements in accounting software, however, have made it easier for hedge fund administrators and accountants to calculate NAV monthly (or daily). In addition, investors have increasingly demanded monthly liquidity and monthly reporting of NAV, which makes it administratively easy to charge the performance fee monthly. Still, an offshore hedge fund might find that charging a performance fee monthly creates a competitive disadvantage in attracting investors.

3. Equalization of Shares

The "equalization of shares" method is more complicated to administer and explain to investors than the foregoing methods and is now rarely used. This method equalizes the investment of an investor admitted when the other shareholders are already subject to an accrued performance fee (because the offshore hedge fund has appreciated) or when the other shareholders have an unrecouped loss and are below their high-water marks (because the offshore hedge fund has depreciated). Without an adjustment, a shareholder who invests during a performance fee period in which the offshore hedge fund has appreciated would immediately suffer a reduction in NAV per share due to the accrued performance fee, even though the shareholder would not have been in the fund to enjoy the appreciation.

To "equalize" such a shareholder's interest in the offshore hedge fund, the shareholder is granted an equalization credit with respect to each of its shares equal to the performance fee percentage multiplied by the difference between the NAV per share at the time the investor invests and the last NAV per share at which a performance fee was charged. The equalization credit appreciates or depreciates based on the offshore hedge fund's performance and ensures that all investors in the offshore hedge fund bear the same degree of risk.

If, on the other hand, a shareholder purchases shares during a performance fee period when shares have decreased in value, the shareholder should equitably pay a performance fee on any appreciation of those shares even though the other investors are charged a lesser fee or no fee. This is accomplished by redeeming, at the end of the performance fee period, for no consideration, a number of the investor's shares with a value equal to the performance fee that should equitably be due from the investor. This procedure is followed until the NAV of the shares matches the previous NAV at which a performance fee was charged to the other shareholders.

4. Rough Justice

As noted above, shareholders that invest when an offshore hedge fund has unrecouped losses and is below the high-water mark receive a windfall because their shares are not assessed a performance fee until the offshore hedge fund makes up those losses, even though they did not participate in those losses. Conversely, shareholders that invest when an offshore hedge fund has appreciated and accrued a performance fee that is not yet payable are penalized, because when the performance fee is paid, the NAV of their shares will be reduced, even though they did not participate in the appreciation.

As the term "rough justice" suggests, in rare cases an offshore hedge fund chooses simply to accept these inequities on the theory that investors should perceive that, over time, they are likely to receive both the benefits and the burdens of the structure. For example, assume that Investor A purchases shares during a performance fee period when the offshore hedge fund has appreciated. Investor A's shares will bear their pro rata portion of the offshore hedge fund's performance fee that is paid at the end of that performance fee period, even though they did not appreciate. If a subsequent Investor B also purchases shares when the offshore hedge fund has accrued a performance fee, Investor A benefits because Investor B's shares will absorb part of the performance fee that otherwise would have been charged to Investor A.

The inevitable inequities of rough justice are unpredictable, and they could affect some investors severely. An investment adviser that uses this approach should take care to disclose fully to investors and prospective investors how the rough justice approach can affect them.[33] Given the sophistication of investors and the ease of applying the other methods (especially the classes and series method), the rough justice method is very rarely used.

§ 15.4 Other Fees Charged by Hedge Funds

1. Soft Lock-Up Fees

Some hedge funds charge a withdrawal fee, typically ranging from 1 to 6 percent of the withdrawal, for withdrawals during a given period, such as 1 year or 3 years, following the investor's investment in the hedge fund. Such a fee replaces or is offered as an alternative to a strict lock-up period during which withdrawals are prohibited. This soft lock-up may be rationalized as compensation for the hedge fund's costs in setting up the new account and unexpectedly liquidating positions to fund the withdrawal.

2. Fees on Special Withdrawals

Hedge funds often charge a fee, typically ranging from 1 to 3 percent of the withdrawal, to an investor that is allowed to withdraw funds at a time other than a prescribed withdrawal date. The fee may be rationalized as compensation for the hedge fund's accounting costs resulting from an extra break-point date, when the hedge fund must value its assets and calculate its liabilities for the purpose of allocating profits and losses. Accordingly, some hedge funds limit the total fee for a special withdrawal to the estimated accounting and other administrative costs associated with a special break-point date.

33. *See* § 15.2.3, *supra*.

§ 15.5 Excessive Fees

The SEC has stated that charging an excessive fee may breach an investment adviser's fiduciary duty to a client and violate Advisers Act section 206(2).[34] Many state securities laws include similar provisions.[35] The Advisers Act fiduciary duty rules apply to all investment advisers, whether or not they are registered or required to be registered with the SEC. In certain circumstances, a high fee (whether asset-based or performance-based) may not breach an investment adviser's fiduciary duty if the investment adviser discloses fully to its clients that the fee exceeds fees customarily charged to accounts of similar size and objectives and that the same or similar services may be available at a lower fee from another investment adviser.[36] In other instances, however, the SEC has found an advisory fee to be so excessive that disclosure could not cure the breach of fiduciary duty.[37] The SEC and some state regulatory authorities have indicated that, depending on the services provided, they may consider an annual asset-based fee in excess of 3 percent of assets under management to be excessive,[38] but they have not provided definitive guidance. State securities law administrators have also stated informally that performance-based fees exceeding 20 percent may invite closer scrutiny.[39]

§ 15.6 Rescission Remedy

Advisers Act section 215[40] provides that a contract for investment advisory services is void if its formation or performance would violate the Advisers Act. An advisory client has a private right of action under this section for restitution of advisory fees paid.[41] Restitution does not include compensation for any diminution in value of the client's account managed by the investment adviser, but such remedies may be available under other federal or state laws.[42]

---

34. Advisers Act § 206(2), 15 U.S.C. § 80b-6(2), makes it unlawful for an investment adviser "to engage in any transaction, practice, or course of business which operates as a fraud or deceit upon any client or prospective client."

35. *See, e.g.*, Cal. Corp. Code § 25238; 10 Cal. Code of Reg. § 260.238(j); 950 Mass. Code of Reg. § 12-205; 3 Colo. Code of Reg. (3 CCR 704-1) § 51-4.8(IA)J.

36. Shareholder Services Corp., SEC No Action Letter (Feb. 3, 1989); *see also* 10 Cal. Code of Reg. § 260.238(j).

37. H & H Investments, SEC No Action Letter (Sep. 17, 1981).

38. *SEC Inspection Manual* (1980) page 15, reprinted in Thomas P. Lemke & Gerald T. Lins, *Regulation of Investment Advisers*, App. F6 (2009); telephone conversation with Meryl Wilson, Cal. Dep't of Corp.

39. Telephone conversation with Colorado Division of Securities.

40. 15 U.S.C. § 80b-15.

41. Advisers Act § 215(b), 15 U.S.C. § 80b-15(b).

42. *See, e.g.,* Transamerica Mortgage Advisors, Inc. v. Lewis, 444 U.S. 11 (1979) (limited private right of action exists under Advisers Act only for restitution of fees paid); Stokes v. Henson, 217 Cal. App. 3d 187 (1990) (granting investors damages equal to rescission for investment adviser's breach of fiduciary duty and constructive fraud); Scalp & Blade, Inc. v. Franger, 2003 N.Y. App. Div. LEXIS 10031 (Oct. 2, 2003) (claim for lost profits is appropriate when alleging investment adviser's breach of fiduciary duty, negligence, breach of contract and fraud, among other claims).

CHAPTER **16**

Tax Considerations

§ 16.1 Federal Income Tax Treatment as a Partnership

This chapter discusses U.S. federal tax treatment of a U.S. hedge fund in sections 16.1 through 16.6, some U.S. federal tax considerations relevant to offshore hedge funds in section 16.7, some U.S. federal tax considerations for the investment adviser to U.S. and offshore hedge funds in section 16.8, and the obligation to file certain reports regarding foreign bank accounts in section 16.9.

1. Election to be Taxed as Partnership

For income tax purposes, U.S. hedge funds generally prefer to be treated as partnerships to obtain "pass-through" tax treatment. Accordingly, most U.S. hedge funds are established as limited partnerships, or occasionally as limited liability companies ("LLCs"), under state law. Treasury Regulations provide that a domestic business entity with two or more members that is not a corporation or one of certain other specified entities under state law may elect for federal income tax purposes to be taxed as either a partnership or an association taxable as a corporation.[1] Thus, a hedge fund with two or more investors established under state law as a limited partnership or LLC will be classified as a partnership unless it files with the IRS an election to be taxed as an association. If it does not file such an election, it will automatically, under the default classification rules, be taxed as a partnership, unless it is deemed to be a publicly traded partnership as discussed in section 16.1.2 below.[2]

2. Publicly Traded Partnerships

Tax Code section 7704[3] treats certain publicly traded partnerships that engage in active business activities as corporations for income tax purposes. A "publicly traded partnership" is a partnership whose interests (a) are traded on an established securities market (including the over-the-counter market), or (b) are readily tradeable on a secondary market or the substantial equivalent

1. Treas. Reg. § 301.7701-3(a), 26 C.F.R. § 301.7701-3(a).
2. Treas. Reg. § 301.7701-3(b), 26 C.F.R. § 301.7701-3(b).
3. 26 U.S.C. § 7704.

thereof. Interests in hedge funds generally are not traded on established securities markets. Under Treasury Regulations, however, interests in a hedge fund could be treated as being readily tradeable on the substantial equivalent of a secondary market if the hedge fund allows such frequent withdrawals and contributions that its liquidity is comparable to that of a security traded on a secondary market.[4] For example, a hedge fund that allows monthly withdrawals and contributions risks being deemed to be tradeable on the equivalent of a secondary market. A hedge fund could also be deemed to be tradeable on the equivalent of a secondary market if it allows frequent assignments of interests in the hedge fund, such as through a matching service.

Tax Code section 7704(c)[5] provides an exception from treatment as a publicly traded partnership for a partnership 90 percent or more of the income of which is certain passive-type income, including interest, dividends and capital gains from disposition of property held to produce dividend or interest income. Treasury Regulations provide that income from notional principal contracts is passive income for this purpose if the property, income or cash flow that measures the amount to which the hedge fund is entitled would give rise to such passive type income.[6] While most hedge funds would meet this test, some hedge funds might engage in investments whose income tax characterization is uncertain, and the IRS may maintain that such investments do not produce qualifying passive-type income.

Even if 10 percent or more of a hedge fund's income in a year does not qualify as passive-type income, the hedge fund may avoid being treated as a publicly traded partnership under Tax Code section 7704 if it qualifies for one or more safe harbors from such treatment provided in the Treasury Regulations. The safe harbor on which hedge funds commonly rely provides that interests in a hedge fund will not be considered readily tradeable on a secondary market or the substantial equivalent thereof if (a) all interests in the partnership were issued in one or more transactions that were not required to be registered under the Securities Act and (b) the partnership does not have more than 100 partners at any time during the taxable year of the partnership.[7] Offerings of interests in hedge funds generally are not required to be registered under the Securities Act.

Generally, an entity that owns a hedge fund interest is treated as only one partner in determining whether the hedge fund has 100 or more partners. If, however, an entity that is a pass-through vehicle for tax purposes invests in a hedge fund, if substantially all of the entity's value is attributable to its interest in the hedge fund, and if a principal purpose of the tiered structure is to avoid the 100-partner limitation, all of the entity's owners are counted as partners in the hedge fund. A hedge fund will not comply with this safe harbor if it relies on Company Act section 3(c)(7)[8] and admits more than 100 partners. A hedge fund that fails to meet one of the safe-harbor requirements is not,

4. Treas. Reg. § 1.7704-1(c)(2), 26 C.F.R. § 1.7704-1(c)(2).
5. 26 U.S.C. § 7704(c).
6. Treas. Reg. § 1.7704-3(a)(1), 26 C.F.R. § 1.7704-3(a)(1).
7. Treas. Reg. § 1.7704-1(h), 26 C.F.R. § 1.7704-1(h).
8. *See* § 3.3, *supra*.

however, necessarily classified as a publicly traded partnership, if its liquidity is sufficiently limited.

§ 16.2 Issues on Formation of Hedge Fund—Capital Contributions

1. Tax Basis

An investor in a hedge fund has a tax "basis" in the investor's interest in the hedge fund. This basis determines whether the investor has taxable gain or loss on a transfer of the investor's interest in the hedge fund, or on receipt of a distribution from the hedge fund. This is commonly called the investor's "outside" basis in the hedge fund. The hedge fund itself also has a tax basis for each asset it holds, which is commonly called the hedge fund's "inside" basis in such asset.

Generally, the initial basis of an investor's interest in a hedge fund equals the amount of money the investor contributed to the hedge fund, plus the adjusted tax basis of any property the investor contributed to the hedge fund, plus the investor's share of the hedge fund's liabilities. If an investor transfers property in kind to a hedge fund, and that transaction is taxable to the investor, the investor's tax basis in the hedge fund increases by the amount of any gain the investor recognizes on the transfer. If any investors are personally liable for any hedge fund liability, only those investors that are personally liable may include their proportionate shares of that liability in their adjusted tax bases. For this purpose, short sales are treated as liabilities.[9]

An investor's basis is increased by the investor's share of hedge fund income and the investor's additional investments in the hedge fund. The investor's basis is reduced (but not below zero) by the investor's share of hedge fund distributions and losses. The initial basis is also decreased by any liabilities of the investor that the hedge fund assumes at the time of investment, although this adjustment typically is not relevant in the hedge fund context.

2. Special Issues on Contribution of Securities

i. Transfer to an "Investment Company"

Generally, a transferor does not recognize taxable gain or loss on the transfer of appreciated or depreciated property to the capital of a partnership. This general rule does not apply, however, and consequently gain will be recognized, if the transfer is to an investment company and results in diversification of the transferor's interests.[10] An entity is an "investment company" for this purpose if: (a) it is a registered investment company (a mutual fund); (b) it is a real

9. Rev. Rul. 95-26, 1995-1 C.B. 131.

10. Tax Code § 721(b), 26 U.S.C. § 721(b); Treas. Reg. § 1.351-1(c)(1), 26 C.F.R. § 1.351-1(c)(1).

estate investment trust (a "REIT"); or (c) more than 80 percent of the value of its assets consist of certain types of property,[11] including money, stocks or other equity interests in a corporation, evidences of indebtedness, options, forward or futures contracts, notional principal contracts and derivatives, foreign currency, interests in precious metals, interests in registered investment companies or REITS, or interests in other noncorporate entities that are convertible into any of such assets.[12] Most hedge funds are treated as investment companies under this 80-percent test.

A transfer will not result in diversification if each transferor transfers identical assets, or only an insignificant amount of the assets transferred by all transferors, in the aggregate, is nonidentical.[13] It is uncertain what percentage of the transferred assets can be nonidentical without causing the transfer to be taxable. Treasury Regulations provide an example in which only 1 percent of the transferred assets are nonidentical and state that such amount is deemed insignificant.[14] The IRS has ruled that 5 percent of the assets being nonidentical is insignificant but that 11 percent is significant.[15] For this purpose, cash is deemed to be nonidentical to a security.

A transfer also will not result in diversification if each transferor contributes a diversified portfolio of assets to the hedge fund.[16] A "diversified portfolio of assets" for this purpose generally is one in which not more than 25 percent of the value of the assets is invested in the stock or securities of one issuer and not more than 50 percent is invested in the stock or securities of 5 or fewer issuers. Cash transferred is generally not included in the numerator or the denominator of this formula. Government securities are included in the denominator but not in the numerator of the formula. It is not clear if short sales should be treated in this formula as liabilities or as security positions. Each transferor must transfer a diversified portfolio; if one transferor transfers a nondiversified portfolio when other transferors transfer diversified portfolios as part of the same transaction, all such transferors will be taxed on the transfer.

Whether a transfer results in diversification is generally determined by reference to the facts existing immediately after the transfer.[17] Treasury Regulations provide, however, that if a plan exists at the time of the transfer to contribute assets at a later date, those transactions can be treated as one transaction.[18]

---

11. Tax Code § 351(e)(1), 26 U.S.C. § 351(e)(1); Treas. Reg. § 1.351-1(c)(1), 26 C.F.R. § 351-1(c)(1).
12. Tax Code § 351(e)(1), 26 U.S.C. § 351(e)(1).
13. Treas. Reg. § 1.351-1(c)(5), 26 C.F.R. § 1.351-1(c)(5).
14. Treas. Reg. § 1.351-1(c)(7) (Example 1), 26 C.F.R. § 1.351-1(c)(7).
15. Priv. Ltr. Rul. 200006008 (Sep. 30, 1999), 1999 PRL LEXIS 1774; Rev. Rul. 87-9, 1987-1 C.B. 133.
16. Treas. Reg. § 1.351-1(c)(6), 26 C.F.R. § 1.351-1(c)(6).
17. Treas. Reg. § 1.351-1(c)(2), 26 C.F.R. § 1.351-1(c)(2).
18. Treas. Reg. §§ 1.351-1(c)(2) and 1.351-1(c)(5), 26 C.F.R. §§ 1.351-1(c)(2) and 1.351-1(c)(5).

Because most hedge funds qualify as investment companies for this purpose, and investors rarely contribute identical assets, an investor who contributes securities to a hedge fund will likely recognize taxable gain, unless that investor, and all other investors who contribute at the same time, contribute diversified portfolios of assets.

ii. Allocation of Gain/Loss to Contributing Partner

If an investor who contributes appreciated or depreciated securities to a hedge fund does not recognize taxable gain at the time of transfer as discussed above in section 16.2.2.i, the hedge fund generally will be required, when it eventually disposes of those contributed securities, to allocate the resulting taxable gain or loss first to the contributing investor to take into account the variation between the adjusted tax basis to the hedge fund of such securities and their fair market value when they were contributed.[19]

iii. Special Rules Regarding Contributed Securities

If a hedge fund distributes a contributed security (which was not taxed at the time of contribution) to an investor other than the contributing investor at any time within 7 years after such contribution, the contributing investor generally will be required to recognize gain or loss at that time based on the unrealized appreciation or depreciation in the security when the contributing investor contributed it to the hedge fund.[20] Moreover, if the hedge fund distributes other property to that contributing investor within 7 years after that investor contributed securities, the contributing investor may be required to recognize gain at the time of the distribution to reflect the unrealized appreciation in the contributed securities at the time of the contribution.[21]

If an investor who contributed a security to a hedge fund in a nontaxable transaction simultaneously or subsequently receives a distribution of cash, the contribution may be treated as if the investor sold the securities to the hedge fund for fair market value, causing the investor to recognize gain on the transfer. Treasury Regulations establish a rebuttable presumption that if an investor receives a distribution within 2 years after contributing securities, the distribution will be deemed to have been part of a disguised sale; the investor must disclose the transaction to the IRS, if it treats the distribution as other than a sale.[22]

If, when the investor made the contribution, it did not intend to receive a distribution of cash in exchange for such contribution, and if the investor's investment in the hedge fund was subject to the appreciation or depreciation of the assets of the hedge fund while invested, the investor should be able to rebut this presumption. Similarly, if an investor receives a security in kind in a distribution within 2 years after contributing cash to the hedge fund, that transaction will be rebuttably presumed to have been a sale of the security by the hedge fund to the investor.[23] Proposed Regulations also provided that any

19. Tax Code § 704(c), 26 U.S.C. § 704(c).
20. Tax Code § 704(c)(1)(B), 26 U.S.C. § 704(c)(1)(B).
21. Tax Code § 737, 26 U.S.C. § 737.
22. Treas. Reg. § 1.707-3(c), 26 C.F.R. § 1.707-3(c).
23. Treas. Reg. § 1.707-6(a), 26 C.F.R. § 1.707-6(a).

transfer of property, money or other consideration by a partner to a partnership would be presumed to be a disguised sale between partners if within 2 years the partnership transfers property, money or other consideration to another partner, unless the facts and circumstances clearly establish otherwise, but those Proposed Regulations were withdrawn.[24]

§ 16.3 Allocations of Profits and Losses for Tax Purposes

1. Pass-Through Tax Treatment

A hedge fund usually receives pass-through tax treatment as a partnership.[25] Thus, the investors in a hedge fund, and not the hedge fund itself, are taxed on the hedge fund's realized income and gains (to the extent that the investors are subject to income tax). This tax liability exists even absent cash distributions. Accordingly, an investor may have taxable income and tax liability from the hedge fund in a fiscal year when the hedge fund distributes no cash to the investor, or even in a fiscal year when such investor's capital account balance is reduced (for example, when the investor's share of net unrealized losses exceeds the investor's share of net realized income and gain for the fiscal year). Most hedge funds do not make annual distributions, even to allow investors to pay their taxes, but instead reinvest all income. Investors are expected to use other assets to pay taxes that arise from their investment in the hedge fund. Most hedge funds have, however, relatively frequent withdrawal rights, such as quarterly or semi-annually, so investors can withdraw funds to pay taxes, but many hedge funds also specify a minimum amount that an investor can withdraw. A hedge fund may grant investors a special withdrawal right to pay taxes in years when the hedge fund's taxable income allocated to investors causes a tax liability that they could not pay without liquidating other investments.

An investor may deduct its share of hedge fund losses only up to the amount of the investor's basis.[26] Losses in excess of adjusted tax basis may be carried over until the investor's outside basis is increased above zero.

The various tax items that pass through to an investor's tax return on a Form 1040, Schedule K-1 (and comparable state tax form) retain their tax character for the investor. Discussed below in this section are some of the typical tax items that pass through to a hedge fund's investors.

2. Special Incentive Profit Allocation

The general partner of most hedge funds receives a share of the profits that is disproportionate to the general partner's capital contributions. Typically, the general partner is allocated 20 percent of the profits otherwise allocable to each

24. Announcement 2009-4, 2009-8 I.R.B. 597.
25. *See* § 16.1, *supra.*
26. *See* § 16.2.1, *supra.*

limited partner in excess of that limited partner's previous losses that have not yet been recouped. The hedge fund usually treats this special incentive profit allocation as an allocation of partnership profits to the general partner rather than as a guaranteed payment under Tax Code section 707(c).[27] Accordingly, such profits allocated to the general partner retain the tax character of the underlying income of the hedge fund (that is, interest, dividends, long-term or short-term capital gains, and unrealized gains).[28] A limited partner's allocable share of profits is correspondingly reduced.

Hedge funds treat this special incentive profit allocation as a partnership allocation rather than as a fee, because the allocation is contingent on the partnership having profits, and is not guaranteed.[29] The IRS has indicated, however, in its Market Segment Specialization Program Guide for Partnerships, designed to assist examiners in examining partnership tax returns, that it believes that such an arrangement could be an improper shifting of the nature of the income for the general partner, and suggests that examiners consider treating it as a payment to a partner in a nonpartner capacity under Tax Code section 707(a),[30] especially if the general partner does not have any of its own capital at risk in the hedge fund.[31]

3. Ordinary Income

Hedge funds generate ordinary income on interest and dividends (other than qualifying dividends) from their investments. The maximum tax rate for individuals and corporations on ordinary income is 39.6 percent. A Medicare tax of 3.8 percent is imposed on individuals on the lesser of their net investment income or their modified adjusted gross income over a threshold amount ($250,000 for joint filers, $125,000 for married filing separately and $200,000 for other types of returns),[32] thus effectively raising the top effective rate to 43.4 percent on investment income other than long-term capital gains.

4. Qualifying Dividends

Hedge funds may generate qualifying dividend income that is taxed to individual partners at a maximum rate of 20 percent.[33] "Qualifying dividend income" generally includes dividends received from U.S. corporations and from certain "qualified foreign corporations," subject to a holding period requirement. To be eligible for the lower tax rate, a hedge fund must hold the stock for more than

---

27. 26 U.S.C. § 707(c); *see* § 15.2.1, *supra*.

28. Bills have been introduced that would change the treatment of all such profits allocated to the general partner to ordinary income. *See, e.g.*, The Carried Interest Fairness Act of 2012, H.R. 4016, 112th Cong. (2012).

29. *See* Rev. Rul. 67-158, 1967-1 C.B. 188.

30. 26 U.S.C. § 707(a).

31. Internal Revenue Service, Market Segment Specialization Program: Partnerships Audit Technique Guide (Sep. 2002), *available at* www.unclefed.com/SurviveIRS/MSSP/partnershipsatg12-16.pdf (last visited May 18, 2013).

32. Tax Code § 1411, 26 U.S.C. 1411

33. Tax Code § 1(h)(11), 26 U.S.C. § 1(h)(11).

60 days during the 120-day period beginning 60 days before the ex-dividend date.[34] With respect to certain preferred stock, the hedge fund must have held the shares more than 90 days during the 180-day period beginning 90 days before the ex-dividend date. The holding period must be satisfied for each dividend payment. Days on which the stock is hedged are generally not included in the holding period.[35] Moreover, the hedge fund must not be obligated to make related payments with respect to positions in substantially similar or related property.[36]

5. Capital Gains and Losses

Hedge funds may generate capital gains on the sale or other disposition of capital assets. The maximum rate of tax for individuals on capital gains from assets held more than a year generally is 20 percent and on capital gains on assets held for a year or less is 39.6 percent. A Medicare tax of 3.8 percent is imposed on individuals on the lesser of their net investment income or their modified adjusted gross income over a threshold amount ($250,000 for joint filers, $125,000 for married filing separately and $200,000 for other types of returns), thus effectively raising the top effective rate to 23.8 percent on long-term capital gains. Individuals are allowed to use capital losses to offset in full capital gains. To the extent that capital losses exceed capital gains in a taxable year, such excess capital losses are also allowed against a maximum of $3,000 of ordinary income. Any capital losses not used in a taxable year may be carried forward.

The current maximum tax rate for corporations on long-term or short-term capital gains is 35 percent. Corporations are allowed to use capital losses to offset in full capital gains but are not allowed to offset ordinary income. Corporations generally may carry capital losses back 3 years and forward 5 years.

Rules relating to straddle transactions may affect a hedge fund's holding period for a security or may otherwise affect whether gain or loss is characterized as short-term or long-term, as well as when gains and losses are recognized.[37] A "straddle" for tax purposes generally arises when a hedge fund holds two or more offsetting positions in stocks, securities, option contracts, futures contracts or forward contracts, which positions, when considered together, have the effect of reducing the hedge fund's risk of loss. Adverse tax consequences may arise from these transactions, such as the deferral of losses on a straddle position and the deferral of interest deductions related to a straddle position. In addition, in determining whether any two or more positions are offsetting, an investor is treated as holding any position held by the hedge fund.[38] Consequently, an investor may be required to treat a position held individually as offsetting a position held by the hedge fund. In such a case, the straddle rules could affect

34. Tax Code § 1(h)(11)(B)(iii), 26 U.S.C. § 1(h)(11)(B)(iii).
35. Tax Code § 246(c)(4), 26 U.S.C. § 246(c)(4).
36. Tax Code § 246(c)(1)(B), 26 U.S.C. § 246(c)(1(B).
37. Tax Code § 1092, 26 U.S.C. § 1092.
38. Tax Code § 1092(d)(4), 26 U.S.C. § 1092(d)(4).

the investor's holding period for the securities involved and may defer the investor's recognition of losses.

6. Gain or Loss from Short Sales

Gain or loss from a short sale of securities is generally considered a capital gain or loss to the extent that the asset used to close the short sale is a capital asset in the hedge fund's hands.[39] Except when the hedge fund has held the securities used to close a short sale for more than a year before entering into the short position, gains on short sales generally are short-term capital gains, subject to less favorable tax rates.[40] A loss on a short sale generally is treated as a long-term capital loss if, on the date of the short sale, the hedge fund has held "substantially identical property" for more than a year.[41] Special rules may also shorten the holding period of any assets held by the hedge fund that are substantially identical to those used to close the short sale.

7. Constructive Sale Transactions

Under Tax Code section 1259,[42] if a hedge fund engages in a constructive sale of an appreciated financial position, the transaction results in recognition of gain. A "constructive sale" for this purpose includes: (a) a short sale of the same or substantially identical property (short sales "against the box"); (b) an offsetting notional principal contract of the same or substantially identical property; (c) a futures or forward contract to deliver the same or substantially identical property; (d) with respect to an appreciated financial position that is one of the above, acquiring the same or substantially identical property; or (e) other transactions provided in Treasury Regulations.[43] A constructive sale does not result in recognition of gain during a taxable year if the offsetting position is closed within 30 days after the end of the taxable year, and the appreciated position is held unhedged for at least 60 days after the closing of the offsetting position.[44] The Treasury has yet to promulgate Treasury Regulations under Tax Code section 1259. In drafting the statute, Congress indicated, however, that it expected that Treasury Regulations would cause transactions such as collars to be treated in some instances as constructive sales.[45]

8. Wash Sales

If a hedge fund sells or disposes of a security for a loss and within the period beginning 30 days before and ending 30 days after such sale or disposition, acquires, or enters into an option or contract to acquire, substantially identical

---

39. Tax Code § 1233(a), 26 U.S.C. § 1233(a).
40. Tax Code § 1233(b), 26 U.S.C. § 1233(b).
41. Tax Code § 1233(d), 26 U.S.C. § 1233(d).
42. 26 U.S.C. § 1259.
43. Tax Code § 1259(c)(1), 26 U.S.C. § 1259(c)(1). No such Treasury Regulations have yet been issued.
44. Tax Code § 1259(c)(3), 26 U.S.C. § 1259(c)(3).
45. Committee Reports on P.L. 105-34, 13 Stand. Fed. Tax Rep. (CCH) ¶ 31,130.67.

securities, the loss will be disallowed.[46] The tax basis of the acquired securities is adjusted generally to reflect the amount of the disallowed loss.

9. Section 1256 Contracts

Tax Code section 1256[47] generally requires that section 1256 contracts held by a partnership at the end of each taxable year be treated as if the partnership sold them for their fair market value on the last business day of such taxable year. A hedge fund must include in its income for the year the net gain or loss from such deemed sales (called "marking to market"), together with any gain or loss from actual sales of section 1256 contracts (adjusted to reflect prior deemed sales). "Section 1256 contracts" include certain regulated futures contracts, foreign currency forward contracts, and options contracts. Forty percent of the capital gains and losses from deemed and actual sales of section 1256 contracts generally is short-term capital gains and losses and the other 60 percent is long-term capital gains and losses.[48] Gains and losses with respect to certain options purchased by options dealers or futures contracts purchased by futures dealers are short-term capital gains and losses to limited partners.[49]

10. Deduction Items

i. Trader vs. Investor

Whether a hedge fund is characterized as an "investor" or as a "trade or business" determines how the investors in the hedge fund may treat the hedge fund's expenses (including the management fee) on their tax returns. A trader for this purpose generally seeks profits from short-term swings in the market. Thus, a trader usually generates little interest, dividends or long-term capital gain income.[50] An investor, on the other hand, purchases and sells securities with the principal purpose of realizing income in the form of interest, dividends and long-term appreciation of securities.[51] The Tax Court has set forth three factors to consider in determining whether a taxpayer trading for its own account is a trader or investor: (a) the taxpayer's investment intent; (b) the nature of the income derived from the activity (long-term capital gains, interest and dividends, as opposed to mainly short-term capital gains); and (c) the frequency, extent and regularity of the taxpayer's securities transactions.[52] Under this last factor, a hedge fund may be deemed to be a trader based on the frequency of its trading, if the portfolio is large enough that it is making daily trades, even if most of its income is derived from long-term capital gains.

---

46. Tax Code § 1091, 26 U.S.C. § 1091.
47. 26 U.S.C. § 1256.
48. Tax Code § 1256(a)(3), 26 U.S.C. § 1256(a)(3).
49. Tax Code § 1256(f)(4), 26 U.S.C. § 1256(f)(4).
50. Chang Hsiao Liang v. Comm'r, 23 T.C. 1040, 1955 Tax Ct. LEXIS 223 (1955).
51. Yaeger Estate v. Comm'r, 55 (CCH) TCM 1101 (1988), aff'd 889 F.2d 29, 89-2 U.S. Tax Cas. (CCH) ¶ 9633 (1989).
52. Hart v. Comm'r, 73 (CCH) TCM 1684 (1997).

A trader's expenses relating to its trade or business are fully deductible in determining adjusted gross income. The deductibility of an investor's expenses is limited. Under Tax Code section 67(c),[53] temporary Treasury Regulations[54] prevent a taxpayer from deducting indirectly, through a pass-through entity such as a partnership, expenses that would not be deductible if paid or incurred directly by the taxpayer. The Tax Code limits a number of deductions characterized as "miscellaneous itemized deductions," including those for expenditures related to investment income or property, which are deductible under Tax Code section 212.[55] Miscellaneous itemized deductions, including those related to investment income or property, are deductible only to the extent that in total they exceed 2 percent of the taxpayer's adjusted gross income.[56] The deductible portion, if any, of such expenditures is further reduced if a partner's adjusted gross income exceeds a specified threshold amount.[57] Miscellaneous itemized deductions are not allowed at all in computing alternative minimum tax.[58]

If the hedge fund is an investor, management fees payable to the hedge fund's investment adviser and other expenses of the hedge fund constitute expenditures related to investment income or property and thus are deductible by a limited partner only to the extent that those expenditures plus the limited partner's other miscellaneous itemized deductions exceed 2 percent of the limited partner's adjusted gross income in any taxable year. If a hedge fund invests solely in other hedge funds (that is, if it is a fund of funds), any management fees paid at the fund of funds level will be treated as investment expenses.[59] If a domestic hedge fund invests in an offshore master fund,[60] management fees paid at the level of the domestic hedge fund may also be deemed investment expenses, even if the master fund qualifies as a trader.

The IRS might also argue that the special incentive profit allocation[61] to the general partner of a hedge fund is an expense, rather than a partnership profit allocation, in which case its deductibility would also be subject to these limits. From time to time, legislation has been introduced in Congress to amend the Tax Code to change the character of the incentive profit allocation to ordinary income. If such an amendment were to be enacted, it might also cause the incentive profit allocation to be treated as an expense allocable to the partners.

If a hedge fund is instead deemed to be engaged in a trade or business, management fees and other expenses are not deemed to be investment expenditures, and their deductibility is not limited as described above.

---

53. 26 U.S.C. § 67(c).
54. Treas. Reg. § 1.67-2T, 26 C.F.R. § 1.67-2T.
55. 26 U.S.C. § 212.
56. Tax Code § 67(a), 26 U.S.C. § 67(a).
57. Tax Code § 68, 26 U.S.C. § 68.
58. Tax Code § 56(b)(1)(A)(i), 26 U.S.C. § 56(b)(1)(A)(i).
59. Rev. Rul. 2008-39, 2008 I.R.B. 252.
60. *See* § 16.7.7, *infra*.
61. *See* § 16.3.2, *supra*.

ii. Interest Expense

Under Tax Code section 163(d),[62] a taxpayer generally may deduct investment interest only to the extent of the taxpayer's net investment income. Interest expense on indebtedness incurred to invest in or hold interests in a hedge fund is subject to the investment interest limitation. Any deduction for investment interest that is disallowed may be carried over to subsequent years to offset net investment income. An investor's share of interest expense incurred by a hedge fund in carrying on its business also should be subject to the investment interest expense limitation.

Tax Code section 265(a)(2)[63] disallows any deduction for interest paid by a taxpayer on indebtedness incurred or continued for the purpose of purchasing or holding tax-exempt obligations. The IRS has announced that such purpose will be deemed to exist with respect to indebtedness incurred to finance a "portfolio investment," and that while a partnership's purpose in incurring indebtedness will be attributed to its general partners, an investment in a hedge fund will be regarded as a portfolio investment. Therefore, if a hedge fund investor owns tax-exempt obligations outside of the hedge fund, the IRS might take the position that any interest the investor pays in connection with the investment in the hedge fund should be viewed as incurred to enable the investor to continue holding those tax-exempt obligations, and that the investor should not be allowed to deduct the investor's full allocable share of such interest.

iii. Organization and Syndication Expenses

No deduction is allowed for expenses paid or incurred to organize a partnership or to promote the sale of, or sell interests in, a partnership.[64] A partnership may, however, elect to deduct $5,000 of organizational expenses (reduced, but not below zero, by organizational expenses in excess of $50,000) in the first year of operation and amortize the remainder over 15 years.[65] Under Treasury Regulations, organizational expenses include filing fees and legal costs of negotiating and preparing the partnership agreement, whereas syndication expenses include brokerage fees related to sales of interests, legal costs of preparing the private placement memorandum, and costs of securities law counseling.[66]

A hedge fund or its general partner may pay a finder a share of the general partner's asset-based management fees or incentive profit allocations for introducing investors to the hedge fund. Such expenses are arguably syndication expenses under these rules and thus may be nondeductible by the hedge fund or its general partner.

---

62. 26 U.S.C. § 163(d).
63. 26 U.S.C. § 265(a)(2).
64. Tax Code § 709, 26 U.S.C. § 709.
65. Tax Code § 709(b), 26 U.S.C. § 709(b).
66. Treas. Reg. § 1.709-2, 26 C.F.R. § 1.709-2.

11. Hedge Funds Are Not Engaged in Passive Activities

A hedge fund generally is not considered to be engaged in a passive activity, and the investors' distributive shares of income, gain or loss are not considered passive income, gain or loss. Temporary Treasury Regulations section 1.469-1T(e)(6)[67] provides that trading personal property, including stocks, bonds and other securities, for the account of owners of the trading entity is not a passive activity, whether or not such trading is a trade or business. Accordingly, an investor's ability to deduct losses of the hedge fund is not limited by the passive loss rule (other limitations may apply, however, as discussed above in sections 16.3.1, 16.3.5, 16.3.8 and 16.3.10). An investor's passive losses from other investment activities are not deductible against the investor's distributive share of the hedge fund's income or gain.

12. Aggregate Allocations versus Layering

Hedge funds maintain capital accounts for book purposes, taking into account unrealized gains and losses as provided in Treasury Regulations.[68] Taking unrealized gains and losses into account is necessary both to reflect gain and loss equitably when partners withdraw or contribute funds and to calculate the general partner's incentive profit allocation. Income tax allocations are, however, calculated by taking into account only realized gains and losses. Accordingly, book allocations of gain or loss may (and typically do) differ each period from tax allocations of gain or loss. A partnership that revalues its capital accounts to reflect unrealized gains and losses must use a reasonable method to take into account any variation between the adjusted tax basis of the property and its revalued value for book purposes.[69] A partnership is not required to use the same method for allocating gain or loss to partners who have contributed property in kind (704(c) allocations) as it does to make allocations with respect to revalued property (reverse 704(c) allocations).

A hedge fund that qualifies as a "securities partnership" under Treasury Regulations can make reverse 704(c) allocations by aggregating gains and losses related to qualified financial assets. To qualify as a securities partnership, a hedge fund must: (a) make its book allocations in proportion to capital account balances (except for reasonable incentive profit allocations to the general partner or investment adviser); (b) on the date of each capital account revaluation, have at least 90 percent of its noncash assets qualify as qualified financial assets; and (c) expect to make revaluations at least annually.[70] "Qualified financial assets" are generally assets that are traded on an established financial market.[71] Accordingly, a hedge fund generally cannot hold more than 10 percent of its

67. 26 C.F.R. § 1.469-1T(e)(6).

68. Treas. Reg. § 1.704-1(b)(2)(iv)(f), 26 C.F.R. § 1.704-1(b)(2)(iv)(f).

69. Treas. Reg. §§ 1.704-3(a) and 1.704-3(a)(6), 26 C.F.R. §§ 1.704-3(a) and 1.704-3(a)(6).

70. Treas. Reg. § 1.704-3(e)(3), 26 C.F.R. § 1.704-3(e)(3).

71. Treas. Reg. § 1.1092(d)-1, 26 C.F.R. § 1.1092(d)-1.

assets as private securities as of any revaluation date (generally the end of each fiscal quarter) if it wants to use an aggregate method of tax allocations. The IRS has ruled that qualified partnerships (as defined in Revenue Procedure 2007-59) can also use the aggregate method of reverse 704(c) allocations.[72] The Treasury Regulations provide examples of permissible aggregate allocation methods, including full netting and partial netting approaches.[73]

A hedge fund that is not permitted to use an aggregate allocation method must allocate taxable gains and losses on a security-by-security basis whenever a particular security is sold or otherwise disposed of and taxable gain or loss is realized, by taking into account which partners' capital accounts were credited or debited for book purposes with appreciation or depreciation of that security ("layering"). Layering is generally more costly for a hedge fund and more difficult to administer than using an aggregate allocation method.

13. Unrelated Business Taxable Income

Tax-exempt investors are taxed on their pro rata shares of any unrelated business taxable income ("UBTI") of a hedge fund.[74] UBTI is generally defined as the gross income from any trade or business unrelated to the tax-exempt business of the entity.[75] If a tax-exempt entity's UBTI, from all sources, less its allocable share of deductions directly connected with carrying on any such trade or business, exceeds $1,000 in any year, the tax-exempt entity is liable for taxes with respect to the excess at tax rates that would apply if the organization were not exempt from taxation.

Generally, hedge funds do not invest in other entities that are themselves engaged in a trade or business and that are structured as pass-through entities for tax purposes. A hedge fund that invests in private securities may, however, occasionally invest in a start-up company that is engaged in a trade or business and structured as a pass-through entity, such as an LLC, which might generate UBTI.

UBTI does not include interest and dividend income, or gains on the sale, exchange or other disposition of assets held for investment.[76] Income from debt-financed property (such as gain from the sale of stock purchased on margin) will, however, constitute UBTI to tax-exempt entities, in the percentage that such property is subject to acquisition indebtedness (the percentage that acquisition indebtedness respecting such property bears to the hedge fund's adjusted tax basis for such property).[77] Generally, "acquisition indebtedness" is indebtedness incurred directly or indirectly in connection with the acquisition or improvement of property. Indebtedness incurred after the acquisition or improvement of any debt-financed property also constitutes acquisition indebtedness,

---

72. Rev. Proc. 2007-59, 2007-2 C.B. 745.
73. Treas. Reg. §§ 1.704-3(e)(iv) and 1.704-3(e)(v), 26 C.F.R. §§ 1.704-3(e)(iv) and 1.704-3(e)(v).
74. Tax Code § 511, 26 U.S.C. § 511.
75. Tax Code § 512(a)(1), 26 U.S.C. § 512(a)(1).
76. Tax Code §§ 512(b)(1) and 512(b)(5), 26 U.S.C. §§ 512(b)(1) and 512(b)(5).
77. Tax Code § 512(b)(4), 26 U.S.C. § 512(b)(4).

if the indebtedness would not have been incurred but for such acquisition or improvement and the incurrence of such indebtedness is reasonably foreseeable at the time of such acquisition or improvement.[78]

Many hedge funds purchase securities through margin accounts and other debt-financed means, and under other circumstances that may be treated as involving acquisition indebtedness. The IRS has ruled, however, that short sales generally are not treated as liabilities for purposes of determining UBTI.[79] The IRS has also privately ruled that investing in commodity futures does not give rise to acquisition indebtedness, even though a margin account is established with a broker.[80] If a tax-exempt entity borrows to invest in a hedge fund, the acquisition financing of the investment may result in the realization of UBTI.

The receipt of UBTI by a tax-exempt entity generally does not affect that entity's tax-exempt status or the exemption of its other income. If a charitable remainder trust, however, receives any UBTI during a taxable year, it is subject to an excise tax equal to the amount of UBTI for that year.[81] Accordingly, charitable remainder trusts ordinarily do not invest in hedge funds that invest on margin. In addition, in some circumstances the continued receipt of UBTI over time may cause some other types of tax-exempt entities to lose their tax exemptions. Tax-exempt entities that want to avoid incurring UBTI with respect to an investment in a hedge fund that trades on margin may consider investing in an offshore hedge fund that is structured as a corporation for U.S. income tax purposes.[82]

14. Marking to Market

A hedge fund that is treated as a trade or business[83] may elect to "mark to market" its portfolio under Tax Code section 475(f).[84] If it makes this election, the hedge fund's securities or commodities on the last business day of each year are treated as though they are sold for tax purposes and the resulting gain or loss is ordinary in character. A hedge fund that is treated as an investor, as opposed to a trade or business, is not permitted to make this election. The election may accelerate recognition of income or loss and convert long-term capital gains to ordinary income. The mark-to-market election simplifies tax accounting, however, and eliminates the need to make many tax adjustments described above (such as wash sales, straddles and constructive sales) because income and character adjustments are done in the aggregate with respect to all securities. A hedge fund that trades frequently and generates little or no long-term capital gain income may benefit from making the election, because it obviates the tracking of those adjustments. A hedge fund that trades in both commodities and securities can make a separate election to mark to market

78. Tax Code § 514(c), 26 U.S.C. § 514(c).
79. Rev. Rul. 95-8, 1995-1 C.B. 107.
80. Priv. Ltr. Rul. 8104098 (Oct. 30, 1980).
81. Tax Code § 664(c), 26 U.S.C. § 664(c).
82. *See* § 16.7.6, *infra*.
83. *See* § 16.3.10.i, *supra*.
84. 26 U.S.C. § 475(f).

either its securities trading activities or its commodities trading activities.[85] Once made, the election remains in effect for all succeeding years (including with respect to securities or commodities purchased in succeeding years) and cannot be revoked without the permission of the IRS.[86]

§ 16.4 Withdrawals

1. Distribution of Cash

An investor is taxed on the taxable income of the hedge fund, whether or not the hedge fund distributes any income or capital to the investor.[87] A partner's adjusted tax basis increases by the amount of any taxable income allocated to it. A cash distribution of the hedge fund's income normally does not result in further taxable income to the investor, except to the extent that the distribution exceeds the investor's adjusted tax basis, in which case it generally is treated as gain from the sale or exchange of an interest in the hedge fund. The taxation of such gain is subject to the same kinds of considerations as are discussed below in section 16.4.3.

2. Distribution of Securities in Kind

Hedge funds sometimes distribute securities in kind. A distribution of marketable securities is treated under Tax Code section 731(c)[88] as a distribution of cash subject to the consequences discussed above in section 16.4.1, unless the distributing partnership qualifies as an investment partnership and the other requirements of Tax Code section 731(c) are met. An "investment partnership" for this purpose is any partnership that has never been engaged in a trade or business (other than as a trader of securities) and substantially all of the assets of which have always consisted of money, stock, notes, bonds and other evidences of indebtedness, interest rate, currency or equity notional principal contracts, foreign currencies and derivatives (including options and forward contracts). "Marketable securities" for this purpose are generally financial instruments and foreign currencies that are treated as actively traded under Tax Code section 1092(d)(1),[89] and certain other assets listed in Tax Code section 731(c)(2)(B).[90] Most hedge funds qualify as investment partnerships and thus their distributions of securities in kind, whether or not marketable, generally should not be treated as distributions of cash, but instead are nontaxable.

When a hedge fund distributes a security in kind in a nontaxable transaction, other than on withdrawal of all of an investor's capital account, the investor's

85. Tax Code § 475(f)(3), 26 U.S.C. § 475(f)(3).
86. *Id.*
87. *See* § 16.3.1, *supra.*
88. 26 U.S.C. § 731(c).
89. 26 U.S.C. § 1092(d)(1).
90. 26 U.S.C. § 731(c)(2)(B).

adjusted tax basis in the security distributed is the lesser of the hedge fund's adjusted tax basis in that security and the investor's adjusted tax basis in the investor's interest in the hedge fund.[91] If a hedge fund distributes a security in kind in a nontaxable transaction on withdrawal of all of an investor's capital account, the investor's adjusted tax basis in the security distributed is the same as the investor's adjusted tax basis in the investor's interest in the hedge fund, reduced by any cash received in the distribution.[92] The investor's gain or loss on a later sale of such asset is the difference between the amount realized on the sale and the investor's adjusted tax basis in the asset. The character of such gain (capital gain or ordinary income) depends on the character of the asset in the hands of the investor. The investor normally may add the hedge fund's holding period to the investor's holding period to determine whether the gain is long-term or short-term.[93]

When an investor withdraws, therefore, a hedge fund can distribute to that investor securities with an aggregate fair market value equal to the investor's capital account, but with a tax basis to the hedge fund less than the investor's adjusted tax basis in its interest in the hedge fund. This effectively reduces the unrealized gains left in the hedge fund for the remaining investors, but could result in a mandatory adjustment to the hedge fund's basis in its securities under Tax Code section 734.[94] Those gains would be realized by the remaining partners ultimately when they withdraw from the hedge fund or the hedge fund dissolves. On the other hand, if the hedge fund distributes to a withdrawing investor securities with an aggregate tax basis higher than the withdrawing investor's adjusted tax basis, the hedge fund increases unrealized gains for the remaining investors, and those remaining investors are more likely to realize a capital loss when they withdraw from the hedge fund or the hedge fund dissolves.

A distribution of securities to an investor who initially contributed securities to the hedge fund, or who has invested in the hedge fund within the last 2 years, is subject to additional tax considerations, as is a distribution of securities originally contributed to the hedge fund by an investor.[95]

If a hedge fund distributes short positions in kind to an investor, the IRS might contend that the transaction is a disguised sale because the investor is assuming a liability of the hedge fund.

3. Sale of Interests

In general, when an investor sells or disposes of its interest in a hedge fund in a taxable transaction, the investor realizes gain or loss equal to the difference between the amount realized on the disposition and the adjusted tax basis of the investor's interest in the hedge fund. If the investor's interest in the hedge fund is a capital asset (as ordinarily is the case), the gain or loss from the sale or other taxable disposition is generally treated as capital gain or loss, and will

91. Tax Code § 732(a), 26 U.S.C. § 732(a).
92. Tax Code § 732(b), 26 U.S.C. § 732(b).
93. Tax Code § 1223, 26 U.S.C. § 1223.
94. 26 U.S.C. § 734; *see* § 16.4.4, *infra.*
95. *See* § 16.2.2.iii, *supra.*

be short-term or long-term depending on whether the investor held that interest for more than a year.

4. Section 754 Election

When an investor transfers an interest in a hedge fund to another investor, including on the transferor's death, the transferee investor's outside tax basis in the interest in the hedge fund may not match the transferee's share of the hedge fund's inside basis in its assets, because the transferee's basis in the interest reflects the hedge fund's unrealized gains or losses. In such case, when those gains or losses are realized, the transferee would be required to pay tax on gains or be allocated losses that effectively occurred before the transferee's investment, even though those gains or losses presumably were reflected in the price paid for the interest.

To avoid these discrepancies, the hedge fund can make an election under Tax Code section 754[96] pursuant to which the basis of the hedge fund's securities is adjusted on a transfer, but only with respect to the new investor. If the hedge fund had unrealized gains at the time of the transfer, and thus the transferee's outside basis is higher than the hedge fund's inside basis in its assets, the election results in an increase in the hedge fund's basis in its assets. On the other hand, if the hedge fund had unrealized losses at the time of the transfer, the election will ordinarily decrease the hedge fund's inside basis in its assets. Accordingly, if a hedge fund's assets have appreciated, the failure to make such an election generally causes a transferee to recognize more taxable income on the disposition of the hedge fund's assets than if such election had been made (although the transferee would then ordinarily receive an offsetting loss when it withdraws from the hedge fund or the hedge fund dissolves). Hence, a transferee may not be willing to pay as much for interests in the hedge fund as the transferee would pay if an election under Tax Code section 754 had been made.

A similar adjustment may be made under Tax Code section 754 when an investor withdraws from a hedge fund and receives a distribution that is more or less than its adjusted tax basis, which also can result in a discrepancy between the hedge fund's aggregate inside basis in its assets and the investors' aggregate outside basis in the hedge fund interest.

As a practical matter, hedge funds rarely make elections under Tax Code section 754, because of the administrative and accounting difficulties that arise in tracking those adjustments with frequent contributions and withdrawals. Once made, a Tax Code section 754 election is irrevocable without the consent of the IRS.[97] As noted above, such an election results in both increases and decreases in the hedge fund's inside basis in its assets, and thus can have both positive and negative results.

Tax Code sections 734 and 743 require a section 754 adjustment on a transfer of a partnership interest with a "substantial" built-in loss (loss of more than $250,000 in the value of partnership property) and on a distribution resulting in a

96. 26 U.S.C. § 754.
97. *Id.*

substantial basis reduction (more than $250,000). For example, if a hedge fund were to distribute securities in kind with a tax basis of $250,000 to a departing partner who has a tax basis in his interest in the hedge fund of $750,000, the departing partner would have a tax basis of $750,000 in the securities going forward, but the hedge fund would be required to decrease the basis of its other assets by $500,000.

Most hedge funds do not permit frequent transfers of interests between parties, so adjustments under Tax Code section 743 are not often required. Tax Code section 743 also provides that an investment partnership can elect not to make the basis adjustment, and instead may disallow losses for the transferee partner from the sale of partnership property, except to the extent that such losses exceed the loss recognized by the transferor. Most hedge funds will not, however, qualify as investment partnerships under this provision and thus will not be able to make this election. To qualify as an "investment partnership" for purposes of Tax Code section 743, a hedge fund must, among other things, (a) have substantive restrictions on each partner's ability to redeem its interests, (b) never have been a trader, as opposed to an investor,[98] (c) have a life of no more than 15 years (20 years for partnerships in existence prior to June 4, 2004), and (d) have issued all of its interests pursuant to a private offering within 24 months of the first capital contribution to the hedge fund.

A hedge fund may be able to avoid mandatory downward basis adjustments on distributions under Tax Code section 734 by using a fill-up provision (discussed below).

5. "Fill-Up" or "Stuffing" Provisions

Instead of making an election under Tax Code section 754, some hedge funds use what is commonly called a "fill-up" or "stuffing" provision to attempt to keep the hedge fund's inside basis in its assets approximately equal to the partners' aggregate outside bases and avoid the discrepancies that occur when an investor withdraws some or all of an investment from the hedge fund when there are unrealized gains or losses. Under a stuffing provision in the hedge fund's partnership agreement, the hedge fund allocates taxable gain and income first to a partner who has withdrawn an amount in excess of the partner's adjusted tax basis in the hedge fund to the extent of such difference. Similarly, a partner who withdraws from a hedge fund when the partner's outside basis exceeds the partner's capital account is allocated taxable losses to the extent of such difference.

While such an allocation generally does not increase or decrease the amount of gain or loss the partner incurs due to withdrawal, it can change the character of the gain for the withdrawing partner. For example, if a partner has held an interest in the hedge fund for more than a year, gain on a withdrawal in excess of the partner's basis would generally be long-term capital gain, but the hedge fund might allocate short-term capital gain and ordinary income to the partner under the stuffing provision, thus changing the character and resulting in a

98. *See* § 16.3.10.i, *supra*.

higher tax rate. Additionally, the stuffing provision could cause a withdrawing partner to recognize gain in the year of withdrawal, rather than the year payment is received.

Absent an election under Tax Code section 754 or a stuffing provision, when a partner withdraws an amount in excess of the partner's adjusted tax basis, the remaining partners could be allocated the taxable gains or income incurred in disposing of assets to fund the withdrawal. Although a stuffing provision arguably should be treated as a reasonable aggregate allocation method for making reverse 704(c) allocations,[99] the IRS has not specifically ruled that such a provision will be respected. The IRS might argue that such a provision is an inappropriate means of avoiding making an election under Tax Code section 754. In addition, the IRS might well challenge such a provision if it were not applied consistently to all withdrawing partners.

§ 16.5 Divisions and Combinations of Hedge Funds

Investment advisers occasionally restructure their hedge funds by, for example, dividing one hedge fund into two or by merging two hedge funds into one. An investment adviser with one hedge fund that relies on the exception from the definition of "investment company" under Company Act section 3(c)(1) might want to establish a second hedge fund that will rely on the exception in Company Act section 3(c)(7), and move the investors who qualify as Qualified Purchasers into the new section 3(c)(7) fund. Similarly, an investment adviser with a section 3(c)(1) hedge fund and a section 3(c)(7) hedge fund may decide that having two hedge funds is unnecessary and combine them.[100]

1. Division of Hedge Funds

At least two alternative methods are available for moving investors into a new hedge fund. First, the hedge fund can distribute assets in kind to the investors who are being moved, and then those investors can contribute those assets to the new hedge fund in exchange for partnership interests. The distribution of securities in kind to the investors generally should not be a taxable event as long as the transaction qualifies under Tax Code section 731[101] as a distribution by an investment partnership, and none of the special circumstances discussed above in section 16.2.2.iii apply (such as a disguised sale of a security to an investor who recently contributed cash, or a distribution of a security that itself was recently contributed to the hedge fund). The subsequent contribution of the securities to the new hedge fund will also not be taxable if the transfer does not result in a diversification of the transferors' interests,[102] either because all of the transferors transfer identical securities and no other transferors transfer

99. *See* § 16.3.12, *supra.*
100. *See generally*, Chapter 3, *supra.*
101. *See* § 16.4.2, *supra.*
102. *See* § 16.2.2.i, *supra.*

nonidentical assets at the same time, or because all transferors transfer diversified portfolios of assets.

Alternatively, the hedge fund could first contribute the assets in kind to the new hedge fund and then distribute interests in the new hedge fund in kind to the investors who are being moved. That transaction will also generally be nontaxable if no diversification occurs on the contribution and the requirements of Tax Code section 731 and other special provisions are met with respect to the subsequent distribution.

The new hedge fund's tax basis in its assets may differ after the transfer under these two approaches. Generally, if the existing hedge fund ("hedge fund 1") fully redeems an investor's interest in hedge fund 1 by distributing to the investor a proportionate share of hedge fund 1's assets, and the investor subsequently recontributes those assets to the new hedge fund ("hedge fund 2") in a nontaxable transaction, hedge fund 2 will receive a basis in the contributed assets equal to the investor's former outside basis in hedge fund 1.

In contrast, if hedge fund 1 contributes its assets to hedge fund 2 in exchange for interests in hedge fund 2 and then distributes those interests in kind to investors in hedge fund 1, hedge fund 2 will receive a basis in the contributed assets equal to hedge fund 1's former inside basis in its assets. Whether one of these options is preferable depends on the difference between the aggregate outside bases of the investors being moved and the inside basis of the hedge fund in the assets being transferred. Absent clear evidence of which approach is being used, the IRS will deem the assets to have first been contributed to the new hedge fund and then interests in that hedge fund to have been distributed in kind to the investors.[103] In addition, the IRS may not respect a transaction that is structured as a distribution of assets followed by a contribution if the investors never formally take title to the assets before transferring them to the new hedge fund.[104]

When a partnership divides into two or more partnerships, and a new partnership is more than 50 percent owned after the transaction by the former partners of the prior partnership, the new partnership is deemed to be a continuation of the prior partnership. Even if the transaction is structured as a formation of a new partnership and the transfer of some partners to that new partnership, the new partnership may be treated for tax purposes as the continuing partnership, and the old partnership as a new entity.[105] The new partnership would thus keep the taxpayer identification number and retain the elections made by the old partnership.

A hedge fund could distribute cash to an investor and then have that investor contribute that cash to the new hedge fund. This would be a taxable event, but may not materially increase the tax liability if the investor is a tax-exempt entity or has little or no gain (or has a loss) in the interest. If an investor with an unrealized loss in a hedge fund interest is distributed cash and contributes that

103. Treas. Reg. § 1.708-1(d)(3), 26 C.F.R. § 1.708-1(d)(3).

104. *Id.*

105. Treas. Reg. § 1.708-1(d), 26 C.F.R. § 1.708-1(d).

cash to the new hedge fund, which holds the same securities as held by the old hedge fund, the wash sale rules[106] would likely disallow deduction of the loss.

2. Combination of Hedge Funds

Two hedge funds can be combined by having one hedge fund either (a) contribute all of its assets to the other hedge fund and then distribute interests of the other hedge fund in kind, or (b) distribute all of its assets to its investors in kind and then have them contribute such assets in kind to the other hedge fund. These transfers would generally have the same consequences as discussed above in section 16.5.1 with respect to divisions of hedge funds, and could result in a different tax basis in the transferred securities for the continuing hedge fund, depending on which form is used.

When two hedge funds are merged or otherwise combined, the combined hedge fund is deemed the continuation of the hedge fund in which the former investors own more than 50 percent of the capital and profits of the combined hedge fund. If the combined hedge fund can be considered to be a continuation of both hedge funds (due to overlap of partners), the hedge fund that contributes the greater amount of assets to the combined hedge fund is deemed to be the continuing hedge fund.[107] Accordingly, even if the transaction is structured for state law purposes as the merger or other combination of hedge fund 1 into hedge fund 2, the IRS may deem the transaction to have been the combination of hedge fund 2 into hedge fund 1. If it is not clear which form of transaction is being used, the IRS will deem the hedge fund that is going out of existence for tax purposes to have contributed its assets to the continuing hedge fund, and then to have distributed the interests in the continuing hedge fund to its partners in dissolution.[108]

§ 16.6 Dissolution

When a hedge fund dissolves, any of its remaining assets normally would be sold, which would cause the investors to realize taxable gain or loss. Distributions of cash in complete liquidation of a hedge fund are generally treated first as a return of capital to the extent of an investor's tax basis in the hedge fund and thereafter as a capital gain, to the extent of the amount of cash distributed. Generally, when a hedge fund liquidates or terminates, an investor recognizes income only to the extent that cash distributed exceeds the investor's adjusted tax basis in the investment at the time of distribution. A distribution of assets on liquidation generally has the results discussed above in section 16.4.2.

106. *See* § 16.3.8, *supra*.
107. Treas. Reg. § 1.708-1(c)(1), 26 C.F.R. § 1.708-1(c)(1).
108. Treas. Reg. § 1.708-1(c)(3), 26 C.F.R. § 1.708-1(c)(3).

§ 16.7 Offshore Hedge Funds

1. General

Except with respect to certain withholding taxes,[109] a hedge fund established under the laws of a jurisdiction outside the United States generally is subject to U.S. income taxation only if it is deemed to be engaged in the conduct of a trade or business within the United States. If the offshore hedge fund is treated as a corporation for U.S. tax purposes, the investors generally are not subject to U.S. tax on their proportionate shares of the income of the entity (subject to special rules discussed below).[110] Most offshore hedge funds are therefore structured to be treated as corporations for U.S. income tax purposes.

Offshore hedge funds are generally marketed to non-U.S. investors and U.S. investors that are exempt from income tax. Non-U.S. investors often prefer to invest in the U.S. securities market through offshore hedge funds, rather than investing directly in U.S. securities or in U.S.-based hedge funds, primarily to limit their exposure to the IRS and other U.S. regulatory authorities, and in some cases to avoid U.S. estate taxes. U.S. tax-exempt entities invest in offshore hedge funds to be able to invest in leveraged portfolios without recognizing UBTI.[111]

2. Classification of Entity

Under Treasury Regulations, a business entity established under the laws of a jurisdiction outside the United States can elect to be treated as a corporation or a partnership for U.S. income tax purposes, unless it is one of certain entities listed by the IRS as "per se" corporations that are automatically treated as corporations.[112]

A non-U.S. entity that is not treated as a per se corporation is classified: (a) as a partnership if it has two or more members and at least one member has unlimited liability; (b) as a corporation if all members have limited liability; or (c) disregarded as an entity separate from its owner if it has only one owner and that owner has unlimited liability.[113] If an entity that is not treated as a per se corporation wants to be classified differently from its treatment under these default rules, the entity must file an election on Form 8832. The election must be filed no earlier than 12 months before and no later than 75 days after the desired effective date.[114]

---

109. *See* § 16.7.5, *infra*.

110. *See* § 16.7.4, *infra*.

111. If the offshore hedge fund is treated as a partnership for U.S. tax purposes, any income, gain, loss or credit of the offshore hedge fund will pass through to the investors, and will be taxable or not to the investors based on their status as nonresident aliens, non-U.S. entities, U.S. taxpayers or U.S. tax-exempt entities. *See also* § 16.7.6, *infra*.

112. Treas. Reg. § 301.7701-2(b)(8), 26 C.F.R. § 301.7701-2(b)(8).

113. Treas. Reg. § 301.7701-3(b)(2), 26 C.F.R. § 301.7701-3(b)(2).

114. Treas. Reg. § 301.7701-3(c), 26 C.F.R. § 301.7701-3(c).

Most offshore hedge funds are entities in which all members have limited liability under the laws of the local jurisdiction, such as exempted limited companies under the laws of the Cayman Islands. These entities are treated as corporations under the default classification rule. Offshore hedge funds that desire to be treated for tax purposes as partnerships, such as master funds,[115] often are structured as limited partnerships under the laws of the offshore jurisdiction, and thus are classified as partnerships under the default rule.

It may be advantageous to form an offshore hedge fund as a partnership under the laws of the offshore jurisdiction, and elect for that entity to be treated as a corporation for U.S. tax purposes, if the offshore hedge fund expects to have significant income subject to U.S. or non-U.S. withholding taxes, because non-U.S. investors may be able to apply for refunds of those taxes under tax treaties between their home jurisdictions and the jurisdictions withholding the taxes. An offshore hedge fund that is uncertain as to the default classification may file a protective Form 8832 on its formation to assure the desired treatment.

3. U.S. Trade or Business

As noted above, an offshore hedge fund is generally not subject to U.S. income taxation (except with respect to certain withholding taxes),[116] if it is not engaged in a U.S. trade or business. Tax Code section 864(b)(2)(A) and Treasury Regulations section 1.864-2(c)(2)(ii) provide that "trade or business within the United States" does not include trading in securities for a taxpayer's own account. "Securities" for this purpose means any note, bond, debenture or other evidence of indebtedness, or any evidence of an interest in or right to purchase any of the above.[117] The volume or frequency of stock transactions in which the offshore hedge fund engages is irrelevant for this determination. It does not matter whether the hedge fund is deemed to be a trader, rather than an investor, as described above.[118]

This exclusion does not apply, however, if the taxpayer is a dealer in stocks or securities.[119] A "dealer" for this purpose is defined as a merchant of stocks or securities with an established place of business regularly engaged in purchasing stocks or securities and selling them to customers with a view to the gains and profits to be derived therefrom.[120] An offshore hedge fund that trades only for its own account and does not purchase and sell securities to customers should not be considered to be a dealer in stocks or securities.

Tax Code section 864(b)(2)(B) provides a similar exclusion from treatment as a U.S. trade or business for an offshore hedge fund that only trades in

---

115. *See* § 16.7.7, *infra*.

116. *See* § 16.7.1, *supra*.

117. Treas. Reg. § 1.864-2(c)(2), 26 C.F.R. § 1.864-2(c)(2).

118. Treas. Reg. § 1.864-2(c)(1), 26 C.F.R. § 1.864-2(c)(1). *See* § 16.3.10.i, *supra*.

119. In some contexts, the Tax Code and Treasury Regulations distinguish "stocks" from "securities," the latter sometimes being confined to various types of debt instruments. The discussion in § 16.7 generally conforms to the terminology of the Tax Code and the Treasury Regulations.

120. Treas. Reg. § 1.864-2(c)(2)(iv), 26 C.F.R. § 1.864-2(c)(2)(iv).

commodities for its own account and is not a dealer in commodities. Proposed Treasury Regulations provide that an "eligible nondealer" that effects transactions in derivatives for its own account is not engaged in a U.S. trade or business.[121]

Before 1997, to avoid being deemed to be engaged in a U.S. trade or business, an offshore hedge fund was required to have its principal place of business outside the United States.[122]

An offshore hedge fund will also be deemed to be engaged in a U.S. trade or business if it invests in U.S. real property interests as defined in Tax Code section 897. U.S. real property investments include fee ownership and co-ownership of land and improvements thereon, leaseholds of land or improvements thereon, options to acquire land or improvements thereon, and options to acquire leaseholds of land and improvements thereon.[123] A U.S. real property interest also includes stock in a corporation, a significant portion of the assets of which are U.S. real property interests.[124]

An offshore hedge fund that owns an interest in a real estate investment trust (a "REIT") must treat distributions by the REIT as gain recognized from the sale or exchange of U.S. real property interests to the extent that the distribution is attributable to gains from the sale or exchange by the REIT of U.S. real property interests. This rule does not apply, however, to a distribution by a REIT with a class of stock that is regularly traded on an established securities market in the United States, if the offshore hedge fund does not own more than 5 percent of that class of stock at any time during the one-year period ended on the distribution date.[125]

If an offshore hedge fund has any U.S. trade or business income, it may fail to satisfy the requirement that it trade for its own account, and in that case arguably all of its income might be taxed in the United States. An offshore hedge fund could have U.S. trade or business income in connection with an investment in a privately held company, for example if it invests in a U.S. start-up company structured as a pass-through vehicle for U.S. tax purposes, or if the offshore hedge fund receives some fee income (such as directors' fees, consulting fees or loan origination fees) with respect to its investment in such company. An offshore hedge fund could encounter a similar result if any of its investments do not qualify as stocks, securities or commodities.

An offshore hedge fund that invests in debt securities could be deemed to be engaged in a U.S. lending or finance business, particularly if it originates the debt, negotiates the terms and receives loan origination or other fees related to the debt securities. An offshore hedge fund that acquires distressed securities, and then restructures the debt, arguably could be deemed to have engaged in lending activities, as could an offshore hedge fund that participates in bank loan syndications.

---

121. Proposed Treas. Reg. § 1.864(b)-1, Proposed 26 C.F.R. § 1.864(b)-1.

122. *See* §§ 4.4.1 and 4.4.5, *supra*, regarding the so-called "ten commandments" that were relevant to the taxation of offshore hedge funds.

123. Tax Code § 897(c)(6)(A), 26 U.S.C. § 897(c)(6)(A).

124. Tax Code § 897(c)(2), 26 U.S.C. § 897(c)(2).

125. Tax Code § 897(h)(1), 26 U.S.C. § 897(h)(1).

4. U.S. Ownership

As noted above, offshore hedge funds that are structured as corporations for U.S. tax purposes are ordinarily marketed to non-U.S. investors and U.S. tax-exempt entities. The passive foreign investment company rules[126] generally make investment in offshore hedge funds structured as corporations for U.S. tax purposes inappropriate for U.S. taxable investors. Offshore hedge funds that have significant U.S. ownership may also be treated as controlled foreign corporations and, as such, subject to special rules.[127]

i. Controlled Foreign Corporations

If U.S. investors own a significant percentage of the shares of an offshore hedge fund structured as a corporation for U.S. tax purposes, the offshore hedge fund may be treated as a controlled foreign corporation (a "CFC") for U.S. income tax purposes. A CFC is generally any non-U.S. corporation of which more than 50 percent of the vote or value of the stock is directly or indirectly owned by U.S. Shareholders.[128] A "U.S. Shareholder" is generally a U.S. person who owns directly or indirectly 10 percent or more of the voting power of the corporation.[129] For example, an offshore hedge fund owned entirely by unrelated U.S. investors, each of whom owns less than 9 percent of the stock, is not a CFC. In addition, an offshore hedge fund held 49 percent by one U.S. investor, 2 percent by another unrelated U.S. investor and 49 percent by non-U.S. persons is not a CFC. On the other hand, an offshore hedge fund held 11 percent by one U.S. investor, 10 percent each by four other U.S. investors and 49 percent by non-U.S. persons would be a CFC. With non-U.S. corporations that have classes of stock with different voting rights, it is often not clear how to measure voting power. Treasury Regulations provide special rules that can result in deemed control when U.S. investors can elect, appoint or replace persons who have power over the corporation similar to that of a U.S. board of directors or who can effectively control such persons.[130]

A U.S. Shareholder of a CFC must include in its income each year its proportionate share of certain types of "tainted" income of the CFC, including foreign personal holding company income. "Foreign personal holding company income" includes dividends, interest and gains from sales of securities. Thus, most income of an offshore hedge fund is foreign personal holding company income. The included amount is treated as a dividend distributed from the CFC and is taxed as ordinary income to the extent of the CFC's earnings and profits, then as a return of basis, and then as gain from the sale of stock. These rules generally should not result, however, in taxable income for U.S. tax-exempt entities, which typically are the only U.S. investors in an offshore hedge fund,

126. *See* § 16.7.4.ii, *infra.*
127. *See* § 16.7.4.i, *infra.*
128. Tax Code § 957, 26 U.S.C. § 957.
129. Tax Code § 951(b), 26 U.S.C. § 951(b).
130. Treas. Reg. § 1.957-1(b); 26 C.F.R. § 1.957-1(b).

even if that offshore hedge fund trades on margin.[131] Nevertheless, the U.S. Shareholders of a CFC must file U.S. information returns and must obtain information from the CFC to complete such forms.[132] To avoid CFC status, an offshore hedge fund generally should assure that U.S. Shareholders never own 50 percent or more of its stock.

ii. Passive Foreign Investment Companies

A U.S. taxpayer who invests in a non-U.S. corporation generally is taxed on dividends received from that corporation at ordinary income rates and is taxed on gain from the sale of the stock of that corporation at capital gain rates. This result is altered, however, if the corporation is a passive foreign investment company (a "PFIC"). A PFIC is generally any non-U.S. corporation if (a) at least 75 percent of the corporation's income is certain passive income (including dividends, interest and gains on the sale of securities) or (b) at least 50 percent of its assets produce such passive income.[133] An offshore hedge fund established to trade stocks and securities for its own account typically is treated as a PFIC, because all of its income is passive and all of its assets generate such income.

A U.S. taxpayer who invests in a PFIC is subject to certain adverse tax consequences under a method of taxation known as the "interest charge" method. These rules apply to any taxable U.S. investor who owns an interest in the PFIC, regardless of the amount of that investor's ownership of the PFIC. A U.S. taxpayer may elect, however, not to be subject to the interest charge rules if the taxpayer elects to treat the PFIC as a Qualified Electing Fund ("QEF") under Tax Code section 1295, or makes a mark-to-market election under Tax Code section 1296. Any U.S. shareholder in a PFIC is required to file an annual information report.[134]

a. Interest Charge Method

As stated above, a U.S. investor in a PFIC is subject to the interest charge method unless the investor makes the mark-to-market or QEF election. Under the interest charge method, the U.S. taxpayer does not report any income with respect to an investment in an offshore fund (the PFIC) until it receives distributions from the offshore hedge fund or sells shares of the offshore hedge fund. If a taxpayer receives an "excess distribution," the taxpayer must treat that excess distribution as being earned ratably over the time the taxpayer held the stock and pay an interest charge as if the taxpayer had reported that income in the previous years but had not paid the tax. These rules are designed to approximate the tax that would have been recognized if the PFIC had distributed

---

131. IRS PLR 9407007 (Nov. 12, 1993); IRS PLR 9024086 (Mar. 22, 1990). While private letter rulings are not binding on the IRS, they are indicative of IRS views. *See also* H.R. Rep. No. 586, 104th Cong. 2d. Sess. F2 (1996), where the House Ways and Means Committee stated in connection with H.R. 3448 that the Committee believed there should be no look-through rule in determining whether dividends from a CFC should be treated as UBTI.

132. Tax Code § 6038(a)(4), 26 U.S.C. § 6038(a)(4).

133. Tax Code § 1297, 26 U.S.C. § 1297.

134. Tax Code § 1298(f), 26 U.S.C. § 1298(f).

all of its income annually, and thus prevent taxpayers from deferring income by investing in offshore corporations.

Whether a distribution is an excess distribution depends on the amount of the distribution in comparison to prior years' distributions. A distribution from the offshore hedge fund is generally an excess distribution only to the extent that the total distributions in a year exceed 125 percent of the average of the distributions received in the prior 3 years.[135] All gain recognized on disposition of PFIC stock (that is, sale of the stock or a redemption of stock by the U.S. person) is treated as an excess distribution.[136]

The aggregate excess distributions for a year are allocated ratably to all of the days the investor held the PFIC stock. Any amounts attributable to a prior year in which the company was a PFIC are treated as taxed at the highest rate (that is, the ordinary income rate) for the year in which earned, and then interest is calculated as if such tax had not been paid in that year.[137] The sum of that tax and interest is then taxable to the investor for the current year, even if the taxpayer has a net operating loss carry forward or other offsetting amounts for the current year.[138] The taxpayer need not, however, file amended tax returns for prior years.

A U.S. taxpayer may invest in a PFIC because of a belief that the PFIC will be able to outperform the IRS interest rate over the course of the investment, so that the tax deferral results in an overall benefit. For this benefit to be realized, the projected outperformance should be analyzed in view of the calculation rules, including that (a) the interest charge is determined as if the gains were earned ratably over the period, whereas ordinarily a larger percentage of the gains would be earned in the later years due to compounding, and (b) all of the gains are taxed as ordinary income rates, whereas if the taxpayer held the securities directly or invested in a pass-through tax vehicle, a portion of the gains may have been taxed at the lower long-term capital gain rate.

b. Qualified Electing Fund

A U.S. taxpayer can avoid being subject to the interest charge method by electing to treat the PFIC as a QEF.[139] The offshore hedge fund must consent to the election and be willing to supply certain information to the U.S. investor, if the investor is audited by the IRS.[140] An offshore hedge fund may not consent to a QEF election, because it involves additional accounting and administrative costs, opens the offshore hedge fund's records to IRS scrutiny, and risks revealing the identities of its other investors.

A taxpayer who makes a QEF election includes in income each year the taxpayer's proportionate share of the QEF's earnings and profits, based on share ownership. This income retains its character as ordinary income or capital gain

135. Tax Code § 1291(b), 26 U.S.C. § 1291(b).
136. Tax Code § 1291(a)(2), 26 U.S.C. § 1291(a)(2).
137. Tax Code § 1291(a), 26 U.S.C. § 1291(a).
138. Tax Code § 1291(a)(1)(C), 26 U.S.C. § 1291(a)(1)(C).
139. Tax Code § 1291(d), 26 U.S.C. § 1291(d).
140. Tax Code § 1295(a), 26 U.S.C. § 1295(a).

income.[141] Thus, for the electing taxpayer, investment in a QEF is similar to investment in a U.S. pass-through vehicle, such as a U.S. partnership. One significant difference is that, if the PFIC has a deficit in earnings and profits for a taxable year, that deficit does not pass through to the investor to offset income from other investments. In addition, if the QEF has net losses in a year followed by profits in the next year, the profits are not offset by the prior year's deficit.[142] Those losses may be offset only on ultimate disposition of the PFIC stock.

One advantage of investing in a PFIC for which a QEF election has been made is that the U.S. taxpayer can elect to defer payment of taxes on the income passed through to the taxpayer until actual distributions are made from the offshore hedge fund, at which time the taxpayer must pay the tax and interest on the deferred amounts.[143] An advantage of this approach over being subject to the interest charge method[144] is that the interest is attributed to the year in which the earnings were actually earned rather than ratably over the period. In addition, for hedge funds that do not qualify as traders, the PFIC structure affords investors greater deductibility of fund fees and expenses. An investor in such a hedge fund that is structured as a partnership might not be able to deduct fully the management fees and other fund expenses.[145] Those fees and expenses, however, reduce the taxable income reportable by an investor in a PFIC for which a QEF election is made.[146]

c. Mark-to-Market Election

Tax Code section 1296 allows a U.S. taxpayer to avoid the interest charge method by electing to mark-to-market marketable stock in a PFIC each year and include the resulting gain or loss in taxable income as ordinary gain or loss. The amount of loss deduction a taxpayer can take each year, however, is limited to the amount of gains previously reported under this election with respect to that stock that have not already been offset.[147] "Marketable stock" is generally stock that (a) is regularly traded on a qualified securities exchange or (b) stock in a PFIC that is similar to a U.S. mutual fund.[148]

Treasury Regulations provide that for a PFIC to be similar to a U.S. mutual fund, among other things: (a) its stock must be redeemable at net asset value; (b) its stock must be available to the general public at its net asset value; (c) its stock must be purchasable by new investors in initial amounts not greater than $10,000; (d) quotations for its shares must be determined and published weekly in a widely available medium; (e) the corporation must be supervised as an investment company by a foreign government or instrumentality; and (f) at all times during the year the corporation must have 100 or more shareholders

---

141. Tax Code § 1293(a), 26 U.S.C. § 1293(a).
142. Tax Code § 1293(a), 26 U.S.C. § 1293(a).
143. Tax Code § 1294, 26 U.S.C. § 1294.
144. *See* § 16.7.4.ii, *supra*.
145. *See* § 16.3.10, *supra*.
146. Tax Code § 1293(e)(1), 26 U.S.C. § 1293(e)(1).
147. Tax Code § 1296(a), 26 U.S.C. § 1296(a).
148. Tax Code § 1296(e)(i), 26 U.S.C. § 1296(e)(i).

with respect to the class of shares at issue.[149] This election is thus not available for investors in most offshore hedge funds, because the stock is not deemed marketable stock.

5. Withholding Taxes on Certain U.S. Income

i. Income Subject to Withholding

Offshore hedge funds generally are subject to U.S. withholding at the rate of 30 percent on the following types of income:

- Dividends from a U.S. corporation;[150]
- Interest from bonds or other securities of a U.S. corporation;[151]
- Interest from other U.S. obligors, except as discussed below; and
- Rents and royalties.[152]

The broker or other payor who has control of the funds generally withholds. An offshore hedge fund structured as a corporation for U.S. tax purposes is required to provide the withholding agent with a Form W-8BEN certifying that it is a non-U.S. entity and is not a pass-through entity for U.S. tax purposes. The 30 percent withholding rate can be reduced under tax treaties, but most offshore hedge funds are established in tax haven jurisdictions with which the United States does not have tax treaties.

For non-U.S. investors investing in U.S. securities through an offshore hedge fund, withholding generally does not reduce their returns, because those investors would generally be subject to the same withholding if they had made the investments in U.S. securities directly. In contrast, a U.S. tax-exempt entity that invests in an offshore hedge fund structured as a corporation for U.S. tax purposes will have its return reduced by the withholding taxes. This disadvantage may be offset by the benefit of avoiding UBTI,[153] if the offshore hedge fund purchases securities on margin.

ii. Exempt Income

The following types of income generally are exempt from withholding:

- Interest on deposits in a bank, including savings accounts, checking accounts and certificates of deposits;
- Interest on deposits in certain qualified savings and loans;

149. Treas. Reg. § 1.1296-2(d), 26 C.F.R. § 1.1296-2(d).

150. A special rule applies to dividends from certain grandfathered U.S. corporations that receive less than 80 percent of their income from an active non-U.S. business; Tax Code § 871(i), 26 U.S.C. § 871(i).

151. A special rule applies to interest from certain grandfathered U.S. corporations that receive less than 80 percent of their income from an active non-U.S. business; Tax Code § 871(i), 26 U.S.C. § 871(i).

152. Tax Code § 1442, 26 U.S.C. § 1442.

153. *See* § 16.7.6, *infra*.

- Distributions from a regulated investment company that constitute "capital gains dividends" under Tax Code section 852(b)(3)(C);[154]
- Exempt interest dividends (as defined in Tax Code section 852(b)(5)(A))[155] from a regulated investment company;
- Interest-related dividends and short-term capital gain dividends (as defined in Tax Code section 871(k)) from a regulated investment company;[156]
- Original issue discount on an obligation payable 183 days or less from the date of original issue; and
- Interest from "portfolio debt investments," defined as (a) certain unregistered debt instruments (bearer bonds) issued prior to March 18, 2012, that meet specific tests to ensure that they are sold only to non-U.S. investors, that state on their face that any U.S. investor that holds that instrument is subject to limitations under U.S. income tax laws, and the interest on which is payable only outside the United States, and (b) as certain obligations in registered form, if the person required to withhold obtains certification (IRS Form W-8 or equivalent) that the beneficial owner (in this case the offshore hedge fund) is not a U.S. investor; an obligation is in "registered form" (i) if it can be transferred only by surrender of the old instrument to the new holder or issuance of a new instrument to the new holder, (ii) if it can be transferred only by a book entry system maintained by the issuer or its agent or (iii) a combination of (i) and (ii).

Many of the U.S. debt instruments in which an offshore hedge fund typically invests qualify as portfolio debt investments. Portfolio debt does not include, however, debt when the holder also owns stock having 10 percent or more of the total combined voting power of the corporate issuer.[157] In addition, portfolio debt does not include certain debt instruments with contingent interest, including debt if the amount of interest due on such debt is contingent on the receipts, sales, cash flow, profits or income of the issuer or a related person, any change in value of the issuer or a related person, or the amount of dividends or other distributions made by the issuer or a related person[158] (provided that the amount and timing of interest can be contingent on factors other than the profits or performance of the issuer, such as other interest rates or indices).[159] Certain types of debt in which an offshore hedge fund might invest, such as distressed securities and bankruptcy claims, also might not qualify as either bearer bonds or registered debt and thus not be considered portfolio debt.

---

154. 26 U.S.C. § 852(b)(3)(C); Treas. Reg. § 1.1441-3(c)(2)(i)(D), 26 C.F.R. § 1.1441-3(c)(2)(i)(D).

155. 26 U.S.C. § 852(b)(5)(A); Treas. Reg. § 1.1441-3(c)(2)(i)(D), 26 C.F.R. § 1.1441-3(c)(2)(i)(D).

156. Tax Code § 871(k); 26 U.S.C. § 871(k).

157. Tax Code § 871(h)(3), 26 U.S.C. § 871(h)(3).

158. Tax Code § 871(h)(4), 26 U.S.C. § 871(h)(4).

159. Tax Code § 871(h)(4)(c), 26 U.S.C. § 871(h)(4)(c).

Income from notional principal contracts ("swaps") are usually sourced to the residence of the recipient, and thus formerly were not subject to withholding.[160] The IRS expressed concern, however, that swaps were being used to avoid withholding on U.S. source dividends.[161] Under current law, dividend equivalent payments are treated as dividends and subject to U.S. withholding, absent different treatment under a treaty or other exemption.[162] A "dividend equivalent payment" is generally any substitute dividend payment made under a securities lending or sale-repurchase transaction or notional principal contract contingent on or determined by reference to payment of a U.S. source dividend. Until January 1, 2014, payments made only under specified notional principal contracts are covered; thereafter, all notional principal contracts will be covered unless the IRS finalizes a rule determining what type of contract does not have the potential for tax avoidance.

iii. Withholding on Foreign Financial Institutions

Any person making a withholdable payment to a foreign financial institution after June 30, 2014, must withhold 30 percent of the payment unless the foreign financial institution agrees to comply with certain disclosure and due diligence requirements regarding accounts held by specified United States persons or United States owned foreign entities.[163] A "withholdable payment" is defined to include most U.S. source payments that are currently subject to withholding, including U.S. source dividends, interest or royalties; it also includes gross proceeds from the sale of U.S. stock or debt.[164] A "foreign financial institution" generally is a foreign entity that accepts deposits in the ordinary course of a banking or similar business or is engaged in the business of holding financial assets for the accounts of others, as well as entities engaged in investing securities or commodities, such as hedge funds, venture funds and private equity funds.[165] Thus, an offshore hedge fund will need to comply with the disclosure and due diligence requirements for certain U.S. account holders to avoid withholding on payments to it.

A "specified United States person" generally is defined as any U.S. person other than tax-exempt organizations, publicly traded corporations, federal, state, or local agencies, banks, REITs, regulated investment companies, common trust funds or tax-exempt trusts.[166] A "United States owned foreign entity" is generally a foreign entity of which specified U.S. persons own 10 percent or more.[167] Since most U.S. investors in offshore hedge funds are tax-exempt,

---

160. Treas. Reg. § 1.863-7(b); 26 C.F.R. § 1.863-7(b).

161. Industry Directive on Total Return Swaps (TRSs) Used to Avoid Dividend Withholding Tax (Jan. 14, 2010), *available at* http://www.irs.gov/Businesses/Corporations/Industry-Directive-on-Total-Return-Swaps-%28%E2%80%9CTRSs%E2%80%9D%29-Used-to-Avoid-Dividend-Withholding-Tax (last visited May 19, 2013).

162. Tax Code § 871(m), 26 U.S.C. § 871(m).

163. Tax Code § 1471, 26 U.S.C. § 1471

164. Tax Code § 1473(1), 26 U.S.C. § 1473(1).

165. Tax Code § 1471(d), 26 U.S.C. § 1471(d).

166. Tax Code § 1473(3), 26 U.S.C. § 1473(3).

167. Tax Code § 1471(d)(3), 26 U.S.C. § 1471(d)(3).

most offshore funds apparently will not need to disclose much information about those investors.

To avoid the 30 percent withholding tax, a foreign financial institution generally must enter into an agreement with the IRS by April 25, 2014, requiring the foreign financial institution to: (a) make annual disclosures to the IRS about its direct and indirect U.S. account holders and their related accounts (including balances, deposits and withdrawals); (b) undertake due diligence to determine direct and indirect U.S. beneficial owners; (c) seek a waiver from each account holder of any non-U.S. law that would prevent reporting the required information and, if such a waiver is not obtained, close the account within a reasonable time; and (d) withhold 30 percent of any distributions to account holders who do not supply required information.[168] With respect to an offshore hedge fund established in a jurisdiction that has entered into an intergovernmental agreement with the IRS, the fund will enter into an agreement with the country in which it is formed to provide the information directly to that government rather than to the IRS. At this writing (mid-2013), the Cayman Islands expects to enter into such an agreement with the IRS.

Subject to certain exceptions, withholding generally is also required on any payments to a non-U.S. entity that is not a foreign financial institution unless the non-U.S. entity certifies that it has no substantial U.S. owners (generally a U.S. person who owns directly or indirectly more than 10 percent of the entity by vote or value) or provides the name, address and taxpayer identification number of each of those owners.[169] For example, a U.S. hedge fund that has a non-U.S. entity investor (that is not a financial institution) might need to withhold on any distribution to such investor (including on proceeds from sales not currently subject to withholding) unless the investor provides the required information.

These withholding requirements are generally effective for payments made after June 30, 2014. A hedge fund's will governing agreement and subscription documents should include provisions to comply with these rules.[170] These rules may make offshore master fund structures less desirable, because an offshore master fund might need to provide this information with respect to the U.S. owners in a U.S. feeder fund. They also may make investing in offshore funds less desirable for non-U.S. investors as their identities become more readily available to the IRS, but some non-U.S. investors might become more willing to invest in U.S. hedge funds.

6. Unrelated Business Taxable Income

As noted above, to avoid recognition of UBTI, U.S. tax-exempt entities may invest in offshore hedge funds structured as corporations for U.S. tax purposes. UBTI is generally defined as the gross income from any trade or business unrelated to the tax-exempt business of the entity.[171] To the extent that UBTI,

168. Tax Code § 1471(b), 26 U.S.C. § 1471(b).

169. Tax Code § 1472, 26 U.S.C. § 1472.

170. The withholding requirements initially were effective for payments made after 2012, but the IRS has extended the effective date.

171. Tax Code § 512(a)(1), 26 U.S.C. § 512(a)(1).

from all sources, of a tax-exempt entity, less its allocable share of deductions directly connected with carrying on any such trade or business, exceeds $1,000 in any year, the tax-exempt entity will incur tax liability with respect to the excess at tax rates that would apply if the organization were not otherwise exempt from taxation. UBTI does not include interest and dividend income, or gains on the sale, exchange or other disposition of assets held for investment.[172] Income from debt-financed property (such as gain from the sale of stock purchased on margin) will, however, constitute UBTI to tax-exempt entities, in the percentage that such property is subject to acquisition indebtedness (the percentage that acquisition indebtedness respecting such property bears to the acquiror's adjusted tax basis for such property).[173]

If a U.S. tax-exempt entity invests in a U.S. hedge fund structured as a partnership that invests on margin, the tax-exempt entity will be required to treat a portion of the income of the hedge fund as debt-financed income giving rise to UBTI, because the character of the income of the hedge fund passes through to the investor.[174] No rules require, however, that a tax-exempt investor in a corporation treat itself as having received an allocable share of the income of the corporation.[175] Accordingly, unless the tax-exempt investor borrows funds to purchase stock of an offshore hedge fund, the investor should not recognize any UBTI from its investment in the offshore hedge fund, even if the offshore hedge fund trades on margin.

Even if a U.S. tax-exempt entity invests in an offshore corporation that is treated as a CFC and trades on margin, it nevertheless should not recognize UBTI. The IRS has ruled that income from the offshore hedge fund retains its character as dividend income and is not treated as a pass-through of debt-financed income.[176]

7. Master Fund Structure

As noted above, offshore hedge funds are usually structured as corporations for U.S. tax purposes. Sometimes the offshore corporation invests all of its assets in another hedge fund organized (generally offshore) as a limited partnership under local law and treated as a partnership for U.S. tax purposes (a "master fund"). Typically, the investment adviser is the general partner of the master fund, and the offshore hedge fund and a U.S. hedge fund are the limited partners (feeders) in the master fund. This structure allows a manager to combine all of the assets of the offshore hedge fund and the U.S. hedge fund into one pool, which can reduce administrative costs and facilitate trades and may be helpful for marketing because the two feeder funds should have identical performance.

Typically, non-U.S. investors and U.S. tax-exempt investors invest through the offshore feeder and U.S. taxable investors invest through the U.S. feeder. With respect to the non-U.S. investors and U.S. tax-exempt investors, the tax

---

172. Tax Code §§ 512(b)(1) and 512(b)(5), 26 U.S.C. §§ 512(b)(1) and 512(b)(5).
173. Tax Code § 512(b)(4), 26 U.S.C. § 512(b)(4).
174. *See* § 16.3.13, *supra*.
175. Tax Code § 512(b)(1), 26 U.S.C. § 512(b)(1).
176. *See* § 16.7.3, *supra*.

results are as discussed above with a typical offshore hedge fund. Thus, U.S. tax-exempt entities retain their protection from UBTI, which usually is their primary motivation for investing in offshore hedge funds.

Under a master fund structure, the manager sometimes receives its compensation at the level of the two feeder entities: as performance fees and asset-based fees from the offshore hedge fund, and as performance allocations and asset-based fees (treated as guaranteed payments) from the U.S. hedge fund. Alternatively, the manager may receive performance allocations and asset-based fees from the master fund, in which case the feeders do not charge any fees or allocations. Under prior law, if the investment adviser was paid a performance fee from the offshore feeder, it may have been able to defer that compensation. Now an adviser generally cannot defer fees from offshore funds.[177] If the master fund generates significant long-term capital gains or qualifying dividend income or has substantial unrealized gains, the investment adviser would prefer for tax reasons to receive performance-based compensation in the form of allocations from the master fund.[178]

Master Funds are typically established under the laws of jurisdictions outside the United States. If a master fund is organized in an offshore jurisdiction, withholding will apply on payments to it.[179] The master fund will need to provide the withholding agent with an IRS form W-8IMY, which must include information regarding what percentage of the master fund is held by non-U.S. investors that should be subject to withholding. For this purpose, the offshore feeder would provide the master fund a Form W-8BEN and would be treated entirely as a non-U.S. investor, even if that feeder has some U.S. tax-exempt investors. If a master fund is established under the laws of a U.S. jurisdiction, payments to the master fund will not be subject to withholding, but the master fund will be required to withhold on the offshore feeder's allocable share of U.S. source dividend and interest income.

8. U.S. Estate Taxes on Non-U.S. Individuals

Non-U.S. individuals may prefer investing in offshore hedge funds to avoid U.S. estate taxes. Tax Code section 2103[180] subjects a non-U.S. individual's gross estate that is situated in the United States to U.S. estate tax. Stock of a corporation incorporated in the United States is deemed to be situated in the United States.[181] Thus, if a nonresident alien dies while holding stock in U.S. corporations directly, the nonresident alien's gross estate for U.S. purposes includes the value of such stock. An investment in a hedge fund structured as a partnership for tax purposes would most likely also be treated as being situated in the United States if the manager or general partner is located in the United States and the hedge fund holds U.S. securities. The IRS generally takes the position that an interest in a partnership is situated where the partnership

177. Tax Code § 457A, 26 U.S.C. § 457A.
178. *See* § 16.8, *infra.*
179. *See* § 16.7.5, *supra.*
180. 26 U.S.C. § 2103.
181. Tax Code § 2104, 26 U.S.C. § 2104.

does business.[182] Stock in a non-U.S. corporation is generally not included in a nonresident alien's estate, however, even if that corporation itself holds U.S. securities. As a result, non-U.S. taxpayers may prefer investing in offshore hedge funds structured as corporations to avoid U.S. estate tax.

§ 16.8 U.S. Taxation of General Partner/ Investment Adviser

1. In General

For nontax reasons, the investment adviser is usually established as an entity with limited liability. Typically, the investment adviser entity is organized as an LLC, a limited partnership, or a corporation that elects to be treated as a Subchapter S corporation. Those entities, unlike Subchapter C corporations, all have the advantage of being subject to a single level of tax. Some investment advisers have two entities: one that receives fee income, such as asset-based fees from hedge funds or separate accounts (including offshore hedge funds), and a second entity that receives performance-based allocations from hedge funds structured as partnerships for tax purposes.

2. Types of Income

An investment adviser typically receives the following types of income: (a) asset-based fees from hedge funds, which are treated as guaranteed payments under Tax Code section 707(c)[183] and taxed as ordinary income; (b) asset-based or performance-based fees from separate accounts (including offshore hedge funds), which are also taxed as ordinary income; (c) performance-based allocations from hedge funds, which retain the tax character of the hedge funds' income;[184] and (d) return on investment of the investment adviser's own proprietary capital, which is taxed as long-term or short-term capital gain, interest or dividend income.

Because the investment adviser is structured as a pass-through entity for income tax purposes, each individual owner of the investment adviser receives a Schedule K-1 from that entity reporting its pro rata share of the income, which retains its tax character as it passes through to such individual. One of the principal tax advantages for the individual owners of the investment adviser is the pass-through of the character of performance-based allocations, based on the activities of the underlying hedge fund. For example, if a manager receives

182. Rev. Rul. 55-701, 1955-2 C.B. 836.

183. 26 U.S.C. § 707(c).

184. *See* § 16.3.2, *supra,* regarding the risk that the IRS might maintain that the performance-based allocation is actually a fee that should be taxed to the investment adviser or its owners as ordinary income. From time to time, bills have been introduced in Congress that would change the treatment of all such profits allocated to the general partner to ordinary income. *See, e.g.*, S. 2075, 113th Cong. (2013).

a 20 percent performance-based allocation as general partner of a hedge fund and the hedge fund has $1,000,000 of gains for the year, comprising $400,000 of realized long-term capital gains, $400,000 of realized short-term capital gains, and $200,000 of gains that have not been realized for tax purposes, the general partner receives a book allocation of profits from the hedge fund of $200,000, which for tax purposes would consist of $80,000 of realized long-term capital gains, $80,000 of realized short-term gains, and $40,000 of unrealized gains.

An individual who owns a 50 percent interest in the investment adviser thus would have his or her capital account credited for book purposes with $100,000 and would receive a Schedule K-1 from the investment adviser reporting $40,000 of long-term capital gains (taxable at rates up to 20 percent) and $40,000 of short-term gains (taxable at rates up to 39.6 percent). In contrast, if the investment adviser were paid a performance-based fee, that individual would have reported $100,000 of ordinary income.

3. Limited Partnerships and Limited Liability Companies

If the investment adviser is a limited partnership or an LLC, it is treated as a partnership for income tax purposes, unless it elects to be taxed as a corporation. References in this section 16.8.3 to "partnerships" and "partners" also refer to LLCs and members. Partnerships offer significantly more flexibility than S corporations, because Subchapter S limits the number of shareholders in S corporations, limits the types of shareholders and restricts an S corporation to one class of stock.[185] Partnerships also generally can make distributions in kind without triggering gain on any appreciation in the assets, and allow the owners to increase their tax bases by their shares of the entity's liabilities. Partnerships also allow more flexibility for admitting new owners without the owners being required either to purchase their interests or to pay tax on receipt of their interests.

i. Flexibility in Allocating Profits

As discussed below in section 16.8.4, an S corporation can only have one class of stock. Accordingly, income and loss must be allocated, and all distributions must be made, in proportion to share ownership. Partnerships (including LLCs) are not similarly restricted. Partnerships can allocate profits in different proportions from capital contributions. Partnerships can divide their income into sources, or baskets, and allocate each source in different proportions, and specially allocate items of income, gain, loss and deduction, as long as the allocations have substantial economic effect.[186]

For example, an investment adviser organized as an LLC may provide in its LLC agreement that income will be divided into four sources: first, return on investment of the investment adviser's own capital (for example when a member invests capital through the investment adviser into the hedge fund)

---

185. Tax Code § 1361, 26 U.S.C. § 1361.
186. Tax Code § 704, 26 U.S.C. § 704.

(the "Investment Source"); second, asset-based management fees from U.S. and offshore hedge funds and performance-based fees from offshore hedge funds and other separate accounts (reduced by the expenses of operating the business) (the "Fee Source"); third, performance-based profit allocations from U.S. hedge funds (the "Performance Source"); and fourth, gain or loss from sale of the business (the Sale Source).

Profits and losses from the Investment Source are generally allocated among the owners of the investment entity in proportion to the amount of capital each invests. The Fee Source, Performance Source and Sale Source may be divided in varying proportions, according to the members' agreement. For example, the principals of the investment adviser may allocate all of the Fee Source to themselves, but allocate shares of the Performance Source and the Sale Source to analysts and others. An individual may benefit from receiving a share of the Performance Source through an allocation from the investment adviser, rather than as a bonus taxable as ordinary income, because allocations of profits from the Performance Source may include long-term capital gains and unrealized gains, depending on the character of the income of the hedge fund.[187] Similarly, if the business is sold, a member who shares in the Sale Source would recognize some capital gain income if a portion of the purchase price is allocated to good will, but if he or she receives a share of the proceeds as a bonus, it would all be ordinary income.

ii. Admission of Partners or Members

When an investment adviser that is structured as a partnership for tax purposes (including an LLC) admits a partner, the tax consequences to the partner depend on whether the partner receives a "capital" or "profits" interest. A capital interest is generally an interest under which the partner receives a capital account balance in excess of the partner's capital contribution, or an interest that would cause the partner to receive proceeds greater than its capital contribution if the partnership were liquidated immediately after the partner is admitted. A profits interest, on the other hand, affords the partner only the right to share in future profits earned, and if the partnership were to be liquidated immediately after the partner receives the interest, the partner would not receive any amounts in excess of capital contributed.

A partner's receipt of a capital interest in exchange for services performed or to be performed results in compensation income for the partner, and presumably a corresponding compensation deduction for the entity. A profits interest generally is not taxable to the partner on receipt; instead, the partner pays income tax on allocations of subsequent profits.[188] Proposed Regulations provide that a partner is taxed on receipt of a profits interest under the general principles of Tax Code section 83, which could cause receipt of a profits interest to be taxable as

---

187. *See* § 16.8.2, *supra*.

188. Rev. Proc. 93-27, 1993-2 C.B. 343. Exceptions to this rule apply if the profits interest relates to a substantially certain stream of income (such as from a long-term net lease) or the partner sells the interest within two years of receipt.

having some initial value, but allow a partnership that meets certain additional conditions to continue to treat a profits interest as having no initial value.[189]

An investment adviser entity typically would not grant a partner an interest with a capital account balance in excess of the amount contributed. A partner might, however, receive a disguised capital interest through the right to share in one of the sources of profits. As noted in section 16.8.3.i above, an investment adviser may divide its income into separate baskets to be allocated separately. A partner would generally be entitled to share in the Investment Source only to the extent of any capital actually contributed. The partner's share of the Fee Source or the Performance Source should generally be treated as a profits interest (unless the IRS were to maintain that the right to the asset-based fee constitutes a substantially certain stream of income) and thus not be taxable on receipt.

If a partner is admitted in the middle of a fiscal period when the assets of the hedge fund have appreciated, however, so that the investment adviser would be entitled to a performance allocation or fee as of that date if the fiscal period were to end, the IRS might maintain that such partner has received a capital interest. Arguably, the partner should not recognize compensation income in that case, because the assets in the hedge fund could depreciate by the end of the measurement period, leaving no amount to be allocated to the new partner. On the other hand, under the definition of "capital interest," if the hedge fund and the investment adviser were both to liquidate as of the admission date, an allocation would typically be due under the partnership agreement for the hedge fund, and the new partner would be allocated some amount in excess of capital contributed.[190]

If a partner is admitted to the investment adviser and is granted a share of the Sale Source at a time when the investment adviser has established good will, the partner would likely be deemed to have received a taxable capital interest. The investment adviser could avoid this result by adjusting its capital accounts before admitting the new partner, to reflect the unrealized appreciation in the investment adviser's assets, so that the new partner only shares in appreciation that occurs after the new partner's admission. Arguably, however, little or no good will attaches to the typical investment adviser that advises only hedge funds, because the business could not be sold without the principals' agreement to enter into employment agreements and covenants not to compete, and thus any good will attaches to the individuals and not the business.[191]

iii. Distributions

The distribution of an asset by a partnership generally does not result in recognition of unrealized appreciation on the asset, in contrast to a distribution

---

189. I.R.S. Notice 2005-43 2005-24 I.R.B. 1221.

190. An election to defer performance-based compensation based on a period of at least 12 months must be made no later than 6 months into the period. Tax Code § 409A, 26 U.S.C. § 409A. By analogy, one could argue that a member admitted to an investment adviser less than 6 months into an annual measurement period for a performance-based allocation should not be deemed to have earned any income on admission.

191. *See* § 16.2.2, *supra*, regarding contributions in kind.

by an S corporation, which results in a deemed sale of the asset for its fair market value.[192] A distribution of marketable securities by a partnership is treated under Tax Code section 731(c)[193] as a distribution of cash unless the distributing partnership qualifies as an investment partnership[194] and the other requirements of Tax Code section 731(c) are met. An investment adviser that only acts as the general partner of hedge funds likely would qualify as an investment partnership.

A partnership is not treated as engaged in a trade or business that would disqualify it as an investment partnership by reason of performing reasonable and customary services to an investment partnership, in which the former partnership holds an interest, in exchange for reasonable and customary fees.[195] If the investment adviser also manages separate accounts, however, such as an offshore hedge fund structured as a corporation, the investment adviser may be deemed to be engaged in a trade or business activity that disqualifies it as an investment partnership. The investment adviser may also be disqualified if it receives other types of fee income, such as director's fees, if they are not incidental to the investment activities.[196]

iv. Departure of Partner or Member

An investment adviser may determine that a departing partner in the investment adviser entity is entitled to receive only his or her capital account on departure, either because the entity has little or no good will or going concern value, or for business reasons relating to the circumstances of the departure. The consequences of a distribution to a departing partner are discussed above.[197] The result may differ if the investment adviser entity agrees to pay a departing partner an amount in excess of his or her capital account, depending on how the transaction is structured.

First, the remaining partners can buy the departing partner's interest directly, in which case the departing partner will generally have capital gain income on the excess of the proceeds over his or her adjusted tax basis (except for the portion of the purchase price allocable to unrealized receivables or inventory under Tax Code section 751).[198]

Second, the investment adviser can pay the departing partner fixed payments for a period of time not based on the income of the partnership, which should be treated as guaranteed payments under Tax Code section 736(a),[199] and which would generally be ordinary income to the withdrawing partner and deductible (subject to other limitations) by the partnership.

Third, the departing partner can remain a partner for a period of time with a declining share of the investment adviser's profits. This should generally

192. *See* § 16.4.2, *supra.*
193. 26 U.S.C. § 731(c).
194. *See* § 16.4.2, *supra.*
195. Treas. Reg. § 1.731-2(e); 26 C.F.R. § 1.731-2(e).
196. *Id.*
197. *See* §§ 16.4 and 16.8.3.iii, *supra.*
198. 26 U.S.C. § 751.
199. 26 U.S.C. § 736(a).

result under Tax Code section 736(a)(1)[200] in that partner's being allocated income in his or her capacity as a partner, effectively causing the payments to be deductible by reducing the remaining partners' allocable shares of the income. An individual who remains a partner or member for income tax purposes might, however, also retain rights as a partner or member under state law, such as the right to inspect books and records.

Finally, the investment adviser could make a distribution to the partner and treat it as a payment under Tax Code section 736(b) if the requirements of that section are met.[201] This would generally result in the departing partner receiving capital gain income and the distribution not being deductible for the remaining partners.

v. *Tax Basis*

A partner's outside tax basis in a partnership interest increases by his or her share of the partnership's liabilities.[202] Short sales are treated as liabilities for this purpose.[203] In contrast, a shareholder's tax basis in shares of an S corporation is not increased by a share of the corporation's liabilities (except that an S corporation shareholder can use the basis of any indebtedness of the corporation to the shareholder to determine the amount of losses or distributions that can be passed through to the shareholder).[204] Distributions from partnerships and S corporations are generally not taxed unless they exceed tax basis, and items of loss and deduction can only be used to the extent of tax basis. For an investment adviser, an increased tax basis can be useful, if an individual member's capital account includes unrealized appreciation in assets invested indirectly in the hedge fund, and if withdrawal of such amounts would otherwise trigger capital gain income.

4. S Corporation Structure

Some investment advisers are structured as S corporations. S corporations are subject to several limitations that do not apply to partnerships. First, an S corporation can only have one class of stock, and distributions and allocations of taxable income must be made in proportion to share ownership.[205] An S corporation cannot divide its income into separate sources and cannot specially allocate specific items of income and loss. An S corporation can effectively divide income into separate baskets only by paying increased salaries and bonuses. If the income used to pay the bonus is long-term capital gain from the performance-based allocation from the hedge fund, the recipient pays tax at the higher ordinary income rates, and the income is subject to self-

200. 26 U.S.C. § 736(a)(1).
201. 26 U.S.C. § 736(b).
202. Tax Code § 752, 26 U.S.C. § 752.
203. *See* § 16.2.1, *supra*.
204. Tax Code § 1366(d)(1), 26 U.S.C. § 1366(d)(1).
205. Tax Code § 1361(b)(1)(D), 26 U.S.C. § 1361(b)(1)(D).

employment taxes (dividends from S corporations generally are not subject to self-employment taxes).[206]

An S corporation cannot have more than 100 shareholders or have any nonresident alien shareholders.[207] With limited exceptions, an S corporation cannot have any entities as owners. This might prohibit an investment adviser from accepting seed capital from an institutional investor.

A person who acquires shares in an S corporation either must pay fair market value for the shares or incur tax liability on the excess of fair market value over the amount paid. An S corporation cannot issue profits interests apart from capital interests.[208] S corporations do offer the advantage, however, of being able to grant incentive stock options as provided in Tax Code section 422.[209] A distribution of an asset in kind by an S corporation, unlike a partnership, results in recognition of any unrealized gain on that asset.[210]

5. Self-Employment Taxes

Self-employment tax is imposed on the self-employment income of each individual. The Social Security tax rate is 12.4 percent of self-employment income, up to the amount provided in Tax Code section 1402(b).[211] The Medicare tax rate is 2.9 percent of all self-employment income, increased to 3.8 percent on self-employment income in excess of $250,000 for a joint return (or $200,000 for other types of returns).[212] A general partner generally pays self-employment tax on the portion of the partnership's income that passes through to that partner and that constitutes income from a trade or business. Capital gains and dividends are generally excluded from self-employment income, so the performance-based allocation that passes through to owners of an investment adviser structured as a partnership should not be subject to self-employment tax, but should be subject to the Medicare tax on net investment income.[213]

In addition, income allocable to limited partners (other than guaranteed payments) is generally exempt from self-employment tax.[214] It is unclear whether passive owners of LLCs constitute general or limited partners for this purpose.[215] Accordingly, owners of an investment adviser structured as a limited partnership might avoid self-employment taxes on the income from asset-based fees, if it is allocated to them as limited partners. The IRS might challenge this

206. Tax Code § 1402(a)(2), 26 U.S.C. § 1402(a)(2). *See* § 16.8.5, *infra.*

207. Tax Code § 1361(b)(1), 26 U.S.C. § 1361(b)(1).

208. *See* § 16.8.3.ii, *supra.*

209. 26 U.S.C. § 422.

210. Tax Code § 1371, 26 U.S.C. § 1371.

211. 26 U.S.C. § 1402(b).

212. Tax Code § 1401, 26 U.S.C. § 1401.

213. Tax Code §§ 1402(a)(2),1402(a)(3), and 1411, 26 U.S.C. §§ 1402(a)(2),1402(a)(3) and 1411. Bills have been introduced that would subject performance-based allocations to self-employment tax. *See, e.g.*, S. 2075, 113th Cong. (2013).

214. Tax Code § 1402(a)(13), 26 U.S.C. § 1402(a)(13).

215. The IRS has proposed regulations on when an individual is a limited partner. Prop. Regs. § 1.1402(a)-2(h), 62 F.R. 1,702 (Jan. 13, 1997).

result, however, for limited partners who actively participate in the business and are not paid a reasonable salary.

Shareholders generally are not subject to the self-employment tax on dividends that they receive from an S corporation. Thus, an S corporation might reduce self-employment taxes on fee income by paying such amounts to its shareholders as dividends. If, however, the shareholders are receiving little or no compensation from the S corporation, the IRS might assert that all or part of the dividends should be subject to self-employment tax, or the IRS might assert that some portion is subject to the Medicare Tax on net investment income.

6. Fee Deferral by Investment Adviser

i. Prior Law

Under prior law, an investment adviser to an offshore hedge fund could often defer receipt of the asset-based fees or performance-based fees otherwise payable by the offshore hedge fund. Typically, the investment adviser and the offshore hedge fund would agree to defer some or all of such fees by treating the fee that would otherwise be due as an unsecured account payable owed by the offshore hedge fund to the investment adviser with a specified maturity date (usually not exceeding 10 years). This account payable was typically adjusted during the deferral period to reflect the subsequent profits and losses of the offshore hedge fund (as if the deferred amount was invested in the offshore hedge fund, except that the offshore hedge fund did not pay fees to the investment adviser on the amount deferred). At the end of the deferral period, the offshore hedge fund paid the fees as adjusted to the investment adviser and the fees were taxable at ordinary income rates. If the assets of the offshore hedge fund appreciated during the deferral period, the investment adviser benefited from not paying tax on the appreciation of the deferred fees during the deferral period.

Complex and detailed rules governed how fee deferrals were structured to avoid being taxable until they were paid. The investment adviser was required to use the cash method of accounting. A partnership that has a C corporation as a partner generally cannot use the cash method of accounting, which could result in precluding any fee deferral by an investment adviser that accepts a C corporation as a partner, such as a seed investor or strategic partner.[216] The investment adviser could not be deemed to have "constructive receipt" of the funds, which generally means that the assets could not be set apart for the investment adviser and the investment adviser could not gain access to the funds. The investment adviser was required to enter into a binding agreement not to receive the fees until the end of the deferral period and could not change its mind. The investment adviser also could not receive any "economic benefit" or cash equivalent for the fees to be deferred for tax purposes. The fees could not be secured or guaranteed, and were required to be available to the creditors of the offshore hedge fund.

---

216. Tax Code § 448, 26 U.S.C. § 448.

Under Tax Code section 409A,[217] the election to defer was required to be made before the beginning of the calendar year in which the services were to be performed. Accordingly, for an investment adviser managing an offshore hedge fund that had a fiscal year that is not the calendar year, the election generally was required to be made before the beginning of the calendar year in which the fiscal year began. For performance-based compensation based on services over a period of at least 12 months, however, the election could have been made no later than 6 months before the end of the service period, which apparently allowed investment advisers to wait to elect to defer annual performance-based fees for up to 6 months into the performance period.

The agreement was required to provide that the fees would not be paid earlier than (a) separation from service, (b) the date the participant becomes disabled, (c) death of the participant, (d) a specified time, (e) to the extent provided in Regulations, a change of ownership or control of the corporation or its assets, or (f) the occurrence of an unforeseeable emergency.[218] These rules on their face address an individual payee. It is unclear how they would be interpreted when the payee is an entity, such as an investment adviser entity.

For example, it is unclear what constitutes separation from service when the provider is an entity. Treasury Regulations section 1.409A-3(i)(6)[219] generally permits a back-to-back arrangement, whereby if there is a deferral arrangement between an investment adviser entity and its employee providing for acceleration of payment of such employee's deferred amounts on the occurrence of a permissible event, such as disability or separation from service, the investment adviser entity can have a corresponding arrangement with the offshore hedge fund providing for acceleration of payment by the offshore hedge fund of such employee's share of any deferred fees. Tax Code section 409A also generally allows deferred fees to be further deferred for a subsequent period, if the election to do so is made more than a year before the first payment is otherwise due and cannot become effective for at least 12 months after it is made and the added deferral period is at least 5 years. Under Tax Code section 457A, all deferred fees for years prior to the enactment of that section generally must be taxable no later than 2017.[220]

Tax Code section 409A provides that if the fees are set aside in an offshore trust or similar arrangement (to be determined under Regulations), the fees will be deemed paid for tax purposes. It is uncertain whether the IRS will attempt to argue that this rule prohibited any deferral of fees payable by an offshore hedge fund. The application of Tax Code section 409A to relationships between partnerships and partners is also unclear, and the Department of the Treasury has not yet issued Regulations addressing that issue.[221] Tax Code section 409A provides for an interest charge and a penalty of 20 percent of the amount deferred with respect to a deferral that does not comply with the rules.

---

217. 26 U.S.C. § 409A.
218. *Id.*
219. 26 C.F.R. § 1.409A-3(i)(6).
220. Tax Code § 457A; 26 U.S.C. § 457A.
221. Treas. Reg. § 1.409A.1(b)(7); 26 C.F.R. § 1.409A.1(b)(7).

ii. Current Law

Effective for amounts deferred that are attributable to services performed after December 31, 2008, Tax Code section 457A provides that compensation deferred from a "nonqualified entity" is included in income when there is no substantial risk of forfeiture of the rights to such compensation. A nonqualified entity is generally any foreign corporation unless substantially all of its income is effectively connected with a U.S. trade or business or subject to a comprehensive foreign income tax, and any partnership unless substantially all of its income is allocated other than to foreign persons or U.S. tax-exempt entities. Most offshore hedge funds and master funds would thus be nonqualified entities and a U.S. investment adviser would be unable to defer fees from such funds.

Under transition guidance issued by the IRS, fees that were deferred for periods prior to 2009 can generally remain deferred but are taxable in the later of (a) the last taxable year beginning before 2018, and (b) the taxable year in which there is no substantial risk of forfeiture.[222] Investment advisers generally could amend plans with respect to deferrals that would be deferred past 2017 to comply with this rule by December 31, 2011. Notice 2009-8 also provides that Tax Code section 457A generally does not apply to stock options or stock appreciation rights that are not subject to Tax Code section 409A, thus providing the possible use of such instruments for deferral of income. Having the investment manager receive stock options also may appeal to investors, because options can result in a longer performance measurement period, depending on when the option is first exercisable.

Tax Code section 457A could apply to performance-based fees that are calculated based on realized gains from sales of illiquid securities, even though the investment adviser did not intend to defer such fees, because they are not paid and due until a later year. One possible solution to this would be for such fees to be subject to a risk of forfeiture if the investment adviser is terminated before those securities are sold.

§ 16.9 State and Local Taxation Issues

Each state has its own system of taxation that could subject all or part of the income of a hedge fund, its investors or its general partner or investment adviser to state tax or obligate them to file information returns or other documents with state tax authorities. Different structures may be used to minimize state and local taxes in different jurisdictions. For example, having an investment adviser entity receive the management fee and a separate entity act as general partner to an onshore fund is common for an investment adviser business located in New York City. Those topics are not addressed in this book.

222. IRS Notice 2009-8, 2009-4 I.R.B. 347.

§ 16.10 Foreign Bank Account Reporting

Every U.S. person or entity that has a financial interest in, or signatory authority over, a financial account in a foreign country in a calendar year must file Form TD F 90-22.1 if the aggregate value of such accounts exceeded $10,000 at any time during that calendar year.[223] The Form must be received by the Department of Treasury by June 30 of the subsequent year. Failure to file the Form when required can result in significant monetary or criminal penalties.[224]

A financial account generally includes any bank, securities, securities derivatives or other financial instruments account. The geographical location of the branch where an account is held, not the nationality of the financial institution where it is held, determines whether an account is foreign.[225] For example, an account with a U.S. bank or brokerage firm is a foreign account if it is located in a foreign office or branch. The term "account" also includes any mutual fund or similar pooled fund that issues shares to the general public and has regular net asset value determinations and redemptions.[226] Thus, an interest in a standard offshore hedge fund would not itself be a foreign account.

A person generally has a financial interest in an account if the person has legal title to it or a beneficial ownership interest in it.[227] Under constructive ownership rules, a U.S. person is deemed to have an interest in accounts held by a corporation in which the U.S. person owns directly or indirectly 50 percent or more of the total value or voting power and accounts held by partnerships in which the U.S. person has a profits interest or capital interest greater than 50 percent. A person is generally considered to have signature authority over an account if the person can control disposition of the account's assets by communicating with the bank or other person maintaining the account (in writing or otherwise).[228]

A U.S. investment management company is required to file Form TD F 90-22.1 if it holds any foreign account directly or owns more than 50 percent of a corporation or partnership that holds such an account. Principals or employees of an investment management company must also file Form TD F 90-22.1 with respect to accounts over which they have signatory authority. A U.S. hedge fund must file Form TD F 90-22.1 if it holds a foreign account directly, or if it owns more than 50 percent of a fund that holds a foreign account. A U.S. investor must file Form TD F 90-22.1 if it owns more than 50 percent of a fund that itself holds foreign accounts.

Form TD F 90-22.1 must be filed annually and is due June 30 of each year with respect to the prior calendar year. In Notice 2009-62, Notice 2010-23, Notice 2011-54 and Notice 2012-2 the Department of the Treasury extended that deadline to file under certain circumstances.

223. 31 U.S.C. § 5314; 31 CFR 1010.350.
224. 31 U.S.C. § 5321.
225. 31 C.F.R. § 1010.350(d).
226. 31 C.F.R. § 1010.350(c)(3)(iv).
227. 31 C.F.R. § 1010.350(e).
228. 31 C.F.R. § 1010.350(f).

The obligation to file Form TD F 90-22.1 is in addition to the obligation imposed under Code section 6038D to file Form 8938. Form 8938 is used to report ownership of certain foreign assets, contains some overlapping information with Form TD F 90-22.1 and must be filed with an individual's federal income tax returns.

Index

R

S

About the Authors

The authors are partners and associates of Shartsis Friese LLP in San Francisco, California. Since its founding in 1975, Shartsis Friese LLP has become one of the nation's preeminent law firms in representing hedge fund managers. Shartsis Friese LLP currently represents several hundred hedge fund managers in all aspects of their businesses, including initial organization, capitalization, employee incentive arrangements, initial licensing and ongoing regulatory compliance (both federal and state), contract negotiation and forms for retail and institutional investors, custodians and broker-dealers, and organization and operation of hedge funds and other investment pools. This practice has developed expertise in the complex and evolving requirements of the Advisers Act, the Company Act, the Exchange Act, the Securities Act, the CEA, the Tax Code, ERISA and other relevant federal laws, and the volumes of rules and regulations of the SEC, CFTC, FINRA, IRS and DOL, as well as myriad comparable (but differing) requirements of state law and regulations.

The Shartsis Friese LLP securities enforcement and litigation group comprises 11 attorneys with expertise in the representation of investment advisers, broker-dealers and other financial services professionals. Two of the group's attorneys worked as enforcement attorneys for the SEC before joining Shartsis Friese LLP.

Douglas L. Hammer, Carolyn S. Reiser, Geoffrey W. Haynes, Neil J. Koren, James J. Frolik and Christina E. Mickelson are partners, and Joan L. Grant and Ellyn T. Roberts are of counsel, of Shartsis Friese LLP. The website is www.sflaw.com.

Amiram J. Givon is a partner of GCA Law Partners LLP in San Francisco, California. Mr. Givon is an expert on ERISA and advises Shartsis Friese LLP and many of its clients on ERISA matters. We are profoundly grateful to Mr. Givon for lending his enormous expertise and wisdom to the preparation of Chapter 11.

We also thank Fernando Marinez, Shartsis Friese LLP's librarian, for his able assistance in preparing the footnotes to this book.